DATE			

Altruism and Helping Behavior

ALTRUISM AND HELPING BEHAVIOR:

Social, Personality, and Developmental Perspectives

Edited by
J. PHILIPPE RUSHTON
RICHARD M. SORRENTINO
The University of Western Ontario

LEA LAWRENCE ERLBAUM ASSOCIATES, PUBLISHERS
1981 Hillsdale, New Jersey

Lawrence Erlbaum Associates, Inc., Publishers
365 Broadway
Hillsdale, New Jersey 07642

Library of Congress Cataloging in Publication Data
Main entry under title:

Altruism and helping behavior.

Includes bibliographies and indexes.
1. Helping behavior—Addresses, essays, lectures.
I. Rushton, J. Philippe. II. Sorrentino, Richard M.
BF637.H4A46   155.2'32   81-9726
ISBN 0-89859-155-4   AACR2

Printed in the United States of America

Contents

PART III: INTERNAL MEDIATORS OF ALTRUISM

viii   CONTENTS

PART V: SOCIAL CONSTRAINTS ON HELPING

PART VI: CONSEQUENCES OF HELPING

List of Contributors

Italics indicate page number of contribution

C. DANIEL BATSON, (*167*), Department of Psychology, University of Kansas, Lawrence, Kansas   66045

JAY S. COKE, (*167*) Department of Psychology, University of Kansas, Lawrence, Kansas   66045

RICHARD DAWKINS, (*19*) Department of Zoology, University of Oxford, Oxford, England 0X1 3YD

BELLA M. DEPAULO, (*367*) Department of Psychology, University of Virginia, Charlottesville, Virginia   22091

CARL H. FELLNER, (*351*) Department of Psychiatry and Behavioral Sciences, University of Washington School of Medicine, Seattle, Washington   98104

JEFFREY D. FISHER, (*367*) Department of Psychology, University of Connecticut, Storrs, Connecticut   06268

JOAN E. GRUSEC, (*65*) Department of Psychology, University of Toronto, Toronto, Ontario, Canada M5S 1A1

KENNETH HARGIS, (*233*) Department of Psychology, Stanford University, Stanford, California   94305

MARTIN L. HOFFMAN, (*41*) Department of Psychology, University of Michigan, Ann Arbor, Michigan   48109

JUDITH A. HOWARD, (*189*) Department of Sociology, University of Wisconsin, Madison, Wisconsin   53706

JERZY KARYLOWSKI, (*233*) Department of Psychology, Polish Academy of Science, Plac Malachowskiego 1, 00-063 Warsaw, Poland

CHARLES KORTE, (*315*) Division of University Studies, North Carolina State University, Raleigh, North Carolina   27650

DENNIS L. KREBS, (*137*) Department of Psychology, Simon Fraser University, Burnaby, British Columbia, Canada V5A 1S6

BIBB LATANÉ, (*287*) Department of Psychology, Ohio State University, Columbus, Ohio 43210

MELVIN J. LERNER, (*213*) Department of Psychology, University of Waterloo, Waterloo, Ontario, Canada N2L 3G1

JOHN R. MARSHALL, (*351*) Department of Psychiatry, University of Wisconsin, Madison, Wisconsin   53792

JAMES R. MEINDL, (*213*) Department of Psychology, University of Waterloo, Waterloo, Ontario, Canada N2L 3G1

ARIE NADLER, (*367*) Department of Psychology, Tel-Aviv University, Ramat-Aviv, Israel

STEVE A. NIDA, (*287*) Department of Psychology, Ohio State University, Columbus, Ohio   43210

MARK RIDLEY, (*19*) Department of Zoology, University of Oxford, Oxford, England OX1 3YD

DAVID L. ROSENHAN, (*233*) Department of Psychology, Stanford University, Stanford, California   94305

J. PHILIPPE RUSHTON, (*3, 91, 251, 425*) Department of Psychology, University of Western Ontario, London, Ontario, Canada N6A 5C2

CRISTINE RUSSELL, (*137*) Department of Psychology, Simon Fraser University, Burnaby, British Columbia, Canada V5A 1S6

PETER SALOVEY, (*233*) Department of Psychology, Stanford University, Stanford, California   94305

SHALOM H. SCHWARTZ, (*189*) Department of Sociology, University of Wisconsin, Madison, Wisconsin   53706 and, Department of Psychology, The Hebrew University, Jerusalem, Israel

RICHARD M. SORRENTINO, (*3, 267, 425*) Department of Psychology, University of Western Ontario, London, Ontario, Canada N6A 5C2

ERVIN STAUB, (*109*) Department of Psychology, University of Massachusetts, Amherst, Massachusetts   01003

F. F. STRAYER, (*331*) Laboratoire D'Ethologie Humaine, Centre Interdisciplinaire de Recherches sur l'Apprentissage et le Developpement en Education, Université du Québec à Montréal, C. P. 8888, Montréal, Québec, Canada H3C 3P8

DAVID W. WILSON, (*287*) Department of Psychology, Texas A & M University, College Station, Texas 77843

Preface

The study of altruism has burgeoned over the past dozen years. The diversity of approaches to the phenomena is greater today than ever, for the field of altruism is currently in a great state of excitement. We felt there was a need for a handbook to provide a forum for these approaches, one that would offer more conceptual focus than highly technical journal articles, and yet be more general than books that offer conceptually integrated reviews. Earlier works (e.g., Macaulay & Berkowitz, 1970) filled this need, but perhaps a measure of the rate of progress in our field is our judgment that such books are now out of date. We have, therefore, assembled a collection of chapters that represent the major approaches to altruism. Here is a diversity of theoretical and methodological orientations at a level of scholarship appropriate for graduate students and professional researchers. We do, however, also expect that the book will be useful to advanced undergraduates, and indeed anyone interested in the phenomena. We believe this volume is an excellent indication of the main research frontier of our science.

The chapters in this book have been organized into seven separate parts. Part I, *Introduction,* consists of a chapter by the editors, that provides an historical background to the study of altruism.

Part II, *The Development of Altruism,* examines the influence of both genes and socialization on the origins of altruistic behavior. In recent years, widespread attention has been given to a new field of enquiry known generally as "sociobiology." It contains the presentation of a genetic component for altruism. The controversy surrounding sociobiology is a heated one. Mark Ridley and Richard Dawkins (Chapter 2), provide a discussion of sociobiology, and comment on its implications for the study and conceptualization of altruism.

Martin Hoffman (Chapter 3), provides an important beginning to a theoretical integration between a genetically-based maturational perspective and that of social learning. He discusses the ontogeny of empathy as a basic motive underlying altruistic behavior. Joan Grusec (Chapter 4), J. Philippe Rushton (Chapter 5), and Ervin Staub (Chapter 6) provide broad social-learning analyses of the socialization of altruism from the perspective of the family, the mass media, and the educational system. The social-learning procedures include such verbal socializing techniques as exhortation and induction, in addition to modeling and reinforcement. Common to all three of these chapters is a concern with the degree to which these principles have broad generalizability to real-life situations.

Part III, *Internal Mediators of Altruism,* contains a variety of hypothetical motives and hypothetical constructs that have been suggested as proximal causes of altruism. In regard to motives, Dennis Krebs and Cristine Russell (Chapter 7) discuss the importance of the development of the ability to take the role of the other and lead us through a critical assessment of the research to date on role-taking and altruism. Daniel Batson and Jay Coke (Chapter 8) summarize their own and others research on empathy and put forward a theoretical model for distinguishing between altruism and egoism. Shalom Schwartz and Judith Howard (Chapter 9) reaffirm and update Schwartz's normative approach to altruism. Their model considers the importance of the situation and distinguishes between personal and social norms. Melvin Lerner and James Meindl (Chapter 10) present a new model of justice and altruism which not only incorporates Lerner's earlier work on the need to believe in a just world but attempts to specify when other types of justice will apply. David Rosenhan, Jerzy Karylowski, Peter Salovey and Kenneth Hargis (Chapter 11) provide an integration of the literature over the last decade on the effects of emotional states and moods on altruism.

Part IV, *Individual Differences in Altruism,* contains two chapters. J. Philippe Rushton (Chapter 12) carries out a reexamination of developmental evidence from over 50 years ago, integrates it with more modern research, and concludes that there is strong evidence for ''an altruistic personality.'' Richard Sorrentino (Chapter 13) presents data on the interaction between a variety of personality characteristics, situations, and the tendency to derogate victims that he relates to understanding the role of mediators of altruism in general.

Part V, *Social Constraints on Helping,* examines social-situational factors that impede, facilitate, or direct the amount of altruism shown. Bibb Latané, Steve Nida, and David Wilson (Chapter 14) provide a thorough review of all the literature on how group size can hinder bystander intervention. They also present an integration of this particular research under a more abstract theoretical model. Charles Korte (Chapter 15) reviews research on the relationship between urban density and helping, and concludes that both personality and situational factors influence the amount of helping found. F. F. Strayer (Chapter 16) provides a naturalistic-observational study of altruism among preschoolers and demonstrates how the very nature of social organization determines the nature and patterning of altruistic behavior.

Part VI, *Consequences of Helping,* examines two often neglected issues. What happens to the donor following an extreme case of helping behavior and how does the recipient feel about being helped? Carl Fellner and John Marshall (Chapter 17) address the former issue by interviewing people who had donated kidneys several years earlier. Jeffrey Fisher, Bella DePaulo and Arie Nadler (Chapter 18) address the latter by presenting a complete review of the extensive and growing body of research examining the mixed consequences of aid on the help recipient.

Part VII, *Overview,* consists of a chapter by the editors, which attempts to highlight some of the major theoretical issues raised in the preceding chapters.

Now, at the close, we would like to express our sincere gratitude to several colleagues. Foremost we must thank the contributors whose book this really is: Without the major care and effort they put into the writing of their chapters, this would not be the valuable source book we feel it has become. We would also like to thank our publisher, Larry Erlbaum, for his encouragement and support from the very beginning. It is a footnote to history that it was Larry Erlbaum, then acquisitions editor at Academic Press, who was responsible for publishing one of the first volumes in the discipline, *Altruism and Helping Behavior* by Macaulay and Berkowitz. Finally we thank colleagues at the University of Western Ontario, and especially Bill Fisher, Mel Goodale, Tory Higgins, Doug Jackson, Cheryl Lawrence, Jim Olson, Clive Seligman, Judy Short, and Neil Vidmar, for a variety of comments and discussions on the ideas in this book.

J. Philippe Rushton
Richard M. Sorrentino
London, Ontario

Altruism and Helping Behavior

INTRODUCTION

1 Altruism and Helping Behavior: An Historical Perspective

J. Philippe Rushton
Richard M. Sorrentino
The University of Western Ontario

In this chapter, an attempt is made to provide some sense of the historical background of the behavioral science approach to altruism. Often it appears in introductory textbooks in, for example, developmental and social psychology, as though the study of altruism only got underway in the mid-1960s—usually, it is suggested, because of either the "Kitty Genovese" incident of 1964 in which 39 bystanders in New York City failed to go to the aid of a young woman being raped and murdered on a city street, or because of the political turmoils in the United States at that time (i.e., Civil Rights for minority groups, and the Vietnam War). Such events undoubtedly spurred individual researchers (e.g., Latané & Darley, 1970). A more accurate picture however is to view the increase of research interest in altruism in the 1960s as part of the general research surge in all aspects of psychological inquiry.

The study of altruism had certainly begun several decades prior to the mid-1960s. Indeed, altruism and helping behavior have always been a major focus of attention for those concerned about the human condition. Although such terms as "altruism" and "prosocial" are of only recent coinage, the behavioral phenomena to which they refer have been examined since time immemorial. Since antiquity attention had centered on altruism via questions such as "what is human nature?" and "how ought people to live their lives?"

In regard to what constitutes "human nature" there have been three main views. The first has been that humans are naturally evil, and that socialization is required to make them social. The second has been that humans are naturally good and that the evil seen is the result of inequitable social conditions and/or too stringent socialization practices. The third has been that human nature is basically "neutral," neither good nor bad. All three views can be traced back at least to the Ancient Greeks and forward to contemporary behavioral scientists.

Among those who have seen human nature as being in some way essentially "bad" (e.g., nonsocial, individualistic, selfish, sinful, and aggressive) might be classed the Sophists (5th and 4th century B.C.), the writers of most of both the old and the new testaments (e.g., St. Paul, 1st century A.D.), Machiavelli (1469–1527), Hobbes (1588–1679), Freud (1856–1939) and Ardrey (1961). Thus Hobbes, in 1651, writing "Of the natural condition of mankind . . ." in his major work, *Leviathan*, stated:

> Hereby it is manifest that, during the time men live without a common power to keep them all in awe, they are in that condition which is called war, and such a war as is of every man against every man. . . . In such condition there is no place for industry . . . no arts, no society, and, which is worst of all, continual fear and danger of violent death, and the life of man is solitary, poor, nasty, brutish, and short.

Among those who have seen human nature as essentially "good" (e.g., social, cooperative, generous, moral, and altruistic) might be put Socrates (5th Century B.C.), Aristotle (384–322 B.C.), Rousseau (1712–1778), Maslow (1908–   ) and Rogers (1902–   ). Thus Aristotle argued that humans are basically social since " . . . man is by nature a political animal." Rousseau argued that humans were born free and equal by nature and juxtaposed "the equality which nature established among men," with "the inequality which men have instituted." Perhaps it is Carl Rogers (1957) who is *most* positive:

> In my experience I have discovered man to have characteristics which seem inherent to his species, and the terms which have at different times seemed to me descriptive of these characteristics are such terms as positive, forward-moving, constructive, realistic, trustworthy . . . whose deepest characteristics tend toward development, differentiation, cooperative relationships; whose life tends fundamentally to move from dependence to independence; whose impulses tend naturally to harmonize into a complex and changing pattern of self-regulation; whose total character is such as to tend to preserve and enhance himself and his species, and perhaps to move it toward its further evolution. [pp. 200–202].

Among those who have conceptualized human nature as basically "neutral" are Epicurus (342–270 BC), Plato (427–374 BC), Locke (1632–1704), Marx (1818–1883), the founder of behaviorism, John B. Watson (1878–1958) and B. F. Skinner (1904–   ). Perhaps the famous quotation from Watson (1924) will suffice:

> Give me a dozen healthy infants, well-formed, and my own specified world to bring them up in and I'll guarantee to take any one at random and train him to become any type of specialist I might select—doctor, lawyer, artist, merchant-chief and, yes, even beggar-man and thief, regardless of his talents, penchants, tenden-

cies, abilities, vocations, and race of his ancestors. I am going beyond my facts and I admit it, but so have the advocates of the contrary and they have been doing it for many thousands of years. Please note that when this experiment is made I am to be allowed to specify the way the children are to be brought up and the type of world they have to live in [p. 104].

Although searchers into the human condition have been divided in regard to what they thought humans *were* like, they have been much less so in terms of what they though they *ought* to be like. "Regard for others" is a virtually universal value within all human societies and forms the basic tenet for most of the world's great religious, social reformist, and revolutionist movements (e.g., Bronfenbrenner, 1970; Whiting & Whiting, 1975; Wilson, 1978). From Christianity, for example, we have the maxims "Do unto others as you would have them do unto you" and "Greater love hath no man than this, that a man lay down his life for his friend."

Although behaving with regard for others is almost universally hailed as a virtue, there have been exceptions. For example, Machiavelli's (1532/1906) counsel for political leaders in his book *The Prince* consisted of such maxims as "To maintain the state a prince is often obliged to act against charity, humanity and religion. . . ." In more modern times the American novelist Ayn Rand (1964) in a book entitled *The Virtue of Selfishness* has asserted that ethical altruism is extremely bad in its consequences for our society because it tends to develop dependent, unenterprising and sentimentalistic personalities and reduces economic progress and political freedom. Overwhelmingly, however, altruism has been viewed through the ages as a valuable, if not indispensable, necessity for the existence and good functioning of society. Certainly in our own culture the importance of altruism as a virtue is stressed. From sermons in the pulpit to lessons in the school; from blandishments in the home to symbolic example from the media hero, citizens are exhorted to altruistic behavior. Indeed institutionalized civic and other awards are provided to help make salient altruism as a virtue. One of the better known of these is perhaps the Carnegie Hero Fund Commission which was established in 1904 to award medals for "outstanding acts of selfless heroism performed in the United States and Canada." The Commission publishes a report annually, listing the awards and the actions that earned it. In 1977 for example, the Commission awarded 56 medals for acts of outstanding heroism (*Carnegie Hero Fund Commission*).

The term "altruism" was originated by the French sociologist Auguste Comte (1798–1857). Comte wrote much about the development of altruism and the "sympathetic instincts." His contributions will be dealt with later in this chapter. Since Comte, other behavioral scientists, including sociologists, anthropologists, developmental, personality, and social psychologists, behavioral biologists and ethologists, and even political scientists and economists, have been actively studying altruistic behaviors. Adam Smith (1759), perhaps the founder of modern capitalist economic theory, for example, began his *The Theory of Moral Sentiments* with:

How selfish soever man be supposed, there are evidently some principles in his nature, which interest him in the fortune of others, and render their happiness necessary to him, though he derives nothing from it, except the pleasure of seeing it. Of this kind is pity or compassion . . . [p. 1].

Nonetheless, this did not stop Smith (1776) from placing self-interest as the fundamental principle of his great work on scientific economics, *The Wealth of Nations:*

It is not from the benevolence of the butcher, the brewer, or the baker, that we expect our dinner, but from their regard to their own interest. We address ourselves not to their humanity but to their self-love, and never talk to them of our own necessities but of their advantages [p. 14].

Smith (1776) felt that ultimately selfish actions led to the good of society through his idea of the "invisible hand":

He (the individual) . . . neither intends to promote the public interest, nor knows how much he is promoting it . . . , he intends only his own gain, and he is in this, as in many other cases, led by an invisible hand to promote an end which was no part of his intention [p. 423].

Indeed, Smith felt that economic prosperity would be better than if people had behaved altruistically:

By pursuing his own interest he frequently promotes that of the society more effectually than when he really intends to promote it [p. 423].

From Adam Smith on, economists have debated whether human behavior was basically selfish and to what extent the laws of economics had to take altruistic motivation into account. The debate continues to this day (e.g., Collard, 1978; Phelps, 1975).

For the remainder of this chapter, a brief review of representative research into altruism from the behavioral sciences is provided. Three general demarcations of inquiry are created to provide organizational coherence to the review. These are the biological, developmental, and social.

1.   A HISTORY OF THE BIOLOGICAL STUDY OF ALTRUISM

Charles Darwin (1809–1882) proposed that humans were biologically disposed to behave socially, cooperatively, and helpfully to one another. He devoted chapters 4 and 5 of his *Descent of Man* (1871) to the moral faculties, speculating that although it was the human beings moral sense that most distinguished human beings from other animals, it arose from two interacting aspects both part of natural selection. The first is a human being's intellectual powers, the second is his or her sociability. Darwin detected such morality in other animal species as well and provided a series of examples of how sociable, cooperative, and helpful animals are to each other. He recognized, however, that to the degree to which altruism evolved through the process of natural selection, a paradox was involved. If the *most* altruistic members of the group were willing to die for others by, for example, sacrificing themselves in battle, then there would be fewer offspring of altruistic self-sacrificing individuals to carry forward the characteristic. How then, is it possible, that altruism could have arisen through the process of natural selection? Altruism remained as something of an anomaly for his theory of evolution and was suitably ignored for some time.

It was not until 1932 that the question was raised again in a serious manner. At this time J. B. S. Haldane wrote an important book integrating the theory of genetics (which had arisen since Darwin's time) with the Darwinian theory of evolution. Haldane raised the specific question of whether there were *genes for altruism,* and, if there were, how these would fare under natural selection. Although Haldane had once again raised the issue, once again however it remained ignored.

It was Wynne-Edwards (1962) who finally brought the issue forward in a manner that required attention. He suggested that evolution occurred through "group selection" rather than "individual selection." Although not a new idea his particular formulation had a major impact on biologists and generated much new research. As it turned out, most of the new studies found evidence against the Wynne-Edwards hypothesis of group selection (Williams, 1966). The concept of group selection however can be applied at a number of different levels. As Ridley and Dawkins discuss in chapter 2 of this volume, it is group selection, through the notion of kin-selection, that solves the paradox of altruism. It does so through the notion of *inclusive fitness* (Hamilton, 1964).

Along with advances in theory came empirical studies—both laboratory and naturalistic. In an early investigation of food sharing in chimpanzees, for example, Nissen and Crawford (1936) carried out the following study. Two cages were set up, side by side in which were placed two hungry chimpanzees. One of the chimpanzees was then given a little food. The question was, would it give any of its food to its hungry companion? The answer was a definite yes. Sometimes the food was passed over without the other's request. On other occasions it was passed over rather ungraciously. Sometimes, when the chimp without food kept up its begging, the chimp with the food would hurl some scraps at the other. Begging elicited giving in even greater amounts when the pair were friends rather than strangers.

Another laboratory study on animal altruism was carried out by Church (1959). He suggested that empathy in rats could be acquired through a conditioning process. In an experiment he demonstrated that rats that had previously experienced shared aversive outcomes with another rat, in the form of electric shock, were markedly affected by the subsequent pain responses of other rats. Animals that had not experienced shared aversive stimulation however showed little "empathic responsiveness" to the pain cues of the other rat.

Many other naturalistic studies carried out over the years have now documented the pervasiveness of altruistic behaviors in animal species as disparate as the social insects, birds, rabbits, deer, elephants, porpoise, and chimpanzees. These include parental behavior, cooperative defense, rescue behavior, cooperative hunting, food sharing, and expressions of affection (see Rushton, 1980; Wilson, 1975, for reviews).

While these ideas were developing in biology, the consequences were not lost on psychologists. In a *Psychological Review* paper, for example, Holmes (1945) discussed the origins of altruism in terms of parental care. He suggested that the affectionate emotions evolved as Nature's way of ensuring that altruistic self-sacrifice would ensue. More recently Campbell (1965) in an article published in the *Nebraska Symposium on Motivation* suggested the possibility that not only had altruistic self-sacrifice evolved in humans, but also such moral traits as *honesty, trust, industriousness, abstinence from indulgence, the ability to save,* and *the willingness to share.* He argued that a priori there was no ruling genetic factors out of account for these traits and he suggested that the genetic basis for these traits increased enormously at the time of the changeover from the basically nomadic hunter-gatherer existence to the complex, interdependent, urban agricultural settlements and civilizations. Interestingly enough, Campbell himself, after considerable reflection, has come to doubt the views he proposed in 1965, i.e., that urban living genetically selected such moral traits in humans as honesty, trust, abstinence from indulgence, etc. He now feels that human genes predispose us toward egoism and that massive socialization is required to overcome this (Campbell, 1972, 1975).

Currently a debate rages as to the status of such ideas (see, Ridley & Dawkins, this volume). It is not our purpose to address this controversy but rather to show that the "modern" ideas of sociobiology and the psychology of animal altruism have roots that go back well over 100 years.

2.   A HISTORY OF THE
DEVELOPMENTAL-PSYCHOLOGICAL STUDY OF
ALTRUISM

A good starting point is the classic "Character Education Inquiry" carried out by Hartshorne and May in the 1920s and published from 1928 to 1930 in three books: *Studies in Deceit; Studies in Service and Self Control;* and *Studies in the Organization of Character.* Hartshorne and May provided 11,000 elementary and high school students with some 33 different behavioral tests of their altruism (referred to as the "service" tests), self-control, and honesty in order to determine whether traits for honesty and altruism existed. Examples of their measures of altruism included:

> *The money-voting test*. In this test, the class had to decide what to do with some money which had been won in a previous contest. Scoring was in terms of the altruistic nature of the choice, ranging from, "Buy something for some hospital child or some family needing help or for some other philanthropy," to "Divide the money equally among the members of the class."

> *The envelopes test*. The children were asked to find jokes, pictures, interesting stories, and the like, for sick children in hospitals, and were given envelopes in which to collect them. The number of articles collected by each child was scored according to a complex scoring system.

At the same time as these behavioral measures were taken, extensive ratings were made of the children's reputations with their teachers and classmates. Hartshorne and May (1928–30) concluded, on the basis of their research, that no moral traits of honesty or altruism existed. Extensive reexamination of their study, however, suggests that, in fact, there are such traits (Rushton, 1980; this volume, Chapter 12). Despite controversy over the conclusions they drew, Hartshorne's and May's (1928–30) study stands as a hallmark historical investigation of altruism by developmental psychologists.

The work of the famous Swiss developmental psychologist Jean Piaget (1896–1980) is the next "classic" in this section. In 1932 Piaget published *The Moral Judgment of the Child* in which he examined the development of children's reasoning about moral dilemmas. Chapter 3 of the book is titled "Cooperation and the Development of the Idea of Justice." Piaget charted the emergence of "true" cooperation around the age of 7 and suggested this occurred because children could now see the world from the perspectives of other people. Such role-playing capacities have long been thought to underlie empathic altruism. Piaget (1932) gave children a variety of stories concerned with generosity. For example:

> Two boys, a little one and a big one, once went for a walk in the mountains. When lunch time came they were very hungry and took their food out of their bags. But they found that there was not enough for both of them. What should be done? Give all the food to the big boy or to the little one, or the same to both? [p. 309].

On the basis of responses to stories such as this, Piaget (1932) described three broad stages of the development of sharing. The first was the *authority* stage based on the demands of elders. Children at this stage of development would be likely to respond to the story in terms of the eldest child having most, simply "because he's the biggest." Next comes the stage of *equality* in which authority is subordinate to the requirements of strict equality of treatment. Thus in the story "both children should have exactly the same." Finally, the *equity* stage sees a shift from a rule of strict equality towards recognition of the relativity of individual needs and circumstances. Thus in the story, either the oldest should have more "because he would have a bigger appetite" *or* the youngest should have the most "because he couldn't manage as well as the other."

Another developmental line of inquiry inspired in part by Piaget is the question of altruism and age. Beatrice Wright (1942) was one of the first to provide evidence for this phenomenon. She found that 8 year olds were more generous than 5 year olds when asked to choose between letting their friend play with the more attractive toy or playing with it themselves. Ugurel-Semin (1952), in another early study, gave Turkish children several nuts to share between themselves and a friend. She found a dramatic increase in generosity as the children became older.

Unfortunately there is not space to consider all the developmental research that occurred during the 1930s, 1940s, and 1950s. Briefly, though, we might mention the largely neglected naturalistic studies of Lois Murphy (Murphy, Murphy, & Newcomb 1937) involving 600 hours of observation, teachers' ratings, experiments, and parent interviews. The observations included detailed 15-minute records of prekindergarten group interactions, and photographing acts of altruism, even among 16-month-old infants. Among her findings, for example, were that 16-month-olds offered toys to even younger playmates; that consistent personality differences in generosity and selfishness were apparent by kindergarten age and that, curiously enough, measures of aggression and sympathy correlated .4 with each other.

Finally, mention might be made of the developmental approaches to the socialization of altruism. Although a smattering of studies occurred prior to the 1950s from a Psychoanalytic perspective, socialization research did not really get underway until the 1950s. At that point many empirically minded psychologists attempted to test theories of socialization, some first translating Freudian concepts into Stimulus-Response terminology (Child, 1954; Kagan, 1958; Mowrer, 1950; Sears, Maccoby, & Levin, 1957).

3.   A HISTORY OF THE SOCIAL-PSYCHOLOGICAL STUDY OF ALTRUISM

The term social-psychological will be used in its widest meaning of how others influence the individual. As Allport (1954) noted, social psychology overlaps political and economic science, cultural anthropology, and sociology, as well as being in many respects indistinguishable from general psychology.

The very term "altruism" was coined by Auguste Comte (1798–1857) who wrote much about the development of altruism and the "sympathetic instincts." He believed that the purpose of an advanced society was to foster the love, and even the worship of, humanity, and that positivistic science, especially the new discipline of sociology (a term he also coined), would produce this new set of values. Comte also believed that he had located the anatomical site of the altruistic motives:

> As to the locality of these three instincts (attachment, veneration, benevolence), Gall's solution, except for the first of them, may be left untouched . . . the great founder of cerebral physiology had been induced to place Attachment in close relation to the egoistic organs and away from the other two sympathetic instincts. But with the organ of Benevolence he was more successful. . . . Allotting (it to) the highest median portion of the frontal division. . . . Venetration should be placed immediately behind it. . . . Attachment I would place laterally to Veneration. Its organ sloping from before backwards connects itself below with that of the Love of Approbation. (*Systems of Positive Polity*, Vol. 1, (1875–1877 p. 569)

Despite the oddness of the above quotation to the modern ear, Comte's contributions to altruism and social psychology is immense. Indeed Allport (1954) credited Comte as the founder of social psychology, as well as the coiner of the terms "sociology" and "altruism." Allport (1954) writes:

> If it were possible to designate a single deliberate "founder" of social psychology as a science we should have to nominate Comte for this honor [p. 7].

The relationship between social psychology and the study of altruism has often been close. In 1908, William McDougall, Reader in Mental Philosophy in the University of Oxford, was the first psychologist to publish a book on Social Psychology. McDougall's book *An Introduction to Social Psychology* expounded an "instinct" approach to human social behavior. Of particular importance is that he emphasized the roles of the "sympathetic instincts" for an understanding of human behavior. He saw in these "the root of all altruism" (1908, p. 69).

This view of altruism was taken issue with by Murphy, Murphy, and Newcomb (1937) in their book *Experimental Social Psychology*. They argued that social factors influenced sympathy suggesting that "the degree of our sympathy depends in part upon the degree of likeness which the individual shows to ourselves [p. 188]." They also implicated the role of conditioning in bringing about attachments and explaining why in some situations we could behave sympathetically and yet in others quite cruelly.

In the developmental section we made brief mention of the naturalistic observational work of Lois Murphy. In *Experimental Social Psychology* much of her work is discussed in chapter 8, the whole of which is given over to a discussion of "Cooperation, friendship, and group activity." In this chapter, social-psychological factors are stressed. For example the child's role in the peer group and his or her friendship patterns are outlined, and, in short, the effects of group structure on altruism. It is interesting to see this as a forerunner to the newer and more "modern" ethological approaches as outlined in the chapter in this volume by Fred Strayer.

Margaret Mead, the anthropologist, also disagreed with the instinct approach to social behavior. In *Sex and Temperament in Three Primitive Societies*, Mead (1935/1950) reported on the altruism of three different tribes in New Guinea: the Arapesh, the Mundugumor, and the Tchambuli. Mead reported that, among the Arapesh, both the men and the women were basically gentle, peaceful, cooperative, unaggressive, and responsive to the needs and demands of others. This was found in the manifestation of sexual desire, for both the men and women. Rape, for example, was virtually unheard of and women and young girls could wander abroad entirely alone in no danger. This tribe, however, lived in marked contrast to that of their neighbors, the Mundugumor. The Mundugumor were cannibals and headhunters. Both men and women were violent, competitive, sexually aggressive, jealous, and ready to avenge the slightest insult. Indeed individuals within this tribe were *so* hostile and jealous of one another that there were virtually no common meeting places, no communal activities, and little cooperative behavior. In turn, both the Arapesh and the Mundugumor differed from the lake-dwelling Tchambuli. Among the Tchambuli, marked sex differences emerged in altruistic behavior. Whereas the women showed a certain jovial solidarity with each other, often sitting around in groups laughing together, the men engaged in a series of unending petty bickering and quarreling. Findings such as these demonstrate that there is a great deal of malleability in human nature, and that norms of appropriate behavior vary from place to place, and person to person.

Social psychologists have been particularly interested in how the transmission of social norms occur, and what effects the presence of other people have on altruistic behavior. McDougall's (1908) early instinct theory, for example, suggested that humans had an instinct to imitate others. This allowed even instinct theories to account for major cultural differences in social altruism. It is interesting that one of the main social psychological variables to emerge during the 1960s and 1970s has been the impact of the behavior of others as "models." It is not always realized however that several modeling studies on altruism were carried out at least as early as the 1950s. Many of these were conducted with adults in naturalistic settings.

Schachter and Hall (1952) showed that modeling could increase the amount of volunteering in class for a psychology experiment. Rosenbaum and Blake (1955) and Rosenbaum (1956) also found that a model who volunteered for an experiment increased volunteering among those who saw a model. These latter investigators also found that a model refusing to volunteer for an experiment decreased the amount of volunteering compared to a group who saw no model. Blake, Rosenbaum, and Dureya (1955) found the amount of money donated to a charity could be increased or decreased as a function of modeling. Finally, Blake, Mouton, and Hain (1956) and Helson, Mouton, and Blake (1958) found that a confederate's compliance with a request to sign either popular or unpopular petitions increased the number of onlookers who were also willing to sign.

The more sociological "social psychology" of the symbolic interactionists might also be mentioned. Symbolic interaction was first labeled so by Blumer (1937). It built on the work of Charles H. Cooley (1902/1956, 1909/1956), a sociologist, and George Herbert Mead (1934), a philosopher. Reacting against both instinctivism and behaviorism, the symbolic interactionists stressed the phenomenology of actors constantly establishing and *negotiating* their mutual relations. Thus social life was viewed as a process by which actors collectively solved problems. Essential to these formulations is (1) the evolution of "mind," (2) the notion of "role-taking," and (3) the idea of actors taking part in various "dramas." Understanding occurs between people when they each take the "role of the other." One influence of the symbolic interactionists was on the "role theorists" (e.g., Sarbin, 1954). Here the number of roles one is capable of playing increases one's potential for empathy. Sarbin (1954) found that those judged as "psychopaths" have few abilities to play roles, whereas high role players are able to predict what other people are feeling or thinking on the basis of minimal cues (e.g., as represented in stick drawings of posture).

Finally, one concept, closely related to sympathy and role taking ability is empathy. This too was of extreme importance to social psychological thinking at the turn of the century. Citing the work of Blanton and Blanton (1927), Lipps (1907), and McDougall (1908), Allport (1954) wrote:

> This process of *empathy* remains a riddle in social psychology. It would seem to be genetically and conceptually basic to social learning and to lie at the heart of any theory of imitation. Some motor mimicry, as we have said, seems reducible to previous conditioning, but in other cases it appears to precede and to be a precondition of learning. The nature of the mechanism is not yet understood [p. 23].

Interestingly, the "riddle" of empathy has taken on renewed interest for many of the contributors in this volume.

Summary

In this chapter an attempt was made to provide some sense of the history of, and concern about, altruism. It was seen that since antiquity attention has centered on altruism via questions such as "what is human nature?" and "how ought people to live their lives?" It was also seen that over the last 100 years active theorizing and research have been continuing in biological, developmental, and social-psychological aspects of the behavioral sciences. It is true, however, that is is only during the last 15 years that the study of human altruism has grown to be of *major* importance. Reviews of the early literature by Berkowitz (1972), Bryan and London (1970), Krebs (1970), Latané and Darley (1970), Macaulay and

Berkowitz (1970), Midlasky (1968), and Wispé, (1972), clearly established altruism as a major topic in the behavioral sciences. Today, many introductory textbooks in, for example, developmental and social psychology, devote a complete chapter to the topic. During the mid-1970s, reviews of research on altruism continued to appear in the literature (e.g., Bryan, 1975; Rushton, 1976; Staub, 1974). Subsequently there has been another spate of reviews, now constituting full books in their own right (Bar-Tal, 1976; Hornstein, 1976; Mussen & Eisenberg-Berg, 1977; Rushton, 1980; Stotland, Mathews, Sherman, Hansson, & Richardson, 1978; Staub, 1978; 1979; Wispé, 1978). In addition, the study of altruism has been broadened immeasurably by analyses from anthropological, biological, and sociological perspectives (Wilson, 1975, 1978).

Now it is time to examine where we stand during the 1980s—perhaps a vital decade for humans to come to understand themselves better.

REFERENCES

Allport, G. W. The historical background of modern social psychology. In G. Lindzey (Ed.), *Handbook of Social Psychology,* Vol. 1. *Theory and Method.* Cambridge, Ma.: Addison-Wesley, 1954.

Bar-Tal, D. *Prosocial behavior: Theory and research.* Washington, D.C.: Hemisphere, 1976.

Berkowitz, L. Social norms, feelings, and other factors affecting helping and altruism. In L. Berkowitz (Ed.), *Advances in experimental social psychology* (Vol. 6). New York: Academic Press, 1972.

Blake, R. R., Mouton, J. S., & Hain, J. D. Social forces in petition signing. *Southwestern Social Science Quarterly,* 1956, *36,* 385–390.

Blake, R. R., Rosenbaum, M., & Duryea, R. Gift-giving as a function of group standards. *Human Relations,* 1955, *8,* 61–73.

Blanton, S., & Blanton, M. *Child guidance.* New York: Century Co., 1927.

Blumer, H. Social Psychology. In E. P. Schmidt (Ed.), *Man and Society.* New York: Prentice-Hall, 1937.

Bronfenbrenner, U. *Two worlds of childhood: U.S. and U.S.S.R.* New York: Russell Sage Foundation, 1970.

Bryan, J. H. Children's cooperation and helping behaviors. In E. M. Hetherington (Ed.), *Review of child development research* (Vol. 5). Chicago: University of Chicago Press, 1975.

Bryan, J. H., & London, P. Altruistic behavior by children. *Psychological Bulletin,* 1970, *73,* 200–211.

Campbell, D. T. Ethnocentric and other altruistic motives. In D. Levine (Ed.), *Nebraska symposium on motivation.* Lincoln: University of Nebraska Press, 1965.

Campbell, D. T. On the genetics of altruism and the counter-hedonic components in human culture. *Journal of Social Issues,* 1972, *28,* 21–37.

Campbell, D. T. On the conflicts between biological and social evolution and between psychology and moral tradition. *American Psychologist,* 1975, *30,* 1103–1126.

Carnegie Hero Fund Commission. Annual Report, 1977. Address: 1932 Oliver Building, Pittsburg, Pennsylvania, 15222, U.S.A.

Child, I. Socialization. In G. Lindzey (Ed.), *Handbook of Social Psychology.* Cambridge, MA.: Addison-Wesley, 1954.

Church, R. M. Emotional reactions of rats to the pain of others. *Journal of Comparative and Physiological Psychology*, 1959, *52*, 132–134.

Collard, D. *Altruism and economy: A study in non-selfish economics*. London: Oxford University Press, 1978.

Comte, A. *System of positive polity*. 4 Vols. London: Longmans, 1875–1877. (Original in French in 1851–1854).

Cooley, C. H. *Human nature and the social order*. (Rev. ed.) In C. H. Cooley, *Two Major Works*. Glencoe, Ill.: Free Press, 1956 (Original 1902).

Cooley, C. H. *Social organization: A study of the larger mind*. In C. H. Cooley, *Two Major Works*. Glencoe, Ill.: Free Press, 1956 (Original 1909).

Darwin, C. *The descent of man*. London: Murray, 1871.

Haldane, J. B. S. *The causes of evolution*. London: Longmans, 1932.

Hamilton, W. D. The genetical evolution of social behavior. I. *Journal of Theoretical Biology*, 1964, *7*, 1–16.

Hartshorne, H., & May, M. A. *Studies in the nature of character*. Vol. 1: *Studies in deceit*. New York: Macmillan, 1928.

Hartshorne, H., May, M. A., & Maller, J. B. *Studies in the nature of character*. Vol. II: *Studies in self-control*. New York: Macmillan, 1929.

Hartshorne, H., May, M. A., & Shuttleworth, F. K. *Studies in the nature of character*. Vol. III: *Studies in the organization of character*. New York: Macmillan, 1930.

Helson, H., Mouton, J. S., & Blake, R. R. Petition signing as adjustment to situational and personality factors. *Journal of Social Psychology*, 1958, *48*, 3–10.

Hobbes, T. *Leviathan*. London: George Routledge & Sons, Ltd., 1651.

Holmes, S. J. The reproductive beginnings of altruism. *Psychological Review*, 1945, *52*, 109–112.

Hornstein, H. A. *Cruelty and Kindness: A new look at aggression and altruism*. Englewood Cliffs, N.J.: Prentice-Hall, 1976.

Kagan, J. The concept of identification. *Psychological Review*, 1958, *65*, 296–305.

Krebs, D. L. Altruism—An examination of the concept and a review of the literature. *Psychological Bulletin*, 1970, *73*, 258–302.

Latané, B., & Darley, J. M. *The unresponsive bystander: Why doesn't he help?* New York: Appleton-Century-Crofts, 1970.

Lipps. T. Das wissen von fremdon Ichen. *Psychologie Untersuchungen*, 1907, *1*, 694–722.

Macaulay, J., & Berkowitz, L. (Eds.). *Altruism and helping behavior: Social psychological studies of some antecedents and consequences*. New York: Academic Press, 1970.

Machiavelli, N. *The prince* [L. Ricci, Trans.]. New York: Oxford University Press, 1906. (Originally published, 1532.)

McDougall, W. *Introduction to social psychology*. London: Methuen, 1908.

Mead, G. H. *Mind self and society from the standpoint of a social behaviorist*. C. W. Morris (Ed.), Chicago: Chicago University Press, 1963. (Original, 1934).

Mead, M. *Sex and temperament in three primitive societies*. New York: Morrow, 1950. (Originally published, 1935.)

Midlarsky, E. Aiding responses: An analysis and review. *Merrill-Palmer Quaterly*, 1968, *14*, 229–260.

Mowrer, O. H. *Learning theory and personality dynamics*. New York: Ronald Press, 1950.

Murphy, G., Murphy, L. B., & Newcomb, T. M. *Experimental Social Psychology* (Revised Edition). New York: Harper & Row, 1937.

Mussen, P., & Eisenberg-Berg, N. *Roots of caring, sharing, and helping: The development of prosocial behavior in children*. San Francisco: W. H. Freeman & Company, 1977.

Nissen, H. W., & Crawford, M. P. A preliminary study of food-sharing behavior in young chimpanzees. *Journal of Comparative Psychology*, 1936, *22*, 383–419.

Phelps, E. S. (Ed.) *Altruism, morality, and economic theory*. Chicago, Il.: Russell Sage, 1975.

Piaget, J. *The moral judgment of the child*. London: Routledge & Kegan Paul, 1932.

Rand, A. *The virtue of selfishness*. New York: NAL, 1964.

Rogers, C. R. A note on "The nature of man." *Journal of Counseling Psychology*, 1957, *4*, 199–203.

Rosenbaum, M. The effect of stimulus and background factors on the volunteering response. *Journal of Abnormal and Social Psychology*, 1956, *53*, 118–121.

Rosenbaum, M., & Blake, R. R. Volunteering as a function of field structure. *Journal of Abnormal and Social Psychology*, 1955, *50*, 193–196.

Rushton, J. P. Socialization and the altruistic behavior of children. *Psychological Bulletin*, 1976, *83*, 898–913.

Rushton, J. P. *Altruism, socialization, and society*. Englewood Cliffs, N.J.: Prentice-Hall, 1980.

Sarbin, T. R. Role Theory. In G. Lindzey (Ed.), *Handbook of Social Psychology*. Vol. I. *Theory and Method*. Cambridge, Ma.: Addison-Wesley, 1954.

Schachter, S., & Hall, R. Group-derived restraints and audience persuasion. *Human Relations*, 1952, *5*, 397–406.

Sears, R. R., Maccoby, E. E., & Levin, H. *Patterns of child rearing*. Evanston, Illinois: Row, Peterson, 1957.

Smith, A. *The theory of moral sentiments*. New York: A. M. Kelley, 1966. (First published 1759.)

Smith, A. *The wealth of nations*. New York: Random House, 1937 (First published, 1776.)

Staub, E. Helping a distressed person: Social, personality, and stimulus determinants. In L. Berkowitz (Ed.), *Advances in experimental social psychology* (Vol. 7). New York: Academic Press, 1974.

Staub, E. *Positive social behavior and morality* (Vol. 1). *Social and personal influences*. New York, Academic Press, 1978.

Staub, E. *Positive social behavior and morality* (Vol. 2). *Socialization and development*. New York, Academic Press, 1979.

Stotland, E., Mathews, K. E., Sherman, S. E., Hansson, R. O., & Richardson, B. Z. *Empathy, Fantasy and Helping*. Beverly Hills, Ca.: Sage, 1978.

Ugurel-Semin, R. Moral behavior and moral judgment of children. *Journal of Abnormal and Social Psychology*, 1952, *47*, 463–474.

Watson, J. B. *Behaviorism*. Chicago: The People's Institute, 1924.

Whiting, B. B., & Whiting, J. W. M. *Children of six cultures: A psychocultural analysis*. Cambridge, Ma.: Harvard University Press, 1975.

Williams, G. C. *Adaptation and natural selection*. Princeton, N.J.: Princeton University Press, 1966.

Wilson, E. O. *Sociobiology: The new synthesis*. Cambridge, Ma.: Harvard University Press, 1975.

Wilson, E. O. *On human nature*. Cambridge, Ma.: Harvard University Press, 1978.

Wispé, L. G. (Ed.). Positive forms of social behavior. *Journal of Social Issues*, 1972, *28*, 3.

Wispé, L. G. (Ed.). *Altruism, sympathy, and helping: Psychological and sociological principles*. New York: Academic Press, 1978.

Wright, B. A. Altruism in children and the perceived conduct of others. *Journal of Abnormal and Social Psychology*, 1942, *37*, 218–233.

Wynne-Edwards, V. C. *Animal dispersion in relation to social behavior*. Edinburgh: Oliver and Boyd, 1962.

DEVELOPMENT OF ALTRUISM

2 The Natural Selection of Altruism

Mark Ridley
Richard Dawkins
University of Oxford

The poisonous sting of a honey bee is an adaptation against hive robbers. Its sharp point is an adaptation to facilitate penetration of the victim's hide, but what are those recurved barbs facing backwards near the tip? The effect of these barbs is that the sting, once inserted, cannot be withdrawn. The whole string is wrenched out of the bee's body and with it some of the bee's vital internal organs. The bee dies as a result, but the sting goes on pumping venom into the victim. The barbs, therefore, enhance the effectiveness of the sting, albeit posthumously. The barbs could be described as instruments of altruistic self-sacrifice.

In evolutionary theory, altruism means self-sacrifice performed for the benefit of others. In everyday speech the world altruism carries connotations of subjective intent. An anonymous donor is often thought more altruistic than one who publicizes his generosity who, we suspect, may have an underlying selfish motive. Rightly or wrongly (Griffin, 1976), zoologists do not concern themselves with such questions of subjective motive. We do not deny that animals have feelings and intentions, but we make more progress in understanding animal behavior if we concentrate on its observable aspects. If we use words like altruism at all, we define them by their effects and do not speculate about the animal's intentions. An altruistic act is one that has the *effect* of increasing the chance of survival (some would prefer to say 'reproductive success') of another organism at the expense of the altruist's. The definition includes, for instance, the feeding of a young cuckoo by its foster parents. There is no intention to be altruistic here: if the foster parent realized what it was doing it would probably kill the cuckoo. The foster-caring behavior is altruistic in its effect, and that is what matters for the definition.

It follows that an indubitably unconscious entity such as a plant, or a gene, is in principle capable of displaying "altruism." An "altruistic" plant might depress its own growth rate and allow neighboring plants to grow accordingly bigger (Seger, 1976). Bethell (1978), however, wrote of the idea of *The Selfish Gene* (Dawkins, 1976b): "This is an ingenious theory but farfetched. There is no reason for imputing the complex emotion of selfishness to molecules . . . [p. 38]." If the theory were as Bethell implies, it would be more than farfetched, it would be downright lunatic. To an ethologist, "the selfish lion" would not imply complex emotion, but, because lions are probably capable of emotion, the ethologist would risk being misunderstood if he used such a phrase without careful qualification. The obvious impossibility of genes' having emotions was one reason for choosing the selfish gene title: it was thought to be immune to that particular misunderstanding! Do physicists have to be careful when speaking of the "charm" of their particles?

It may be objected that if biologists mean so little by selfishness and altruism they are leaving out all that is interesting. This is a different kind of criticism, and one against which we shall not offer a defense: different people are interested in different things. Darwinism may not throw light on altruism and selfishness in their conscious, subjective senses; but Darwinism can give a different kind of illumination which, in our opinion, has a fascination of its own. Indeed, a widespread interest is indicated by the large number of publications on sociobiology that are appearing (Barlow & Silverberg, 1980; Blurton Jones, 1976; Caplan, 1978). When Campbell gave his presidential address to the American Psychological Association (Campbell, 1975) on a similar theme to the present essay, large sections of two journals were subsequently devoted to discussing it (*Zygon* 11 (3), 1976 and *American Psychologist* 31 (5), 1976).

Our definition of altruism was taken from Wilson's *Sociobiology* (1975). Wilson has gone so far as to name altruism as "the central theoretical problem of sociobiology." Sociobiology is in the tradition of evolutionary ethology which has, ever since Lorenz's work beginning in the 1930s, and especially Tinbergen's in the 1950s and 1960s, sought to elucidate the adaptive significance of behavior. Darwin himself took this approach in both *On the Origin of Species* and *The Expression of Emotions in Man and Animals*. The recent revival of interest in the adaptive significance of behavior has been inspired by new ideas from Hamilton, Williams, Maynard Smith, Trivers and others, building on those of Fisher, Haldane and Darwin himself.

NATURAL SELECTION

Ethologists are interested in the evolution of altruism, not just for what it can tell us about our own nature but because it is a paradox for the Darwinian theory. The paradox is this. By definition, altruists would be expected to have a lower reproductive success than the selfish rivals whom they help. Altruistic behavior should, therefore, disappear from the population. It shouldn't exist, yet apparently it does.

Some people think that the answer to this paradox is that although altruism is disadvantageous to the altruist it makes up for this by its advantage to the group or species to which the altruist belongs. Groups possessing altruistic members are less likely to go extinct than wholly selfish groups; hence altruistic behavior survives in the world. This is the theory of group selection, a theory which has had a curious history. It was explicitly named and powerfully advocated by Wynne-Edwards (1962), but this event came almost at the end of its long history, indeed it may have precipitated the end. The group selection theory had earlier exerted a long hold over the subconscious reasoning of biologists (Williams, 1966, and Ghiselin, 1974, give powerful critiques). Why this should have been so is a fascinating question for philosophers and historians of science, which does not seem to have been tackled. Darwin himself in general had nothing to do with group selection. He firmly placed the individual organism as the object of natural selection (see Ghiselin, 1969 for a perceptive analysis of Darwin's thought). Darwin might have approved of Ghiselin's (1974) own much quoted rhetoric on the subject of animal society, although he would have wished for a gentler tone.

> The evolution of society fits the Darwinian paradigm in its most individualistic form. Nothing in it cries out to be otherwise explained. The economy of nature is competitive from beginning to end. Understand that economy, and how it works, and the underlying reasons for social phenomena are manifest. They are the means by which one organism gains some advantage to the detriment of another. No hint of genuine charity ameliorates our vision of society, once sentimentalism has been laid aside. What passes for cooperation turns out to be a mixture of opportunism and exploitation. The impulses that lead one animal to sacrifice himself for another turn out to have their ultimate rationale in gaining advantage over a third; and acts 'for the good' of one society turn out to be performed to the detriment of the rest. Where it is in his own interest, every organism may reasonably be expected to aid his fellows. Where he has no alternative, he submits to the yoke of communal servitude. Yet given a full chance to act in his own interest, nothing but expediency will restrain him from brutalizing, from maiming, from murdering—his brother, his mate, his parent, or his child. Scratch an 'altruist,' and watch a 'hypocrite' bleed [p. 247].

The objections to the group selection theory have been frequently explained in the literature (Maynard Smith, 1964, 1976; Williams, 1966; Dawkins, 1976b), and will be given only the briefest mention here. Group selection certainly happens, in the sense that some groups go extinct. The problem is whether such differential extinction can be used to explain anything. In Williams' (1975) words:

No one is likely to deny . . . that a population's gene frequencies may have some effect on its persistence. This does not justify Levins' position that if group selection is real it deserves attention from a busy biological community. To deserve attention it needs some minimal degree of importance. The problem is not: Is it there? but rather: Has it produced important effects? [p. 157].

If group selection had produced any important effects, these would probably fall under the general heading of altruism. Imagine a set of groups, some of which have altruistic members, others of which have only selfish members. Selfish groups are more likely to go extinct than groups containing altruists, who sacrifice themselves to save the group. So differential group extinction, group selection, will tend to preserve altruistic behavior in the world. But unfortunately it isn't as simple as that. Selection *within* groups will favor selfish organisms over altruists because the selfish organisms will tend to have more offspring. It seems, then, that we have selection at two levels pushing in opposite directions. Which of the two selective forces will win, group selection in favor of altruism or individual level selection against it? Mathematical models show that, except in very special conditions which are almost never realized in nature, group selection will lose because it is so slow. Differential group extinction (or production of emigrants) is almost necessarily a slower kind of natural selection than differential death (or reproduction) of organisms.

Fortunately, we can very well do without group selection. The explanation of altruistic behavior without recourse to group selection is a theoretical triumph that we owe mainly to W. D. Hamilton. We shall now explain the theory of natural selection in a way that is a little controversial, but which is not fundamentally unorthodox and which makes Hamilton's ideas very easy to introduce. We shall look at natural selection from the points of view of the gene rather than the individual (Dawkins, 1976b). (The truth of Hamilton's ideas, however, is not dependent on this particular way of expressing the theory of natural selection.)

Natural selection is a process of differential survival. What are the entities that differentially survive; are they, perhaps, individual organisms? It is certainly true that some organisms are more likely to die than others, but survival itself is important only because it is a prerequisite to reproduction. An organism that consumed all the food it gathered, instead of feeding some of it to children, might well live a long time, but it would not pass on its selfish tendencies to future generations. Natural selection is not, then, a process of differential survival of organisms. Over evolutionary time, what survives is not the organism but the tendency, say, to feed children rather than the tendency to feed only oneself. Natural selection is differential survival of tendencies or characteristics of organisms. But how are characteristics passed on? Cultural inheritance is one possible way, but by far the most obvious way is genetic inheritance. Gene frequencies in populations are what really change in evolution. As Williams (1966) has cogently argued, therefore, we may regard the gene as the fundamental unit of natural selection. On this understanding of natural selection, it is convenient to explain adaptations by considering hypothetical "genes." The approach, crudely epitomized, is to postulate a gene that has a certain effect on individual phenotypes and then inquire whether such a gene would be favored by natural selection.

Many critics have had difficulty understanding what is meant by postulating a gene "for" some trait, especially, for some reason, if that trait is a behavioral one. As Campbell (1975) has written:

Aware that there are millions of genes, each with multiple effects and interactions, population geneticists assume that an unspecified subset is available to influence any behavioral trait in any direction. Then, for simplicity's sake, they plot the hypothetical fate in a population of a single gene, for example one determining self-sacrificial altruism in the form of bravery in group defense. This is apt to seem a totally unacceptable form of speculation to psychologists. One of the reasons why is our incredulity that a behavioral tendency as abstract and polymorphic as 'bravery' could be influenced by a single gene. [p. 1110].

How *could* a single gene specify the whole developmental program of something as complex as altruistic behavior? Does not such postulation imply an ineluctable genetic determinism as well as a hopelessly naive oversimplification of the processes of development? What of the environment and its effects?

These are all nonproblems. When Darwinians postulate a gene "for," say, altruistic behavior, irrevocable determination by single, unaided genes never even enters their heads. Accuse them of "genetic determinism" and you will simply bewilder them. A gene "for" any phenotypic trait is really a gene for a *difference* between individuals. This has always been implicit in classical genetics. Geneticists happily speak of genes "for" brown eyes, yet you will never catch a geneticist rearing animals in an altered environment to see how the environment influences the color of their eyes. Unlike embryologists, geneticists are simply not interested in the myriad of environmental and genetic factors that go to make up eye pigment itself. They care only that this individual has brown eyes whereas that individual has blue. They are concerned only with the determination of differences.

And differences are exactly what Darwinians are concerned with too. In their thought experiments they postulate two kinds of individual: altruistic and selfish, say; or perhaps they postulate a quantitative continuum of altruism/selfishness, influenced by the additive effects of polygenes in the same way as the continuum of height or weight. Maybe they postulate pairs of genes, alleles, that, when compared with each other, tend to exert different effects on individual behavior; and they ask which, of each pair, is likely to be evolutionarily stable against invasion by the other. Never does it occur to them that the genes they are postulating might exert their effects in isolation from other genes and from the environment. Never does it occur to them that the effects of the genes that they postulate might be thought to be irreversibly deterministic.

Few people have difficulty in accepting parental care as a Darwinian adaptation. On this assumption the behavior must have been favored by natural selection. Natural selection had to have something to choose between. This can only have come about if there were genes specifying differences between organisms that were more rather than less inclined to show parental care. Now it is easy to imagine that there is only a slight quantitative difference between caring for one's own offspring and caring for someone else's, a difference that could easily be influenced genetically. There is therefore nothing unrealistic in performing a thought experiment in which we compare the fates of two genes, one "for" parental altruism, the other "for" indiscriminate altruism. Both these genes would exert their effects in a simple quantitative way on an existing, highly complex, developmental process. In the same way, nitrate exerts a simple quantitative effect on the growth of wheat; nobody should be tempted to suppose that nitrate, alone and unaided, can make something as complex as a wheat plant, nor that the effects of nitrate on wheat growth are irreversibly deterministic!

These, then, are the terms in which we pose the Darwinian problem of alturism. Under what conditions might a gene that tends to make organisms behave altruistically spread through a population at the expense of a rival gene for selfishness? Present day theory recognizes three main ways in which natural selection can favor altruistic behavior. These are the subject of the next section.

THREE EVOLUTIONARY ROUTES TO ALTRUISM

1. Relatedness

As we have seen, there is no difficulty in seeing parental care as an adaptation. Parents with a genetic predisposition to care for their offspring are directly preserving copies of the genes concerned. However, it is not only parents and offspring that share genes "identical by descent" (i.e., copied from a common ancestor): *all relatives do to some extent.* Thus altruism between any relatives can be favored by selection; parental care is only a special case. Darwin (1859, pp. 237–238) must have appreciated this in a qualitative way when he suggested "family selection" as an explanation for the otherwise puzzling evolution of sterile workers in social insects. Quantitative formulation was not possible until the advent of Mendelism. Fisher's (1930, pp. 177–181) discussion of the evolution of warning coloration, and Haldane's incomplete model (1932, p. 207) and some casual remarks in a popular article (Haldane, 1955), indicate an understanding of the connection between relatedness and altruism. But it is Hamilton who, in a series of papers (1964; 1970; 1971; 1972; 1975; 1979) has developed nearly all the important ideas about the evolution of altruism between relatives.

It is not essential, but it is convenient to begin by oversimplifying the argument by considering only genes that are rare in the population as a whole. If we are to calculate whether some altruistic act towards a relative will be favored by natural selection we need to know the probability of that relative's sharing that altruist's gene. For simple cases, this probability can easily be deduced from elementary genetics. In most species of animals each individual receives one set of genes from its father and one set from its mother. If a gene is rare in the population it is most unlikely that both parents would possess it. So if a single rare gene is in an offspring, there is a probability of one half that it is in its mother, and one half that it is in its father. Similarly, if a single rare gene is in a mother, there is a probability of one half that it is in a particular offspring; and likewise for a gene in a father. Now consider the probability that an organism shares a gene with a full sibling. The probability that the organism shared the gene with its mother is one half, and the probability that the mother shares a gene with the other offspring is another half. The total probability that two full siblings share a maternal gene is therefore a quarter. The same reasoning gives the probability of sharing a paternal gene as a quarter. The total probability that the siblings share a single rare gene is obtained by adding the maternal and paternal probabilities and so is one half. This simple reasoning can be extended to any pair of relatives, and the results for various relatives are given in Table 2.1.

Genes, then, can be favored by natural selection not only if they cause their bearers to leave more offspring, but also if they cause their bearers to increase the survival of their other genetic relatives. If the loss in reproduction of the gene in the altruist is more than compensated by the gain in reproduction of that gene in the beneficiary, then the gene for altruism will be favored by natural selection. Therefore, other things being equal, we expect an individual to behave altruistically toward a relative if C, the cost to the altruist, is less than B, the benefit to the recipient, multiplied by the appropriate coefficient of relatedness, r. (Genes

TABLE 2.1

Coefficients of Relatedness (r) between an Organism and the Specified Relative. (Diploidy assumed.)

Relative	r
Parent	1/2
Offspring	1/2
Full sibling	1/2
Half sibling	1/4
Grandparent	1/4
Grandchild	1/4
First cousin	1/8
Nephew or niece	1/4
Uncle or aunt	1/4
Second cousin	1/32

that cause altruism are favored when $rB > C$, or $K > 1/r$ where K is the benefit to cost ratio.) Thus we expect altruism between full siblings when $B/C > 2$, between first cousins when $B/C > 8$, and so on. This, in brief, is Hamilton's theory of the evolution of altruism. It has come to be known by a name not of his own choosing, "kin selection" (Maynard Smith, 1964).

In Hamilton's theory there is really no fundamental difference between caring for offspring and caring for any other kind of relative. When natural selection favors genes for altruism among relatives, that process is the same whether the relatives in question are cousins, offspring, great-aunts or some mixture of them. However, parental care was understood long before it was shown to be a special case of kin selection. This has led to the widespread misconception that kin selection is concerned with relatives specifically *other* than offspring. (This is only one of several simple misunderstandings plaguing the literature on kin selection: Dawkins (1979) discusses twelve of them.)

As Hamilton (1975) has emphasized, kin selection is not the only kind of selection leading to altruism between individuals especially likely to share genes. The "Green Beard Effect" (Dawkins, 1976b, p. 96) is a wholly fanciful thought experiment that illustrates the point in an extreme way. Genes frequently have more than one effect on phenotypes. Imagine a gene that has two effects: it causes individuals possessing it to have a green beard, and it also causes them to behave altruistically towards green-bearded individuals. Clearly such a gene might be very successful in the population, and this kind of altruism could therefore occur with no necessity for the individuals concerned to be related. The green beard serves as a recognition cue (not necessarily conscious recognition of course) for the altruistic gene. No examples of this effect are ever likely to be discovered in nature, but it is an instructive possibility.

Another though experiment along this line is that the very act of altruism itself could serve as a recognition cue for other would-be altruists (Dawkins, 1976b, p. 96). A gene that tended to make individuals care for any other individuals seen caring for a third party might well be caring for copies of itself. This is *not* the same as "reciprocal altruism," which is the subject of the next major section.

There is no space here to review all the evidence of altruism among relatives. Parental care, of course, provides the most numerous and the most extreme examples. Much of the evidence on this and other kinds of kin-selected altruism has been discussed by Hamilton (1964, 1972, 1979), Brown (1975), Wilson (1971, 1975), and others. We shall choose a few examples of nonparental care of relatives.

Aphids are small insects that live on plants. (Green aphids are often termed "greenflies.") They normally feed by sucking juices out of plants through their mouth-parts, which are shaped rather like a drinking straw. Aphids can reproduce both sexually and asexually. During a period of asexual reproduction, all of the sisters in a clone are genetically identical ($r = 1$). Theoretically, therefore, we should not be surprised to see individuals sacrificing themselves, or foregoing their own reproduction in the interests of clone mates. Intriguingly, Aoki (1977) has discovered a "soldier caste" in the Japanese aphid *Colphina clematis*. Clones consist of two distinct kinds of individual, the difference being, of course nongenetic. Type A individuals develop normally and eventually reproduce. Type B individuals are retarded at an early stage of development, and so never reproduce; they develop fighting jaws, quite unlike the normal aphid plant-sucking mouthparts that characterize Type A individuals. With these jaws they protect their Type A sisters from predators. Their fighting jaws are unsuitable for the normal aphid method of feeding, and it is not known how they feed. It would be fascinating to know whether they are fed by their Type A sisters.

Sterile casters are, of course, the salient feature of truly social insects: termites, ants, social bees and wasps. The members of a colony of these insects are not a genetically identical clone, but they may be genetically especially close, either because of inbreeding or for other reasons (Hamilton, 1972). The genetic system (haplodiploidy) of the Hymenoptera (the ants, bees and wasps) causes the relatedness between sisters to be 3/4, which is higher than the relatedness of a mother to her daughter ($\frac{1}{2}$). Females might, therefore, be selected to rear sisters rather than daughters. However, females are more closely related to their sons ($r = \frac{1}{2}$) than their brothers ($r = \frac{1}{4}$ under haplodiploidy), so it is likely that females would only evolve social habits if they can rear their sisters while discriminating against their brothers (Hamilton, 1964; Trivers & Hare, 1976). This kin selection theory of the evolution of sociality in insects is still highly problematic and controversial.

More and more examples are being found among vertebrates of care of young by relatives other than parents, usually elder siblings (Brown, 1978; Emlen, 1978; Hrdy, 1976; MacRoberts & MacRoberts, 1976). Kin-selection is not the only possible reason for the evolution of such "helping at the nest"; for instance, the helpers may gain experience in the art of child-rearing which they put to good use later when they have children of their own. If the helpers are only obtaining experience in child-rearing it would not matter, for the evolution of the trait, whether the helpers were related to the children they care for. The "aunts" of the primate literature provide a similar example. "Aunts" are females that, more or less completely, care for infants other than their own. Despite their name, "aunts" are not particularly likely to be real genetic aunts, and in this case as well the behavior may be selfish, not altruistic. The aunts obtain practice in child-rearing but the infant sometimes may not benefit because of the incompetence of the aunt (Hrdy, 1976, 1977).

Attempts at a genetic interpretation of quantitative data on altruistic behavior in animals are those of Kurland (1977) on Japanese monkeys, and of Bertram (1976) on lions. Female lions sometimes suckle the offspring of other females of the pride, and Bertram has shown the females of a statistically average pride to be related, r being approximately .15. He reckoned males in a typical pride to be related to each other by about $r = .22$, but to be virtually unrelated to females in the pride. Males cooperate with each other, notably in initially taking over the pride by overthrowing the previously incumbent males. Newly usurping males are, of course, unrelated to existing cubs in the pride, and it is therefore not surprising that infanticide by incoming males is common (apparently analogous infanticide by langurs is discussed by Hrdy, 1977). Bertram rightly emphasizes that what is important is not how closely related two individuals actually are, but how closely related lions in their position are statistically likely to be. Nobody is suggesting that animals have a cognitive awareness of how best to benefit their genes. Rather, natural selection favors unconscious behavioral "rules of thumb" that in average statistical conditions tend to have the *effect* of benefiting the individual's genes.

Skeptics rightly raise barriers of suspicion when they are presented with neat examples which appear to be compatible with a neat theory. What about all the examples that don't fit the theory? What about predictions of the theory that are not met in nature? We share this skepticism with respect to particular examples. However, the theory of kin selection itself does not stand or fall by its predictions; only the extent of its operation in nature is open to question. If you accept the neo-Darwinian theory of natural selection, you have no option but to accept kin selection, because one follows logically and necessarily from the other. Although the logical argument of kin selection cannot be wrong, it could easily be irrelevant if its premises do not obtain in nature. The detailed selection pressures that, in practice, have shaped the evolution of any particular adaptation are complex and subject to empirical investigation. It may be that the selection that favored helping at the nest by Florida Scrub Jays had nothing to do with the fact that the helpers are normally siblings of the helped (Woolfenden, 1975). But the theory of kin selection itself is not under test, or rather it is only under test in the same sense as the whole neo-Darwinian theory may be under test. Nowadays few biologists doubt the basic truth of neo-Darwinism. They accept it as a truth, and use that truth to unravel details. The theory of kin selection should be treated similarly.

2. Reciprocal Altruism

Over a lifetime, an altruist may do better than a nonaltruist if recipients are later kind to altruists rather than nonaltruists. If an altruist saves a drowning organism then the rescued organism may later save that altruist in return, and so both would benefit. This is reciprocal altruism; for the natural selection of reciprocal altruism the altruist and recipient need not be relatives. With reciprocal altruism, natural selection favors altruistic *acts* but not altruistic *lives*.

In *The Descent of Man* (1871, Chapter V), Darwin suggested reciprocal altruism as one way in which natural selection could favor altruism in humans: "if he aided his fellow men, he would commonly received aid in return [p. 131, 1894 edition]." Darwin called this a "low motive," but, as Williams (1966, pp.

93–96) pointed out in rediscussing reciprocal altruism, no conscious motive need occur. All that matters is that *in fact* recipients of altruism repay. Trivers (1971) has given the most extensive discussion of the evolution of reciprocal altruism. The present exposition follows Dawkins (1976b, pp. 197–202), but uses a more recently published example (Packer, 1977). When a male olive baboon (*Papio anubis*) is consorting with a female, it is hard for a single male to supplant him, but relatively easy for two in coalition to do so. Packer observed that pairs of unrelated males joined forces in this way. On any particular occasion, one of the two males copulates while the other, the "altruist," does not. Later, when another female comes into oestrus, the same two males are likely to get together again, but this time their roles are reversed; the former beneficiary is now the altruist. Such cooperation pays only if two males are more than twice as effective in gaining copulations as one.

There is a further problem, which applies to all reciprocal altruism. This is its vulnerability to cheating. A male that had been helped by another male and had copulated would presumably be better off not helping that other male in return. Let us do a thought experiment to see how reciprocal altruism can be evolutionarily stable. Imagine that there are some males called "suckers" who indiscriminately help other males. A population of suckers would be vulnerable to invasion by "cheats" who accept help but do not reciprocate; cheats take the benefits but do not incur the costs and so are favored over suckers by natural selection. Now imagine a third kind of behavior called "grudger." Grudgers only help others who have not yet cheated them. Thus a grudger will help suckers and other grudgers, but will only help an individual cheat once. After being cheated, the grudger remembers and does not help that cheat again. There are two evolutionarily stable kinds of population that can emerge from this model depending on the initial frequencies of the behavioral types (Dawkins, 1976b). One is a population of grudgers; the other is a population of cheats. Roughly, if the initial proportion of cheats is high, grudgers cannot invade because they are unlikely to meet a given cheat more than once; but if the grudgers start at more than a critical frequency they increase, and cheats cannot invade because grudgers mainly help each other rather than cheats. Although grudgers are not favored when rare there are a variety of nonselective processes known in theoretical population genetics (stochastic changes of gene frequency in small populations, migration, etc.) that can increase the frequency of a rare trait. And once grudgers break through the critical frequency (20% in one model, Dawkins, 1976b) they are uninvadable; they form an evolutionarily stable population.

For reciprocal altruism to evolve, the organisms must either be capable of recognizing each other individually or they must be able to discriminate in favor of other reciprocators (grudgers) in some analogous way. As an example of reciprocation without true individual recognition, consider the case of the cleaner fish (Trivers, 1971). Cleaning parasites off large fish is a way of life that has evolved independently among a number of groups of small fish and shrimps. The cleaner benefits by eating the parasites; the cleaned fish benefits by losing them, but in a sense the cleaned fish could be said to show altruism. It could easily eat the cleaner after the cleaner has finished removing all the parasites, but it refrains from doing so and even lets the cleaner escape after entering its mouth to pick its teeth. At the moment when it decides not to eat the cleaner, what has the cleaned fish to gain by its restraint? The answer is probably that it stands to be cleaned by the same individual cleaner later, when it has accumulated a further burden of parasites. This is made possible by the fact that the cleaners are site-tenacious. Each individual cleaner has a home base at a certain spot in the reef, and individual clients call back again and again to be attended by the same individual cleaner. Here, site recognition takes the place of individual recognition, but *some* kind of recognition is essential for the theory to work. If there was no statistical tendency for the same individual cleaner to attend the same individual fish repeatedly, natural selection would not favor altruistic restraint on the part of the larger fish, and a newly cleaned large fish would eat its benefactor, because by doing so it would harm its genetic rivals no less than it would harm itself.

3. Manipulating Others to Behave Altruistically towards You

A phrase commonly encountered in the literature about adaptation is that animals maximize their fitness, or their inclusive fitness. The phrase is misleading for a variety of reasons, one of which is that natural selection can cause an organism to behave not in the interests of its own inclusive fitness, but of someone else's (Dawkins, 1978; Dawkins & Krebs, 1978). It is easy to see why natural selection favors an organism that selfishly manipulates the behavior or physiology of another organism. A predator can save the energy of catching its prey by manipulating the behavior of the prey, causing it to come to the predator; thus are male fireflies lured by the false sexual flashes of *femmes fatales,* who eat them (Lloyd, 1975). Or the predator might drug its prey (Wilson, 1971, p. 413). Cuckoos manipulate the behavior of their foster-parents to obtain food, and there is a large literature on how parasites manipulate the behavior of their hosts (Holmes & Bethell, 1972). In all of these cases the manipulated animal behaves altruistically. Prey that approach predators decrease their own chances of survival while increasing that of the predators. Here one would certainly not want to think of the altruist as having altruistic intentions; but nevertheless the behavior is altruistic by our definition in terms of behavioral effects.

Manipulation can evolve because animals make decisions by rules of thumb. For example, small fish might recognize their prey as "small, wriggling and worm-shaped." Given that the fish has to use such a pattern, or cue, in the environment, there is the possibility of mimicking these patterns and therefore deceiving the fish. Some predatory angler fishes have lures that look like worms; any fish that approaches this "prey" will be eaten. Presumably there is selection on the prey fish to improve its definition of "worm" but so also is there selection on the angler fish to improve its mimicry. Here, as in all cases of manipulation, an evolutionary "arms race" exists (Dawkins & Krebs, 1979).

Most of the cases of manipulation that have been discovered so far are inter-specific, though there are possible examples of intraspecific manipulation (Daw-kins & Krebs, 1978). There are two likely reasons for this disparity. First, students of animal communication have tended to work in the paradigm that animal signals communicate *information,* which will often have blinded them from seeing examples of signals that *deceive.* Second, there may be a real difference between the case where both manipulator and manipulated are in the same gene pool and the case where they are in different gene pools; from this difference it is expected that intraspecific manipulation will be less extreme (Dawkins & Krebs, 1978; Wallace, 1973) than interspecific manipulation, though not entirely absent.

Many of Trivers' papers (1971, 1972, 1974) comment on possible psycholog-ical implications of his theories of conflict and cooperation between organisms. Take, for instance, his interesting analysis of parent-offspring conflict (1974). The argument is deduced from the theory of kin selection. A parent is related equally to all of its offspring, but any one offspring is more "related" to itself than to any of its siblings. It follows (though this is not the full argument) that there will be conflict between parent and offspring over the amount of parental care. Trivers suggests this theory as an explanation of (among other things) weaning conflict. Although the parents might be thought to be all-powerful when in conflict with their offspring, Trivers argues that the offspring psychologically manipulate their parents, so increasing the amount of parental care. For instance, at weaning time the offspring might act as if it were younger than it is.

Most previous discussion of the evolution of manipulation have been of the parental manipulation of offspring (Alexander, 1974; Ghiselin, 1974; cf. Daw-kins, 1976b, pp. 146–147; Parker & MacNair, 1978). As has been argued in the present section, the process is of much greater generality.

ADAPTATION AND ALTRUISM IN HUMANS

A striking feature of the opposition to Darwinism in the 19th century, and of the current opposition to "sociobiology," is the extend to which it concentrates on one primate species, *Homo sapiens. The Origin of Species* virtually never men-tioned this species and it occupies a fittingly small part of *Sociobiology;* yet essentially all of the more baleful criticism of both books has been inspired by an unwillingness to see *Homo sapiens* as "just an animal." Reluctant as we are to pander to such transparently wishful thinking, we have to admit that *Homo sapiens* really is a rather unique species. It has transformed the environment at a greater rate, if not to a greater extent, than the plants of the Precambrian which put the oxygen into the atmosphere, or than the corals which built reefs visible from the moon. It is a species whose main mode of evolution is now nongenetic and whose behavior it will be impossible to understand only by an evolutionary genetic approach. The evolutionary uniqueness of man is that he is uniquely inscrutable to biologists interested in adaptation.

A biologist, looking at an animal and trying to interpret the way it is in terms of Darwinian adaptation, assumes that the animal can be regarded as a machine designed to preserve copies of the genes inside it. But following a change in any species' environment (and that includes evolutionary changes in other species with which it interacts), there is an inevitable time-lag before the prior degree of adaptation is restored. All species are probably at least slightly "behind" their environment, but this must apply *a fortiori* to *Homo sapiens,* a species whose ecological and social environment changes visibly and progressively year by year. This is one reason why we must be wary of explaining modern human behavior in terms of Darwinian evolution. We come into the world designed, in body and brain, for survival on the Pleistocene plains of Africa. What that brain does today might bear some relation to the roles for which it was originally selected, but the connection is tenuous and needs to be interpreted with subtlety and care. The human brain has taken off on a nongenetic evolutionary trip, and if there are vestiges of our everyday behavior that are still simply explicable in ordinary Darwinian terms we have no right to expect this to be so as a rule. Therefore when, as frequently happens, people challenge Darwinians to "explain" the love of a woman for her adopted child, say, it is often sensible not to accept the challenge. Civilized human behavior has about as much connection with natural selection as does the behavior of a circus bear on a unicycle. And if that sounds unduly negative, it is not intended in that spirit. The analogy is rather apt. The tricks of circus animals usually turn out to be founded upon the natural behavioral repertory of the species (Breland & Breland, 1961), but we still have to be cautious about interpreting such antics in a simple Darwinian way. Similarly, there probably is a connection to be found between civilized human behavior and natural selection, but it is unlikely to be ovbious on the surface. This problem is likely to be less acute if we confine our attention to "primitive" peoples who have lived in the same cultural environment for many generations, and we shall give some examples later.

Meanwhile, there are other problems. As explained earlier, the phrase "gene for" implies a genetic influence on the differences between individuals in some specified environment. The last three words are important. Change the environment, and you may well change the expression of a gene; it may well become a gene "for" something quite different. We shall take homosexuality as an example. (Weinrich [1976] has given an extensive sociobiological treatment of homosexuality.)

There is some evidence that homosexuality in western males is heritable. Thus Kallman (1952) found that of about 40 homosexual males who had identical (monozygotic) twins, every single one of their twins was also homosexual (see also Friedmann, Green & Spitzer, 1976; Heston & Shields, 1968). Twin studies cannot provide conclusive evidence of causality (Kempthorne, 1978), but as far as it goes the evidence is suggestive. It suggests the existence of genes "for" homoxesuality in the sense in which we are using the expression. Now, homosexuality is not particularly rare, so the Darwinian seems to be faced with a puzzle. Homosexual behavior does not seem, on the face of it, an effective way of passing on genes. If, therefore, there are indeed large numbers of "homosexual genes" in human populations, why are they there?

Trivers (1974), Wilson (1975, 1978) and Weinrich (1976) have hypothesized that homosexuality in humans may be an adaptation analogous to worker sterility in social insects. Human homosexuals, it is argued, may have helped rear other relatives rather than offspring of their own, passing on the homosexual genes indirectly. There is at present no evidence for this hypothesis; but the point we are making now is that this kind of explanation may be entirely superfluous. There may be nothing to explain. Let us accept, for the sake of argument, that there are truly genes "for" homosexuality in our gene pool. The important point is that like any other genes, they will manifest a particular phenotypic expression only in certain environments. It may be, for instance, that males that are genetically predisposed to homosexuality will actually become homosexual only if brought up in a certain way, say if they are bottle-fed, or if they sleep in their own bed rather than with their parents. If, in the Pleistocene, infants never slept alone (remember this examples is just for the sake of argument), the very same "homosexual" genes might never have found expression in homosexual behavior. Indeed, the genes would not then have been genes for homosexuality at all; they might have been genes for something quite different, like hunting skill.

These cautious provisos are worth stating, because we do not want to give the impression that human sociobiology will be straightforward. Taking them as read, we now examine some of the interesting suggestions that have been made about human altruism. Kin selected altruism in humans has been discussed by a number of authors (Alexander, 1975, 1977; Campbell, 1975; Chagnon & Irons, 1979; Greene, 1978; Hamilton, 1975; Sahlins, 1976; van den Berghe & Barash, 1978; Wilson, 1975, 1978). Parental care is an uncontroversial example. The theory of kin selection is a fairly recent invention so most of its applications to humans have been reanalyses of existing data rather than new work stimulated by theoretical predictions from kin selection. It can, therefore, be anticipated that the most exciting work on human behavior and kin selection has yet to be done. Work done so far certainly demonstrates how old data can be looked at in new ways, and so new insights gained. Alexander (1977), for example, suggests that some of the differences in patterns of altruism between different cultures conform to predictions from kin selection theory. For instance, in some cultures "paternal" care is practiced by the mother's brother, not by the mother's husband. Alexander (1974, 1977) and Greene (1978) both argue that the theory of kin selection predicts that "mother's brother" altruism will be found in cultures in which the father's certainty of paternity is so low that the expected relatedness of a maternal uncle to an offspring is higher than that of the offspring's mother's husband. There is some evidence supporting this prediction.

There seems to be three ways in which patterns such as this could have evolved. First, there might be genetic differences between the peoples, their different cultural environments having set up the conditions for the selection of different genes. This is very unlikely because the cultures concerned have probably not been in separate stable existence for long enough. Second, it might be that all people in different cultures are genetically programmed to develop different appropriate behavior patterns in different environments: the genetic program is conditional. Third, humans are intelligent and work out how to behave such that they benefit their genes. Here the genes would presumably confer on people a fondness for relatives, analogous to, and as introspectively mysterious as, sexual desire. Just as humans may exercise rational intelligence in the pursuit of irrational sexual lust, so might they harness their rational intelligence in the service of nepotism.

It is indeed a striking fact about all human cultures that they are obsessed with kinship. It seems plausible to explain this general obsession as an adaptation, although the minutiae of differences between cultures reflect the cognitive working out of this obsession in manners that may or may not be what would be predicted from a naive application of the theory of kin selection.

If kin selection theory is applicable to humans, it should also predict patterns of variation in altruistic behavior within cultures. Other things being equal, it would be expected that given a choice between behaving altruistically towards one of two relatives, the one with the higher expected coefficient of relatedness would be preferred. Let us reemphasize that this does not imply that humans can calculate, and have cognitive knowledge of, expected coefficients of relatedness to all potential beneficiaries. All that matters is that the simple behavioral rules used result in altruism mainly being directed towards closer relatives. Indeed, Chagnon (1979, p. 87) "was always struck with the degree to which actual genealogical relatedness, as distinct from 'fictive' kinship, seemed to be important to the Yanamanö": The Yanamanö, a South American tribe, behave as if they understood relatedness better than they say they do. Hames (1979) has examined the association between relatedness and "interaction" within village populations, and his data, although preliminary as he admits, suggests a correlation. Furthermore, kin relatedness predicts interaction frequency better than more geographical proximity does. So closer relatives living further apart interact more than distant relatives that live closer together. This latter result is important because the predictions about humans that have been derived so far from the theory of kin selection are not all that precise or counter-intuitive: One often feels that many other models besides kin selection could predict more altruism between closer relatives.

Chagnon and Bugos (1979) have examined a more specific problem. They have reanalysed extensive data on an ax fight that occurred in a Yanamanö village in 1971. About 30 individuals were in this fight, in two opposing groups. Chagnon and Bugos (1979) had extensive genealogical information about the combatants and were able to estimate the relatedness between all pairs of individuals in the fight. They could thus estimate the mean relatedness within each of the groups and also the mean relatedness of the individuals in the different groups. The actual figures were .2 and .09 for the within-group mean relatednesses, both of which are higher than .06 which is the mean relatedness of pairs in different groups. The overall mean relatedness for all combatants was .079— higher than the between-group mean but lower than both the within-group means. The data suggest that the two fighting groups are nonrandom genetic samples from the total population of villagers, although relatedness was not the only factor determining which group each individual joined.

Turning now to reciprocal altruism, Trivers' (1971) paper contains many speculations on the human psychological implications of this theory. As we saw above, reciprocal altruism is highly vulnerable to cheating, and in humans we can envisage subtle cheats who consistently give slightly less than they receive. Trivers suggests that many human psychological characteristics such as envy, guilt and moralistic aggressiveness may result from the natural selection of individuals to perfect their subtle cheating and their resistance to cheating by others.

Third, manipulation: Of all the subjects in this essay, it may be manipulation that holds the best possibilities for useful interaction between evolutionary ethology and social psychology, albeit this kind of "altruism" lies furthest from the everyday common sense meaning of the word. Already some findings of social psychologists in this area have passed into the ethological literature (Dawkins & Krebs, 1978). Of particular interest are social psychological studies of persuasion, manifested not so much in verbally expressed attitudes as in actual behavior. Probably ethologists have more to learn from social psychologists in this area.

THE CRITICISM OF HUMAN SOCIOBIOLOGY

Ever since Darwin enunciated his ideas attempts have been made to apply them to humans. One line of notorious misapplication is that now termed social Darwinism. Social Darwinism now means the attempt to justify the human suffering that results from economic competition by arguing that natural evolution is caused by a bloody struggle for existence. By its association with social Darwinism, the idea of natural selection has been unpopular in the social sciences. More recently, Darwinism has suffered by the enthusiasm for swallowing other disciplines that has marked sociobiology's more evangelistic texts. Thus Wilson (1975) has written:

> Let us consider man in the free spirit of natural history, as though we were zoologists from another planet completing a catalog of social species on Earth. In this macroscopic view the humanities and social sciences shrink to specialized branches of biology; history, biography and fiction are the research protocols of human ethology; and anthropology and sociology together constitute the sociobiology of a single primate species [p. 547].

Although the first sentence of this quotation will nowadays offend few, the remainder of the passage can hardly be expected to win friends in the social sciences, much as we as biologists may enjoy it. Coming from another background, we ourselves did not take kindly to "ethology . . . and . . . comparative psychology . . . are destined to be cannibalized by neurophysiology and sensory physiology from one end and sociobiology and behavioral ecology from the other" (Wilson, 1975, p. 6). As for "The transition from purely phenomenological to fundamental theory in sociology must await a full, neuronal explanation of the human brain" (Wilson, 1975, p. 575), you could write "ethology" for "sociology" and "seagull" for "human," and it would still seem hopelessly unrealistic, the doomed pipedream of "the neurophysiologist's nirvana" (Dawkins, 1976a; see also Nelson, 1973).

It would be a shame if such talk of cannibalism, such brash overestimation of the explanatory power of evolutionary biology, were to blind social scientists to the importance of Darwinism for their subject. Enough damage has already been done by the social Darwinists; let us not compound this by being too tactless and bold in our enthusiasm for the new Darwinism. Human sociobiology is not social Darwinism all over again, and social scientists cannot shrug it off as a new incarnation of a long-discredited geneticism with fascistic learnings. The following is a notorious and ill-mannered attempt to link human sociobiology with the worst excesses of social Darwinism (the quotation is from a letter to *New York Review of Books,* November 13, 1975, signed by 16 authors):

> John D. Rockefeller, Sr. said 'The growth of a large business is merely a survival of the fittest . . . It is merely the working out of a law of nature and a law of God.' These theories provided an important basis for the enactment of sterilization laws and restrictive immigration laws by the United States between 1910 and 1930 and also for the eugenics policies which led to the establishment of gas chambers in Nazi Germany. . . . The latest attempt to reinvigorate these tired theories comes with the alleged creation of a new discipline, sociobiology.

In fact, the prescriptions of illiberal political action by Rockefeller and the social Darwinists have no support from modern sociobiologists. Modern Darwinian ethologists or sociobiologists are usually at pains to emphasize the distinction between what is and what ought to be, and they may even argue that a full understanding of Darwinian selection is a good basis for a political fight against its action in our own species (Dawkins, 1976b; Hamilton, 1971). Thus, if biologists come up with an evolutionary explanation of, say, female exploitation by males or vice versa (Trivers, 1972), it does *not* mean they approve of the exploitation. On the contrary, as Trivers (1976) has written, "Darwinian social theory . . . should . . . give us a deeper understanding of the many roots of our suffering."

Lewontin (1970) correctly wrote that " . . . insufficient attention has been given by social scientists to the findings of geneticists [p. 4–5]." Ruse (1979) justly proposes that "Human sociobiology should be given the chance to prove its worth. If it cannot deliver on its promises, it will collapse soon enough [p. 214]." We applaud Campbell's (1975) suggestion that "psychologists interested in 'human nature' pay attention, however skeptically, to this rich source of hypotheses [pp. 1110–1111]." It is in this spirit that we conclude our exposition of the natural selection of altruism.

REFERENCES

Alexander, R. D. The evolution of social behavior. *Annual Review of Ecology and Systematics,* 1974, *5,* 325–382.

Alexander, R. D. The search for a general theory of behavior. *Behavioral Science,* 1975, *20,* 77–100.

Alexander, R. D. Natural selection and the analysis of human sociality. In C. E. Goulden (Ed.), *Changing scenes in the natural sciences.* Philadelphia: Academy of Natural Sciences, 1977.

Aoki, S. *Colophina clematis* (Homoptera; Pemphigidae), an aphid species with 'soldiers.' *Kontyu,* 1977, *45,* 276–282.

Barlow, G. W., & Silverberg, J. (Eds.), *Sociobiology—beyond nature/nurture.* Boulder, Colorado: Westview Press, 1980.

Bertram, B. C. R. Kin selection in lions and in evoltuion. In P. P. G. Bateson & R. A. Hinde (Eds.), *Growing points in ethology.* Cambridge, Eng.: Cambridge University Press, 1976.

Bethell, T. Burning Darwin to save Marx. *Harper's,* December 1978, *257,* 31–38, 91–92.

Blurton Jones, N. G. Growing points in human ethology: Another link between ethology and the social sciences? In P. P. G. Bateson & R. A. Hinde (Eds.), *Growing points in ethology.* Cambridge, Eng.: Cambridge University Press, 1976.

Breland, K., & Breland, M. The misbehavior of animals. *American Psychologist,* 1961, *16,* 681–684.

Brown, J. L. *The evolution of behavior.* New York: Norton, 1975.

Brown, J. L. Avian communal breeding system. *Annual Review of Ecology and Systematics,* 1978, *9,* 123–155.

Campbell, D. T. On the conflicts between biological and social evolution and between psychology and moral tradition. *American Psychologist,* 1975, *30,* 1103–1126.

Caplan, A. *The sociobiology debate.* New York: Harper & Row, 1978.

Chagnon, N. A. Mate competition, favoring close kin, and village fissioning among the Yanomanö Indians. In N. A. Chagnon & W. Irons (Eds.), *Evolutionary biology and human social behavior.* North Scituate, Mass.: Duxbury Press, 1979.

Chagnon, N. A., & Bugos, P. E. Kin selection and conflict: An analysis of a Yanomanö ax fight. In

N. A. Chagnon & W. Irons (Eds.), *Evolutionary biology and human social behavior*. North Scituate, Mass.: Duxbury Press, 1979.

Chagnon, N. A., & Irons, W. *Evolutionary biology and human social behavior: An anthropological perspective*. North Scituate, Mass.: Duxbury Press, 1979.

Darwin, C. R. *On the origin of species*. London: John Murray, 1859.

Darwin, C. R. *The descent of man*. London: John Murray, 1871.

Darwin, C. R. *The expression of the emotions in man and animals*. London: John Murray, 1872.

Dawkins, R. Hierarchical organization: A candidate principle for ethology. In P. P. G. Bateson & R. A. Hinde (Eds.), *Growing points in ethology*. Cambridge, Eng.: Cambridge University Press, 1976.

Dawkins, R. *The selfish gene*. Oxford: Oxford University Press, 1976 (b).

Dawkins, R. Replicator selection and the extended phenotype. *Zeitschrift für Tierpsychologie*, 1978, *47*, 61–76.

Dawkins, R. Twelve misunderstandings of natural selection. *Zeitschrift für Tierpsychologie*, 1979, *51*, 184–200.

Dawkins, R. Good strategy or evolutionarily stable strategy? In G. W. Barlow & J. Silverberg (Eds.), *Sociobiology—beyond Nature/nurture*. Boulder, Colorado: Westview Press, 1980.

Dawkins, R., & Krebs, J. R. Animal signals: Information or manipulation? In J. R. Krebs & N. B. Davies (Eds.), *Behavioural ecology*. Oxford: Blackwell, 1978.

Dawkins, R., & Krebs, J. R. Arms races between and within species. *Proceedings of the Royal Society of London, B*, 1979, *205*, 489–511.

Emlen, S. T. The evolution of cooperative breeding in birds. In J. R. Krebs & N. B. Davies (Eds.), *Behavioural ecology*. Oxford: Blackwell, 1978.

Fisher, R. A. *The genetical theory of natural selection*. Oxford: Clarendon Press, 1930.

Friedmann, R. C., Green, R., & Spitzer, R. L. Reassessment of homosexuality and transsexualism. *Annual Review of Medicine*, 1976, *27*, 57–62.

Ghiselin, M. T. *The triumph of the Darwinian method*. Berkeley: University of California Press, 1969.

Ghiselin, M. T. *The economy of nature and the evolution of sex*. Berkeley: University of California Press, 1974.

Greene, P. J. Promiscuity, paternity and culture. *American Ethnologist*, 1978, *5*, 151–159.

Griffin, D. R. *The question of animal awareness*. New York: Rockefeller University Press, 1976.

Haldane, J. B. S. *The causes of evolution*. London: Longmans Green, 1932. (Reprinted in paperback: Ithaca, N.Y.: Cornell University Press, 1966.)

Haldane, J. B. S. Population genetics. *New Biology*, 1955, *18*, 34–51.

Hames, R. B. Relatedness and interaction among the Ye'kwana: A preliminary analysis. In N. A. Chagnon & W. Irons (Eds.), *Evolutionary biology and human social behavior*. North Scituate, Mass.: Duxbury Press, 1979.

Hamilton, W. D. The genetical evolution of social behaviour. *Journal of Theoretical Biology*, 1964, *7*, 1–52.

Hamilton, W. D. Selfish and spiteful behaviour in an evolutionary model. *Nature*, 1970, *228*, 1218–1220.

Hamilton, W. D. Selection of selfish and altruistic behavior in some extreme models. In J. F. Eisenberg & W. S. Dillon (Eds.), *Man and beast: Comparative social behavior*. Washington, D.C.: Smithsonian Institution Press, 1971.

Hamilton, W. D. Altruism and related phenomena, mainly in social insects. *Annual Review of Ecology and Systematics*, 1972, *3*, 193–232.

Hamilton, W. D. Innate social aptitudes in man: An approach from evolutionary genetics. In R. Fox (Ed.), *Biosocial anthropology*. London: Malaby Press, 1975.

Hamilton, W. D. Wingless and fighting males in fig wasps and other insects. In M. S. Blum & N. A. Blum (Eds.), *Reproductive competition and sexual selection in insects*. New York: Academic Press, 1979.

Heston, L. L., & Shields, J. Homosexuality in twins. *Archives of General Psychiatry*, 1968, *18*, 149–160.

Holmes, J. C., & Bethell, M. W. Modification of intermediate host behaviour by parasites. In E. V. Canning & C. A. Wright (Eds.), *Behavioural aspects of parasite transmission*. London: Academic Press, 1972.

Hrdy, S. B. Care and exploitation of nonhuman primate infants by conspecifics other than the mother. *Advances in the Study of Behavior*, 1976, *6*, 101–158.

Hrdy, S. B. *The Langurs of Abu*. Cambridge, Mass.: Harvard University Press, 1977.

Kallman, F. J. Twin and sibship studies of overt male homosexuality. *American Journal of Human Genetics*, 1952, *4*, 136–146.

Kempthorne, O. Logical, epistemological and statistical aspects of nature-nature data interpretation. *Biometrics*, 1978, *34*, 1–23.

Kurland, J. A. Kin selection in the Japanese monkey. *Contributions to Primatology*, 1977, *12*.

Lewontin, R. C. Race and intelligence. *Bulletin of the Atomic Scientists*, 1970, *26* (March), 2–8.

Lloyd, J. E. Aggressive mimicry in Photuris fireflies: Signal repertoires by femmes fatales. *Science*, 1975, *187*, 452–453.

MacRoberts, M. H., & MacRoberts, B. R. Social organization and behavior of the acorn woodpecker in central coastal California. *Ornithological Monographs*, 1976, *21*, 1–115.

Maynard Smith, J. Group selection and kin selection. *Nature*, 1964, *201*, 1145–1147.

Maynard Smith, J. Group selection. *Quarterly Review of Biology*, 1976, *51*, 277–283.

Nelson, K. Does the holistic study of behavior have a future? In P. P. G. Bateson & P. H. Klopfer (Eds.), *Perspectives in ethology*. New York: Plenum, 1973.

Packer, C. Reciprocal altruism in *Papio anubis*. *Nature*, 1977, *265*, 441–443.

Parker, G. A., & MacNair, M. R. Models of parent-offspring conflict. I. Monogamy. *Animal Behaviour*, 1978, *26*, 97–110.

Ruse, M. *Sociobiology: Sense or nonsense?* Dordrecht, Holland: D. Reidel, 1979.

Sahlins, M. *The use and abuse of biology*. Ann Arbor: University of Michigan, 1976.

Seger, J. Evolution of responses to relative homozygosity. *Nature*, 1976, *262*, 578–580.

Trivers, R. L. The evolution of reciprocal altruism. *Quarterly Review of Biology*, 1971, *46*, 35–57.

Trivers, R. L. Parental investment and sexual selection. In B. Campbell (Ed.), *Sexual selection and the descent of man*. Chicago: Aldine, 1972.

Trivers, R. L. Parent-offspring conflict. *American Zoologist*, 1974, *14*, 249–264.

Trivers, R. L. Foreward to R. Dawkins, *The selfish gene*. Oxford: Oxford University Press, 1976.

Trivers, R. L., & Hare, H. Haplodiploidy and the evolution of social insects. *Science*, 1976, *191*, 249–263.

van den Berghe, P. L., & Barash, D. P. Inclusive fitness and human family structure. *Current Anthropology*, 1977, *79*, 809–823.

Wallace, B. Misinformation, fitness and selection. *American Naturalist*, 1973, *107*, 1–7.

Weinrich, J. D. *Human reproductive strategy: The importance of income unpredictability, and the evolution of non-reproduction*. Ph.D. Dissertation, Harvard University, 1976.

Williams, G. C. *Adaptation and natural selection*. Princeton, N.J.: Princeton University Press, 1966.

Williams, G. C. *Sex and evolution*. Princeton, N.J.: Princeton University Press, 1975.

Wilson, E. O. *The insect societies*. Cambridge, Mass.: Harvard University Press, 1971.

Wilson, E. O. *Sociobiology: The new synthesis*. Cambridge, Mass.: Harvard University Press, 1975.

Wilson, E. O. *On human nature*. Cambridge, Mass.: Harvard University Press, 1978.

Woolfenden, G. E. Florida scrub jay helpers at the nest. *Auk*, 1975, *92*, 1–15.

Wynne-Edwards, V. C. *Animal dispersion in relation to social behaviour*. Edinburgh: Oliver & Boyd, 1962.

3 The Development of Empathy

Martin L. Hoffman
University of Michigan

Although interest in altruism has burgeoned in recent years, the developmental aspect has received little attention. One reason may be that most of the research has a social-learning orientation which seems to imply that the learning process, whether based on conditioning, reward, or exposure to the words or deeds of models, is the same regardless of age. I have for several years been working on a developmental theory of an altruistic motive, empathy, that may not be dependent on learning in the usual sense of the term (Hoffman, 1963, 1970, 1975, 1977b). What I will do here is first argue briefly for the plausibility of an altruistic motive that is independent of egoistic motives and then present the current version of the theory.

The doctrinaire view in psychology has long been that altruism can ultimately be explained in terms of egoistic, self-serving motives. Empirical evidence for this view has not been advanced, perhaps because the conception of egoistic humans seems so obvious that evidence is unnecessary. Then, too, it is always possible, when viewing an example of human action that appears to be motivated by an interest in the welfare of others, to adduce a hidden, unconscious, or tacit self-regarding motive (e.g., social approval, self-esteem) as constituting the *real* source of such behavior. This inference is plausible and it fits so well with our Western conception of man that it is easy to forget that it is just an ad hoc hypothesis, not evidence, and the burden of proof rests as much on an egoistic interpretation as on an interpretation that humans are by nature altruistic.

The issues are complex and clear-cut evidence is lacking, but several convergent lines of evidence—biological and behavioral—which I have pulled together elsewhere seem to suggest that it is as reasonable to assume that humans have an independent motive to help others, as it is to postulate an egoistic motive base for

41

all helping behavior. For lack of space, I will only briefly summarize the argument. See Hoffman (1981) for a detailed treatment, including references.

Behavioral Evidence

The behavioral evidence for an independent altruistic motive, necessarily circumstantial, is as follows: First, it is clear from the research that most people of all ages try to help others in distress, particularly when no other witness is present. Second, though their motive for helping might theoretically be egoistic, if this were true we would expect people to be less likely rather than more likely to help when there are no other witnesses. Furthermore, if people helped, say, for social approval, we would expect a positive correlation between arousal of approval needs and helping. What is found is the opposite: People are *less* likely to help when approval needs are aroused, and more likely to help when approval needs are fulfilled. The available evidence suggests, then, that social approval may not be the usual motive for helping.

Third, though altruistic action is often preceded by a time consuming process of decision-making (e.g., in donating a kidney), there are times when a speedy response is necessary. Evidence for a speedy altruistic response can be found in the few studies of bystander reactions in emergencies in which data on speed of helping were obtained. For example, in several experiments in which a person appears to have an epileptic fit, or falls and cries out in pain, over 90% of the subjects rushed to help the victim; and the average reaction time was 5–10 seconds. It is hard to tell how fast this is without a proper standard of comparison. I searched, and I think I found a good one. In the Botswana society in Africa an infant's crying is treated as an emergency to be responded to as quickly as possible. Konner, Devore, and Konner (1974) reported that the average reaction time for the mother to get to a crying baby is 6 seconds. This suggests that the 5-10 seconds latency in the innocent-bystander research is indeed short. These findings, then, suggest that even in an indivudalistic society like ours, distress cues from a total stranger can sometimes have an immediate, compelling quality. I find it hard to believe that this can be explained entirely by culture or socialization. I think it is more compatible with the view that there may be a powerful action tendency or motive in humans that is triggered by appropriate stimuli. (The evidence that empathy may be the basis for this motive will be presented later.)

The Biology of Altruism

According to the prevailing concept in evolutionary biology, inclusive fitness (Hamilton, 1964, 1971), an individual's genetic fitness is measured not only by his and his offspring's genetic fitness but also by the enhancement of the fitness of other relatives who share his genes. Thus natural selection favored genetic tendencies to perform altruistic acts if the recipients were closely enough related for a net increase in the actor's genes to result. An important extension of the concept was made by Eberhard (1975) who showed mathematically that the degree of relatedness need only be above average for the population and, fur- thermore, that the probability of altruism is increased if the beneficiary stands to gain a great deal (e.g., in emergencies), if the cost is low (e.g., if the altruist is excluded from reproducing on his own or controls an abundant resource), if the donor is efficient at giving aid, or the beneficiary efficent at using it. Altruism toward quite distant relatives is thus encompassed by inclusive fitness. If we add to this the concept of reciprocal altruism (Trivers, 1971), which states that natural selection favored altruism to totally unrelated members of one's group, because such altruism will be paid back in the future and thus contribute to the propagation of one's own genes, then clearly a good case for a biological basis for altruism in humans can be made.

The case may appear limited since the donor's genes ultimately benefit. But if we think of the donor as a total organism, not just a carrier of genes, then the physical or psychological cost of the act to the donor may clearly mark it as altruistic. The problem may thus be a confusion of conceptual levels of analysis, due in part to a narrow view of inclusive fitness. Though inclusive fitness implies that natural selection occurs at the level of genes and that genes are therefore "selfish," it does not imply that gene propagation is the prime mover in evolu- tion and that changes in the total organism are merely the consequences. As noted by Gould (1977), ". . . Selection simply cannot see genes and pick among them directly . . . Selection view bodies. It favors some because they are stronger, better insulated, etc. [p. 24]." Furthermore, because there are no particular genes for particular body parts, selection cannot operate directly on genes through body parts coordinated to them. It is the total organism that confronts the persistent ecological pressures and is directly involved in the strug- gle for existence. Organisms that adapt well are likely to survive, mate, pass their genes to offspring and thus create new individuals carrying the physical charac- teristics and underlying gene formations that made survival possible. Organisms that adapt poorly are less likely to survive and reproduce, and the maladaptive characteristics and gene formation eventually disappear. In short, it is in the process of *organisms* changing and adapting to persistent ecological pressures that structures, *genotypes as well as phenotypes,* are selected and maintained to become part of the biological inheritance of the species. It follows that if survival required altruism as well as egoism, as inclusive fitness suggests, then a be- havioral disposition toward altruism must have been built into the evolving human organism.

What might this mechanism be? Natural selection requires a mechanism that is reliable yet also flexible. One possibility is a mechanism for internalizing social norms. Given the ancient interdependence of people, such a mechanism probably did evolve, and it would have the advantage of letting local circum- stances dictate which norms are chosen by groups to inculcate into members. But because local circumstances, hence social norms, very enormously, a mechanism for internalizing norms would probably not be reliable enough to assure the level of altruism required by inclusive fitness. At the other extreme, an automatic helping response (fixed action pattern) is not tenable because it would not allow the flexibility needed for survival. Furthermore, as survival requires the ability to respond either egoistically or altruistically, depending on circumstances, inclusive fitness also dictates the presence of mechanisms for distinguishing when one or the other is appropriate. For example, it must be possible for some kind of assessment to be made wherein the degree of kinship and the benefits versus the costs of helping are considered. What therefore must have been acquired through natural selection is a predisposition or motive to help, which, though biologically based, is nevertheless amendable to control by perceptual or cognitive processes. Thus it was not altruistic action but *mediators* of altruistic action that were selected because this provided the necessary flexibility and enabled the most effective (in terms of inclusive fitness) determination of whether or not an altruistic act should occur.

These evolutionary requirements appear to be fulfilled by empathy, defined as a vicarious affective response to others, that is, an affective response appropriate to someone else's situation rather than one's own. Thus there is considerable evidence that people of all ages, even 12-month-old infants, respond empathically to another person in distress whether physiological arousal, facial expression, or verbal report is used as the index of empathic arousal (see review by Hoffman, 1977b; also Main, Weston, & Wakeling, 1972.) There is also evidence that empathy may be largely involuntary, so long as one pays attention to the victim. The research indicates, for example, that it is hard for people to avoid empathizing with someone in pain or distress unless they engage in certain perceptual or cognitive strategies such as looking away from the victim or trying hard to think about other things. And, finally, there may be reason to believe that a neural basis has existed, since the early days of human evolution, for empathic affect arousal as well as the necessary cognitive intervention between arousal and action (e.g., MacLean, 1973).

DEVELOPMENT OF EMPATHIC AND SYMPATHETIC DISTRESS

In this theoretical model empathy has affective, cognitive, and motivational components. The focus is on empathic distress, which is pertinent to altruistic motivation, although the model may also bear on other empathically aroused affects.

Modes of Empathic Arousal

There are at least six distinct modes of empathic arousal. They vary in degree of perceptual and cognitive involvement, type of eliciting stimulus (e.g., facial, situational, symbolic), and amount and kind of past experience required. They are presented here roughly in order of their appearance developmentally.

1. Reactive Newborn Cry.   It has long been known that infants cry to the sound of someone else's cry. The first controlled study of this reactive cry was done by Simner (1971), who found it in 2- and 3-day-olds. He also established that the cry was not simply a response to a noxious physical stimulus, as the infants did not cry as much to equally loud and intense nonhuman sounds. There thus appears to be something especially unpleasant about the sound of the human cry. Simner's findings have been replicated in 1-day-olds by Sagi and Hoffman (1976) who report in addition that the subject's cry is not a simple imitative vocal response lacking an affective component. Rather, it is vigorous, intense, and indistinguishable from the spontaneous cry of an infant who is in actual distress. No one yet knows the reason for this reactive cry—whether it is innate, learned, or a primary circular reaction resulting from the infant's confusion between the sound of his own and someone else's cry. Regardless of the explanation, the fact remains that infants respond to a cue of distress in others by experiencing distress themselves. This reactive cry must therefore be considered as a possible early precursor of empathy, thought not a full empathic response because it lacks any awareness of what is happening. Furthermore, the co-occurence of another's cry and distress in the self may lead to an association between distress cues from others and distress in the self. This leads to the next mode of empathic arousal.

2. Classical Conditioning.   The second mode, which requires some perceptual discrimination capability and therefore appears a bit later than the reactive new born cry, is a type of direct classical conditioning of empathy that results from the experience of observing the distress of another person at the same time that one is having a direct experience of distress. The result is that distress cues from others become conditioned stimuli that evoke feelings of distress in the self. Aronfreed and Paskal (1965) created the necessary co-occurrence of distress in the child and distress cues from someone else by subjecting the child to an aversive sound at the same time that the experimenter (who presumably heard an even more aversive sound, through earphones), showed a pained expression. This may seem like a contrived way to achieve the needed co-occurrence between distress in self and distress cue from another but the co-occurrence also happens in real life, as just noted, in connection with the newborn's reactive cry. Another example, which also occurs in infancy, involves the bodily transfer of the caretaker's affective state to the infant through physical handling. For example, if the mother feels anxious or tense, her body may stiffen and the child may also experience distress. Subsequently, the mother's facial and verbal expressions that accompanied her distress can serve as conditioned stimuli that evoke distress in the child even in the absence of physical contact. Furthermore, through stimulus generalization, similar expressions by other persons may evoke distress feelings in the child. This mechanism may explain the behaviors fitting Sullivan's (1940) definition of empathy as a form of ''nonverbal contagion and communion'' between mother and infant.

3. Direct Association. The third mode was described some time ago by Humphrey (1922). When we observe someone experiencing an emotion, his facial expression, his voice, posture, or any other cue in the situation that reminds us of past situations in which we experienced that emotion, may evoke a similar emotion in us. The usual example cited is the boy who sees another child cut himself and cry. The sight of the blood, the sound of the cry, or any cue from the victim or the situation that reminds the boy of his own past experiences of pain may evoke an empathic distress response. This mode does not require the co-occurence of distress in self and distress cues from others. The only requirement is that the observer have *past* experiences of pain or discomfort. The feelings of distress that accompanied those past experiences are then evoked by distress cues from the victim that call up any of them. It is thus a far more general associative mechanism than conditioning, one which may provide the basis for a variety of distress experiences with which children and adults as well, may empathize.

4. Mimicry. A fourth mode of empathic arousal was described over 70 years ago by Lipps (1906). For Lipps, empathy is an innate, isomorphic response to another person's expression of emotion. There are two steps: The observer automatically imitates the other with slight movements in facial expression and posture ("mother mimicry"). This then creates inner kinesthetic cues in the observer that contribute (through afferent feedback) to the observer's understanding and feeling the same emotion. This conception of empathy has been neglected in the literature probably because it seemed too much like an instinctive explanation. There is some recent research (reviewed by Hoffman, 1977b), however, suggesting its plausibility.

5. Symbolic Association. The fifth mode, like the third, is based on the association between the victim's distress cues and the observer's past distress. In this case, though, the victim's distress cues evoke empathic distress not because of their physical or expressive properties but because they symbolically indicate the victim's feelings. For example, one can respond empathically to someone when reading a letter from him, or hearing someone else describe what happened to him. This is obviously a relatively advanced mode of arousal as it requires language. It is still largely involuntary, however, and the language serves mainly as a mediator between the victim's distress and the observer's empathic response. Once the observer comprehends the victim's situation he can be expected to respond empathically.

6. Role-taking. The previous modes are largely involuntary and minimally cognitive, requiring only enough perceptual and cognitive discrimination ability to detect the relevant cues from the model (e.g., mimicry) or the model's situation (e.g., association). In the sixth mode, which is clearly the most advanced developmentally, the person imagines how he or she would feel if in the other's place. The pertinent research has been done mainly by Stotland and his associates. In the most relevant study (Stotland, 1969), one group of subjects were instructed to imagine how they would feel and what sensations they would have in their hands if exposed to the same painful heat treatment that was being applied to another person. These subjects gave more evidence of empathic distress both physiologically and verbally, than (a) subjects instructed to attend closely to the other person's physical movements and (b) subjects instructed to imagine how the other person felt when he or she was undergoing the treatment. The first finding indicates simply that imagining oneself in the other's place is more empathy arousing than observing another's movements. The second finding, however, suggests that empathic affect is most likely to be generated when the focus of attention is not on the model's feeling but on the model's situation and on how the self would feel in that situation. That is, we imagine how we would feel if the stimuli impinging on the model were impinging on the self. Cognitively, the process resembles that in which we imagine how we would feel in a hypothetical situation having nothing to do with another person. The difference of course is that when we know that we are responding to what is happening to someone else, rather than what might happen to us, we experience some of what the other person is feeling.

Why should focusing on the stimuli impinging on the model evoke affect in the observer? An obvious answer is that associative connections may be made between these stimuli and similar stimulus events in the observer's own past. That is, imagining oneself in the other's place may produce an empathic response because it has the power to evoke associations with real events in one's own past in which one actually experienced the affect in question. Thus, the process may have much in common with the associative modes discussed earlier. The important difference is that in this case the evoking stimulus is the mental representation of oneself in the other's situation. That is, the arousal is triggered by a cognitive restructuring of events (what is happening to the other is viewed as happening to the self) and is thus more subject to conscious control.

These six modes of empathic arousal do not form a stage sequence in the sense of each one encompassing and replacing the preceding. The first mode typically drops out after infancy, owing to controls against crying, although even adults feel sad on hearing a cry and sometimes feel like crying themselves. The last mode, being deliberate, is probably infrequent—used at times, for example, mainly by some parents and therapists. The intermediate four modes, however, enter in at different points in development and may continue to operate through the life span. Which modes operate at a particular time depends on the cues in the situation. For example, the predominant mode may be mimicry when expressive cues from the victim are salient, and conditioning or association when situational cues are salient.

It is important to note that since both expressive and situational cues are often present (and the arousal modes are largely involuntary) empathy may well be an overdetermined response. It may also be self-reinforcing because every time it occurs the connection between distress in self and distress cues from others is strengthened. This may explain why empathy is so prevalent in humans.

Cognitive Transformation of Empathy

Though empathy may usually be aroused by the predominantly simple, involuntary mechanisms just described, the subjective experience of empathy is rather complex. The literature on empathy often stops with the idea that the observer feels vicariously what the model feels through direct experience. This is the essential feature of empathy, to be sure, but a mature adult who observes another person in pain, for example, may also feel sympathy for the victim and a desire to reduce the victim's distress. More importantly for present purposes, the experience of empathy also has a significant cognitive component, at least in older children and adults. Thus, regardless of the arousal mechanism, the mature empathizer knows that this arousal is due to a stimulus event that is impinging on someone else and he has some idea of what the other person is feeling. Young children who lack the distinction between self and other may be empathically aroused without these cognitions. In other words, how people experience empathy depends on the level at which they cognize others. This suggests that the development of empathic distress must correspond at least partly to the development of a cognitive sense of the other, which undergoes dramatic changes developmentally and thus provides a conceptual basis for a developmental scheme for empathy.

Though extensive work has been done on role-taking, there is as yet no formal literature on a broader, life-span conception of a cognitive sense of the other. I have pieced together four stages pertinent to such a conception, with an approximate time-table, from several different bodies of research (Hoffman, 1975). Briefly, (1) for most of the first year children appear to experience a fusion of self and other. (2) By about 12 months, they attain "person permanence" and become aware of others as physical entities distinct from the self. (3) By 2 or 3 years, they acquire a rudimentary sense of others as having inner states (thoughts, perceptions, feelings) independent of their own, although they cannot yet discern the other's inner states. This is the initial step in role-taking. Later they become able to discern what the other's inner states are, progressing from simple to complex states. (4) By late childhood or early adolescence, they become aware of others as having personal identities and life experiences beyond the immediate situation.

Empathy may thus be viewed as having an affective component that is experienced differently as the child progresses through these four social-cognitive stages. I will now describe four hypothetical levels of empathic distress that may result from this coalescence of empathic affect and the cognitive sense of the other, as exemplified by empathizing with another person in distress.

1. Global Empathy. For most of the first year, before the child has acquired "person permanence," distress cues from others may elicit a global empathic distress response—a fusion of unpleasant feelings and of stimuli that come from the infant's own body, from the dimly perceived "other," and from the situation. Because infants cannot yet differentiate themselves from the other, they must often be unclear as to who is experiencing any distress that they witness, and they may at times behave as though what is happening to the other is happening to them. For example, a colleague's 11-month-old daughter who saw another child fall and cry responded as follows: She first stared at the victim, looking as though she were about to cry herself, and then put her thumb in her mouth and buried her head in her mother's lap, which is what she does when she hurts herself. Kaplan (1977) reports a very similar response in a 9-month-old girl.

The transition to the second level begins as the child approaches person permanence. At first, children are probably only vaguely and momentarily aware of the other person as distinct from the self; and the mental image of the other, being transitory, may often slip in and out of focus. Consequently, children at this intermediate stage probably react to another's distress as though the dimly perceived self and the dimly perceived other were somehow simultaneously, or alternately, in distress. This is a difficult concept to grasp, and examples may help. One child I know, whose typical response to his own distress, and to distress in others, beginning late in the first year, was to suck his thumb with one hand and pull his ear with the other—an example of level "1" functioning. Something new happened at 12 months. On seeing a sad look on his father's face, he proceeded to look sad and suck his thumb, while pulling on his father's ear—as though he was just beginning to recognize the difference between self-in-distress and other-in-distress but the distinction was not yet clear. In a similar example, Zahn-Waxler, Radke-Yarrow, and King (1979) describe a child whose first positive overture to someone in distress, at 12 months, involved alternating between gently touching the victim and gently touching himself.

2. "Egocentric" Empathy. The second level is clearly established when the child is fully aware of the self and other as distinct physical entities, and thus able for the first time to experience empathic distress while also being aware that another person, and not the self, is the victim. The child cannot yet fully distinguish between his own and the other person's inner states, however, and is apt to confuse them with his own, as illustrated by his efforts to help others, which consist chiefly of giving the other person what he himself finds most comforting. Examples are a 13-month-old who responded with a distressed look to an adult who looked sad and then offered the adult his beloved doll; and another who ran to fetch his own mother to comfort a crying friend, even though the friend's mother was equally available. In labeling this empathic level, I used quotations because the term "egocentric" is not entirely accurate. Although the child's attempts to help indicate a confusion between what comforts him and what comforts the other, these same acts, nevertheless, together with his facial responses, indicate that he is also responding with appropriate empathic affect.

3. Empathy for Another's Feelings.   With the beginning of a role-taking capability, at about 2 or 3 years, the child becomes aware that other people's feelings may sometimes differ from his and their perspectives are based on their own needs and interpretation of events. More important, because the child now knows that the real world and his perception of it are not the same, and that the feelings of others are independent of his, he becomes more responsive to cues about what the other is feeling. By 3 years, even in artificial laboratory situations, children can recognize and respond empathically to happiness or sadness in others in simple situations (e.g., Borke, 1971). And, with the development of language, which enables children for the first time to derive meaning from symbolic cues of affect, not just its facial and other physical expressions, they can begin to empathize with a wide range of feelings including for example not only the victim's need for help but also his pride and desire *not* to be helped at times. And, finally, children can eventually be aroused empathically by information pertinent to someone's feelings even in that person's absence. This leads to the fourt empathic level.

4. Empathy for Another's General Plight.   By late childhood, owing to the emerging conception of self and other as continuous persons with separate histories and identities, one becomes aware that others have feelings beyond the immediate situation. Consequently, though one may continue to be empathically aroused by another's immediate distress, one's empathic concern is intensified when one knows that the other's distress is not transitory but chronic. This fourth level, then, consists of empathically aroused affect combined with an image of another's general plight (typical level of distress or deprivation, opportunities available or denied, future prospects, etc.). If this image contradicts the immediate expressive or situational cues, these cues may lose their force for the observer who knows they are only transitory. Consider a laughing, playing child who does not know that he has a terminal illness. A mature observer who does know may respond more with sadness than joy, whereas a more youthful observer will do the reverse. In other words, if the image of the other falls short of the observer's standard of well being, an empathic distress response may result even if contradicted by the other's apparent momentary state, that is, the image may override contradictory situational cues. (A certain amount of distancing is implied here, as one responds to a mental image rather than the immediate stimulus presented by the other.)

To summarize, empathy is the coalescence of vicariously aroused affect and a mental representation of the other, at whatever level the observer is capable. Individuals who progress through the four stages become capable of a high level of empathic distress. They can process various types of information—that gained from their own vicarious affective reaction, from the immediate situational cues, and from their general knowledge about the other's life. They can act out in their minds the emotions and experiences suggested by this information, and introspect on all of this. They may thus gain an understanding, and respond affectively, in terms of the circumstances, feelings, and wishes of the other, while maintaining the sense that this is a separate person from themselves.

As an extension of the fourth level, children can eventually be empathically aroused by the plight of an entire group or class of people (e.g., poor, oppressed, outcast, retarded). Because of different backgrounds, one's specific distress experience may differ from theirs. All distress experiences probably have a common affective core, however, and this together with the individual's high cognitive level allows for a generalized empathic distress capability. The combination of empathic affect and the perceived plight of an unfortunate group may be the developmentally most advanced form of empathic distress. It may also provide a motive base, especially in adolescence, for the development of certain social and political ideologies centered around alleviation of the plight of unfortunate groups (Hoffman, 1980).

Sympathetic Distress.   Thus far, I have suggested that empathic distress includes both an affective component and a cognitive component that is derived from the observer's cognitive sense of the other. Many affect theorists, notably Schachter and Singer (1962) and Mandler (1975), suggest that how a person labels or experiences an affect is heavily influenced by certain pertinent cognitions. ("One labels, interprets, and identifies this stirred-up state in terms of the characteristics of the situation and one's apperceptive mass . . .," Schachter & Singer, 1962, p. 380). These writers are explaining how we distinguish among different affects (e.g., anger, joy, fear) aroused *directly*. Quite apart from this issue (Other writers argue that the differentiation of affects has a neural rather than a cognitive basis), the cognitive sense of others appears to be so intrinsic to *empathically* aroused affect as to alter the very quality of the observer's affective experience. More specifically, once people are aware of the other as distinct from the self, their own empathic distress, which is a parallel response—a more or less exact replication of the victim's actual feelings of distress—may be transformed at least in part into a more reciprocal feeling of concern for the victim. That is, they continue to respond in a purely empathic, quasiegoistic manner—to feel uncomfortable and highly distressed themselves—but they also experience a feeling of compassion or what I call sympathetic distress for the victim, along with a conscious desire to help because they feel sorry for him or her and not just to relieve their own empathic distress. In short, I am suggesting that the affective and cognitive components of empathy combine to produce a qualitatively different feeling in the observer. The developmental process involved may be the one pertaining to the co-occurrence of distress in the emerging "self" and the emerging "other," discussed earlier.

This transformation hypothesis is difficult to test. As yet the evidence is circumstantial: as already noted, (1) children seem to progress developmentally from responding to someone's distress first by seeking comfort for the self, and later by trying to help the victim and not the self; and (2) there appears to be an in-between stage, in which they feel sad and comfort both the victim and the self, which occurs at about the same time that they gain person permanence. Insofar as this transformation does occur, the four levels previously described may be said to apply to sympathetic as well as empathic distress. (From here on, the term empathic distress will be used generically to refer to both empathic and sympathetic distress).

Empathy as Motive

The relevance of empathic distress to altruism of course is that it is assumed to form the basis of a motive to help others. This is not a new idea, going back at least two centuries to writers like Hume, Rousseau, Shelley, and Adam Smith who wrote about its importance in cooperative social life. Why should empathic distress lead to helping? The answer may simply be that empathic distress is unpleasant and helping the victim is usually the best way to get rid of the source. One can also accomplish this by directing one's attention elsewhere and avoiding the expressive and situational cues from the victim. Such a strategy may work with children but provides limited relief for mature observers who do not need these cues to be empathically aroused, as discussed earlier.

In the earliest empirical study, Murphy (1937) found a positive correlation between empathic behaviors such as "responding to another child's distress by staring with an anxious expression," and behaving in a comforting manner. Empathy also related positively to aggression, however. Murphy suggested the pattern may simply reflect the child's social activity level: Highly active children are more empathic, helpful, and aggressive. Feshbach and Feshbach (1969), in a more controlled study, replicated Murphy's aggression findings for boys: 4- to 5-year-old boys who obtained high empathy scores on a measure in which subjects report how they feel after looking at story slides depicting children in situations representing different emotions (Feshbach & Roe, 1968), were rated as more aggressive by nursery school teachers than boys with low empathy scores. For 6- to 7-year-old boys there was a negative relation between empathy and teacher ratings of aggressiveness, which suggests that by this age empathy may have begun to take hold as an inhibitor of aggression. There was no relation between empathy and aggression for girls at either age.

Levine and Hoffman (1975) examined the relation in 4-year-olds between the Feshbach-and-Roe measure of empathy and a modified version of Kagan and Madsen's (1971) measure of cooperation. No correlation was found between empathy and cooperation, for either sex. In this study the cooperative subjects were asked why they cooperated. Only a few answered in empathic terms (e.g.,

"Because he wanted me to help him," or "Because he would cry if I didn't"); most referred to the requirements of the game, or to reciprocity. Thus, the emotional state of the other child was not salient during the game, which suggests that young children's empathic capability may sometimes not be engaged because their attention is easily captured by task demands and other irrelevant stimuli.

In a study of kindergarten boys, Kameya (1976) examined the relation between the Feshbach-and-Roe measure and several indices of helping behavior which included helping an experimenter who dropped a pile of paper clips and expressed pain after bumping his knee, donating candy to poor children, and volunteering to color pictures for hospitalized children. Empathy did not correlate with any of these behaviors. Among subjects who did volunteer to color pictures for hospitalized children, however, those who actually took the pictures with them and showed signs of following through on their promise had higher empathy scores than those who showed no signs of following through. This "follow through" behavior is the only altruism index involving considerable self-sacrifice over a prolonged period (the subjects were told they would have to do the coloring during two successive recess periods while the other children were outside playing). This suggests that although empathy may not often be engaged in young children, when it is engaged it may serve as a rather effective prosocial motive.

These somewhat inconsistent correlational findings stand in contrast to the rather clear pattern that seems to be emerging in naturalistic observations (Main et al., 1979; Murphy, 1937; Sawin, 1979; Zahn-Waxler et al., 1979) and experimental research. Thus during the first year children tend to cry in response to distress cues from others, including unfamiliar adults. This empathic cry decreases during the second year and the decrease appears to be closely associated with an increase in overt attempts to comfort the victim, although many children this age do nothing, probably because they lack the necessary coping skills. By 3- or 4-years of age most children show both empathic distress and some form of helpful action. And, there is also evidence that children (9-year-olds) who respond empathically (show a sad look on their face) are more apt to make a sacrifice to help a victim than those who do not respond empathically (Lieman, 1978). Finally, the experimental research on adults also shows a clear pattern (see review by Hoffman, 1977b): When exposed to someone in distress, adults are invariably aroused empathically (as indexed physiologically); the arousal is typically followed by helping action; and the latency of the act decreases with both the intensity of empathic arousal and magnitude of the pain cues from the victim.

Why is there a discrepancy between the correlational and other research? For one thing, the Feshbach-Roe measure, which was used in all the correlational studies, has problems which I have noted elsewhere (Hoffman, 1977b, in press c). The main problem lies in the assumption that empathy is a unitary trait, which underlies a scoring system in which responses reflecting empathic fear, anger, sadness, and happiness are summed to produce a subject's empathy score. A measure specifically of empathic sadness or distress might yield more consistent findings. The results obtained by Main et al. (1979) and Sawin (1979) fit this view: Main found that 12-month-old infants who showed empathic sadness in response to the cry of an adult stranger in a laboratory situation were described by their parents as actively attempting to comfort distressed persons in the home environment. Sawin used the Feshbach-Roe measure and found that whereas the overall empathy score did not relate to helping in first and third grade children, the subscore for empathic sadness did, significantly for the first-grade group. The correlational method may thus be consistent, after all, with the naturalistic and experimental, adding credence to the generalization that empathy leads to helping action.

When the findings are arranged developmentally the result is a neat package: In response to someone's being hurt, children below a year of age cry empathically; in the second year they cry less but show empathic distress in their facial responses and occasionally attempt to help; by 3 or 4 years they continue to show empathic distress and in most instances can be counted upon to make some attempt to help. Beyond the preschool years, people continue to respond empathically and with more consistently appropriate helping behavior, the latency of the helping act increasing with the intensity of the victim's distress cues, and helping action being followed by a drop in empathic arousal. These findings all fit the pattern to be expected if empathic distress were a prosocial motive.

Empathic Overarousal

There is evidence that altruistic action may require a certain amount of need fulfillment in observers, so as to reduce their self-preoccupation and leave them open and responsive to cues signifying the other's affect and need for help. For example, the arousal of deprived need states such as concerns about failure, social approval, and even physical discomfort due to noise has been found to interfere with altruistic action (e.g., Mathews & Canon, 1975; Moore, Underwood & Rosenhan, 1973; Murphy, 1937; Staub & Sherk, 1970; Wine, 1975). Because empathic distress may itself be extremely aversive under certain conditions, it may at times direct the attention of observers to themselves and thus actually decrease the likelihood of an altruistic act. Consider one of the experimental groups in the study of kindergartners by Kameya (1976) who were presented with several stories involving children who were ill, deprived, in pain, or combinations of these. The subjects took turns playing each of the roles and then discussed the feelings of the story children. In this group empathy was found to relate *negatively* to one of several helping behaviors (it did not relate to the others). These results suggest that the experimental treatment, though designed to improve role-taking skills, may have instead evoked extreme empathic distress, especially in the high-empathy subjects. These subjects may then have attended to their own distress, thus accounting for the negative relation. Perhaps there is an optimal range of empathic arousal—determined by people's levels of distress tolerance—within which they are most responsive to others. Beyond this range, they may be too preoccupied with their own aversive state to help anyone else.

Another possibility is that once over their threshold of distress tolerance, observers may employ certain mechanisms to reduce the level of arousal itself. They might avoid interacting with people in pain, like the empathic nursing students in a study by Stotland, Mathews, Sherman, Hansson, & Richardson (1979). They might employ certain perceptual and cognitive strategies such as looking away from the victim or thinking about other things, as did Bandura and Rosenthal's (1966) subjects who were given a strong dose of epinephrine before observing someone receive electric shocks. Or, they might even derogate the victim, for example, by making negative attributions about his motives or blaming him for his plight. Like other motives, then, empathic distress may operate as a prosocial motive only within certain intensity limits. Beyond that point, it may be transformed into an egoistic motive.

The apparent egoistic element in empathic overarousal must not be overdrawn. First of all, avoidance of overarousal may have been adaptive in human evolution because it often occurred when the victim's situation was hopeless. This would reduce the benefit/cost ratio virtually to zero, and the situation would then not provide a valid test of altruism. Secondly, in preserving one's energies rather than helping when the situation is hopeless, the individual continues to be available to help others when helping will be more effective, that is, when the benefit/cost ratio is clearly above zero.

Is Empathy Altruistic or Egoistic?

Empathy is uniquely well suited for bridging the gap between egoism and altruism, as it has the property of transforming another person's misfortune into one's own distress and thus has elements of both egoism and altruism. Because it is an aversive state that can often best be alleviated by giving help to the victim, some writers treat it as an egoistic motive (e.g., Piliavin, Rodin, & Piliavin, 1969; Gaertner, & Dovidio, 1977). Undoubtedly people do feel good after helping someone but what these writers seem to overlook is the difference between the consequence of an act and its aim. Because a person has a satisfied feeling afterwards does not necessarily mean that he acted in order to have that feeling. When subjects, whether adults or children, are asked why they helped or what crossed their minds when they encountered a victim, they give a variety of answers, which rarely pertain to their own distress (Darley & Latane, 1969; Eisenberg-Berg & Neal, C., 1979; Latane & Rodin, 1969). This is in keeping with the view that with the partial transformation of empathic into sympathetic distress the conscious aim of a person's action is gradually changed, at least in part, from relieving their *own* empathic distress to relieving the victim's distress.

An unconscious egoistic motive may of course be operating but there is as yet no evidence for this.

The more fundamental point is that even if there were no sympathetic component and people did help only to relieve their own empathic distress, to conclude that empathic distress is egoistic is to overlook the fact that *all* motives prompt action that is potentially satisfying to the actor. If a satisfied feeling afterwards is characteristic of all motives, then it cannot be used as the defining criterion of a particular class of motives (e.g., egoistic motives). If a satisfied feeling results from action triggered by empathic distress, then this satisfied feeling cannot be reason enough to define empathic distress as egoistic. To do this would eliminate the possibility of altruistic motivation by defining it out of existence. It would also obscure certain profound differences between empathic distress and other motives. Aside from its egoistic element, empathic distress has certain dimensions that clearly mark it as an altruistic motive: First, it is aroused by another's misfortune, not just one's own; second, a major goal of the ensuing action is to help the other, not just the self; and third, the potential for gratification in the actor is contingent on his doing something to reduce the other's distress. It is thus more appropriate to designate empathic distress as an altruistic motive—perhaps, with a quasiegoistic component—than to group it with such obviously self serving motives as material gain, social approval, and competitive success.

Perhaps there are more subtle forms of egoistic motivation that can do what empathy can do. Bandura (1977) argues, for example, that people may engage in any act to gain self-reward. This certainly seems plausible, as what one rewards oneself for depends largely on the cultural norms guiding one's socialization; and there seems to be an infinite variety of such norms. Thus self-reward might very well mediate helping behavior if one were appropriately socialized. And because children in our society are often encouraged to help others, they may be expected to reward themselves when they help. It must be noted, however, that there is nothing *intrinsically* prosocial about self-reward, as there is about empathy (the arousal of affect in common with that of the victim). It therefore seems unlikely that self-reward would be reliably aroused by another's misfortune and that one's gratification. would be contingent on helping the victim. Indeed, in an individualistic competitive society like ours, self-reward would seem at least as likely to mediate egoistic, as altruistic behavior. We must tentatively conclude that self-reward is a far less reliable motive base for prosocial action than is empathy.

Two qualifications are in order. The first is the phenomenon of overarousal, discussed earlier, which suggests that beyond a certain point empathic distress may become so aversive that one's attention is directed to the self and not the victim. The second is the evidence that empathic distress and helping are positively related to perceived similarity between observer and victim. Thus, children respond more empathically to others of the same race or sex (Feshbach & Roe, 1968; Klein, 1971). And adults have been found to empathize more to others perceived as similar to themselves in abstract terms (e.g., similar "personality traits'') (Krebs, 1975). These findings indicate that empathic morality may be particularistic, applied more to one's group than to others, although the findings are also compatible with the idea that moral education programs which point up the similarities among people, at the appropriate level of abstraction, may help foster a more universalistic morality.

Before moving on, it is necessary to point out that empathic distress must be viewed in the perspective of all the emotional responses a person may make when observing someone in distress. In focusing on empathy, it is easy to lose sight of the fact that an observer's emotional response to a victim may not always be empathic. For example, it may be a direct reaction to something noxious, such as the sight of the victim's blood. It may be a startle response to sudden movements by the victim. It may be due to feeling afraid that what happened to the victim might happen to the self. It may be due to feeling threatened by the victim's distress because one is highly dependent on the victim, as when one is a child and the victim is one's parent. Still another possibility, as noted in discussing empathic overarousal, is that the observer's empathic distress may be so aversive that his attention is redirected toward his own discomfort rather than the victim's; though he appears distressed, his concern is mainly for his own upset state.

Finally, the research on attribution points up still another influence on how people respond to victims. That is, people tend to make causal inferences about events. We may therefore expect a person who encounters someone in distress, to make inferences about the cause of the victim's plight. The nature of the inference depends on the cues relevant to causality, and the inferences may then serve as a cognitive input, in addition to the observer's sense of the other, that helps shape the observer's affective experience. Thus, if the cues signify that the victim is responsible for his own plight, this may neutralize the empathic distress, and the observer may end up feeling indifferent or even derogating the victim. If the cues indicate that a third person is to blame, the person may feel anger at that person because he sympathizes with the victim or because he empathizes and therefore feels attacked himself. It is only when the cues indicate it was an illness or accident over which the victim had no control that the analysis of empathic distress I outlined, including the partial transformation of empathic into sympathic distress, may apply. Culture can play a role in all of this: If the victim belongs to an outcast group, for example, his misery may be responded to with indifference.

People may also make causal attributions about the victim's plight for reasons not based on situational cues. For example, as noted, they may use perceptual or cognitive strategies including blaming the victim as ways of reducing the discomfort of overarousal. These tendencies may be a function of individual differences in personality, although Lerner and Simmons (1966) claim evidence for a widespread tendency to respond with a derogatory attitude toward victims. There is some evidence that their findings may be due to the instructions given the subjects (Aderman, Brehm, & Katz, 1974). If the findings do reflect a real phenomenon, however, they must somehow be reconciled with the extensive research summarized earlier indicating that people of all ages typically respond empathically and with some attempt to help the victim. Perhaps the different findings can be explained by differences in research design. More likely, there may be no contradiction at all. People may have negative attitudes towards a victim, and still be empathically aroused and motivated to help him in the immediate situation.

Empathy is thus one component of the observer's affective response to someone's plight. It is probably in general a large component, given all the evidence that an affective response to another's plight typically leads to a disposition to help. Nevertheless our analysis suggests that empathy should be treated as a component of one's response to others, and studies of empathy should be designed to rule out or control the nonempathic components insofar as possible.

Empathy and Guilt

Thus far in my analysis, the observer is an innocent bystander. A special case of interest is that in which the cues indicate that the observer is the cause of the other's distress. It seems reasonable to assume, when one feels empathic distress, that if the cues indicate one has caused the victim's distress one's empathic distress will be transformed by the self-blame attribution into a feeling of guilt. That is, the temporal conjunction of empathy for someone in distress and the attribution of one's own personal responsibility for that distress will produce guilt.

I have elsewhere presented a theory and some research bearing on this type of guilt (which differs from the Freudian version)—its relation to empathy, its developmental course, its function as an altruistic motive, and the role of socialization (Hoffman, 1976, in press a, in press b; Thompson & Hoffman, 1980). For now I will just summarize briefly the developmental parallels between guilt and empathic distress. First, as discussed earlier, once the child becomes aware of others as separate physical entities, he experiences empathic distress when observing someone who is physically hurt; his empathic distress may be transformed into guilt, however, if his own actions were responsible for the hurt. Similarly, once the child becomes aware that others have inner states, the empathic distress that he experiences in the presence of someone having painful or unhappy feelings may be transformed into guilt if his actions were responsible for those feelings. And, finally, once he becomes aware of the identity of others beyond the immediate situation, his empathic response to their general plight may be transformed into guilt if he feels responsible for their plight.

The relation between empathic distress and guilt may go one step further, once the child develops the capacity to feel guilty not only over harm that he has done but also over ommission or inaction, for example, not helping someone in need. Guilt may thus become part of his subsequent affective responses to another's distress even when he is not to blame—at least in situations in which he might have helped but did not. That is, from then on, even as an innocent bystander, he may rarely experience empathic distress without some guilt. The line between empathic distress and guilt thus becomes very fine, and being an innocent bystander is a matter of degree. To the degree that one realizes that one could have acted to help but did not, one may never feel totally innocent. This is another way of saying that empathy and guilt may be the quintessential social motives, because they may transform another's pain into one's own discomfort and make one feel partly responsible for the other's plight whether or not one has actually done anything to cause it.

THE ROLE OF SOCIALIZATION

The discussion so far has dealt with the natural processes of empathy development assumed to occur under ordinary conditions in most cultures because of the tendency of humans to respond vicariously to others. People also have egoistic needs, however, which must not be overlooked, and socialization, which in part reflects the larger themes in society, may build upon the child's empathic or egoistic proclivities in varying degrees. I have suggested elsewhere (Hoffman, 1970b) that there may be little conflict between empathic and egoistic socialization in early childhood, even in individualistic societies like ours. At some point in life the two may begin to clash, however, sometimes dramatically, as one becomes aware that the society's resources are limited and one's access to them is largely contingent on how well one competes with others. Parents know this, and it may affect their childrearing goals. For this and other reasons (e.g., their patience with the child, their own personal needs and the stresses under which they operate), wide variations in childrearing practices, hence in children's capacity for empathy, can be expected.

There is little research on socialization and empathy but if we assume that helping another in distress reflects on empathic response—which seems reasonable in view of the findings relating empathy to helping—then we can find modest support for speculations based on our theoretical model.

First, we would expect that if the child is allowed the normal run of distress experiences, instead of being shielded from them, this should expand his empathic range. To date the only evidence for this hypothesis is that preschool children who cry a lot themselves are more empathic than children who do not often cry (Lenrow, 1965). There is a theoretical limitation to this hypothesis: certain extremely painful situations might be repressed, resulting in an inability to empathize with the emotions involved.

A second expectation is that because empathy is largely involuntary its development should be fostered by socialization experiences that direct the child's attention to other people's inner states. In situations in which the child has harmed others, we would therefore expect that the parent's use of discipline techniques that call attention to the victim's pain or injury or encourage the child to imagine himself in the victim's place—inductive techniques—should help put the feelings of others into the child's consciousness and thus enhance his empathic potential. The positive correlation between inductive techniques and helping in older children has long been known (see review by Hoffman, 1977a); and the same thing has recently been reported in children under 2 years (Zahn-Waxler et al., 1979).

Third, we would expect role-taking opportunities to help sharpen the child's cognitive sense of others and increase the likelihood that he will pay attention to others, thus extending his empathic capability. Because role-taking is affectively neutral, however, useful in manipulating as well as helping others, role-taking opportunities in positive social contexts should be a more reliable contributor to empathy and helping, than role-taking in competitive or neutral contexts. The research provides modest support for this expectation: Role-taking training in prosocial contexts has been found to increase helping behavior in children and adults; the research on role-taking in neutral or competitive contexts, all of it correlational, shows a lack of relation between role-taking and helping (see review by Hoffman, in press a).

Finally, we would expect that giving the child a lot of affection would help keep him open to the needs of others and empathic, rather than absorbed in his own needs. And, we would also expect that exposing the child to models who act altruistically and express their sympathetic feelings would contribute to the child's acting empathically rather than making counter-empathic attributions about the cause of people's distress. Both these expectations have been borne out by the research (see review by Hoffman, in press a).

It thus appears that empathy and helping may be fostered by relatively benign, nonpunitive socialization experiences. These experiences may be effective because empathy develops naturally, as I suggested, and is to some extent present at an early age. It may thus serve as a potential ally to parents and others with prosocial childrearing goals for the child, something to be encouraged and nurtured rather than punished as egoistic motives must sometimes be. And, besides benefitting from the child's existing empathic tendencies, these same socialization experiences may also help enhance the empathic tendencies. In other words, there may be a mutually supportive interaction between naturally developing empathy and these socialization experiences.

CONCLUDING REMARKS

A theoretical model of empathic arousal, its developmental course, its transformation into guilt and other related affects, and its implications for altruistic motivation has been presented. Its distinctive feature is the stress on an emotion—empathic distress—and the interaction between affective and cognitive processes in the development of that emotion. The affective component pertains to the arousal and motivational properties of the emotion. The cognitive component pertains to the shaping and transformation of the affective experience that results from the actor's awareness that the event is happening to someone else, and the actor's causal attributions concerning the event. The affective and cognitive components develop through different but constantly interacting processes and are experienced not as separate states but as fusion, a "hot" cognition.

Though as yet loose and tentative, the model appears to provide a broad integrative framework for ordering existing knowledge about altruistic behavior. This includes findings such as these:

1. People generally respond to another's distress with an empathic affective response as well as a tendency to help.

2. At least up to a point, the speed of the helping response increases with the intensity of empathic affect and severity of the victim's distress.

3. Empathic affect appear to subside more quickly when the observer engages in a helpful act than when he does not.

4. Young children appear to experience empathic distress; and whether they act appropriately or inappropriately, or not at all, is related to the level at which they can cognize others. (Reinforcement and imitation theories might have difficulty explaining this, since socialization agents are unlikely to reward or provide models for inappropriate action or inaction.)

5. People are more apt to help others when their approvals need are satisfied rather than aroused.

6. The findings summarized in the discussion of socialization are in keeping with the model.

Though the model may thus encompass much of what is known about people's response to distress, a true assessment of it awaits the test of hypotheses derived specifically from it.

REFERENCES

Aderman, D., Brehm, S. S., & Katz, L. B. Empathic observation of an innocent victim: The just world revisited. *Journal of Personality and Social Psychology,* 1974, *29,* 342–347.

Aronfreed, J., & Paskal, V. *Altruism, empathy, and the conditioning of positive affect.* Unpublished manuscript, University of Pennsylvania, 1965.

Bandura, A. *Social Learning Theory.* Englewood Cliffs, N.J.: Prentice Hall, 1977.

Bandura, H., & Rosenthal, L. Vicarious classical conditioning as a function of arousal level. *Journal of Personality and Social Psychology,* 1966, *3,* 54–62.

Borke, H. Interpersonal perception of young children: Ego-centrism or empathy? *Developmental Psychology,* 1971, *5,* 263–269.

Darley, J. M., & Latane, B. Bystander intervention in emergencies: Diffusion of responsibility. *Journal of Personality and Social Psychology,* 1968, *8,* 177–383.

Eberhard, M. J. The evolution of social behavior by kin selection. *Quarterly Review of Biology,* 1975, *50,* 1–33.

Eisenberg-Berg, N., & Neal, C. Children's moral reasoning about their own prosocial behavior. *Developmental Psychology,* 1979, *15,* 228–229.

Feshbach, N. D., & Feshbach, S. The relationship between empathy and aggression in two age groups. *Developmental Psychology,* 1969, *1,* 102–107.

Feshbach, N. D., & Roe, K. Empathy in 6- and 7-year-olds. *Child Development,* 1968, *39,* 133–145.

Gaertner, S. L., & Dovidio, J. F. The subtlety of white racism, arousal and helping behavior, *Journal of Personality and Social Psychology,* 1977, *35,* 691–707.

Gould, S. J. Caring groups and selfish genes. *Natural History,* Dec. 1977, 20–24.

Hamilton, W. D. The genetic evolution of social behavior. *Journal of Theoretical Biology,* 1964, *7,* 1–52.

Hamilton, W. D. Selection of selfish and altruistic behavior in some extreme models. In J. F. Eisenberg & W. S. Sillon (Eds.), *Man and beast: Comparative social behavior,* Washington, D.C.: Smithsonian Institution Press, 1971.

Hoffman, M. L. Parent discipline and the child's consideration for others. *Child Development,* 1963, *34,* 573–588.

Hoffman, M. L. Conscience, personality, and socialization techniques. *Human Development,* 1970, *13,* 90–126.

Hoffman, M. L. Developmental synthesis of affect and cognition and its implications for altruistic motivation. *Developmental Psychology,* 1975, *11,* 607–622.

Hoffman, M. L. Parental discipline and moral internalization: A theoretical analysis. *Developmental Report No. 85,* University of Michigan, 1976.

Hoffman, M. L. Moral internalization: Current theory and research. In L. Berkowitz (Ed.), *Advances in experimental social psychology, Vol. 10.* New York: Academic Press, 1977, 86–135. (a)

Hoffman, M. L. Empathy, its development and prosocial implications. In C. B. Keasey (Ed.), *Nebraska Symposium on Motivation: Vol. 25,* University of Nebraska Press, 1977, 169–218. (b)

Hoffman, M. L. Adolescent morality in developmental perspective. In J. Adelson (Ed.), *Handbook of adolescent psychology,* New York: Wiley Interscience, 1980.

Hoffman, M. L. Is altruism part of human nature? *Journal of Personality and Social Psychology,* 1981, *40,* 121–137.

Hoffman, M. L. Empathy, guilt, and social cognition. In W. F. Overton (Ed.), *Relations Between Social and Cognitive Development.* Hillsdale, N.J.: Lawrence Erlbaum Associates, in press. (a)

Hoffman, M. L. Affective and cognitive processes in moral internalization: An information processing approach. In E. T. Higgins, D. Ruble, & S. W. Hartup (Eds.), *Advances in social cognitive development.* New York: Cambridge University Press, in press. (b)

Hoffman, M. L. The measurement of empathy. In C. Izard (Ed.), *The Measurement of Emotion in Childhood.* New York: Cambridge University Press, in press. (c)

Humphrey, G. The conditioned reflex and the elementary social reaction. *Journal of Abnormal and Social Psychology,* 1922, *17,* 113–19.

Kagan, S., & Madsen, M. Cooperation and competition of Mexican, Mexican-American, and Anglo-American children of two ages under four instructional sets. *Developmental Psychology,* 1971, *5,* 32–39.

Kameya, L. I. *The effect of empathy level and role-taking training upon prosocial behavior.* Unpublished doctoral dissertation, University of Michigan, 1976.

Kaplan, L. J. The basic dialogue and the capacity for empathy. In N. Freedman & S. Grand (Eds.), *Communicative structures and psychic structures.* New York: Plenum, 1977.

Klein, R. Some factors influencing empathy in six and seven year old children varying in ethnic background. *Dissertation Abstracts,* 1971, *31,* 3960A. (University Microfilms No. 71-3862).

Konner, M., Dovore, I., & Konner, M. Infancy in hunter-gatherer life: An ethological perspective. In N. White (Ed.), *Ethology and Psychiatry*. Toronto: University of Toronto Press, 1974.

Krebs, D. L. Empathy and altruism. *Journal of Personality and Social Psychology*, 1975, *32*, 1124–1146.

Lenrow, P. B. Studies in sympathy. In S. S. Tomkins & C. E. Izard (Eds.), *Affect, cognition and personality*. New York: Springer, 1965.

Lerner, M. J., & Simmons, C. Observer's reaction to the innocent victim: Compassion or rejection? *Journal of Personality and Social Psychology*, 1966, *4*, 203–210.

Lieman, B. *Affective empathy and subsequent altruism in kindergartners and first graders*. Paper presented at meetings of the American Psychological Association, Toronto, September 1978.

Levine, L. E., & Hoffman, M. L. Empathy and Cooperation in 4-Year-olds. *Developmental Psychology*, 1975, *11*, 533–534.

Lipps, T. Das Wissen von fremden Ichen. *Psychologische Untersuchungen*, 1906, *1*, 694–722.

MacLean, P. D. *A Triune concept of the brain and behavior*. Toronto: University of Toronto Press, 1973.

Main, M., Weston, D. R., & Wakeling, S. "Concerned attention" to the crying of an adult actor in infancy. Paper presented at meetings of the Society for Research in Child Development, San Francisco, March 1979.

Mandler, G. *Mind and emotion*. New York: Wiley, 1975.

Matthews, K. E., & Canon, L. K. Environmental noise level as a determinant of helping behavior. *Journal of Personality and Social Psychology*, 1975, *32*, 571–577.

Moore, B. S., Underwood, B. & Rosenhan, D. L. Affect and altruism. *Developmental Psychology*, 1973, *8*, 99–104.

Murphy, L. B. *Social Behavior and child personality*. New York: Columbia University Press, 1937.

Piliavin, I. M., Rodin, J., & Piliavin, J. A. Good samaritanism: A underground phenomenon. *Journal of Personality and Social Psychology*, 1969, *13*, 289–299.

Sagi, A., & Hoffman, M. L. Empathic distress in newborns. *Developmental Psychology*, 1976, *12*, 175–176.

Sawin, D. B. Assessing empathy in children: A search for an elusive construct. Paper presented at meetings of the Society for Research in Child Development, San Francisco, March 1979.

Schachter, S. & Singer, J. E. Cognitive, social and physiological determinants of emotional state. *Psychological Review*, 1962, *69*, 379–399.

Simner, M. L. Newborn's response to the cry of another infant. *Developmental Psychology*, 1971, *5*, 136–150.

Staub, E., & Sherk, L. Need for approval, children's sharing behavior, and reciprocity in sharing. *Child Development*, 1970, *41*, 243–253.

Stotland, E. Exploratory investigations of empathy. In L. Berkowitz (Ed.), *Advances in experimental social psychology* (Vol. 4). New York: Academic Press, 1969.

Stotland, E., Mathews, K. E., Sherman, S. E., Hansson, R., & Richardson, B. Z. *Empathy, fantasy and helping*. Beverly Hills, Calif.: Sage, 1979.

Thompson, R., & Hoffman, M. L. Empathy and the arousal of guilt in children. *Developmental Psychology*, 1980, *15*, 155–156.

Trivers, R. L. The evolution of reciprocal altruism. *Quarterly Review of Biology*, 1971, *46*, 35–57.

Wine, J. D. Test anxiety and helping behavior. *Canadian Journal of Behavioral Science*, 1975, 216–222.

Zahn-Waxler, C., Radke-Yarrow, M., & King, R. A. Childrearing and children's prosocial initiations towards victims of distress. *Child Development*, 1979, *50*, 319–330.

4 Socialization Processes and the Development of Altruism

Joan E. Grusec
University of Toronto

Perhaps altruism is a built-in characteristic of the human species, waiting to reveal itself at the first available opportunity. To the extent that it is not, however, it must be fostered. Society must intervene, either to nourish a basic predisposition, build an altruistic motive from virtually whole cloth, or suppress base desires and replace them with prosocial urges and behaviors. Clearly the agents of socialization comprise members of many different groups—parents, peers, teachers, the media. This chapter will focus primarily on the role of adult socializing agents in fostering helping, sharing, and co-operation.

One of the major goals of socialization is the *internalization* of important societal values in young children. Thus parents hope that their offspring will eventually conform to parental dictates and wishes in the absence of surveillance by some external agent. Some behaviors may not need to be internalized as they are annoying only when parents have knowledge of their occurrence, e.g., failing to take out the garbage, bickering with siblings. But behaviors like stealing, lying, and concern for the welfare of others cannot always be monitored and so must be the object of internalization. In the survey that follows, then, one must consider which techniques of socialization are particularly conducive to long-term facilitation of altruism, i.e., the development of consideration for others which no longer depends on external surveillance.

It can, of course, be questioned whether internalization is really possible. As Hoffman (1970) points out, internalization is a middle class concept, necessary amongst a group of individuals who have a great deal at stake in maintenance of the social order and where direct supervision of activity is not the norm. Internalization may, in fact, be a fiction promulgated in order to help us maintain behavior we might prefer not to maintain. If behavior were always believed to be solely governable by its external consequences there would no doubt be less

65

inclination to exhibit it when the possibility of external consequences was less visible. On the other hand, if one *believes* in conscience and inner drives for goodness, one might be more likely to continue moral behavior in the absence of external surveillance.

MECHANISMS OF ACQUISITION

Overview

Except for the work of Lois Murphy during the 1930s, psychologists have studied altruism intensively for only the last 15 or so years. Thus developmental studies of altruism reflect changes in emphasis and methodology that have taken place in the area of social and personality development during that period. Early studies were concerned with the role of various discipline techniques—power assertion (physical punishment, verbal censure, etc.), withdrawal of love, and reasoning—in the fostering of morality. Subsequently interest focused on the roles of modeling and positive reinforcement in the induction of concern for others, and a multitude of studies assessed the mechanisms through which these procedures worked. As interest grew during the 70s in the child's cognitions about the social world, so too did interest shift in the mechanisms which might facilitate altruism. Now researchers began to focus on the child's ability to understand how others were thinking and feeling, and to explore the role of empathy as a mediator in the development of concern for others. While the role of reasoning continued to be of interest, concern was also extended to other verbal techniques such as preaching or moral exhortation. Recent extensions of attribution theory from the domain of social psychology to that of developmental psychology appear to hold some promise for the study of altruism, and a discussion of them is included at the end of this chapter.

As well as changes in content, the altruism research also reflects changing methodological approaches that have predominated at different times in the recent history of social development research. Early studies were correlational in nature, relying on parent and child assessments of child-rearing experiences and/or attitudes. During the 60s researchers began to turn toward the laboratory experiment in order to achieve greater control over the variables they were studying, as well as to enable themselves to make inferences about causality. The laboratory experiment, while achieving these important goals, has not been without its critics. Concern with problems of demand characteristics, and whether or not brief laboratory manipulations provide sufficient information about the long-term effects of daily and repeated adult-child interactions, has led to the introduction of a variety of methodological innovations—field experiments, observational studies of altruism in natural settings, continued interest in the assessment through interview of child-rearing approaches and their effects, as well as evaluation of the effects of laboratory manipulations outside the specific setting in which they were conducted. Each approach, of course, has its own set of strengths and weaknesses. Used in concert, however, these various approaches appear to be giving us some valuable insights into the processes whereby the altruism of young children can be encouraged.

The Growth of Concern for Others.   When do children first start to reveal an interest in and reaction to the needs of others? Zahn-Waxler and Radke-Yarrow (1979) have provided some fascinating insights into the development of this facility. By training mothers to report on the reactions of their children to distress in others, these investigators were able to establish that children as early as 12 months of age show strong reactions when others are in need of help. One 12-month-old child ran to her mother who was crying, patted her face, and then buried her own face in her mother's lap, apparently both providing and requesting comfort. At the age of 17 months this same child physically comforted another child, although she no longer demanded comfort herself. Whereas children obviously become increasingly more adept at responding to and dealing with the distress of others as they grow older, Zahn-Waxler and Radke-Yarrow were struck by the similarities in altruism between 2- and 7-year-olds: Even very young children are proficient at making inferences about the feelings of others and in helping them. As well, they noted within a given child the great consistency in the nature of his or her reaction to distress in others over the years. Thus some children could be characterized as intensely emotional and compassionate, some as intellectual and analytical, some as avoidant and unable to tolerate emotional needs in others, and some as nonresponsive or nondescript in their reactions. About two-thirds of the children showed the same patterns of responding when they were 7 years old as they had shown when they were 2 years old. The child just described who comforted another child no doubt as her mother had comforted her, at the age of 7 spontaneously gave her sandals to a younger friend to protect her feet from burning as the two of them walked together on a hot sidewalk. A boy at the age of 2 pushed a bothersome child into a swimming pool in order to protect a friend: At the age of 7 he attacked an adult who had pushed ahead of his grandmother in the grocery line. An 18-month-old child ran away or plugged her ears when she heard crying or angry voices and, when she was 7, complained that she could just not take any more of someone's crying. As Zahn-Waxler and Radke-Yarrow (1979) point out, if such distinctive orientations can be seen so early, then these early years may be an especially important time for parents and teachers to either strengthen or attempt to modify existing behavior.

Response Consequences

One of the first and obvious places to look for the antecedents of altruism is in the kinds of consequences that altruistic behavior produces in the environment. Certainly researchers have established that reinforcement and punishment are powerful determinants of behavior. A child who is rewarded for altruism through the application of verbal approval and/or receipt of material items and privileges contingent on the display of concern for others should subsequently be more likely to display altruism. Similarly, punishment for the failure to be altruistic (verbal disapproval, withdrawal of privileges and material rewards) should lead to less altruistic behavior in the future.

But what happens to altruism when rewards or punishments are no longer forthcoming? Socializing agents may cease to administer them either because they no longer feel this should be necessary, or because they are not around to do so. If altruism were to continue nevertheless, this would be evidence that the behavior had been internalized. However, there is really no reason to believe that such an outcome *would* occur—the evidence indicates that when reinforcement or punishment are no longer administered, or when discriminative stimuli associated with their presence (e.g., the socializing agent) are removed, the behavior will not be maintained.

Fischer (1963), Azrin and Lindsley (1956), Gelfand, Hartmann, Cromer, Smith, and Page (1975), and Hartmann, Gelfand, Smith, Paul, Cromer, Page, and Lebenta (1976) have shown that helping or sharing or cooperation can all be increased with the appropriate use of rewards or punishments. There is no evidence in these studies, however, that altruism continues once response consequences are no longer in effect, or in the absence of the experimenter. In one study Altman (1971) did report that children who were reinforced for cooperation were subsequently more friendly and less hostile during free-play periods. This outcome may point up a beneficial side-effect of altruism. Although cooperation may not have been directly internalized in the Altman study, simply "forcing" children to engage in prosocial behavior may have exposed them to its benefits (for example, social approval from the peer group) and these benefits may have been instrumental in maintaining the behavior.

Recently, a number of investigators (e.g., Garbarino, 1975; Lepper, Greene, & Nisbett, 1973) have reported that if children are performing an activity at a moderately high rate in the absence of any obviously discernible reinforcement, and then are given material reinforcement contingent on the activity, they subsequently spend *less* time engaging in the behavior when the reward is withdrawn. The introduction of external and salient incentives appears to undermine the child's basic interest in the behavior that has been reinforced. Explanations for this phenomenon are diverse. Lepper et al. (1973) suggest that the introduction of external incentives leads children to attribute their interest in the activity to the external incentives and to believe they have less interest once those incentives are removed. Others (e.g., Reiss & Sushinsky, 1975) propose that the presence of salient incentives distracts children from the activity and hence interferes with their interest in it. Perry, Bussey, and Redman (1977) have proposed that the frustration induced by the withdrawn reward produces negative affect which interferes with the behavior. The "overjustification effect," as it has been dubbed, occurs only under certain circumstances (Ross, 1976). Nevertheless it serves as a warning to those involved in the training of altruism. If one were to take a child who was generally behaving to others in a kind and considerate fashion, and were to attempt to increase the occurence of this considerate behavior by drawing attention to it with salient reinforcement, the procedure could well backfire. Rather than making the child even more altruistic some of this basic altruism could be destroyed.

It is not clear that overjustification effects occur with social reinforcement. Recently, Smith, Gelfand, Hartmann, and Partlow (1979) reported that 7- and 8-year-old children who were praised for sharing or verbally rebuked for not sharing were likely to attribute their sharing to a desire to help or a concern for the welfare of the child with whom they shared. On the other hand, those given penny rewards or fined, stated that they had shared in order to get a reward or to avoid losing money. If behavior which is followed by social consequences ("That was a fine thing you did" or "It's too bad you didn't help") is seen by a child to be compelled by some inner desire or value system, whereas that followed by material or physical consequences is attributed to external pressure from adults, then the use of social consequences ought to be a more efficient way of promoting internalization of altruistic values. Indeed, some support for this is provided by Rushton and Teachman (1978) who found that social reinforcement for sharing ("good for you," "That's really nice of you") increased sharing even when the experimenter was no longer present.

It has been argued that moderate punishment is a necessary part of the socialization process (Walters & Grusec, 1977). We shall see later that parents who exert firm pressure on their children to comply with their wishes are more successful in gaining compliance than those who do not. And a component of this firm pressure is surely some threat of negative consequences which the child perceives to be genuine. It is also evident, however, that punishment cannot be exerted baldly so that compliance is easily attributable to external pressures.

Modeling

According to personality theorists, one of the major ways in which children acquire the value systems of society is through identification. By identifying with their parents they adopt parental attitudes and behaviors, including those related to altruism. With this theoretical background it is not surprising that such a major part of the research on altruism has been concerned with the role of modeling or imitation in the acquisition of concern for others. Included in this concern has been an interest in the effects of different characteristics of models on the willingness of children to imitate. Most of the modeling research has been carried out in the context of the laboratory experiment, although a few field experiments and observational studies have generally corroborated the findings of the laboratory experiments.

Simply stated, children imitate the altruistic behavior of those they observe (Bryan & Walbek, 1970; Elliot & Vasta, 1970; Grusec, 1971; Grusec & Skubiski, 1970; Rushton, 1976; Rutherford & Mussen, 1968; Staub, 1971a; Yarrow & Scott, 1972). Although White (1972) suggests that some practice in actual sharing, in the presence of an adult, is necessary in order to facilitate the effects of the model, a number of studies have demonstrated quite substantial effects of modeling even in the absence of mediating practice. Rice and Grusec (1975), for example, had children and an adult model play a miniature bowling game where they received tokens, exchangeable for prizes, when they bowled winning scores. Near the game was a sign requesting donations for poor children, and a bowl in which tokens could be placed. Children observed the adult donate half of his or her winnings to the poor children, and then were left alone to play the game and were observed, through a one-way mirror, to see whether or not they donated any tokens. In those conditions in which no permissive reference to the possibility of donation had been made by the experimenter, matching of the model's amount of donation was virtually perfect. In other conditions, where children and models had been told they could share if they wished, but did not have to, the matching of behavior was not so perfect, although substantial amounts of donating did occur. It would appear, then, that children will follow the lead of a model in charitable behavior, and that they will match that lead especially closely in a situation where alternative courses of action have not been spelled out for them.

Though laboratory studies have provided much useful information about the socialization of altruism, they have not, to date, sampled a wide variety of situations. Donation and aid to others (e.g., Staub, 1971a) have been the primary altruistic behaviors studied. Most manipulations of modeling have been brief, most models have been strangers to the child, and most measurements of modeling effects have taken place in the training situation (albeit, usually in the absence of the experimenter and/or model, when the child was apparently alone and unobserved). Yarrow, Scott, and Waxler (1973) have expanded on this basic modeling paradigm. These investigators exposed preschoolers to an adult for a half hour a day for five days, spaced over a two-week period. During this time the adult was either nurturant—helpful, supportive, sympathetic, and protective—for half the children, or, for the other half, nonnurturant—aloof, detached, and minimally helpful. Subsequently, the adult modeled altruism through the use of imaginary situations, which involved the presentation of three-dimensional scenes of people or animals in difficulty, e.g., a monkey in a cage trying to reach a banana beyond its grasp. Some children received more extensive training which additionally involved behavioral incidents in which the model actually, rather than symbolically, aided others in distress, e.g., another adult came into the room where the model and child were sitting and accidentally banged her head against the table. In this study the model also accompanied her examples of altruism with numerous comments in which she verbalized her awareness of and sympathy for the animal or person's distress, described the necessary aid and the pleasure she felt at providing that aid, and used the word "help" to summarize what had been done. In the extended training, the model's confederate also provided approval for altruism. It should be noted, then, that whatever results Yarrow et al. obtained could be attributable either to modeling, verbalizations, approval, or some combination of these. They found that symbolic modeling (and its various accompaniments)—the "lesson"-type setting—increased helping in the same and similar situations, e.g., children verbalized helping statements and actions in imaginary situations. Only extended training, however, by a nurturant model, produced an increase in real-life helping, and this was revealed only two weeks later. Thus Yarrow et al. concluded that only adults who manifest altruism at every level, both in principle as well as in their practice toward the child (nurturance) and toward others, will be successful as socializers of prosocial behavior.

Model Characteristics.   One part of the research on modeling and altruism has focused, as did the Yarrow et al. (1973) study, on the role played by characteristics of the model. The two major characteristics (dictated by theories of identification) that have been studied are the nurturance (warmth, concern, interest) and the power (prestige, control of resources) of the model. Both have been assumed to facilitate a child's willingness to emulate a model's altruism, although research support for the importance of nurturance has been equivocal. In laboratory studies, for example, nurturance appears to have no effect on, or to actually *decrease,* the willingness of children to imitate an adult's donation of tokens to others who are less fortunate, although it increases their willingness to help others whose cries of distress are heard coming from the next room (Grusec, 1971; Grusec & Skubiski, 1970; Staub, 1971a; Weissbrod, 1976). The typical manipulation of nurturance, in this case, involves a brief (10 to 15 min) interaction between model and child in which the model behaves in either a pleasant and friendly fashion to the child, or is aloof and cool. The model's friendly behavior may well be alleviating children's anxiety about behaving "properly" in the experimental situation, encouraging them to keep more tokens for themselves in the case of donation, or to investigate events in other rooms in order to help someone in obvious distress. What these studies do, then, is to point out the importance of children's perception of a situation where altruism is demanded. Do they feel free or not to do as they wish (keep rewards for themselves, or move to another room)—freedoms that obviously interact with the form of altruism demanded. The studies are less pertinent, however, to a hypothesis that children identify with the altruistic values of loving and affectionate caretakers.

Nonlaboratory studies have supported a relationship between nurturance and altruism. Rutherford and Mussen (1968) reported that boys who were generous perceived their fathers as nurturant and warm, and as models of generosity, sympathy, and compassion. Recall also that Yarrow et al. (1973) found greater behavioral altruism on the part of children who had interacted with a nurturant adult, although the model's nurturance did not facilitate symbolic altruism. Rosenhan (1969) interviewed workers in the Civil Rights Movement of the late 50s and 60s and asked them to describe their parents. Those workers who were fully committed to the movement and who made extensive personal sacrifice in order to be involved described their parents as vigorous workers in the cause of justice and as warm and loving. Contrasted with this was the description of parents of only partially committed workers who were seen as paying mere lip service to moral causes and as cool and aloof, even avoidant.

How does nurturance facilitate altruism (if it does so)? It could be that in behaving nurturantly to children, adults are displaying altruistic behaviors of helping and concern—a nurturant parent is much more likely to model just this class of behaviors than is a nonnurturant parent. Children who are emotionally secure because they have loving and accepting parents may be better able to direct their attention outward and thereby be receptive to the needs of others. Yarrow et al. (1973) do stress, however, that nurturance must be accompanied by specific teaching. And one would wish to define more clearly the component parts of nurturance and to inquire if it is physical contact, sympathy, concern, interest, empathy, example, acceptance, or some combination of these which is especially important in altruism's development. Moreover, nurturance, or some forms of nurturance, may be less conducive to the growth of concern for others. It was noted earlier that children given brief periods of nurturance may be less inclined to aid others. Parents who are too loving and nurturant, in the sense of being noncontingently accepting of all their child does, may consequently fail to demand high standards of achievement in the moral domain for their children, even though they themselves behave in a moral way. Mischel and Liebert (1966), for example, found that models who set high standards of reward for themselves but who required less in the way of achievement from the children observing them caused the children to quickly adopt the lower standard for themselves.

Another model characteristic affecting the imitation of altruism is power. Children are more likely to imitate the donating of a model who is in a position to decide whether or not they will be chosen for a special trip than one who has no such influence (Grusec, 1971). It may be that children learn through experience that it is wise to do what powerful people might wish them to do in order to maximize their chances of reward. Indeed, the failure to find an effect of power when the model is described as the child's future teacher suggests that models may need to be in direct control as agents of reinforcement (Bryan, 1975).

Generalization of Modeling Effects. There is no doubt that modeling is a powerful determinant of altruism. In the absence of example, children are denied the opportunity to observe exactly how altruistic dispositions can be translated into action. The child who hugs and pats another child who is upset and crying was highly likely hugged and patted himself when in distress. The child who offers to help someone pick up items that have accidentally been dropped probably had a parent who helped her under similar circumstances in the past. Without the presence of examples of prosocial behavior children's altruistic repertoires would be greatly limited.

One can inquire, however, as to the extent to which examples of altruistic behavior generalize behond the specific acts which have been modeled. Obviously such generalization is desirable in order to make the effects of socialization more efficient, for to model every possible occasion when altruism might be appropriate would be impossible. It has been argued that observation of models allows children to generate abstract rules that govern future behavior in dissimilar situations (e.g., Rosenthal & Zimmerman, 1978). The data on the modeling of altruism, however, seem to be somewhat equivocal on this point.

Rice and Grusec (1975) and Rushton (1975) have demonstrated that the effects of modeling show great durability, being evident in retests over a 2- to 4-month period. In other laboratory experiments, Elliott and Vasta (1970) and Midlarsky and Byran (1972) reported generalization of modeling to slightly different situations (e.g., sharing candy and sharing pennies, donation of candy solicited by two different adults in two different settings). Generalization to more distant settings, however, does not appear to be the rule. Elliott and Vasta did not find that children trained to share candies gave up a preferred toy to a stranger. Nor did Grusec, Saas-Kortsaak, and Simutis (1978) find that children who had imitated a model who gave up game winnings to poor children were any more likely to share pennies they had won with fellow schoolmates, or to collect craft materials for sick children. Thus it appears that the effects of modeling do not generalize to situations somewhat discrepant from the original training situation. And by this is not meant extremely diverse situations, e.g., donation and physical comforting of others, where it would be rather surprising to find generalization, but situations where two kinds of relatively impersonal aid to others are required.

In these studies, of course, training for altruism was of limited duration, usually lasting only a few minutes. But other studies, where training h•. been more extensive, have not provided evidence for generalization either. As noted previously, Yarrow et al. (1973) failed to find that the effects of symbolic modeling of altruism generalized to real-life altruism. It is not even clear whether the effects they *did* find may not have been mediated at least partially by the direct teaching their subjects received in the form of verbalizations about helping. This possibility is strengthened by the findings of another field experiment (Friedrich & Stein, 1975). In the Friedrich and Stein study children saw a series of prosocial films—four segments from the television show "Misterogers' Neighbourhood." After this exposure children showed increments in helping on a fantasy measure which involved play with puppets. Generalization to real-life altruism occurred, however, only when modeling was combined with training in pretending to be, or taking the role of, the distressed other. Limitations of the generalizability of modeling effects are evident in yet another study (Yarrow & Scott, 1972). Preschoolers in a nursery school setting observed nurturant or nonnurturant adults who modeled either gentleness and warmth, or roughness and punitiveness, to play animals. Although the children imitated the nurturant behaviors of the nurturant model there was no evidence that these effects generalized to the children's helpful interactions with their peers.

In light of these various studies, it seems reasonable to conclude that although the effects of modeling generalize to some extent, they certainly do not generalize very far beyond the specific training situation. In real life, of course, children are provided with a variety of models who display a variety of prosocial behaviors. And the more examples of altruism provided the easier it should be for children to abstract a general rule about the importance of showing concern for others. But how efficiently is this accomplished? Interestingly enough, comments on cross-cultural differences in approaches to education suggest it may not be that easy. Thus observers have distinguished between systems of informal and formal education, and the cognitive consequences of these two approaches for the acquisition of knowledge. In the case of informal education, learning occurs in the course of every-day adult activities in which the young participate as they are able. One of the major mechanisms for acquiring knowledge is observational learning—learning by looking—or imitation. Formal education, on the other hand, involves didactic teaching, is out of context, and relies on language and direct instruction for the communication of information. These two approaches have quite different consequences. One consequence is that learning in a formal setting encourages the generalization of rules and operations across a number of problems, whereas learning in an informal setting is concrete, situation-bound, and unable to provide principles that could govern behavior in related settings (Scribner & Cole, 1973). The extension of this analysis to the realm of altruism would suggest, then, that techniques of socialization that promote the development of general principles of concern for others may be necessary in addition to the provision of specific example. We shall now turn to some of these techniques.

Verbal Persuasion

Although parents may wait for altruism to occur in order to reinforce it, or may try to encourage the behavior by engaging in it themselves, there are other techniques of socialization that require less patience and are less indirect. It is probably faster to get children to conform, at least immediately, by instructing or exhorting them to do so, than by using any other technique of socialization. Mothers recognize this fact. In a recent study (Grusec & Kuczynski, 1980), mothers of 4- and 7-year-olds were asked to describe the various disciplinary techniques they would use when their children had misbehaved. Of 40 mothers interviewed, 95% reported that on one or more occasions they would use strong verbal pressure in order to force their child to engage in appropriate behavior.

How effective *is* some form of forced appropriate behavior in the production of altruism? A number of investigators (e.g., Bryan, 1975; Midlarsky & Bryan, 1972; Rushton, 1975; Staub, 1972; Yates, 1974) have compared the effects of modeling and verbal pressure to comply (moral exhortation or preaching) on such indices of self-control as altruism and the ability to delay gratification. Bryan's work, and that of his coinvestigators, has been invaluable in pointing out the dangers of hypocrisy on the part of socializing agents—that those who preach altruism and practise greed produce greedy children. If we consider only prosocial exhortations and prosocial modeling, however, the research tends to suggest that extensive exhortations may be as effective as example, although short ones (e.g., "it's good to give") are not.

Grusec, Saas-Kortsaak, and Simutis (1978) exposed children to two different kinds of exhortation: a specific one emphasizing the importance of charity (sharing with those less fortunate) and a general one which emphasized the importance of helping others whenever possible. The effects of these exhortations and that of modeling of donation (giving tokens to poor children in order to purchase gifts for them) were compared on a number of measures. Thus children were observed to see how many tokens they donated both immediately after the training manipulation and three weeks later, as well as whether or not they helped the experimenter pick up a number of objects she had "accidentally" knocked over. They were then given the opportunity to share gifts (pencils) with other children in the school who would not be able to participate in the research. Finally, more than a month after their original training, the children were visited in their classrooms by a man whom they had never seen before. He asked them to make drawings and collect craft articles such as margarine tubs and pieces of fabric for children who were in the hospital and needed the drawings to cheer them up, and the craft materials to help occupy their time. All these tests, except for helping the experimenter pick up objects she had dropped, were conducted when the child was alone (e.g., donating was observed from behind a one-way mirror) or so that the child's anonymity was apparently maintained.

It was predicted that moral exhortations containing a general message would have greater effect on the various tests of generalized altruism than would moral exhortations of a more specific kind ("give half your tokens to the poor children since it would be a good thing to make them happy by doing this"): The specific content would require that children themselves generalize from a given behavior to related ones, while a general content would ensure that this was already done. Similarly, it was predicted that modeling, or example, would be relatively ineffective in the production of generalized altruism because it would require children themselves to extract from their training the general principle that one should show concern for others. Finally, however, it was predicted that exhortation would produce psychological reactance, at least for a short time after training. (Staub, 1971b, found that children who were preached to about the need for helping others were subsequently less likely to help the experimenter.) The effects of reactance were expected to dissipate with time, however, so that the benefits of exhortation might finally reveal themselves.

The results of this study are summarized in Table 4.1. Example was more effective in the immediate donation test than was exhortation, although this difference disappeared in the delayed test. This change may have occurred because children's memory of whether they had seen someone donate or had merely heard them praise the virtues of donation become blurred over time; indeed, we found that even immediately after training, although children could accurately recall that the model had donated in the example condition, many erroneously recalled that the model had donated in the exhortation condition. Some evidence of reactance after preaching can be seen on the helping measure, although this is confused by evidence of reactance after example as well. Boys who had been exhorted to share (the specific exhortation) shared more pencils than boys who had been exhorted to help others, and somewhat more ($p < .10$) than boys who had been exposed to neither example nor exhortation. And finally, children who had been exposed to a general exhortation collected more craft articles for the sick children than did those who had received no treatment at all.

Although the results were sometimes inconsistent (e.g., why did children in the example-general exhortation group not collect more craft materials than those in the control condition) they do suggest that exhortation can be effective, at least in the long run, whereas (as discussed earlier) the effects of example or modeling may be confined to the training situation. Our tentative suggestion was that exhortation is encoded into memory as a statement of what ought to be done, whereas example is encoded as a description of what once happened. This

TABLE 4.1
Number of Children Who Donated Tokens Immediately
and Three Weeks Later, Number of Children Who Helped,
Mean Number of Pencils Shared, and Number of Children
Returning Craft Items. N = 16 Per Group.

	Example			*No Example*		
Preaching	Specific	General	None	Specific	General	None
Donation:						
immediate	13	12	11	4	6	0
delayed	5(15*)	3(14*)	4(14*)	2(13*)	3(13*)	0(15*)
Helping	7	4	2	3	4	9
Sharing:						
boys	3.62	1.62	2.25	3.50	1.37	2.62
girls	2.50	3.00	2.37	1.37	2.37	2.62
Craft items	4	2	3	4	9	2

*Number of children available for the follow-up

distinction is similar to that made by Tulving (1972) between episodic and semantic memory, i.e., between memories of specific events and of knowledge produced by the event, with the latter not tied to the situation in which it was first acquired. Material encoded in semantic memory should have a greater element of compulsion attached to it since it more nearly resembles a prescribed norm of behavior: In the case of example, attached as it is to a specific situation, there is less of an element of coercion.

Several other studies indicate that children will conform to verbal pressures of varying degrees of intensity. Adults who merely suggest that sharing is the appropriate and expected behavior in a given situation are often just as effective as those who model sharing behavior, particularly if children have not been told that they do not have to share if they do not wish to (Grusec, 1972; Rice & Grusec, 1975); moreover, the effects of these indirect and gentle admonitions last for at least four months. Similarly, White (1972) and White and Burnham (1975) found that children who were told that the experimenter would like them to donate some pennies they won to poor children gave more than those told they could give if they wished but that they did not have to, an effect which endured at least one week. In a naturalistic study of parents' child-rearing practices Baumrind (1973) reported that warm and reasonable parents who placed demands on their children to display prosocial behavior, and who firmly enforced these demands, had children who were cooperative and friendly. Zahn-Waxler, Radke-Yarrow, and King (1979) trained mothers to record their reactions to their 1 ½- to 2 ½-year-old-children when these children had been the cause of distress to others; mothers were also instructed to record their children's behavior when the children were bystanders to distress in others (the latter a measure of altruism). These investigators found that the children who showed the greatest amounts of altruism—physical and verbal sympathy ("all better now?", hugging), providing objects (e.g., bandaids), finding someone else to help, protecting, giving physical assistance—had mothers who responded to their deviations, i.e., to situations in which the children caused distress to others, with explanations as to why they should not have done what they did. These explanations had a strong affective character, (the punitive element considered in the earlier discussion of response consequences), with the most effective being those having a large component of moralizing ("You made Doug cry. It's not nice to bite," "It was bad for Jim to hit Mary"). As well, mothers who suggested positive action after their child's deviation ("Why don't you give Jeffy your ball?") also had children who were highly altruistic.

In a later chapter Ervin Staub (Chapter 6) describes some of his research and theorizing about the antecedents of prosocial behavior. He suggests that parents and other socializing agents who focus responsibility on children to behave prosocially and who actually influence them to participate in prosocial behavior are using an important technique for promoting altruism. He discusses several different types of participation. Thus children can be asked or told to do certain things, i.e., assigned responsibility. If pressure to perform prosocial acts is not too great, children may eventually come to see their behavior as self-caused, and this could then lead to the development of beliefs and values consistent with that behavior. Another type of participation involves role-playing. It can lead to the learning of specific altruistic acts, and the performance of these acts may, as in the case of assigned responsibility, lead to the perception of altruism as self-caused. Also role-playing enables the child to see the point of view of the distressed other, an important condition for the activation of prosocial values. Participation can also be embodied in the form of teaching other children. Here the child-teacher engages in a meaningful prosocial activity, and the procedure has the advantage of being indirect, i.e., children are not forced to be prosocial. Essentially, then, Staub is emphasizing the importance of influencing children rather directly to perform prosocial behavior—one way of accomplishing this, provided it is not too coercive, is through the use of verbal instruction.

In conclusion, instructing children to be helpful, suggesting that they might be helpful, and even preaching to them about the virtues of concern for others, all have beneficial effects on their altrustic behavior. Although it makes intuitive sense that such behavior might backfire on socializing agents, the evidence is not that clear. Interactions between age of subjects and subtlety of verbal direction no doubt exist, and these remain to be explicated.

Empathy and Perspective-Taking

The ability to understand another person's thoughts and feelings has been hypothesized to play a central role in the mediation of concern for others. The relationship between empathy, perspective-taking, and altruism is discussed at length in other chapters (Hoffman, Krebs, Batson & Coke) and so the relevant literature will be only briefly surveyed here.

Empathy—the experiencing of another's emotional state—is supposed to facilitate altruism, because any action to reduce another's distress should also reduce one's own, empathically-experienced, distress. And the ability to know how others are thinking and feeling (cognitive and affective perspective or role-taking) should put one in a better position to intervene on their behalf. Some correlational studies have confirmed the anticipated relationships between altruism, empathy, and perspective- or role-taking ability, while others have not. If one groups those studies that were successful in showing predicted relationships, and those that were not, by age, an interesting pattern emerges—empathy, altruism, and perspective-taking ability are more likely to be related in younger children than they are in older children. Thus Rubin and Schneider (1973) found willingness to help and share with others was positively correlated with the ability to communicate in a nonegocentric manner—their subjects were 7 years old. Buckley, Siegel, and Ness (1979) found that 3- to 8-year-old children who could correctly rotate a display so that they had the same view as someone else (a measure of perspective-taking ability) helped and shared more with a peer than those who were less adept at seeing the perspective of others. They also found that children who were altruistic could identify the emotion of a character in a story better than children who were less altruistic. Sawin (1979) measured empathy by observing children's facial expressions of emotion as they watched slides of other children in situations that were emotion-arousing. He found that, for 6-year-olds, this measure correlated with willingness to donate tokens to other children who could not participate in the study.

On the other hand, Rushton and Wiener (1975) did not find a relationship between a series of role-taking tasks and generosity to charity or generosity to a friend—their subjects were 7- to 11-year-olds. Sawin found no relationship between empathy and altruism in 8-year-olds. Iannotti (1978) provides equivocal evidence: Role-taking and altruism were correlated while empathy and altruism were not. His subjects were 6- and 9-year-olds, however, neither as young as those of Buckley et al. (1979), nor as old as those of Rushton and Wiener. And Zahn-Waxler, Radke-Yarrow, and Brady-Smith (1977) found no relationship between perspective-taking ability and altruism in 3- to 8-year-olds. They measured altruism directed toward an adult, however, rather than toward other children, and it is possible that children may have perceived the adult to be quite capable of looking after herself.

Although this hypothesized relationship between age and correlations of empathy and role-taking ability with altruism remains to be adequately tested, it does bring some order to the results of existing studies. It may well be that older children have experiences that mask or overcome the link between the ability to understand another's emotions and point of view and altruism.

If empathy, role-taking ability, and altruism are related, it should be possible to facilitate the development of altruism by training children (at least younger ones) to be more empathic and more able to understand other people's point of view. And this is indeed the case. Staub (1971b) trained kindergarten children to play the role of both a child who needed help (e.g., because she had fallen and hurt herself) and the role of someone who helped that child, in several different situations. Twenty-four hours later children were brought to a playroom where they heard apparent cries of distress (actually a recording) coming from an adjacent room. Girls who had had practice in role-taking responded more frequently to the distress than did those who had had no training. Boys showed generalized effects, sharing candy more than did those with no training. And these effects endured for at least one week. Iannotti (1978) asked 6- and 9-year-old boys to take either one role or to switch roles in a series of skits, with training going on for 25 minutes a day for ten days. In one skit, for example, several boys who were in need of money found a wallet with valuables inside and subjects acted out several solutions to the dilemma. During the training the boys were asked questions about the motives, feelings, and thoughts of the character they were playing. A control group met for the same length of time to discuss the stories, but did not act them out. Six-year-olds who had had role-playing experience subsequently shared more candy than those in the control group, with the most sharing observed in those who had switched roles. No effect of training was found, however, for 9-year-olds (a further confirmation of the age hypothesis). Finally, Friedrich and Stein (1975) reported that preschoolers, especially boys, who used puppets to rehearse altruistic events they had seen in a television film, were more helpful in real-life situations.

A word of caution must be introduced in the evaluation of these and similar studies. Sometimes it is difficult to know whether role-playing itself is responsible for changes in the dependent measure. Staub (1971b) and also Friedrich and Stein (1975), for example, gave mild verbal reinforcement to subjects for playing helpfully, and this may have been responsible for at least some of the increases in altruism that they observed. In addition, the enactment of prosocial roles, as well as providing experience in understanding how others are thinking and feeling, may also be providing subjects with practice in behaving helpfully.

It was noted earlier that parental reactions to their children's deviations can have implications for their children's altruism (Zahn-Waxler, Radke-Yarrow, & King, 1979). One parental disciplinary technique, which Hoffman has singled out as particularly instrumental in the development of altruism, is reasoning which stresses the effects a child's behavior has on others. Hoffman suggests that this form of reasoning—what he terms "other-oriented induction"—is particularly effective in moral development because, among other consequences, it elicits the child's natural proclivities to be empathic. Hoffman and Saltzstein (1967) found that the parents of seventh grade girls who reported that they used induction had daughters who were rated by their peers as being considerate. For boys, however, consideration of others was unrelated to induction; moreover, it was positively related to parental use of power assertion (physical punishment, withdrawal of privileges, verbal censure, etc.). In a later study with fifth graders, Hoffman (1975) assessed parents' explicit suggestion of reparation after deviation (which presumably give their children actual experience in helping others), their encouragement of apology, and their expression of concern for the victim's feelings. He found that this discipline approach correlated with peer ratings of consideration, although only when it was used by the parent of the opposite sex. Dlugokinski and Firestone (1974), studying 10- and 13-year-olds, found that those who reported that their mothers frequently used inductive discipline were seen by their classmates as more considerate, attached more importance to other-centered values (e.g., "getting a job that helps others" rather than "having a life of pleasure and comfort"), and donated more money to charity. And finally, Eisenberg-Berg and Geisheker (1979) reported that 8- and 9-year-old children were more influenced by empathic exhortations which emphasized how happy and excited recipients of sharing would be than they were by normative exhortations which emphasized that people ought to share.

The data are mixed and questions remain to be answered. Nevertheless, empathy and role-taking ability appear to assume some importance in the development of concern for others. One must ask, of course, how empathy and role-taking ability transform themselves into actual helping behavior. Here practice, verbal exhortation, and observation of others' helpfulness—to name a few—must surely be part of the experiences to which the child has been exposed.

Attribution of Prosocial Characteristics

In recent years attribution theorists (e.g., Nisbett & Valins, 1971) have impressed upon psychologists that the reasons people give to account for their own behavior will affect whether or not they continue to behave that way. If the cause of behavior is perceived to be external (e.g., "I shared my toys because my mother would be angry with me if I didn't") then the chance that sharing will continue when mother is not around to be angry are lessened. If the reason is perceived to be internal ("I shared for no immediate external reason that I can perceive. Therefore I must like to share") then behavior is more likely to endure. Attribution theory provides, then, a potentially interesting mechanism for the internalization of behavior and has, in fact, been used to account for the inhibition of socially undesirable behavior (e.g., Dienstbier, Hillman, Lehnhoff, Hillman, & Valkenaar, 1975; Lepper, 1973; Walters & Grusec, 1977).

Attribution theorists have focused on situations in which people themselves speculate about the causes of their own behavior. Some psychologists (e.g., Jensen & Moore, 1977; Miller, Brickman, & Bolen, 1975, as well as my own colleagues and I) have looked at situations in which causes of their behavior are supplied to children by others. Presumably, if children are given labels or attributions of charitability and helpfulness, these could be effective in governing their future behavior—if they see themselves as altruistic persons they should continue to behave in accord with such a self-concept. Perry, Perry, Bussey, English, and Arnold (1980) have suggested that this is so because failure to live up to attributed prosocial characteristics leads to heightened self-criticism. To avoid this self-criticism, then, children behave prosocially.

In one study (Grusec, Kuczynski, Rushton, & Simutis, 1978) 7- to 10-year-old children were induced to donate some of their winnings from a game to poor children and were told "You shared quite a bit." To this statement was added the suggestion that they did so because they were the kind of people who liked to help others (internal-attribution condition) or that they did so because the experimenter had expected them to (external-attribution condition). Other children were not provided with an explanation for their behavior (no-attribution condition). Donating had been induced in one of two ways—either by having the children observe a model who donated or by instructing them to donate. In the first case it was hypothesized that children would be unsure as to why they had donated (researchers have enough difficulty understanding why children imitate—perhaps children have little more insight into this aspect of their behavior) and so they could be influenced by the reasons given them. In the second case we thought they would be less affected as the real reason for their behavior was quite obvious—an adult had instructed them to share, and had watched to make sure they complied.

Our hypothesis was confirmed. When later left alone, children in the modeling condition donated more if they had been in the internal or self-attribution condition than if they had been in the external-attribution condition, an effect which endured when subjects were retested two weeks later (see Table 4.2). Attributions had no effect in the direct-instruction condition, although the high level of donation maintained in this condition attests to the effectiveness of instructing or forcing children to engage in prosocial behaviors.

Children were also asked at the end of the first experimental session to share some pencils they had been given with other children in the school who would not be able to play the game. Here we observed only an effect of attribution, with greater sharing in the self-attribution than in the external-attribution and no-attribution conditions. The effects of attributions generalized beyond the training situation, then, even when the attributions did not modify original behavior. Thus the potential effectiveness of attributions was later fulfilled—when coercion no longer existed, behavior was modified.

The results of this study suggested that socializing agents who attribute prosocial characteristics to helpful children will increase their helpfulness. It coincidentally provided another illustration of the power of instruction. One wonders about the relative effectiveness of attribution and instruction—although children in the modeling plus self-attribution condition donated more than children in the instruction plus no-attribution condition, this difference only approached statistical significance ($p < .08$, one-tailed). Miller et al. (1975), however, have found evidence for the superiority of attribution over a form of instruction. They told children they were neat and tidy individuals and found this to be more effective in reducing their littering than telling children they *ought* to be neat and tidy. Both approaches were more effective than no treatment at all. There is a difference, of

TABLE 4.2
Mean Number of Tokens Donated Privately in Each Condition.
N = 14 Per Group.

	Immediate Test		Delayed Test	
Condition	*Modeling*	*Instruction*	*Modeling*	*Instruction*
Self-attribution	6.07(14)	5.64(12)	4.43(13)	5.21(11)
No attribution	4.14(11)	4.36(11)	5.14(12)	4.50(10)
External attribution	2.72(10)	4.78(13)	2.92 (7)	4.22(10)

Note: Numbers in parentheses represent number of children donating.

course, between telling someone to do something and telling them they *ought* to do it. The complexities of verbal direction remain to be sorted out.

Attribution vs. Social Reinforcement.   Although the attribution of prosocial characteristics may promote altruism by leading children to believe that they are altruistic individuals, an alternative explanation is possible. In the Grusec, Kuczynski, Rushton, & Simutis (1978) study we may simply have been reinforcing children for donating, perhaps enabling them to generalize altruism to a related situation by emphasizing in our verbalizations the dimension of helping. Lepper (1973) has reported that children who presumably attributed honest behavior to internal causes subsequently rated themselves as somewhat more honest, a suggestion that their self-concepts had indeed been modified. But what of the situation in which attributions come from an external agent?

Accordingly, we set out to compare the effects of attribution of prosocial characteristics with social reinforcement for prosocial behavior (Grusec & Redler, 1980). We believed that both would be equally effective in promoting the future occurrence of the behavior to which they were directed, but that they would differ in ther effectiveness on tests of generalized altruism. If attributions affect self-concept their effect should generalize (helpful people help in all situations) whereas social reinforcement, given for a specific behavior, should have less pervasive effects.

Eight-year-old boys and girls came individually to a research trailer parked in the school yard and were told they could donate winnings from a game to poor children if they wished (this suggestion was designed to be less coercive than direct instruction, yet it was most effective in inducing children to share). After they had shared, all children were told in a neutral tone of voice, "Gee, you shared quite a bit." This was followed in the attribution condition by "I guess you're the kind of person who likes to help others whenever you can. Yes, you are a very nice and helpful person," in the social reinforcement condition by "It was good that you gave your marbles (tokens) to those poor children. Yes, that was a nice and helpful thing to do," and in the control condition by nothing at all. Children were then left alone to play the game and their donation was observed through a one-way mirror. At the end of the session they were given the opportunity to share, anonymously, some pencils they had been given for participation with other children in the school who would not be able to come to the trailer.

One week later the children returned, individually, to another room in the trailer where an adult, whom they had never seen before, asked them to help fold some cardboard for roofs she was making for toy houses. After the child had complied he or she was thanked by the adult who then commented in the attribution condition that the child was evidently a nice person who was helpful whenever possible and in the reinforcement condition that the child had done a nice thing and that it was good that he or she had helped with the work. Children were then given a Viewmaster and several packages of slides and told they could either play with the Viewmaster or fold some more cardboard roofs while the experimenter was out of the room.

One to two weeks later children were visited in their classrooms by an unknown man and asked to make drawings and collect craft materials for the Hopsital for Sick Children.

In Table 4.3 the results of prosocial attributions and reinforcement on various measures are summarized. On every measure our hypothesis about the relative effects of attribution and reinforcement was confirmed. Prosocial attribution and social reinforcement were equally effective in facilitating donation—the behavior to which they had originally been applied. On the various generalization tests (sharing pencils, folding cards rather than playing with the Viewmaster, drawing, and collecting craft materials), however, prosocial attribution continued to have an effect whereas there was now no difference between the reinforcement condition and the control condition.

The Developmental Question.   The effects of prosocial attribution appear to be more pervasive than those of social reinforcement and, in light of the earlier discussion, perhaps more pervasive than those of modeling. The attributional approach, however, has its own set of limitations. One of these limitations may be of a developmental nature. Telling children they are helpful should make them more helpful only to the extent that they think of themselves as having stable dispositional characteristics and only to the extent that they act in accord with these. Livesley and Bromley (1973) and Peevers and Secord (1973) suggest that this is a condition that may not exist until children are 7 to 8 years old, with a quite abrupt shift at this point from their thinking of themselves and others in terms of surface traits to their thinking in terms of more enduring dispositional traits.

To assess this possibility Grusec and Redler (1980), in a second study, included 4- to 5-year-olds as well as 8-year-olds as subjects. Again, for 8-

TABLE 4.3

Mean Number of Tokens Donated, Pencils Shared, Cardboard Roofs Folded, Drawings Made, and Craft Materials Collected in Each Condition.

N = 20 Per Group.

	Attribution	Reinforcement	Control
Marbles	7.7	6.4	3.3
Pencils	5.8	2.8	2.3
Cardboard roofs	4.6(16)	1.8(9)	2.1(10)
Drawings	2.7	1.6	1.4
Craft material	(9)	(2)	(4)

Note: Numbers in parentheses represent numbers of children in each condition who folded roofs and returned craft material.

year-olds, prosocial attributions were more effective than social reinforcement on tests of generalized altruism. For the younger children, however, this was not the case. Although more of them donated tokens in both the attribution and social reinforcement conditions than in the control condition, there was no effect at all of either treatment manipulation on any generalization test. Evidently, then, the use of labeling as a way of promoting changes in children's behavior may be a technique that depends to some extent on their cognitive capacities.

One wonders if there is some kind of critical period in the development of a child's altruistic self-concept. Our data suggest that labeling may not have much of an effect if it is done before the age of 7 or 8. Are there ways in which attributions could be made to have an effect earlier in the developmental sequence? Since the onset of dispositional thinking appears to be relatively sudden, are there crucial years in which self-concepts develop? Once children begin to think of themselves as having certain characteristics (e.g., as being smart, stupid, clumsy, amusing, helpful, stingy, compliant) how difficult is it to modify this self-image?

All these are questions remaining to be answered. We have, however, one additional piece of evidence relevant to the developmental problem. We wondered if it might be more difficult to manipulate the beliefs of 10-year-olds about their potential for helpfulness, since they should already have a relatively fixed perception of their own altruistic nature. Contrary to our expectations, however, attributions were effective both on the training test and on a generalization test (Grusec & Redler, 1980). In the same study we also manipulated social reinforcement. Unlike 8-year-olds, 10-year-olds showed an effect of this variable even on a generalization test. Thus, while 8-year-olds discriminated between statements about their acts and statements about their dispositions, 10-year-olds appeared to be more flexible—they were willing to extrapolate from evaluations of acts to inferences about their own characteristics. Evidence for such a cognitive change has been recently presented by Nelson and Nelson (1978). They noted that children's concepts develop through a series of stages in which they swing from great breadth of inclusion to rigid inflexible application of rules to more flexible extension of rules. In the area of prosocial attribution 8-year-olds may be in the rigid stage whereas 10-year-olds may have moved to the stage of flexible extension.

SOME FINAL THOUGHTS

The variety of techniques that can be employed to promote altruistic behavior is great indeed, including reinforcement, punishment, modeling, exhortation, direction, role-playing and empathy training, and prosocial attribution. Each, of course, has its advantages and each its limitations. No doubt there are other techniques which parents use and which remain to be discovered and investigated by psychologists.

There are two issues which are frequently addressed in discussions of altruism. One has to do with whether or not altruism can be considered a unitary trait—is an individual cooperative and helpful in all situations, or cooperative and helpful in only some situations? Are some individuals more consistently altruistic than others? One answer to this question could lie in a consideration of the techniques used to socialize altruism. Modeling and exhortations involving specific references to specific situations may foster situation-specific altruism. Techniques that promote a wide range of altruistic behaviors—the attribution of prosocial characteristics, general exhortations about the importance of helping others whenever possible, and the encouragement of empathy—may be more likely to produce a child who shows greater consistency in helpfulness across a variety of situations. Such a relationship is easily testable.

A second issue pertains, essentially, to a consideration of when altruism is appropriately displayed and when it is not. A given behavior, for example, can be helpful or not depending on the situation in which it is expressed, the person to whom it is directed, the mood of the recipient, and so on. There are occasions when help is unwanted, inappropriate, or, in the long run, detrimental to the welfare of the recipient. These are situations that children must be trained to recognize and amongst which they must learn to discriminate. (The fact that adults often do not give aid when they ought to may reflect, in part, a failure on their part to have learned adequately when help is appropriate and when it is not.) Some socialization techniques may be more useful in this regard than others. Take, for example, techniques which encourage empathy. To the extent that they are successful in orienting children to the feelings and reactions of others they may make them sensitive to when help is needed and when it is not. Contrast these techniques, which focus the child's attention on others, with that of prosocial attribution, which focuses the child's attention on him or herself. In the case of the latter techniques children could be expected to be less affected by the external effects of their altruism than they would be in the case of empathically-oriented techniques. On the other hand, the attributional approach may promote a principled approach to altruism that is relatively independent of immediate consequences and which, under some conditions, could be quite desirable.

Clearly, any technique employed in isolation is not going to be as effective in the training of altruism as will a group of techniques used together. Modeling must be amplified by accompanying statements of principle, the ability to empathize is not much good in the absence of knowledge about what one might do to translate that concern into action, knowledge no doubt best acquired through watching the actions of others. Although we have much left to learn—what combinations of techniques are peculiarly effective, what are the best kinds of exhortations (simple statements, suggestions or commands, statements referring to norms of concern for others, empathy-based statements), what interactions occur between age and technique—we have made considerable progress in understanding the best ways to socialize altruism in children.

REFERENCES

Altman, K. Effects of cooperative response acquisition on social behavior during free play. *Journal of Experimental Child Psychology*, 1971, *12*, 387–395.

Azrin, N., & Lindsley, O. The reinforcement of cooperation between children. *Journal of Abnormal and Social Psychology*, 1956, *2*, 100–102.

Baumrind, D. The development of instrumental competence through socialization. In A. D. Pick (Ed.), *Minnesota Symposia on Motivation*. Vol. 7. Minneapolis: University of Minnesota Press, 1973.

Bryan, J. H. Children's cooperation and helping behaviors. In E. M. Hetherington (Ed.), *Review of child development research*, Vol. 5. Chicago: The University of Chicago Press, 1975.

Bryan, J. H., & Walbek, N. Preaching and practicing generosity: Children's actions and reactions. *Child Development*, 1970, *41*, 329–353.

Buckley, N., Siegel, L. S., & Ness, S. Egocentrism, empathy, and altruistic behavior in young children. *Developmental Psychology*, 1979, *15*, 329–330.

Dienstbier, R. A., Hillman, D., Lehnhoff, J., Hillman, J., & Valkenaar, M. C. An emotion-attribution approach to moral behavior: Interfacing cognitive and avoidance theories of moral development. *Psychological Review*, 1975, *82*, 299–315.

Dlugokinski, E. L., & Firestone, I. J. Other centeredness and susceptibility to charitable appeals: Effects of perceived discipline. *Developmental Psychology*, 1974, *10*, 21–28.

Eisenberg-Berg, N., & Geisheker, E. Content of preachings and power of the model/preacher: The effect on children's generosity. *Developmental Psychology*, 1979, *15*, 168–175.

Elliot, R., & Vasta, R. The modeling of sharing: Effects associated with vicarious reinforcement, symbolization, age, and generalization. *Journal of Experimental Child Psychology*, 1970, *10*, 8–15.

Fischer, W. F. Sharing in preschool children as a function of amount and type of reinforcement. *Genetic Psychology Monographs*, 1963, *68*, 215–245.

Friedrich, L. K., & Stein, A. H. Prosocial television and young children: The effects of verbal labeling and role playing on learning and behavior. *Child Development*, 1975, *46*, 27–38.

Garbarino, J. The impact of anticipated reward upon cross-age tutoring. *Journal of Personality and Social Psychology*, 1975, *32*, 421–428.

Gelfand, D. M., Hartmann, D. P., Cromer, C. C., Smith, C. L., & Page, B. C. The effects of instructional prompts and praise on children's donation rates. *Child Development*, 1975, *46*, 980–983.

Grusec, J. E. Power and the internalization of aversive behaviors. *Child Development*, 1971, *42*, 93–105.

Grusec, J. E. Demand characteristics of the modeling experiment: Altruism as a function of age and aggression. *Journal of Personality and Social Psychology*, 1972, *22*, 139–148.

Grusec, J. E., & Kuczynski, L. Direction of effect in socialization: A comparison of the parent vs. the child's behavior as determinants of disciplinary techniques. *Developmental Psychology*, 1980, *16*, 1–9.

Grusec, J. E., & Redler, E. Attribution, reinforcement, and altruism. *Developmental Psychology*, 1980, *16*, 525–534.

Grusec, J. E., Kuczynski, L., Rushton, J. P., & Simutis, Z. Modeling, direct instruction, and attributions: Effects on altruism. *Developmental Psychology*, 1978, *14*, 51-57.

Grusec, J. E., Saas-Kortsaak, P., & Simutis, Z. M. The role of example and moral exhortation in the training of altruism. *Child Development*, 1978, *49*, 920-923.

Grusec, J. E., & Skubiski, S. L. Model nurturance, demand characteristics of the modeling experiment and altruism. *Journal of Personality and Social Psychology*, 1970, *14*, 352-359.

Hartmann, D. P., Gelfand, D. M., Smith, C. L., Paul, S. C., Cromer, C. C., Page, B. C., & Lebenta, D. V. Factors affecting the acquisition and elimination of children's donating behavior. *Journal of Experimental Child Psychology*, 1976, *21*, 328-338.

Hoffman, M. L. Moral development. In P. H. Mussen (Ed.), *Manual of child psychology*. New York: Wiley, 1970.

Hoffman, M. L. Altruistic behavior and the parent-child relationship. *Journal of Personality and Social Psychology*, 1975, *31*, 937-943.

Hoffman, M. L., & Saltzstein, H. D. Parent discipline and the child's moral development. *Journal of Personality and Social Psychology*, 1967, *5*, 45-57.

Iannotti, R. J. Effect of role-taking experiences on role taking, empathy, altruism, and aggression. *Developmental Psychology*, 1978, *14*, 119-124.

Jensen, A. M., & Moore, S. G. The effect of attribute statements on cooperativeness and competitiveness in school-age boys. *Child Development*, 1977, *48*, 305-307.

Lepper, M. R. Dissonance, self-perception, and honesty in children. *Journal of Personality and Social Psychology*, 1973, *25*, 65-74.

Lepper, M., Greene, D., & Nisbett, R. Undermining children's intrinsic interest with extrinsic reward: A test of the "overjustification" hypothesis. *Journal of Personality and Social Psychology*, 1973, *28*, 129-137.

Livesley, W. J., & Bromley, D. B. *Person perception in childhood and adolescence*. London: Wiley, 1973.

Midlarsky, E., & Bryan, J. H. Affect expressions and children's imitative altruism. *Journal of Experimental Research in Personality*, 1972, *6*, 195-203.

Miller, R. L., Brickman, P., & Bolen, D. Attribution versus persuasion as a means for modifying behavior. *Journal of Personality and Social Psychology*, 1975, *31*, 430-441.

Mischel, W., & Liebert, R. M. Effects of discrepancies between observed and imposed reward criteria on their acquisition and transmission. *Journal of Personality and Social Psychology*, 1966, *3*, 45-53.

Mowrer, O. H. *Learning theory and the symbolic processes*. New York: Wiley, 1960.

Murphy, L. *Social behavior and child personality: An exploratory study of some roots of sympathy*. New York: Columbia University Press, 1937.

Nelson, K. E., & Nelson, K. Cognitive pendulums and their linguistic realization. In K. E. Nelson (Ed.), *Children's language*. Vol. 1. New York: Gardner Press, 1978.

Nisbett, R. E., & Valins, S. *Perceiving the causes of one's own behavior*. Morristown, N.J.: General Learning Press, 1971.

Peevers, B. H., & Secord, P. F. Developmental changes in attribution of descriptive concepts to persons. *Journal of Personality and Social Psychology*, 1973, *27*, 120-128.

Perry, D. G., Bussey, K., & Redman, J. Reward-induced decreased play effects: Reattribution of motivation, competing responses, or avoiding frustration. *Child Development*, 1977, *48*, 1369-1374.

Perry, D. G., Perry, L. C., Bussey, K., English, D., & Arnold, G. Processes of attribution and children's self-punishment following misbehavior. *Child Development*, 1980, *51*, 545-552.

Reiss, S., & Sushinsky, L. Overjustification, competing responses, and the acquisition of intrinsic interest. *Journal of Personality and Social Psychology*, 1975, *31*, 1116-1125.

Rice, M. E., & Grusec, J. E. Saying and doing: Effects on observer performance. *Journal of Personality and Social Psychology*, 1975, *32*, 584-593.

Rosenhan, D. Some origins of concern for others. In P. H. Mussen, J. Langer, & M. Covington (Eds.), *Trends and issues in developmental psychology,* New York: Holt, Rinehart, & Winston, 1969.

Rosenthal, T. L., & Zimmerman, B. W. *Social learning and cognition.* New York: Academic Press, 1978.

Ross, M. The self perception of intrinsic motivation. In J. H. Harvey, W. J. Ickes, & R. F. Kidd (Eds.), *New directions in attribution research.* Vol. 1. Hillsdale, New Jersey: Lawrence Erlbaum Assoc., 1976.

Rubin, K. H., & Schneider, F. W. The relationship between moral judgment, egocentrism, and altruistic behavior. *Child Development,* 1973, *44,* 661–665.

Rushton, J. P. Generosity in children: Immediate and long-term effects of modeling, preaching, and moral judgment. *Journal of Personality and Social Psychology,* 1975, *31,* 459–466.

Rushton, J. P. Socialization and the altruistic behavior of children. *Psychological Bulletin,* 1976, *83,* 898–913.

Rushton, J. P., & Teachman, G. The effects of positive reinforcement, attributions, and punishment on model induced altruism in children. *Personality and Social Psychology Bulletin,* 1978, *4,* 322–325.

Rushton, J. P., & Wiener, J. Altruism and cognitive development in children. *British Journal of Social and Clinical Psychology,* 1975, *14,* 341–349.

Rutherford, E., & Mussen, P. Generosity in nursery school boys. *Child Development,* 1968, *39,* 755–765.

Sawin, D. B. *Assessing empathy in children: A search for an elusive construct.* Paper presented at the biannual meeting of the Society for Research in Child Development, San Francisco, March 1979.

Scribner, S., & Cole, M. Cognitive consequences of formal and informal education. *Science,* 1973, *182,* 553–559.

Smith, C. L., Gelfand, D. M., Hartmann, D. P., & Partlow, M. E. Y. Children's causal attributions regarding help-giving. *Child Development,* 1979, *50,* 203–210.

Staub, E. A child in distress: The influence of nurturance and modeling on children's attempts to help. *Developmental Psychology,* 1971, *5,* 124–132. (a)

Staub, E. The use of role playing and induction in children's learning of helping and sharing behavior. *Child Development,* 1971, *42,* 805–817. (b)

Staub, E. Effects of persuasion and modeling on delay of gratification. *Developmental Psychology,* 1972, *6,* 166–177.

Tulving, E. Episodic and semantic memory. In E. Tulving & W. Donaldson (Eds.), *Organization and memory.* New York: Academic Press, 1972.

Walters, G. C., & Grusec, J. E. *Punishment.* San Francisco: Freeman, 1977.

Weissbrod, C. S. Noncontingent warmth induction, cognitive style, and children's imitative donation and rescue effort behaviors. *Journal of Personality and Social Psychology,* 1976, *34,* 274–281.

White, G. M. Immediate and deferred effects of model observation and guided and unguided rehearsal on donating and stealing. *Journal of Personality and Social Psychology,* 1972, *21,* 139–148.

White, G. M., & Burnham, M. A. Socially cued altruism: Effects of modeling, instructions, and age on public and private donations. *Child Development,* 1975, *46,* 559–563.

Yarrow, M. R., & Scott, P. M. Imitation of nurturant and nonnurturant models. *Journal of Personality and Social Psychology,* 1972, *23,* 259–270.

Yarrow, M. R., Scott, P. M., & Waxler, C. Z. Learning concern for others. *Developmental Psychology,* 1973, *8,* 240–260.

Yates, G. C. R. Influence of televised modeling and verbalization on children's delay of gratification. *Journal of Experimental Child Psychology,* 1974, *18,* 333–339.

Zahn-Waxler, C., & Radke-Yarrow, M. *A developmental analysis of children's responses to emotions in others*. Paper presented at the biannual meeting of the Society for Research in Child Development, San Francisco, March, 1979.

Zahn-Waxler, C., Radke-Yarrow, M., & Brady-Smith, J. Perspective-taking and prosocial behavior. *Developmental Psychology, 1977, 13,* 87–88.

Zahn-Waxler, C., Radke-Yarrow, M., & King, R. A. Child rearing and children's prosocial initiations toward victims of distress. *Child Development, 1979, 50,* 319–330.

5 Television as a Socializer

J. Philippe Rushton
The University of Western Ontario

The results of many surveys have now shown that, in North America (1) almost every family has at least one television set, (2) the television is turned on for almost 6 hours per day in the average household, (3) both children and adults watch, on the average, over 3 hours of television daily, (4) about 40% of all leisure time is spent with television, and (5) television ranks third (behind sleep and work) as a consumer of time (e.g., *Ontario,* 1977). The figures relating to children are particularly interesting. Children begin watching television on a regular basis 3 or 4 years before entering Grade One and most children watch television every day. It has been estimated that by the time the child is 16 years of age—he or she will have spent more time with television than will ever be spent in any kind of classroom. Another comparison also demonstrates perspective: By the time a child is 5 and reaches kindergarten, he or she has spent more time watching television than a liberal arts student spends in the classroom throughout his or her 4 years at a university!

An important question that arises from such considerations is: Can the content of what is watched influence viewers' behavior? It is certainly true that people learn by watching others. Indeed, this is one of the most fundamental ways by which people learn new behavior. By watching others, people who enter new occupations learn skills and attitudes necessary to their new job. Also by watching others, people can learn the complex skills involved in new sports and leisure-time activities. Such learning often involves a great deal of effort and concentration. Other such learning, however, takes place quite automatically. Think of speech as an example. The majority of words we use are learned without conscious effort. Simply by observing others, people acquire the vocabulary and many of the rules of grammar that they use. People also acquire their accents and styles of delivery by observing others. Thus whether people use a wide or a more limited range of expressive gestures when they talk will depend to a large extent on the particular models they watched when they were learning the language. Much of this learning took place without their even being aware of it.

Children are particularly likely to learn by watching others. They are at a most formative period in their lives where they are striving to gain some understanding and mastery of the social world that they inhabit. By watching others and then imitating what they have seen they can learn the "rules" of social behavior. Although adults have very often learned to distinguish between who is appropriate and who is inappropriate to watch and learn from, young children very often have not made this distinction.

Of particular importance for the current purpose is the research that confirms that watching others leads to learning the norms and emotional responses that people have for each other (Rushton, 1980). One of the most important implications of this pertains to television. If one of the main ways in which people learn is by observing others, then it follows that people can learn a great deal from viewing others on television. This has been a question of concern for more than two decades now (Himmelweit, Oppenheim & Vince, 1958).

In recent years, concern has focused primarily on whether violence on television contributes to the amount of violence in society. Many governmental inquiries as well as scholarly researchers have investigated this question and a vast literature has come into being. Although there are still dissenters (e.g., Halloran, 1978; Kaplan & Singer, 1976), the weight of the evidence appears to demonstrate that television portrayals of violence do increase the amount of antisocial behavior in society. For example, a recent Canadian Royal Commission of inquiry into the problem concluded:

> If the amount of depicted violence that exists in the North American intellectual environment could be expressed in terms of a potentially dangerous food or drink additive . . . there is little doubt that society long since would have demanded a stop to it . . . [*Ontario,* Vol. 1, 1977, p. 51].

Other recent reviews have also concluded that the portrayal of violence on television increases antisocial behaviors (Comstock, Chaffee, Katzman, McCombs, & Roberts, 1978; Liebert & Schwartzberg, 1977; Murray & Kippax, 1979; Parke, Berkowitz, Leyens, West & Sebastian, 1977; Rushton, 1980).

It is not the intention in this chapter to consider this evidence yet again; rather it is to focus on television as a force for good. Although there has long been a research interest in the possible harmful effects of media violence, the other side of the coin, the potential for good has only recently been investigated. Notwithstanding its recency, this research literature is now burgeoning. It demonstrates that television can have quite diverse effects, including the power to influence prosocial behavior. (The term "prosocial" is used to specify that which is socially desirable and which in some ways benefits another person or society at large.) This definition will involve a value judgment based on the wider social context. The present chapter reviews some of the key studies in this more recent line of inquiry into television effects. It borrows heavily from the outline and content I have followed in previous discussion of this same literature (Rushton, 1977, 1979, 1980).

This chapter investigates the consequences of showing five types of television content to viewers. The first type of programming is altruistic in nature, and includes such behaviors as generosity, helping, and cooperation. The second concerns showing friendly behavior. The third involves showing self-control behaviors such as resisting temptation and delaying gratification. The fourth involves showing both adults and children coping with their fears. Finally the portrayal of occupational, ethnic group, and sex roles is examined. Some of the studies examined the television effects in laboratory situations and others used more naturalistic environments. As we shall see the results from both settings come to similar conclusions. Nonetheless throughout the review a clear demarcation is made between the two types of testing environments. The term television is used here in the widest sense; i.e., it will include specially constructed videotapes used purely for experimental or therapeutic purposes in addition to commercial television programs. The nature of the programming is clearly specified throughout the review.

THE EFFECTS OF SHOWING ALTRUISTIC BEHAVIORS ON TELEVISION

Laboratory Studies

In a series of experiments, reviewed by Bryan (1975) several hundred 6- to 9-year-old children, of both sexes, were shown specially constructed 5-minute videotape film of a model who played on a bowling game, won gift certificates, and donated or did not donate some of these gift certificates to a charity. Subsequently, the child was watched through a one-way mirror to see how much of his or her winnings he or she donated to a similar charity. The results showed that children were strongly influenced by what they had seen the models doing on TV. Children who had watched generosity on the videotape gave more of their certificates to the charity than did those children who had watched selfishness portrayed. Other studies, using similar procedures, have replicated Bryan's findings. Elliot and Vasta (1970) showed that 5- to 7-year-old children were influenced by television models to share both candy and money. Rushton and Owen (1975) found that 8- to 10-year-old British children were influenced to donate tokens to a charity by watching TV models do so.

The film material used in these studies was not like that produced for commercial purposes however. It lasted for only 5 minutes and showed one person acting a number of times in just one way (e.g., being generous) in one highly specific situation. In addition the child who watched was then tested in exactly the same situation in which he or she had seen the model act. Sprafkin, Liebert, and Poulos (1975) went further than the aforementioned studies and conceptually replicated the previous findings with a highly successful commercial television program, *Lassie*. They divided 30 5-year-old white middle-class children into three groups and showed each group one of three half-hour television films, complete with commercials. A prosocial *Lassie* program involved Jeff, Lassie's master, risking his life by hanging over the edge of a mine shaft to rescue Lassie's pup. A neutral *Lassie* film and a neutral non*Lassie* film made up two control groups. After watching the programs the children were taken to another room where they could earn points toward a prize by playing on a game. During the course of playing the game they had an opportunity to aid puppies in distress by calling for help by pressing a Help button. Pressing the Help button, however, would interfere with earning points toward the prize. The average time spent pressing the Help button for children who had watched the prosocial Lassie was 93 seconds, whereas in the two neutral conditions it was 52 and 38 seconds respectively. Thus this study supported the previous laboratory studies using a program from a highly successful commercial series.

Collins and Getz (1976) also carried out a laboratory investigation using a regular program complete with commercials. They edited a television action-adventure drama made for adults such that in one version a model responded constructively to an interpersonal conflict while in another he responded aggressively. Fourth, seventh, and tenth graders saw one of these versions or a wildlife documentary control. They were then given an opportunity to either help or hurt a fictitious peer who was apparently completing a task by either pressing a "help" button which shut off a distracting noise or a "hurt" button which increased it. Children of all ages who had seen models of constructive coping showed greater prosocial responding than subjects in the other two conditions, i.e., they gave more help responses than children who viewed either the aggression or the control programs.

Naturalistic Studies

Friedrich and Stein (1973) carried out a study with 97 nursery school children. First, the children's naturally occurring free play behavior was coded into categories such as "aggressive," prosocial," and "self-control." The children were then randomly assigned to one of three groups and exposed to 4 weeks of selected television. The first group watched aggressive television films such as *Batman* and *Superman* cartoons. A second group watched "neutral" films such as children working on a farm, and a third group watched *Mister Rogers' Neighborhood,* a prosocial education television program that stresses cooperation, sharing, sympathy, affection and friendship. During the 4-week exposure to one of the three television diets, the children's free play behavior was recorded by observers who were "blind" as to experimental condition.

The results of this experiment demonstrated that the programs did have some effect on the children's subsequent aggressive or prosocial behavior. The aggressive television content led to increased interpersonal aggression for those children who were above average in such aggression at baseline. However the effects did not generalize to a 2-week retest. Although exposure to the prosocial television content led to increased prosocial behavior, it did so only in the children from the lower half of the socioeconomic status distribution. Here too, however, the results failed to extend to the 2-week retest. Both the aggressive and prosocial films had stronger effects on the measures of self-control as we shall see when we come to that section.

In a subsequent study with *Mister Rogers' Neighborhood,* Friedrich and Stein (1975) randomly assigned 73 preschoolers to one of five conditions. One group of children watched four "neutral" programs about nature and other topics unrelated to interpersonal behavior. The other four groups saw four programs from *Mister Rogers' Neighborhood* chosen to form a dramatic sequence. In this sequence, a crisis arose in which one of the characters feared that she would be replaced by a fancy new visitor. Action centered on the attempts of friends to understand her feelings, reassure her of her uniqueness, and help her. Children watched the television programs in groups of three or four over 4 days. Results indicated that when children were asked questions such as "How do friends show they like you?" those who had watched the prosocial television films reported more ways of showing how friends demonstrated affection than children who had watched neutral films. This was true both in situations that were similar to those in the *Mister Rogers' Neighborhood* program and also to those that involved new situations. On another test a behavioral measure of helping another child in a quite different context; while there were no overall differences between those children who had watched prosocial television programs and those who had watched the neutral television programs, it was found that if watching the prosocial television had been paired with direct training to be helpful through "role-playing" techniques, then children in this condition were more helpful than those who had been given the training but no diet of prosocial television. This suggests the possibility that prosocial television might be used as an adjunct to other training procedures when attempting to teach or enhance prosocial tendencies in children—as nursery school teachers and parents might well wish to do.

This latter conclusion gains additional credence from a study by Friedrich-Cofer, Huston-Stein, Kipnis, Susman, and Clewett (1979). They found that even 8 weeks of prosocial television, by itself, did not influence the behavior of urban poor children. However, if the prosocial television was augmented with themes from *Mister Rogers' Neighborhood* acted out in class, then significant behavioral gains in prosocial behavior were found compared to control groups.

A particularly ambitious and realistic study was carried out by Moriarty and McCabe (1977) with 259 children and youth engaged in organized team sports. Participants in Little League baseball, lacrosse and ice-hockey were included. Both the antisocial and prosocial behavior of the players on the field, before, during, and after experimental treatment were measured. The experimental treatment consisted of providing antisocial, prosocial, and control video presentations of the relevant sport to the randomly assigned teams. The prosocial material consisted of (1) altruism—helping, encouraging, and team work; (2) sympathy—compassion, pity, and caring for another's plight; (3) courtesy—displays of respect; (4) reparation—correcting a wrong, or apologizing; and (5) affection—any overt expression of positive feelings towards another. The results indicated that exposure to the prosocial content clearly increased the level of prosocial behavior for the hockey and lacrosse players, although not for baseball players. The showing of the antisocial programs had no effect in this particular study.

Finally a study might be reported that assessed the relative influence of role-playing and prosocial television content in facilitating altruism. Ahammer and Murray (1979) showed Australian kindergarten children television programs such as *Lassie, I Love Lucy, The Brady Bunch* and *Father Knows Best*. On the basis of a content analysis some of these programs were designated as high in prosocial television while others were designated as neutral. The prosocial programs had a high frequency of expressing concern for others' feelings, sympathy, task persistence, and explaining feelings of self or others. The children were either assigned as a class to a "prosocial" viewing condition or to a "neutral" viewing condition. The viewing took place ½ hour per day, 5 days per week, for 4 weeks. The children were pretested on a variety of measures one week prior to the onset of television viewing and were posttested on these same measures one week after the conclusion of training. The results indicated that the prosocial television condition was associated with increases in a situational test of helping (for boys only) and increases in a test of cooperation (for both boys and girls). Helping had been measured by the child's willingness to forego playing with some attractive toys in order to help another absent child complete a task which consisted of placing marbles in a box one at a time. Cooperation was indexed by the number of candies that the child won in contrast to his or her partner, while playing on a Madsen cooperation/competition table. Thus observation of standard television programs in which the main characters displayed concern for others, could be effective in facilitating altruism in specific situational tests quite dissimilar from the situations seen on the programs. Of interest in this study was the finding that role-playing techniques were even more effective in facilitating altruism than was the prosocial television. This latter finding, of course, does not detract from the fact that prosocial television had independent effects.

THE EFFECTS OF SHOWING FRIENDLY BEHAVIORS ON TELEVISION

Laboratory Studies

Fryrear and Thelen (1969) assigned boys and girls of nursery school age to one of two main television viewing groups: one which observed an adult demonstrating "affectionate" behavior toward a small stuffed clown, and a control group. Children were subsequently given an opportunity to play with a group of toys which included the small clown. An observer sat in the back of the room and watched to see whether the child imitated the affectionate behavior toward the toy. Children who watched television films of affectionate behavior were subsequently more likely to express similar affection than children who had not seen such behavior on television.

Gorn, Goldberg and Kanungo (1976) carried out a study in Canada to investigate whether prosocial television content could increase nursery school children's friendliness toward ethnic minorities. After being exposed to special "Sesame Street" inserts containing nonwhite children, a sample of 3- to 5-year old white children showed a strong preference for playing with nonwhites as opposed to whites. This sharply contrasted with the preferences of a control group not exposed to these inserts.

Naturalistic Studies

O'Connor (1969) conducted a dramatic and potentially important study to see if television programs could be used to enhance social interaction among those nursery school children who tended to isolate themselves from their peers. Thirteen severely solitary children were chosen for the study. These children were interacting on fewer than five of 32 possible interactions reliably observed over an 8-day period. One group of these isolated children was then shown a specially prepared sound-color film shown over a television console. This film portrayed a graduated sequence of 11 scenes in which children interacted in a nursery school setting with reinforcing consequences ensuing. All the scenes were accompanied by a female narrator describing the actions of the model and the responses of the other children. For comparison purposes, a second group of children were shown a film of dolphins engaging in acrobatic feats.

The results were quite dramatic. Children who had watched the specially made film about others engaging in social interaction increased from their baseline score of an average of nearly 2 interactions out of the 32 possible to an average of nearly 12 interactions out of the possible 32. The control group showed no increase over their baseline scores. Furthermore, a follow-up at the end of the school year showed that the changes were durable over time.

In a subsequent study, O'Connor (1972) selected 33 social isolates from four nursery school populations according to both teacher ratings and behavioral samples obtained by trained observers. In a 2 × 2 factorial design, half of the children viewed a specially constructed 23-min modeling film depicting appropriate social behavior, while the other half viewed a control film. Half of the subjects in each film condition then received social reinforcement contingent upon the performance of peer interaction behaviors. Modeling was shown to be a more rapid modification procedure than was shaping-through-reinforcement, and resulted in more stable social interaction patterns over time, with or without the attendant social reinforcement. In the follow-up assessments, modeling subjects remained at the original baseline level of nonisolates, while social reinforcement and control subjects returned to isolate baseline level.

In a study of similar nature, Keller and Carlson (1974) showed 19 socially isolated preschoolers either four 5-minute videotapes in which social skills (e.g., how to socially reinforce peers) were modeled (treatment) or 4 sequences of a nature film (control). The frequency with which subjects dispensed and received social reinforcement and the frequency of social interaction were rated by observers pre- and post-treatment and at follow-up. Results indicated that treatment produced increases in all 3 dependent measures for the treatment group.

Coates, Pusser, and Goodman (1976) assessed the effects of both *Sesame Street* and *Mister Rogers' Neighborhood* on 32 preschool children. The frequency of these children's behaviors were recorded into one of three categories:

> (1) *Positive reinforcement:* giving positive attention such as praise and approval, sympathy, reassurance, and smiling and laughing; giving affectionate physical contact such as hugging, kissing, and holding hands; giving tangible reinforcement such as tokens, prizes and other objects; (2) *Punishment:* giving verbal criticism and rejection such as criticism, negative greetings, obvious ignorings, and sarcasm; giving negative physical contact such as hitting, biting, and kicking; withdrawing or refusing tangible reinforcement such as taking away a toy; and (3) *Social contact:* any physical or verbal contact between a child and another child or adult.

Following these baseline measures children watched either 15 minutes of *Sesame Street* or 15 minutes of *Mister Rogers' Neighborhood* for each of four days. These programs had previously been content analyzed for the frequency of occurrence of positive reinforcement and punishment. After watching the programs, the children were observed and the frequency with which they behaved in any of the categories mentioned above was recorded. In addition, a four day follow-up was undertaken. The results showed that the television programs affected the children's social behavior in a significant manner, particularly on the immediate post-viewing tests. For all children *Mister Rogers' Neighborhood* significantly increased the giving of positive reinforcement to, and social contacts with, both other children and adults. For *Sesame Street* the effects were only found for children who had low baseline scores.

THE EFFECTS OF SHOWING SELF-CONTROL
BEHAVIORS ON TELEVISION

Laboratory Studies

Stein and Bryan (1972) explained to 80 8- and 9-year-old girls the rules by which they could win money by playing an electronic bowling game. Before playing the game the children watched a television program in which they saw a same sex peer playing the same game. This peer model either behaved in violation of these rules or in accordance with them. Children who observed the transgressing model cheated more than twice as much as those who observed a model adhering to the rules.

Wolf and Cheyne (1972) carried out an experiment with 7- to 8-year-old boys. First the children were taken to a games room and allowed to play with some toys. They were forbidden, however, to touch or play with one particularly attractive toy. It was found that an average of 4 minutes and 40 seconds would go by before an average boy in this situation would touch the toy. However, if the boy had watched a TV program of another same-age boy playing with similar toys and this TV child had *not* touched the toy, then the average boy would wait nearly 8 minutes before transgressing. If, on the other hand, the TV program had shown another boy violating the rule and touching the forbidden toy, then the subject would be likely to touch the toy in less than 3 minutes. Very similar results were found when the measure of the child's resistance to temptation was based on the *length* of time he played with the toy. The average boy would play with the forbidden toy for about 1 minute out of the 10 that was observed. If he watched a TV program depicting violation of the rules then he would play with the forbidden toy for nearly 4 out of 10 minutes. If however, he watched a TV program showing adherence to the rules then he would touch the forbidden toy for only about 7 seconds. Wolf and Cheyne (1972) brought the boys back one month later and put them into the same situation. The results still showed an effect for the television program. Whereas children who had seen no television film one month earlier managed to resist the temptation for nearly 6 minutes, boys who had seen a model giving in to the temptation, only resisted for 4 minutes. In this 4-week retest no effect was found for the "self-controlled" model however. These results were replicated by Wolf (1973).

Another form of self-control is the ability to delay gratification to a later point in time. Yates (1974) carried out a study with 72 8-year-old New Zealand children. Baselines were established by asking children if they would prefer a small reward such as money immediately, or a larger one by waiting for 7 days. Some time later, some of the children watched television programs of an adult female model exemplify high-delay behavior and/or verbalize reasons for delaying gratification. Other children did not watch such programs. Compared to controls, children who had watched the television programs showing delay of gratification were subsequently more likely themselves to choose to delay their gratification for a larger reward later. Furthermore, when the children were retested 4 weeks later their behavior still showed the effects of the exposure to the television film.

Naturalistic Studies

In a study described previously in the section on altruistic behavior (Friedrich & Stein, 1973), either the prosocial television program *Mister Rogers' Neighborhood*, the aggressive television programs of *Superman* and *Batman,* or neutral fare was shown to 93 4-year-old nursery school children for a 4-week period. During this time their naturally occurring free-play behavior was observed. Three categories of self-control behavior had been recorded. These were: obedience to rules, tolerance of delay, and persisting at task. In regard to the obedience to rules category, aggressive films decreased this behavior in relation to neutral films, whereas the prosocial films increased it, producing an overall difference. In regard to tolerating delay, the aggressive films significantly decreased such behaviors over both the neutral and prosocial conditions that did not differ from one another. Furthermore these particular effects were maintained across the 2-week retest. Finally the prosocial television content increased persistence at tasks over the neutral and aggressive films on both immediate and later observations.

THE EFFECTS OF SHOWING PEOPLE COPING WITH THEIR FEARS ON TELEVISION

Laboratory Studies

The first study to be reported concerns young children who were inappropriately afraid of dogs. Bandura and Menlove (1968) first measured 3- to 5-year-old children's willingness to approach and play with a cocker spaniel on a number of occasions, to determine which children were afraid of dogs. Some children were then shown eight specially prepared 3-minute film programs over an 8-day period in which they saw other children playing with dogs. Another group of fearful children were shown movies of Disneyland instead. After watching these films, the children were given opportunities to approach live dogs. Previously fearful children who had watched other children showing courage were now much more likely to approach and play with the dogs than the children in the control group were. Furthermore, this reduction in fear generalized to dogs quite different from those seen in the film, and was maintained over a 4-week retest period.

A study by Bandura, Blanchard, and Ritter (1971) investigated whether film programming could help adolescents and adults reduce their fear of snakes. Only those who reported having a severe fear of snakes took part. For example, their dread of snakes had actually to be so severe as to interfere with their ability to do gardening or go camping. These people were then shown films of young children, adolescents, and adults engaging in progressively threatening interactions with a large king snake for 35 minutes. Behavioral measures were then taken in the presence of live snakes. The findings were clear. People who had watched the film significantly reduced their fears. It might be mentioned that the behavioral measures were quite stringent and included actually holding the snake in the hands. The ultimate test (which 33% of the subjects performed) including allowing the snake to lie in their laps while they held their hands passively at their sides.

Weissbrod and Bryan (1973) attempted to see whether similar techniques would succeed with 8- to 9-year-old children who had indicated an extreme fear of snakes on a fear inventory, and also refused to pet a snake during a pretest. These children watched a 2 ½ min videotaped sequence involving a model either approaching a live 4-ft. boa constrictor (the experimental group) or a stuffed 5-ft. toy snake (the comparison condition). All children watched their respective films twice through and then, 2 days later, watched them twice through again. Following this second showing of the film the children were taken to an aquarium that housed a 4-ft. boa constrictor and asked to touch, then pet, and then hold the snake. The experimental group were able to go further into the sequence than the control comparison group, and furthermore, maintained their superiority on another test taken 2 weeks later. For example, although none of the ten children in the control were able to actually handle the snake 2 weeks after watching a "neutral" film, 11 out of the 40 children in the experimental condition could.

Naturalistic Studies

Melamed and Siegel (1975) showed 60 children aged 4 to 12 who were about to undergo elective surgery for hernias, tonsillectomies, or urinary-genital tract difficulties, either a relevant peer modeling film of a child being hospitalized and receiving surgery or an unrelated control film. The experimental film was 16 minutes in length and consisted of 15 scenes showing various events that most children hospitalized for elective surgery encounter. Both groups received extensive preparation by the hospital staff. State measures of anxiety, including self-report, behavioral observation, and Palmar Sweat Index, revealed a significant reduction of preoperative (night before) and postoperative (3-4 week postsurgery examination) fear arousal in the experimental as compared to the control film group. In addition parents reported more problem behavior in the children who had not seen the modeling film.

Effects for the therapeutic value of film modeling have been demonstrated in a number of other studies. O'Connor (1969, 1972) used film models to decrease children's fear of social interaction. Jaffe and Carlson (1972) and Mann (1972) treated test-anxious university and high school students with videtaped modeling procedures and found significant improvement on performance measures. Shaw and Thoresen (1974) demonstrated that specially constructed films can effectively reduce adults' fears of dental treatment. These authors used actual visits to the dentist for treatment as their measure of success. Video desensitization has also been successfully applied to the treatment of sexual dysfunction among women (Wincze & Caird, 1976).

Only a very few of the many studies that have used modeling films to systematically diminish anxiety in therapeutic contexts have been reviewed here. Major reviews of this particular literature have been carried out by Rosenthal and Bandura (1978) and Thelen, Fry, Fehrenbach and Frantschi (1979). Both reviews conclude that such films have vast therapeutic potential.

THE EFFECTS OF SHOWING OCCUPATIONAL, ETHNIC GROUP, AND SEX ROLE BEHAVIOR ON TELEVISION

To what extent are our conceptions about occupations, ethnic groups, and sex roles influenced by how we see them portrayed on television? Given the power of television to alter both viewer's aggressive and prosocial behavior, it might well be expected that such expectations *would* be readily influenced. Strangely enough, far less research has been aimed at this particular question. Although researchers have carried out several content analyses of the social roles portrayed on television they have not, in the main, carried out research to see whether these particular portrayals are subsequently mirrored in viewers' perceptions. Let us examine the content analyses.

In regard to occupational roles, Smythe (1954) in an early study, found that teachers were portrayed as the kindest and fairest, journalists the most honest, and scientists the least kind, the most unfair, and the least honest of all the occupations he looked at. DeFleur (1964) found that television portrayed the police as generally hardened and often brutal; private investigators as resourceful and more capable than the police; salesmen as glib; journalists as callous; and truck drivers as aggressive. In a more recent study, Williams, Zabrack and Joy (1977) found that the police were portrayed as powerful, interesting, satisfied with their lives, and overwhelmingly emotionally stable. This was similar to a finding by Dominick (1978) who also found that television police were far more efficient than are police in real life. Dominick (1978) also noted that the portrayal of law enforcement on prime time television had increased dramatically over the years from 7% in 1953 to 27% in 1977.

Psychiatrists and their mentally ill patients have also been represented in different ways from earlier times to more recent ones. Winick (1978) found, for example, in an analysis of 151 movies made from 1919 to 1978 that there was an increasing trend that as mental illness and its treatment became more accepted, there was a tendency to make the patient and his therapist less exotic, magical, frightening, and more human.

In regard to ethnic groups, the characters portrayed on North American television are overwhelmingly young, white, middle class, and American (Williams *et al.*, 1977). Most ethnic minorities and citizens of foreign countries are ignored. When they are presented they are often made to look either ridiculous or villainous and this has been a source of hurt and irritation to groups as far flung as Chinese, Italians, Mexicans, and perhaps particularly, Native Peoples. Even Canadians have sometimes been concerned at the way in which they have been portrayed, particularly in Hollywood movies (Berton, 1975). In response to black American protest, portrayals of black Americans seem to have shifted somewhat in recent years, so that they are now presented both more frequently and in higher-status positions. In a recent content analysis, Donagher, Poulos, Liebert, and Davidson (1975) found that black males, for example, were usually portrayed as nonaggressive, persistent, altruistic, and more likely to make reparation for injury than any other group. Black women expressed a high ability to explain feelings in order to increase understanding, resolve strife, and reassure others. Unfortunately, as mentioned, very few studies have actually been carried out to see whether television portrayals are ever mirrored in viewer's perceptions.

One interesting study that did look at viewers perceptions was carried out by Vidmar and Rokeach (1974). These authors investigated racially prejudiced and nonprejudiced viewers perceptions of Archie Bunker, the chief protagonist in the comedy satire *All in the Family*. Archie Bunker is a conservative, superpatriotic working-class American who engages in a great deal of racial and ethnic prejudice but who is at the same time very endearing in many ways, especially when everything goes wrong for him (as it often does). One of the stated aims of the program is to bring racial bigotry into the open and make fun of it, thus serving to reduce it. Vidmar and Rokeach (1974) found however that how the viewers perceived the program depended on their preexisting attitudes. High prejudiced viewers, as measured by a questionnaire, were more likely to perceive Archie as admirable and to make better sense and win arguments than low prejudiced viewers. Thus, the authors concluded, the program may inadvertently be reinforcing prejudice and racism in those already prejudiced. The selectivity of preception was further documented by Vidmar and Rokeach (1974) by some data these authors had collected about another program *Sanford and Son*. This is a situation comedy modeled after *All in the Family* about a black junk dealer who is prejudiced against whites. Sanford, the junk dealer, is lazy, lives in a junkyard, and throws his beer cans out the front door. On the other hand, his son Lamont is ambitious and hard working. The authors found that high prejudiced persons were significantly more likely to perceive Sanford as typical of blacks than were low prejudiced viewers.

Although studies such as that by Vidmar and Rokeach (1974) clearly demonstrate that television content is perceived differently by different types of people, they do not speak directly to the question of whether television programs can modify prejudiced attitudes. At least two such studies have been carried out directly on this question. One very early British study did find that television could increase children's knowledge about foreigners (Himmelweit, Oppenheim & Vince, 1958). A recent Canadian study found that children's play preferences could be made more favorable to minority groups after viewing special inserts on *Sesame Street* (Gorn, Goldberg, & Kanungo, 1976).

In regard to the portrayal of sex roles, some concern has been expressed in regard to the way females have been portrayed. A study by Sternglanz and Serbin (1974) provided support for this concern. These authors content analyzed a number of children's programs that had high Nielsen ratings. They found, first of all, that males were portrayed nearly twice as often as females. There were also major differences between the sexes in the types of behavior portrayed. Males, for instance, were more often portrayed as aggressive and constructive (e.g., building, planning) than females, while females were more likely to be shown as deferent and passive. In addition, the consequences that males and females received for emitting behavior were different, with males more often being rewarded and females more often receiving no consequence. An exception to this was that females were more often punished for high levels of activity than were males. On the other hand, at least when women were portrayed they were presented as ''interesting'' and ''emotionally stable'' (Williams et al., 1977).

Finally, Silverman, Sprafkin & Rubinstein (1979) in an analysis of sexual behavior on prime time TV, found, that sexual innuendos have dramatically increased in frequency in recent years; while the TV viewer in 1975 could hear an average of about one innuendo per hour, in 1977 he or she could hear about seven. Interestingly enough it was white females who were disproportionately responsible for the physically suggestive behaviors. (Black females affectionately touched children; males engaged in aggression!)

It appears that commercially produced television programs are carrying quite different messages about the appropriate behavior for males and females. Given the general evidence on the powerful effectiveness of modeling on television as a means of teaching behavior, television may well be an important source in the learning of stereotyped sex roles.

SUMMARY AND CONCLUSION: UNDERSTANDING TELEVISION EFFECTS.

People learn norms, the ''rules'' of social behavior, from watching others. This is the key to understanding the effects of television. Television is much more than mere entertainment; it is also a major source of observational learning experiences, a setter of norms. It determines what people will judge to be appropriate behavior in a variety of situations.

In this chapter, over two dozen experimental investigations were reviewed from an even larger body of data. These studies, from both laboratory and naturalistic settings, demonstrated that television programming can modify viewers' social behavior in a prosocial direction. Generosity, helping, cooperation, friendliness, adhering to rules, delaying gratification, and a lack of fear can all be increased by television material. This suggests that television is an effective agent of socialization; that television entertainment is modifying the viewers perception of the world and how to live in it.

From the present vantage point, therefore, it would appear that television does act as a socializer. The evidence suggests that it influences the social behavior of viewers in the direction the content of the programs dictate. If, on the one hand, prosocial helping and kindness make up the content of television programming, then this is what may be learned by viewers as appropriate, normative behavior. If, on the other hand, antisocial behaviors and uncontrolled aggression are shown, then these are what viewers may learn to be the norm. This view will fit well with the fact that billions of dollars are spent annually by advertisers on North American television. Advertisers believe, correctly, that brief, 30 second exposures of their product, repeated over and over, will significantly modify the viewing public's behavior in regard to those products. The message therefore seems clear: People learn from watching television and what they learn will depend on what they watch. As discussed in detail elsewhere (Rushton, 1980), it might very well be that television has become one of the major agencies of socialization that our society currently possesses.

REFERENCES

Ahammer, I. M., & Murray, J. P. Kindness in the kindergarten: The relative influence of role playing and prosocial television in facilitating altruism. *International Journal of Behavioral Development*, 1979, *2*, 133–157.

Bandura, A., Blanchard, E. B., & Ritter, B. The relative efficacy of desensitization and modeling approaches for inducing behavioral, affective and attitudinal changes. *Journal of Personality and Social Psychology*, 1971, *13*, 113–199.

Bandura, A., & Menlove, F. L. Factors determining vicarious extinction of avoidance behavior through symbolic modeling. *Journal of Personality and Social Psychology*, 1968, *8*, 99–108.

Berton, P. *Hollywood's Canada*. Toronto: McClelland and Stewart, 1975.

Bryan, J. H. Children's cooperation and helping behaviors. In E. M. Hetherington (Ed.), *Review of child development research* (Vol. 5). Chicago: University of Chicago Press, 1975.

Coates, B., Pusser, H. E., & Goodman, I. The influence of "Sesame Street" and "Mister Rogers' Neighborhood" on children's social behavior in the preschool. *Child Development*, 1976, *47*, 138–144.

Collins, W. A., & Getz, S. K. Children's social responses following modeled reactions to provocation: Prosocial effects of a television drama. *Journal of Personality*, 1976, *44*, 488–500.

Comstock, G., Chaffee, S., Katzman, N., McCombs, M., & Roberts, D. *Television and human behavior*. New York: Columbia University Press, 1978.

DeFleur, M. L. Occupational roles as portrayed on television. *Public Opinion Quarterly*, 1964, *28*, 57–74.

Dominick, J. R. Crime and law enforcement in the mass media. In C. Winick (Ed.), *Sage Annual Reviews of Studies in Deviance*, Vol. 2 *Deviance and Mass Media*. Beverly Hills, Ca.: Sage Publications, Inc., 1978.

Donagher, P. C., Poulos, R. W., Liebert, R. M., & Davidson, E. S. Race, sex and social example: An analysis of character portrayals on interracial television entertainment. *Psychological Reports*, 1975, *37*, 1023–1034.

Elliot, R., & Vasta, R. The modeling of sharing: Effects associated with vicarious reinforcement, symbolization, age, and generalization. *Journal of Experimental Child Psychology*, 1970, *10*, 8–15.

Friedrich, L. K., & Stein, A. H. Aggressive and prosocial television programs and the natural behavior of preschool children. *Monographs of the Society for Research in Child Development*, 1973, *38* (4, Serial No. 151).

Friedrich, L. K., & Stein, A. H. Prosocial television and young children: The effects of verbal labeling and role playing on learning and behavior. *Child Development*, 1975, *46*, 27–38.

Friedrich-Cofer, L. K., Huston-Stein, A., Kipnis, D. M., Susman, E. J., & Clewett, A. S. Environmental enhancement of prosocial television content: Effects of interpersonal behavior, imaginative play, and self-regulation in a natural setting. *Developmental Psychology*, 1979, *15*, 637–646.

Fryrear, J. L., & Thelen, M. H. Effect of sex of model and sex of observer on the imitation of affectionate behavior. *Developmental Psychology*, 1969, *1*, 298.

Gorn, G. J., Goldberg, M. E., & Kanungo, R. N. The role of educational television in changing the intergroup attitudes of children. *Child Development*, 1976, *47*, 277–280.

Halloran, J. D. Studying violence and the media: A sociological approach. In C. Winick (Ed.), *Sage Annual Reviews of Studies in Deviance*. Vol. 2. *Deviance and Mass Media*. Beverly Hills, Ca.: Sage Publications, Inc., 1978.

Himmelweit, H., Oppenheim, A. N., & Vince, P. *Television and the child: An empirical study of the effects of television on the young*. London: Oxford University Press, 1958.

Jaffe, P. G., & Carlson, P. M. Modeling therapy for test anxiety: The role of model affect and consequences. *Behavior Research and Therapy*, 1972, *10*, 329–339.

Kaplan, R. M., & Singer, R. D. Television violence and viewer aggression: A re-examination of the evidence. *Journal of Social Issues*, 1976, *32*(4), 35–70.

Keller, M. F., & Carlson, P. M. Social skills in preschool children with low levels of social responsiveness. *Child Development*, 1974, *45*, 912–919.

Liebert, R. M., & Schwartzberg, N. S. Effects of mass media. *Annual Review of Psychology*, 1977, *28*, 141–173.

Mann, J. Vicarious desensitization of test anxiety through observation of videotaped treatment. *Journal of Counseling Psychology*, 1972, *19*, 1–7.

Melamed, B. G., & Siegel, L. J. Reduction of anxiety in children facing hospitalization and surgery by use of filmed modeling. *Journal of Consulting and Clinical Psychology*, 1975, *43*, 511–521.

Moriarty, D., & McCabe, A. E. Studies of television and youth sport. In *Ontario. Royal Commission on Violence in the Communications Industry. Report* (Vol. 5). *Learning from the Media*. (Research Reports) Toronto: Queen's Printer for Ontario, 1977.

Murray, J. P., & Kippax, S. From the early window to the late night show: A cross-national review of television's impact on children and adults. In L. Berkowitz (Ed.), *Advances in Experimental Social Psychology* (Vol. 12). New York: Academic Press, 1979.

O'Connor, R. D. Modification of social withdrawal through symbolic modeling. *Journal of Applied Behavior Analysis*, 1969, *2*, 15–22.

O'Connor, R. D. Relative efficacy of modeling, shaping, and the combined procedures for modification of social withdrawal. *Journal of Abnormal Psychology*, 1972, *79*, 327–334.

Ontario. Royal Commission on Violence in the Communications Industry. Report. Vol. 1. *Approaches, conclusions and recommendations* Vol. 2. *Violence and the media: A bibliography*

Vol. 3. *Violence in television, films and news* Vol. 4. *Violence in print and music* Vol. 5. *Learning from the media* Vol. 6. *Vulnerability to media effects* Vol. 7. *The media industries: From here to where?* Toronto, Ontario: Queen's Printer for Ontario, 1977.

Parke, R. D., Berkowitz, L., Leyens, J. P., West, S., & Sebastian, R. J. Some effects of violent and nonviolent movies on the behavior of juvenile delinquents. In L. Berkowitz (Ed.), *Advances in experimental social psychology* (Vol. 10). New York: Academic Press, 1977.

Rosenthal, T. L., & Bandura, A. Psychological modeling: Theory and practice. In S. L. Garfield & A. E. Bergin (Eds.), *Handbook of Psychotherapy and Behavior Change*. New York: Wiley, 1978.

Rushton, J. P. Television and prosocial behavior. In *Ontario. Royal Commission on Violence in the Communications Industry. Report.* (Vol. 5). Toronto: Queen's Printer for Ontario, 1977.

Rushton, J. P. The effects of prosocial television and film material on the behavior of viewers. In L. Berkowitz (Ed.), *Advances in Experimental Social Psychology* (Vol. 12). New York: Academic Press, 1979.

Rushton, J. P. *Altruism, socialization, and society.* Englewood Cliffs, N.J.: Prentice-Hall, 1980.

Rushton, J. P., & Owen, D. Immediate and delayed effects of TV modeling and preaching on children's generosity. *British Journal of Social and Clinical Psychology,* 1975, *14,* 309–310.

Shaw, D. W., & Thoresen, C. E. Effects of modeling and desensitization in reducing dental phobia. *Journal of Counseling Psychology,* 1974, *21,* 415–420.

Silverman, L. T., Sprafkin, J. N., & Rubinstein, E. A. Physical contact and sexual behavior on prime-time TV. *Journal of Communication,* 1979, *29,* 33–43.

Smythe, D. W. Reality as presented by television. *Public Opinion Quarterly,* 1954, *18,* 143–156.

Sprafkin, J. M., Liebert, R. M., & Poulos, R. W. Effects of a prosocial example on children's helping. *Journal of Experimental Child Psychology,* 1975, *20,* 119–126.

Stein, G. M., & Bryan, J. H. The effect of a televised model upon rule adoption behavior of children. *Child Development,* 1972, *43,* 268–273.

Sternglanz, S. H., & Serbin, L. A. Sex role stereotyping in children's television programs. *Developmental Psychology,* 1974, *10,* 710–715.

Thelen, M. H., Fry, R. A., Fehrenbach, P. A., & Frantschi, N. M. Therapeutic videotape and film modeling: A Review. *Psychological Bulletin,* 1979, *86,* 701–720.

Vidmar, N., & Rokeach, M. Archie Bunker's bigotry: A study in selective perception and exposure. *Journal of Communication,* 1974, *24,* 36–47.

Weissbrod, C. S., & Bryan, J. H. Filmed treatment as an effective fear-reduction technique. *Journal of Abnormal Child Psychology,* 1973, *1,* 196–201.

Williams, T. B., Zabrack, M. L., & Joy, L. A. A content analysis of entertainment television programming. In *Ontario: Royal Commission on Violence in the Communications Industry. Report* (Vol. 3). *Violence in Television Films and News.* Toronto: Queen's Printer for Ontario, 1977.

Wincze, J. P., & Caird, W. K. The effects of systematic desensitization and video desensitization in the treatment of essential sexual dysfunction in women. *Behavior Therapy,* 1976, *7,* 335–342.

Winick, C. Mental illness and psychiatrists in movies. In C. Winick (Ed.), *Sage Annual Reviews of Studies in Deviance.* Vol. 2. *Deviance and Mass Media.* Beverly Hills, Ca.: Sage Publications, Inc., 1978.

Wolf, T. M. Effects of televised modeled verbalizations and behavior on resistance to deviation. *Developmental Psychology,* 1973, *8,* 51–56.

Wolf, T. M., & Cheyne, J. A. Persistence of effects of live behavioral, televised behavioral, and live verbal models on resistance to deviation. *Child Development,* 1972, *43,* 1429–1436.

Yates, G. C. R. Influence of televised modeling and verbalization on children's delay of gratification. *Journal of Experimental Child Psychology,* 1974, *18,* 333–339.

6

Promoting Positive Behavior in Schools, in Other Educational Settings, and in the Home

Ervin Staub
University of Massachusetts, Amherst

A substantial amount of research and theoretical writing has accumulated about how parental child-rearing and other adult influences contribute to the development of positive behavior in children (Staub, 1979). Can we, on the basis of research findings and related theory, suggest specific practices that teachers, educators and parents can use to develop children's positive behavior? Can we suggest social conditions such as the nature and rules of the school environment and the peer group that would promote helping, sharing, kindness, cooperation, and positive interpersonal behavior? In this chapter I discuss principles of change and practices and envrionmental conditions that would promote change, which are suggested or implied by research findings and theory reviewed in this volume and elsewhere (Staub, 1978a, 1979). Although the role of educational settings is stressed, these principles and practices are also applicable to the home.

A basic issue about promoting positive conduct is whether the desire or motivation exists among adults to do so. We may be in the process of developing reasonable knowledge of how to do it, but will parents and educators want to apply such knowledge? For many people the notion that societal agencies, such as schools, would intentionally promote characteristics in children that are either "moral" in nature or somehow related to morality still represents a threat of interference with their rights as parents. An even more profound issue is whether parents as well as educators regard positive behavior as desirable—as qualities to be promoted. Many may consider the tendency for kindness, helpfulness, generosity, and willingness to make sacrifices for the sake of others, as counterproductive to individuals promoting their own interests. Competitiveness and looking out for "you know who" can be seen as characteristics to be promoted in one's children, if they are to survive in a tough world—and with some justification. Beyond these considerations, we live in a world of uncertain morality, where to many people what is right and wrong is unclear, with society providing limited direction as to the right conduct and the right character; and offering less guidance than did earlier, more tradition-directed societies.

I will not attend in detail here to the desirability of positive conduct and the value of characteristics that promote such conduct. Nonetheless, I will briefly make a few generalizations, based on the many research findings (reviewed in this book and Staub, 1978a; 1979), which may reduce worries about the undesirable consequences of our children becoming kind, prosocial individuals, First, to develop values, beliefs, and emotional relationships that lead to positive behavior does not mean that children and adults do not also develop "self-promoting" personal motives. Moreover, several characteristics that are important in promoting positive behavior are such that they make it likely that prosocial individuals will be able to reasonably weigh other people's claims to their help, attention, or to material goods, and respond only when legitimate claims exist, while at other times pursue their own goals and the satisfaction of their own needs. Second, rather than being submissive, weak persons, who could easily be exploited by others, the people most likely to respond to others' needs are individuals with at least moderately positive self-esteem: they are competent and trust their competence (see the following section). These and other characteristics that promote positive behavior seem also optimal from the standpoint of how effectively a person pursues his or her *own* interests. Finally, interactions among peers tend to be reciprocal, and positive behavior toward others tends to beget positive behavior. Thus, positive relationships to other people, and personal adjustment and happiness, may be promoted by the tendency to engage in positive conduct. With many people showing such a tendency, harmonious functioning of groups and harmonious relationships among members of groups may follow.

Personality and Positive Behavior

The preceding discussion implied an important assumption: that positive behavior is an expression of the child's personality, of varied personal characteristics that make such behavior more or less likely. If so, we need to concern ourselves with what personal characteristics promote and inhibit positive behavior. Extensive research findings and related theory suggest what such characteristics are (see Staub, 1978a), and having specified them we can ask how these characteristics and the positive behavior associated with them might be promoted.

In previous papers I elaborated a model specifying how personal characteristics and the nature of circumstances that surround a person interact in determining social behavior (Staub, 1978a; 1978b). In order for a child to act prosocially under varied circumstances, to show at least a moderate degree of cross-situational consistency in positive behavior, the child will have to have a strong motivation for positive action. Such motivation can be conceptualized as personal goals (Staub, 1978a; 1978b). Personal goals have varied components: they specify desired outcomes or end-products of behavior; they have a cognitive network associated with them that is involved in the evaluation of relevant outcomes and associated circumstances. Upon activation of a personal goal by an aspect of the environment tension is aroused, which gets reduced upon reaching or satisfying the goal.

Traditionally, internalized values, norms, and empathy have been regarded as the primary personal motivators of positive behavior. In my conception values, norms and empathy are subsumed under or integrated in personal goals. Positive behavior is motivated by two different prosocial goals, which are based on two different value orientations. *Prosocial orientation* is characterized by a positive orientation towards other people, concern about others' welfare, and feeling of personal responsibility for others' welfare. Prosocial orientation would motivate people to benefit others; to increase their welfare or reduce their distress. Another value orientation may be called orientation toward *duty or obligation*. Such an orientation would lead to a desire to act according to socially appropriate standards, to do what is right. Although wanting to do one's duty might frequently motivate positive behavior, under certain circumstances doing what is *right* according to some impersonal social or moral values or norms (e.g., justice) may interfere with helping another person. Sometimes deviation from societal dictates or even from abstract moral absolutes is required to respond to someone's need.

Value orientations of these kind can provide the motivational base for positive behavior. Such value orientations can be the basis of constructing *standards* of behavior appropriate to specific circumstances that a person faces. In addition, individuals who possess a strong prosocial orientation are likely to react to other people's needs with *empathy*. The manner of their perception and evaluation of others' needs is likely to give rise to corresponding empathic emotion.

Other types of motives, for example, need for approval, can also lead to positive behavior, but the desired outcome is not to promote another's welfare, or to do one's duty by helping, but to gain approval. Although such *extraneous* motives can sometimes promote positive behavior (when such behavior is likely to lead to approval), at other times they may diminish its likelihood (when helping might bring disapproval or one needs to engage in other kinds of behavior to gain approval).

A strong personal goal will not necessarily give rise to positive behavior on any one occasion. First, other characteristics are also important in determining whether people will or will not behave in positive ways. They include varied types of competencies: the perception by a person of his or her ability to provide help or support to another, the actual knowledge of how to help, or the capacity to generate plans of action. Perceptual tendencies, such as the capacity to view events from another's point of view, to consider or perceive another's needs and feelings—that is, affective role-taking—is important, as many research findings indicate. While a strong prosocial orientation is likely to be associated with the capacity for affective role-taking, the two are not identical. It is possible to understand how others feel without feeling with them, or to want to benefit others without being good at perceiving or identifying how they feel or what they need.

The person's self-conception, and particularly self-esteem, is also important. How people perceive the relationship between themselves and others depends not only on their orientation toward others, embodied in prosocial orientation, but also on their orientation toward themselves. Negative self-esteem, permanent, or temporary—brought about by specific experiences or events—can decrease helping, whereas positive self-esteem and positive moods often increase helping. People's self-esteem probably affects their experience of the connection or bond to others: the extent they attend to others' needs, their evaluation of other human beings, and their concern for others' welfare. Whether a person's customary self-esteem is high or low is likely to affect how he or she responds to specific experiences that potentially influence temporary or current self-esteem (Staub, 1978a).

In summary, in order to consider how we might promote positive behavior, we need to be aware that a variety of personal characteristics are involved in affecting its occurrence. But even if a person possesses all the relevant characteristics, he or she will not always respond to others' needs, or promote others' goals. Every person has varied personal goals, and sometimes circumstances or situations will activate those goals that cause conflict with responding to others. The *activation potential* of a situation may be very high for an achievement goal, or some other goal. Sometimes both an achievement goal and a prosocial goal can be satisfied through the same kind of action: a person might excel by helping others (Feinberg, 1977; described in Staub, 1978a, Chapter 2; 1978b). Another time an achievement goal might only be pursued if a person does not respond to someone's need. People with a strong achievement goal may choose to pursue the activities that will satisfy their achievement goal, even if they possess strong motivation to promote others' welfare. Thus, the nature of a person's goals, other relevant characteristics, and the nature of surrounding circumstances all need to be considered if we are to accurately predict how a person will behave on a specific occasion.

The above model suggests, nonetheless, that people, children or adults, who possess strong prosocial goals, and supporting characteristics, will tend to behave positively under varied (although certainly not all) circumstances, in comparison to children or adults who have weak prosocial goals and/or weak supporting characteristics. Consequently, one primary question is how can such goals and supporting characteristics be promoted.

With this brief conceptual overview, I embark on the task of specifying: (1) what behaviors directed at children; (2) what activities that children are led to engage in or experiences that they are exposed to; and (3) what environmental rules or structures, will promote positive behavior. I will only discuss related research to a very limited degree: usually I will summarize research findings that I extensively reviewed elsewhere (Staub, 1978a, 1979) in brief generalizations. In the next few pages there will be some overlap, inevitably, with material presented in other chapters (mainly in Joan Grusec's). Our understanding of how we can promote positive behavior comes, in part, from knowledge gained through research on parent-child relations and its laboratory analogues. The similarity will decline as we examine "natural socialization," the influence of the peer group, and the school environment, and discuss moral education efforts.

BEHAVIORS DIRECTED AT THE CHILD: RELATIONSHIPS AND TRANSACTIONS BETWEEN ADULTS AND CHILDREN

Warmth and Nurturance

The relationship between adults and children provides a framework for specific childrearing techniques used by the adult for promoting certain kinds of behavior and inhibiting other kinds. Extensive research shows that a positive relationship between adults and children—warmth, affection, nurturance and love, promotes positive behavior. In contrast, hostility and anger between parents and children were found to be associated with negative behavior and aggression by the children (Bandura & Walters, 1959; Lefkowitz, Eron, Walder, Huesmann, 1977).

The division of the adult-child interaction into specific components, such as the relationship aspect, and the specific practices adults employ in raising children, in exacting obedience and in educating them, is useful for coming to understand how each component affects the child's development. Such a division can be misleading, however, without the recognition that the influence of a specific component will depend on the pattern of practices of which it is a part (Baumrind, 1975; Staub, 1979). To highlight this point, consider that children in laboratory experiments were found to engage less in positive behavior when this resulted in a sacrifice by them of material goods—such as candy or gift certificates—after exposure to warm, nurturing models, in contrast to exposure to nonnurturant models. In the laboratory setting, a brief exposure to the nurturant models may have implied permissiveness and lack of punitiveness. Without an established relationship with the adult, children used this to their own advantage. In the view of several writers, if children are to be effectively socialized—if they are to learn or internalize standards of behavior that adults promote, reasonable control is necessary, in addition to nurturance. The issue of control and forms of discipline that adults use will be discussed in the next section.

Why is warmth and affection by adults important? First, they create an atmosphere in which children are most likely to learn what adults try to teach them, verbally, or through their own example. Second, a warm nurturant relationship with an adult is likely to make the child want to be like that adult, and to imitate that adult's example, and can lead to the adoption of values and behaviors of the adult to a greater degree; it is likely to lead children to identify with the adult and to internalize values and standards. Third, having the experience of a benevolent environment, one that treats them well, children are more likely to be benevolently oriented to their environment and the people in it; to assume that other people are kind rather than unkind, to desire contact with others rather than to avoid them. Finally, warmth and affection are likely to make children more confident of their actions and make them less concerned with the possible negative consequences of initiating action that could benefit others.

A further consequence of warmth and affection by adults has profound implications. In a study by Yarrow and Scott (1972) children were supervised either by warm adults, or by indifferent, matter-of-fact adults. They observed the adult enact scenes with small doll figures, in which the characters engaged in both positive and negative behaviors. Children supervised by the warm adult remembered more of the positive behaviors that the adult performed with the figures, whereas children supervised by the indifferent adult remembered more negative, aggressive behaviors performed with the figures. The findings suggest the important possibility that children are more likely to perceive or remember the behaviors of adults that are consistent with the kind of relationship they have with them.

Is it possible to train adults—teachers in schools, and in general people in educational settings—to relate to children in a nurturant, affectionate way? In two studies Yarrow, Scott and Waxler (1973) and Yarrow and Scott (1972) trained the same individuals to interact with children in either a warm, affectionate way or in a distant, indifferent manner. Seemingly the training was effective in leading these adults to behave in different ways toward the preschool children they supervised.

In order to effectively train adults to be warm and nurturant it is necessary to consider what these terms refer to. Frequently, warmth and nurturance are treated as unitary dmensions, which they are unlikely to be. Yarrow and Scott (1972) wrote: "Warmth generally refers to a pervasive quality in the relationship of mother and child. It includes feelings of love, demonstrations of affection, ministering to the child's needs, providing expectations of acceptance and help, etc. [p. 260]." Obviously, warmth can vary in degree. It can also vary in its qualitative aspects. An important aspect or dimension of warmth can be sensitivity by adults to the child's feelings, moods, or needs (Staub, 1979). An adult can be generally warm and affectionate without a special capacity to perceive and thus to effectively respond to the child's psychological needs, to his or her feelings. In order to train adults to relate to children in a warm or nurturant way one may want to break these aspects down into several components, such as showing interest in the child; showing affection; responsiveness to the child's needs; sensitivity in perceiving the child's psychological states; and others.

Might there be limits to "trainability"? The personality of an adult, his or her orientation toward children, as well as the general life circumstances and psychological well-being of a person, may place limits on how far the person has the capacity for, interest in, and affection and warmth toward children. Although limits may sometimes not be surmountable without extensive intervention in the adult's life, at other times certain types of training may be helpful. Clinical experience with training parents to effectively guide and discipline their children suggests that the capacity by formerly ineffective adults to exert reasonable but effective control over their children generates warmth and affection. When parents who face highly uncooperative children [which generates strong negative feelings in parents] learn skills to induce cooperation and obedience, their feelings of agency and control is accompanied by renewed feelings of warmth and affection toward the children. This suggests that training educators in nurturance toward children may best be accompanied by training them in reasonable and effective ways of exerting influence or control. Training them to use positive reinforcement to increase the likelihood of desirable behaviors may be especially important; positive reinforcement can generate feelings of warmth and affection in the child, and withholding reinforcement can be effective in diminishing undesirable behaviors.

In training adults it is important to help them become aware of the children's capacity to elicit varied behaviors. The relationship between adults and children is inevitably transactional, with children frequently having great power in modifying or manipulating adult conduct. Without an awareness of this, children who need warmth and nurturance most may not receive it, either because they limit their contact with adults, or because they generate emotions and behaviors of a contrary nature. How to limit negative behavior while still acting in a nurturant manner is a difficult but important aspect of such training. The adults, ideally, would learn to move a child from a transactional relationship which they learned in the past—the child engaging in aggressive or disruptive behaviors that would elicit negative and repressive consequences from adults—to one with increasingly more benevolent "entries" by each partner. Such changes would presumably also affect the child's interactions with his or her peers.

Reasonable Control and Forms of Discipline

A basic aspect of adult orientation toward children is the extent to which adults exercise effective control over children's behavior. To do so is likely to be important for effective socialization in general and for the development of positive behavior in particular (Baumrind, 1971; 1975; Staub, 1979). Sometimes the term control has negative conotations. I am using it simply to refer to adult insistence that children carry out important directives and adhere to rules that adults consider important. Control does not imply that children are not allowed autonomy. The directives that parents or adults consider important and the rules that they insist that children abide by may be few in number, related to limited domains. Beyond these domains, and increasingly as the child gets older, adults can allow greater and greater self-control, decision-making, and autonomy. However, affection and warmth without a reasonable degree of control are likely to lead to license rather than socialized, positive behavior.

The manner of control is highly important. Obviously, violent means of control, or highly punitive ones, are discrepant from and incongruent with an affectionate environment. There is strong evidence that the frequent use of physical punishment by parents results in aggression, hostility, and resistance by children (Aronfreed, 1968; Eron, Walder, & Lefkowitz, 1971). The least coercive techniques that bring about desired behavior or stop misbehavior seem the most useful. It is necessary, however, that adults be willing to follow noncoercive attempts at control with punishment, if they are to lead children to engage in the required or desirable behavior, which is the essence of control.

Reasoning with children, explaining to them why certain behaviors are desirable and others undesirable, is itself a form of control, often effective even at a very young age. Children seem to respond to the very process of reasoning, apart from its content. (Some forms of reasoning as means of promoting positive behavior will be discussed in the next section.) Explaining to children both general principles about why certain behaviors are expected and others prohibited, as well as providing specific reasons at specific times, is likely to be the most effective.

Sometimes, however, reasoning is not enough. Children's desires and adults' expectations frequently conflict. How can control and discipline be affected? There is extensive literature on these issues (Baumrind, 1975; Staub, 1979), and I will restrict myself here to a few comments. We may distinguish between practices that aim at bringing about a desired behavior and practices that aim at prohibiting undesirable behavior, or prescriptive and proscriptive emphases in raising children (Olejnik & McKinney, 1973; Staub, 1979). A prescriptive orientation, as the limited research shows, tends to be associated with more prosocial behavior. Practices that aim at promoting or bringing about desirable behavior are likely to be associated with reasoning with the child, with explaining why the child should, or might like to, or would find it worthwhile or rewarding to do something. Thus, inherent in a prescriptive orientation is the valuing of certain behaviors and associated outcomes. Progressively, a prosocial orientation may develop in children exposed to prescriptive practices.

But how can desirable behavior be brought about on occasions when requests by adults and reasoning are ineffective? The use of threats, particularly mild threats, may be an effective practice. On the whole, research on child rearing practices paid little attention to the use and effectiveness of threats as a means of influencing children. Some studies found that the use of mild threats in prohibiting children from playing with particular toys has greater effects than severe threats, in that mild threats lead to the devaluation of the desired objects (see

Aronfreed, 1968, for a review). Consistent with reasoning derived from cognitive dissonance theory, following mild threats children might attribute the reason for either engaging in some behavior or inhibiting some action to themselves rather than to external forces. They may subsequently perceive themselves differently. Their evaluation of the behavior or its outcome may also be affected.

A proscriptive emphasis, or prohibiting of undesirable behavior, may more likely be associated with a tendency to use punishment than reward. Rewards seem more consistent with promoting interest in positive behavior and a positive orientation toward other people than the use of punishments. A focus on punishing undesirable behavior, through love withdrawal, or by other means, may give rise to a value orientation that is concerned with duty and obligation and with the inhibition of undesirable impulses in general (Hoffman, 1970b).

It seems important to carefully train adults to use various techniques of control and discipline, rather than simply throwing them in with children, and to develop an orientation in educators toward discipline where they will escalate only as necessary, from reason and responsiveness to other techniques. Training adults to make children in the group responsible for each other's conduct can also be useful. Children assuming responsibility for behavior that affects the welfare of the group or any one person in it can provide a way of learning by doing, a form of "natural socialization," which will be discussed later.

Induction and Other Verbal Communications to Children

I noted the importance of explaining to children the desirability or undesirability of varied forms of conduct. In the realm of moral behavior Hoffman (1970a) focused attention on a specific form of reasoning, induction, which refers to communicating to children the consequences of their behavior on other people. I distinguished between negative induction, explaining the harmful consequences of undesirable behavior, and positive induction, explaining the beneficial consequences of positive behavior (Staub, 1971, 1979). An extensive amount of research examined the effects on children's behavior of both induction and other types of verbal communications promoting positive behavior. When parents are asked to describe how they treat their children or when children are asked to describe how parents treat them, reports of the use of indication are associated with positive behavior by children. In most existing studies this positive behavior was not directly observed, but information was provided by peers, who tend to describe children who receive induction as concerned about others' welfare, as considerate and helpful (Hoffman, 1975; Hoffman & Saltzstein, 1967).

In contrast, experimental studies in which a strange adult makes a statement or communication to the child to promote positive behavior showed variable effects. There may be many reasons for this discrepancy in findings (see Staub, 1979, pp. 170–171). An important one is that parents have continuing control over the child, and parents who reason with the child may also insist that the child behave in a manner consistent with what the parents say. In contrast, in most experimental studies it is implied that the adults will have little more to do with the child after the verbal communication. Thus reasoning and control are not combined. In an educational setting, of course, adults have continuing control and can progressively build a relationship with the child.

Another issue is the kind of verbal communication that is used. Several different kinds have been employed in experimental studies. Preaching to the child (telling the child that sharing or other kinds of positive behavior is good, a nice thing to do, and so on) usually has no effect on children's willingness to donate to others. Children may continuously hear such communications from an early age on, and may learn to disregard them (or even to act in opposition to them). Another kind of verbal communication, explicitly telling children what is expected of them—for example, stating a behavioral rule or norm for sharing or donating—appears effective. Children tend to abide by such communications. Frequently such communications lead them to behave in a positive way in an adult's presence, and later they continue to act positively in the adult's absence. A third type of verbal communication, positive induction, had variable effects. Several studies found that positive induction does not by itself enhance later positive behavior (Sims, 1974, 1978; Staub, 1971). In other studies induction increased children's positive acts (Eisenberg-Berg & Geisheker, 1979; Midlarsky & Bryan, 1972).

Most likely, as Dlugokinski and Firestone (1973) found, at least initially the effects of induction will be a function of prior experiences of children with reasoning by parents and other adults. In their study, induction increased the generosity of children who reported that parents practiced induction with them at home, but power-assertive type statements affected generosity by children who reported that their parents tended to use power-assertive verbal communications. "Embedded Induction" may be most effective in promoting positive behavior (Staub, 1979, pp. 171–173). The term refers to induction in conjunction with some positive behavior that children engage in, so that children can associate the thoughts and reasons they are provided with their actual behavior. Such a combination of verbal communication with the children's own actions may also be useful in calling the attention of children to induction statements. (Especially of those children who are not accustomed to induction and have not previously learned to respond to them with related behaviors.)

Finally, attributing characteristics or behavior tendencies to children—for example, suggesting to them that the reason they have engaged in some positive behavior is because they are generous or kind or helpful—has been found to increase later positive behavior (Staub, 1978, p. 222). Note again that here a verbal communication is associated with some actual behavior of the child.

One important question is how or why induction and other verbal communications increase later positive conduct. Induction is likely to provide a cognitive network, a way of thinking, with emphasis on other people's feelings and desires, and an emphasis on the association between others' needs and one's own actions. Such thinking, which is a component of prosocial orientation as I conceptualized it, places value on others' welfare, leads to interpretations that can give rise to empathic emotion, and in general can serve as self-guidance to action that would benefit other people.

A potential danger in various kinds of verbal communications is that they give rise to psychological reactance in children, a feeling of pressure to act in a certain way, and a feeling of limitation of freedom by the child to decide what to do. Verbal communications that promote positive behavior invoke moral norms and values that have an obligatory character. The resulting psychological reactance can lead to opposition in children which leads them to act contrary to the pressure they perceive. This seems more likely to happen with boys: in a number of studies, my associates and I found that extensive inductive statements about positive behavior that children were engaging in increased girls' positive behavior but did not affect and sometimes even decreased boys' positive actions (Staub & Feinberg, 1978; Staub & Fotta, see Staub, 1979, Chapter 6). A potentially important unrecognized issue in socialization and in educational efforts is that many children may receive adult directives, including verbal communications, with a readiness to resist and oppose. Reasonable but firm control by adults, and inducing children to engage in the desired behavior may be important to get beyond resistance and to affect children's thoughts and feelings about the behavior in question.

Other kinds of verbal communications that prescribe positive action might be effective because they lead children to engage in positive conduct. Participation in positive actions appears to increase later positive behavior. This will be discussed in the next section. At that time reasons for the effectiveness of attributing positive characteristics to children will also be considered.

In summary,[1] in verbal communications, there may be three steps which can be useful in increasing positive actions, each using a different kind of communication. To schematically indicate their nature, let's imagine Johnny, who is very good at playing with marbles and wins many of them from other children. A first step may be a prescriptive communication, like the following, "Johnny, you are extremely good at playing with marbles—whenever you win five, share two with another child who has none, so that he can also play." The second step might be an inductive communication: (as they share) "when you share your marbles the (other child) feels good that you care for him/her and that he/she can participate in the play." The third communication may be attributive: (after sharing) "Johnny, you are really generous and kind for sharing your marbles." This example simply intends to schematically present what kind of verbal communica-

---

[1] A verbal influence on children different from those discussed so far is embodied in the discussion of moral dilemmas with children, aimed at advancing their level of moral reasoning. This will be considered in the section on moral education.

tions may be effective, and if used together, in what sequence might they be useful. However, tentative as the findings are (Staub, 1975b, 1979) they suggest that one can say too much, and thus as a rule one may want to use one or two such communications, but not all of them together. Also, the issue of manipulativeness in providing verbal communications in such a sequence has to be considered.

The effectiveness of induction and other types of verbal communications can depend on the past experience of the child at home. Children who are accustomed to induction may gain from it. Children who are accustomed to power-assertive practices and power-assertive verbal communications may initially not take inductive statements seriously, because they have not learned that adults will insist that they act consistently with such statements. They may need gradual training in taking such communications seriously. Having received such training from teachers and others, they may begin to attend to inductive statements and learn self-guidance from them.

NATURAL SOCIALIZATION: LEARNING BY DOING, BY PARTICIPATION

In a variety of publications Staub (1975a, 1975b, 1979) suggested that children learn to behave positively through their actual participation in positive behavior. There is cross-cultural evidence (Whiting & Whiting, 1975), as well as some experimental research that attempted to directly test this hypothesis (Staub & Fotta; Staub, Levy, & Shortsleeves; Staub & Jancaterino; Staub & Feinberg; see Staub, 1975b; 1979, Chapter 6). In addition, in a variety of experiments, children were induced to engage in some positive behavior with an increase in that behavior on a later occasion (Staub, 1979, Chapter 6). The conditions surrounding children's engagement in positive behavior—for example, the extent to which they receive reinforcement for it, whether verbal communications, which can provide a cognitive network, accompany it, and whether participation is effective in making a contribution to others' welfare—are all likely to be important in determining whether it increases later positive actions. Participation with appropriate supporting conditions may result in children developing values and beliefs that promote positive behavior. In the course of participation interpretations previously heard may be applied to the positive behavior, to its outcome, or to the value of benefiting others, and children may also engage in self-attribution of both positive intent and of characteristics that lead them to engage in positive acts.

Learning by participation is a natural way for children to develop positive behavioral tendencies in educational settings. There are varied ways that children can help others: tending animals, watching over younger siblings (Whiting & Whiting, 1975), taking care of pets (Bathurst, 1933), making toys for hospitalized children, or making toys to help an art teacher determine what are the best materials to use in art classes, as well as children teaching other children (see Staub, 1975b; 1979, Chapter 6) all appear useful in increasing children's later positive behavior. The more important and meaningful the tasks or opportunities to provide help or assume responsibility for others' welfare, the more likely it is that participation will be effective. The combination of a feeling of importance by children and of benefiting others may be important. Cleaning up rooms or classrooms can promote a feeling of responsibility, but by itself probably is not a prosocial tendency. On the other hand, overwhelming children with demands for participation in positive action, expecting and demanding self-sacrifice when other children are free to do fun-filled activities, can lead to resentment and opposition (Bossard & Boll, 1956; see Staub, 1979, Chapter 6).

An important issue is how children are induced to participate. In educational settings, as well as at home, children can usually be naturally guided to activities that benefit others. These activities can truthfully be presented as important, allowing participation as showing trust in the child, and sometimes as enjoyment and fun. Positive reinforcement in the course of the initial steps can be useful. Although there is no relevant evidence, it would seem that relatively forceful, power-assertive ways of getting children initially involved in positive actions, may also lead to learning to value other's welfare and assuming responsibility for others, if power or force is diminished over time, so that the child can progressively see himself or herself as an agent (rather than a pawn) in engaging in positive action.

As noted earlier, procedures that directly induced children to engage in some positive behavior (Grusec, Kuczynski, Rushton, & Simutis, 1978; Rosenhan & White, 1967; White, 1972; White & Burnam, 1975) increased their later positive behavior, usually to the authors' surprise. In these studies children were either directly instructed to donate some material possessions in the first phase of the study or they were told to follow the example of a model who donated, and were observed doing so in the model's presence. Subsequently they shared more than control subjects and as much or more than children in experimental groups who were expected to share more. These studies suggest procedures for one kind of participatory learning, where specific guidance or inducement is provided to children.

Further support for the importance of learning by doing, and examples of procedures, comes from research that was guided by a behavior modification approach. Barton and Osborne (1978) employed "positive practice" to induce sharing in five children with moderate to severe hearing loss and poor speech communication. The positive practice procedure required children to practice the desirable behavior (verbal sharing) when it did not occur. The teacher instructed children how to verbally initiate and accept sharing, modeled this to children, and then had children practice these roles. Substantial increase in physical sharing resulted from this procedure, which lasted following a 15-week period. The term sharing in this study referred to the cooperative use of play materials. In another study by Barton and Ascione (1979), the experimenter explained to the child why sharing was desirable and how it can be done appropriately; modeled the behavior for a specific child; had the child rehearse the behavior with the experimenter; and prompted and praised rehearsal. The other children were to imitate the first child's behavior. Physical sharing increased from both verbal practice, and physical combined with verbal practice, and had durable and generalized effects. Both of these procedures provide examples of how cooperative play behavior, children using the same resources and materials together, can be increased among young children. According to the view elaborated above a crucial aspect of the effectiveness of these procedures is the children's actual participation in the activity. While the rehearsal of the activity can be regarded as a form of role playing, the behaviors that are practiced can immediately be applied to "real" interactions.

Although there are opportunities to induce positive *interactive* behaviors, a major difficulty is to find meaningful activities for children to benefit others in need. Our society is so organized that children's opportunites for prosocial action are somewhat limited. Some of the activities listed above may be useful. An important form of participation in prosocial behavior may be for children to take responsibility for each other. Older ones can help younger ones, children who know something better can show others how to do it, and in other ways children may be induced to mutually promote and assume responsibility for each other's welfare. These suggestions are consistant with recent speculations about the importance for children of experiences in mixed age groups (Konner, 1975).

ROLE PLAYING: "AS IF" PARTICIPATION

A number of experiments have shown that children's participation in role playing—in the course of which they perform either the role of helpers, or the role of children to be helped, or both, exchanging roles—can increase their later positive behavior (Iannotti, 1977; Staub, 1971). Role playing in an enactive mode of learning, that appears useful with adults as well, and has been used extensively in varied forms of psychotherapy. Because it is enactive, what is done in the course of role playing appears to function—and to be experienced by people—as similar to the actual performance of behavior. Thus, it may be regarded as "as if" participation. Even role playing of a general kind, children enacting various experiences and problems in their everyday life, can affect relevant conduct. For example, it can decrease children's participation in delinquent activities (Chandler, 1973).

Role playing can contribute to children's capacity for role taking, for viewing events from other people's perspective. It can also contribute to children learning specific actions that may be helpful to others. Role playing may also help children to develop cognitive skills, so that they can develop plans of actions when somebody is in need.

Role playing is an easy and natural way in educational settings to promote children's positive behavior. Even very young children are usually willing and interested in enacting various roles, and if they are initially shy, the observation of another child can help them get involved. Providing children initially with specific things to say and do in the course of role playing can also help overcome their initial reluctance to enact roles. An advantage of learning through role playing is that anything can be enacted. It is thus possible to involve in role playing all aspects of thought, feeling and action that one considers relevant to learning concern for others and helping others.

MODELING, AND THE INFLUENCE OF TELEVISION

As extensively demonstrated in many domains, the example of other people is a powerful influence on our behavior. Modeling can lead to generous and helpful action, as many experiments showed. Staub's analysis (1978a, pp. 205–207) of the influence of models suggests that when observers attribute positive motives and intentions to a model, unselfishness and the desire to benefit others, they are likely to imitate the model's behavior. Perceiving the actor's intention as consistent with his motives may lead to positive evaluation of a prosocial action and the attribution of free choice to him; consequently, corresponding motives may be aroused in an observer. When circumstances lead people to attribute selfish purposes or intentions, models are not likely to be imitated. These generalizations are based primarily on research with adults. It is possible that young children are less affected by differences in models motives, particularly if such motives are subtly expressed. Children are also likely to imitate models because the model's behavior defines expectations as well as communicates appropriate actions, sets standards, and points to ideals.

Our knowledge about the influence of models has been extended in research showing how the observation of television programs can also increase positive behavior. For example, Friedrich and Stein (1973, 1975) found that exposing nursery school children to prosocial television programs increased the interactive prosocial behaviors of children who tended to watch primarily aggressive television programs at home. Exposure to prosocial television also resulted in more constructive problem solving and greater delay of gratification by children in their task-related activities. The example of models, television shows, and more generally the observation of events in their environment, must affect children's understanding of the world, their views of appropriate and effective ways of coping, and of relating to other people. They learn, for example, whether discussion and compromise or aggression are the best ways to deal with conflict. The structure of children's environment, and examples in them, educate them about options they have and reasonable plans for actions, and communicate values to them. For example, children in the Friedrich and Stein (1973) study may have learned prosocial strategies of interpersonal interaction through their exposure to prosocial television programs.

Having children watch prosocial in place of antisocial television shows is something that educational environments can promote. Adults can directly expose preschoolers to prosocial television. Alternatively, through homework assignments or through discussions in class of specific shows, adults can both lead children to watch prosocial rather than aggressive television programs at home, and bring about cognitive rehearsal of what was seen. Observation, cognitive rehearsal, and the opportunity to rehearse observed behavior in the school setting are a combination of influences that appear highly effective in increasing positive behavior (Friedrich-Cofer, Huston-Stein, Kipnis, Susman, & Clewett, 1979; Staub, 1979).

In other words, the exposure of children to prosocial television programs in conjunction with their everyday experience in an educational setting seems particularly important. The setting provides children with the opportunity to try out what they learn from observation in their own interactions with other children. Such enactive use of observed and thus indirectly experienced ways of behaving may be crucial for changes in behavior and in related thoughts and feelings. One might call this conjunction of observation and action "embedded modeling." As an active mode of learning, it may be particularly effective (Staub, 1979, pp. 153–160. The extent to which embedded modeling occurs will be affected by the nature of the social environment, its rules and structure. Recent research findings show that certain kinds of play materials can be provided and teachers can be trained to facilitate the enactive use of what children see on television both in play activities and in interpersonal interaction (Friedrich-Cofer et al., 1979). (For further information on the effects of television on behavior see Rushton's chapter in this volume.)

THE NATURE OF THE PEER GROUP, THE CLASSROOM, THE SCHOOL, THE LARGER ENVIRONMENT

Children's environments can be conceptualized at various levels. These different levels of environments have their own rules, which affect the way children behave and what they learn.

With regard to the peer group, I suggested (Staub, 1979) that children receive extensive socialization in the course of their interactions with peers. There is evidence that interactions among peers is guided by both reciprocity and complementarity. Reciprocity refers to the tendency of children to be recipients of the kinds of behaviors they direct towards others. Children who behave aggressively tend to have aggressive behavior directed towards them. Children who behave positvely tend to be recipients of positive behaviors. Complementarity refers to the fact that children's behavior fits with, or matches behaviors directed towards them. For example, children who are generally responsive to others, but who tend not to provide specific help, are the recipients of generally positive behavior, but they receive few requests for help. The child's behavior and the behavior directed toward the child complement each other (Staub, 1979, Chapter 7; Staub & Feinberg, 1978).

The apparent significance of peer socialization is enhanced if you consider that some children may develop consistent negative patterns of interaction with others. This must affect how they think about themselves (as being disliked or incompetent in social interactions), and how they think and feel about others (as being hostile, unpleasant, negative, difficult to interact with). Habitual patterns that children develop in approaching and interacting with others, and thus their long-term adjustment and personality, may be affected (Cowen, Pederson, Babigan, Izzo, & Frost, 1973; Roff, Sells & Golden, 1972). The extent to which children behave aggressively towards each other, resolve conflict through aggressive means, isolate some while favor others, is likely to be affected by the rules adults establish for the group. Basic rules can be provided which limit aggression and conflict, while at the same time allow children considerable autonomy. Autonomy is likely to be more constructively used if basic rules minimize negative behavior. As with regard to control and discipline of individual children, discussed earlier, it would seem that the less force is applied to bring about effective control and adherence to basic, minimal rules, the more beneficial the effects. Less force creates less negativity, hostility, and opposition toward adults and allows children to regard their own positive behaviors and that of others, and the constructive nature of the group, as self-caused or peer-caused, rather than adult imposed.

Rules are not simply imposed, of course. They are created partly by the way the group is organized, and by the adults' behavior and example. A long time ago Lewin, Lippitt, and White (1939) demonstrated that different leadership styles by adults had substantially different effects on the behavior and experience of children in groups. In groups of 5- to 10-year-old boys who had a democractic leader the products of the boys' activities had a higher quality, and they were happier both with their group and their leader, and less hostile to each other, than groups led by a laissez-faire adult (permissive leadership), which experienced disorganization, boredom, and conflict, or groups led by authoritarian leaders in which boys were either passive or rebellious and aggressive in peer interaction, as well as inefficient in their work in the leader's absence. More such research is needed to delineate dimensions of group organization and of rules, and their varied effects on peer interaction. Conditions that lead to cooperation, in contrast to conflict and anatagonism, are likely to have important socializing effects. Cooperation appears to engender positive feelings among members of dyads, and small groups, not only toward other members of the group, but also toward outsiders, such as peers in the children's classroom (Staub, 1978a, Chapter 9; see below).

Cooperative Learning in Schools

Recently a number of investigators demonstrated that learning in a cooperative fashion can affect children's success in mastering academic material, and/or their self concept and/or their liking for others and other aspects of their orientation toward others. Aronson and his associates (Aronson & Bridgeman, 1979; Aronson, Stephan, Sikes, Blaney, & Snapp, 1978) noted that desegregation efforts did not have the desired consequences; studies of desegregation showed few if any beneficial effects. In fact, in 25% of the studies desegregation was followed by a decrease in the self-esteem of young minority children. They reasoned that they can overcome the established views that children in different groups hold of themselves and of each other by providing minority children with the opportunity to act as experts. In this, they followed Cohen and Roper (1972) who found that when black children were instructed to build radios and taught this to white children, subsequently in small groups "equal status" interactions were found. This did not happen in a control group. (Note the similarity between this procedure and the research on teaching others that was mentioned in the earlier section on natural socialization.)

Aronson and his associates developed the "jigsaw" technique to provide an *interdependent* learning environment, in contrast to the competitive learning environment which, in their view, is common to American schools. The "students are placed in six person learning groups. The day's lesson is divided into 6 paragraphs such that each student has one and only one segment of the written material. Each student has a unique and vital part of the information which, like the pieces of a jigsaw puzzle, must be put together for any of the students to learn the whole picture. The individual must learn his/her own section to teach it to the other members of the groups (Aronson & Bridgeman, 1977, pp. 440–441)."

This procedure appears to provide equal status, allows each child to play the role of the expert, and in the researchers' view teaches children that old competitive behaviors are inappropriate and leads them to learn to listen to others, and to ask appropriate questions. In one study (Blaney, Stephan, Rosefield, Aronson, & Sikes, 1977) the experimental classes met in jigsaw groups for about 45 min a day, 3 days a week for 6 weeks. The students in these groups, in contrast to control groups, showed both increased self-esteem, and increase in their liking for their groupmates of both the same and different ethnic origins. Other studies showed similar results, with evidence for better learning of academic content by minority students in jigsaw classes than in traditional classes, and the same level of learning for white children in the two kinds of classes (Lucker, Rosefield, Sikes, & Arsonson, 1977).

Aronson and Bridgeman propose that the changes are due to: more active involvement by children in the learning process; increase in empathic role-taking. Bridgeman (1977) demonstrated, using a revised version of Chandler's (1973) role-taking cartoon series, that the jigsaw experiences enabled students to consider to a greater degree what information was or was not available to another. Perhaps due to increased role-taking, individuals who engaged in the interdependent tasks also tended to explain their own and others' success and failure the same way, making the same attributions. In addition to the work of Aronson and associates, others have recently also demonstrated that learning in various forms of cooperative structures has some of the positive consequences noted here (Johnson & Johnson, 1975; Lazarowitz & Sharan, 1980).

One of the most basic human tendencies, whether completely culturally acquired or supported by some genetically determined inclination (or based on the early experience of close relationship to a small group—the family), is to separate people into an ingroup and an outgroup, into *us* and *them*. Some people we recognize as similar to ourselves, as sharing our basic humanity, as having legitimate needs, hopes and desires. Others we identify and/or experience as separate, different, as belonging to an outgroup. Even if a person possesses a prosocial value orientation, this may not be applied to those in the outgroup. The schools have perhaps the most basic potential to extend children's awareness of the communality between their own and others' needs, hopes, and desires, to diminish the likelihood that others will be defined as them rather than us, or to stretch the circle and lead children to allow more rather than fewer people into their psychological ingroup. Interrelatedness in the course of meaningful cooperative work may help accomplish these goals. Setting children shared common goals, "superordinate" (Sherif, Harvey, Hood, & Sherif, 1961) to their individual goals, may make cooperation highly meaningful, and contribute to its effectiveness.

With regard to practical application, it is important that in most of the research studies noted earlier engagement in cooperative or interdependent learning part of the time was sufficient for beneficial results. Some of the successful cooperative activities were even organized in the context of between-group competition (DeVries, Edwards, & Slavin, 1979). To make children's learning and interaction with others universally cooperative would be a tall order indeed, and would not represent their general life experience. To provide children with meaningful cooperative tasks and learning activities should, in contrast, be feasible in all schools.

School Size and Experiential Learning

A study by Barker and Gump (1964) showed another aspect of the environment that is important: school size substantially affected children's participation in varied activities, such as music festivals, dramatic and journalistic competitions, and student government. In smaller schools a much larger percentage of children participated, and held responsible positions within the school.

Barker and Gump (1964) wrote that children in small schools reported:

> ... more satisfaction related to the development of competence, to being challenged, to engage in important actions, to being involved in group activities and to achieving moral and cultural values (while larger school students reported) more satisfaction dealing with vicarious enjoyment, with large entity affiliation, with learning about their school's persons and affairs and with gaining 'points' via participation [p. 197].

Because participation in varied activities should lead to learning through natural socialization, as discussed earlier, and participation that places responsibility on a person for other people's welfare should lead to the learning of prosocial values and behavior, one would expect important differences to result from education in a small rather than a large school. The conditions in the small school would provide children with more opportunities for role taking in interaction with peers, and thus, according to a cognitive developmental perspective, would contribute to the development of moral reasoning. Although some schools are large and no immediate steps can be taken to alter their size, it may be possible to create even in large schools the conditions that appeared to affect the natural socializing experiences of children in smaller schools. It should be possible to create opportunities for children to participate in varied activities, and to develop ways to entice them to participate. Participation may often be regarded as an honor. While volunteering to partcipate requires initative, overcoming shyness, and a certain degree of self-assertion, particularly in an environment where most children are relatively anonymous, special opportunities and invitations to participate may be pleasing to many children. Children can themselves organize many activities with a little initial help, so that much staff effort is not needed. These include school plays, craft or art fairs, sport events, and activities that specifically aim to benefit other people.

Moral Education in the Schools

In the last decade, psychologists and educators have engaged in research and demonstration projects on moral education in the schools, using varied procedures, based on different theoretical orientations. Common to these approaches is the focus on chainging children's thinking: their reasoning about right and wrong conduct, that is, their moral reasoning; their beliefs and values; how they go about making decisions about moral issues.

Because the focus of these approaches has been cognitive change, an important question is the extent to which such procedures can be expected to bring about change in positive behavior. As the discussion at the beginning of the chapter implies, we can expect behavior change to result from moral education efforts if they produce a change in children's motivation—for example, the motivation to benefit others, or to do what is right by others, or to believe that by benefiting others one also benefits oneself. Given an existing motivation for positive behavior a greater awareness of others' needs can also lead to increased prosocial behavior. However, we cannot expect that procedures that bring about change in thinking or verbal expression will automatically bring about behavior change as well.

Cognitive Developmental Education.   An extremely important aspect of the cognitive developmental approach is to establish the existing level of children's reasoning. Cognitive developmental psychologists have attempted to advance the level or stage of children's moral reasoning by exposing them to reasoning about moral dilemmas that are one stage above their own, and/or by engaging them in group discussion about dilemmas. Exposure to a higher stage of reasoning is expected to stimulate "disequilibrium" in children's thinking, which can be resolved, and a new equilibrium created, when children move to what is regarded as a developmentally more advanced stage of reasoning (Kohlberg, 1969).

In an early study Turiel (1966) found that exposing children to thinking one stage above their own increased their subsequent usage of such thinking. (However, this change was only slightly greater than the increase in children's usage of reasoning one stage below their own following exposure to such reasoning.) The treatments consisted of exposure to advice by an adult experimenter about the resolution of two hypothetical moral dilemmas.

In an early study conducted in the schools Blatt (1970) had sixth-grade children participate in a program of classroom discussion of moral dilemmas, three times a week for 3 months. According to Kohlberg, 1969: "Blatt's procedure was to elucidate the arguments of the Stage 3 children as against the Stage 2 children on hypothetical moral conflicts, then to pit the Stage 3's against the Stage 4's, and finally to himself present Stage 5 arguments [p. 403]." The reasoning of 45% of the children moved up one stage, in contrast to 8% in the control group. A majority of Stage 2 children moved up to Stage 3, and a majority of Stage 3 children moved up to Stage 4. There was little change from Stage 4 to Stage 5.

These studies were followed by others: Evidence of the effectiveness of these procedures is somewhat mixed, on the whole. Grimes (1974) engaged students in the discussion of moral dilemmas and in creating and role playing original dilemmas in a course on moral education. The children's mothers also participated in the course, which, as it was found in some Head Start projects, may be of crucial importance. The sixth-grade children in the experimental class moved from preconventional (Stage 1 and 2) to conventional (Stage 3 and 4) moral reasoning. Sullivan (1975), on the other hand, reported that in similar moral reasoning courses there was change in stage of reasoning in one school, not in another. In Lickona's (1978) view, so far, the Kohlbergian interventions have produced only modest gains in moral reasoning. In high school social projects in Boston and Pittsburgh, for example, only half of the teachers conducting moral discussions were able to stimulate upward stage-change in their students over the course of the academic year, and the size of the change was only from one-quarter to one-half a stage.

Many theoretical and practical issues exist with regard to this type of intervention. Apart from questions about the theory that can be and have been raised, how change comes about has not yet been established. Modeling of moral reasoning by adults has produced change in several studies (for a review see Staub, 1978, pp. 174–176). What is the contribution of instruction from and exposure by adults, and participation by children, that produces the experiential mix necessary for change? Practical issues also exist. For example, the system is highly complex, and extensive training of teachers may be required to be sufficiently familiar with the system and to be well prepared to guide discussion.

Several other approaches have been and are currently being explored for stimulating moral reasoning. They include role-taking experiences (Paolitto, 1975) and peer counseling. Both adolescents (Dowell, 1972) and prison inmates (Lorish, 1974) have been taught to act as peer counselors, and then engaged in peer counseling. This experience did result in significant advances in moral reasoning. Peer counseling seems a form of experiential learning, which provides the counselor with an important, self-enhancing role, in the course of which he or she can benefit another. It also involves exchange of views and feedback from peers, and thus the opportunity for role taking. The previous discussion on experiential learning suggests that such an experience can be expected to increase prosocial behavior. A further approach to stimulate moral reasoning has been to create and have students participate in fair and democratic social arrangements. The term "just community" has been applied to such efforts.

The evidence is not yet clear how to best contribute to change in moral reasoning. In this chapter, which is about promoting prosocial behavior, it is important to stress that change in moral reasoning will not necessarily be accompanied by increased prosocial behavior (see Staub, 1978, pp. 258–264). Having children in schools engage in moral reasoning under adult guidance might be most effective in increasing positive behavior (and probably even moral reasoning itself) if it is accompanied by or ideally even embedded in participation in positive action. For example, in preparation for or during participation in prosocial action by members of a class reasons for such action can be explored in class discussion, partly set up in the form of moral dilemmas.

Summary and Conclusions

This chapter intends to suggest some ways in which persons who work with children in educational settings may contribute to the development of a prosocial value orientation, prosocial goals, and a tendency to behave positively—through play-type activities such as role playing, through promoting children's participation in varied activities, and through their own relationships to children. The manner in which the organization of the peer group and of a school can affect the development of prosocial tendencies is also noted. In every domain that this chapter discusses further elaboration and specification is needed—and research, to enable us to justifiably make such specifications and elaborations.

ACKNOWLEDGMENT

The preparation of this chapter and some of the research reported in it were supported by NIMH Grant No. 23886 to the author.

REFERENCES

Aronfreed, J. *Conduct and conscience.* New York: Academic Press, 1968.

Aronson, E., & Bridgeman, D. Jigsaw groups and the desegregated classroom: In pursuit of common goals. *Personality and Social Psychology Bulletin, 1979, 5,* 438–446.

Aronson, E., Stephan, C., Sikes, J., Blaney, N., & Snapp, M. *The jigsaw classroom.* Beverly Hills, Calif.: Sage Publications, Inc., 1978.

Bandura, A., & Walters, R. H. *Adolescent aggression: A study of the influence of child training practices and family interrelationship.* New York: Ronald Press, 1959.

Barker, R. G., & Gump, P. V. *Big school, small school.* Stanford, Calif.: Stanford University Press, 1964.

Barton, E. J., & Ascione, F. R. Sharing in pre-school children: Facilitation, stimulus generalization, response generalization, and maintenance. *Journal of Applied Behavior Analysis, 1979, 12,* 417–430.

Barton, E. J., & Osborne, J. G. The development of classroom sharing by a teacher using positive practice. *Behavior Modification, 1978, 2,* 231–251.

Bathurst, J. E. A study in sympathy and resistance among children. *Psychological* Bulletin, 1933, *0,* 625.

Baumrind, D. Current patterns of parental authority. *Developmental Psychology,* 1971, *4,* 1–101.

Baumrind, D. *Early socialization and the discipline controversy.* Morristown, N.J.: General Learning Press, 1975.

Blaney, N. T., Stephan, C., Rosefield, D., Aronson, E., & Sikes, J. Interdependence in the classroom: A field study. *Journal of Educational Psychology,* 1977, *69,* 139–146.

Blatt, M. *Studies on the effects of classroom discussion upon children's moral development.* Unpublished doctoral dissertation, University of Chicago, 1970.

Bossard, J. H.S., & Boll, E. S. *The large family system.* Philadelphia: University of Pennsylvania Press, 1956.

Bridgemann, D. L. *The influence of cooperative, interdependent learning on role taking and moral reasoning: A theoretical and empirical field study with fifth grade students.* Unpublished Doctoral Dissertation, University of California, Santa Cruz, 1977.

Chandler, M. J. Egocentrism and antisocial behavior: The assessment and training of social perspective-talking skills. *Developmental Psychology,* 1973, *9* 326–332.

Cohen, E., & Roper, S. Modification of interracial interaction disability: An application of status characteristics theory. *American Sociological Review, 1972, 6,* 543–657.

Cowen, E. L., Pederson, A., Babigan, H., Izzo, L. D., & Frost, M. A. Long term follow-up of early detected vulnerable children. *Journal of Consulting and Clinical Psychology,* 1973, *41,* 438–446.

DeVries, D. L., Edwards, K. J., & Slavin, R. E. Bi-racial learning teams and race relations in the classroom: Four filed experiments on Teams-Games-Tournament. *Journal of Educational Psychology,* in press.

Dlugokinski, E. L., & Firestone, I. J. Congruence among four methods of measuring other-centerdness. *Child Development,* 1973, *44,* 304–308.

Dowell, R. *A curriculum in ego counseling for adolescents.* Unpublished doctoral dissertation, Harvard University, 1972.

Eisenberg-Berg, N., & Geisheker, E. Content of preachings and power of the model/preacher: The effect on children's generosity. *Developmental Psychology,* 1979, *15,* 168–175.

Eron, L., Walder, L. O., & Leftkowitz, M. M. *Learning of aggression in children.* Boston: Little, Brown, 1971.

Feinberg, H. K. *Anatomy of a helping situation: Some personality and situational determinants of helping in a conflict situation involving another's psychological distress.* Unpublished doctoral dissertation, University of Massachusetts, Amherst, 1977.

Friedrich-Cofer, L. K., Huston-Stein, A., Kipnis, D. M., Susman, E. J., & Clewett, A. S. Environmental enhancement of prosocial television content: Effects on interpersonal behavior, imaginative play, and self-regulation in a natural setting. *Developmental Psychology,* 1979, *15,* 637–647.

Friedrich, L. K., & Stein, A. H. Aggressive and prosocial television programs and the natural behavior of preschool children. *Monographs of the Society for Research in Child Development,* 1973, *38, (4,* Serial No. 151).

Friedrich, L. K., & Stein, A. H. Prosocial television and young children: The effects of verbal labeling and role playing on learning and behavior. *Child Development,* 1975, *46,* 27–38.

Grimes, P. Teaching moral reasoning to eleven year olds and their mothers: A means of promoting moral development. Unpublished doctoral dissertation, Boston University, School of Education, 1974.

Grusec, J. E., Kuczynski, L., Rushton, J. P., & Simutis, Z. M. Modeling, direct instruction, and attributions: Effects on altruism. *Developmental Psychology,* 1978, *14,* 51–57.

Hoffman, M. L. Moral development. In P. H. Mussen (Ed.), *Carmichael's manual of child development.* New York: Wiley, 1970. (a)

Hoffman, M. L. Conscience, personality, and socialization technique. *Human Development,* 1970, 13, 90–126. (b)

Hoffman, M. L. Altruistic behavior and the parent-child relationship. *Journal of Personality and Social Psychology,* 1975, *31,* 937–943.

Hoffman, M. L., & Saltzstein, H. D. Parent discipline and the child's moral development. *Journal of Personality & Social Psychology,* 1967, *5,* 45–57.

Iannotti, R. J. Effects of role-taking experiences on role taking, empathy, altruism and aggression. *Developmental Psychology,* 1977, *13,* 274–281.

Johnson, D. W., & Johnson, R. T. *Learning together and alone.* Englewood Cliffs, New Jersey: Prentice-Hall, 1975.

Kohlberg, L. Stage and sequence: The cognitive-developmental approach to socialization. In D. Goslin (Ed.), *Handbook of socialization theory and research.* Chicago: Rand McNally, 1969.

Konner, M. Relations among infants and juveniles in comparative perspective, In M. Lewis & L. Rosenblum (Eds.), *Friendship and peer relations.* New York: Wiley, 1975.

Lazarowitz, R. H. and Sharan, S. Enhancing prosocial behavior through small-group teaching in school. Paper presented at the International Conference on The Development and Maintenance of Prosocial Behavior, Warsaw, Poland, 1980.

Lefkowitz, M. M., Eron, L. D., Walder, L. O., & Huesmann, L. R. *Growing up to be violent: A longitudinal study of the development of aggression.* New York: Pergamon Press, 1977.

Lewin, L., Lippitt, R., & White, R. K. Patterns of aggressive behavior in experimentally created "social climates." *Journal of Social Psychology,* 1939, *10,* 271–299.

Lickona, T. The developmental theorists' approach to moral/citizenship education. *Research for Better Schools,* Inc., 1978.

Lorish, R. *Teaching counseling to disadvantaged young adults.* Unpublished doctoral dissertation, Boston University, School of Education, 1974.

Lucker, G. W., Rosefield, D., Sikes, J., & Aronson, E. Performance in interdependent classroom: A field study. *American Educational Research Journal, 1977, 13,* 115–123.

Midlarsky, E., & Bryan, J. H. Affect expressions and children's imitative altruism. *Journal of Experimental Research in Personality, 1972, 6,* 195–203.

Olejnik, A. B., & McKinney, J. P. Parental value orientation and generosity in children. *Developmental Psychology, 1973, 8,* 311.

Paolitto, D. *Role-taking opportunities for early adolescents: A program in moral education.* Unpublished doctoral dissertation, Boston University, School of Education, 1975.

Roff, M., Sells, S. B., & Golden, M. M. *Social adjustment and personality development in children.* Minneapolis: University of Minnesota Press, 1972.

Rosenhan, D., & White, G. Observation and rehearsal as determinants of prosocial behavior. *Journal of Personality & Social Psychology, 1967, 5,* 424–431.

Sherif, M., Harvey, O. J., Hood, W., & Sherif, C. *Intergroup conflict and cooperation: The robber's cave experiment.* Norman, Oklahoma: University of Oklahoma Institute of Intergroup Relations, 1961.

Sims, S. *Socialization and situational determinants of sharing in black children.* Unpublished doctoral dissertation, University of Michigan, 1974.

Sims, S. A. *Induction, self-induction and children's donation behavior.* Paper presented at the 49th Annual Meeting of the Eastern Psychological Association, Washington D.C., March 1978.

Staub, E. The use of role playing and induction in children's learning of helping and sharing behavior. *Child Development, 1971, 42,* 805–817.

Staub, E. *The development of prosocial behavior in children.* Morristown, New Jersey: General Learning Press, 1975. (a)

Staub, E. To rear a prosocial child: Reasoning, learning by doing, and learning by teaching others. In D. DePalma & J. Folley (Eds.), *Moral development: Current theory and research.* Hillsdale, New Jersey: Larence Erlbaum Associates, 1975. (b)

Staub, E. *Positive social behavior and morality, Vol. 1: Social and personal influences.* New York: Academic Press, 1978. (a)

Staub, E. Predicting prosocial behavior: A model for specifying the nature of personality-situation interaction. In L. Pervin & M. Lewis (Eds.), *Internal determinents of behavior.* New York: Plenum Press, 1978 (b).

Staub, E. *Positive social behavior and morality, Vol. 2: Socialization and development.* New York: Academic Press, 1979.

Staub, E., & Feinberg, H. *Positive and negative peer interaction and some of their personality correlates.* Unpublished research, University of Massachusetts, Amherst, 1978.

Sullivan, E. V. *Moral learning: Findings, issues, and questions.* New York: Paulist Press, 1975.

Turiel, E. An experimental test of the sequentiality of developmental stages. *Journal of Personality and Social Development, 1966, 3,* 611–618.

Whiting, J. W. M., & Whiting, B. *Children of six cultures.* Cambridge, Massachusetts: Harvard University Press, 1975.

White, G. M. Immediate and deferred effects of model observation and guided and unguided rehearsal on donating and staling. *Journal of Personality & Social Psychology, 1972, 21,* 139–148.

White, G. M., & Burnam, M. A. Socially cued altruism: Effects of modeling, instructions, and age on public and private donations. *Child Development, 1975, 46,* 559–563.

Yarrow, M. R., & Scott, P. M. Imitation of nurturant and non-nurturant models. *Journal of Personality & Social Psychology, 1972, 23,* 259–270.

Yarrow, M. R., Scott, P. M., & Waxler, C. Z. Learning concern for others. *Developmental Psychology, 1973, 8,* 240–261.

III INTERNAL MEDIATORS OF ALTRUISM

7 Role-Taking and Altruism: When you put yourself in the shoes of another, will they take you to their owner's aid?

Dennis Krebs
Cristine Russell
Simon Fraser University

Interviewer: "If you knew how someone else felt, would you be more likely to help them than if you didn't?"

Adam: "Oh yes, what you do is, you forget everything else that's in your head, and then you make your mind into their mind. Then you know how they're feeling, so you know how to help them. Some kids can't do that because they think everybody's always thinking the same things."

According to 8 year old Adam, a process we might call role-taking mediates altruism. A number of psychologists feel the same way. The relationship between role-taking and altruism makes sense: we see a friend in sorrow, feel bad, and try to help; we drive by a hitchhiker, remember how we felt in a similar situation, and stop to offer a lift. However, intuitive plausibility holds small currency in the harsh domain of scientific verification. Our purpose in this chapter is to examine the conceptual flirtation between role-taking and altruism with a view toward appraising its qualifications for an empirically-sanctioned relationship.

Psychological Research on Role-Taking and Altruism

Kurdek (1978) summarized the results of 10 studies that investigated the relationship between role-taking and altruism. Since Kurdek's review, at least 6 additional studies have been reported (see Table 7.1). Considered as a whole, the findings from these 16 studies are woefully inconclusive. Approximately half of them found a positive relationship; approximately half failed to find a significant relationship; and three studies found some evidence for a negative correlation

TABLE 7.1

Studies on Role-Taking and Altruism

Study	Subjects	Role-taking Tasks	Altruism Tasks	Outcome
Barrett & Yarrow 1977	79/5 to 8 years	"Inferential ability"	Naturalistic comforting, sharing, helping in summer camp	Negative correlation for low assertive boys (-.51) N.S. positive for high assertive children (.36-.38)
Buckley, Siegel, & Ness (1979)	41/3½ to 9 years	Perceptual Affective Congruent ("empathy")	Either helping peer retrieve spilled pegs or sharing cookie with peer	Perceptual r-t & altruism .46 (age partialled) Affective & perceptual r-t both sig. different for altruists vs. nonaltruists
Eisenberg-Berg & Lennon (1979)	51/4 & 5 years	Congruent Empathy Congruent Affective role-taking ("social comprehension")	Naturalistic observations in preschool setting of solicited & unsolicited total sharing, comforting, & helping of peers	*Affective role-taking* N.S. except with solicited sharing: .27 (p < .06) *Empathy* negative with total spontaneous pro-social (from -.29 to -.47)
Emler & Rushton (1974)	60/7 to 13 years	7 pictures 5 ¢ - 10 ¢	Donate tokens to fund	n.s.
Green (1975)	40/kindergarten	Affective Congruent	Retrieve "dropped" papers Help older girl sort tickets	.70 retrieving (girls only) n.s. sorting
Iannotti (1975)	60/6 and 9 years	Composite Cognitive Affective Incongruent	Share candy with needy child	Composite cognitive .66 Affective -.45

Study	N/Age	Measures	Prosocial behavior	Results
Iannotti (1978)	60/4-5 & 8-9 years	Selman 5¢-10¢ Incongruent Empathy	Donating candy to "needy child"	Role-taking predicted altruism with age held constant (step-down F regression produced sig. higher altruism scores for 6-year-olds, but not for 9-year-olds)
Iannotti (1979)	80/6 to 10 years	Selman 5¢-10¢ Incongruent Empathy	Sharing candy with "needy child"	Ss above Stage 2 role-taking and 63% accuracy on empathy measure shared sig. more than Ss above criterion on only one measure with groups matched on age
Krebs & Sturrup (1974)	24/Grades 2 and 3	7 pictures 5¢-10¢	Naturalistic suggesting, offering help, supporting: composite measure; teacher's ratings	.47 7 pictures and composite .52 5¢-10¢ and composite .42 7 pictures and teacher's rating .57 5¢-10¢ and teacher's rating
Kurdek (1978b)	96/Grades 1 through 4	Chandler 5¢-10¢ Feffer Selman	Teacher-rated help classmates	N.S.
Leckie (1975)[1]	160/3-8 years	Perceptual, Cognitive Affective	Retrieve "dropped" papers donate to fund	N.S. except .33 for cognitive with 8-year-olds
Olejnik (1975)[1]	160/Grades kindergarten through 3	Composite Cognitive	Share candy with friend Share candy with stranger	With friend .66 With stranger .24

(Continued)

Study	Age/N	Task	Measure	Results
Rubin & Schneider (1973)	55/7 years	Referential communication	Help younger child stack tickets Donate candy to poor children	.64 with M.A. partialled .29 with M.A. partialled
Rushton & Wiener (1975)	30/7 years 30/11 years	Perceptual Referential communication	Donate to charity Share with friends	All n.s. except: perceptual and share with friend (.40)
Strayer & Christophe (1978) (extended and published as Strayer, in press)	14/5 years	Affective Incongruent Perceptual	Naturalistic observations of "empathic" prosocial responses in day care centre (comforting, help-giving) Donating pennies to "needy child"	*Affective r-t* .42 (spontaneous) ($p < .10$) *Perceptual r-t* .40 (solicited) .48 (donating)
Zahn-Waxler, Radke-Yarrow, & Brady-Smith (1979)	108/3 to 7 years	4 perceptual tasks 7 simple own-other perceptual distinguishing tasks	6 naturalistic measures of helping, sharing, and comforting	N.S.

[1]Adapted from Kurdek (1978a).

between the two measures. In short, empirical research on the relationship between role-taking and altruism supplies distressingly little support for the budding intuitions of little Adam and the assumptions of the person on the street.

As revealed in Table 7.1, investigators have selected a wide array of operations to represent both role-taking and altruism. The variability among measures may be responsible for the inconsistencies in the findings: different measures of role-taking may assess different processes; different helping behaviors may stem from different sources; and different combinations of measures may give rise to qualitatively different relationships. Thus, this chapter is devoted to an examination of first, the construct of role-taking, second, the construct of altruism, and finally, the nature of the relationship between the two.

THE CONSTRUCT OF ROLE-TAKING

It seems reasonable to assume that investigators would obtain a clear idea of what role-taking is before they select or develop tests to assess it. However, this seemingly sensible assumption is largely unfounded. There is little consensus among psychologists about the nature of role-taking. One problem concerns the relationship between role-taking and empathy. To some investigators the constructs denote qualitatively different processes. To others they are interchangeable. Deutsche and Madle summarize some of the other conceptual problems with the construct. Employing the term "empathy," but using it to refer to processes commonly denoted by the term role-taking, Deutsche and Madle (1975) conclude that:

> Although numerous definitions of empathy have been advanced during the past century (Gompertz, 1960), several issues have not been clarified within an historic framework: whether an empathic response is a shared emotional experience, an understanding of affect, or both; whether an empathic response is a response to an object, another's affect, and/or circumstance; whether one process or several explain how one is empathic; and whether self-other differentiation is required by various definitions of empathy [p. 267].

By and large, psychologists have invested little energy in clarifying the concepts of role-taking and empathy. In the words of Urberg and Docherty (1976) "Researchers have generally devised their own tasks and often assumed that their tasks defined the essence of role-taking behavior [p. 198]." Investigators who have attempted to organize existing measures of role-taking and empathy have made the distinctions summarized in Fig. 7.1 (see Shantz, 1975; Kurdek, 1978a). The nature of the operations involved in each "type" of role-taking, and a sample of the tasks that have been used to assess them are displayed in Table 7.2.

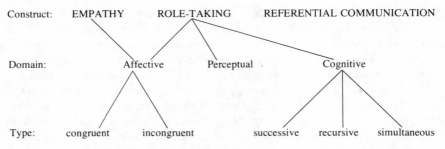

FIG. 7.1. A rough classification of measures of role-taking and related processes.

The existence of different tests purporting to measure the same or similar phenomena raises a number of pressing questions. Do all tests supply an equally valid measure of role-taking? Are the distinctions that have been made between types of role-taking and between role-taking and related processes such as empathy the most meaningful ones? How are the different types of role-taking related? Before we can hope to explain the inconsistencies in studies that have tested the relationship between role-taking and altruism, we must answer these questions. Two main approaches are available—(1) examining the conceptual distinctiveness and overlap among measures of role-taking, empathy, and related processes; and (2) examining the empirical relationships among them. There is distinct paucity of conceptual work in the area. Most research has been empirical. Although we believe that there are a number of conceptual problems with the definition and categorization of types of role-taking, space does not permit us to go into them here. We turn, therefore, to an examination of empirical research on the issue.

Empirical Research on the Relationship among Measures of Role-taking

In examining the empirical relationship among measures of role-taking, researchers typically compute the correlation between scores on two or more tests that purport to assess the phenomenon. Occasionally, they factor analyse scores from a number of tests. It is important to recognize at the outset that although analyses of this kind may supply a basis for determining the extent to which different tests assess the same underlying processes (and, thus, whether they are assessing the same or different, unitary or multidimensional constructs), they are not equipped to establish the construct validity of individual tests of role-taking.

In an attempt to evaluate the relationship among measures of role-taking, we undertook a review of the findings from relevant studies. Independently, and coincidentally, Ford (1979) undertook a similar analysis. The way in which we classified measures and the first-order conclusions we reached were remarkably

TABLE 7.2
Tests of Empathy, Role-taking, and Referential Communication

Tasks	Description
Empathy	
Feshbach & Roe Empathy Test (Feshbach & Roe, 1968)	Subject is shown slide sequences, accompanied by a narrative, in which a child of similar age and sex is shown in situations likely to elicit happiness, sadness, anger, or fear. After viewing, the subject is asked "How do *you* feel?"
Modifications of affective role-taking tasks (e.g., Iannotti, 1978)	Subjects are given an affective role-taking task, but the subject's own responses are scored rather than their judgments of the story characters' feelings.
A variety of psychophysiological measures (e.g., Stotland, 1969, Stotland et al. 1978; Krebs, 1975)	Subjects' heart rate, blood pressure, GSR, etc. are assessed as they observe others undergoing emotional experiences.
Adult pencil and paper tests (Hogan, 1969; Merehbian & Epstein, 1972)	Traditional psychometric tests.

What is Measured: Empathy tasks assess the subject's ability to *feel* the way another person feels. Empathy differs from affective role-taking, which involves *understanding* how others feel (see Hoffman, 1975; Krebs, 1975). In affective role-taking tasks the subject is asked—"How does the story character feel?"—while in empathy tasks the subject is asked, "How do *you* feel?" As is the case for affective role-taking tasks, some empathy tasks use stories in which the story character's affect is incongruent with the situation in which the character is presented, in order to minimize the likelihood that subjects will respond on the basis of projection rather than on the basis of their own emotional responses to the accurately-perceived emotions of the characters.

Tasks	Description
Affective Role-Taking	
Congruent Affect Tasks	
Rothenberg Affect Inference (Rothenberg, 1970)	Tape recordings of dyadic interactions between adults depicting happiness, anger, sadness, & distress/anxiety are presented. Subject must describe how one actor felt and explain the basis of his or her actions.

(Continued)

143

(Continued)

Borke's Affect Inference
(Borke, 1971)

Stories are presented in which emotion is elicited in a story character, either as the result of the subject's hypothetical actions or otherwise. Subject must select a picture of a face (happy, sad, angry, or afraid) depicting the emotions of the story character.

Incongruent Affect Tasks
Modifications of Borke Task
(e.g., Kurdek & Rodgon, 1975)

Borke's stories, or similar stories, are modified so that the affect of the story character is incongruent with the situation in which the character is depicted (e.g., a sad child at a birthday party).

What is Measured: Affective role-taking tasks assess the subjects' ability to identify how another person feels (without necessarily reporting that they themselves are experiencing a similar emotion). Early tasks presented story characters similar in age and sex to the subjects, in situations likely to be familiar to them (e.g., Borke, 1971). To minimize the likelihood that subjects would be able to correctly identify the story characters' emotions on the basis of projection, later investigators (e.g., Kurdek & Rodgon, 1975) modified the tasks to create incongruity between the story characters' emotions and the situations in which they were presented.

Perceptual Role-Taking

Three Mountains Task
(Piaget & Inhelder, 1956)

An array representing three mountains is placed on a table. Subject must choose the view seen by a doll in a different position.

Modifications: Several tasks use simpler arrays and/or vary response requirements. In some tasks, the subject moves around a stationary array; in others, the subject remains stationary while the array is revolved.

Flavell et al., Tasks (Flavell, Botkin, Fry, Wright, & Jarvis, 1968)

Variety of tasks requiring subject to choose the perspective of an object or array of objects seen by another person.

Masangkay, et al., Tasks (Masangkay, McCluskey, McIntyre, Sims-Knight, Vaughn, & Flavell, 1974)

Tasks requiring subject to indicate which object is seen by another, rather than to indicate the perspective of object (s) seen by the other. Used with subjects as young as three years.

What is Measured: Perceptual or visual-spatial role-taking tasks measure the ability to perceive physical displays from the viewpoint of another. In all tests the perspective of the other is incongruent with the perspective of the observer. The main ways in which different tests of perceptual role-taking differ is in terms of the complexity of the physical display, the method of assessing children's responses, and the degree of disparity between the perspective of the subject and the perspective of the other.

144

Successive Decentering Tasks

Feffer's Role-Taking Task
(Feffer & Gourevitch, 1960)

Pictures are presented in which three Characters interact (e.g. a woman hitting a child while an opposite-sex child looks on). The subject must tell a story based on the picture, then retell it from the viewpoint of each of the three characters.

Selman's Social-Moral Dilemmas
(Selman & Byrne, 1974)

Audiovisual filmstrips present dilemmas in which a main character interacts with one or more other characters. Standardized questions assess the degree to which the subject understands the characters' differing viewpoints and understands that two characters could consider each other's viewpoints.

Simultaneous Decentering Tasks

Chandler's Bystander Cartoons
(Chandler & Greenspan, 1972)

Cartoon sequences are presented in which the story character is exposed to situations that would result in particular emotional reactions.

The subject must identify a late-arriving bystander's thoughts about the story characters' emotional reaction and its cause. The subject must ignore his or her own privileged information in order to take the viewpoint of the bystander.

Feffer and Selman tests
(Feffer & Gourevitch, 1960; Selman & Byrne, 1974)

Scored for adopting a third person, "generalized other" perspective.

Recursive Role-Taking Tasks

Flavell's Nickel-Dime Game
(Flavell et al., 1968)

Subjects play a game in which they must hide money under one of two boxes, labelled 5¢ and 10¢, between which an opponent will choose. Responses are scored on the degree to which the subjects' justifications for their game strategies reflect a consideration of the other child's likely strategies, and a consideration that the other child might employ cognitions about the subject's own strategies in deciding which choice to make.

(Continued)

145

(Continued)

Miller et al.'s Recursive Cartoons
(Miller, Kessel, & Flavell, 1970)

Cartoon sequences are presented in which what characters say is put in smooth cartoon clouds, and what they think in scalloped cartoon clouds. Subjects must indicate awareness that one person may be the subject of another person's thoughts, and follow this procedure through different numbers of iterations: "She is thinking that he is thinking that she is thinking. . . ."

What is Measured: Three main types of tests have been employed to assess the ability to understand what another is thinking—tests of successive or sequential role-taking, recursive role-taking, and simultaneous or coordinated role-taking. *Successive* or *sequential* role-taking tests assess people's ability to understand that the same events may be interpreted differently by different people. In some tests, subjects are required to characterize a situation from the point of view of two or more different people in succession. In other tests, subjects are not required to indicate explicitly what others are thinking; rather, they are asked to make choices that would follow from the others' trains of thought. For example, they might be asked to select a birthday gift first for their mother then for an opposite sex peer. The term *simultaneous* role-taking has been used to refer to a number of different processes. According to Kurdek (1978) simultaneous role-taking is assessed by *privileged information* tasks such as Flavell's 7 picture task and Chandler's cartoons. Theorists such as Feffer, Selman, and Kohlberg discuss simultaneous role-taking in terms of the ability to synthesize two or more points of view simultaneously. Thus, rather than alternating between first one person's point of view, then another's, a subject might view the situation from an overriding perspective; saying, for example, "These two people realize that they are in *conflict*, they are searching for a *compromise*." The perspective of each person is taken into account, as well as the relationship between them ("conflict," "compromise"), and there is an implicit recognition that each of the parties is able to view the situation from the point of view of the other. *Recursive* role-taking involves the ability to understand that role-takers can take one another's roles simultaneously. In this regard it is similar to simultaneous role-taking. In addition, however, recursive role-taking may undergo any number of iterations. Tests such as those of Feffer and Selman may elicit sequential, recursive, and simultaneous role-taking.

Referential Communication

Glucksberg et al., blocks
(Glucksberg, Krauss, & Weisberg, 1966).

The subject must convey to a silent "listener" on the other side of a screen how to construct a stack of blocks identical to one in front of the subject. (The blocks differ from each other along more than one dimension). Scoring is based on the degree to which the subject's speech is egocentric (use of pronouns with unstated referents, the number of pieces of information conveyed, etc.).

Nahir & Yussen Communication Task (1977)

Subjects are shown pictures of common objects along with standard statements. The task is to communicate this information about the object separately to both an adult and a child listener (hypothetical). Measures such as MLU and complexity are compared for the two narratives as an index of the degree to which the subject adapts speech to the characteristics of the listener.

What is Measured: Referential communication tasks assess the ability to "construct a message that enables someone else to know what that message refers to" (Glucksberg, Krauss, & Higgins, 1975, p. 305). In most tests, this involves conveying privileged information to a person who possesses a different perspective. The information usually relates to the appearance of a physical stimulus such as a pattern of blocks or a picture that is visible to the subject, but not to the other. Referential communication involves decentration in the child's verbal communication with others. Thus it is closely related to the egocentric phenomenon of private speech, in which, for example, a child playing by herself out of view of her parent might nonetheless ask the parent, "What is this?".

similar. In the interest of space, we will not present the results of our analysis here.[1] Like Ford, we found that the relationship among many types of role-taking had not been investigated. And, like Ford, we found two main trends among those that had. First, tests of "affective" role-taking did not appear to relate to tests of "perceptual" and "cognitive" role-taking, suggesting that the affective processes may be independent from the others, and, inasmuch as empathy is defined as an affective response, supplying a basis for distinguishing between role-taking and empathy. Second, perceptual role-taking appeared to relate to (a) referential communication and (b) cognitive simultaneous role-taking (see Table 7.2). Indeed, there was even the suggestion of a *menage a trois* among the three.

There are two reasons why we might expect measures of perceptual role-taking to relate to measures of referential communication. First, the subject matter on both tasks is visual-spatial in nature—subjects must describe how static objects look in relation to one another. Second, the cognitive operations are similar structurally. Both types of tests assess subjects' ability (a) to understand that physical displays look different when they are viewed from a different position, (b) to recognize how the displays would look from another position, and (c) to distinguish between the two perspectives. The major difference between the tasks relates to the necessity in referential communication to instruct another and to deal with sequences of action (see Glucksberg, Krauss, & Higgins, 1975). But these points do not account for the association between these tests and cognitive simultaneous role-taking.

An alternative explanation—one that might account for the relationship among all three types of role-taking tasks—is that they require the subject to take a point of view that conflicts with his or her own viewpoint. In this sense, all three are "simultaneous" role-taking tasks in which subjects must overcome the compelling immediacy of their own perspectives.

Ford (1979) also found evidence for an association among these measures, but he attributed them to "other explanatory constructs," such as a child's "general level of cognitive, perceptual, or linguistic development [p. 1185]." Focusing on the general failure of measures of role-taking to interrelate, Ford entertained two conclusions: That "some or all of the tests are not good measures of the construct, [and that] the theory (Piagetian) that specifies the meaning of the construct is incorrect [p. 1185]." Ford favored the latter interpretation; however, in our view the problem lies less with the correctness of Piagetian theory, and more with the absence of a fully developed theory of egocentricity and role-taking. It is largely due to the absence of an overriding theory, we contend, that studies have failed to conduct valid tests of the relationship among measures. Let us look at some evidence that supports this contention.

---

[1]The table summarizing our findings on the relationship among measures of role-taking is available from the senior author upon request.

Methodological Problems: Research on Role-taking

Correlational research is susceptible to two opposing dangers—concluding that two or more tests are related when the correlation between them is really due to third factors ("false positives"), and concluding that a nonsignificant correlation between two or more tests establishes that they are not associated ("false negatives").

False Positives

A number of studies have found that tests of role-taking correlative positively with tests of intelligence and cognitive development; and other studies have found that role-taking correlates with moral development (see Krebs & Gillmore, in press, for a review of relevant studies). Similarly, researchers investigating perceptual perspective-taking have found evidence that this skill involves cognitive spatial abilities (Coie, Costanzo, & Farnill, 1973; Hoy, 1974). Findings such as these raise the possibility that a third factor is responsible for the observed positive associations among measures. In the words of Ford (1979):

> Perspective-taking ability may account for little of the variance (in performance on role-taking tests) after age 4 or 5 . . . More plausible sources of variance include (a) general intelligence . . . (b) verbal comprehension . . . (c) specific cognitive factors such as spacial or perceptual abilities, depending on the complexity and/or familiarity of the task stimuli . . . (d) characteristics specific to the type of response required (e.g. verbal vs. nonverbal; symbolic vs. concrete) . . . and (e) variables highly specific to the task, such as whether a real person or a doll is sitting in the position in which a visual/spacial perspective must be inferred [p. 1185].

Although Ford's points clearly are well-taken, they may overstate the case. The task of finding variables that are theoretically unrelated to role-taking cannot be undertaken thoroughly until we have a better idea of what role-taking is. Clearly role-taking should bear some relationship to cognitive development—it is an intrinsically cognitive process. Therefore, whether the correlation between role-taking and other abilities is evidence against the discriminant validity of role-taking tests or in favor of their convergent validity is an open question.

False Negatives

There are countless methodological pitfalls that may conspire to mask valid relationships—oversights while running experiments, errors in scoring test results, mistakes in the analysis of data. Most of them are general to all psychological research. However, there are at least two methodological oversights that are particularly problematic in research on role-taking; (1) insensitivity to task difficulty and (2) insensitivity to the developmental level of subjects.

Task Difficulty.   Studies have found that perceptual role-taking is influenced by the complexity and discreteness of objects (Borke, 1975; Brodzinsky &

Jackson, 1972; Cox, 1977; Masangkay, McCluskey, McIntyre, Sims-Knight, Vaughn, & Flavell, 1974), the perspective of the other (Shantz & Wilson, 1972), the mode of identification (Borke, 1975; Fishbein, Lewis, & Keiffer, 1972), and other variables (see Piaget & Inhelder, 1970; Shantz, 1975). Similarly, Brandt (1978) reported that when three types of questions (asking what a bystander would think, giving a choice between egocentric and decentered responses, and specifically asking if the bystander knew about privileged information), were used on privileged information tasks, the correlations between the tasks ranged from .29 to .82. Spilton and Lee (1977) reported different effectiveness in referential communication tasks depending on the quantity of listener feedback; and Deutsch (1975) found that children performed better on affective role-taking tasks when subject and story character were of the same rather than opposite sex.

The variability produced by differences in task demands and testing situations complicates immensely the task of assessing the relationship between different types of role-taking. When an investigator gives a group of subjects two types of role-taking tests and fails to find a significant association between the scores, it is difficult to determine whether the disparity was caused by differences in task demands or differences in underlying processes. Thus, the goal of researchers in this area seems better defined as comparing the amount of variance accounted for by task demands and type of role-taking than testing the association between types of role-taking that may vary in task demands.

Developmental Level. The problem of insensitivity to task difficulty is related to the problem of insensitivity to the developmental level of subjects. Measures of chronological and mental age typically relate positively to measures of role-taking (see Perry & Krebs, 1980). To some investigators, these relationships are theoretically insignificant. Consider, for example, the position adopted by Ford (1979): "Since there are age differences in measures with some cognitive content . . . this kind of information is not as decisive or as discriminating as some other kinds of evidence might be . . . For the same reasons, studies of change over time might be less useful for answering questions about the construct validity of egocentrism . . . [p. 1170]." We disagree. We believe that egocentricity is best viewed in developmental context, as a form of social thought that normally undergoes a number of qualitative changes with age.

From a Piagetian perspective, different role-taking tests should assess abilities that relate to one another in a logically progressive, hierarchical way, with the tasks understood only by old children comprising more advanced forms of role-taking than tasks understood by both young and old children. In this view, the practice of giving children at different stages of development the same test of role-taking and concluding that those who do not pass it cannot role-take is equivalent to giving a group of adults a complex test of logic, and concluding that those who can't solve it can't think. There is ample evidence to suggest that the failure of two role-taking tests to correlate among children at one developmental level supplies no indication that the tests do not validly assess role-taking skills that are acquired at other stages.

From a cognitive-developmental perspective, the tasks of an investigator is not only to determine whether different operations (scores on tests) reflect the same type of role-taking (i.e., are linearly correlated), but also to determine whether the clusters of correlated operations that define different types of role-taking follow one another in an invariant sequence. There may be developmental hierarchies within cognitive, perceptual and affective role-taking. There may be developmental hierarchies between types, with, for example, children acquiring affective role-taking skills first, then perceptual role-taking skills, then the cognitive type. And there may be hierarchies that consist of intersections within and between types of role-taking.

There is little evidence on hierarchical cross-domain relationships; and there is little evidence for a developmental progression of affective role-taking or empathy. However, there is evidence that both perceptual and cognitive role-taking abilities undergo a number of qualitative transformations with development. Flavell (1974, 1977), Masangkay et al. (1974), and Lempers, Flavell & Flavell (1977) have obtained evidence for a hierarchical progression in perceptual role-taking. At the first level, the child realizes that other people can see some objects but not others. At the second level, the child realizes that different people viewing the same event from different perspectives may have different visual experiences. Other investigators have outlined developmental progressions in cognitive role-taking ability. For example, Feffer and Gourevitch (1960) supplied evidence that children pass through three stages, defined by (1) lack of the ability to decenter, (2) the ability to conceptualize a situation from different points of view in succession, and (3) the ability to coordinate two or more points of view simultaneously. Selman and Byrne (1974) offered a similar empirically-based developmental hierarchy of ''perspective taking,'' consisting of an egocentric level, ''subjective role-taking,'' ''self-reflective role-taking,'' and ''mutual role-taking.''

The empirical support for existing hierarchies of role-taking is based almost exclusively on their originators' own tests. Such schemes would go a great deal further in elucidating the construct of role-taking and organizing research in the area if they could account for the abilities assessed by the tests developed by others. A modest start toward this end was made by Perry and Krebs (1980) who interpreted the 7-pictures and nickel and dime tests popularized by Flavell, Botkin, Fry, Wright, and Jarvis (1968) in terms of Selman and Byrne's (1974) model (see Table 7.3). In a more elaborate study, Urberg and Docherty (1976) performed an analysis of role-taking tests that were developed by themselves and several other investigators, and gave the tests to a group of young children. The results supported the models of Feffer and Selman, showing, in the words of Urberg and Docherty (1976), ''a fundamental structural difference—sequential vs. simultaneous decentering [p. 198].''

TABLE 7.3
Operational Definitions of Role-Taking Stages

Selman's social role-taking stage	Criterion on Flavell's role-taking tests
Stage 0—Egocentric viewpoing (age range 3-6) Child has a sense of differentiation of self and others, but fails to distinguish between the social perspective (thoughts and feelings) of other and self. Child can label other's overt feelings, but does not see the cause and effect relation of reasons to social actions.	Either no conception that another child would tell a different story to 4 pictures; or the belief that another child would pick whatever cup the S would pick, usually the one that covers the larger amount of money.

Stage 1—Social informational role-taking (age range 6-8)
    Child is aware that other has a social perspective based on other's own reasoning, which may or may not be similar to child's. However, child tends to focus on one perspective rather than coordinating viewpoints.
	I A (Emergent)
	    Sense that another child would see a different story with 4 pictures, but some confusion about the difference in the two perspectives; belief that another child would pick the cup that appears to contain the larger amount of money.
	
	1 B (Consolidated)
	    Full differentiation of perspectives on the 7 pictures test; the realization that another child might attempt to fool the guesser in the nickel-and-dime game by putting the nickel under the dime cup.

Stage 2—Self-reflective role-taking (age range 8-10) Child is conscious that each individual is aware of the other's perspective and that this awareness influences self and other's view of each other. Putting self in other's place is a way of judging his intentions, purposes, and actions. Child can form a coordinated chain of perspectives, but cannot yet abstract from this process to the level of simultaneous mutuality.	Evidence of the ability to take the roles of both actors in the nickel-and-dime game, and to realize that each could attempt to outwit the other by anticipating his moves.

Note: Theoretical definitions from Selman & Byrne (1974); from Perry & Krebs (1980)

The developmental perspective contains the potential to bring considerable order to the classification of role-taking tests. It introduces a vertical, hierarchical dimension that interesects with the existing horizontal typology, at least for tests of perceptual and cognitive role-taking. However, the potential of this perspective seems largely uncultivated. In our view, research on role-taking would benefit from a longitudinal empirical-conceptual bootstrapping approach similar to the one employed by Kohlberg and his colleagues in the study of moral development (see Colby, 1978). First, investigators would construct some reasonable theory of what operations are involved in role-taking, how they interrelate, and how they change with development. Next, they would borrow, adapt, and invent measures to assess them. Then they would test a sample of children repeatedly over a span of years, revise their conceptions and measures of role-taking in accordance with their findings, and so on, over as many iterations as necessary to produce an empirically and conceptually consistent synthesis.

At present almost all conceptual models of role-taking pertain only to the cognitive or perceptual domains. Ultimately they must also include the affective types. A promising beginning toward a synthesis of the affective, perceptual, and cognitive aspects of role-taking and empathy has been presented by Hoffman (1975, 1979). In Hoffman's (1975) model, inborn or early acquired empathic emotions become structured by increasingly complex stages of role-taking ability. In the beginning, an infant experiences "empathic distress" that is "presumably a fusion of unpleasant feelings and stimuli from his own body, the dimly perceived "other," and the situation [p. 612]." As infants acquire the ability to understand object permanence and to distinguish between self and other, the "affective portion of the child's global empathic distress . . . is extended to the separate self and other that emerge [p. 615]." Later, with "the emerging awareness that others have independent inner states,the affect aroused in (the child) by another's distress may be presumed to motivate more active efforts to put himself in the other's place and find the true source of his distress [p. 616]." Finally, with advancing role-taking ability, the child becomes able to "comprehend the plight not only of an individual but also of an entire group or class of people . . . provid(ing) the requisites for a generalized empathic distress [p. 617]."

Recapitulation

Perhaps it is time to take account of where we are in our exploration of role-taking and altruism. We opened by discovering that in spite of the intuitive plausibility of the association between these two phenomena, studies that have tested it have obtained mixed results. Noting that different studies have employed different measures of role-taking, we entertained the idea that the inconsistency in findings is associated with differences among measures. We turned to an examination of research on the relationship among measures of role-taking, but found it sparse and poorly equipped to answer our questions. We ended by discussing some methodological problems with research in the area, exploring the value of a cognitive-developmental perspective, and advocating the development of more comprehensive conceptual models.

In all of this we have given altruism rather short shrift. It is now time to make up for this relative neglect. We will examine the construct of altruism in roughly the same way we have examined the construct of role-taking—reviewing some conceptual definitions, looking at the ways in which it has been operationalized, and exploring the possibility that differences in measures of altruism can help account for the inconsistencies in finding on the relationship between role-taking and altruism.

THE CONSTRUCT OF ALTRUISM

One of the classic issues in philosophy concerns the role of altruism in human nature. People help one another all the time. In fact, so also do the members of many other species. But that doesn't mean they are altruistic—i.e., that the primary motive behind their behavior is to benefit another. In the words of Hatfield, Walster, and Piliavin (1978), "the majority of scientists . . . interpret altruism in cost-benefit terms, assuming that individuals, altruists included, learn to perform those acts that are rewarded . . . and to avoid those acts that are not [pp. 128–129]." We all get invited out to lunch; but is there, as skeptics through the ages have asked, any such thing as a *free* lunch?

Conceptual Definitions of Altruism

The question of whether people are capable of altruism depends, of course, on how altruism is defined. Although there is general agreement on the rough profile of altruism among psychologists, there is little consensus about its finer features. For example, Krebs (1970) defined altruism as "self-sacrificial other oriented behavior," and Wispé (1972) defined it as "a regard for the interest of others without concern for one's self-interest." Severy (1974) disagreed with these conceptual definitions, and argued that altruism should be defined as "helping motivated by the other person's being in need [p. 190]." According to Severy, "the essence of altruism lies in the reason motivating the aiding behavior [p. 193]." Krebs and Wispé (1974) agreed that a critical criterion of altruism is its motivation base, but questioned whether the perception of need in another is sufficient to motivate altruistic behavior. Ultimately they concluded that "To argue about the final definition of altruism in the absence of a theoretical context and without an empirical input is to indulge in little more than an intellectual pillow fight [p. 196]."

Operational Definitions of Prosocial Behavior

As Krebs (1975, 1978) and Krebs and Wispé (1974) have pointed out, most investigators in the area avoid the problems associated with establishing the validity of measures of altruism by labeling the behaviors in which they are interested "prosocial," and defining them operationally. Faced with the task of selecting a prosocial behavior, the typical investigator appears to be guided more by practical facility than concern with conceptual appropriateness. Most of the measures of prosocial behavior employed in contemporary research are easily quantifiable and readily adaptable to laboratory settings—measures such as donating money or tokens to charity, sharing candy or some other resource, helping an experimenter or confederate in an experimental situation, or behaving generously in an experimental game—although, in recent years investigators have become increasingly inclined to investigate naturalistic helping behaviors.

Like different role-taking tasks, different measures of prosocial behavior share a certain general quality. However, as with tests of role-taking, the assumption that different measures of prosocial behavior are interchangeable is a tenuous one. Indeed, even measures that purport to assess the same type of prosocial behavior may contain subtle but significant differences. Consider donating to charity for example. It may well make a difference (a) whether a child wins the money he or she is asked to donate, or is simply given some money, (b) whether the child is given chips, pennies, or candies, (c) whether a subject is given resources hours before or immediately preceding the opportunity to donate, or (d) whether the recipient is a poor child, a number of poor children, a friend, or a stranger. In addition, subtle differences in the way subjects are apprised of the opportunity to donate could have powerful effects on their behavior, and, to complicate matters even further, variables such as these may either have a direct effect or interact with other variables, such as role-taking ability, to produce differential effects. For example, showing the picture of the child who will receive a donation may be necessary to engage the role-taking abilities of young, but not old children (see Krebs, 1978).

The Empirical Relationship Among Measures of Prosocial Behavior

In the same way that investigators have examined the empirical relationship among tests that purport to assess role-taking, so also have investigators assessed the empirical relationship among measures of prosocial behavior. And, just as the overall picture from studies on role-taking failed to assume a coherent form, so also have studies on prosocial behavior failed to produce consistent results. A number of studies have found weak positive relationships among different prosocial measures (e.g., Dlugokinski & Firestone, 1974; Krebs & Sturrup, in press; Rubin & Schneider, 1973) but other studies have not (e.g., Green & Schneider, 1974). Rushton reviewed the research on the correlation between unitary measures of altruism in 1976, and concluded that: "Mischel's (1968) magic number of .30 once again emerges as the overall representative intercorrelation [p. 901]." The general picture appears to be the same today. However, there are a couple of noteworthy trends.

Among recent studies, the evidence indicates that naturalistic measures of prosocial behavior do not tend to correlate positively with laboratory measures. For example, Strayer (in press) failed to find a significant relationship between measures of either solicited or unsolicited naturally-occurring prosocial behavior and an experimental measure of donating. And Mussen, Rutherford, Harris, and Keasey (1970) failed to find any relationship between a sociometric measure of altruism and generosity in a prisoners' dilemma game. However, there is some indication that naturally-occurring prosocial behaviors that are elicited by emotional displays in others might relate to one another. Strayer and Christophe (1978) found a significant positive correlation between daycare children's naturally-occurring spontaneous and naturally-occurring solicited prosocial responses to emotional displays in their peers. Yarrow and Waxler (1976) found a low but significant positive correlation between serminaturalistic acts of sharing and comforting (and neither measure correlated significantly with measures of helping). Yarrow & Waxler (1976) concluded that ''the relatively impersonal utilitarian 'helping' of an inconvenienced person seems to tap a different kind of behavior from that involved in responding to the emotions of another person, or in reacting to hurt or sadness [p. 123].'' However, it must be noted that the association between sharing and comforting did not hold up in their study in a purely natural setting.

Rushton (1980, this volume) considers the evidence on the consistency of altruism within individuals as it relates to the issue of an ''altruistic personality.'' Rushton finds a respectable amount of evidence for a trait of altruism. Although agreeing with Rushton's general conclusion, we nevertheless remain skeptical about the comparability of measures of altruism. Indeed, it is our suspicion that if more appropriate measures of altruism were employed more prevalently, the evidence favoring a general trait would be strengthened considerably. To this end, we would like to offer four suggestions.

First, measures of prosocial behavior should have ecological validity—i.e., they should reflect the types of behaviors displayed by subjects in their everyday lives. Naturalistic observations accomplish this most adequately. Seminaturalistic measures, in which an experimenter arranges a real life situation, also help meet this requirement (see Yarrow & Waxler, 1976). It is, of course, also possible to devise ecologically valid experimental measures; but we must ask, for example, how many 3- to 12-year-old children are asked to donate tokens to charity outside of a psychologist's lab?

Our second point is similar to one we made about role-taking. Investigators must maintain a sensitivity to the developmental level of their subjects. If someone tells you that he or she conducted a study that employed sharing candies as a measure of altruism, you could be quite sure that the subjects were young children. When the daughter of one of the present authors gives her sister candy, it appears to involve a monumental sacrifice. However, the only time he offered his wife candy during the last year was when she was struggling to maintain a diet. (Significantly, when she reacted in a most ungrateful manner, he received a great deal of gratuitous sympathy from his youngest daughter.)

Third, "altruism" involves an *alter,* other, or recipient. In general, people are more strongly disposed to give to friends than strangers, people they like rather than people they dislike, people who are similar to them rather than different from them, etc. (see Krebs, 1970; Staub, 1978). As mentioned earlier, small variations in characteristics of the recipient may induce large differences in prosocial behavior.

Finally, single measures of prosocial behavior are severely limited for most purposes. When we consider an issue such as the nature of the relationship between role-taking and altruism, we are ultimately interested in the relationship between two general qualities. We would not expect children with even the most advanced role-taking skills to behave altruistically all the time—in every situation. Rather, we would expect them to behave more altruistically than the average child over the course of a day or a week, across an array of situations involving different people, different types of help, and different constraints. Thus, the limitations on samples of behavior intrinsic to most laboratory research may mitigate against the discovery of existing relationships. If an investigator really wants to obtain a valid measure of altruism, it would seem incumbent on him or her to obtain a sample of the child's behavior in a number of different situations. As noted by Rushton (1976, 1980) multiple measures of altruism have been found to correlate with one another more positively than single measures.

With this discussion of research on altruism, we have completed two-thirds of the task we set for ourselves. We have pursued the question "What is role-taking?" in considerable detail; and we have explored the meaning and measurement of altruism. It is now time to turn to the core of our concern—a consideration of the nature of the relationship between the two constructs.

THE RELATIONSHIP BETWEEN ROLE-TAKING AND ALTRUISM

In view of the fact that some of the studies that have investigated the relationship between role-taking and altruism have obtained positive results, and others have not, we might ask whether there are any systematic differences in other aspects of these studies that could explain the differences in their results. For example, studies that assess one type of role-taking might consistently obtain positive results, whereas studies that assess another type might not; or a particular type of role-taking might relate only to a particular type of altruism in subjects of a particular age. Let us, therefore, return to the studies summarized in Table 7.1, examine those that have employed similar measures, and search for commonalities in their results. We will focus first on the findings of studies that have employed measures of affective role-taking and empathy, then turn to an examination of those that have employed measures of the perceptual and cognitive types.

Affective Role-taking and Empathy. Some of the findings in most of the studies on the relationship between affective role-taking, empathy, and altruism were significant. The subjects in the studies typically were relatively young, but the age range was highly variable (from 3 ½ to 9–10 years old). There was little comparability among measures of prosocial behavior.

Conceptually, we would expect affective role-taking to relate most strongly to prosocial behaviors involving expressions of affect in other individuals. There is some suggestive support for this expectation. Strayer and Christophe (1978) found a tendency for affective role-taking to relate to a naturalistic measure of unsolicited comforting, helping, and supporting more strongly than to an impersonal measure involving a donation. In addition, two of the other studies that reported positive associations employed measures of face-to-face helping such as retrieving dropped papers (Green, 1975), picking up spilled puzzle parts, or sharing a cookie (Buckley, Siegel, & Ness, 1979). However, this trend was not consistent across all studies (see Table 7.1).

The most interesting findings on affective role-taking and empathy were opposite to what we would expect. Iannotti (1975), and Eisenberg-Berg and Lennon (1979) found evidence for a negative relationship between these measures and prosocial behavior. It may be significant that the subjects in both the Iannotti and Eisenberg-Berg and Lennon studies were preschool children—children we would expect to be relatively egocentric. Ironically, the measures of "empathy" employed by these investigators actually may have assessed a form of egocentricity. In the Eisenberg-Berg and Lennon study, children were simply asked to indicate how they felt after hearing an affect-laden story, with no obligation to distinguish between their own and the character's perspective. And although employing an incongruent affect test, Iannotti (1978) found a significant negative relationship between his measure of empathy and both cognitive simultaneous role-taking and age. The negative relationship between measures of empathy such as these and prosocial behavior may occur because young children who score high on them may become engulfed by their own emotional reactions, and, lacking the ability to distinguish between their perspective and that of someone who needs help, fail to realize that they can be an agent of assistance. This explanation receives some support from a recent finding by Barnett, King, and Howard (1979). Children who related unpleasant experiences involving themselves subsequently shared less than children who related sad incidents involving others. (For evidence on the relationship between the ability to identify how characters feel [affective role-taking] and feeling similarly, see Feshbach & Roe, 1968 and Mood, Johnson, & Shantz, 1974; and for an explanation of these and other findings that is consistent with ours, see Iannotti, 1979.)

Perceptual Role-taking.   In view of the impersonal nature of the subject matter assessed in most perceptual role-taking tests, we might expect this type of role-taking to relate to impersonal types of prosocial behavior. There was a vaguely suggestive tendency for perceptual role-taking to relate to one of the most impersonal measures of altruism—donating to charity (Strayer & Christophe, 1978). However, in general, there appears to be little consistency in the findings of studies that have employed measures of perceptual role-taking.

Cognitive Role-taking.   A significant feature of measures of cognitive role-taking such as those of Feffer, Flavell, and Selman is that they assess not one but several levels or types of role-taking. Thus, the goal of testing becomes not to divide children into role-takers and non role-takers, or even to give subjects a quantitative score on one type of role-taking; rather, it is to discover what types of role-taking abilities each child possesses. Studies that have employed cognitive role-taking tests capable of assessing different types of role-taking have tended to obtain positive results (see, for example Iannotti, 1975, 1978, 1979; Krebs & Sturrup, in press; Olejnik, 1975). Subjects in these studies mainly fall within the 6 to 11 range—the period when role-taking ability is believed to undergo a qualitative transformation (from the ability to engage in sequential to the ability to engage in coordinated role-taking).

Such findings are promising. They suggest that studies that are sensitive to the developmental level of subjects and employ tests that tap both immature and mature types of role-taking may relate more consistently to measures of altruism than those that do not. The significant relationship for only one age group (9 year olds) and not another (6 year olds) reported by Iannotti (1978) indicates the importance of employing role-taking tests appropriate to childrens' developmental level. Differences in measures of prosocial behavior do not appear to exert any systematic effect on the results.

Role-taking: Capacity vs. Application

Two studies found that cognitive role-taking related to prosocial behavior only when it interacted with other variables, such as sympathy (Emler & Rushton, 1974) and empathy (Iannotti, 1979). Finding that role-taking relates to prosocial behavior only under particular conditions raises a rather compelling point. When we consider the relationship between role-taking and altruism, we typically think of people putting themselves in the shoes of others, understanding that the others need assistance, and helping them. But in all the studies we considered, *not one* tested whether their subjects took the role of the person they were given an opportunity to help! None of them assessed role-taking in the helping situation. Rather, they assessed their subjects' *ability* to role-take in some other context—usually an experimental one bereft of any relevant social interaction.

Although children who are unable to role-take obviously won't, there is no guarantee that those who can will. Role-taking processes must be *engaged* and *applied* in the helping situation before they can be expected to mediate altruism. The sympathy manipulation in the Emler & Rushton (1974) study and the empathy interaction in the Iannotti (1979) study may have helped engage the role-taking capacities of subjects who possessed them. It is interesting to wonder whether a reanalysis of studies in the area would reveal that most of the variance is accounted for by the failure of children who do not possess adequate role-taking abilities to behave prosocially, with much more inconsistency among subjects who possess the capacity, but in whom it may or may not have been engaged in the experimental situation.

The Relationship Between Role-taking and Altruism: In Pursuit of a Proper Definition.

By now it has become abundantly (and perhaps painfully) clear that there is much more to the constructs of role-taking and altruism than initially may meet the eye. In a sense, the opposite is true of the relationship between them—there is less. In our view the relationship between these fickle forces is highly conditional. Role-taking ability is at most a necessary (and never a sufficient) condition for, at best, a certain type of altruism. Role-taking may mediate any number of nonaltruistic, or even antisocial behaviors; and any number of other factors may mediate altruism.

In order to determine whether an act of helping is altruistic, we must satisfy at least two conditions. First, we must discover the forces that motivate it; then we must assess the extent to which the motivating forces are intrinsically altruistic—that is to say, the extent to which they give rise to the intention to benefit another at some cost to self, and are devoid of self-interest. The motivation intrinsic to role-taking is to obtain knowledge (c.f., Turiel, 1977). It is similar in function to asking people questions about themselves. You see someone with a longing look on his or her face, and you wonder what the person wants. You could ask the person, but this approach isn't always available. An alternative approach is to engage in role-taking. The motivation intrinsic to this process is to gather information, to improve understanding, to enhance knowledge; not to behave altruistically.

Interestingly, the case may be quite different for the types of vicarious affective responses commonly called empathy. Inasmuch as empathy involves feeling (vs. understanding) how another feels, it may produce an intrinsically altruistic motive. Feeling bad because another feels bad or feeling good because another feels good may contain a much greater impetus to optimize the affective state of the other than understanding how he or she feels (see Krebs, 1975).

This is not to deny that role-taking bears a special conceptual relationship to altruism. Although a vast array of experiences may affect a wide variety of prosocial behaviors—experiences such as guilt, observation of someone else helping, feeling like a member of a crowd, or receiving a favor—the types of helping to which these experiences give rise are most plausibly characterized in other terms, such as expiation, conformity, or reciprocity. In contrast, role-taking appears to contain the sort of nonegoistic, or *alter* orientation that is intrinsic to the concept of altruism. Nevertheless, the use to which role-taking is put need not necessarily be altruistic. A con artist may take the role of a potential mark in order to anticipate the mark's reaction to one of his or her ploys.

How, then, does role-taking relate to altruism? In our view role-taking may produce a cognitive state that is conductive to altruism in at least two interrelated ways. First, the knowledge obtained through role-taking may produce a state of cognitive disequilibrium, which may be resolved by helping another. The salient recognition that a person needs help evokes in most people an uncomfortable state akin to a lack of closure or a sense of cognitive inconsistency that presses for resolution. Helping is one way to resolve this type of cognitive discomfort. Closing one's eyes to the need, leaving the scene, telling oneself that someone else will help are other alternatives.

Secondly, recognizing that a person needs help may stimulate a sense of moral responsibility. Most people believe they *should* help those in need. Some investigators have defined this belief in terms of norms such as the *norm of social responsibility* (Berkowitz & Daniels, 1963). Other investigators have defined it in terms of *equity* (Walster, Walster, & Berscheid, 1978). And other investigators have defined it in terms of *moral judgment and reasoning* (Kohlberg, 1976). Believing that a course of action is right contains an intrinsic motivation to foster it; the sense of *ought* contains a press toward action. If role-taking exerts its effect through moral reasoning, we would expect moral reasoning to correlate more positively with altruistic behavior (when it is the moral alternative) than role-taking ability. Some evidence supports this general expectation (see Emler & Rushton, 1974; Blasi, 1980).

In many situations the decision to help another appears to be affected by whether we believe that the other deserves to be helped or not, and whether or not we feel that we are responsible for helping the person. Conclusions about deserving and responsibility may be mediated by more abstract types of role-taking than putting ourselves in the shoes of a person who needs help. A person might ask not only, "How is that other person feeling," but also "What would I want someone to do if I were in his or her place?" Thus, the type of indirect hypothetical role-taking involved in moral reasoning may supply an additional impetus (or resistance) to altruistic behavior.

To summarize the present discussion: we have been arguing that role-taking is an information-gathering process that is not in itself intrinsically altruistic, but that the cognitive states it produces and the moral reasoning it mediates may give rise to altruistic motivation.

Of course even if we were able to bridge the gap between the psychological states produced by role-taking and the motivation to behave altruistically, there would still be a significant distance to go. Namely, we would still have to get from the motivational state to altruistic behavior. For the most part, we must skirt this difficult issue here. As discussed in detail elsewhere (Krebs, in preparation), the path from role-taking (a cognitive process) to a desire to act (a motivational state) to altruistic or moral behavior is one with many detours. People who want to help others often lack the courage, initiative, opportunity, and resources to help. A full analysis of the relationship between role-taking and altruism must specify the mechanisms that engage both role-taking abilities and behavior. Empirically, this calls for a greater sensitivity to interactions. For example, in a recent study, Barrett and Yarrow (1977) failed to find any relationship between social "inferential ability" and naturally-occurring altruism in their sample of subjects as a whole. However, when they divided their subjects into high- and low-assertive groups, they found that role-taking related positively to prosocial behavior among highly assertive children, but negatively among unassertive children. In the words of Barrett and Yarrow (1977) "Perhaps sensitive comprehension of others' experiences results in higher affective arousal which in the socially courageous child leads to prosocial intervention. The same sensitivities and arousal in the more timid, nonassertive children might have an inhibiting effect [p. 480]."

Conclusion

By way of general conclusion, we can say that when people put themselves in the shoes of others, they may become more inclined to render them aid. But the shoes of others do not fit all people equally well, and getting into them is never enough. The path from role-taking to altruism is tortuous and indirect. Conceptually, there is little agreement about the processes involved in role-taking; and, empirically, the relationship among different tests has failed to form a consistent pattern. So also is the case with altruism: There is disagreement about the nature of the phenomenon, and a pervasive tendency for investigators to operationalize it in terms of convenient measures. No one has as yet outlined a coherent model of how role-taking should relate to altruism. In view of the variability among measures of both role-taking and prosocial behavior and the absence of an overriding theory about how they should go together, it is not surprising that studies that have investigated their relationship have produced inconsistent results.

REFERENCES

Barnett, M. A., King, L. M., & Howard, J. A. Inducing affect about self or other: Effects on generosity in children. *Developmental Psychology*, 1979, *15*, 164–167.

Barrett, D. E., & Yarrow, M. R. Prosocial behavior, social inferential ability, and assertiveness in children. *Child Development*, 1977, *48*, 475–481.

Berkowitz, L., & Daniels, L. Responsibility and dependency. *Journal of Abnormal and Social Psychology*, 1963, *66*, 429–436.

Blasi, A. Bridging moral cognition and moral action: A critical review of the literature. *Psychological Bulletin*, 1980, *88*, 1–45.

Borke, H. Interpersonal perception of young children: Egocentrism or empathy? *Developmental Psychology*, 1971, *5*, 163–269.

Borke, H. Piaget's mountains revisited: Changes in the egocentric landscape. *Developmental Psychology*, 1975, *11*, 240–244.

Brandt, M. M. Relations between cognitive role-taking performance and age, task presentation, and response requirements. *Developmental Psychology*, 1978, *14*, 206–213.

Brodzinsky, D. M., Jackson, J. P., & Overton, W. F. Effects of perceptual shielding in the development of spatial perspectives. *Child Development*, 1972, *43*, 1041–1046.

Buckley, N., Siegel, L. S., & Ness, S. Egocentrism, empathy and altruistic behavior in young children. *Developmental Psychology*, 1979, *15*, 329–330.

Chandler, M. J., & Greenspan, S. Ersatz egocentrism: A reply to H. Borke. *Developmental Psychology*, 1972, *7*, 104–106.

Coie, J. D., Constanzo, P. R., & Farnill, D. Specific transitions in the development of spatial perspective-taking ability. *Developmental Psychology*, 1973, *9*, 167–177.

Colby, A. Evolution of a moral-developmental theory. In W. Damon (Ed.), *Moral development: New directions for child development*. San Francisco, Ca.: Jossey-Bass, 1978.

Cox, M. V. Perspective ability: The conditions of change. *Child Development*, 1977, *48*, 1724–1727.

Deutsch, F. The effects of sex of subject and story character on preschooler's perceptions of affective responses and intrapersonal behavior in story sequences. *Developmental Psychology*, 1975, *11*, 112–113.

Deutsch, F., & Madle, R. A. Empathy: Historic and current conceptualizations, measurement, and a cognitive theoretical perspective. *Human Development*, 1975, *18*, 267–287.

Dlugokinski, E. L., & Firestone, I. J. Other centeredness and susceptibility to charitable appeals: Effects of perceived discipline. *Developmental Psychology*, 1974, *10*, 21–28.

Eisenberg-Berg, N., & Lennon, R. *Altruism and the assessment of empathy in the preschool years*. Paper presented at meeting of the Society for Research in Child Development, San Francisco, March 1979.

Emler, N. P., & Rushton, J. P. Cognitive-developmental factors in children's generosity. *British Journal of Social and Clinical Psychology*, 1974, *13*, 277–281.

Feffer, M. H., & Gourevitch, V. Cognitive aspects of role-taking in children. *Journal of Personality*, 1960, *28*, 383–396.

Feshbach, N. D., & Roe, K. Empathy in six and seven year olds. *Child Development*, 1968, *39*, 133–145.

Fishbein, H. D., Lewis, S., & Keiffer, K. Children's understanding of spatial relations: Coordination of perspectives. *Developmental Psychology*, 1972, *7*, 21–33.

Flavell, J. H. The development of inferences about others. In T. Mischel (Ed.), *Understanding other persons*. Oxford: Blackwell, Basil, Mott, 1974.

Flavell, J. H. *Cognitve development*. Englewood Cliffs, N.J.: Prentice-Hall, 1977.

Flavell, J. H., Botkin, P. T., Fry, C. L., Wright, J. W., & Jarvis, P. E. *The development of role-taking and communication skills in children*. New York: Wiley, 1968.

Ford, M. E. The construct validity of egocentrism. *Psychological Bulletin*, 1979, *86*, 1169–1188.

Glucksberg, S., Krauss, R. M., & Higgins, R. The development of referential communication skills. In F. D. Horowitz (Ed.), *Review of child development research* (Vol. 4). Chicago: University of Chicago Press, 1975.

Glucksberg, S., Krauss, R. M., & Weisberg, R. Referential communication in nursery school children: Method and some preliminary findings. *Journal of Experimental Child Psychology*, 1966, *3*, 333–342.

Green, F. P., & Schneider, F. W. Age differences in the behavior of boys on three measures of altruism. *Child Development*, 1974, *45*, 248–251.

Green, S. K. *Causal attribution of emotion and its relationship to role-taking and helping behavior in children*. Unpublished doctoral dissertation, Loyola University of Chicago, 1975.

Hatfield, E., Walster, G. W., & Piliavin, J. A. Equity theory and helping relationships. In L. Wispe (Ed.), *Altruism, sympathy, and helping.* New York: Academic Press, 1978.

Hoffman, M. L. Developmental synthesis of affect and cognition and its implications for altruistic motivation. *Developmental Psychology,* 1975, *11,* 607-622.

Hoffman, M. Development of moral thought, feeling, and behavior. *American Psychologist,* 1979, *34,* 958-966.

Hogan, R. Development of an empathy scale. *Journal of Consulting & Clinical Psychology,* 1969, *33,* 307-316.

Hoy, E. A. Predicting another's visual perspective: A unitary skill? *Developmental Psychology,* 1974, *10,* 462.

Iannotti, R. J. *The effect of role-taking experience on role-taking, altruism, empathy, and aggression.* Paper presented at the meetings of the Society for Research in Child Development, Denver, April 1975.

Iannotti, R. J. Effect of role-taking experiences on role-taking, empathy, altruism, and aggression. *Developmental Psychology,* 1978, *14,* 119-124.

Iannotti, R. J. *The elements of empathy.* Paper presented at meetings of the Society for Research in Child Development, San Francisco, March 1979.

Kohlberg, L. Moral stages and moralization: The cognitive-developmental approach. In T. Lickona (Ed.), *Moral development and behavior.* New York: Holt, 1976.

Krebs, D. L. Altruism—An examination of the concept and a review of the literature. *Psychological Bulletin,* 1970, *73,* 258-302.

Krebs, D. L. Empathy and altruism. *Journal of Personality and Social Psychology,* 1975, *32,* 1134-1146.

Krebs, D. L. A cognitive-developmental approach to altruism. In L. Wispé (Ed.), *Altruism, sympathy, and helping.* New York: Academic Press, 1978.

Krebs, D. L. *Moral knowledge and moral action.* In preparation.

Krebs, D. L., & Gillmore, J. The relationship among the first stages of cognitive development, role-taking, and moral development. *Child Development,* in press.

Krebs D. L., & Sturrup, B. Role-taking ability and altruistic behavior in elementary school children. *Journal of Moral Education,* in press.

Krebs, D. L., & Wispé, L. On defining altruism. *Journal of Social Issues,* 1974, *30,* 194-201.

Kurdek, L. A. Perspective taking as the cognitive basis of children's moral development: A review of the literature. *Merrill-Palmer Quarterly,* 1978, *24,* 3-24. (a)

Kurdek, L. A. Relationship between cognitive perspective taking and teachers' ratings of childrens' classroom behavior in grades one through four. *Journal of Genetic Psychology,* 1978, *132,* 21-27. (b)

Kurdek, L. A., & Rodgon, M. M. Perceptual, cognitive, and affective perspective taking in kindergarten through sixth-grade children. *Developmental Psyhcology,* 1975, *11,* 643-650.

Leckie, G. *Ontwikkeling van sociale cogniti: Een ontwikkelingsmodel voor rolnemongsvaardigheld bij kindren.* Unpublished doctoral dissertation, University of Nijmegen, 1975.

Lempers, J. D., Flavell, E. R., & Flavell, J. H. The development in very young children of tacit knowledge concerning visual perception. *Genetic Psychology Monographs,* 1977, *95,* 3-53.

Masangkay, Z. S., McCluskey, K. A., McIntyre, C. W., Sims-Knight, J., Vaughn, B. E., & Flavell, J. H. The early development of inferences about the visual percepts of others. *Child Development,* 1974, *45,* 357-366.

Mehrabian, A., & Epstein, N. A. A measure of emotional empathy. *Journal of Personality,* 1972, *40,* 523-543.

Miller, P. H., Kessel, F. S., & Flavell, J. H. Thinking about people thinking about people thinking about . . . : A study of social cognitive development. *Child Development,* 1970, *41,* 613-623.

Mood, D., Johnson, J., & Shantz, C. U. *Affective and cognitive components of empathy in young children.* Paper presented at the southeast regional meeting of the Society for Research in Child Development, Chapel Hill, N. C., 1974.

Mussen, P., Rutherford, E., Harris, S., & Keasey, C. B. Honesty and altruism among preadolescents. *Developmental Psychology*, 1970, *3*, 169–194.

Nahir, H. T., & Yussen, S. R. The performance of kibbutz- and city-reared Israeli children on two role-taking tasks. *Developmental Psychology*, 1977, *13*, 450–455.

Olejnik, A. B. *Developmental changes and interrelationships among role-taking, moral judgments, and children's sharing.* Paper presented at the meetings of the Society for Research in Child Development, Denver, April 1975.

Perry, J. E. & Krebs, D. Role-taking, moral development, and mental retardation. *The Journal of Genetic Psychology*, 1980, *136*, 95–108.

Piaget, J., & Inhelder, B. *The child's conception of space.* London: Routledge & Kegan Paul, 1956.

Piaget, J., & Inhelder, B. *Mental imagery in the child.* New York: Basic Books, 1970.

Rothenberg, B. B. Children's social sensitivity and the relationship to interpersonal competence, intrapersonal comfort, and intellectual level. *Developmental Psychology*, 1970, *2*, 335–350.

Rubin, K. H., & Schneider, F. W. The relationship between moral judgment, egocentrism, and altruistic behavior. *Child Development*, 1973, *44*, 661–665.

Rushton, J. P. Socialization and the altruistic behavior of children. *Psychological Bulletin*, 1976, *83*, 898–913.

Rushton, J. P. *Altruism, socialization, and society.* Englewood Cliffs, N.J.: Prentice-Hall, 1980.

Rushton, J. P., & Wiener, J. Altruism and cognitive development in children. *British Journal of Social and Clinical Psychology*, 1975, *14*, 341–349.

Selman, R. L., & Byrne, D. F. A structural-developmental analysis of levels of role-taking in middle childhood. *Child Development*, 1974, *45*, 803–806.

Severy, L. J. Comment on: Positive forms of social behavior: An overview. *Journal of Social Issues*, 1974, *30*, 189–194.

Shantz, C. U. The development of social cognition. In E. M. Hetherington (Ed.), *Review of Child Development Research*, Vol. 5. Chicago: University of Chicago Press, 1975.

Shantz, C. U., & Wilson, K. E. Training communication skills in young children. *Child Development*, 1972, *43*, 693–698.

Spilton, D., & Lee, L. C. Some determinants of effective communication in four-year-olds. *Child Development*, 1977, *48*, 968–977.

Staub, E. *Positive social behavior and morality* (Vol. 2). New York: Academic Press, 1978.

Stotland, E. Exploratory studies of empathy. In L. Berkowitz (Ed.), *Advances in experimental social psychology* (Vol. 4). New York: Academic Press, 1969.

Stotland, E., Mathews, K. E., Sherman, S. E., Hansson, R. O., & Richardson, B. Z. *Empathy, fantasy, and helping.* Beverly Hills: Sage Publications, 1978.

Strayer, J. A naturalistic study of empathic behaviors and their relation to affective states and perspective-taking skills in preschool children. *Developmental Psychology*, in press.

Strayer, J., & Christophe, C. *Empathy and egocentrism in preschoolers.* Paper presented at the meetings of the Canadian Psychological Association, Ottawa, June 1978.

Turiel, E. Distinct conceptual and developmental domains: Social-conventional and morality. In C. B. Keasey (Ed.), *Nebraska symposium on motivation, 1977*. Lincoln: University of Nebraska Press, 1977.

Urberg, K. A., & Docherty, E. M. Development of role-taking skills in young children. *Developmental Psychology*, 1976, *12*, 198–203.

Walster, E., Walster, G. W., & Berscheid, E. *Equity: Theory and research.* Boston: Allyn & Bacon, 1978.

Wispé, L. Positive forms of social behavior: An overview. *Journal of Social Issues*, 1972, *28*, 1–20.

Yarrow, M. R., & Waxler, C. Z. Dimensions and correlates of prosocial behavior in young children. *Child Development*, 1976, *47*, 118–125.

Zahn-Waxler, C., Radke-Yarrow, M., & Brady-Smith, J. Perspective-taking and prosocial behavior. *Developmental Psychology*, 1977, *13*, 87–88.

8
Empathy:
A Source of Altruistic
Motivation for Helping?*

C. Daniel Batson
Jay S. Coke
University of Kansas

Imagine that you are jogging down a quiet, country road. Rounding a corner, you come upon a horrible scene. A sports car is on its side, half in and half out of the ditch. On the pavement is the driver, a young woman. She is lying on her back, eyes closed, barely moving. Her face is bloody and bruised; her left leg, clearly broken, is twisted at a grotesque angle.

What do you do? The answer is likely obvious: You help. You rush to her side, or you race off to find a telephone and call the police or an ambulance. Few of us would not expect to help in this situation—the need is great and unambiguous; there is no one else to help; helping is not likely to bring personal danger; and so on. Not only is helping in this situation consistent with our expectations, it is consistent with a large body of research on situational factors that make helping more or less likely (see Krebs, 1970; Staub, 1978, for reviews). But in this chapter we wish to move beyond the question of whether you would help to address a different question: Why did you help?

An answer suggested by a number of psychologists during the past decade (Aronfreed, 1970; Batson, Darley, & Coke, 1978; Coke, Batson, & McDavis, 1978; Hoffman, 1975; Krebs, 1975; Mehrabian & Epstein, 1972; Piliavin & Piliavin, 1973; Stotland, Matthews, Sherman, Hansson, & Richardson, 1978) is that an empathic emotional response can lead to motivation to help. These researchers suggest that observing another's distress tends to produce vicarious physiological arousal in the observer. If this vicarious arousal is cognitively labeled as concern for the person in distress, the observer will experience empathic emotion (Schachter, 1964; Stotland, 1969). And empathic emotion, it is

---

*Jack Brehm made helpful comments on an earlier draft of this chapter.

167

claimed, can trigger motivation to help. Thus, one answer to the question of why you helped the young woman is that, in response to her distress, you felt empathic concern, and this emotional response led to motivation to see her distress reduced.

But this answer, even if valid, raises a further question: What is the *nature* of the motivation evoked by empathic emotion? Several researchers (Aronfreed, 1970; Batson et al., 1978; Hoffman, 1975, 1976; Krebs, 1975) have recently speculated that empathic emotion might produce motivation to help that is truly altruistic, that is, motivation directed toward the end-state goal of reducing the other's distress. If this is so, it would have broad theoretical implications, for few if any major psychological theories of motivation allow for the possibility of truly altruistic motivation (cf. Bolles, 1975, for a review). Current theories tend to be egoistic; they are built on the assumption that everything we do is ultimately directed toward the end-state goal of benefitting ourselves.

To find that empathy produces altruistic motivation could also have wide-ranging practical implications. It would suggest a very different approach to socialization for prosocial behavior than the currently dominant approach of inhibition of egoistic impulses through discipline, shaping, modeling, and internalized guilt. For if altruistic impulses are also present in the individual, socialization programs should probably try to encourage these impulses as well as discourage egoistic ones.

Whether truly altruistic motivation ever exists in humans was a central question for many 19th and early 20th century social philosophers and social scientists (see, for example, Comte, 1875; Kropotkin, 1902; McDougall, 1908; Mill, 1863; Spencer, 1872). By around 1920, however, theories of motivation based on behaviorism or psychoanalysis were sufficiently sophisticated to provide an egoistic account of any behavior that might appear to be altruistically motivated. As a result, the question of the existence of altruism was shelved by mainstream psychologists; it was assumed to be either clearly answered in the negative or clearly unanswerable. Continued dominance of psychology by modern descendents of these early egoistic theories of motivation may explain why the recent upsurge of interest in helping behavior has not led to a parallel upsurge of interest in the classic question of whether at least some helping might be altruistically motivated. Those who have suggested that empathic emotion leads to altruistic motivation have brought this classic question to the fore once again.

Even raising the question of altruism opens a Pandora's box of complex issues and conceptual traps. Yet, with some trepidation, we believe that the time has come for social psychologists interested in helping to lift the lid and face these issues. The potential for getting caught in one or more of the traps is great, but the importance of the question is also great.

Of course, the egoistic orientation of modern psychology should not be dismissed lightly; it has prevailed for decades, and it can easily account for what might appear to be altruistic motivation arising from empathic emotion. To illustrate, you may have answered the question of why you helped the young auto-accident victim in other-directed, altruistic terms—you felt sorry for her and wished to reduce her distress. But this apparently altruistic concern to reduce her distress may not have been the end-state goal of your action. It may only have been an intermediate means to the ultimate end of reducing *your own* distress, distress arising from the unpleasant emotions you experienced as a result of seeing her lying on the pavement (shock, disgust, fear, or grief) and the increase in unpleasant emotion you anticipated if you did not help (guilt or shame). Interpreted in this way, your helping was not altruistic; it was an instrumental egoistic response. You acted to reduce her distress because that reduced your own distress.

Thus, although the suggestion that empathic emotion produces altruistic motivation deserves careful consideration, it also deserves stringent scepticism. Any contemporary consideration of the existence of altruism cannot simply turn the clock back to the naively optimistic pre-1920 assertions of human goodness and innate concern for others. If one is to take seriously the claim that empathic emotion evokes altruistic motivation, one must also take seriously modern egoistic explanations for the motivation evoked by empathy.[1]

EMPATHY

Before considering whether empathy evokes truly altruistic motivation, we need to say a little about empathy as a concept. For a relatively new term (apparently coined by Titchener in 1909 to translate the German "Einfühlung"), empathy has seen a wide range of definitions (cf. Wispé, 1968). Not only has its meaning varied, but its relation to associated concepts such as sympathy has also varied. Because empathy has been used by different people in contradictory ways, it would be impossible to propose a definition that would capture its essence. We can only try to make clear what we mean by the term.

A Definition of Empathy

Empathy, as we shall use it, is *an emotional response elicited by and congruent with the perceived welfare of someone else.* Empathy has often been defined as an emotional response to the emotion of another. We have chosen to focus

---

[1]In focusing our attention on the possibility that empathic emotion leads to altruistic rather than egoistic motivation for helping, we are not meaning to imply that empathy is the only possible source of altruistic motivation or that altruistic motivation is the only possible consequence of empathic emotion.

instead on emotional response to the perceived welfare of another because, while the other's welfare is often reflected in his or her emotional state, it is not always (as, for example, when an accident victim is unconscious). We believe that to feel concern and compassion in response to the perceived distress of an unconscious victim, as presumably the Good Samaritan did, should be included in our definition of empathy.

When we say that empathic emotion is *congruent* with the perceived welfare of the other, we mean that empathy involves experiencing positive emotion when the other's lot is desirable and negative emotion when it is undesirable. A similar relationship exists for anticipated changes in the lot of the other. Empathic emotion should become more positive to changes that one perceives the other to desire and more negative to changes the other wants to avoid. In our view, empathy typically does not involve experiencing the same lot as the other, only a congruent reaction to that lot. Someone else's triumph is not likely to evoke a sense of triumph but a more subdued sense of happiness; another's suffering and distress is not likely to evoke the same sense of suffering or pain but feelings such as compassion or concern. As Solomon Asch (1952) put it, "It is because we become aware of the situation and experience of others that we can feel *with* them. The mere duplication of an observed reaction may in fact be a sign of an inadequate social relation. There are times when the sight of suffering merely reminds a person of his own suffering; when this is so, he has simply lost social contact [p. 172, italics in original]."

Our conception of empathy does not always permit a clear distinction between empathy and sympathy. Empathy as we are defining it includes congruent reactions to another's pleasure as well as to another's pain. Sympathy is not usually applied to congruent emotional reactions to another's pleasure, but it is often applied to reactions to another's pain. So, congruent emotion elicited by witnessing another in distress in a helping situation could appropriately be called sympathy instead of empathy, as has been done by, for example, Heider (1958). Our reason for preferring the term empathy is that it has typically been the term used by social psychologists during the past decade.

We must also admit that our conception of empathy does not always permit a clear determination of whether an emotional reaction is empathic. In those cases in which the other's lot is clearly desirable and the emotional reaction is positive, or clearly undesirable and the emotional reaction is negative, we may say with confidence that the emotional reaction is congruent and therefore empathic. But as the lot of the other or the emotional response becomes more ambiguous, we enter a large gray area in which it is difficult to say whether or to what degree the reaction is empathic. On the other side of this gray area are reactions that clearly are not congruent and so not empathic, as for example when one feels negative emotion in reaction to another's triumph (jealousy or envy) or positive emotion in reaction to another's tragedy (malicious joy). Researchers studying empathy have sought to work with situations in which the lot of the other is clearly desirable or clearly undesirable, allowing them to infer with some confidence whether an emotional reaction to this lot is congruent, and so empathic.

Evidence that Empathy Exists

Of course, to provide a definition carries no assurance that what is defined actually exists. Before we can say that empathy as we have defined it exists, we must be satisfied (1) that perceptions of the welfare of another person can trigger vicarious emotional responses; (2) that these vicarious emotions are congruent with the presumed welfare of the other. To provide evidence for the first of these two criteria, it is necessary to show that witnessing a target person having a desirable or undesirable experience can cause an emotional reaction in an observer even when it is clear that the stimuli causing the target's experience are not, and will not be, impinging on the observer.

To provide such evidence, Berger (1962) had people observe a target person performing a task and led them to believe that following the onset of a visual signal the target person either was receiving electric shock (electric shock condition) or was not receiving electric shock (no shock condition). Further, the target person either jerked his arm following the visual signal (movement condition) or did not jerk his arm (no movement condition). All research participants were told that they themselves would not be shocked during the study.

Berger reasoned, first, that both a painful stimulus in the environment (shock) and a distress response (movement) were necessary for an observer to infer that the target person was experiencing pain. He reasoned, second, that if participants in his experiment were responding vicariously, they should display a physiological reaction to watching the target person only when they inferred that he was experiencing pain. Therefore, Berger predicted that participants in the shock-movement condition would display the most physiological arousal, because only they would infer that the target person was experiencing pain and so only they would show a vicarious emotional response. For participants in each of the other three conditions, either the painful stimulus or the target's distress response was missing. Results followed the predicted pattern. Consistent with the assumption that people can experience vicarious emotion as a result of perceiving another in pain, participants in the shock-movement condition were more physiologically aroused while observing the target person than were participants in the other three conditions. Subsequent research (Bandura & Rosenthal, 1966; Craig & Lowrey, 1969; Craig & Wood, 1969; Lazarus, Opton, Nomikos, & Rankin, 1965) has provided additional evidence for this first criterion, including evidence that people can experience vicarious emotion (reflected in measures of physiological arousal) as a result of perceiving another in a desirable as well as an undesirable state (Krebs, 1975; Stotland, 1969).

Subsequent research has also provided evidence (Bandura & Rosenthal, 1966; Hygge, 1976; Krebs, 1975; Staub, 1978; Stotland, 1969) for the second criterion, that the vicarious emotions experienced are typically, although not always, congruent with the current and anticipated perceived welfare of the target person. Stotland and Sherman (reported in Stotland, 1969) found that people who responded with vicarious emotion to witnessing another undergoing what they perceived to be a painful experience, reported their own emotional state to be one of increased tension and nervousness; they were also more likely than people in control conditions to report that they found participating in the study a relatively unpleasant experience. In contrast, people who responded vicariously to another undergoing what they perceived to be a pleasurable experience reported, relative to controls, that they found participating in the study to be a pleasant experience. Similarly, Krebs (1975) found that observers reported feeling relatively badly when watching someone whom they thought was about to receive an electric shock and relatively good when watching someone about to receive a reward.

Although self-reports of the sort used in these studies might easily result from a desire to *appear* empathic rather than from a true empathic response, it is important to note that in both the Stotland and Sherman and the Krebs studies these reports occurred in conjunction with evidence of increased vicarious emotion on physiological measures. In control conditions in which it would have been just as desirable to appear empathic, neither the physiological measures nor the self-reports provided evidence of an empathic response. This convergence of physiological and self-report data provides reasonably strong evidence that participants in these studies actually were experiencing emotions congruent with the perceived welfare of the other, and not simply saying that they were. Empathy as we have defined it apparently can exist.

A SOURCE OF ALTRUISTIC MOTIVATION FOR HELPING?

There is reasonably clear evidence that empathy as we have defined it can motivate helping (cf. Aderman & Berkowitz, 1970; Aronfreed & Paskal, cited in Aronfreed, 1970; Coke et al., 1978; Harris & Huang, 1973; Krebs, 1975). But is there any basis for assuming that this motivation is in any degree altruistic? Certainly the list of researchers claiming that it is has grown over the past few years (cf. Aronfreed, 1970; Batson et al., 1978; Hoffman, 1976; Krebs, 1975). One cannot, however, base a case on the popularity of the idea. And when one looks for empirical evidence to back up these researchers' claim, one finds very little. The problem is that it is extremely difficult—impossible, some would say (including us at times, though we wish now to recant somewhat)—to find evidence for altruistic motivation that cannot also be interpreted as evidence for instrumental egoistic motivation. Recall the ease with which we provided an egoistic interpretation of the apparently altruistic act of helping the young auto-

Chicago Public Library
Harold Washington - HWLC
9/25/2012   11:34:12 AM
-Patron Receipt-

ITEMS BORROWED:

1:
Title: Altruism and helping behavior : socia
Item #: R0030253829
Due Date: 10/16/2012

2:
Title: Message-attitude-behavior relationsh
Item #: R0034123898
Due Date: 10/16/2012

-Please retain for your records-

EICHELBE

accident victim encountered while jogging. Most of the supposed empirical evidence for altruism can be reinterpreted just as easily. And if some helping act can equally plausibly be interpreted as altruistically or egoistically motivated, parsimony would seem clearly to be on the side of an egoistic interpretation.

The difficulty in determining whether empathic motivation is egoistic or altruistic is, of course, that egoism and altruism are motivational concepts, and we cannot directly observe motivation, only behavior. Therefore, to provide empirical evidence that empathic motivation for helping is altruistic, we need to identify some point at which the egoistic and altruistic interpretations differ at a behavioral level. If no such point can be found, then we must conclude that the claim that empathy evokes altruistic motivation is of no real theoretical or practical significance.

Conceptual Distinction Between Egoism and Altruism

In an attempt to find a point of behavioral difference, it is important, first, to be clear about the points of conceptual difference. Therefore, let us say exactly what we mean by egoistic and altruistic motivation for helping. A person's helping is egoistic to the degree that he or she helps from a desire for personal gain (e.g., material rewards, praise, or enhanced self-esteem) or a desire to avoid personal pain (e.g., punishment, social castigation, private guilt, or shame). That is, *egoistically-motivated helping is directed toward the end-state goal of increasing the helper's own welfare.* In contrast, a person's helping is altruistic to the degree that he or she helps from a desire to reduce the distress or increase the benefit of the person in need. That is, *altruistically-motivated helping is directed toward the end-state goal of increasing the other's welfare.*

This distinction between egoism and altruism leads to three observations:

1. Helping, as a behavior, can be either egoistically or altruistically motivated; it is the end-state goal, not the behavior, that distniguishes an act as altruistic.
2. Motivation for helping can be a mixture of altruism and egoism; it need not be solely or even primarily altruistic to have an altruistic component.
3. Increasing the other's welfare is both necessary and sufficient to attain an altruistic end-state goal.

To the degree that helping is altruistically as opposed to egoistically motivated, increasing the other's welfare is not an intermediate, instrumental response directed toward increasing one's own welfare; it is an end in itself. Although one's own welfare may be increased by altruistically motivated helping (for example, it may produce feelings of personal satisfaction or relief), personal gain must be an unintended by-product and not the goal of the behavior. This conception of altruism and of the distinction between it and egoism seems quite consistent not only with Auguste Comte's (1875) initial use of the term but also with modern dictionary defintions, e.g., "unselfish concern for the welfare of others" (Webster's).

Empirical Distinction Between Egoism and Altruism: A Schematic Analysis

Equipped with this conceptual distinction between egoistic and altruistic motivation for helping, we may return to the problem of making an empirical distinction between them. As we have said, all we can directly observe is the behavior, helping. The challenge is somehow to use the behavior to provide a basis for inferring whether the motivation underlying it is egoistic or altruistic.

We believe that we have, in fact, developed a technique for doing this. The key to our technique lies not in trying to identify the motivation behind any single behavioral response but in inferring motivation on the basis of a *pattern* of responses across a series of systematically varied situations. We cannot, of course, claim originality for this general technique; it is a standard approach in the empirical study of complex human motivation (cf. for example, the use of the forced compliance paradigm to detect the motivational state of cognitive dissonance—Festinger, 1957). To our knowledge, however, this approach has not previously been applied to the problem of determining whether empathic motivation for helping is egoistic or altruistic.

Building upon Piliavin and Piliavin's (1973) general analysis of the role of emotional arousal in motivating helping, we first developed a schematic analysis of egoistic and altruistic motivation for helping. The analysis reflected the difficulties in distinguishing empirically between egoistic and altruistic motivation, but it also suggested how such a distinction might be possible. A model summarizing the analysis appears in Fig. 8.1. We shall go through the model in Fig. 8.1 level by level, considering first the potential helper's possible goals, then possible behaviors, and finally, the costs associated with these behaviors.

Goals

As we have noted, much research suggests that bystanders can become empathically aroused when confronted with a person in distress. As we have also noted, either of two motives might be generated by this empathic response. One possibility is that the empathic arousal is experienced as unpleasant and leads to a desire to increase one's own welfare by reducing this unpleasant emotional state (Goal B in Fig. 8.1). The other possibility is that the emotional arousal leads to a desire to increase the other's welfare by reducing his or her need (Goal A). According to our definitions of egoism and altruism, if the aroused bystander's end-state goal is B, then the motivation is egoistic; if it is A, then the motivation

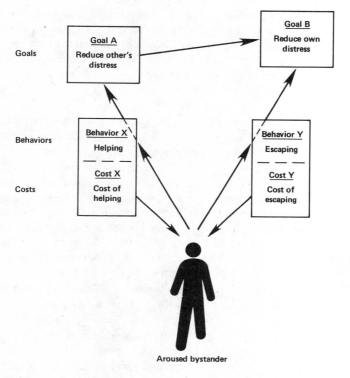

FIG. 8.1.   Schematic model of egoistic and altruistic motivation for helping.

is altruistic. This part of the model is simply a schematic representation of our conceptual distinction between egoism and altruism.

Behaviors

Moving to the level of behaviors, Behavior X, helping the person in distress, leads directly to Goal A, and Behavior Y, escaping from the need situation, leads directly to Goal B. To observe Behavior X, however, does not justify the inference that the bystander's end-state goal is A, that his or her motivation is altruistic. Note the arrow leading from Goal A to Goal B. Consistent with modern egoistic theories of motivation, this arrow represents the possibility of an instrumental egoistic response, i.e., of pursuing Goal A as an intermediate step on the way to Goal B. As we discovered when imagining why one might have helped the young auto-accident victim, if removing another's distress removes the cause of one's own distress, helping can serve as a means of reaching end-state goal B. And to the degree that a helper's end-state goal is B, his or her motivation is egoistic.

Our schematic model reflects, then, the confounding of motives and behaviors noted previously. One can display helping behavior (X) because of either egoistic (Goal B) or altruistic (Goal A) motives. In order to determine whether helping is directed toward Goal A or Goal B it is necessary to consider another set of variables, the costs associated with each of the possible behaviors.

Costs

As Piliavin and Piliavin (1973) have pointed out, both helping and escaping carry costs. The costs of helping (x) include the physical effort involved, the unpleasantness endured as a result of continued exposure to the other's distress, the unpleasant possibilities of becoming vulnerable to subsequent requests for help or enmeshed in long legal proceedings, and so forth. The costs of escaping (y) include the physical effort involved in escaping from the need situation (often minimal) and, more importantly, the feelings of guilt and shame one anticipates as a result of knowing that the person in need is continuing to suffer. Each set of costs reduces the likelihood that the bystander will engage in the related behavior, either helping or escaping, even if that behavior would lead to a desired goal.

Although it may not be immediately apparent, this simple schematic model suggests a way to distinguish empirically whether a bystander's motivation is egoistic or altruistic. Here is how. If the bystander's motivation is egoistic, by definition the goal is to reduce his or her own distress (Goal B). As the schematic makes clear, this goal can be reached either by helping (X) and so removing the cause of one's own distress or by escaping (Y) and so removing contact with the cause. Because either behavior can lead to the desired goal, the likelihood that the egoistically-motivated bystander will *help* should be an inverse function of the cost of helping (x) and a direct function of the cost of escaping (y). Thus, if the bystander were egoistically motivated and all other variables in the schematic were held constant, increasing the costs of escaping (y) by, for example, preventing the bystander from leaving the scene of the accident and so making it harder to ignore the continuing distress of the unhelped victim should increase the rate of helping. Conversely, reducing the costs of escaping by, for example, making it easy for the bystander to leave the scene of the accident and thus to avoid thinking about the victim's continuing distress should decrease the rate of helping.

If, on the other hand, the bystander's motivation is altruistic, by definition his or her goal is to reduce the other's distress (Goal A). As the schematic makes clear, one can reach this goal by helping (X) but not by escaping (Y). The fact that escaping will not reduce the other's distress leads to different predictions for the effect of the cost variables on helping. The likelihood that the altruistically motivated bystander will help is still an inverse function of the cost of helping (x), but it is independent of the cost of escaping (y), because escaping is a goal-irrelevant behavior. Increasing or decreasing the cost of escaping should have no effect on the rate of helping; the rate should remain as high when escaping is easy as when it is difficult.

We would, therefore, expect the cost of helping variable (x) to have the same effect on helping when the potential helper's motivation is altruistic as it does when the motivation is egoistic.[2] We would not, however, expect the cost of escaping variable (y) to have the same effect. To the extent that the bystander's motivation is egoistic, reducing the cost of escaping should decrease the rate of helping; to the extent that the bystander's motivation is altruistic, reducing the cost of escaping should not affect the rate of helping.

These predictions suggest a way of determining whether the motivation for helping is egositc or altruistic. Although the motivation cannot be inferred from any single behavioral response, it can be inferred from the *pattern* of helping responses presented in Table 8.1. To the extent that the motivation for helping is egoistic, the helping rate should be affected by the difficulty of escaping; the easier it is to escape continued exposure to the need situation, the lower the cost of escaping, and the less likely a bystander should be to help. But to the extent that the motivation for helping is altruistic, the helping rate should be unaffected by the difficulty of escaping; it should be just as high when escape is easy as when escape is difficult.

---

[2]If one wishes to consider the costs of helping (x) as reflecting an egoistic desire to keep personal costs at a minimum, the suggestion that costs of helping should affect the rate of helping (X) even when the helper's motivation is altruistic (Goal A) simply underscores the point made earlier that the bystander's·motivation need not be exclusively altruistic to have an altruistic component. The bystander may have the end-state goal of seeing the other's need reduced and, at the same time, have a second, independent end-state goal of enduring as little personal pain as possible. These two motives, one altruistic and the other egoistic, may exist simultaneously.

This observation suggests not only the complexity of the motives involved in a potential helping situation, but it also suggests the futility of trying to demonstrate empirically the existence of altruism by focusing on the costs of helping (x). It has often been assumed that for an empirical demonstration of altruism, one must observe a willingness to help regardless of the costs to self. In terms of our schematic this would mean that the likelihood of a bystander helping (X) should be independent of variation in the costs of helping (x). But, as we have just observed, this independence is not required by our conception of altruism. Although in certain extreme cases, such as a mother's reaction to the distress of a child, one might find helping even in the face of very high costs to self, our schematic suggests that, in most cases, the altruistically motivated bystander will still be sensitive to the costs of helping; the greater the costs, the less the likelihood of helping. Moreover, the special case of maternal behavior seems best dealt with not as one in which the cost of helping is irrelevant but as one in which the threshold for x is very high, so high that even extremely high costs cannot deter the decision to act. In less extreme cases, it seems perfectly reasonable to expect an altruistically motivated individual also to have the egoistic concern to minimize his or her own costs. If this is true, the popular suggestion of manipulating the costs of helping (x) to detect altruism is misguided; it will not enable one to distinguish egoistic motivation from altruistic motivation. For, regardless of the nature of the motivation, the likelihood of helping will be an inverse function of x.

TABLE 8.1
Rate of Helping When Difficulty of Escaping (y)
is Varied and Motivation is Egoistic or Altruistic

Cost (Difficulty) of Escaping	Type of Motivation (Emotion)	
	Egoistic (Personal Distress)	Altruistic (Empathic Concern)
Easy	Low	High
Difficult	High	High

Conceptual Distinction Between Personal Distress and Empathic Emotions

Now let us apply this general technique for discriminating between egoistic and altruistic motivation for helping to the specific question of whether empathic motivation is altruistic. As Piliavin and Piliavin (1973) have suggested, a number of emotions can be experienced as a result of witnessing the distress of another person. Besides empathy, a bystander can experience shock, alarm, disgust, shame, and fear. Building upon this suggestion, we would propose that at least two functionally different emotional states can be produced by witnessing another's distress: (1) *empathic concern*, made up of emotions such as compassion, concern, warmth, and softheartedness, and (2) *personal distress*, made up of emotions such as shock, alarm, disgust, shame, and fear. We would further suggest that people experience these two emotional states as phenomenologically distinct. Finally, we would suggest that feelings of personal distress elicit egoistic motivation to reduce one's own distress, whereas feelings of empathic concern elicit altruistic motivation to reduce the other's distress.

To the extent that these suggestions are correct, one can relabel the columns in Table 8.1, as has been done in parentheses. Experiencing personal distress emotions as a result of witnessing another person in distress should lead to egoistic motivation directed toward reducing one's own distress, and the likelihood that this motivation will lead the bystander to help should be a direct function of the difficulty of escaping (Column 1 of Table 8.1). In contrast, experiencing empathic concern should lead to altruistic motivation directed toward reducing the other's distress, and this motivation should lead to increased helping regardless of the difficulty of escaping (Column 2).

If, however, we are wrong and the motivation to help resulting from empathic emotion is egoistic rather than altruistic, helping motivated by empathy should follow the pattern predicted in Column 1. Although the absolute level of helping might be higher for people experiencing empathic concern, the rate of helping should be a direct function of the difficulty of escaping, just as for people experiencing personal distress.

Note that the entire pattern depicted in Table 8.1 is important if one is to provide evidence that empathic emotion evokes altruistic rather than egoistic motivation for helping. If, for example, one were to compare the easy and difficult escape cells only in the column marked altruistic (empathic) motivation, the altruistic prediction is for no difference in the rate of helping. Such a result could easily occur simply because the escape manipulation was too weak to affect behavior or the behavioral measure was insensitive. If, however, an escape manipulation does have a significant effect on helping when a bystander responds to the other's need in terms of personal distress emotions but does not have a significant effect on helping when a bystander's response is empathic, the evidence that empathic emotion evokes altruistic motivation is much stronger. Then the evidence cannot be dismissed as being the result of a weak escape manipulation or an insensitive measure.

It should also be noted that our reasoning rests on the assumption that people make a reasonably clear distinction between the personal distress and empathic emotions that may result from witnessing another's distress. Therefore, before considering how each of these emotional states relates to helping when escape is easy and difficult, we need to have some empirical evidence that they are qualitatively distinct.

Empirical Distinction Between Personal Distress and Empathic Emotions

Evidence that personal distress and empathic emotions are qualitatively distinct has been found in four different studies (Batson, Cowles, & Coke, 1979; Batson, McDavis, Felix, Goering, & Goldman, 1976; Coke, 1979; Coke et al., 1978, Experiment 2). Although the four studies varied in detail, participants in each were asked to indicate their emotional response to a radio broadcast in which they learned about a person in need (either the victim of a tragic automobile accident or a graduate student in education seeking people to partcipate in her master's thesis research). In each study, after participants had heard the broadcast they completed a questionnaire designed to assess their emotional response to it. The questionnaire consisted of adjectives describing emotional states, and for each adjective participants were asked to indicate the degree to which they had experienced that emotion on a scale from 1 (not at all) to 7 (extremely). Included in the questionnaire were some adjectives assumed to represent the concept of personal distress and others assumed to represent the concept of empathic concern.

In order to assess the structure of emotional responses to the target person's distress, factor analyses (principal components analyses with varimax rotation) were performed on participants' ratings of the emotion adjectives. As might be expected, the factor structures across the four studies differed in detail, but in all four studies the factor structure suggested that subjects experienced personal distress and empathic concern as qualitatively different emotional states. Five adjectives that were assumed to reflect the concept of personal distress all loaded highly on the same factor: upset (4 studies), troubled (3 studies), alarmed (4 studies), disturbed (3 studies), and distressed (3 studies). Five adjectives that were assumed to reflect the concept of empathic concern loaded highly on a second, orthogonal factor: empathic (3 studies), concerned (3 studies), warm (4 studies), softhearted (4 studies), and compassionate (3 studies). Based on the factor analyses, it seems clear that participants in these studies made a qualitative distinction between the emotional states of personal distress and empathic concern, suggesting that people do experience these two emotional states as phenomenologically distinct. Knowing this permits us to consider the nature of the motivation to help evoked by each and, particularly, to consider whether empathic concern leads to altruistic motivation.

Evidence Concerning the Nature of the Motivation to Help Evoked by Personal Distress and Empathic Concern

We know of only four studies to date that provide empirical evidence relevant to the predictions in Table 8.1. Moreover, two of these studies provide only incomplete evidence, because the difficulty of escaping was not manipulated; the need situation was always presented in such a way that escape was easy. Therefore, these two studies involved only the two cells in the top row of Table 8.1, and so, although they can provide results consistent with the predicted difference in helping caused by personal distress and empathic concern, they cannot provide strong support. Fortunately, two other experiments have recently been completed in which difficulty of escaping was manipulated. Each of these experiments provides data for all four cells of Table 8.1, permitting a more direct test of the hypothesis that empathic emotion evokes altruistic motivation to help.

Let us look first at the studies in which difficulty of escaping was not manipulated. In Experiment 2 reported by Coke et al. (1978), constraints against psychologically escaping from the need situation were purposely made weak. Participants learned of a graduate student's need for research participants indirectly by listening to a taped radio broadcast, and all that was necessary to escape continued exposure to the need situation was to lay aside the subsequent appeal for help and forget it. Only volunteering to help would lead to further exposure to the graduate student's need.

Results indicated that in this situation greater self-perceived empathic concern correlated positively with helping but greater self-perceived personal distress did not. This pattern was entirely consistent with that predicted in Table 8.1. Presumably, relatively high personal distress led to an increased desire to reduce one's own distress; but because escape was easy, this egoistic motivation led to no increase in helping. In contrast, even though escape was easy, relatively high empathic concern did lead to increased helping. This was precisely what would be expected if the motivation evoked by empathic concern was altruistic (see Row 1 of Table 8.1).

The lack of evidence in this experiment that self-perceived personal distress correlated positively with helping was entirely consistent with the prediction in Table 8.1. But this lack of evidence could also have been an artifact of an overall low amount of personal distress evoked by the procedure used. After all, hearing a graduate student say that she needs participants for her Master's thesis research is not likely to be very distressing. The results of a subsequent correlational study reported by Batson, Cowles, and Coke (1979), however, provided additional evidence that greater self-reported empathic concern correlates positively with helping when escape is easy, whereas greater personal distress does not. In this second study the need situation described in the taped radio broadcast presented the results of a rather gory automobile accident. There was evidence that this tape evoked relatively high levels of both personal distress and empathic concern in listeners. Constraints against psychologically escaping from the need situation were again made weak by using the same technique used by Coke et al. (1978, Experiment 2). And once again, consistent with the predictions in the top row of Table 8.1, greater self-reported empathic concern correlated positively with helping but greater self-reported personal distress did not.

Still, in both of these studies it was simply assumed that the need situations used were ones in which escape was easy enough that increased egoistic motivation would not lead to any increase in helping, whereas increased altruistic motivation would. Far stronger evidence that empathic concern evokes altruistic motivation to help would be provided by a design in which both the degree of empathic concern and the difficulty of escape were manipulated, i.e., in which all four cells in Table 8.1 were represented. Two experiments have recently been completed using this design, and each provides support for the hypothesis that empathic concern leads to altruistic motivation to help.

The procedures used in these two experiments (reported by Batson, Duncan, Ackerman, Buckley, & Birch, 1981) were quite similar. In each, participants were exposed to a need situation designed to have the capacity to elicit both personal distress and empathic concern. Participants observed a young woman, Elaine, supposedly receiving mild but unpleasant electical shocks as she participated in an experiment concerned with learning under aversive conditions. After the learning task was explained to Elaine, participants heard her tell the research assistant that she had been thrown from a horse and against an electrical fence when she was young; the doctor had said that this traumatic experience might lead her to react quite strongly even to mild electric shock in the future. Elaine's reactions while performing the learning task made it clear that she did indeed find the shocks extremely unpleasant.

In Experiment 1, participants (all female) were told that their task was to observe Elaine over closed-circuit TV (actually all participants saw the same prerecorded video tape) and to form an impression of her while she performed the learning task. Following Stotland (1969) and Krebs (1975) the degree of empathic concern that participants felt for Elaine was manipulated by varying their apparent similarity to Elaine. This was done by having the participants and, supposedly, Elaine complete an attitude questionnaire at an initial session several weeks prior to the actual experiment. Ostensibly to help them in forming an impression of Elaine, participants were given an opportunity to see her responses to the questionnaire prior to watching her perform the learning task. Responses on Elaine's questionnaire had been prepared by someone other than the experimenter in such a way that they were either very similar to the participant's (similar condition) or very dissimilar (dissimilar condition). To manipulate difficulty of escaping, participants were informed that Elaine would be completing ten short trials in the learning task. They were also informed either that they would be observing only the first two trials (easy escape condition) or that they would be observing all ten trials (difficult escape condition).

During the second trial, Elaine began reacting so strongly to the shocks that the research assistant suggested that the experiment should be terminated. Explaining that she did not wish to ruin the research, Elaine said that even though the shocks were very unpleasant she wanted to try to continue. Then the assistant hit upon an idea: perhaps the observer (i.e., the research participant) and Elaine could exchange places. Soon after the participant overheard the assistant suggest this possibility to Elaine, the experimenter entered the participant's room and asked her whether she would be willing to take Elaine's place in the shock experiment. At this point, participants in the easy escape condition believed that their exposure to Elaine's distress was going to be terminated whether they helped or not. Participants in the difficult escape condition believed that they could terminate their exposure to Elaine's distress only by helping.

Batson et al. (1981) reasoned that observing Elaine receive the shocks should, typically, lead a person to experience both feelings of personal distress and empathic concern. The relative degree of these two emotions experienced by participants in this experiment was, however, expected to be a function of the similarity manipulation. Participants in the dissimilar condition should experience a relatively low degree of empathy and so a predominance of personal distress. In contrast, participants in the similar condition should experience a relatively high degree of empathy and so a predominance of empathic concern. If personal distress leads to egoistic motivation, participants in the dissimilar condition should display a high rate of helping only when escape was difficult. And if empathic concern leads to altruistic motivation, participants in the similar condition should display a high rate of helping regardless of ease or difficulty of escape. This reasoning, based on the predictions in Table 8.1, suggested that there would be a relatively high rate of helping in all but the dissimilar–easy escape condition. And this is exactly what was observed: Participants in the dissimilar–easy escape condition were significantly less likely to offer to change places with Elaine than were participants in each of the other three conditions; in these conditions helping was consistently high (not so high, however, that the absence of differences among these three conditions could be accounted for by a ceiling effect).

Moreover, Elaine's need was perceived to be relatively high in all conditions, and although participants' perceived liking for Elaine was greater in the high similarity than in the low similarity conditions, there was no evidence that differences in perceived liking accounted for the differences in helping. In sum, the results conformed exactly to the pattern that, according to Table 8.1, would be expected if empathic concern led to altruistic motivation; they did not conform to the pattern that would be expected if empathic concern led to egoistic motivation.

Experiment 2 reported by Batson et al. (1981) provided a generalized replication of Experiment 1, using a different manipulation of the degree of empathic concern. The similarity manipulation employed in Experiment 1, although effective according to manipulation check questions, provided only an indirect manipulation of empathy. In Experiment 2, Batson et al. attempted to manipulate both empathic concern and personal distress more directly. This was done by using an emotion-specific misattribution technique. In the context of what was supposedly a separate experiment, participants (all female) were given a capsule just before they viewed Elaine receiving shocks in the learning task. Half of the participants were told that the capsule—actually a placebo—produced as a side-effect a feeling of warmth and sensitivity (warm side-effect condition). The other participants were told that the capsule produced as a side-effect a feeling of distress and uneasiness (distress side-effect condition). Thus, unlike the typical placebo-misattribution manipulation in which some people are told that the placebo will arouse them and some are told that it will not, or some are told that the placebo will produce side-effects that are relevant to the arousal they are experiencing and others are told to expect side-effects that are irrelevant, all participants in Experiment 2 were told that the placebo would produce relevant arousal. What was manipulated was the *nature* of the arousal the placebo would produce.

Batson et al. reasoned that witnessing Elaine's plight would cause all participants to experience both empathic concern and personal distress. Those in the warm side-effect condition, however, were expected to misattribute at least some of their feelings of empathic concern to the capsule. As a result, they were expected to attribute primarily feelings of personal distress to Elaine's plight. Participants in the distress side-effect condition were expected to do the opposite; they were expected to misattribute at least some of their feelings of personal distress to the capsule and so to attribute primarily feelings of empathic concern to Elaine's plight. Manipulation checks indicated that participants in the two side-effect conditions did, indeed, make the expected differential attributions of the two emotional states to the capsule and to observing Elaine. Further, there was no evidence that the overall level of arousal attributed to observing Elaine differed across the two conditions; only the perceived nature of the arousal differed.

To manipulate difficulty of escape, all participants in Experiment 2 were told that Elaine would perform two learning trials under the aversive conditions. Half of the participants in each side-effect condition were told that they would be observing both trials (difficult escape condition); the others were told that they would observe only the first (easy escape condition).

Paralleling the procedure in Experiment 1, Elaine's reactions during the first trial made it clear that she found the shocks extremely unpleasant. And after participants had viewed the first trial, they were given an unexpected opportunity to help Elaine by taking her place for the second trial.

Consistent with the pattern in Table 8.1, Batson et al. predicted that people in the warm side-effect–easy escape condition would be least likely to help Elaine. These people should have been egoistically motivated to reduce their personal distress, and inasmuch as they did not have to watch the second trial, escape rather than helping should have been the easier way to do this. People in the warm side-effect–difficult escape condition should also have been egoistically motivated to reduce personal distress, but for them, as they would have to watch Elaine undergo the second trial if they did not help, helping should have been the easier way to do it. People in the distress side-effect condition should have perceived their response to Elaine to be relatively empathic and, as a result, been relatively altruistically motivated to reduce her distress. Since this goal could be achieved only by helping, the rate of helping was expected to be high in the distress side-effect condition regardless of whether escape was easy or difficult.

Results again followed the predicted pattern. People in the warm side-effect–easy condition were significantly less likely to offer help than were people in the other three conditions; in these conditions helping was consistently high. And once again, this pattern of results could not be accounted for by a ceiling effect. Nor could it be accounted for by differences in perceived need or by differential liking for Elaine, for checks on each of these factors revealed no reliable differences between conditions. Instead, it seemed that, as in Experiment 1, a relative preponderance of empathic emotion as opposed to personal distress produced a pattern of helping that suggested that the underlying motivation was altruistic rather than egoistic.

CONCLUSIONS

As noted earlier, the idea that empathic emotion produces genuinely altruistic motivation contradicts the egoistic assumption of most, if not all, current psychological theories of motivation. Because egoism is a widely held and basic assumption, it is only prudent to require that the evidence supporting altruism be strong before it is accepted.

If our schematic analysis is conceptually valid, the four studies that we have summarized seem to make an initial step toward providing such evidence. The results of these studies suggest that empathic concern motivates helping whether escape from the need situation is easy or difficult. In contrast, an emotional response of personal distress motivates helping only when escape from the need situation is difficult. This is precisely the pattern of results one would expect if empathic emotion but not personal distress elicits genuinely altruistic motivation to see another's need reduced.

Still, four studies are not many on which to base so radical a change in our view of human motivation, especially when these studies have at least two limitations. First, in each of the four studies the person in need was female, and because it seemed likely that research participants would be more emotionally aroused by the need of a same-sex target person, only female research participants were used. Although there is evidence of sex differences in quantity of empathic responding (Hoffman, 1977), we know of no evidence nor any a priori reason to believe that empathy would elicit qualitatively different kinds of motivation in males and females. Still, future research should assess this possibility. Second, each of the four studies came out of one laboratory—ours. Confidence in the hypothesis that empathic concern elicits altruistic motivation would certainly be strengthened by converging evidence from other laboratories, especially ones with perspectives different from our own.

It may be, then, too early to conclude that empathic emotion can lead to altruistic motivation to help. But if future research produces the same pattern of results as that found in the studies reported here, this conclusion, with all its theoretical and practical implications, would seem not only possible but necessary. For now, the research to date convinces us of the legitimacy of *suggesting* that the motivation to help evoked by empathic emotion may be truly altruistic. In doing so, it leaves us far less confident than we were of contemporary egoistic reinterpretations of apparently altruistically-motivated helping. To return to the example with which we began the chapter, even though an egoistic interpretation is possible, perhaps your motivation for helping the auto-accident victim really *was* in some degree altruistic, namely, to the degree that it was evoked by empathic concern for the young woman.

REFERENCES

Aderman, D., & Berkowitz, L. Observational set, empathy, and helping. *Journal of Personality and Social Psychology*, 1970, *14*, 141-148.

Aronfreed, J. M. The socialization of altruistic and sympathetic behavior: Some theoretical and experimental analyses. In J. Macaulay & L. Berkowitz (Eds.), *Altruism and helping behavior*. New York: Academic Press, 1970.

Asch, S. E. *Social psychology*. New York: Prentice-Hall, 1952.

Bandura, A., & Rosenthal, T. L. Vicarious classical conditioning as a function of arousal level. *Journal of Personality and Social Psychology*, 1966, *3*, 54-62.

Batson, C. D., Cowles, C., & Coke, J. S. Empathic mediation of helping: Egoistic or altruistic? Unpublished manuscript, University of Kansas, 1979.

Batson, C. D., Darley, J. M., & Coke, J. S. Altruism and human kindness: Internal and external determinants of helping behavior. In L. Pervin & M. Lewis (Eds), *Perspectives in interactional psychology.* New York: Plenum Press, 1978.

Batson, C. D., Duncan, B., Ackerman, P., Buckley, T., & Birch, K. Is empathic emotion a source of altruistic motivation? *Journal of Personality and Social Psychology,* 1981, *40,* 290–302.

Batson, C. D., McDavis, K., Felix, R., Goering, B., & Goldman, R. Effects of false feedback of arousal on perceived emotional state and helping. Unpublished manuscript, University of Kansas, 1976.

Berger, S. M. Conditioning through vicarious instigation. *Psychological Review,* 1962, *69,* 450–466.

Bolles, R. D. *Theory of motivation* (2nd ed.). New York: Harper & Row, 1975.

Coke, J. S. *Empathic mediation of helping: Egoistic or altruistic?* Unpublished Ph.D. dissertation, University of Kansas, 1979.

Coke, J. S., Batson, C. D., & McDavis, K. Empathic mediation of helping: A two-stage model. *Journal of Personality and Social Psychology,* 1978, *36,* 752–766.

Comte, I. A. *System of positive polity* (Vol. 1). London: Longmans, Green, & Co., 1875.

Craig, K. D., & Lowrey, J. H. Heart rate components of conditioned vicarious autonomic responses. *Journal of Personality and Social Psychology,* 1969, *11,* 381–387.

Craig, K. D., & Wood, K. Psychophysiological differentiation of direct and vicarious affective arousal. *Canadian Journal of Behavioral Science,* 1969, *1,* 98–105.

Festinger, L. *A theory of cognitive dissonance.* Palo Alto: Stanford University Press, 1957.

Harris, M. B., & Huang, L. C. Helping and the attribution process. *Journal of Social Psychology,* 1973, *90,* 291–297.

Heider, F. *The Psychology of interpersonal relations.* New York: Wiley, 1958.

Hoffman, M. L. Developmental synthesis of affect and cognition and its implications for altruistic motivation. *Developmental Psychology,* 1975, *11,* 607–622.

Hoffman, M. L. Empathy, roletaking, guilt, and development of altruistic motives. In T. Lickona (Ed.), *Moral development and behavior.* New York: Holt, 1976.

Hoffman, M. L. Sex differences in empathy and related behaviors. *Psychological Bulletin,* 1977, *84,* 712–722.

Hygge, S. Information about the model's unconditioned stimulus and response in vicarious classical conditioning. *Journal of Personality and Social Psychology,* 1976, *33,* 764–771.

Krebs, D. L. Altruism—An examination of the concept and a review of the literature. *Psychological Bulletin,* 1970, *73,* 258–302.

Krebs, D. L. Empathy and altruism. *Journal of Personality and Social Psychology,* 1975, *32,* 1134–1146.

Kropotkin, P. *Mutual aid, a factor of evolution.* New York: McClure, Phillips, 1902.

Lazarus, R., Opton, E. M., Nomikos, M. S., & Rankin, N. O. The principle of short-circuiting of threat: Further evidence. *Journal of Personality,* 1965, *33,* 622–635.

McDougall, W. *Introduction to social psychology.* London: Methuen, 1908.

Mehrabian, A., & Epstein, N. A measure of emotional empathy. *Journal of Personality,* 1972, *40,* 525–543.

Mill, J. S. *Utilitarianism.* London: Parker, Son, & Bourn, 1863.

Piliavin, J. A., & Piliavin, I. M. The Good Samaritan: Why *does* he help? Unpublished manuscript, University of Wisconsin, 1973.

Schachter, S. The interaction of cognitive and physiological determinants of emotional state. In L. Berkowitz (Ed.), *Advances in experimental social psychology* (Vol. 1). New York: Academic Press, 1964.

Spencer, H. *The principles of psychology* (Vol. 2; 2nd ed.). London: Williams & Norgate, 1872.

Staub, E. *Positive social behavior and morality* (Vol. 1). New York: Academic Press, 1978.

Stotland, E. Exploratory investigations of empathy. In L. Berkowitz (Ed.), *Advances in experimental social psychology* (Vol. 3). New York: Academic Press, 1969.

Stotland, E., Matthews, K. E., Sherman, S. E., Hansson, R. O., & Richardson, B. Z. *Empathy, fantasy, and helping.* Beverly Hills, Calif.: Sage Publications, 1978.

Wispé, L. G. Sympathy and empathy. In D. L. Sills (Ed.), *International encyclopedia of the social sciences* (Vol. 15). New York: Free Press, 1968, 441–447.

9 A Normative Decision-Making Model of Altruism

Shalom H. Schwartz
Judith A. Howard
University of Wisconsin-Madison

When social psychologists talk about norms, they typically have in mind a set of social dos and don'ts—shared expectations about how we should act, backed by the threat of group sanctions or the promise of rewards. Failure to help the victim of an assault elicits condemnation, for example, whereas generosity to service organizations ($40 billion from Americans in 1978) elicits praise. In any society there are social rewards for selfless acts that benefit others and social punishments for selfish acts. Altruistic norms are social expectations to perform selflessly and to refrain from selfish acts towards others. Norms relevant to helping are sometimes conceptualized much more broadly. Theorists refer to norms of giving (Leeds, 1963), of reciprocity (Gouldner, 1960), of social responsibility (Berkowitz, 1972), of justice (Lerner, 1975), of equity (Homans, 1961).

When the concept of norms is applied to explain altruistic behavior, however, numerous problems arise. As first noted by Latané and Darley (1970), different and even contradictory social norms may be relevant simultaneously. Coming upon a battling couple, what do social norms enjoin? Should we protect the weak? Mind our own business? Take responsibility for others' welfare? Respect the family's right to privacy?

With enough detailed information about this situation each of us might be able to decide which norm should take priority. To reach this decision, however, it is often necessary to specify so much about the situation that helping could be viewed as controlled by the immediate situational influences identified, rather than by social norms. Moreover, individuals differ not only in their knowledge of social norms, but also in which norms they accept as relevant. Even when people agree about the relevance of particular social norms, individual differences in responsiveness to group sanctions may lead to disagreement about priorities among those norms.

A viable normative explanation of helping must circumvent these problems. In introducing such an explanation we note a fundamental contradiction between the idea that people help in order to conform with social norms and the notion of altruism. Altruism refers to self-sacrificial acts intended to benefit others regardless of material or social outcomes for the actor, whereas helping refers to any acts that benefit others. Acts may be helpful regardless of the actor's motivation, but they are altruistic only if motivated by a desire to benefit others rather than to gain social or material rewards. By definition then, helping acts motivated only by the desire to conform with social norms are not altruistic, because the purpose of helping is to optimize external sanctions. To be useful for explaining *altruism*, a normative explanation must point to internalized motivation.

One tradition in psychology and sociology views social norms as important influences on behavior primarily because these norms are the main source of internalized values and self-expectations (Freud, 1933; Mead, 1962; Parsons, 1952). The core notion of this tradition is that individuals come to accept social expectations as self-expectations, social values as personal values. How does this occur? The symbolic interactionist explanation suggests that the very existence of a self is a product of "role-taking," adopting the perspective of others on the world in general and on oneself in particular (Mead, 1962). Learning and abstracting from the perspectives of many others leads over time to the development of a "generalized other." The generalized other is an internalized composite, representing the set of perspectives on the self and external reality common to one's group.

The concept of internalizing social values is ubiquitous in socialization theories. Social learning theory suggests that children adopt social values through identifying with their parents as the mediators of rewards and punishments (Bandura, 1977). Cognitive developmental theories see the development of role-taking capacities as central to the person's recognition of social expectations, which then stimulates growth and reorganization of internal values (Piaget, 1948; cf. Krebs, Ch. 6).

The various explanations of internalization have two elements in common. One is the recognition of individual differences in internalized values as a function of different socialization experiences. Thus, adults may differ substantially in the particular values they have internalized, especially in heterogeneous, complex societies. One person may donate blood only because of peer pressures, whereas another is motivated by internalized values. A third donates initially in response to perceived social norms but returns from a sense of internalized obligation. A second common element is the concept of self-reinforcement. Prior to internalization of a value, reinforcement for behavior relevant to that value is administered by others. In contrast, once internalized, a value is used as a standard to evaluate one's own behavior, as a basis for rewarding or punishing oneself.

Shifting the focus of normative explanations from social norms to internalized, self-reinforced standards resolves the contradiction between altruism and normative influences. The altruist is motivated by anticipated self-reinforcement tied to his or her own internalized values. To hide a Jew from the Nazis as an affirmation of one's own values, for example, is an altruistic act under the control of internalized, though socially acquired, standards. To perform this act for social approval, for 10,000 zloty, or for the thrill of defying danger is not altruism, however helpful it may be.

Although internalized values are appropriate for the explanation of altruism, several of the aforementioned problems associated with normative explanations remain unsolved. One does not know which of many possible expectations will be relevant in a situation, which will enter awareness and take priority for the actor, which are in fact internalized rather than anchored in social sanctions. There is, moreover, the added difficulty of measuring internalized motivation.

The theory of normative influences and the methodology presented in this chapter seek to overcome these problems and to identify the conditions under which norms influence behavior and the processes through which this influence is exercised. This theory recognizes that a mixtrue of altruistic and nonaltruistic motivations often influence decisions regarding helping. Consequently, we present a general model of the relationships among internalized and social normative influences as they join with other factors to influence behavioral decision-making.

Thus far we have treated values both as general sources of expectations and as referring to specific behavior. Values are usually conceptualized (Rokeach, 1973) as general preferences for particular endstates (e.g., equality) or modes of behavior (e.g., compassion). If internalized values are general and abstract, however, they can give no precise guidance to behavioral decisions made in concrete situations with unique characteristics. One does not donate to an abstract concept labeled charity. One responds instead to such specifics as the tone of a solicitation letter, the perceived sincerity of an appeal, and other details. Only if an encyclopedic collection of specific social norms were internalized could the multitude of specific situations we encounter be covered. Such a process of internalization seems unlikely.

The concept of "personal norms" has been proposed as the link between general internalized values and specific self-expectations in concrete situations (Schwartz, 1973, 1977). This concept and its role in normative decision-making are explicated later in detail. Briefly, it is assumed that when people face behavioral choices, their value systems are activated. That is, they weigh the implications of the available action alternatives for that set of internalized values which they perceive as relevant. This cognitive process of comparison and evaluation (which may occur either with or without self-conscious awareness) results in the generation of personal norms, feelings of moral obligation to perform or refrain from specific actions. Personal norms include both a cognitive component of self-based expectations directing behavior and an emotional component of anticipatory self-satisfaction or dissatisfaction. Thus, personal norms are situated, self-based standards for specific behavior generated from internalized values during the process of behavioral decision-making.

Feelings of moral obligation are emotionally arousing. This arousal—experienced as anticipatory pride or guilt, self-affirmation or deprecation—motivates behavior based on internalized values. A person may refrain from acting altruistically even when both the anticipated moral benefits and self-satisfaction associated with action and the moral costs and self-deprecation for inaction are high. Inaction may be due to the social or material costs associated with altruistic acts. Thus one who witnesses a stranger stealing clothes from a laundromat machine may refrain from intervening despite his feelings of moral obligation, because he perceives that the social and physical costs of intervention are high.

When substantial costs oppose a morally valued act, emotional conflict results. This conflict may evoke defensive reactions aimed at reducing the self-based costs of inaction by modifying self-expectations. The relative intensity of this arousal, a function of the moral versus nonmoral implications of an action, determines the strength of motivation to behave altruistically or to defend against value-based self-expectations.

Our model is one of several recent theoretical models which reemphasize the influence of emotional arousal on social behavior. Rokeach's (1979) model of value change asserts that the recognition of inconsistency among values or between values and behavior induces feelings of self-dissatisfaction. These feelings lead to value change and consequently influence behavior. Similarly, in discussing the impact of causal attributions for success or failure on subsequent behavior, Weiner (1978) emphasizes the importance of the emotional arousal associated with the causal attributions. Like our personal norms model, both these models stress the role of emotions associated with self-based evaluative standards in shaping behavior.

Theories that emphasize arousal have also been developed explicitly to explain helping behavior. Batson (Ch. 7; Coke, Batson & McDavis, 1978) distinguishes two types of arousal elicited by observing another's suffering. Feelings of *empathic concern* are tied to another's welfare, hence they are relieved only by reducing the other's suffering. Feelings of *personal distress,* while evoked by the other's plight, induce attention to one's own discomfort. Such feelings are relieved not only by providing help but also by actions that merely divert attention from suffering. Although personal distress can lead to helping, Batson asserts that the crucial mediator of *altruism* is empathic concern.

We agree with this distinction, though we view empathic concern as an emotional response elicited only when reactions to another's plight have implications for one's internalized values. People experience empathic concern only toward those whose welfare is relevant to their own internalized values. Whether we view an aborted fetus as a human being, for example, so that our moral values about taking human life are relevant, determines whether we feel empathic concern toward this fetus.

A NORMATIVE MODEL OF HELPING

Overview

We have proposed that personal norms serve as the link between general internalized values and specific self-expectations in concrete situations. The model we present describes a decision-making process through which personal and social norms mediate the influence of general values on altruistic and/or helping behavior. This process includes five sequential stages: Attention, Motivation, Evaluation, Defense and Behavior. To illustrate these stages, consider the example of two graduate students, Ben and Abbie, who pass a man crouched on a step, apparently in pain, while they are enroute to a class. Ben keeps walking, but Abbie stops to help. Why? 1. *Attention:* Particular aspects of the immediate situation are attended to, resulting in perceptions about need, potential action, and ability. For example, Abbie may notice the man but Ben may not. Alternatively, both may note the man's need, think of an action which could help (e.g., inquiring if he is OK), and see themselves as capable of this action. 2. *Motivation:* This set of perceptions activates the individual's unique internal value system, generating feelings of moral obligation to perform or refrain from specific acts. Thus, even if Ben and Abbie both think they can help, the implications of this act for their internalized systems of values may generate quite different personal norms. Ben's internalized values may call for helping friends but refraining from interfering with strangers. The personal norm he constructs in this situation may therefore enjoin him to leave this stranger alone and threaten self-deprecation for meddling. Abbie, on the other hand, may have strong values favoring action to support the welfare of both strangers and friends. The implications of these values lead to construction of a specific self-expectation to offer help in this situation, accompanied by feelings of moral obligation. 3. *Evaluation:* The potential moral and nonmoral costs and benefits of engaging in specific behaviors are evaluated. Perhaps both Ben and Abbie have relevant values and generate personal norms enjoining help. In evaluating the pros and cons of helping, however, Abbie may feel the moral benefits of action clearly outweigh the social or nonmoral psychological costs, whereas Ben does not. She anticipates feelings of self-affirmation for helping, no public criticism for meddling, and only weak revulsion if the man is drunk. Moreover, she is strongly motivated by the anticipated moral costs of not helping; if the man is badly hurt, she will feel terrible if she fails even to ask about his condition. 4. *Defense:* This step follows if evaluation indicates that costs and benefits are relatively balanced. Because it is easier to distort our own perceptions than to control the material and social outcomes of action, defenses usually reduce conflict by weakening our own feelings of moral obligation. This is accomplished by redefining some element of the situation perceived in stages 1 or 2, that is, by changing perceptions of need, of potential actions, of ability, or of the relevance of one's moral values. With this new definition, the person recycles through subsequent steps in the decision-making process until evaluation of costs and benefits points to a clearly preferable action (including no action).

For Ben the anticipated costs of talking to a stranger and of losing face if his help is rejected may outweigh both the moral benefits of self-affirmation and the moral costs of violating any sense of obligation. To defend against moral self-deprecation, Ben may redefine the situation: The man is not really ill; talking to him won't help. By denying the reality of need or efficacy of action, Ben can ignore the man with minimal moral costs. 4. *Behavior:* Overt helping or inaction follows from the preceding evaluation. Ben proceeds to class while Abbie stops to assist, both feeling satisfied with their decisions. Nonetheless, each may experience lingering feelings of dissatisfaction. Ben's redefinition of the situation may not totally convince him that he has no moral obligation to help, and Abbie may feel anxious about her instructor's reactions when she shows up late.

In sum, our model describes a sequential process activated by the perception of need. This in turn generates value-based self-expectations for behavior and associated feelings of moral obligation. The moral and nonmoral costs and benefits of action are evaluated, producing either a behavioral decision or conflict. Conflict leads to defensive reactions which weaken feelings of moral obligation and facilitate attainment of a behavioral decision. Helping or inaction follows from this decision.

Although the example highlights those cognitive processes that may mediate the initial perception of need and the final behavioral decision, self-conscious awareness is not necessary to this process. In fact, the actor's focus of attention is likely to oscillate between those external situational cues which initially activate attention and the internalized value structure used to evaluate behavior.

The example demonstrates that the same behavioral outcome can emerge from different underlying cognitions and emotions. Because self-conscious awareness is not necessary for this process, people cannot be relied upon to report these cognitions and emotions accurately. This raises the question whether one can test which of the many possible paths through the normative decision-making process an individual will take. As we now elaborate the model, we will point to the types of analyses suitable for establishing an empirical base for our view of normative decision-making.

The Elaborated Model

The complete model illustrates the specific steps that occur in each stage of this normative decision-making process. The decision-maker's progress through these steps is influenced both by aspects of the situation and by individual characteristics. Situation and person variables determine the initial activation of the internalized value structure, the perceived relevance of social norms, and the viability of defenses against feelings of obligation. Thus these variables moderate the impact of feelings of internalized moral obligation and of social norms on behavior. For each stage in the model, important personal and situation variables are identified, and available empirical evidence for their operation is cited. No single study has tested the full causal process represented in the complete model, but tests of connections among various parts have been reported.

Attention

During the attention stage the actor becomes aware of those characteristics of the specific situation that determine whether a decision is needed. Perceptions of this specific situation determine the appropriateness of particular actions. If the need for a decision becomes apparent, and actions which address the need can be identified and executed, then those actions defined as appropriate determine which internalized values are relevant for this decision. There are three steps in the attention stage (see Fig. 9.1.)

Awareness of a Person in a State of Need.   This step requires first that the person in need be noticed and second that his or her state be defined as needy. Becoming aware of need contradicts our general expectation that the welfare of those around us will be relatively satisfactory. The undesirable discrepancy between this expectation and the perceived present state of affairs motivates action to reduce this discrepancy. Thus the "motor" of this normative decision-making model, like other cognitive discrepancy models of motivation (e.g., Reykowski, 1975; Deci, 1975), is the need to reduce perceived discrepancies between actual and desired conditions.

Two situational factors, salience and clarity of need, influence both the initial noticing of need and the definition of the perceived need as serious. Salience and clarity of need increase, for example, as the physical distance between an ob-

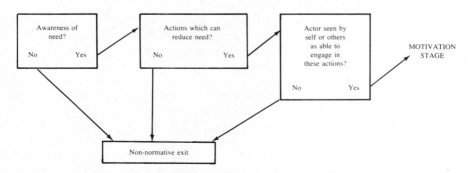

FIG. 9.1.   ATTENTION Stage: Activation of relevant cognitions.

server and a victim decreases; thus victims of an emergency are more likely to be helped by those physically nearby (Piliavin & Piliavin, 1975). In a very different setting, spelling out the detailed needs of the family of a woman requiring a bone marrow transplant made need more salient and clear, eliciting more volunteering (Schwartz, 1970).

Situational cues regarding seriousness of another's need influence whether this need will be defined as sufficiently serious to warrant remedial action. For example, passersby are more likely to offer aid when a victim appears to collapse from a heart attack rather than an injured knee, presumably because a heart attack is defined as more serious (Staub & Baer, 1974). Moreover, the seriousness of perceived need also influences the evaluation and defense stages of the model. Mistaken interference in another's affairs may provoke attempts to justify one's error by invoking either social norms or internalized values. The success of such attempts increases if one can claim that the victim's need appeared serious.

Individual differences in receptivity to situational need cues have also been found to influence the awareness of need and hence helping behavior. Awareness of the specific negative consequences for others of remaining in their current needy state is critical to this normative decision-making process. Awareness of these negative consequences heightens the perceived discrepancy between actual and desired conditions.

The Awareness of Consequences Scale (AC, Schwartz, 1968a) measures this tendency to become aware of the consequences for others of remaining in their current state. Respondents to the AC scale read short stories and describe the thoughts of the central characters as they decide what to do. Responses are coded for the extent to which the needs of others enter into the decision process. The following is a sample item: "Dick was happy he could drive home a little faster than usual because traffic was light at this hour. He had promised his wife he'd be early, so they could make it during the visiting hours at the hospital to see her father tonight. As he turns to exit from the highway, Dick sees a car some 50 yards ahead of him suddenly veer off the road into a ditch and turn over. As he approaches the place where the other car left the road, what thoughts and feelings are running through Dick's mind?"

In situations where the moral desirability of a behavior is widely accepted, AC is positively associated with that behavior. Students who were especially likely to be aware of others' needs (high AC), for example, were also more likely to be helpful and considerate toward their peers in residential groups (Schwartz, 1968a). There is also evidence that awareness of a person in need is influenced by the interaction among situation and person factors (Schwartz, 1974). When the needs underlying a Head Start campaign were not spelled out, the volunteering behavior of college women depended upon their individual tendency to show spontaneous awareness of others' needs (AC). When serious need was described, this individual tendency did not influence helping behavior. Presumably the situational salience of need made women sufficiently aware, rendering superfluous any further impact of their individual tendency to become aware of need.

Identification of Actions Which Might Relieve This Need.   Once the awareness of a person in need is activated, identification of particular actions which can relieve this need is necessary to continuation of the decision-making process. Those situational factors which influence the awareness and definition of need also define the scope of actions relevant to need. The choice of actions, in turn, determines which values will be activated. If situational cues suggest that a collapsed person has suffered a heart attack, certain actions are seen as appropriate (e.g., placing a blanket around his body) whereas others are not (e.g., rousing him to physical exercise). It is the necessity of choice among these actions that takes us to the next step in the normative decision-making model. If no actions are recognized as appropriate, the decision process terminates; the actor does not proceed to generate personal norms or to assess social expectations.

Recognition of Own Ability to Engage in These Actions.   Once potentially helpful actions are recognized, internalized values become relevant only for those actions a person feels able to execute. If a woman with a heart condition herself witnessed the heart attack, for example, she might feel incapable of helping. Her failure to intervene would not have implications for her internalized moral values because no personal norms would be generated. Bystanders' perceived ability to help was manipulated directly in a study in which a woman was threatened by a dangerous rat (Schwartz & Ben David, 1976). Students persuaded they were unable to handle rats helped substantially less than those persuaded they were able, presumably because relevant values were less likely to be activated in the low-ability group.

Perceived ability may also influence decision-making during later steps in the model. Attributions of ability are associated with general feelings of competence, satisfaction, confidence (Weiner, 1978), and good mood (Rosenhan, Ch. 10). These feelings affect both the anticipated social and physical costs for helping (Isen, Shalker, Clark, & Karp, 1978) and the evaluation of these costs. Students who believed themselves unable to handle the dangerous rat, for example, were more likely to anticipate that they could deflect social criticism by claiming inability as well as to expect failure if they tried to intervene.

Thus far we have focused on the sequence of steps which activate perceptions required for normative decision-making. The individual actor may not generate each of these perceptions. The perceived severity of need may be insufficient to stimulate a search for actions that might reduce this need. Alternatively, no such actions may be recognized, or relevant actions may be missing from the actor's repertoire. If each of these perceptions is not activated in turn, the decision-making process ends prior to norm construction. The objective result is inaction. Unlike inaction at a later stage, however, this decision not to act is not based on internalized values. Thus relevant perceptions of need, actions, and personal ability are requisite to the generation of morally relevant behavioral decisions.

Generation of Feelings of Obligation

If a person perceives actions as relevant to another's need and feels capable of performing these actions, implications of the actions are considered. We distinguish three types of implications: (1) physical, material and psychological implications that follow directly from the action; (2) implications for the actor's internalized moral values; (3) social implications, that is, outcomes dependent upon the reactions of other people (see Fig. 9.2).

Every act requires some effort and time; thus there are always at least some physical and material outcomes of behavior. Many acts also have direct psychological consequences not based in moral values. Leaping into the sea to rescue a drowning stranger, for example is dangerous (physical costs), will ruin one's clothes (material costs), and will provide a thrill (nonmoral psychological benefits). This first type of implication is not sharply delimited here because, although it is weighed together with normative considerations, it is not uniquely important for a model of normative decision-making. Our central concern is with the special class of psychological implications actions have for people's internalized moral value systems. Social implications are also important for a normative decision-making model insofar as people use perceived social norms as cues to the social responses that acts will elicit.

Internalized Moral Values and Personal Norms.   Internalized values form an organized cognitive structure. Values vary in their importance to the self, their specificity or generality, their interconnections, and their relationships to experience and to overt expression (Bem, 1970; Rokeach, 1973; Schwartz, 1977; Rosenberg, 1979). The positions of particular values in the cognitive structure (e.g., compassion, equality, wisdom) may be quite different for one person than

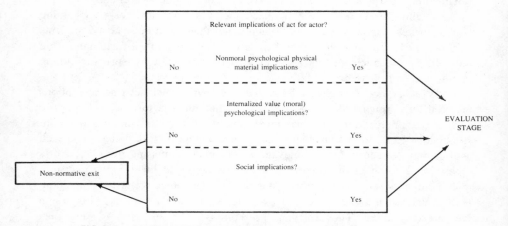

FIG. 9.2.   MOTIVATION Stage: Generation of feelings of (moral) obligation.

for another. Hence, the value implications of engaging in a specific behavior vary across people.

Among the most important values for altruistic helping are equity and justice. Equity and justice are undoubtedly invoked as legitimate social expectations in order to induce compliant helping, so that they might be viewed as general social norms (e.g., Berkowitz & Walster, 1976; Lerner, Ch. 9). But most social psychological analyses of the influences of equity and justice on individual behavior are best interpreted as treating equity and justice as internalized values from which specific personal norms are generated in the behavioral situation (e.g., Greenberg, 1978).

A personal norm is constructed for each potential action focused upon throughout the attention stage of the model. Personal norms are constructed by scanning the implications of these actions for one's relevant internalized values. In other words, the actor asks herself whether she is morally responsible for these actions in this situation, given her own general internalized values. As noted above, personal norms consist of cognitive and affective components—a self-expectation for behavior and emotions associated with this expectation.

The more central to one's self-evaluation the values implicated by an action, the stronger the emotional arousal. Anticipated compliance elicits feelings of self-satisfaction and anticipated inaction elicits feelings of self-deprecation. Thus the sanctions attached to personal norms are based in the self-concept. Because the stimuli that activate the scanning of internalized values are situationally variable, the personal norms generated are momentary, rather than enduring standards. Although values are relatively enduring preferences for general outcomes or modes of behavior, personal norms are situation-specific reflections of the cognitive and affective implications of a person's values for specific actions.

Measurement of Personal Norms. Because personal norms are conceptualized as constructed in the choice situation, measuring personal norms in advance of behavioral choice is problematic. Measuring relatively stable underlying values may reveal little about personal norms. We cannot know what feelings of obligation will actually be generated from a person's unique complex of values without knowing what aspects of a situation are attended to and what specific actions considered. We have approached this problem by asking people to describe the feelings of moral obligation they would feel if faced with specified behavioral choices. The validity of this procedure depends on the extent to which respondents actually project themselves into the hypothetical situations described in the personal norm items. A typical format is: "The following questions ask whether you personally would feel a moral obligation to be a transplant donor under various circumstances. Do you think that this is something you ought to do or something you should *not* do? . . . If a close relative of yours needed a bone marrow transplant and you were a suitable donor, would you feel a moral obligation to donate bone marrow?"

Although personal norms may be constructed for any value-relevant behavior, they have been measured primarily with reference to unusual, nonrecurrent actions in hypothetical situations (e.g., organ donation, volunteering to tutor blind children). This invalidates the alternative explanation that a relationship between personal norms and behavior emerges because prior behavior leads to construction of norms that appear consistent with and justify the behavior.

Social Norms.   If the perceptions activated in the attention stage of the model point to the existence of general social expectations for particular actions, these perceived social norms may also influence the behavioral decision. Here the actor asks himself whether he is responsible for action in terms of social norms. Like personal norms, social norms have a cognitive and an affective component. Perceived social norms include an awareness of a social standard for behavior and feelings of anxiety, fear, pride, etc., in anticipation of others' reactions to the behavior. Both the informal and formal sanctions associated with such norms are socially based, rather than based in internalized values.

People comply with social norms to maximize socially mediated external reinforcements. For social norms to influence behavioral decisions requires first that the group of which the actor is a member share a relevant behavioral expectation (i.e., that a social norm exists), and second that the actor attend to that shared expectation when reaching the decision. Research seldom establishes the existence of these conditions. Moreover, what may appear as compliance with general social norms is often a response to specific anticipated social influence attempts—threats, promises, or direct reinforcements. Many an electric drill or cup of flour changes hands specifically to avoid a neighbor's angry stares, for example, rather than to avoid violating social norms.

Measurement of Social Norms.   To measure social norms consistently with our normative decision-making model entails determining whether the actor perceives that others share specific expectations for behavior in a situation. We therefore measure *perceived* social norms by asking about the social obligations people believe that others would hold for them in concrete situations. The typical format asks how "the people whose opinions you value most would react if you discussed with them whether you should be a transplant donor under various circumstances. *Regardless of your personal views,* would these people think that this is something you ought to do or something you should *not* do?"

Reference group theory (Shibutani, 1955) leads one to inquire about the perceived norms of significant others—those whose perspectives a person adopts as his own. Several studies indicate, however, that the perceived norms of significant others add little to prediction of behavior from personal norms (Schwartz, 1977). The norms of significant others may directly influence the construction of personal norms, thus influencing behavior indirectly through internalization by the person in question. Alternatively one might measure the actor's perception of the social norms held by people who would learn of an act and sanction it. The danger of this approach is that it may tap specific social influences rather than social norms. In all events, the one study using this approach also found little influence of perceived social norms on behavior beyond that of personal norms (Schwartz & Fleishman, 1979).

Empirical Evidence. Evidence that behavior is dependent on the personal norms constructed from internalized values is provided by significant correlations between personal norms and a variety of subsequent behaviors: volunteering to donate bone marrow ($r = .24$, Schwartz, 1973), pledging to take University class notes for Army Reservists ($r = .26$, Rothstein, 1974), donating blood ($r = .43$, Pomazal, 1974; $r = .24$, Zuckerman & Reis, 1978) volunteering to tutor blind children ($r = .26$, Schwartz, 1978), volunteering time for elderly welfare recipients ($r = .30$, Schwartz & Fleishman, 1979). Evidence for the influence of perceived social norms is both weaker and less diverse. A significant correlation has been observed with volunteering time for elderly welfare recipients ($r = .15$). Positive but nonsignificant correlations were found with donating blood ($r = .09$ in both studies), with volunteering to donate bone marrow ($r = .12$), and with everyday considerateness and helpfulness ($r = .09$, data from study reported in Schwartz, 1968a).

Although many of these correlations are significant, they are not particularly strong. This is consistent with the assumption of the normative decision-making model that the strength of the associations between norms and behavior depends on the moderating effects of attention conditions. Evidence for such moderating effects was obtained in the study of everyday helpfulness and considerateness among peers (Schwartz, 1968a). As expected from the model, personal norms were substantially correlated with behavior for students who tend to take note spontaneously of others' need ($r = .44$, high AC quartile), but not for those who tend to overlook others' need ($r = -.01$, low AC quartile).

There was also some indication that AC moderates the impact of perceived social norms. Behavior correlated significantly with perceived social norms for the high AC quartile ($r = .27$) but not for the low AC quartile ($r = -.05$). Thus whether people consider the relevance of social norms for their potential actions may also be a function of the individual tendency to take note spontaneously of others' need.

Anticipatory Evaluation

Subsequent to identification of the physical, moral and social outcomes implied by specific helping behaviors, the anticipated costs and benefits of these outcomes are evaluated (see Fig. 9.3). Both situation and person factors influence the assessment of costs and benefits. Thus the salience of social costs and benefits may be increased by a situational cue such as the presence of referent

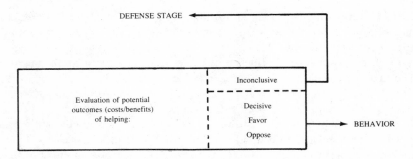

FIG. 9.3.   ANTICIPATORY EVALUATION Stage.

others (Ewens & Ehrlich, 1972). Anticipated physical costs of intervention may be increased, for example, by witnessing a rescuer injured in a fire.

Among person factors that affect the evaluation of moral outcomes is the centrality of the values implicated in a behavior for the person's overall self-evaluation. The impact of a personal norm on a behavior is stronger for people whose self-evaluation is closely tied to the values from which the personal norm is constructed. Thus the correlation between personal norms for considerateness and everyday considerateness behavior was significantly stronger for students who ranked considerateness as one of their most central values ($r = .32$) than for students who viewed it as less central ($r = .04$, Schwartz, 1977).

Minimal physical costs of effort and time are inherent in any action, but the presence of social and moral implications is less certain. There are behaviors that have no moral relevance for some people; because these behaviors are unrelated to internalized values, no personal norms are constructed. In the absence of internalized moral implications, social costs and benefits may have considerable influence on behavioral decisions.

The balancing of social and moral implications is illustrated in a study of volunteering to aid elderly welfare recipients in need (Schwartz & Fleishman, 1978). An appeal for help invoked the social expectation that women should offer aid, but varied the legitimacy of this expectation by describing the need as due either to the elderly persons' lack of trustworthiness or to arbitrary events beyond their control. Women who had indicated feelings of moral obligation either to aid elderly persons or to oppose such aid responded consistently with their premeasured personal norms, regardless of the legitimacy of need: For these women the moral costs and benefits outweighed the social. On the other hand, women who had reported no personal norm regarding this issue were significantly influenced by the legitimacy of need, volunteering twice as much when the social expectation invoked was legitimate rather than illegitimate.

The outcome of the evaluation of anticipated costs and benefits determines which step in the model follows next. If moral and nonmoral considerations favor the same helping action, a decision is reached and the defense step is skipped. If the various costs and benefits of available actions are evaluated as relatively balanced, however, and the outcomes of these actions are not trivial, conflict is experienced. The decision is delayed while the person defensively redefines the situation. Living in some sections of Johannesburg one might hesitate to sign an ad denouncing apartheid, anticipating excessive social and material costs, regardless of how favorable one's personal norms. How is this conflict resolved?

Defense

The most common method for reducing decisional conflict is to weaken one's feelings of moral obligation through redefining the situation. The preferred defense is to redefine one's own perceptions and interpretations, because physical and social outcomes of action are less easily controlled. Four types of denial, each implied by one of the earlier steps in the model, can reduce feelings of obligation: denial of need, denial of effective actions, denial of ability, and denial of responsibility. The actor cycles back through the decision-making process in order to generate a new definition of the situation which may facilitate a clear-cut behavioral decision. Where the new cycle begins depends on the form of denial employed (see Fig. 9.4).

Denial of Need. The first step in the model is to become aware of a person in need. Faced with the costs of acting on a recognized need, a person may reexamine the situation defensively to find cues that permit denial of the need or at least a reduction in its perceived severity. Thus one who feels she should donate bone marrow but fears the physical pain of a transplant may seek a rationale for denying the recipient's need.

Ambiguity of need cues and individual insensitivity to such cues enhance the probability of effective denial. An actor who totally denies the reality of need can exit from the decision-making process after step one of the second cycle without incurring moral costs. If the perceived severity of need is only weakened, decision-making continues through the subsequent steps. The reduction in perceived severity of need may lead, however, to weaker personal norms or to a lower estimate of moral or social costs. The new cost/benefit ratio may permit a clear decision not to help.

Denial of Effective Action. If need is perceived as serious enough to merit attention, the actor may defend against the conflict by concluding that the action would not be effective. Bystanders may conclude that intervening to protect a woman from a beating by her husband won't work. Instead, another line of action may be defined as more appropriate (e.g., calling the police). This action may then be evaluated in subsequent steps in the decision-making process. Choice of the action to be undertaken is a function of the relative conflict aroused

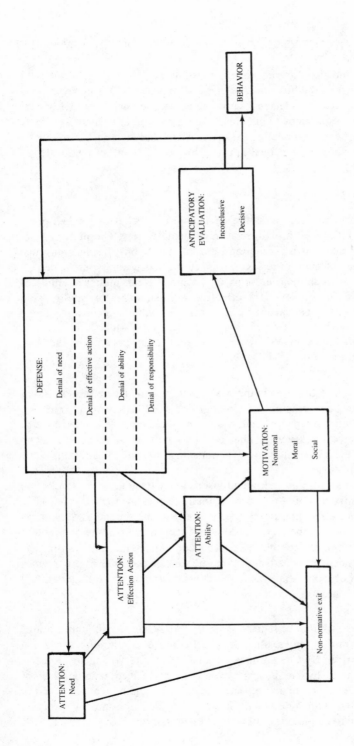

ATTENTION: → MOTIVATION: → ANTICIPATORY → BEHAVIOR
Activation of   Generation   EVALUATION
Relevant Cognitions of Feelings

ATTENTION: → MOTIVATION: → ANTICIPATORY → (DEFENSE) → BEHAVIOR
                              EVALUATION

FIG. 9.4. DEFENSE Stage: Defensive recycling through a normative decision-making model.

by evaluation of the set of social, physical and moral implications associated with each of the possible actions.

Denial of effective actions may also operate in conjunction with changes in perceived need. Newly recognized needs suggest alternative actions that may be less conflictual. Some alternative actions may reduce nonmoral costs (e.g., giving money for a dialysis machine rather than donating one's kidney). Other alternatives may reduce the moral costs of inaction. A woman might refuse to be a foster parent for runaways with little moral cost, if she decides that foster parenting is much less effective than preventing teens from running away.

Denial of Personal Ability.   Another mode of defense is to deny one's ability or competence to perform the necessary actions. If redefinition of need points to new effective actions, the actor may now simply conclude that he lacks the requisite abilities. Or, defensive recycling may commence with reevaluation of the actor's personal competence. In a current study, for example, we have been amazed at the number of women whose arthritis renders them unable to distribute pamphlets in their neighborhoods. This mode of defense is especially effective for deflecting the social costs of ignoring social norms invoked in appeals.

Denial of Responsibility.   The final mode of defense is denial of responsibility to conform with normative obligations. That is, actors reject their liability for violating the personal or social norms activated in the motivation stage, claiming that under the circumstances the norms do not apply to them. As with the other defenses, both person and situation variables influence the use of responsibility denial.

The responsibility denial scale (RD) (Schwartz, 1968b; Schwartz & Howard, 1980) measures the individual tendency to accept or reject rationales that reduce personal responsibility for the interpersonal consequences of one's actions. RD is measured by 28 items that provide various rationales—provocation, lack of intentionality, overriding pressures, job obligations. The following sample item is coded for acceptance of the rationale: "When a person is nasty to me, I feel very little responsibility to treat him well." (Agree).

Responsibility denial has mediated the personal norm-behavior relationship in several studies. Personal norms were not correlated with volunteering to donate bone marrow for Wisconsin women high on RD ($r = .01$), for example, but the correlation was substantial for women low on RD ($r = .44$, Schwartz, 1973). Similarly, personal norms did not predict volunteering to tutor blind children for Israeli undergraduates high on RD ($r = -.03$), but the correlation was strong for those low on RD ($r = .72$, Schwartz & Howard, 1980). Thus those likely to deny their responsibility do not behave consistently with their feelings of moral obligation, while those who accept personal responsibility do behave consistently.

The same pattern of mediation by RD has been observed for everyday helpfulness and considerateness (Schwartz, 1968b) and for volunteering to aid elderly welfare recipients (Schwartz & Fleishman, 1979). RD does not mediate the impact of perceived social norms on behavior, however, probably because denying responsibility to oneself fails to reduce the anticipated costs of violating social expectations (Schwartz & Fleishman, 1979).

Situational factors also influence whether one can successfully deny personal responsibility. Any factor that initially increases the salience of a person's special liability for the fate of a needy other also increases the difficulty of subsequently denying responsibility. Students helped the woman endangered by an escaped rat significantly more if they were directly blamed for causing the escape than if it was the woman's own fault (Schwartz & Ben David, 1976). Presumably those blamed for the accident were less able to deny personal responsibility for its consequences.

Salience of responsibility should also mediate the relationship between personal norms and behavior, because it should block responsibility denial. In the only test of this mediating effect, however, the results were opposite the prediction. This anomalous finding has stimulated refinements to the theory, discussed in the following section.

In sum, decisional conflict produced by evaluating the anticipated costs and benefits of an action elicits defenses against the feelings of moral obligation to perform that action. If these defenses succeed, actors may either exit from the system before new personal norms are constructed, or they may construct new personal norms and reach a behavioral decision on the basis of the reevaluated social, physical and moral outcomes.

If further conflict is generated, recycling through the decision-making process may continue, though there are factors that prevent repeated iterations. Particularly in emergencies, the rapid intensification of need tends to short-circuit multiple iterations, because the passage of time itself increases the moral costs of inaction. Even in nonemergency situations, the passage of time leads eventually to changes that end this process: Need may dissipate, or attention may be drawn elsewhere by new stimuli. If delay in response is prolonged, both the personal and the social costs of helping rise, because acting now implies that action was appropriate from the outset, hence that the actor was derelict.

Behavior

Once a behavioral decision is reached, the helping act is performed or not. Both action and inaction modify the situation and thus have potential for changing its meaning for the actor. New needs may become salient, new actions may be recognized, perceived responsibility may shift. Dissatisfactions may linger because decisions rarely permit avoidance of all costs. Thus a new sequence of decision-making may occur. Moreover, the outcomes of the behavior enacted may change the structure of internalized values and perceived social norms, and the assessment of physical and material costs. Consequently, future behavior in objectively similar situations may differ considerably from past behavior.

BOOMERANG EFFECTS

The empirical data presented suggest that situation and person factors conducive to norm activation increase the association between personal norms and behavior, and the absence of such factors decreases this association. Although most of the available findings support this key hypothesis of the normative decision-making model, anomalous results have also been obtained. Specifically, in the presence of factors presumed *most* conducive to activating norms favoring helping, decreased rates of helping behavior have sometimes been obtained. We term this a boomerang effect. Much of our current research examines this effect in order to refine and extend the theory.

A boomerang effect was first found in the study of bone marrow donation. Personal norms and behavior were significantly associated in all conditions but the one most conducive to norm activation, the high responsibility/high salience of need condition. Although this is the only study with a boomerang effect in which personal norms were measured, two other studies produced results that may reflect a similar phenomenon. In one (Schwartz, 1970), the volunteering rate increased when the salience of need was increased from low to moderate among people told there was a 1/25 chance they would provide an adequate match for a bone marrow transplant, but volunteering boomeranged to its lowest level when need was most salient. A similar unexpected finding was obtained in the bake sale study (Schwartz, 1974): When exposed to high seriousness of need, students with the highest scores on the spontaneous tendency to attend to others' need (AC) volunteered significantly less than those with moderate and low AC scores.

Given the worthy causes involved in these two studies, we can safely assume that most participants felt some moral obligation to volunteer. The unexpected drops in volunteering may therefore be interpreted as showing that personal norms had the least impact on behavior in precisely those circumstances hypothesized to be most conducive to norm activation.

Three plausible explanations suggest that the boomerang effect stems from a loss of internal value-based motivation to behave altruistically. The explanations are complementary, and all are consistent with the process of personal norm construction presented here. First, when an appeal is framed in a highly pressuring manner (e.g., by including excessive or dramatic statements of need), the target of the appeal may become suspicious of the motives of the person seeking help or of the true severity of need. This suspicion may elicit denial of need, so that feelings of moral obligation are not generated and helping behavior is therefore reduced.

A second explanation maintains that the perception of manipulativeness in an appeal elicits reactance, stimulating a need to retain behavioral freedom by resisting the pressure to help (Brehm, 1966). Even though subjects accept the reality of need, their feelings of reactance may lead them to exercise behavioral freedom by refusing to volunteer. In general, complying with an appeal may produce nonmoral psychological costs that weigh against any moral benefits of acting on one's feelings of moral obligation. Moreover, the threat to behavioral freedom is strongest for people with positive personal norms: Because they stand to benefit most from self-affirmation, they experience the strongest reactance. This explanation is currently under examination in a study of the effect of salience of need and disavowal of intention to pressure on the relationship between personal norms to help runaway teenagers and subsequent volunteering.

A third explanation of boomerang effects suggests that external pressures to provide aid undermine the internalized motivation to perform altruistic actions. We have argued that the benefit of altruistic acts is affirmation of one's internalized values. Making salient external reasons to engage in helping behaviors may deprive otherwise internally motivated actors of the opportunity to see themselves as guided by their own values. People exposed to conditions that heighten the salience of external reasons for helping (e.g., social pressure, money) may actually help, but their help may be a function of external rewards rather than of internalized values. A question deriving from this explanation is currently under study: Can personal norms be undermined by offering external rewards (money) for behavior which conforms with these norms? If personal norms tap one form of intrinsic motivation, as is implicit in the internalized value approach, they should indeed become less positive when pronormative behavior is induced by external rewards (cf. Deci, 1975; Lepper & Greene, 1978).

CONCLUSION

This chapter presents a general model of normative influences on the decision-making that underlies helping behavior. This model specifies how social, material and psychological (including moral) influences on helping combine in concrete situations. While the model delineates situational impacts on helping, it treats the person as an active perceiver and interpreter of situational cues. Thus the model also specifies the types of person variables that influence the perception, interpretation and defensive redefinition of situations that call for helping responses.

By focusing on the influence of personal norms—situated representations of internalized values—this model avoids problems associated with social normative explanations that have led to critiques of normative explanations in general. Social norm approaches have difficulty accounting for the situational specificity of behavior, because social norms are conceptualized in general terms. Because personal norms are constructed on the basis of situational cues, explanations using personal norms can be situationally specific without assuming the internalization of a multitude of specific norms. Furthermore, social normative approaches generally assume rather than measure the prevalence of the norms they invoke. They tend to ignore the fact that people vary both in their perception of social norms as relevant and in the sanctions they associate with particular social norms. The personal norm approach addresses these factors explicitly, assessing the relevance of particular actions for the values of each individual and the strength of the sanctions which that individual attaches to value-relevant actions.

The concept of internalized moral norms permits one to distinguish altruism as a special subtype of helping. Altruism, according to our model, is a product of self-based motivation: Altruistic helping is motivated by feelings of moral obligation generated when individuals evaluate the implications of action alternatives for their internalized values.

This model of personal normative influence also addresses questions left untouched by empathy explanations of helping. Empathy theories hold that one of the types of emotional arousal elicited by witnessing suffering leads to helping. When the type of arousal labeled empathy emerges and why it leads to helping are not described. We suggest that empathic arousal occurs only when responses to the need of another have relevance for one's internalized values. Because one values the other's welfare, the emotion elicited is directed toward actions that aid the other.

The concept of personal norms as a link between general values and specific behaviors points to methods for measuring the internalized motivation likely to be relevant when behavioral decisions are made. Currently available data support the utility of this concept for understanding and predicting altruism. Research is needed on how the structure and content of internalized values influence the construction of personal norms. Many of the more interesting hypotheses regarding the moderating effects of situation and person variables on the relationship between internalized motivation and altruistic behavior have yet to be studied. Explanations of the boomerang findings discussed earlier enrich the theory by suggesting how situation and person variables may combine interactively to affect the personal norm-behavior relationship. Empirical examination of these explanations is currently underway.

The normative model presented here emphasizes personal norms, but it also specifies how social norms may be implicated in the stages of the decision-making process. Social normative explanations have been rightly criticized, and past studies have failed to demonstrate consistent relationships between social norms and helping behavior. Future research with social norms would benefit by considering the relevance of each stage of the model for social normative impacts, that is by identifying the conditions which draw attention to social expectations, lead actors to perceive these as applicable to themselves, and prevent or promote the success of defenses against social sanctions. These conditions could then be investigated as potential moderators of the relationship between explicitly measured social norms and helping behavior.

ACKNOWLEDGMENT

Preparation of this manuscript was supported by NSF grant BNS 77-23287 to the first author.

REFERENCES

Bandura, A. *Social learning theory*. Englewood Cliffs, N.J.: Prentice-Hall, 1977.

Bem, D. *Beliefs, attitudes and human affairs*. Belmont, California: Brooks/Cole, 1970.

Berkowitz, L. Social norms, feelings and other factors affecting helping and altruism. In L. Berkowitz (Ed.), *Advances in experimental social psychology* (Vol. 6). New York: Academic Press, 1972.

Berkowitz, L., & Walster, E. (Eds.), *Advances in experimental social psychology (Vol. 9)*. New York: Academic Press, 1976.

Brehm, J. W. *A theory of psychological reactance*. New York: Academic Press, 1966.

Coke, J. S., Batson, C. D., & McDavis, K. Empathic mediation of helping: A two-stage model. *Journal of Personality and Social Psychology*, 1978, *36*, 752–766.

Deci, E. L. *Intrinsic motivation*. New York: Plenum Press, 1975.

Ewens, W. L., & Ehrlich, H. J. Reference–other support and ethnic attitudes as predictors of intergroup behavior. *Sociological Quarterly*, 1972, *13*, 348–360.

Freud, S. *New introductory lectures on psychoanalysis*. New York: Norton, 1933.

Gouldner, A. W. The norm of reciprocity: A preliminary statement. *American Sociological Review*, 1960, *25*, 161–178.

Greenberg, J. Effects of reward value and retaliative power on allocation decisions: Justice, generosity, or greed? *Journal of Personality and Social Psychology*, 1978, *36*, 367–379.

Homans, G. C. *Social behavior: Its elementary forms*. New York: Harcourt-Brace, 1961.

Isen, A. M., Shalker, T. E., Clark, M., & Karp, L. Affect, accessibility of material in memory, and behavior: A cognitive loop? *Journal of Personality and Social Psychology*, 1978, *36*, 1–12.

Latané, B., & Darley, J. M. *The unresponsive bystander: Why doesn't he help?* New York: Appleton, 1970.

Leeds, R. Altruism and the norm of giving. *Merrill-Palmer Quarterly*, 1963, *9*, 229–240.

Lepper, N. R., & Greene, D. (Eds.), *The hidden costs of reward*. Hillsdale, N.J.: Lawrence Erlbaum Associates, 1978.

Lerner, M. J. The justice motive in social behavior: Introduction. *Journal of Social Issues*, 1975, *31*, 1–19.

Mead, G. H. *Mind, self and society*. Chicago: University of Chicago Press, 1962.

Parsons, T. The superego and the theory of social systems. *Psychiatry*, 1952, *15*. Reprinted in T. Parsons, *Social structure and personality*. Glencoe, Illinois: Free Press, 1964.

Piaget, J. *The moral judgment of the child*. Glencoe, Illinois: Free Press, 1948. (Originally published in 1932.)

Piliavin, J. A., & Piliavin, I. M. *Good samaritan—Why does he help?* Unpublished manuscript, University of Wisconsin, 1975.

Pomazal, R. J. *Attitudes, normative beliefs, and altruism: Help for helping behavior.* Unpublished doctoral dissertation, University of Illinois, 1974.

Reykowski, J. Prosocial orientation and self-structure. In J. Reykowski (Ed.), *Studies on the mechanisms of prosocial behavior.* Warsaw: Warsaw University Press, 1975.

Rokeach, M. *The nature of human values.* New York: Free Press, 1973.

Rokeach, M. Value theory and communication research. In D. Nimmo (Ed.), *Communication yearbook III,* Transaction Books, 1979.

Rosenberg, M. *Conceiving the self.* New York: Basic Books, 1979.

Rothstein, H. R. *Attitudes and behavior: The effects of perceived payoffs and facilitating intrapersonal conditions.* Unpublished master's thesis, Hebrew University of Jerusalem, 1974.

Shibutani, T. Reference groups as perspectives. *American Journal of Sociology,* 1955, *60,* 562–569.

Staub, E., & Baer, R. S., Jr. Stimulus characteristics of a sufferer and difficulty of escape as determinants of helping. *Journal of Personality and Social Psychology,* 1974, *30,* 279–284.

Schwartz, S. H. Awareness of consequences and the influence of moral norms on interpersonal behavior. *Sociometry,* 1968, *31,* 355–369. (a)

Schwartz, S. H. Words, deeds, and the perception of consequences and responsibility in action situations. *Journal of Personality and Social Psychology,* 1968, *10,* 232–242. (b)

Schwartz, S. H. Elicitation of moral obligation and self-sacrificing behavior. *Journal of Personality and Social Psychology,* 1970, *15,* 283–293.

Schwartz, S. H. Normative explanations of helping behavior: A critique, proposal, and empirical test. *Journal of Experimental Social Psychology,* 1973, *9,* 349–364.

Schwartz, S. H. Awareness of interpersonal consequences, responsibility denial and volunteering. *Journal of Personality and Social Psychology,* 1974, *30,* 57–63.

Schwartz, S. H. Normative influences on altruism. In L. Berkowitz (Ed.), *Advances in experimental social psychology* (Vol. 10). New York: Academic Press, 1977.

Schwartz, S. H. Temporal instability as a moderator of the attitude-behavior relationship. *Journal of Personality and Social Psychology,* 1978, *36,* 715–724.

Schwartz, S. H., & Ben David, A. Responsibility and helping in an emergency: Effects of blame, ability and denial of responsibility. *Sociometry,* 1976, *39,* 406–415.

Schwartz, S. H., & Fleishman, J. A. Personal norms and the mediation of legitimacy effects on helping. *Social Psychology,* 1978, *41,* 306–315.

Schwartz, S. H., & Fleishman, J. A. *Personal norms as a distinctive attitudinal variable.* Unpublished manuscript, University of Wisconsin-Madison, 1979.

Schwartz, S. H., & Howard, J. A. Explanations for the moderating effect of responsibility denial on the personal norms-behavior relationship. *Social Psychology Quarterly,* 1980, *43,* 441–446.

Weiner, B., Russell, D., & Lerman, D. Affective consequences of causal ascriptions. In J. H. Harvey, W. Ickes, & R. F. Kidd, *New directions in attribution research* (Vol. 2). Hillsdale, N.J.: Laurence Erlbaum Associates, 1978.

Zuckerman, M., & Reis, H. T. Comparison of three models for predicting altruistic behavior. *Journal of Personality and Social Psychology,* 1978, *36,* 498–510.

10 Justice and Altruism

Melvin J. Lerner
James R. Meindl
University of Waterloo

THE SELF-SERVING ORIGINS OF ALTRUISM AND JUSTICE

Why do people give money to the poor . . . care for their children . . . risk their lives in war . . . help the lady who drops her groceries . . . help someone who collapses in the subway . . . leave the room to tell the experimenter that someone appears to be having an epileptic fit? Why would some people devote their lives to healing the sick, serving the poor and the mentally retarded?

If our assumptions about human nature require us to construe acts which seem to benefit others as instrumental in origin and purpose, then the answers and implications are clear: Although such behavior includes some greater or lesser benefits to others, they are all designed to meet the best interests of the actor. The benefits to others are secondary and coincidental. Invariably these actions are performed because they are seen as the most desirable, least painful, or most rewarding way to behave. If the payoff structures were different, these people would probably have acted otherwise (Darley & Latané, 1968; Schwartz, 1975; Walster & Piliavin, 1972).

There may be value in viewing some helping behavior this way, but what has happened to "altruism" as a particular class of social acts? What is clearly implied by this approach is that if we wish to understand and predict the conditions under which someone will or will not act in ways which might involve some benefit to another person, we must first understand the ways in which these "acts" are tied to the actor's private motives and goals. That is not only the direction that "altruism" research has taken, it is also what has happened in the efforts of most social psychologists to understand the way in which the theme of justice appears in human encounters. It has been assumed that people act according to the rules of "justice" if and when they believe them to be the most profitable, least costly way for them to behave (Walster & Walster, 1975). The costs and profits are determined by the gains and losses measured in terms of other more desired resources (Walster, Walster, & Berscheid, 1978). In one form or another, these assumptions have achieved the level of truisms in most contemporary approaches in the study of justice (Deutsch, 1975; Leventhal, 1976a; Walster et al., 1978).

Much of the early just world research grew out of similar assumptions—that people cared about what happens to others because of the implications of other people's fate for their own security and sanity (Lerner, 1965). This motivational base, which is generated exclusively out of self concern, was assumed to shape the ways in which we react to any given instance of injustice in our world. Presumably, I care about how just your fate is not because of any intrinsic interest in you, but because if an injustice can happen to you—someone in my "world"—who is similar to me in relevant ways—then I may also be vulnerable to the same malevolent forces. How can I then continue to work, plan, and have confidence in my world? How am I to feel secure now and in the future (Lerner, 1980; Lerner & Simmons, 1966; Lerner & Whitehead, in press)? According to most systematic analyses, what we do when we become aware of an injustice is the direct result of a "cost-accounting" among the perceived available alternatives. The general rule is that we elect the course of action which is least costly to us, not the victims (Schwartz, 1975; Walster & Piliavin, 1972). Whether we walk away from or derogate the victim; whether we engage in great efforts of compensation, punish the inflictor, or for that matter, only rant and rave about the injustice of it all, is determined by which of these alternatives (alone or in concert) involves the best payoffs for us—the observers. If acting to correct an injustice is too costly, the observer may derogate the victim; and if that is too costly, the observer may invent a fantasy solution, possibly with the belief that injustice will be corrected in the "here-after" (Lerner & Miller, 1978).

INITIAL STAGES IN THE DEVELOPMENT
OF JUSTICE MOTIVE THEORY:
THE "PERSONAL CONTRACT"

The Psychological Basis of the Personal Contract

The psychology of deserving and justice has been construed by most social scientists as emotionally "conditioned" and a cognitively represented consequence of growing up in a justice-oriented society. In more recent forms of this model it is assumed that the social unit, out of its collective wisdom, was able to recognize that living by the rules of justice was to the long term benefit of all.

The social unit created social institutions to ensure that people followed these rules and that children came to believe in them—despite the fact that we are unremittingly selfish in our constant efforts to "maximize our outcomes" (Campbell, 1972; Walster et al., 1978). Once the relevant belief system are implanted in and become a part of the child's psychological makeup, other processes such as "dissonance reduction," cognitive balance, and the need to believe in a "Just World" (Lerner, 1980) provide additional incentives to keep the selfish appetites in line with the requirements of fairness (Leventhal, 1976a).

All of this might be true. It certainly fits familiar ways of viewing social behavior. But is it the most plausible representation of why people care about justice? There are at least two reasons why one might search for other alternatives. First, if you are at all impressed with phenomenological data, then the cost-minimization view of why people care about justice for themselves or others simply does not correspond with what people experience. Most people seem to act according to the rules of justice simply because it is the "natural" thing to do. There are no internally administered or anticipated future "pellets" or successful "avoidance of shocks" that one can detect.

Secondly, it seems much more plausible that the transformation of raw self-interest into more effectively organized rules of conduct requires the kind of intelligence, symbolic processes, memory, and problem solving capability that could only be located in the individual "psyche." No social device contains the processes required for the "collective wisdom" needed to invent or shape the "social contract." On the other hand, it is possible to see the development of the "sense of justice" in each child and the continual reinvention of the meaningful variations of the "social contract" by children at play (Freud, 1930, Piaget, 1965).

A composite picture can be pieced together from the remarkably convergent and at times complementary observations generated by social scientists of diverse theoretical stripes. For example, children seem to begin life as biologically dominated organisms. Their behavior is characterized by rather unmoderated and direct expressions of impulses to reduce biological tensions. They seem to do that which feels best at that moment with little awareness or regard for the future consequences of their acts. Certainly any significant interruption or delay of gratification sets off an emotional display indicating some mixture of pain and aggression.

Later, the child controls this impulsive behavior, and is able to tolerate the frustration of the impulse to obtain immediate gratification in order to engage in an activity designed to be more profitable in the long run. As the developmental process unfolds, increasingly greater parts of the child's activities reflect this change from a "pleasure" to a "reality" principle. A developing cognitive structure would make this possible. In any given situation the child could remember alternative sequences of activities with attendant consequences. Given the ability to anticipate various outcomes and their costs in terms of efforts, risks, etc., the child can elect the desired course of action. The growing capacity to retain and abstract from past experiences, and the ability to use these to generate "alternative futures" symbolically, sets the stage for the child to make a rationally self-interested choice. As children mature they can recognize that their interests would be best served in the long run by planned efforts to cope with the situational contingencies and environmental demands. Of course whether or not the child does in fact elect to behave more rationally will depend on the willingness to forego more immediate gratifications in order to engage in activities that may not only be relatively unpleasant, but may also involve costly efforts.

When will the child do all of this? The answers that have been generated lead us to the themes of justice and deserving. Apparently, what is required for the willingness to delay immediate gratification of long-term benefits is a sufficient trust that one's environment is so constructed that the initial stages of an activity, which involve the investment of effort and cost in goals denied will in fact lead to the expected, more desirable outcomes in the future. Also required are the appropriate psychological mechanisms to control the internal demand for the immediate expression of desires—letting go and doing just what feels good at the moment. The former we have described metaphorically as the "belief in a just world," (Lerner, 1980) without which, we have suggested, people could not function effectively. And the latter is the "personal contract" that portrays the continuing inner dialogue between the more rational aspect of the self and the immediately experienced impulses.

The terms of the "contract" arise from the promise to one's self that the long-term benefits will in fact be worth the costs of postponing the gratification of more immediate desires and the investment of time and effort. The "intelligent" part of the self maintains control over the "impulsive" part by erecting the psychological structure of the personal contract. The sense of entitlement derives from the promisory nature of this "contract." The person comes to expect the latter, more desirable outcomes. Any failure to acquire those outcomes generates a sense of betrayal, of a promise to one's self unfulfilled. The experience of entitlement is the cognitive-affective representation of this inner conflict and the conditional quality of its resolution. In this manner the inner-dialogue generates the psychological roots of the sense of deserving—of being entitled to a particular set of outcomes by virtue of what one has done, one has invested.

One implication of these assumptions is that given a reasonably stable environment involving clear contingencies between various acts and outcomes, the developing human organism with its cognitive potential and experiential demands would generate a psychology of entitlement-deserving without the necessary proesence of other people. Presumably the solitary, feral child would grow up to recognize how to build a hut in order to stay warm and dry, and that it would be worth going through the efforts to do it. If, after the work is completed the hut is unexpectedly trampled by elephants or destroyed by lightning, the reaction would not be simply the expression of negative effect. There is good reason to expect that the adult's imagination would create and name "forces" that not only explain what happened, but make it seem both "appropriate" and avoidable given the right "magic" (Kelsen, 1946).

What we have said up to this point is that in the "normal" course of development the child will place increasingly greater areas of goal-seeking activities within the structure of a "personal contract" which orients the child to "deserving" the desired outcomes. The viability of this "contract" is never absolute. The person must generate sufficient trust in the "justness" of the world in order to maintain control over the impulsive urges which demand more immediate gratification. In any case, we are positing the creation of a psychological "structure" out of the blending of intelligence with self-interest, which remains at the service of and vulnerable to the person's self-interest. The introduction of other people in to the person's attempts to organize goal-seeking around the theme of deserving leads to the construction of the "social contract." In order to be able to "deserve" one's own outcomes the person must adopt procedures that both enable and require the other's in one's world to do likewise. From this perspective the concern with justice for others and the forms it takes are derived from and shaped by everyone's enlightened self-interested desire to organize their own goal-seeking around "deserving" what they desire.

The Development of the "Personal Contract" and the Psychology of Entitlement

The research concerned with the development of justice and the commitment to deserving has employed a procedure developed by Walt Mischel (1973) to assess the willingness to "delay gratification" as a rough, indirect way of approximating the extent to which children were committed to their "personal contract". That research had shown that fourth grade children could be roughly separated by a median split on the basis of their reactions to that measure into those who seemed strongly committed to an equity rule of deserving even when it was costly for them (High DG), and those (Low DG) who understood this rule of deserving but whenever they were not threatened with public sanctions acted on the basis of immediate, direct self interest (Braband & Lerner, 1975; Long & Lerner, 1974).

More recent research (Lerner & Meindl, 1980) suggests that apparently, the third-fourth grade ages are a pivotal period for the private commitments to a justice of equity based upon the assessment of relative contribution and a justice of equality or parity where each member deserves the same amount. For example, we know from other research that as early as grade 1 or before very young children know these two rules of justice. They are aware of the normative expectations concerning the appropriate use of one or the other rule; and they are particularly sensitive to these norms will regard to their relationships to others who are likely to benefit or be harmed by their actions (Anderson & Butzin, 1978; Lerner, 1974a; Nelson & Dweck, 1977). We found, however, that it is not until approximately the fourth grade that children make a strong private commitment to the "equity" form of justice (Lerner & Meindl, 1980). The High DG fourth-grade children who, theoretically, had the stronger commitment to a "personal contract" followed a contributions rule—justice of equity when they were "coworkers"—and a justice of parity when they were "team members," *regardless of whether that meant they would have less or more of the pay*. And they did this whether they were under public scrutiny or annonymous. The Low DG fourth-grade children who presumably had a less well developed "personal contract" followed either of these rules of justice in their allocations only under conditions of adult surveillance or when it allowed them to keep more money.

The third grade children who were only a year younger revealed an intriguingly different pattern under conditions of anonymity. They appeared to be fixated on one or another form of justice. For example, the Low DG children divided their pay equally with other children even at greater cost to themselves and even when they had made the larger contribution. They did this whether they were team-members of coworkers. The High DG children also ignored their relation to the other child-worker and allocated the pay completely on the basis of relative contribution. Thus, it appears quite plausible that the pivotal process in the child's commitment to a contributions rule of justice (equity) is the development of various degrees of commitment to the "personal contract."

A summary of this line of research indicates quite clearly that *the awareness of the appropriate social norms occurs earlier than the psychological commitment in rules of deserving;* and that among the younger children, the assessed *willingness or ability to defer immediate gratification co-occurs with and is roughly predictive of the commitment to deserving in their behavior*. What ever determines the development of the processes and structure metaphorically described as *the "personal contract," occurs with or mediates the child's willingness to accept and comply with the terms of the "social contract"*—to be fair to others as well as one's self.

The "Personal Contract" and Adult Behavior

The metaphor of the "personal contract" and the psychological processes associated with it have also proven valuable in enabling us to take another look at the way adults respond to the needs of others—the opportunity to be altruistic. The personal contract is essentially a description of a psychological structure which reflects the shaping and guiding of self-interest by the emergence of human intelligence. The sense of deserving and entitlement appears in our lives as the experiential representation of this shaping and guiding process. The promisory quality implicit in the experience of "entitlement" derives from an implicit dialogue between the appetitive and the intelligent aspects of the self.

The most ambitious theoretical derivation from these assumptions is that in the normal course of development, given reasonably stable environment, people will organize their goal-seeking around the related concerns of deserving and justice. The desire to maximize one's outcomes or minimize costs is translated into the desire to gain as much as possible for one's self within the terms of and while maintaining the commitment to the personal contract, striving to deserve what one wants. The assumption is that although the person in highly invested in maintaining the commitment to the personal contract, there are two kinds of potential threats to the ability to maintain that commitment. *Internally,* there is always the greater or lesser impulse to do just that which feels good, regardless of any notions of deserving. This internal threat is exacerbated by any *evidence from the environment* that the contract is not viable. Consequently, the concern with justice for others who are a part of one's psychological world is an intelligent derivative of this commitment to the personal contract for one's self. The clear inference is that, other things being equal, my own "deserving" takes precedence over my concern for yours. And in fact, if there were no implicit or explcit contingencies between our fates, i.e., implications for the viability of my personal contract, my well being and deserving, from what happens to you, I would not be concerned at all with your suffering, deprivation, etc. Or I might be concerned to the extent I see your fate as the occasion to act out some other valued agendas, e.g., express my superiority, establish claim to special statuses in our society, etc. In accordance with this perspective, research has found that coming to the aid of a victim and sensitivity to their deservingness will occur if such responsiveness does not pose a threat to the actor's own deservingness (Holmes, Miller, & Lerner, 1974; Miller, 1977, a, 1977b; Miller & Smith, in press). For example, Miller (1977b) illustrated the dynamics associated with the person's commitment to the "personal contract." An opportunity to eliminate the undeserved suffering of others—an injustice—that also required them to have less than they deserved operated as a deterrent to work on a task for which they would be paid. They were less willing to work under those circumstances than when they could keep the money they deserved for themselves. However when there was sufficient money for them to meet the requirements of their own deserving, while providing additional money to correct an injustice for others, that became a strong incentive to work—even stronger than if they could have kept all of the money for themselves.

So, clearly and once again, both justice and altruism are portrayed as instrumental devices to further our self-interest, and maximize our outcomes. They are personal and social tools invented to increase one's general level of satisfaction. By implication, at least, that is equivalent to Walster et al.'s assertion that people will follow the rules of justice only so long as that offers the promise of greatest profit (Walster et al., 1978). If it appears to be more profitable to act in some other way—even unjustly—people will do so.

But that is probably not true.

JUSTICE MOTIVE THEORY II:
A NEW LOOK AT WHY AND HOW PEOPLE
CARE ABOUT JUSTICE

Self-interest as a Trivial Motive in Comparison With Justice

Unless we are willing to stretch the meaning of "profit," "self-interest," and "maximize outcomes" to the point where they lose all substantive meaning and can be defined only tautologically, then there is ample evidence that this instrumental conception of how we act accounts for only a minor part of our behavior.

There is considerable evidence that people place the concern for others welfare—their justice—ahead of their own deserving. There are probably complex social psychological processes involved in getting young men to go to war—interrupt what they had worked for and deserved in order to risk their lives—for "them." However, this is a clear example of where, for a large number of people, the concern for the common good or its symbolic representation, takes precedence over all their other goals, including their own deserving.

Actually, for most adults in our society the greater part of their efforts are designed *manifestly* to benefit others, and whatever benefits accrue to themselves is indirect and derivative. What one does at work to acquire desired resources, how one allocates these resources, and how one expends whatever additional resources, time energy is *explicitly* directed toward benefiting others either directly or toward meeting one's obligations to the social unit. The only way one can possibly rescue the self-serving assumption is by construing all social behavior as essentially an "exchange" where everyone anticipates and receives compensation *later,* for their manifestly other-oriented acts. That may be an accurate interpretation of the strategy underlying a greater or lesser part of human behavior; however, the important point here is that the exchange proposition is a theoretical invention to explain, or explain away, the overwhelming evidence that contradicts the common assumption that people are motivated by self-serving ends. In fact, for the most part, people *do not act* in obviously self-serving ways. As citizens, parents, spouses, good employees, etc. we devote most of what we have and our efforts for the benefit of others; and we do it as naturally, if not more so, than what we might do for "ourselves." For the most part, considerations of entitlement and deserving shape these other-oriented activities.

Probably the most eloquent testimony to the power of the theme of justice appears in the way victims of injustice handle their own fates. There is every reason for victims to resist actively, emotionally what has happened to them. Although many do, many others do not and it is the latter reaction that is most fascinating. There is, on the one hand, the victim's desire to believe that people get what they deserve. So why not accept what has happened and find justice in the event? To do that would jeopordize their ability to act in their own behalf to eliminate their suffering and deprivation. That would also threaten their self-concept with the implication they are weak, inferior, and undesirable. It is rather amazing then that various investigators have shown that often the threat to the victim's sense of self worth is of less consequence than the importance of finding justice in their fate (Beck, 1967; Bulman & Wortman, 1977; Chodoff, Friedman, & Hamburg, 1964; Kubler-Ross, 1969). The more carefully documented experimental findings are, if anything, more dramatic.

Rubin and Peplau (1975), for example, found a measurable lowering of self-esteem among young men who had learned that there was a high probability that they were the victims of the draft lottery. Could they allow themselves to believe that the ''chance'' drawing of a slip was all that distinguished them from the others who would not have to suffer that terrible fate? Apparently not, and among other reactions they saw themselves as less desirable people. In an even more carefully constructed situation, Comer and Laird (1975) showed that people who were by chance assigned to the very unpleasant task of having to eat a caterpillar while others would do something much more pleasant, not only engaged in self-derogation, but this experimentally induced effect persisted for some time. This was revealed by their subsequently being released from their initial unpleasant fate and then given the chance to suffer electric shocks or not. Remarkably enough, those initially deemed as victims tended to perpetuate this assigned fate by voluntarily electing the shock.

One implication of all this is clear. *If the commitment to justice is an instrumental derivative of self-interest then there is overwhelming evidence that, for adults, it has assumed the "functionally autonomous" status as the dominant goal in the person's life.*

But even this derivative interpretation is less plausible in light of what we see with very young children. We have described the developmental process which presumably mediates the appearance of differing degrees of commitment to certain kinds of justice (e.g., an equity form based upon relative contributions or inputs) and the personal contract. It is also evident, however, that the commitment to justice per se appears very early in the child's life. At that time the commitment seems to be based upon status—who one is. As early as 3 and 4 years of age, children apply status-based rules of entitlement in their allocations (Damon, 1976; Nelson & Dweck, 1977). Of course, even at that early age, one cannot rule out the causal role of prior conditioning. But clearly it strains credulity to impute an instrumental strategy base to the very young child's justice-dominated acts. We know that children are not that foresighted or guileful at that age. Their judgments of and reactions to entitlement are much more automatic than is implied by any of the instrumental models of justice.

So where do these observations and findings lead us? What have we learned from this analysis? One conclusion is that *our attempts to understand ''justice'' oriented or altruistic behavior have led to their translation into events and processes that fit prior assumptions about human behavior generally.* Certainly in retrospect that is quite obvious; what else could we have done? That brings us to the second conclusion: *every such translation has generated a poor fit.* They have done violence to the available data by ignoring or retranslating the most obvious evidence into awkward derivations to make them fit prior assumptions.

Guidelines for a Theory of Justice in Human Affairs

More constructively, what we have learned from this analysis can serve as potential guidelines for a more adequate model of justice and altruistic behavior. In the first place, it simply does not make sense to approach such enormous and important parts of our lives as if they were derivative or instrumental derivatives of other underlying, more powerful, or basic personal agendas. There appears to be no more powerful and ubiquitous theme in human affairs than the personal and institutionalized concern with justice and deserving. Also, people voluntarily, if that term has any meaning at all, give away most of their resources and gain most of their "satisfaction" from doing for others. If this is true then it is highly doubtful that social psychologists will be able to invent a mechanism or set of mechanisms that provide a satisfactory explanation for how the weak and peripheral desires in our lives generate and control those events that dominate our private and social world.

Perhaps the best clue that we might gain from our past efforts is that we should avoid trying to treat altruistic and justice-dominated behaviors as if they were derivative and instrumental. Instead, *we should reexamine and modify our underlying model of the psychology of social relations in light of what we have learned about the civilized aspects of human behavior, the concern with justice, and one's relation to others.*

There is one other highly germaine set of observations that has not been discussed here. It is an important fact of our social life that what people view as just and deserved varies from situation to situation. This variability is not random or idiosyncratic but systematic in fashion. There are clear patterns to the forms that justice and deserving take in any given context. For example, it has been pointed out that very often one can see a "Justice of Need" appear in the way parents allocate resources among family members. A "Justice of Equality" often dominates the relationship between friends, or those who want to maintain harmonious relations, whereas a justice based upon the assessment of proportional contributions occurs most frequently in situations where there is an emphasis on productivity—a work milieu. And, in the situations where everyone has the desire for a scarce resource, a rule of Justified Self Interest appears whereby every member is entitled to compete on their own behalf (Lerner, 1974b). Not only have there been attempts to organize these forms of justice into a coherent framework (Deutsch, 1975; Lerner, 1974a, 1975, 1977; Lerner et al., 1976; Leventhal, 1976a; Sampson, 1975; Walster & Walster, 1975), early experimental efforts have yielded valuable data delineating and specific interpersonal and situational cues which elicit a particular form of justice (Lerner, 1974b).

In the most general sense, what we have learned is that *the operative judgments of "who" is entitled to "what" depend directly on the perceived relation among the participants in the encounter.* More importantly, there is a clear pattern to the appearance of these perceptions. For all intents and purposes once a "relationship" is perceived there is an organized quality to the person's construction of the event. The various elements, including the judgments of entitlement they take on a sense of "appropriateness" or "requiredness" as described by Gestalt theorists (Asch, 1946; Kohler, 1929). That, of course, would help to explain why people experience the sense of justice or injustice in such immediate and direct ways. For example, when confronted with a violation of the "required" event, we experience immediate and compelling demands. This occurs even though there was no awareness of an explicit concern with justice, much less a set of rules that we were applying in our calculations of who deserved what. What is also interesting to reflect upon at this point is what could be the source of the often powerful motivation we experience when confronted with an injustice? Cahn (1949) tried to capture the strength and the immediacy of the reaction by describing it as the experience of a direct assault upon one's self. And maybe it is, in a sense. In any case, we can now move on to the recasting of the social psychology of justice and altruism.

JUSTICE MOTIVE THEORY II: THE PSYCHOLOGICAL CONSTRUCTION OF SOCIAL ENCOUNTERS

Relevant Developmental and Cognitive Processes

It is not possible to describe the proposed model fully, but for the purposes of this chapter we should be able to provide an outline of the basic assumptions from which most of the remaining hypotheses can be inferred.

A core set of assumptions is that people organize their experiences, not only in the historical sense but more importantly in the dynamics of each encounter. They create meaning, which provides continuity and stability to their activities. Obviously, then, the person is supremely invested in maintaining an organized structure of the environment. Given an invested structure, new information is processed and fit within the organizing framework. The central motivational force probably stems from the need to protect the integrity of this organizational structure. If one is looking for functional bases of this force, it could easily be posited that in order to operate effectively on the environment the person needs the order and stability generated by this organized structure.

These assumptions are not at all radical or unfamiliar, but if we are to generate a usable model we need to provide more information about the nature of the psychological structures and processes that determine the way the person organizes the perceptual imputs. Our initial efforts to find patterns in social judgments of deserving and justice yielded evidence for three kinds of relations that appear in the way we view others. These were defined roughly as: (1) an *Identity* relation, where we are psychologically indistinguishable from the other and we experience that which we perceive they are experiencing; (2) a *Unit* relation where we perceive ourselves as distinct but similar to the other on relevant dimensions; and (3) *Nonunit* relation based upon the perception of being different than they in ways that are meaningful and have value (Lerner, 1975, 1977).

We also described important developmental events whereby the child learns and is able to manipulate sequences of activities that generate a conception of impersonal "processes"—ways of acting and producing outcomes which are independant of any given individual. Not only does this enable the child-adult to develop a "personal contract" orientation to deserving their outcomes but, in addition, it provides them with a way of viewing their own and others activities. People can be seen in "positional" terms, as actors, located at one or another stage in an impersonal activity. Once the child understands and can make use of the information that there are alternative ways of acting in any given context, then the behavior of others can be assessed in terms of their choice in electing a given sequence. In addition, their behavior at any given moment can be viewed as reflecting their position in an elected or imposed process (Lerner, 1975; Piaget, 1965).

At this point, we can begin to think of the cognitive structuring of social relations from a developmental perspective. We will assume that the child seeks to generate an organized construction of the world. The patterns of early experiences, especially those associated with important and enduring consequences provide the outline of this construction. Given the child's investment in creating order and continuity, these early outlines provide the integrative structure for processing new information. Thus, with additional experience they will remain viable if they are sufficiently "valid" and effective so that their integrity does not disintegrate in the face of overwhelmingly "surprising," or contravening experiences.

Interestingly enough, one can find plausible scenarios for the appearance of developmental analogues for these three "kinds of relations" in the typical experiences of growing up in our culture. The earliest would be the persistent and powerful empathic experience of sharing the emotional state of others. In particular this reaction is most likely to appear when others transmit certain affective cues. There are even stronger associations of this "identity" reaction with others with whom one has been closely associated during this early period, such as members of one's family, etc. That is one kind of relation with others.

The other two appear somewhat later as the child interacts in various contexts with others with whom there is a perception of similarities and differences. Important areas of their lives become organized, defined in terms of this kind of judgment. How they are treated by others in their world—parents, peers, etc. is determined in patterned ways. They come to experience the same outcomes as those who are treated and defined as the same: same age, same sex, same neighborhood, etc. They are given "more or less," treated more or less well than those who are "different" than they. The "similar" ones are more likely to generate positive affect, act cooperatively whereas the "different" ones are the competitors, hindrances, to what one wants. Conceivably, these early, preceptually contingent experiences would generate the prevalent tendency among humans to favor one's own kind versus "them" on almost any dimension of similarity-difference. Tajfel (1970) has referred to this as the "Generic Norm."

Presumably then, these three interpersonally contingent kinds of early experiences provide the basic templates for the way people define and view their relations to others. Initially the various meaning elements appeared together. The perception of others as "identical," "similar," or "different" are combined with ways of treating one another: respectively, they would be nurturant and vicarious, generally cooperative, or generally hindering and competitive. There are also appropriate sets of outcomes: increase "their–our" sense of well-being, share equally, and have more or less.

In the course of maturation the experiences of a child engaging in more extended goal acquisition engenders an elaboration on this structure. The comprehension and use of impersonal processes in goal acquisition enables the child to separate the activities associated with the three kinds of relations. In other words, the child learns that it is possible to work cooperatively with one of "them" and to compete with one of "us," and, at times, to engage in "identity" based activities with anyone. The "identity" activities are those activities designed to allow another person to acquire a desired resource. Our only "acquisition" of the resource in question under these circumstances occurs vicariously, as we experience some form of that which the other who having gained the resource, is experiencing (see Table 10.1).

In any given situation, however, the person resynthesizes the perceived relation to the other, and task-relevant acquisition process into an organized construction of the event. In the synthesis either the perceived relation or acquisition process assumes dominance as "figure," whereas the other becomes "ground." Once constructed the resultant cognitions, affect, and activities emerge. They appear in the stream of actions with one another, having the experiential concommitant of a "good Gestalt," a sense of requiredness, appropriateness. As portrayed here, the assessment of "who" is entitled to "what" is no less an inherent aspect of any encounter than the recognition of the activities I must engage in to get what I want, and my perception of who the other person is and how they help or hinder me. *The term "emergent activities" is intended to*

TABLE 10.1
Perceived Relationship and Associated Cognitive Elements[a]

Associated cognitive elements	Perceived Relationship		
	Identity	*Unit*	*Non-Unit*
Person perception	same 'me"	similar "us"	different "them"
Activity relation to goal	vicarious; dependency	mutually facilitative;	hindering; divergent
Outcomes	need; welfare	equality; equivalence	more/less

[a](adapted from Lerner, 1978; Lerner and Whitehead, 1980).

capture the elements of immediacy and requiredness associated with the person's organized construction of an interpersonal encounter. The construction includes acts, actors, and assessments of appropriate outcomes. The net result of "Who does what," "with," "to," or "for whom," emerges out of three factors:

1. *the perceived relation to the other(s),*
2. *process involved in goal acquisition, and*
3. *the relative salience of these (figure-ground). The resultant organized construction is experienced as a demand, an integrated impulse to act and feel and think in a particular way.*

What is being proposed, then, is that in any encounter with another person we attend to and process cues of *who they are* in terms of identity, similar, or different, and *where we stand in relation to what we want:* I can only experience my goals vicariously through you, or our goals are convergent, or our goals are divergent requiring contravening acts. The proposition that *these are integrated* so that the *more salient aspect generates the focus of organization* whereas the other provides the limiting conditions leads to 18 rather than nine ways in which we construe our interpersonal encounters.

Some Examples of "Emergent Activities"

If there is any validity to this conceptual system we should be able to take even these crude definitial statements and propositions and, by using some of the familiar meaning elements associated with these terms, generate recognizable descriptions of these *Emergent Activities*. Unfortunately, we simply do not have an adequate language system for designating more precisely those processes subsumed under the labels of *"Vicarious Dependent,"* or *"Unit Related-Convergent Goals,"* or *"Nonunit Divergent Goals."* Nor can we do any better at this point with the perceptual categories which frame how we perceive others—*Identity, Unit, or Nonunit.* Fortunately we do have enough understanding of these structural elements and the processes to begin generating meaningful descriptions of each of the ways in which they can appear in our lives (see Table 10.2).

Although it will not be possible to attempt a complete explication of each *Emergent Activity* it should be evident from the descriptive labels alone that "altruistic-like" behaviors occur in a variety of interpersonal contexts involving rather distinct psychological constructions. For example, some of the more familiar acts occur under conditions where there is a scarce resource (Nonunit Process) and we identify with the other(s) involved (Identity Relation) (see the upper right cell in Table 10.2). Under these conditions, if the empathic tie is dominant it would be natural for us to engage in acts which we or others might label as self-sacrificial or martydom. However, with that emotional bond we of course vicariously share in their fate. We experience their pain or rescue. When the acquisition process—the resources in question—is the focus of our construction then our identification with the other(s) is viewed in a more impersonal way. From the problem-solving perspective that emerges, the sense of identity with other(s) leads us to attempts to minimize the overall amount of deprivation that we would incur collectively over an extended time span. We perceive ourselves and others as occupants of various positions in the relevant process, and our reactions reflect a psychological representation of a utilitarian decision.

As one scans Table 10.2 it is easy to detect contexts in which other altruistic-like acts appear with all the requiredness of an "entitlement." This is particularly obvious in any of the "Identity" relations (top row in Table 10.2). However, when I perceive you as similar to me, more or less equivalent in essential respects (Unit Relation) (middle row in Table 10.2), then "altruistic" acts appear most often when you are dependent on me for the acquisition of a desired resource. If, as in *Identity Process* situations I cannot directly share in the resource, our perceived equivalence leads to the anticipation of the *same* outcomes. This entitlement takes the shape of the appropriateness of reciprocal acts, either in an immediate and direct way (as occurs when Relation is dominant) or in a more functional, adaptive way, over a longer time span as is characteristic of the problem-solving perspective that appears when Process is dominant (middle cell, first column in Table 10.2).

And finally, some of the most important, or at least, dramatic altruistic-like acts often appear when there is the perception of both *Nonunit Process* and *Nonunit Relation* where Relation is dominant (see the bottom right cell in Table 10.2). In this context, the activities that emerge include the sacrifice of one's own resources in the apparent service of one's own kind who have directly or

TABLE 10.2
Summary of Emergent Activities[a]

Relation to Other	Process		
	Identity (vicarious; dependent)	Unit (convergent goals)	Nonunit (divergent goals)
Identity ("same")	nurturant concern for other's welfare / meeting other's needs	collective orientation / individual oriented commune	utilitarian decisions / martyrdom, self sacrifice
Unit ("similar")	mutual responsiveness / reciprocity	cooperation, relative contribution equity / team effort, parity	parallel competition, justified self-interest / formal contest
Nonunit ("different")	evaluating other's acts (corresponds with individual's goals) / judging other's personal worth (corresponds with individual's values)	contractual relations, mock equity / status consistent division of labour	regulated conflict, maximizing legal outcomes / "fight," maximize differential outcomes

[a]Note: In the upper right half of the cell, process is dominant; In the lower left half of the cell, relation is dominant.

symbolically been harmed or demeaned by "them." Who could be considered more altruistic than the warrior who lays down his life and fortune for his country, or the boyfriend who risks getting his nose broken to regain the honor of his fair damsel? Although this form of heroics may appear to have some of the same selfless elements as described earlier in the self-sacrifical behavior that occurs in Identity Relations, it is quite distinct psychologically in terms of motives and goals. This form of heroics is designed to maintain the Nonunit relationship to "them." The issue here is a conflict over the scarce resource of superior status. The person's sacrifice is designed to protect the image of one's own kind as better than "them." Actually an active program of research has been generated recently to document and test many of the implications of the underlying dynamics involved in heroically based altruism and aggression (Meindl & Lerner, 1980).

A Final Word on "Strategies" and the Appearance of Selfish Behavior

One last word about important aspects of the theory that have not yet been described here. We have described elsewhere the ways in which people develop strategies and metastrategies for managing the experienced demands which occur with the Emergent Activities (Lerner & Whitehead, 1980). The need for strategies arises from the realization that each encounter has implications for the actor's future interactions with others. My own desires for a given resource and the way I allocate it is shaped by my remembered and anticipated relations with many other people, including those in my family, work group, etc. Also, in our culture most acquisitional efforts involve a considerable time span with a variety of others, each of whom is capable of eliciting any of the three kinds of Relations on the basis of the cues they emit. They could display important qualities of similarity, or difference, or elicit an empathic reaction. In order to act effectively in a "work" context for example, we develop strategies, as individuals and as part of our social institutions to govern and control our perceived relations to others.

   Probably the most easily described strategy of particular relevance to our understanding of what we can see happening around is the prevalence in our culture, both institutionalized and private, of the use of "Mock-Equity" (Nonunit Relation, Unit Process, Process dominant) as an initial orientation to new encounters. The "Mock-Equity" strategy is highly functional in that it enables us to interact cooperatively with others while maintaining our perception that they are really "different" from us. With that perception we are able to act essentially in our own behalf without regard for the other(s) whenever the circumstances permit. The familiar "Equity" form that this kind of contractual based cooperation takes probably stems from its similarity to the "personal contract" where each person's outcomes resembles their efforts and deprivations, at least on a proportional basis. Unfortunately, the prevalence of this strategy in our culture, particularly in work relationships has led social scientists to believe the dynamics and form of "Mock Equity" are the only strategy by which people determine entitlements and justice (Homans, 1961; Walster et al., 1978). This belief has gained considerable support primarily because most of the research, virtually all of it, that has been done in this area has occurred in an employment-work context. And of course, it is in those contexts that we have instititionalized *the norms which dictate that we can and should do whatever is legitimate to serve our own ends.*

And that observation of course brings us back to the beginning of this chapter.

ACKNOWLEDGMENT

The writing of this chapter was facilitated by Canada Council Grant 573-0194 and Social Sciences and Humanities Research Council Grant 410-77-0601-X1 to Melvin J. Lerner.

REFERENCES

Anderson, N. H., & Butzin, C. A. Integration theory applied to children's judgments of equity. *Developmental Psychology,* 1978, *14,* 593–606.

Asch, S. Forming impressions of personality. *Journal of Abnormal and Social Psychology,* 1946, *41,* 258–290.

Beck, A. T. *Depression: Clinical, experimental, and theoretical aspects.* New York: Harper & Row, 1967.

Braband, J., & Lerner, M. J. "A little time and effort"—Who deserves what from whom? *Personality and Social Psychology Bulletin,* 1975, *1,* 177–181.

Bulman, R. J., & Wortman, C. B. Attributions of blame and coping in the "real world": Severe accident victims react to their lot. *Journal of Personality and Social Psychology,* 1977, *35,* 351–363.

Cahn, E. *The sense of injustice,* New York: N.Y.U., 1949.

Campbell, D. T. Ethnocentricsm and other altruistic motives. In D. Levine (Ed.), *Nebraska Symposium on Motivation.* Lincoln, Nebraska: University of Nebraska Press, 1972.

Comer, R., & Laird, J. D. Choosing to suffer as a consequence of expecting to suffer: Why do people do it? *Journal of Personality and Social Psychology,* 1975, *32,* 92–101.

Chodoff, P., Friedman, S. B., & Hamburg, D. A. Stress, defenses and coping behavior: Observations in parents of children with malignant diseases. *American Journal of Psychiatry,* 1964, *120,* 743–749.

Damon, W. *The social world of the child.* San Francisco: Jossey-Bass, 1976.

Darley, J. M., & Latané, B. Bystander intervention in emergencies: Diffusion of responsibility. *Journal of Personality and Social Psychology,* 1968, *8,* 377–383.

Deutsch, M. Equity, equality, and need: What determines which value will be used as the basis of distributive justice? *Journal of Social Issues,* 1975, *31,* 137–149.

Freud, S. *Civilization and its discontents.* London: Hogarth, 1930.

Holmes, J. G., Miller, D. T., & Lerner, M. J. *Symbolic threat in helping situations: The "exchange fiction."* Unpublished manuscript, University of Waterloo, 1974.

Homans, G. C. *Social behavior: Its elementary forms.* New York: Harcourt & Brace, 1961.

Kelsen, H. *Society and nature: A sociological inquiry*. London: Kegan Paul, 1946.

Kohler, W. *Gestalt psychology*. New York: Liveright, 1929.

Kubler-Ross, E. *On death and dying*. New York: MacMillan, 1969.

Lerner, M. J. Evaluation of performances as a function of performer's reward and attractiveness. *Journal of Personality and Social Psychology*, 1965, *1*, 355-360.

Lerner, M. J. *Children's acceptance or rejection of a martyr*. Unpublished manuscript, University of Kentucky, 1968.

Lerner, M. J. The justice motive: "Equity" and "parity" among children. *Journal of Personality and Social Psychology*, 1974, *29*, 539-550. (a)

Lerner, M. J. Social psychology of justice and interpersonal attraction. In T. Huston (Ed.), *Foundations of Interpersonal Attraction*. New York: Academic Press, 1974. (b)

Lerner, M. J. The justice motive in social behavior. *Journal of Social Issues*, 1975, *31*, 1-19.

Lerner, M. J. The justice motive: Some hypotheses as to its origins and forms. *Journal of Personality*, 1977, *45*, 1-52.

Lerner, M. J. *The justice motive in social behaviour: hypotheses as to its origins and form II*. Social Sciences and Humanities Research Council Grant Proposal, 1978.

Lerner, M. J. *The belief in a just World: A fundamental delusion*. New York: Plenum, 1980.

Lerner, W. J., & Meindl, J. R. *The justice motive and self interest: Some factors influencing the emergence of "equity" and "parity" among children*. Manuscript submitted for publication, 1980.

Lerner, M. J., & Miller, D. T. Just world research and the attribution process: Looking back and ahead. *Psychological Bulletin*, 1978, *85*, 1030-1051.

Lerner, M. J. & Simmons, C. H. The observer's reaction to the "innocent victim": Compassion or rejection. *Journal of Personality and Social Psychology*, 1966, *4*, 203-210.

Lerner, M. J., & Whitehead, L. A. Procedural justice viewed in the context of justice motive theory. In G. Mikula (Ed.), *Justice in Social Interaction*. Bern: Huber, 1980.

Leventhal, G. S. Fairness in social relationships. In J. W. Thibaut, J. T. Spence, & R. C. Carson (Eds.), *Contemporary topics in social psychology*. Morristown, N.J.: General Learning Press, 1976. (a)

Leventhal, G. S. The distribution of rewards and resources in groups and organizations. In L. Berkowitz & E. Walster (Eds.), *Advances in Experimental Social Psychology*, Vol. 9, New York: Academic Press, 1976. (b)

Long, G. T., & Lerner, M. L. Deserving, the "personal contract," and altruistic behavior by children. *Journal of Personality and Social Psychology*, 1974, *29*, 551-556.

Meindl, J. R., & Lerner, M. J. *Heroics in an interpersonal situation*. Manuscript submitted for publication, 1980.

Miller, D. T. Altruism and threat to a belief in a just world. *Journal of Experimental Social Psychology*, 1977, *13*, 113-124. (a)

Miller, D. T. Personal deserving versus justice for others: An exploration of the justice motive. *Journal of Experimental Social Psychology*, 1977, *13*, 1-13. (b)

Miller, D. T., & Smith, J. The effects of own deservingness and deservingness of others on children's helping behavior. *Child Development*, in press.

Mischel, W. Processes in delay of gratification. In L. Berkowitz (Ed.), *Advances in experimental social psychology* (vol. 7). New York: Academic Press, 1973.

Nelson, S. A., & Dweck, C. S. Motivation and competence as determinants of young children's reward allocation. *Developmental Psychology*, 1977, *13*, 192-197.

Piaget, J. *The moral development of the child*. New York: Free Press, 1965.

Rubin, Z., & Peplau, A. Who believes in a just world? *Journal of Social Issues*, 1975, (3), 65-89.

Sampson, E. E. On justice as social equality. *Journal of Social Issues*, 1975, *31*, 46-64.

Schwartz, S. The justice of need and the activation of humanitarian norms. *Journal of Social Issues*, 1975, *31*, 111-136.

Tajfel, H. Experiments in intergroup discrimination. *Scientific American,* 1970, *223,* 96–102.

Walster, E., & Piliavin, J. A. Equity and the innocent bystander. *Journal of Social Issues,* 1972, *28,* 165–189.

Walster, E., & Walster, G. W. Equity and social justice: An essay. *Journal of Social Issues,* 1975, *31,* 21–44.

Walster, E., Walster, G. W., & Berscheid, E. *Equity: Theory and research.* Boston: Allyn & Bacon, 1978.

11 Emotion and Altruism

David L. Rosenhan
Stanford University

Peter Salovey
Stanford University

Jerzy Karylowski*
Polish Academy of Science, Warsaw

Kenneth Hargis
Stanford University

In this chapter we review and integrate the experimental and theoretical literature on the effects of emotion on altruism. Expect the worst! The task is hazardous, the road often dark and tortured, and your guides quite possibly confused! In part, difficulties arise from the fact that the relevant literatures are often foggy and conflicting. In further measure, the very meanings of emotion, as well as the traditional dichotomies between positive and negative emotion, are all in question. Finally, you will have already read enough of this book to understand that the meaning of altruism is also subject to dispute.

It is in the context of these shifting sands and moving targets then, that we attempt to take aim on the relations between emotion and altruism. We begin by briefly asserting, with little elaboration, a framework for understanding the nature and influence of emotion. We then turn to the experimental literature, examining what is known about the impact of positive and negative affects on altruism. That done, we look into the relevance of these experiments for a variety of theories that attempt to explain the relations between affect and altruism.

*This chapter was prepared when Jerzy Karylowski was at the Department of Psychology, Stanford University, as an American Studies Research Fellow of the American Council of Learned Societies.

233

THE EFFECTS OF EMOTIONS

Emotions intensify attention and magnify cognition: that is their primary psychological function. When emotion is experienced, attention narrows and becomes anchored on those stimuli that appear to provoke the emotion. One probable result of this attentional anchor is that emotion itself is amplified in a feedback loop. Another is that cognitions appropriate to that emotion are triggered. The general pool of available cognitions is reduced and focused: emotion-appropriate cognitions become available and themselves amplify emotion. A third result is that behaviors that are relevant to the emotion and its resultant cognitions are rendered more likely to occur.

Although this sounds like quite a theoretical mouthful, examples are easily come by and make the matter more comprehensible. Recall your exquisite sensitivity towards someone you love, and compare it to your responsiveness to someone whom you don't in the least dislike. In the former instance, the attention and cognitions are intensified, and generate behaviors that are unlikely to occur in the latter case. The presence of emotion distinguishes, cognitively and behaviorally, fighting for keeps from shadow boxing; kissing someone toward whom one feels intense passion, from kissing a sibling with whom one gets along perfectly well; writing a paper to which one has long looked forward, from writing one which merely fulfills a hastily given word.

One simple test of the presence and power of emotion is whether the laws of reinforcement are violated or at least momentarily suspended. It is here that the relation between emotion and altruism acquires its strong theoretical significance (Rosenhan, 1978). The ordinary laws of reinforcement seek to maximize rewards to the self. Technically speaking, they forbid altruism, which by definition is behavior directed towards the welfare of others at the expense of one's own welfare, even of one's life (London, 1970; Rosenhan, 1970). As we shall see, certain affects are the fulcra upon which the ordinary laws of reinforcement are violated. While experiencing those affects, people are led away from stances that maximize their own rewards and find instead that their attention, cognitions, and behaviors are directed towards the needs of others, often without regard for the quid pro quo. Formally (and only formally) altruism is paradoxical in the same sense that neurosis is paradoxical (cf. Mowrer, 1950): Both violate the ordinary laws of reinforcement because of the presence of affect.

With the possible exception of fear, the significance of affect for personality theory and social psychology has been relatively unexplored. In largest part, this omission arises from the inability to induce powerful emotions in the laboratory (fear again excepted). The laboratory has been a relatively sterile place, not the sort of place in which your typical subject would be likely to experience intense affect. Recent advances in the subtlety and skill with which specific affects can be induced promise to change all that and to render the experimental study of emotion more accessible.

Further difficulty is imposed by the very categories of emotion that have been established historically: positive and negative affect. We continue to use those rubrics here. Yet our own belief is that the various negative affects have much less in common than their simple phrase implies: Indeed, their differences may outweigh their similarities. Consider for a moment shame and anger. Both are negative affects. Yet it is hard to think of a set of cognitions or behaviors that they might share in common, and easy to conjure up cognitions and behaviors that would distinguish them. Rather than pooling the "negative affects" by fiat, as it were, it is an important experimental task for the future to disentangle them, to locate their specific commonalities and their significant differences. Perhaps then a psychology of affect, which traces its connections to cognition and behavior will be possible.

That said, we turn now to examine the impact of positive affect on altruism.

THE POSITIVE AFFECTS

Certain positive mood states have been often and powerfully linked to increases in altruism, a fact known to fundraisers long before it was explored experimentally. The earliest laboratory finding in this area is by Berkowitz and Connor (1966) who induced success experiences in adults and found them more willing to help a supervisor make envelopes than were those who failed success orientation, or controls. Isen (1970), using less constrained tasks, found that adults would be more helpful and more charitable following a success induction. Both investigators were struck by the emotional overtones of such experiences with success. Berkowitz and Connor explained their results in terms of the "glow of goodwill" which is generated by success and which makes people more tolerant of the costs of helping. Isen's "warm glow of success" similarly emphasizes the emotional aspects of a success experience.

The "feel good, do good" phenomenon is not limited to success, by any means. Kazdin and Bryan (1971) varied perceived competance and found that subjects who believed themselves more competent were more willing to donate blood in an ongoing drive than those who felt less competent. Similar findings were obtained by Midlarsky and Midlarsky (1973).

Simple, even accidental, good fortune of the most trivial sort, apparently has effects that are similar to those of success and competence. Receiving a cookie for no apparent reason other than spontaneous kindness, finding a dime in a telephone booth (Isen & Levin, 1972) or being given free stationery (Isen, Clark & Schwartz, 1976) predisposes people to help. Such helpfulness, it should be noted, is not directed toward the cookie- or stationery-donor—that would be a quid pro quo—but towards third parties who were not involved in the gift-giving, a matter to which we return shortly.

Success, competence, and good luck are complex mixtures of cognition and emotion. Yet, until recently, investigators in this area believed that it is the affective aspects of these experiences that are significant for altruism. Support for that view has come from a variety of studies. Aderman (1972), for example, asked subjects to read and experience a set of statements taken from Velten (1968). These statements described feelings of "elation" for one group of subjects, and feelings of "depression" for another. Those who were elated were much more willing to volunteer subsequently for an unpleasant experiment than those who were depressed.

What is true for adults has been true for children, and with remarkable consistency: Positive affect promotes helpfulness, sharing, and charitability. Such positive affect may arise from success (Isen, Horn, & Rosenhan, 1973; Rushton & Littlefield, 1979) or from happy memories of an unspecified sort (Moore, Underwood & Rosenhan, 1973; Rosenhan, Underwood & Moore, 1974) but the effects are strikingly positive for altruistic behavior.

Why?   Why should positive affect have such striking effects on prosocial behavior? One possibility is that the experiences that generate positive affect simultaneously have an effect on the way one evaluates one's resources. One is more willing to contribute to charity, for example, because the value of money is lowered after experiencing positive affect. Such a possibility was entertained in two experiments by Isen, Horn & Rosenhan (1973), but unsuccessfully.

Another possibility is that positive affect makes one more attentive to occurrences outside the self, whereas negative affect directs the eye inward. Thus, it can be argued that the effects of positive affect are attentional. Children and adults who experience positive affect are more likely to notice the needs of others than are control subjects or those experiencing negative affect. This hypothesis too, has received serious attention by Underwood, Froming and Moore (1977) but unfortunately, has failed to be confirmed.

One further possibility for which there is increasingly strong and confirming evidence, is that positive affects make available, and intensify, cognitions that are appropriate to those affects. Such a view is taken by Isen, Shalker, Clark and Karp (1978). In one experiment, they demonstrate that subjects who have experienced mere good fortune tend to assess the performance of products which they owned more favorably than those who had not experienced such a fortuitous encounter. In a second study, subjects who had succeeded in a computer game called Star Trek were much more able than those who failed to retrieve words from recently acquired memory. Successful subjects, moreover, recalled more words that were associated with positive personality traits than did subjects who failed.

These findings by Isen and her colleagues (1978) are significant for the relations they establish between affect and cognition. Further work needs to be done in this area before the affect-cognition linkage, and its relation to behavior, is fully understood. There is already some evidence that attentional processes are implicated here. Rosenhan, Salovey and Hargis (in press) induced joy in two groups of subjects. The first group experienced joy for themselves—an egocentric joy. The second group experienced empathic joy for a close friend. Those who experienced egocentric joy were markedly more altruistic towards a third party than those who experienced empathic joy. Indeed, the latter were less altruistic than a comparable control group which did not experience these affects.

Attention, to the self or the other—and that is what is involved in egocentric or empathic experiences—is surely significant for cognition. Thinking of another's joy simply does not signal cognitions about the other's needs: Obviously, if someone is joyful they cannot simultaneously be experiencing the need to which altruism is directed. But why should egocentric joy trigger altruistic behavior? One possibility is that egocentric joy, operating through social comparison processes, expands one's sense of relative efficacy. One feels relatively fortunate, relatively resource-laden, and therefore feels more willing to share with others. We discuss the potential role of relative efficacy in altruistic behavior later in the chapter. For the present, however, we note that evidence is accumulating that cognitive processes mediate the relationship between positive affect and prosocial behavior.

THE NEGATIVE AFFECTS

There is a sweet consistency of findings with regard to positive affect that is almost entirely missing when one considers the effects of negative affect on altruistic behavior. There, empirical findings seem to conflict with each other in ways that make the organization of this section an Herculean task. We shall attempt to organize these materials according to the presumed mediating variables—guilt, shame, sympathy, and the like—in the hope of elucidating the underlying theoretical issues. We make no strong case for a particular view of these data. Indeed, we have come to believe that a variety of mechanisms may gird the relationship between negative affect and altruism. We guarantee the reader, however, that the area is both rich and complex.

Guilt. Although the psychoanalytic adage that guilt underlies all altruistic behavior (Freud, 1937; Glover, 1925) is likely untrue, there is little question that under certain conditions guilt can elucidate altruistic behavior. Indeed, the common interpretation of harm-doing experiments wherein the subject is made to feel responsible for breaking, say, an expensive piece of equipment and is therefore more willing to volunteer in a different painful experiment (cf. Wallace & Sadella, 1966), is that the subject feels guilty for his behavior. His subsequent altruistic behavior serves to alleviate that guilt and, possibly, to bolster self-esteem.

The effects of transgression on altruism are robust. They hold for a variety of transgressions, such as shocking a confederate, killing a laboratory animal, or knocking over a box of sequenced index cards. And they hold for a variety of altruistic behaviors, including helping to score exams, participating in subsequent experiments, even donating blood. Altruism is increased regardless of whether the transgression is intentional (e.g., Carlsmith & Gross, 1969; Freedman, Wallington & Bless, 1967; Keating & Brock, 1976; McMillan, 1970, 1971; McMillan & Austin, 1971) or unintentional (Cialdini, Darby & Vincent, 1973; Cunningham, Seinberg & Grev, in press; Darlington & Macker, 1966; Freedman, Wallington & Bless, 1967; Harris & Samrotte, 1976; Konecni, 1972; Rawlings, 1968; J. W. Regan, 1971; D. Regan, 1971; Wallace & Sadalla, 1966). It hardly matters whether the harm-doing is public and known (e.g., Carlsmith & Gross, 1969; Cialdini, Darby & Vincent, 1973; Darlington & Macker, 1966; Keating & Brock, 1976) or quite private (Freedman, Wallington & Bless, 1967; McMillan, 1970, 1971). It does not matter whether the requisite altruism is directly requested (cf. Carlsmith & Gross, 1969; Cialdini, Darby & Vincent, 1973; Darlington & Macker, 1966; McMillan, 1970, 1971; J. W. Regan, 1971) or not directly requested (cf. Keating & Brock, 1976; Konecni, 1972; Rawlings, 1968; D. Regan, 1972). The prosocial behavior can be of direct benefit to the victim (e.g., Carlsmith & Gross, 1969; Harris & Samerrotte, 1976; Keating & Brock, 1976; Konecni, 1972; McMillan, 1970, 1971; McMillan & Austin, 1971) or of benefit to an uninvolved third party (e.g., Carlsmith & Gross, 1969; Darlington & Macker, 1966; Freedman, Wallington & Bless, 1967; Rawlings, 1968; J. W. Regan, 1971; D. T. Regan, 1972). With the possible exception of J. W. Regan (1971), all of the requisite prosocial behavior was of a public rather than private sort, although in most cases subjects were led to believe that those who were monitoring or observing their prosocial behavior had no prior knowledge of their transgressions. Finally, the findings hold both in the laboratory and in field settings (Harris & Samerotte, 1976; Konecni, 1972; Regan, Williams & Sparling, 1972.)

The view that guilt is the variable which mediates the effects of harmdoing on prosocial behavior, gains credence from a series of studies which have examined the role of confusion. Harris, Benson and Hall (1975) found that church-goers are less likely to contribute to charity following confession than prior to it. In another study, subjects who transgressed and were then given an opportunity to confess to the experimenter were subsequently less prosocial than those who had not confessed (Carlsmith, Ellsworth & Whiteside, cited in Freedman, 1970). Similar findings are reported by J. W. Regan (1971). Her study however, is interesting for several additional reasons. First, confession reduced the prosocial behavior of harmdoers, but not of observers. Such a finding is strongly consistent with a guilt interpretation of harm-doing data. Moreover, the effects of confession were strongest on those who transgressed most. Finally, the more harmdoers (but not observers) talked about their feelings and behaviors during confession, the less prosocially they subsequently behaved. Taken together, these findings strongly support the view that guilt is the mediating variable in the harmdoing–altruism sequence.

Although the findings are self-evidently robust, their interpretation is not entirely unambiguous. At first blush, it would seem that the presumed presence of guilt adequately accounts for these phenomena. But if that were the case, then merely observing harm-doing (as opposed to doing the harm oneself) would hardly result in subsequent altruistic behavior. But in fact, observing harmdoing results in a level of prosocial behavior that is indistinguishable from that induced by actually doing the harm oneself. Indeed, in two studies (Konecni, 1972; J. W. Regan, 1971) the prosocial behavior of observers was slightly higher than that of the harmdoers.

Sympathy. How shall we account for the observer findings? Why is it that when observers witness harm being done to others they are often more altruistic than even the harmdoers themselves? One possibility is that observers experience anticipatory guilt (Rawlings, 1968). Ordinarily, the ascription of guilt is reactive and quite literally, means guilt regarding our own behaviors. But there is a broader kind of guilt that is aroused whenever internal standards are violated, regardless of who does the violating. Such anticipatory guilt alerts even an observer to norms of responsibility and restitution which are consequent to harm-doing.

The notion of anticipatory guilt however, seems strained to us. It seems simpler and more direct to assume a two-factor view: that harmdoers are motivated by guilt while observers are motivated either by sympathy or by attempts to bolster their beliefs in a just world (J. W. Regan, 1971).

The view that feelings of sympathy are elicited in those who observe harmdoing, and that these feelings directly promote the altruistic behavior of observers, gains credence indirectly from the two studies (Carlsmith & Gross, 1969; Freedman, Wallington & Bless, 1967) in which merely observing a harm *failed* to induce prosocial behavior. In both studies (and only in those studies) subjects had absolutely no feedback about the victim's feelings. Indeed, in Carlsmith and Gross (1969), they had never even seen the victim. Thus, a critical ingredient for the arousal of sympathy—feedback from the victim—was missing and consequently, prosocial behavior was not aroused. In contrast, in those studies where observers were found to engage in a higher level of prosocial behavior than even the harmdoers themselves (Konecni, 1972; J. W. Regan, 1971) observers were exposed to a full and ample range of feedback. They could fully observe the reactions of the victim, and could therefore empathize more profoundly.

Obviously, feedback from the victim cuts very differently according to whether one is an observer or a harmdoer. Otherwise, harmdoing would always eventuate in a *higher* degree of prosocial behavior than observing because potentially harmdoers can experience *both* guilt and sympathy, whereas observers experience only sympathy. One senses, however, that the sympathy felt for the victim that one has harmed may be mitigated by an opposing tendency to derogate the victim and thereby reduce one's guilt. Such a tendency, as might be expected, is stronger when the harmdoer is responsible for the harmdoing than when he is not responsible.

Aderman and Berkowitz (1970) in a complex experiment, found that a condition that yielded the highest incidence of help for an experimenter was one in which subjects attended to the plight of a student who needed help but was not helped. The student's need aroused a sympathy for the needy, they argued, one which generalized strongly to the needs of the experimenter. Thompson, Cowan and Rosenhan (1980) asked subjects to imagine that a close friend was dying of cancer. In addition, these subjects attended to the feelings of the dying person. Compared to subjects who attended to their own feelings and to controls, those who attended to the feelings of the sufferer were considerably more helpful to a third party. Again, a sympathy interpretation seems appropriate to these data. Sympathy then, is a general arouser for altruistic behavior. It arouses prosocial behavior not only for the victim with whom one sympathizes, but also for needy third parties.

Shame. When transgression occurs publicly, it is difficult to distinguish whether the subsequent prosociality arises from feelings of guilt, or from those feelings of shame. There is considerable evidence that the experience of shame itself facilitates prosociality. Apsler (1975) found that embarrassment increases altruistic behavior. That increase, moreover, occurs regardless of whether the request for help is made by someone who observed the embarrassing incident or by someone who is unaware of it. Thus, it is the subjective feeling of embarrassment that promotes altruism, rather than the image-repair that might flow from it. In a similar vein, the self derogation which arises from either obtaining deviant personality scores (Freedman & Doob, 1968) or from being called derogatory names (Steele, 1975) results in increased helping.

The cognitions that accompany a transgression—indeed, the manner in which people are socialized to view transgression can have important affective consequences which in turn, are dispositive for prosocial behavior. In a significant study, Dienstbier and his colleagues (Dienstbier, Hillman, Hillman, Lehnhoff, & Valkenaar, 1975) induced children to believe that the negative feelings they experienced following transgression arose either because that transgression was public and therefore shameful, or because the children felt they had done something wrong and were therefore feeling guilty. Subsequently, the children were led to believe they were entirely alone, and were given the opportunity to transgress. As might be expected, those who attributed their negative feelings to guilt behaved more prosocially than those whose attributions were to shame. The latter group presumably required a public, rather than private forum for controlling that behavior.

Sadness, Failure and Self-concern. Feelings of sadness, of personal rejection, and of failure appear to have quite different effects from the negative affects we have just considered in that, by and large, they retard or simply do not affect prosocial behavior. Because they constitute general exceptions to the stated rule of "feel bad, do good" and because those exceptions have theoretical implications, they require some detailed examination.

In a series of studies, young children who were asked to reminisce on things that had made them sad, were either less or no more charitable than controls, and considerably less charitable than those who had been instructed to think about happy things (Cialdini & Kenrick, 1976; Moore, Underwood & Rosenhan, 1973; Rosenhan, Underwood & Moore, 1974). Similar findings have obtained among adults. Aderman (1972) induced sad feelings among adults by having them read the Velten (1968) statements, and found such subjects less willing to perform favors for the experimenter than were elated subjects. Finally, in a naturalistic setting, people who attended a saddening movie were less likely to donate money at a charity booth than controls who had watched an affectively neutral movie (Underwood, Berenson, Berenson, Cheng, Wilson, Kulik, Moore & Wenzel, 1977).

What holds true for sadness applies also to the experience of failure—and, indeed, quite probably to the experience of any negative affect wherein attention is focused on the self. Thus, several studies (Berkowitz & Connor, 1966; Berkowitz, 1972; Isen, 1970; Isen, Horn & Rosenhan, 1973) confirm that failure either retards prosocial behavior or makes it indistinguishable from controls. For example, Isen, Horn and Rosenhan (1973) found that task failure led to fewer (though not significantly fewer) anonymous contributions than did a neutral outcome task. Similarly, evaluation apprehension (Johnson, Hildebrand & Berkowitz, cited in Berkowitz, 1972) and hearing one's own voice on a tape recorder (Gibbons, 1978) leads to decrements in helping behavior.

The findings with regard to sadness however, are not without exception. Cialdini and Kenrick (1976) asked children in three age groups to think about things which made them sad. As indicated above, young children were somewhat (but not significantly) less altruistic than controls of the same age. But older children were more altruistic generally, and more altruistic than same-age controls. Cialdini and Kenrick argue that the nexus between negative affect and prosocial behavior is acquired through socialization. Young children are insufficiently socialized and therefore are not altruistic when sad. But older children, they argue, understand both the reward value and the nature of altruism and so, when they are sad, are more helpful than comparable controls.

HOW DOES AFFECT EFFECT ALTRUISM?

We have alluded to minitheories that account for the relation between affect and altruism—such as sympathy, image repair, guilt, and such—but have thus far neglected to examine significant overarching theories. Such theories tend variously to be motivational or cognitive, and tend to fit some of the data well, but not all of it comfortably. It may well be that the smaller explanations do less violence to the data than the overarching views, at least at present. We leave that judgment to the reader.

Negative State Relief Model.   Cialdini and his associates (Cialdini, Darby & Vincent, 1973; Cialdini & Kenrick, 1976; Kenrick, Baumann & Cialdini, 1979) have argued that negative states, particularly sorrow and depression, facilitate altruism because by being generous to others people make themselves feel better. Their theory, called the Negative State Relief Model, holds that people experiencing a negative mood are motivated to terminate it. Because we are socialized to view altruistic acts as personally gratifying, being altruistic is one way people can relieve negative moods. Accordingly, altruistic acts are self-therapeutics, which are more likely to occur during negative-mood states.

To test this theory directly, Cialdini, Darby and Vincent (1973) predicted that witnessing or committing a transgression would fail to produce increased altruism when an event designed to reduce negative affect was interposed between the transgression and an opportunity to be altruistic. Consistent with this prediction, they found that subjects who witnessed or caused harm to an experimental confederate were subsequently more altruistic unless an unexpected positive event (receiving money or praise) was interposed between the transgression and the altruism opportunity. Cialdini et al. (1973) have argued that these data strongly support the notion that negative affect makes people more altruistic.

We have already seen however, that there are some negative states that seem not to encourage altruism, and that indeed, there are some states that directly discourage it. Such data are discordant with Cialdini's view. Data from young children can be rationalized by asserting, as Cialdini and Kenrick (1976) do, that a certain degree of socialization is necessary before altruism is given the hedonic cast which enables it to ameliorate negative affect. But data from adult subjects which also fail to find increased altruism (e.g., Isen, 1970; Thompson, Cowan & Rosenhan, 1980; Underwood et al., 1977) are more difficult to integrate into the model.

The Cost-benefit Model.   A second model that has been suggested to reconcile the seemingly conflicting data on negative affect and altruism is Weyant's (1978) cost-benefit (perceived reward value for helping) model. Weyant suggests that the decision to help or not to help is the result of an evaluation of the costs and benefits expected. In an experiment with college students, Weyant induced either positive or negative mood by varying the difficulty of a phony aptitude test. Benefits for helping were manipulated by asking subjects to either collect money for a worthwhile charity (the American Cancer Society) or a less worthwhile charity (Little League Baseball). In the high-costs for helping condition, subjects were asked to solicit donations door-to-door, whereas in the low-costs for helping condition subjects were asked to simply sit at a table and collect donations. As predicted by his model, Weyant found that positive-mood subjects volunteered more than affectively neutral subjects, but negative-mood subjects volunteered more than neutrals in the high-benefit/low-cost condition and less than neutrals in the low-benefit/high-cost condition. Thus, Weyant suggests the conflicting results seen among the negative affect studies can be explained by examining the interactions of mood states with the costs and benefits for helping.

Although Weyant's model explains his own data clearly, it is difficult to apply his theory to the findings of others, because it is hard to determine which of the previous studies involved high- or low-costs and benefits for helping.

Focus of Attention.   A third model that attempts to explain both the positive and negative effects of negative affect on helping behavior has been proposed by Thompson, Cowan and Rosenhan (1980). They suggest that focus of attention may mediate the impact of negative affect on altruism. Often, in studies where subjects focus on the problems and misfortunes of others, negative affect results in increased altruism. On the other hand, negative affect inhibits and even decreases altruism in many of the studies that have subjects experience negative moods that are focused on themselves. Thus, it is expected that when subjects are made to feel sad because someone else is transgressed against, their subsequent helping would be augmented. But, when subjects feel sad because they fail at a task, read depressing statements, or think about past unhappy experiences, altruistic behavior is inhibited and, in many studies, decreased.

Thompson et al. tested this hypothesis by manipulating subjects' focus of attention while they were experiencing negative affect. Subjects listened to a tape that solemnly described their friend's tragic death from cancer. Subjects were directed to attend either to the worry, anxiety, and intense pain of their dying friend or to their own pain and sorrow caused by their friend's death. Subjects in a control condition listened to a boring, emotionally "neutral" tape. Both other- and self-oriented subjects were much sadder than the controls (but did not differ from each other). However, as predicted, subjects who attended to the thoughts and feelings of their friend were significantly more helpful than the self-focused or control subjects. Thus, Thompson et al. (1980) state that "negative moods . . . facilitate altruism only among people who are attending to the problems of others, but not among people who attend to their own needs, concerns and losses [p. 291]."

Why should that be? Why should such differential effects obtain for negative affect according to whether one is focused on one's own feelings or on another person's? Thompson et al. speculate that focus of attention operates on the first few cognitions that come to mind (Karylowski, 1977; Taylor & Fiske, 1978). Focus of attention can affect these cognitions either by priming subjects' interpretations of reality (cf. Bransford & Johnson, 1973), or by increasing the accessibility of behavior-relevant cognitions (Isen, Shalker, Clark & Karp, 1978). Confronted with the decision to help, a person who has attended to the plight of another may quite literally, think first about the problems and needs of others. People focused on their own difficulties by contrast, may think first of themselves and their own needs.

Although focus of attention explains some phenomena quite well in our view, it is inadequate as a full explanation for the effects of negative affect on prosocial behavior. In studies where subjects have been embarrassed (Apsler, 1975) or derogated (Steele, 1975) attention would appear to be directed toward self, yet such manipulations increase altruism. Nor does the focus of attention view adequately account for the promotive effects of guilt and shame, which presumably make subjects attend to themselves and their own behaviors on altruism.

Comparative Efficacy.   A final, and in our opinion, more fruitful theoretical view of these diverse data holds that affect can momentarily but powerfully alter one's tacit perceptions of the relative wealth or efficacy (cf. Bandura, 1977) of oneself or others. Because altruism is, by definition, behavior intended to benefit another without the expectation of quid pro quo, it seems reasonable that altruism should occur only when there is a perceived imbalance of resources between self and other, and when that imbalance is weighted in favor of the self. Mood, focus of attention, and other cognitions affect the perception of that balance. Thus, in the Thompson, Cowan and Rosenhan (1980) experiment, subjects who attended to the plight of the victim tacitly felt more fortunate. That imbalance of resources in favor of self led them to feel that they had something extra to contribute. Thus, they were helpful. On the other hand, subjects who attended to their own feelings of loss, tacitly experienced a resource imbalance, which led them to see others as more fortunate than themselves. Under those conditions they were understandably less altruistic.

If this view is correct, then focus of attention should interact with positive affect in precisely the opposite direction from negative affect. This is to say that much as focusing on the plight of another tacitly makes one feel more fortunate (and therefore more altruistic), focusing on the good fortune of another should make one feel correspondingly impoverished, and therefore less inclined towards altruism. This is precisely what was found in a recent experiment by Rosenhan, Salovey and Hargis (in press) which was discussed ealier. Subjects heard an audio tape that described the joy experienced on a wonderful holiday in Hawaii. In one condition, the joy was the subject's: They imagined themselves on the holiday. In another condition, the joy was experienced by the subject's best friend. Consistent with previous findings, when subjects experienced the joy for themselves, they were enormously helpful. But when they experienced the joy for a close friend, they were less helpful than controls.

This comparative efficacy view enables us also to understand the guilt data: Those who are themselves harmdoers, or who observe harmdoing, tacitly experience their comparative enrichment at the expense of another. It also explains the public shame data: Those who have lost face in public through such experiences as shame or failure, will seek to regain their comparative status through prosocial behavior, because such behavior makes one look good. But they will engage in such behavior only publicly, not privately, because in private there is no image repair, on the one hand, and the experience of shame makes them feel relatively impoverished, on the other (cf. Isen, Horn & Rosenhan, 1973).

SUMMARY

The effects of mood on behavior have long been thought to be powerful (cf. Tomkins, 1963). It should not surprise us, therefore, that mood has strong effects on prosocial behavior. The effects of positive moods are relatively straightforward. With few exceptions, positive moods promote altruism. The significant requirement of this view is that the positive affect be experienced for the self. Reverse effects can be obtained when the affect is experienced for another.

The effects of negative mood are more complex. Some negative moods, such as guilt seem generally to facilitate prosocial behaviors, whereas others, such as sadness, retard it. The data, however, are less concordant than those for positive affect, suggesting that a finer theoretical comb needs to be applied here.

We have reviewed several theoretical views, though by no means all of them. Each of these views seems promising, but none is yet powerful enough to accommodate all of the data. The reader may feel as some of us do, that neither the phenomena of altruism nor those of affect yet lend themselves to a single overarching theory.

ACKNOWLEDGMENT

Research for this work was supported in part by the Kenneth and Harle Montgomery Research Fund.

REFERENCES

Aderman, D. Elation, depression and helping behavior. *Journal of Personality and Social Psychology,* 1972, *24,* 91.

Aderman, D., & Berkowitz, L. Observational set, empathy and helping. *Journal of Personality and Social Psychology,* 1970, *14,* 141–148.

Apsler, R. Effects of embarrassment on behavior toward others. *Journal of Personality and Social Psychology,* 1975, *32,* 145–153.

Bandura, A. Self-efficacy: Toward a unifying theory of behavioral change. *Psychological Review,* 1977, *84,* 191–215.

Berkowitz, L. Social norms, feelings and other factors affecting helping behavior and altruism. In L. Berkowitz (Ed.), *Advances in experimental social psychology,* Vol. 6. New York: Academic Press, 1972.

Berkowitz, L., & Connor, W. H. Success, failure, and social responsibility. *Journal of Personality and Social Psychology*, 1966, *4*, 664–669.

Bransford, J. D., & Johnson, M. K. Consideration of some problems in comprehension. In W. G. Chase (Ed.), *Visual information processing*. New York: Academic Press, 1973, 383–438.

Carlsmith, J. M., & Gross, A. E. Some effects of guilt on compliance. *Journal of Personality and Social Psychology*, 1969, *11*, 232–239.

Cialdini, R. B., Darby, B. L., & Vincent, J. E. Transgression and altruism: A case for hedonism. *Journal of Experimental Social Psychology*, 1973, *9*, 502–516.

Cialdini, R. B., & Kenrick, D. T. Altruism as hedonism: A social development perspective on the relationship of negative mood state and helping. *Journal of Personality and Social Psychology*, 1976, *34*, 907–914.

Cunningham, M. R., Seinberg, J., & Grev, R. Wanting to and having to help: Separate motivations for positive mood and guilt induced helping. *Journal of Personality and Social Psychology*, in press.

Darlington, R. B., & Macker, C. E. Displacement of guilt-produced altruistic behavior. *Journal of Personality and Social Psychology*, 1966, *4*, 442–443.

Dienstbier, R. A., Hillman, D., Hillman, J., Lehnhoff, J., & Valkenaar, M. C. An emotional-attribution approach to moral behavior: Interfacing cognitive and avoidance theories of moral development. *Psychology Review*, 1975, *82*, 299–315.

Freedman, J. L. Transgression, compliance, and guilt. In J. R. Macaulay & L. Berkowitz (Eds.), *Altruism and Helping Behavior*. New York: Academic Press, 1970, 155–161.

Freedman, J. L., & Doob, A. N. *Deviance: The psychology of being different*. New York: Academic Press, 1968.

Freedman, J. L., Wallington, S. A., & Bless, E. Compliance without pressure: The effects of guilt. *Journal of Personality and Social Psychology*, 1967, *7*, 117–124.

Freud, A. *The ego and the mechanisms of defense*. London: Hogarth, 1937.

Gibbons, F. X. *Self-awareness, self-concern and pro-social behavior*. Paper presented at the meeting of the American Psychological Association, Toronto, August 1978.

Glover, E. Notes on oral character formation. *International Journal of Psychoanalysis*, 1925, *6*, 131–154.

Harris, M. B., Benson, S. M., & Hall, C. *The effects of confession on altruism*. *Journal of Social Psychology*, 1975, *96*, 187–192.

Harris, M. B., & Samerotte, G. C. The effects of actual and attempted theft, need, and a previous favor on altruism. *Journal of Social Psychology*, 1976, *99*, 193–202.

Isen, A. M. Success, failure, attention and reaction to others: The warm glow of success. *Journal of Personality and Social Psychology*, 1970, *15*, 294–301.

Isen, A. M., Clark, M., & Schwartz, M. F. Duration of the effect of good mood on helping: "Footprints in the sands of time." *Journal of Personality and Social Psychology*, 1976, *34*, 385–393.

Isen, A. M., Horn, N., & Rosenhan, D. L. Effects of success and failure on children's generosity. *Journal of Personality and Social Psychology*, 1973, *27*, 239–248.

Isen, A. M., & Levin, P. F. The effect of feeling good on helping: Cookies and kindness. *Journal of Personality and Social Psychology*, 1972, *21*, 384–388.

Isen, A. M., Shalker, T. E., Clark, M., & Karp, L. Affect accessibility of material in memory and behavior: A cognitive loop? *Journal of Personality and Social Psychology*, 1978, *36*, 1–12.

Karylowski, J. Explaining altruistic behavior: A review. *Polish Psychological Bulletin*, 1977, *8*, 27–34.

Kazdin, A. E., & Bryan, J. H. Competance and volunteering. *Journal of Experimental Social Psychology*, 1971, *7*, 87–97.

Keating, J. P., & Brock, T. C. The effects of prior reward and punishment on subsequent reward and punishment: Guilt versus consistency. *Journal of Personality and Social Psychology*, 1976, *34*, 327–333.

Kenrick, D. T., Baumann, D. J., & Cialdini, R. B. A step in the socialization of altruism as hedonism: Effects of negative mood on children's generosity under public and private conditions. *Journal of Personality and Social Psychology*, 1979, *37*, 747–755.

Konecni, V. J. Some effects of guilt on compliance: A field replication. *Journal of Personality and Social Psychology*, 1972, *23*, 30–32.

London, P. The rescuers: Motivational hypothesis about Christians who saved Jews from the Nazis. In J. Macauley & L. Berkowitz (Eds.), *Altruism and Helping Behavior*. New York: Academic Press, 1970.

McMillan, D. L. Transgression, fate control and compliant behavior. *Psychonometric Science*, 1970, *21*, 103–104.

McMillan, D. L. Transgression, self-image and compliant behavior. *Journal of Personality and Social Psychology*, 1971, *20*, 176–179.

McMillan, D. L., & Austin, J. B. Effect of positive feedback on compliance following transgression. *Psychonometric Science*, 1971, *24*, 59–61.

Midlarsky, E., & Midlarsky, M. Some determinants of aiding under experimentally induced stress. *Journal of Personality*, 1973, *41*, 305–327.

Midlarsky, M., & Midlarsky, E. Status inconsistency, aggressive attitude, and helping behavior. *Journal of Personality*, 1976, *44*, 371–391.

Moore, B., Underwood, B., & Rosenhan, D. L. Affect and altruism. *Developmental Psychology*, 1973, *8*, 99–104.

Mowrer, O. H. *Learning Theory and Behavior*. New York: Wiley, 1950.

Rawlings, E. I. Witnessing harm to others: A reassessment of the role of guilt in altruistic behavior. *Journal of Personality and Social Psychology*, 1968, *10*, 337–380.

Regan, D. T. Effects of a favor and liking on compliance. *Journal of Personality and Social Psychology*, 1971, *7*, 627–639.

Regan, D., Williams, M., & Sparling, S. Voluntary expiation of guilt: A field replication. *Journal of Personality and Social Psychology*, 1972, *24*, 42.

Regan, J. W. Guilt, perceived injustice and altruistic behavior. *Journal of Personality and Social Psychology*, 1971, *18*, 124–132.

Rosenhan, D. The natural socialization of altruistic autonomy. In J. Macauley & L. Berkowitz (Eds.), *Altruism and Helping Behavior*. New York: Academic Press, 1970.

Rosenhan, D. L. Toward resolving the altruism paradox: Affect, self-reinforcement, and cognition. In L. Wispe (Ed.), *Altruism, Sympathy and Learning*. New York: Academic Press, 1978.

Rosenhan, D. L., Salovey, P., & Hargis, K. The joys of helping: Focus of attention mediates the impact of positve affect on altruism. *Journal of Personality and Soical Psychology*, in press.

Rosenhan, D. L., Underwood, B., & Moore, B. Affect moderates self-gratification and altruism. *Journal of Personality and Social Psychology*, 1974, *30*, 546–552.

Rushton, J. P., & Littlefield, C. The effects of age, amount of modelling, and a success experience on seven-to eleven-year-old children's generosity. *Journal of Moral Education*, 1979, *9*, 55–56.

Steele, C. M. Name-calling and compliance. *Journal of Personality and Social Psychology*, 1975, *31*, 361–369.

Taylor, S. E., & Fiske, S. T. Salience, attention and attribution: Top of the head phenomena. In L. Berkowitz (Ed.), *Advances in Experimental Social Psychology*, Vol. 12. New York: Academic Press, 1978.

Thompson, W. C., Cowan, C. L., & Rosenhan, D. L. Focus of attention mediates the impact of negative affect on altruism. *Journal of Personality and Social Psychology*, 1980, *38*, 291–300.

Tomkins, S. S. *Affect, imagery, consciousness, Vol. II: The positive affects*. New York: Springer, 1963.

Underwood, B., Berenson, J. F., Berenson, R. J., Chenge, K. K., Wenzel, G., Kulik, J., & Moore, B. S. Attention, negative affect and altruism: An ecological validation. *Personality and Social Psychology Bulletin*, 1977, *3*, 54-58.

Underwood, B., Froming, W. J., & Moore, B. S. Mood, attention, and altruism: A search for mediating variables. *Developmental Psychology*, 1977, *13*, 541-542.

Velten, E. A. A laboratory task for induction of mood states. *Behavior Research and Therapy*, 1968, *6*, 473-482.

Wallace, L., & Sadalla, E. Behavioral consequences of transgression. 1: The effects of social recognition. *Journal of Experimental Research in Personality*, 1966, *1*, 187-194.

Weyant, J. M. Effects of mood states, coasts, and benefits on helping. *Journal of Personality and Social Psychology*, 1978, *36*, 1169-1176.

IV
INDIVIDUAL DIFFERENCES IN
ALTRUISM

12 The Altruistic Personality

J. Philippe Rushton
The University of Western Ontario

This chapter will attempt two things. First, to demonstrate that there is a great deal more consistency to altruistic behavior across situations than might often be supposed, i.e., that there is a "trait" of altruism—indeed one sufficiently broad to warrant the concept of "the altruistic personality." Second, to suggest that the motivations underlying "the altruistic personality" are (a) a person's empathy and/or (b) a person's internalized norms of appropriate behavior. Evidence will be provided that individual differences in paper-and-pencil measures of the above constructs predict situational altruism.

1. THE GENERALITY VERSUS SPECIFICITY OF ALTRUISTIC BEHAVIOR

If a survey were to be taken of researchers in the field of altruism as to whether they believed there was such a clearly defined entity as "the altruistic personality," it is probable that the overwhelming majority would answer with a resounding "no." There are very few, if any, programs of research in operation on "consistent patterns of individual differences" in altruistic behavior although just about every other conceivable research approach has been used (to which this volume partially attests). No, researchers do not study the altruistic personality for the fairly compelling reason that they don't believe there is such a thing. They have even said so in print. For example, Dennis Krebs (1978) recently wrote:

As Hartshorne and May showed a half century ago, just about everyone will help in some situations; just about nobody will help in other contexts; and the same people who help in some situations will not help in others.

and

There is little basis for resisting Gergen, et al.'s characterization of personality research on altruism as "a quagmire of evanescent relations among variables, conflicting findings, and low order correlation coefficients (Gergen, et al., 1972, p. 113) [p. 142].

Krebs is certainly not alone in his view. For example, Latané's and Darley's (1970) now classic monograph concluded:

There are . . . reasons why personality should be rather unimportant in determining people's reactions to the emergency. For one thing, the situational forces affecting a person's decision are so strong. . . . .
A second reason why personality differences may not lead to differences in overt behavior in an emergency is that they may operate in opposing ways at different stages of the intervention process [p. 115].

Even those as positively disposed toward the possibility of an altruistic personality as Paul Mussen and Nancy Eisenberg-Berg (1977) recently concluded on a pessimistic note:

To researchers in personality development, it seems intuitively reasonable to hypothesize that prosocial dispositions are . . . connected with personal characteristics and with deep-lying motives. However a critical review of relevant empirical studies shows only a partial support for this hypothesis. In many instances, the data yield no confirmation, and the findings of some studies contradict the results of others. In view of these facts, conclusions must be regarded as tentative and suggestive at best [p. 68].

Later, they state:

This is unfortunate, for the discovery of clear-cut and direct connections between personality characteristics and prosocial behavior would have many theoretical and practical implications [p. 77].

The only major researcher who approaches the conclusion that there is an altruistic personality is Ervin Staub. Staub (1978, 1979) has suggested that people differ to the degree to which they have a general "prosocial orientation." He emphasizes however, the "interactionist approach" in which "general values" interact with "specific norms" to determine behavior in accord with both the demands of particular situations and still other personality characteristics of the actor (e.g., his or her ''competence'' and ''need for achievement''). Thus some people are altruistic in some situations but not in others whereas others are altruistic in the latter but not in the former. Staub comments favorably on Mischel's (1968) review of the evidence on consistency. According to Staub (1978):

> Mischel . . . reviewed evidence that led him to conclude that consistency is in the eye of the beholder, that consistency is not real but is illusory. We are motivated to believe that the world around us is predictable, so we perceive our own behavior and that of others as consistent . . . consistency in interpersonal and social behavior is low. Mischel points out that correlations in behavior under different circumstances, or between personality test scores and behavior, seem to reach a maximum of about .30. . . . Mischel's reasoning clearly implies that a person who is helpful at one time need not be expected to be helpful another time . . .
>
> The underlying assumption in the reasoning that follows is that consistency in behavior is limited. Most behavior is determined in a complex manner [pp. 40–41].

In a review of the generality of children's altruistic behavior published in the 1976 *Psychological Bulletin* Rushton (1976), too, was persuaded by the Mischel (1968) review and concluded:

> It would appear from the studies reporting data on the generality of altruistic behavior that Mischel's (1968) magic number of .3 once again emerges as the overall representative correlation [p. 901].

Since then the matter has been looked into more thoroughly (Rushton, 1980, Chapter 4). The result is quite amazing. All of the quotations cited earlier would probably never have occurred if we had all thoroughly considered more fully the Hartshorne and May (1928-30) studies in the original! Other researchers such as Burton (1976) and Eysenck (1977) have clearly pointed the way in this respect. Let us consider the Hartshorne and May (1928-30) study in some detail, for it is the largest study of the question ever undertaken, raises most of the major points of interest, and has been seriously misinterpreted in the past.

The classic study of the ''specificity versus generality of behavior'' controversy was the enormous ''Character Education Enquiry'' carried out by Hartshorne and May in the 1920's and published from 1928 to 1930 in three volumes: *Studies in Deceit, Studies in Service and Self Control,* and *Studies in the Organization of Character.* These investigators gave 11,000 elementary and high school students some 33 different behavioral tests of their altruism (referred to as the ''service'' tests), self-control, and honesty in home, classroom, church, play and athletic contexts. At the same time extensive ratings of the children's reputations with their teachers and their classmates were taken in all these areas. By intercorrelating the children's scores on all these tests it was possible to discover whether the children's behavior was specific to situations or generalizable across them. If the children's behavior is specific to situations then the correlations across situations should be extremely low or even nonexistent. If the children's behavior is generalizable across situations, then the correlations should be substantial. There is, thus, a crucial test of the generality hypothesis.

Altruism

Consider first the tests of altruism in which the students were given opportunities to help others. Five tests were given, making up a battery that Hartshorne and May called the "service" tests. These included:

1. *The self or class test.* A spelling contest was set up in which each student could compete for one of two sets of prizes, one for the winning class and one for the winning individual. No one could enter both contests. Each had to choose whether his or her score was to count for him or herself or for the class.

2. *The money-voting test.* In this test, the class had to decide what to do with some money which might be, or actually had been, won in the previous contest. Scoring was in terms of the altruistic nature of the choice, ranging from, "Buy something for some hospital child or some family needing help or for some other philanthropy," to "Divide the money equally among the members of the class."

3. *The learning exercises.* This test attempted to measure the amount of effort that would be expended to work for the Red Cross, for the class or for oneself, on a mental abilities test, using as scores, gains from the basic, un-motivated score obtained on the first day.

4. *The school kit test.* Each child was provided with a pencil case containing ten articles which came, "as a present from a friend of the school." It was then suggested to them that they might give away any part or all of the kit in an inconspicuous way, in order to help make up some kits for children who had no interesting things of this kind.

5. *The envelopes test.* The children were asked to find jokes, pictures, interesting stories, and the like, for sick children in hospitals, and were given envelopes in which to collect them. The number of articles collected by each child was scored according to a complex scoring system.

Techniques similar to those used in the study of altruistic behavior were applied in the study of honest behavior and behavior involving self-control. Here students were tempted to cheat, lie, steal, and maintain self-control in a variety of circumstances. For example:

Honesty

Included among the battery of tasks were the following:

1. *The "duplicating technique".* Students were given, for example, paper-and-pencil tests of knowledge in a school subject; the papers were collected, and

a photocopy made of the answers. At a later session of the class the original papers were returned and each student was told to score his or her own paper according to an answer key provided. Cheating consisted of illegitimately increasing the score by copying answers from the key. By comparing changes in the student's answer booklet with photocopies of the original booklets, such deception could readily be ascertained.

2. *The "double-testing technique"*. With this method, students were tested twice on alternate versions of a given test. On one of the occasions, they were given the opportunity to cheat, and on the others there was strict supervision and no opportunity to cheat. Any differences found between the scores made on the two occasions served as the measure of cheating. This particular technique was used to demonstrate deception in work done at home as well as in the classroom. It also lent itself to testing in a quite different context, namely, athletics. The achievement of the student on such activities as pull-ups, chinning, and broad jumping could be measured when the test was self-administered and again when administered by the examiner.

Self-control

Here the several tasks included:

1. *Resisting the candy temptation*. Several candies were put on each child's desk. The children were told that the experimenter would prefer them not to eat the candies for a lengthy time period, during which a paper-and-pencil test was given. Self-control consisted of inhibiting the tendency to eat the candy.

2. *The "wooden face" test*. The children were told to try and not make any change in their faces while the examiner tickled them with feathers, showed them jokes, and placed bad odours under their noses. Self-control consisted of not showing any change of expression.

Knowledge of Moral Rules

In addition to all the above situational tests, a number of questionnaires were given to the students assessing such things as their knowledge of moral rules. For example they were asked their opinion as to (a) whether it was a student's duty to engage in such activities as helping a slower child with his lessons and (b) whether another child should be punished for taking a few apples from a fruit stand. These were given on different occasions in different settings. One battery of such tests were called the "information tests." They included for example the *Cause-effect Test* consisting of true-false forced-choice questions to items such as "Good marks are chiefly a matter of luck" and "Ministers' sons and deacons' daughters usually go wrong." Criteria of what constituted the "correct" answer was that more than 75% of graduate students thought it to be correct.

Reputational Ratings

In addition to the batteries of tests already described, both the student's teachers and their classmates were asked to make ratings of all children as to their altruism, honesty, self-control, persistence, etc. One concerned with altruism, for example, was the "Guess Who" test. Here, very short descriptions of a person were provided (e.g., "Here is someone who is kind to younger children, helps them on with their wraps, helps them across the street, etc." and "Here is the class athlete . . ."). The children were asked to write down the names of any boys or girls in their class who fitted each description. This test was given to both children and teachers.

What were the results from this extremely large and intensive study? First, let us consider the measures of altruism. The behavioral measures intercorrelated a low average of +.23 with each other, thus suggesting support for the specificity viewpoint. However if the five measures were combined into a battery, they correlated a much higher +.61 with the measures of the child's reputation for altruism among his or her teachers and classmates. Furthermore, the teacher's perceptions of the student's altruism agreed extremely highly (r = +.80) with that of the student's peers on the "Guess Who" test. These latter results indicate a considerable degree of generality and consistency in altruistic behavior.

Virtually identical results as the above were found for the measures of honesty and self-control. Any one behavioral test correlated, on average, only a lowly +.20 with any one other behavioral test. If, however, the measures were combined into batteries, then much higher relationships were found with either the teachers' ratings of the children or with any single measure taken alone. Typically these correlations were of the fairly high order of +.50 and +.60. Thus, depending on whether the focus is on the relationship between just two of the behavioral measures or whether it is instead on the broader relationship between averaged groups of situations, the notions of both specificity *and* generality are supported. The question then becomes, which of these two focal points is the more useful or accurate?

Hartshorne and May (1928-30) focused overwhelmingly on the specific correlations of +.20 and +.30 rather than those of +.50 and +.60 gained from combining the individual tests. This led them to conclude in favor of the doctrine of specificity. For example, they stated:

> . . . neither deceit nor its opposite, 'honesty' are unified character traits, but rather specific functions of life situations. Most children will deceive in certain situations and not in others. Lying, cheating, and stealing as measured by the test situations used in these studies are only very loosely related [p.411, 1928].

Other writers have sided with Hartshorne and May. In a very influential review, for example, Mischel (1968) extolled again the notion of specificity in behavior, pointing out that the average validity coefficient of personality is +.30. Persons, therefore, are said to exhibit "discriminative facility" between situations. Mischel (1968) selectively reviewed some of Hartshorne's and May's work in order to demonstrate how behavior changed from situation to situation. Thus, if children took alternate forms of one of the paper-and-pencil tests in diverse social settings—such as at home, in Sunday school, at club meetings, as well as in the classroom—the test-retest correlations fell from a relatively high +.70 in the *same* situation, to +.40 in a *different* situation.

This doctrine of "specificity" is correct in what it argues, i.e., that situations are important, that people acquire different ways of dealing with different situations, and that the old idea of a trait as some "inner entity operating independently of the situation in which the individual is placed [Hartshorne & May, 1928, p. 385]," is quite incorrect. Unfortunately, some have interpreted this as meaning that consistency does not exist. This is quite wrong. The evidence is very solid that there are quite stable and consistent patterns of individual differences across situations. Hartshorne's and May's conclusions were much too suggestive of specificity. By focusing on correlations of +.20 and +.30 between any two items, rather than those of +.50 and +.60 based on a battery of items they created a very misleading impression. A much more accurate picture of reality is found by looking at the predictability achieved from sampling a number of behavioral examples. This greater predictability occurs because there is always a fair amount of randomness in any one situation. By combining and averaging over situations the randomness (called "error variance") itself is averaged out leaving a clearer view of a person's true behavior. These expectations are made explicit in psychometric theory in which, for example, in educational and personality testing, the more items there are on a test, the higher the reliability is. Thus any one behavioral test ought to be considered similar to any one item on an educational or personality test.

Imagine how highly inappropriate it would be for professors to assess the knowledge of the students in their courses on the basis of two or three multiple-choice items. The intercorrelations between such items is typically around +.20. Taking the student's answers to several such questions together, however, does allow for a true picture of their attainment to occur. This is also true in measuring altruism and, as we have seen, combining individual tasks in the Hartshorne and May (1928-30) studies led to substantial predictability. Correlations of +.50 and +.60 allow for the accounting for 25% to 36% of the variance in a set of scores. This is really quite high and supports the view that there is generality in altruistic behavior.

A great deal of further evidence for this conclusion is to be found in Hartshorne's and May's data. Indeed, examination of the relationships between the total scores on the battery of altruism tests with those of the batteries concerned with honesty, self-control, persistence and moral knowledge, suggest that the generality of behavior is not limited to altruism. There is instead evidence for a general moral trait. This conclusion rests on the relationship between the batteries of altruism, self-control, honesty, and persistence which Hartshorne and May found to intercorrelate an average of +.31. Furthermore, measures of moral knowledge intercorrelated an average of +.37 with the four batteries of behavioral tests. Thus, knowledge of how children endorse items such as "most of the things you learn in school never do you any good anyway," "clean speech is a sign of being a 'goody-goody,'" and "I feel it is a student's duty to help a slow or dull child with his lessons," allows a greater than chance prediction of such diverse behaviors as: voting to give money to a charity rather than to oneself; not cheating on either a game or an exam when given the opportunity; controlling the tendency to make a face when smelling a bad odor or being tickled with a feather; and not being distracted from an arithmetic test by a page full of interesting drawings. All the above could also be predicted by better than chance by knowledge of whether the students were rated as conscientious by their classmates.

All of the above supports the idea of a pervasive general factor of "moral character." This also has been the conclusion of many subsequent researchers. Burton (1963), for example, reanalyzed much of the original Hartshorne and May data and subjected them to more sophisticated statistical analyses. A factor analysis revealed a first general factor that accounted for between 35 and 40% of the common variance, a figure strongly suggesting the existence of "moral character." This has since been replicated using other children and other tests (e.g., Nelsen, Grinder & Mutterer, 1969) and reviewed by Burton (1976).

Despite the conclusions of Hartshorne and May themselves about the specificity of behavior, they carried out several analyses that almost necessarily assumed that there was consistency across situations. They studied, for example, *individual differences in consistency* across situations, arguing that such differences suggested integration of personality and, even, Rushton (1980) suggested "integrity." In this account, integrity would exist when a person's behavior could be predicted from both his or her past behavior and from knowledge of his or her moral principles. Hartshorne and May found a distinct relationship between "integrity" and acting in a prosocial manner. For example, although altruism and honesty were characteristics which could be predicted from one situation to another, dishonesty, lying, cheating, and the whole range of antisocial activities tended to be unpredictable and unintegrated. Thus, the behavior of the person lacking in integrity tended to be inconsistent, undependable, unpredictable, and even contradictory. Such a person would be at the mercy of the varying temptations of every situation. It is interesting too that Hartshorne and May found distinct relationships between integrity and emotional stability, and also among both of these and persistence and resistance to suggestion. There appears to be a general prosocial, moral person characterized by what has often been labeled, rather vaguely, elsewhere, "ego strength."

Since the pioneering work of Hartshorne and May (1928-30) many other studies have also provided data that speak directly to the "specificity versus generality" of altruism. As has been reviewed elsewhere (Rushton, 1976, 1980) the typical correlation between any two behavioral indices is about +.30. Combining measures, on the other hand, again led to a substantially greater degree of predictability. Let us consider briefly some of this additional evidence.

To test the hypothesis that generosity was part of a pattern of prosocial moral characteristics including kindness and cooperation, Rutherford and Mussen (1968) initially sampled 63 middle-class 4-year-old boys. A generosity score was found for each child based on the number of candies given away to a friend. On this basis, the initial sample of 63 was divided into 14 nongenerous children who gave no candies away at all and 17 highly generous children who gave away a large proportion of their candies. These extreme groups then were found to differ in a variety of ways. Specifically, teachers rated the generous children as more generous, more kind, less competitive, less quarrelsome, and less aggressive than the nongenerous children. Highly generous children also were more generous and less hostile in objectively scored, semistructured projective doll play. In addition, a behavioral measure of competitiveness based on a car-racing game showed the generous group to be less competitive than the nongenerous group.

Dlugokinski and Firestone (1973) took four measures from 164 children aged 10 to 13: a pencil-and-paper measure of how one understood the meanings of kindness; a pencil-and-paper measure of the relative importance of altruistic as opposed to selfish values; judgments from their classmates of how considerate or selfish they were viewed to be; and a behavioral measure concerned with donating money to a charity. The six possible correlations were all positive and ranged from $+.19$ to $+.38$. Further, the authors reported, multiple correlations of any three variables as predictors of the fourth ranged from $+.42$ to $+.51$. In a later paper, Dlugokinski and Firestone (1974) replicated these relationships.

Recent studies have examined the relations among children's naturally occurring altruism. Krebs and Sturrup (1974) reported a study of 23 children aged 7 and 8. Three altruistic coding categories were used: offering help, offering support, and suggesting responsibly. Offering help was found to correlate $+.21$ with offering support and $+.09$ with suggesting responsibly, which in turn correlated $+.24$ with offering support. A somewhat higher correlation was obtained when a composite behavioral altruism score was calculated on the basis of the three preceding measures. This composite score correlated $+.47$ with an independently derived, teacher's rating of the child's overall altruism. In an extensive study of children's freeplay behavior in a natural setting, Strayer, Wareing, and Rushton (1979) studied 26 children over a 30-hour period. These authors found relationships of $+.50$ and $+.60$ between such coded altruism as donating and sharing objects, cooperation, and helping.

On the basis of this evidence it would seem that there is a ''trait'' of altruism. Some people are consistently more generous, helping, and kinder than others. Furthermore, such people are readily *perceived* as more altruistic, as is demonstrated by the several studies showing positive relationships among behavioral altruism and peers' and teachers' ratings of how altruistic a person seems (Dlugokinski & Firestone, 1973, 1974; Krebs & Sturrup, 1974; Rutherford & Mussen, 1968). It may be remembered that Hartshorne and May (1928-30) also found a solid relationship between the students' reputations for being kind and considerate and how altruistic they actually were on behavioral tests.

We now have achieved the preliminary objective specified at the beginning of this chapter; that is, to demonstrate that there is far greater consistency to altruistic behavior than is generally supposed. The typical coefficient of consistency is +.50 and +.60—double the figures of +.20 and +.30 that are usually put about. To be sure correlations of +.20 and +.30 are to be found between individual "items," which is in fact quite high given the error variance involved in single item tests. However it is no more sensible to measure "altruism" by one task than it is to assess students' ability in a subject by asking them only one question. Students' abilities tend to be quite stable and consistent when adequately assessed—so also is their altruism. The view that greater consistency occurs with the more measures taken has been recently demonstrated by Epstein (1979, 1980) using a variety of self-report measures even including such measures as "moods." He found that stability coefficients reliably increased from +.20 from one day to the next to +.70 and higher when averaged from one week to the next. Block (1971) has shown that personality is stable over *decades* when measured reliably.

2.   MOTIVATIONS UNDERLYING "THE ALTRUISTIC PERSONALITY"

If there *is* an "altruistic personality," a number of questions immediately spring to mind: What is he or she like? What motivates such a person? From where did he or she gain such a personality? How could we get more people to acquire such personalities? How is it that sometimes even altruistic personalities are often *un*altruistic? For the remainder of this chapter let us consider the hypothesis that there are stable individual differences in *motivation* to behave altruistically.

Many motivational constructs have been suggested as explanations of altruistic behavior. These have included, among others, altruistic "attitudes," "beliefs," "opinions," "values," and "goals"; "empathy," "sympathy," and "role-taking abilities," and moral "principles," "rules," "norms" and "standards." As Rushton (1980) suggested in detail, however, much of the research literature and terminology concerned with the motivations to be altruistic can be usefully understood in terms of (a) a person's empathy and/or (b) a person's internalized norms of appropriate behavior.

Empathy

Empathy may be defined as experiencing the emotional state of another. A state of empathy is said to exist between A and B when A matches his or her feelings with those of B. This matching of emotion can result from either (1) cues given off *directly* by B or (2) A's conscious knowledge of B's situation. Both animals and extremely young infants experience empathy on the basis of direct cues. Furthermore, direct cues undoubtedly will continue to be important to eliciting altruism throughout the life span. Among humans, however, cognitive abilities come into play as age increases, which vastly extend the capacity for empathic responding. What we refer to as "role-taking" abilities—that is, the focusing of A's attention on B's situation and the attempt to imagine what that is like—provides the capacity to empathize, even with individuals who lived thousands of years ago or who are still to be born.

Norms of Appropriate Behavior

A *norm* may be defined as a *standard by which events are judged and on that basis approved or disapproved.* An individual might apply such standards to evaluate good from bad, right from wrong, appropriate from inappropriate, beauty from ugliness, or truth from falsehood. Standards vary in the degree to which they are internalized. Norms that are held strongly enough to be considered "oughts" are called moral principles. Those norms held more abstractly are referred to as values, and norms held tentatively and found arbitrary, may be called social rules. For our purposes, the notion of a norm, defined as an internal standard, will encompass all constructs such as goals, principles, rules, and values.

There are many norms concerned with prosocial behavior. For example there are (1) norms of social responsibility, (2) norms of equity, and (3) norms of reciprocity. These have in common the fact that they all are internal standards against which events are judged. If one's own behavior does not match up, one censures oneself, which produces an aversive state requiring redress.

The motivational systems of empathy on the one hand and norms of social responsibility, equity, and reciprocity on the other, are "hypothetical constructs," that is, they cannot be observed directly. They are postulated in order to explain the regularities in behavior that can be observed. The danger of such constructs, though, is that they end up being postdictive rather than predictive, thus giving us only pseudo explanations, that is, an instance of helping behavior occurs, and then we "explain" it by saying that empathy or a norm to help must have been in operation. We can break the circle however, and solve some of these problems, in a number of ways. It must be recognized, for example that empathy and norms are properties of *individuals,* which bring us directly back to the theme of this chapter—"the altruistic personality." If there is an altruistic personality, and if these motivations really are the important ones, then there ought to be consistent patterns of individual differences in empathy and norms, that is, some people should be either more empathic and/or have higher moral standards than others. This allows us a direct test of the adequacy of these motivational constructs. For example, compared to people who are relatively low in empathy, people who are highly empathic should (a) register more physiological distress at the sight of another's suffering, (b) perceive themselves as more empathic, (c) be perceived by others as more empathic, and (d) behave more to reduce the unhappiness or the suffering of another. Similarly, persons who have high moral standards should (a) endorse rules based on those norms more than do individuals who have not internalized the same norms, (b) behave more in accord with those norms than do people who have not internalized them, (c) be able and willing to verbalize rules based on those norms to others, and (d) apply sanctions to individuals who violate the norms.

Let us then examine the two motivation systems from the perspective of individual differences. In regard to empathy several studies have supported the view that paper-and-pencil measures predict situational altruism (e.g., Eisenberg-Berg & Mussen, 1978; House & Milligan, 1976; Liebhart, 1972; Mehrabian & Epstein, 1972). To discuss but one of these, Mehrabian and Epstein (1972) found that university students' empathy scores predicted both a refusal to administer high levels of shock to another person and agreement to volunteer time to help an emotionally upset confederate of the experimenter. Empathy was assessed by a 33-item questionnaire with such positively keyed items as "It makes me sad to see a lonely stranger in a group" and "I really get involved with the feelings of the character in a novel," and such negatively keyed items as "I find it silly for people to cry out of happiness" and "I often find that I can remain cool in spite of the excitement around me."

In regard to internalized standards, it is suggested that some people have internalized them more fully than others. Perhaps the most direct test of this hypothesis is to see whether observed differences in altruistic behavior are correlated with paper-and-pencil measures of a person's knowledge of, and agreement with, moral norms. A wide range of studies have demonstrated this to be the case. Individuals with high scores on paper-and-pencil or verbal measures of social responsibility, other-oriented values, or moral reasoning tasks, were more likely to engage in prosocial behavior than those with lower scores on the same tests (e.g., Anchor & Cross, 1974; Berkowitz & Daniels, 1964; Berkowitz & Lutterman, 1968; Dlugokinski & Firestone, 1973, 1974; Eisenberg-Berg, 1979; Eisenberg-Berg & Hand, 1979; Emler & Rushton, 1974; Haan, Smith & Block, 1968; Harris, Mussen & Rutherford, 1976; Krebs & Rosenwald, 1977; Midlarsky & Bryan, 1972; Rubin & Schneider, 1973; Rushton, 1975; Staub, 1974; and Willis & Goethals, 1973).

For example, in regard to "social responsibility," Berkowitz and Daniels (1964) found that high scorers on this dimension behaved more altruistically than low scorers did. Their measure of altruism consisted of the number of cardboard boxes made for another person who was allegedly dependent on the subject for his or her help. Social responsibility was measured by the degree to which subjects endorsed such items as "I am the kind of person people can count on." Staub (1974), in a major undertaking, had his students fill out a large number of scales, including the measure of "social responsibility" just discussed. In addition he gave (1) a measure of social *irresponsibility:* Machiavellianism (Christie & Geis, 1968). Sample items included agreement with "Anyone who completely trusts anyone else is asking for trouble" and disagreement with "Most men are brave"; (2) a measure of how high a person rank ordered such values as "helpful" and "equality" in a long list of alternative values (Rokeach, 1973), and (3) a measure of moral reasoning based on Kohlberg's (1976) dilemmas. In a test of whether any of these measures predicted helping behavior, Staub (1974) gave all the subjects the opportunity to intervene in an emergency situation some weeks after completing all the questionnaires. The results of this study were very interesting. All the different questionnaire measures, that is, social responsibility, Machiavellianism, high levels of moral reasoning ability, and having helpful values, grouped significantly and positively together on a single factor in a factor analysis, along with high scores on measures of helping behavior. Thus, a broad, prosocial orientation emerged that had manifested itself in a variety of ways.

Of interest in the Staub (1974) study was the finding that an individual's level of moral reasoning correlated both with the more traditional questionnaires of moral attitudes and with measures of altruistic behavior. This is a highly interesting finding and strongly supports the notion of an altruistic personality based on internalized personal norms. At least nine other published studies have also found that individuals with "high" levels of moral judgment as assessed on either Piagetian (1932) or Kohlbergian (1976) moral reasoning tasks behave more altruistically than those who are low (Anchor & Cross, 1974; Eisenberg-Berg, 1979; Eisenberg-Berg & Hand, 1979; Emler & Rushton, 1974; Haan, Smith & Block, 1968; Harris, Mussen & Rutherford, 1976; Krebs & Rosenwald, 1977; Rubin & Schneider, 1973; Rushton, 1975). These measures differed considerably from each other in the age range tested, the measure of moral judgment used, and the indices of altruistic behavior assessed.

Emler and Rushton (1974) used two moral judgment stories from Piaget (1932), and found that predictions of 60 7- to 13-year old children's anonymous donations to a charity could be made with better than chance results with knowledge of the children's level of moral judgment. Furthermore, this finding was maintained when the effect of age was covaried from the analysis. In a subsequent study, Rushton (1975) replicated this with 140 7- to 11-year-olds and, furthermore, showed that the relation between moral judgment and altruism held up over a 2-month retest.

The findings are not limited to laboratory measures. For example, Harris, Mussen, and Rutherford (1976) used peer ratings of the children's prosocial disposition and found correlates with moral judgment. These authors gave 33 boys, 10 and 11 years old, the Kohlberg test of moral judgment and found that maturity of moral judgment was significantly correlated with resisting a temptation in a situational test as well as with a reputation among their peers for being concerned with the welfare of others.

Similar studies have been carried out with adults. For example, Krebs and Rosenwald (1977) demonstrated a significant, positive relationship between the moral reasoning of adults as measured by Kohlberg's test of moral development and their altruism. The test of altruism was whether subjects would mail a questionnaire back to the experimenter at some minor inconvenience to themselves. Although over 90% of those at Stages 4 and 5 helped in this way, only 40% of those at Stages 2 and 3 did so. Finally, Eisenberg-Berg (1979) found that high school students' responses to prosocial moral dilemmas predicted their subsequent altruistic behavior. For males such scores predicted their completion of a dull experimental task 2 to 3 weeks later, whereas for females they predicted humanitarian sociopolitical attitudes.

Summary

It would seem that there is an altruistic personality and that it can be described as follows: This person is more motivated to engage in altruistic acts. He or she has internalized higher and more universal standards of justice, social responsibility, and modes of moral reasoning, judgment, and knowledge, and/or he or she is more empathic to the feelings and sufferings of others and able to see the world from their emotional and motivational perspective. On the basis of such motivations, this person is likely to value, and to engage in, a great variety of altruistic behaviors—from giving to people more needy than themselves, to comforting others, to rescuing others from aversive situations. Altruists also behave consistently more honestly, persistently, and with greater self-control than do nonaltruists. As a result of his or her altruistic activity, this person will have a *reputation* for being altruistic among his or her peers and colleagues. Furthermore, the consistently altruistic person is likely to have an integrated personality, strong feelings of personal efficacy and well-being, and what generally might be called "integrity."

REFERENCES

Anchor, K. N., & Cross, H. J. Maladaptive aggression, moral perspective, and the socialization process. *Journal of Personality and Social Psychology,* 1974, *30,* 163–168.

Berkowitz, L., & Daniels, L. R. Affecting the salience of the social responsibility norm: Effects of past help on the response to dependency relationships. *Journal of Abnormal and Social Psychology,* 1964, *68,* 275–281.

Berkowitz, L., & Lutterman, K. G. The traditional socially responsible personality. *Public Opinion Quarterly,* 1968, *32,* 169–185.

Block, J. *Lives through time.* Berkeley, Calif.: Bancroft Books, 1971.

Burton, R. V. Generality of honesty reconsidered. *Psychological Review,* 1963, *70,* 481–499.

Burton, R. V. Honesty and dishonesty. In T. Lickona (Ed.), *Moral development and behavior: Theory, research and social issues.* New York: Holt, Rinehart & Winston, 1976.

Christie, R., & Geis, G. (Eds.). *Studies in Machiavellianism.* New York: Academic Press, 1968.

Dlugokinski, E. L., & Firestone, I. J. Congruence among four methods of measuring other-centeredness. *Child Development,* 1973, *44,* 304–308.

Dlugokinski, E. L., & Firestone, I. J. Other centeredness and susceptibility to charitable appeals: Effects of perceived discipline. *Developmental Psychology,* 1974, *10,* 21–28.

Eisenberg-Berg, N. Relationship of prosocial moral reasoning to altruism, political liberalism, and intelligence. *Developmental Psychology,* 1979, *15,* 87–89.

Eisenberg-Berg, N., & Hand, M. The relationship of preschoolers' reasoning about prosocial moral conflicts to prosocial behavior. *Child Development,* 1979, *50,* 356–363.

Eisenberg-Berg, N., & Mussen, P. Empathy and moral development in adolescence. *Developmental Psychology,* 1978, *14,* 185–186.

Emler, N. P., & Rushton, J. P. Cognitive-developmental factors in children's generosity. *British Journal of Social and Clinical Psychology,* 1974, *13,* 277–281.

Epstein, S. The stability of behavior: 1. On predicting most of the people much of the time. *Journal of Personality and Social Psychology,* 1979, *37,* 1097–1126.

Epstein, S. The stability of behavior. II. Implications for psychological research. *American Psychologist,* 1980, *35,* 790–806.

Eysenck, H. J. *Crime and personality* (3rd edition). St. Albans, Hertfordshire, England: Granada Publishing Ltd., 1977.

Haan, N., Smith, M. B., & Block, J. Moral reasoning of young adults: Political-social behavior, family background, and personality correlates. *Journal of Personality and Social Psychology,* 1968, *10,* 183–201.

Harris, S., Mussen, P., & Rutherford, E. Some cognitive, behavioral and personality correlates of maturity of moral judgment. *Journal of Genetic Psychology,* 1976, *128,* 123–135.

Hartshorne, H., & May, M. A. *Studies in the nature of character.* Vol. 1: *Studies in deceit.* New York: Macmillan, 1928.

Hartshorne, H., May, M. A., & Maller, J. B. *Studies in the nature of Character.* Vol II: *Studies in self-control.* New York: Macmillan, 1929.

Hartshorne, H., May, M. A., & Shuttleworth, F. K. *Studies in the nature of character.* Vol. III: *Studies in the organization of character.* New York: Macmillan, 1930.

House, T. H., & Milligan, W. L. Autonomic responses to modeled distress in prison psychopaths. *Journal of Personality and Social Psychology,* 1976, *34,* 556–560.

Kohlberg, L. Moral stages and moralization: The cognitive-developmental approach. In T. Lickona (Ed.), *Moral development and behavior: Theory, research, and social issues.* New York: Holt, Rinehart & Winston, 1976.

Krebs, D. L. A cognitive-developmental approach to altruism. In L. Wispé (Ed.), *Altruism, sympathy, and helping: Psychological and sociological principles.* New York: Academic Press, 1978.

Krebs, D. L., & Rosenwald, A. Moral reasoning and moral behavior in conventional adults. *Merrill-Palmer Quarterly of Behavior and Development,* 1977, *23,* 77–87.

Krebs, D. L., & Sturrup, B. Role-taking ability and altruistic behavior in elementary school children. *Personality and Social Psychology Bulletin,* 1974, *1,* 407–409.

Latané, B., & Darley, J. M. *The unresponsive bystander: Why doesn't he help?* New York: Appleton-Century-Crofts, 1970.

Liebhart, E. H. Empathy and emergency helping: The effects of personality, self-concern, and acquaintance. *Journal of Experimental Social Psychology,* 1972, *8,* 404–411.

Mehrabian, A., & Epstein, N. A measure of emotional empathy. *Journal of Personality,* 1972, *40,* 525–543.

Midlarsky, E., & Bryan, J. H. Affect expressions and children's imitative altruism. *Journal of Experimental Research in Personality,* 1972, *6,* 195–203.

Mischel, W. *Personality and assessment.* New York: Wiley, 1968.

Mussen, P., & Eisenberg-Berg, N. *Roots of caring, sharing, and helping: The development of prosocial behavior in children.* San Francisco: W. H. Freeman & Company, Publishers, 1977.

Nelsen, E. A., Grinder, R. E., & Mutterer, M. L. Sources of variance in behavioral measures of honesty in temptation situations: Methodological analyses. *Developmental Psychology*, 1969, *1*, 265–279.

Piaget, J. *The moral judgment of the child*. London: Routledge & Kegan Paul, 1932.

Rokeach, M. *The nature of human values*. New York: Free Press, 1973.

Rubin, K. H., & Schneider, F. W. The relationship between moral judgment, egocentrism, and altruistic behavior. *Child Development*, 1973, *44*, 661–665.

Rushton, J. P. Generosity in children: Immediate and long-term effects of modeling, preaching, and moral judgment. *Journal of Personality and Social Psychology*, 1975, *31*, 459–466.

Rushton, J. P. Socialization and the altruistic behavior of children. *Psychological Bulletin*, 1976, *83*, 898–913.

Rushton, J. P. *Altruism, socialization, and society*. Englewood Cliffs, N.J.: Prentice-Hall, 1980.

Rutherford, E., & Mussen, P. Generosity in nursery school boys. *Child Development*, 1968, *39*, 755–765.

Staub, E. Helping a distressed person: Social, personality, and stimulus determinants. In L. Berkowitz (Ed.), *Advances in experimental social psychology* (Vol. 7). New York: Academic Press, 1974.

Staub, E. *Positive social behavior and morality* (Vol. 1). *Social and personal influences*. New York: Academic Press, 1978.

Staub, E. *Positive social behavior and morality* (Vol. 2). *Socialization and development*. New York, Academic Press, 1979.

Strayer, F. F., Wareing, S., & Rushton, J. P. Social constraints on naturally occurring preschool altruism. *Ethology and Sociobiology*, 1979, *1*, 3–11.

Willis, J. A., & Goethals, G. R. Social responsibility and threat to behavioral freedom as determinants of altruistic behavior. *Journal of Personality*, 1973, *41*, 376–384.

13 Derogation of an Innocently Suffering Victim: So Who's the "Good Guy"?

Richard M. Sorrentino
The University of Western Ontario

In 1970, Lerner presented some rather startling evidence indicating that the more innocent victims appear to be in their suffering, the more observers will devalue or derogate those victims. The paradigm employed in most of these studies involved a learner (confererate), who received electric shocks for making errors in a paired-associates learning task. Subjects, whose role was to evaluate the effectiveness of the teaching method, were found to take a rather negative view of the learner. Rather than rate the victim positively or at least neutrally on evaluative dimensions, their ratings were found to be lower than their rating of a confederate who did not receive electric shocks or where the learner later received compensation for her suffering. Perhaps most surprising of all, in one study, the greatest derogation of the victim occurred in the martyr condition, where the observers were led to believe that the victim, after expressing fear of the shock and reluctance to participate, had agreed to undergo the shock so that they, the observers, might receive their needed credit for participating in the experiment.

These and the results of many other conditions reported by Lerner (1970), are all supportive of Lerner's just world hypothesis. Lerner writes:

> What I am postulating here is that for their own security, if for no other reason, people want to believe they live in a just world where people get what they deserve. Any evidence of undeserved suffering threatens this belief. The observer then will attempt to reestablish justice. One way of accomplishing this is by acting to compensate the victim; another is by persuading himself that the victim deserved to suffer, after all. In our culture, and probably many others, suffering is seen as deserved if the person behaved poorly or if he is inherently "bad" or undesirable. It is also reasonable to conjecture that most observers would prefer to attribute suffer-

ing to something the victim did rather than to his personal worth. The assumption here is that attaching responsibility to behavior provides us with the greater security—we can do something to avoid such a state [p.208].

Hence it is the situation of injustice that threatens one's belief in a just world. To the extent that the victim is suffering innocently and cannot be compensated for his or her suffering, one is motivated to derogate the victim. In so doing, that is, by persuading one's self that the victim deserved to suffer, a person's belief in a just world is restored. Where the learner later receives money for her suffering, justice is restored and there is no need to derogate her. Conversely, where the learner is perceived to be a martyr, she is even more innocent in her suffering, and derogation is greater.

Although not without its critics (e.g., Chaikin & Darley, 1973; Godfrey & Lowe, 1975; Sorrentino & Boutilier, 1974) since the writing of the Lerner (1970) chapter, considerable evidence in support of the just world hypothesis has also accrued (see Lerner & Miller, 1978). Several studies, for example, have addressed the issue of derogation of rape victims. Indeed, as one would predict from the just world hypothesis, subjects were more likely to hold the victim responsible if she were a virgin or a married woman than a divorcée (Jones & Aronson, 1973). In another study (Smith, Keating, Hester, & Mitchell, 1976) rape victims were found to be held more responsible if they were unacquainted with the assailant than if they were acquainted. Interestingly this included such victims as social workers and even nuns! Thus even when it comes to rape, the more innocent a victim appears to be, the more she will be held responsible in order for one to preserve a belief in a just world.

Another interesting extension of the just world hypothesis has been to the area of self-derogation. It appears that when persons themselves suffer due to chance events, they may restore justice by regarding themselves as deserving of their fate. This ranges from being randomly assigned a number in the 1971 U.S. draft lottery—i.e., where induction into the armed services is likely (Rubin & Peplau, 1975), to being randomly assigned as subjects required to eat caterpillars (Foxman & Radtke, 1970) or worms (Comer & Laird, 1975).

A thorough review of research, criticisms and replies to criticisms exists elsewhere (e.g., Lerner & Miller, 1978). The present chapter is devoted to an issue that seems to have fallen behind in research investigating the just world hypothesis. This is the role of individual differences.

THE ROLE OF INDIVIDUAL DIFFERENCES IN VICTIM DEROGATION

One of the most highly cited studies reporting individual differences relevant to the just world hypothesis is that by Rubin and Peplau (1975). These authors proposed that, "... there are relatively enduring individual differences in the extent to which people perceive others (and perhaps themselves) as deserving their fates in a wide range of situations [p. 69]." As a result they devised a "Just World Scale" consisting of 20 items such as "basically the world is a just place," and "by and large, people deserve what they get." The predictive utility of the scale was established in their study, cited earlier, of students in the 1971 national draft lottery, and by a number of other studies (Flowers, 1973; Miller, Smith, Ferree, & Taylor, 1973; Zuckerman, Gerbasi, Kravitz, & Wheeler, 1974). These studies are all consistent with Rubin and Peplau's (1975) assumption that, people who believe most strongly in a just world are most likely to see victims as meriting their misfortune and/or asking for trouble.

Research on the Just World Scale then, not only supports the predictive utility of the scale, but adds further credence to the just world hypothesis. What we find particularly interesting in terms of the present chapter, however, is the relationship of the Just World Scale with other personality measures. Rubin and Peplau (1975) reported that belief in a just world correlates positively with religiousness, authoritarianism, and internality as measured on Rotter's (1966) Locus of Control Scale. These authors expected the correlation with religiousness, "because the major Western religions endorse the belief in a just world, (Rubin & Peplau, 1975, p. 78)." The correlation with authoritarianism was hypothesized because:

> The link between the belief in a just world and authoritarianism is consistent both with their common cultural content (e.g., the tendency to describe leaders in idealized terms) and with the logic of Piaget's and Kohlberg's cognitive-developmental models. The two constructs converge on the themes that strong and powerful people are good and that weak and powerless people are bad. Moreover, authoritarianism has been shown to be related to intolerance for cognitive inconsistency (Steiner and Johnson, 1963) and to hostility toward handicapped and underprivileged persons and groups (Centers, 1963; Christie, 1954; Noonan, Barry, and Davis, 1970), tendencies which would also be expected to follow from the belief in a just world [p. 77].

Internals were hypothesized to have a greater belief in a just world than externals on the basis that internals have the expectation that one can determine one's own rewards and punishments, rather than being at the mercy of external forces (Rotter, 1966).

On the basis of the correlational evidence, then, one might expect that religious persons, authoritarians, and internals are more likely than their counterparts (nonreligious persons, nonauthoritarians, externals) to derogate an innocently suffering victim. Rubin and Peplau (1975) are careful to point out, however, that authoritarianism may be conceptually distinct from belief in a just world (see for example, Lerner, 1978), and that the internal-external reasoning may not hold given that there may be people who believe in a just world governed by external forces, as Kübler-Ross (1969) suggests. The critical question, however, remains. That is, what happens when persons who differ on the three dimensions of religiousness, authoritarianism and locus of control actually observe a victim suffering innocently? Three studies are presented here which bear on this issue. Two have been published previously and the third is based on data from an unpublished Honors Thesis done in collaboration with the present author. The studies by no means represent a systematic program of research as they were run purely for interest's sake. In addition, following the presentation of the results of the three studies, the reader may find him or herself in the midst of a complex maze of reasoning as derogation of a victim is not as straightforward as we or others might have thought. On the other hand, the reader should be made aware that such complexity is indeed the state of the art at this point. Finally, those of you who prefer to believe there are "good guys" and desire to espouse the evils of belief in a just world, religiousness, authoritarianism, and possibly internality, as some authors have done, should proceed with caution.

STUDY 1: RELIGIOUSNESS AND DEROGATION (SORRENTINO AND HARDY, 1974)

As with Rubin and Peplau (1975), we too hypothesized that religious persons would be more likely to derogate an innocently suffering victim than nonreligious persons. Certainly, previous research would suggest that religious persons were likely candidates for this nonmeritorious role. Early research in psychology was quick to point out the apparent hypocrisy between religious dogma and actual behavior (e.g., Allport & Kramer, 1946; Kirkpatrick, 1949). In perhaps the most condemning statements, Rokeach (1969) wrote, "Most disturbing are those findings that show religious-devoutness to be positively rather than negatively related to bigotry, authoritarianism, dogmatism and antihumanitarianism [p. 4]."

Rokeach (1969) himself found dramatic evidence in support of this statement. In his study, 1400 adult Americans were interviewed immediately after the assassination of Dr. Martin Luther King, Jr. He found that subjects who rated salvation (an index of religiosity) high were significantly less likely than those who rated salvation less high to show compassion for deprived persons in American society (e.g., the poor, welfare recipients, blacks). Perhaps most importantly, with reference to Martin Luther King, those who rated salvation high were more likely to conclude that Dr. King brought his death on himself, or they expressed fear, whereas those who rated salvation less high were more likely to express compassion. Because the ranking of salvation relative to other values was found to correlate highly and positively with church attendance and ratings of religious importance, Rokeach concluded that strongly religious people indeed demonstrate less compassion than less religious or nonreligious people.

Given the apparent lack of compassion evidenced by religious persons, along with arguments similar to Rubin and Peplau (1975) that religious persons should have a greater need to believe in a just world than nonreligious persons, the present study hypothesized that religious persons would be more likely to derogate an innocently suffering victim than those who were nonreligious persons.

METHOD

Subjects

A total of 80 summer school students (37 males, 43 females) enrolled at the University of Western Ontario were recruited. They ranged in age from 18- to 28-years-old.

Procedure

Students reported to a lecture room that contained two television monitors and a videotape playback system which was disguised by a cabinet. Among the students was the confederate of the experimenter. The experimenter began by leading the subjects to believe that they would be participating in two separate experiments. Under the guise of the first experiment, pre-experimental measures were taken. Specifically, subjects were asked to rate on a 9-point scale the extent to which they felt religion was important in their everyday life.[1] Subjects scoring above the median constituted the High religious group and those below, the Low religious group. In addition, subjects were asked to respond on a 9-point scale (from agree to disagree) to five questions that were adopted directly, or modified somewhat, from Rokeach's (1969) study. These were intended to measure attitudes toward socially relevant issues. Finally, in order to discern whether there is a correlation between religiousness and a belief in a just world, subjects were asked to indicate on a 9-point scale the extent to which they believed in a just world.[2]

After completing the pre-experimental questionnaire, subjects were told that they would now begin the second experiment. They were led to believe that they would watch a live experiment in progress and afterwards respond to a questionnaire designed to gauge their reactions to psychological experiments. Subjects were told they would observe a "serial learning task" being conducted by another psychologist. The experimenter further explained that because the actual experimental room was extremely small a camera had been installed in the experimental room and the subjects would view the experiment by means of the television monitor. Next, they were informed that one of them would be requested to be a subject in the serial learning experiment. The experimenter, as if in a random fashion, selected a female sitting toward the front of the room, who in reality was the confederate of the experimenter. The confederate was given directions to the experimental room and left the lecture room.

---

[1]Measures of degree of church attendance and ranking of the value of salvation were also obtained. Results on these measures, though not as strong (distributions were highly skewed), were similar to those for importance of religion. The correlation between importance of religion and salvation was .71 ($p < .01$) and was .73 ($p < .01$) between importance of religion and church attendance.

[2]"The Belief in a Just World Scale" was unknown to us at this time.

At this stage, the experimenter said that he would switch on the camera in the experimental room. In reality, he turned on the videotape machine and subjects viewed either the "Experimental" or "Control" videotape, depending on which session they were in. On both tapes the confederate proceeded to learn a series of 11 nonsense syllables to criterion in eight trials. The two tapes were identical except for the experimental manipulation. In the Experimental tape, the situation was presented such that the confederate appeared to receive a rather painful electric shock whenever she made an error. In the Control tape, the confederate was merely informed of her mistakes and, consequently, did not portray any signs of suffering.

After the confederate had successfully mastered the serial learning task, the subjects were informed that she would take a 5-minute break and then repeat a similar task. At this stage, subjects were requested to answer a questionnaire on what they had observed of the experiment up to this point. This was actually the postexperimental questionnaire. Among "filler" items, this questionnaire required subjects to evaluate the confederate by means of 10 seven-point rating scales containing highly evaluative bipolar adjectives such as "attractive-unattractive" and "likeable-unlikeable" from a list by Kirby and Gardner (1972). The primary dependent measure, evaluation of the victim, was derived by summing over the subject's scores on these items.

RESULTS

A significant positive correlation between the importance of religion item and the one on belief in a just world was found ($r(78) = .38$, p $< .01$), thus replicating Rubin and Peplau's (1975) finding. In addition, results on the social issue items, as shown in Table 13.1, are consistent with Rokeach's findings on a similar scale. That is High religious persons appear to show less compassion (or at least less desire to help) for deprived persons in Canadian society than Low religious persons, $t(78) = 1.98$, p $< .05$, as measured by the composite index.

Up to this point then, our results appear to be consistent with the notion from previous research that it is the High religious persons who are the "bad guys" and this could be due to a need to believe in a just world.

Let us look, however, at the responses of subjects where they actually observe an innocently suffering victim. Analysis of variance reveals a significant main effect for Conditions, $F(1,76) = 6.67$, p $< .025$; and a significant Religiousness $\times$ Conditions interaction, $F(1,76) = 5.65$, p $< .025$; on victim evaluation scores. The Conditions main effect replicates a study reported by Lerner (1970), with subjects in the standard shock condition showing greater derogation of the learner, $\bar{X} = 48.53$, than subjects in the Control condition, X $= 52.75$. The Religiousness $\times$ Conditions pattern of interaction is shown in Table 13.2. Note there is *no evidence* that high religiousness persons are more likely to derogate an innocently suffering victim than low religiousness persons. In fact, quite the

TABLE 13.1
Individual Means and Composite Mean of the Five Social
Items for High versus Low Religiousness Subjects[a]

Item	High Religiousness	Low Religiousness
1. Immigration should be limited to only professional people.	5.15	6.23
2. Free dental care should be given to those who can't afford it.	6.17	6.76
3. French Canadians are demanding more than they are entitled to.	5.32	5.57
4. Every person has the right to adequate housing.	6.91	7.26
5. Canadian Indians can learn just as well as whites given same education.	7.91	8.10
Composite mean	31.40	34.20*

[a]The higher the mean, the more favorable the attitude toward the social issue.
*p. < .05

contrary was found. As seen in Table 13.2, although the Low Religiousness subjects do give higher evaluations than High Religiousness subjects in the Control condition, it is they who derogate the learner where she receives electric shocks (Experimental condition).[3] The High religious subjects, in fact, *do not vary* in their evaluations. In other words, to religious persons it made little difference whether the learner was suffering or not.

The crux of the paradox now becomes clear. Religious persons show less compassion as evidenced by their endorsement of social indices and have a greater need to believe in a just world than less religious persons. Yet, when a person is receiving painful electric shocks, it is the Low religious group who wear the black hats! Out attempt at explaining this paradox is reserved for later. Let us first examine our remaining correlates of a need to believe in a just world.

STUDY II: AUTHORITARIANISM AND DEROGATION (SORRENTINO, HANCOCK, AND FUNG, 1979)

As with religiousness, there is considerable evidence to suggest that authoritarians should be more likely to derogate an innocently suffering victim than nonauthoritarians. Authoritarians have repeatedly been found to be prejudiced and bigoted (e.g., Adorno, Frenkel-Brunswik, Levinson, & Sanford, 1950;

[3]Throughout the three studies this condition well be referred to secondarily as the "standard shock condition" for purposes of comparison.

TABLE 13.2
Mean Evaluation Scores for
Religiousness x Conditions Combinations on Evaluation of the Learner

	Condition			
	Experimental (Standard shock)		*Control*	
Group	M	n	M	n
High Religious	50.10*	21	50.50	22
Low Religious	46.80	19	55.50	18

*The higher the score the more positive the evaluation.

Vidmar & Rokeach, 1974), as well as punitive and retributive (e.g., Epstein, 1965; Mitchell & Byrne 1972; Vidmar, 1975). Given the correlation between authoritarianism and belief in a just world (Rubin & Peplau, 1975) as well, perhaps here, unlike religiousness, we will find our "bad guys."

METHOD

Two experiments were run in this study. The second, run nearly a year later and with a different experimenter, was a replication of the first experiment. Each experiment had two conditions: the standard shock condition, here called the Noninvolved condition, run in Study 1; and the Involved condition. This latter condition was adapted from Lerner and Matthews (1967), where the subject is made to believe that he or she is in some way responsible for the victim's suffering. This is done by having the subject pick a card that will determine the learner—which turns out to be the confederate. Lerner and Matthews (1967) felt that derogation should be even greater in this condition as observers would also be inclined to ward off or deny the possibility that they are responsible for the victim's suffering. Other than the addition of this condition, procedural details are essentially similar to Study I.

Levels of authoritarianism were inferred from a median split (High vs. Low) of subjects' scores on the Byrne and Lamberth (1971) acquiescent-free measure of authoritarianism. Fifty-three male and female college students participated as subjects in each of these experiments. Evaluation of the learner, using Lerner's 15 evaluative nine-point scales (Lerner, 1971), constituted the primary dependent measure.

If one follows the rationale that a greater belief in a just world leads to greater derogation, then one should expect in these experiments that High authoritarians should show higher derogation than Low authoritarians, and this difference will be greater in the Involved than Noninvolved condition. In actual fact, we did not make this prediction, as will be discussed later, but let us first see what happened.

RESULTS

Analyses of variance revealed significant authoritarianism $\times$ involvement interactions on evaluation of the learner in both experiments, $F(1,49) = 4.91$, p $< .03$; $F(1,49) = 6.70$, p $< .01$ (no main effects were significant). The patterns of these interactions are shown in Table 13.3. Note that in both experiments, where the subject is made to feel responsible for the victim's suffering (Involved condition), High authoritarians are more negative in their evaluations of the learner than Low authoritarians, but in the standard shock condition (Noninvolved condition), the reverse occurs. As in Study I, it is the Lows and not the Highs who are more likely to derogate an innocently suffering victim using the standard Lerner and Simmons (1966) paradigm.

Once again, then, it is the "good guys" who are wearing the "black hats," in the typical derogation condition. High authoritarians do, however, wear the "black hat" in the Involved condition, but here we must raise the question, is making a person feel responsible for someone's suffering conceptually the same as threatening his or her belief in a just world? If not, then we must assume: (1) so far we have no evidence that the greater the belief in a just world (as evidenced by religiousness and authoritarianism) the greater the derogation of an innocently suffering victim, and (2) some mechanism other than belief in a just world may also lead to derogation of an innocently suffering victim when one is made responsible for the victim's suffering.

Before rushing to conclusions of these points, let us take a glimpse at the final character in our trilogy, the internal. Surely, here, we will find evidence that internals are more likely to derogate an innocently suffering victim than externals. The next study suggests that this indeed is the case—or maybe not.

TABLE 13.3
Mean Evaluation of the Learner Scores for Authoritarianism
x Involvement Combinations in the Two Experiments

Group	Experiment I Condition		Experiment II Condition	
	Involved	Noninvolved (Standard Shock)	Involved	Noninvolved (Standard Shock)
High Authoritarian	69.36* (n = 14)	74.46 (n = 13)	67.92 (n = 12)	78.87 (n = 15)
Low Authoritarian	74.93 (n = 14)	65.00 (n = 12)	81.64 (n = 14)	72.42 (n = 12)

*The higher the score the more positive the evaluation.

STUDY III: THE EFFECTS OF INTERNAL CONTROL ON
VICTIM DEROGATION
(BOUTILIER, 1973)

In an M.A. thesis by Hardy (1972) upon which Study I is based, the Rotter Internal-External control Scale (I-E Scale) was also administered. No relation, however, was found between I-E scores and derogation of a victim. This led us to conjecture whether only one of the two factors that in fact make up the scale (Lao, 1970), may be related to victim derogation. One factor, that of "Personal Control," measures the amount of control persons believe that they personally possess. The other factor, "Control Ideology," measures the amount of control one believes most people in society possess. Using only the "Personal Control" factor as a measure of Internal-External control, the present study assesses the degree to which Internals would be more likely to derogate an innocently suffering victim than Externals.

Another interesting feature of this study is that Boutilier considered the effects of contingent vs. noncontingent shock on the performance of the learner. In all previous research using the Lerner "teacher-learner" paradigm, even though the learner was assigned her fate due to chance events, the amount of her suffering was, in a sense, contingent upon her performance. That is, she received electric shock only when her answers were incorrect. In examining this issue, Boutilier felt that if the learner received noncontingent shock (i.e., random shock) she would be even more innocent in her suffering, and should, according to the just world hypothesis, receive even greater derogation from observers. Boutilier hypothesized therefore that: (1) persons who score High on the personal control scale should derogate an innocently suffering victim more than those who score Low; (2) these differences should be greater in a Noncontingent than Contingent shock condition; and (3) these differences should be greater than in appropriate control conditions where no electric shock was administered.

METHOD

Subjects

Thirty-three female and 15 male introductory psychology students participated as part of their course requirement. (As I-E Scale scores for personal control were already available for 800 students the sample was drawn from this population.) Counterbalanced pairs of conditions were then randomly assigned to one of six sessions.

Materials

Four versions of black and white videotape depicted a female subject learning a list of nonsense syllables in serial order. Each version took approximately 6.5 minutes to play. The videotaped experimenter presenting the list was portrayed as a graduate student working on his master's thesis. In the experimental conditions shocks were delivered either, contingently, upon wrong responses or, noncontingently, at random intervals throughout the learning task. A buzzer sounded for the duration of the shock delivery. The control conditions were identical except that no shock was administered, that is, the confederate playing the role of the learner-victim did not react as if she were being shocked when the buzzer sounded. All conditions contained an equal number of buzzer presentations. The videotaped experimenter-perpetrator was clearly shown pulling a switch on a box in front of him each time he sounded the buzzer and, in the experimental conditions, delivered a simultaneous electric shock.

The postexperimental questionnaire included Lerner's (1971) victim evaluation items also used in Study II. Other than differences in experimental conditions, the procedure was similar to that of Study I.

RESULTS

Before proceeding further, the reader should be cautioned that a 2(I-E) × 2(Shock-No Shock) × 2(Contingent-Noncontingent) unequal n experimental design with N = 35 results in an extremely small n per cell (n = 3 to 6 per cell). Despite this small n, however (perhaps there is a just world after all), the study did manage to obtain highly significant results. This is due to the fact that although subjects did derogate the learner significantly more in the Shock than Buzzer condition, $F(1,28) = 5.95$, $p < .025$, the pattern of interaction between levels of Internal and External control and Contingent vs. Noncontingent reinforcement was identical within the Buzzer and Shock condition (apparently, the administration of the Buzzer was of sufficient repugnance to elicit similar differences). This yielded a significant I-E × Contingent-Noncontingent pattern of interaction on evaluation of the victim, $F(1,28) = 7.41$, $p < .02$.

Table 13.4 presents the mean evaluation score of the learner for the significant personal control × contingency interaction as well as the means within the Shock vs. Buzzer condition. It can be seen that either across or within the Shock vs. Buzzer condition, results conform to expectations within the Contingent condition. That is, Internals made lower evaluations of the learner than Externals. Note, however, that within the Noncontingent condition, a reversal of predictions occurs with Externals making lower evaluations of the learner than Internals. This is seen both across and within Shock vs. Buzzer conditions.

TABLE 13.4

Mean Evaluation Scores of the Learner as a Function
of Personal Control and Contingency
across and within Electric Shock plus Buzzer vs. Buzzer Conditions

Across Conditions		Contingent	Noncontingent
	Internal Control	89.40* (n = 10)	96.00 (n = 8)
	External Control	100.25 (n = 9)	83.48 (n = 8)

Within Conditions	Buzzer Only		Shock plus Buzzer	
	Contingent	Noncontingent	Contingent (Standard Shock)	Noncontingent
Internal Control	96.20 (n = 5)	106.50 (n = 4)	82.60 (n = 5)	85.50 (n = 4)
External Control	99.20 (n = 6)	88.20 (n = 5)	101.30 (n = 3)	78.80 (n = 4)

*The higher the score the more positive the evaluation.

DISCUSSION

The significant ($p < .02$) personal control $\times$ contingency pattern of interaction on evaluation of the learner again challenges previous assumptions regarding correlates of belief in a just world. Although it seemed logical that internals would be more likely to derogate an innocently suffering victim than externals, and the difference should be greater where the victim has even less control of her fate, the results do not support this hypothesis. Instead, the pattern of interaction suggests that internals derogate more where the victim still has some control over her own fate, whereas externals derogate more where the victim has little or no control.

GENERAL DISCUSSION

The three studies presented here, each with respect to one of Rubin and Peplau's (1975) personality correlates of belief in a just world, show results that do not follow along lines consistent with that belief. Using the condition which most closely follows the experimental paradigm employed by Lerner and Simmons (1966), that is, the Experimental condition in Study I; the Noninvolved condition in Study II, and the Contingent shock condition in Study III, we find only the latter study supportive of previous expectations. In Study I, it is the Low and not the High religious subjects, and in Study II, it is the Low and not the High authoritarian subjects, who are more likely to derogate an innocently suffering victim. Study III, on the other hand, does show Internals more likely to derogate than Externals as measured by the personal control factor of the I-E scale. Yet, even here results vis-a-vis the Noncontingent shock condition do not follow as the Noncontingent condition should have accentuated rather than reversed the expected results. The remainder of this section offers an interpretation of the results of these three studies.

Study I. One plausible *post hoc* explanation of these results was that the High religious subjects were simply ignoring situational determinants in making their evaluations of the learner. This would explain why their evaluations did not differ between conditions. In contrast, the Low religious subjects might have taken situational determinants into account when making their evaluations. Note in Table 13.2 that they not only gave the learner lower evaluations in the Experimental condition than High religious subjects, but higher evaluations in the Control condition. Hence in the Experimental condition, the Low religious subjects derogated the learner because they attended to her suffering. In the Control condition they may have attended to the learner's succeeding at the task and positively evaluated her. The High religious persons simply ignored these aspects.

This then could explain the crux of the paradox. Although High religious persons do have a greater need to believe in a just world than Low religious persons, they are less likely to derogate because they are not attending to the fact that the victim is suffering innocently. If they are ignoring this fact, then obviously there is no threat to their need. Ironically, because Low religious persons do attend to this fact, their need is threatened and they must derogate the victim in order to remove this threat.

This would also explain why religious persons do appear to be less compassionate in other situations (e.g., Table 13.1, Study I; Rokeach, 1969). That is, because they do not consider situational determinants in evaluating others, they can see no reason why those less fortunate than themselves should be given special treatment, nor would they feel sorry for them. In essence, if one ignores the situation, one is likely to conclude that people bring on their own fortune or misfortune and they should neither be helped nor derogated.

Although we felt that this explanation fit the data nicely, the question, why should High religious subjects be less likely to attend to situational determinants than Low religious subjects, remained. One possibility is that it is not religiousness per se which is accounting for these results, but rather the strong correlate of religiousness and authoritarianism. This view is supported not only by the fact that many studies have repeatedly found high correlations between religiousness and authoritarianism (see Kirscht & Dillehay, 1967, pp. 67-72) but several studies suggest that high authoritarians are more likely to attend to a person's attitudes or character whereas low authoritarians are more likely to attend to situational factors as well in making judgments about the causes of one's behavior (see Centers, Shomer & Rodrigues, 1970; Mitchell & Byrne, 1973; Berg & Vidmar, 1975).

Study II.   The two experiments run here were an outgrowth of Study I. If the results on religiousness were actually due to authoritarianism, then we should also expect Low Authoritarians and *not* High Authoritarians to be the "bad guys" in the standard derogation paradigm. This is indeed what we found in the Noninvolved condition as we had predicted. But what of the Involved condition where the High authoritarians do in fact derogate more than the Lows? In attempting to account for this latter finding, we suggest that because authoritarians are traditionally assumed to be ego-defensive (e.g., Adorno et al., 1950; Kirscht & Dillehay, 1967), they may be attempting to ward off guilt or avoidance of self-blame. Chaikin and Darley (1973) and Sorrentino and Boutilier (1974) have previously argued that avoidance of self-blame may be another mechanism that leads to derogation of a suffering victim. By derogating the victim, observers can hold the victim responsible for her suffering and deny their own responsibility.

The interaction between authoritarianism and involvement on derogating the learner in these studies then, appears to be explainable. The Noninvolved condition primarily arouses a threat to one's need to believe in a just world. Those who are more likely to attend to the innocence of the victim are more likely to derogate the victim in order to preserve their belief. Thus, the Low authoritarians derogate the victim more than the High authoritarians. The Involved condition, on the other hand, primarily arouses avoidance of self-blame. Those who are more likely to be ego-defensive are more likely to derogate the victim in order to ward off any feelings of self-blame for the victim's suffering.

Finally, as the two experiments in Study II were stimulated by Study I concerning religiousness and victim derogation, the second experiment also examined this relationship. As reported elsewhere (Sorrentino et al., 1979), we did find evidence suggestive of the fact that it is not religiousness per se, but authoritarianism leading to victim derogation in the Involved shock condition. Future research, then, might pursue the possibility that when the effects of authoritarianism are partialled out, the effects of religiousness may well lead to different conclusions than those which suggest religious persons are less compassionate than nonreligious persons.

Study III.   Although the reversal of derogation scores for the Internals vs. Externals in the Noncontingent shock condition at first appears to go against the just world hypothesis, a *post hoc* interpretation consistent with the hypothesis is possible. If we assume, following from scores on the Belief in a Just World scale, that Internals are more likely to perceive the world as just, where one can have control over the environment, then it is the Contingent shock condition that is the greater threat to internals. Here, the Internal is reminded that even where one has some control over the environment (i.e., the learner can avoid electric shock by learning the list), injustice can occur. The Noncontingent shock condition, on the other hand, does not have the same personal relevance to the Internal, as "things like that simply don't happen in the real world." The converse, of course, happens for the External. Believing that things do happen due to chance (or external forces) and the world isn't necessarily just, the Noncontingent shock condition is of greater personal relevance to the External. It implies that chance events can be bad (or external forces, malevolent).

In a sense, then, the Contingent and Noncontingent shock conditions may serve as a microcosm of society for the Internal and External, respectively. Beliefs about the world, *whether just or unjust,* are threatened and derogation occurs.

CONCLUSIONS

Three areas of investigation of individual differences on derogation of an innocently suffering victim were presented here. None of them yielded results consistent with predictions made from knowledge of the positive correlation of these measures with belief in a just world. We cannot make the simple assumption that the greater the belief in a just world the greater will be the derogation of an innocently suffering victim. Nor would we recommend that therapy for just world believers commence immediately. Some other implications of the present results are as follows:

1. To reiterate the above, belief in a just world may not necessarily lead to derogation of an innocently suffering victim. Three correlates of the belief: religiousness, authoritarianism, and internal control; lead either to opposite results or take on more complex dimensions. Given these findings we would also be cautious of results which use only a belief in a just world scale.

2. Mechanisms other than preservation of a need to believe in a just world may be aroused when observing a victim suffer innocently. The derogation by the Authoritarians in the Involved condition (Study II) raises the possibility that avoidance of guilt or self-blame is aroused. The derogation by the Externals in the Noncontingent condition offers the speculation that they will derogate if bad things do happen in a world governed by chance events. Also, in conjunction with other chapters in this book either norms to help and/or empathy may be aroused.

3. Lerner (see Chapter 10) has now gone beyond the derogation of victims due to a belief in a just world by providing a model of altruism based on justice notions. Here too, however, the role of individual differences might be considered. If, for example, we are correct in our assumption that authoritarians are not compelled to question the victim's suffering vis-a-vis their belief in the just

world, then it is also possible that they would not follow some of the core assumptions of the new justice model. This model is also built around processing information and fitting it within one's organizing framework.

4. Finally, what of our title caption, "So who are the good guys"? Our answer is, there are no good guys or bad guys. As Brown (1965) noted, what the Nazis considered to be the "good" "J" personality turned out to be our culture's "bad" authoritarian personality. Perhaps we should not make value judgments. A more fruitful approach might be to recognize that, given the *right* situation, anyone would come to derogate (*or help*) an innocently suffering victim.

REFERENCES

Adorno, T., Frenkel-Brunswik, E., Levinson, D., & Sanford, R. *The authoritarian personality.* New York: Harper, 1950.

Allport, G. W., & Kramer, B. Some roots of prejudice. *Journal of Psychology,* 1946, *22,* 9–39.

Berg, K. S., & Vidmar, N. Authoritarianism and recall of evidence about criminal behaviour. *Journal of Research in Personality,* 1975, *9,* 147–157.

Boutilier, R. *Does inequity anxiety motivate victim devaluation?* Honours B. A. Thesis, University of Western Ontario, 1973.

Brown, R. *Social psychology.* New York: The Free Press, 1965.

Byrne, D., & Lamberth, J. *The effect of erotic stimuli on sex arousal, evaluative responses, and subsequent behavior.* Technical reports of the Commission of Obscenity and Pornography (Vol. 8). Washington, D.C.: U.S. Government Printing Office, 1971.

Centers, R. Authoritarianism and misogyny. *Journal of Social Psychology,* 1963, *61,* 81–85.

Centers, R., Shomer, R. W., & Rodrigues, A. A field experiment in interpersonal persuasion using authoritative influences. *Journal of Personality,* 1970, *38,* 392–403.

Chaikin, A. L., & Darley, J. M. Victim or perpetrator? Defensive attribution of responsibility and the need for order and justice. *Journal of Personality and Social Psychology,* 1973, *25,* 268–275.

Christie, R. Authoritarianism re-examined. In R. Christie & M. Jahoda (Eds.), *Studies in the scope and method of the authoritarian personality.* Glencoe, Ill.: Free Press, 1954.

Comer, R., & Laird, J. D. Choosing to suffer as a consequence of expecting to suffer: Why do people do it? *Journal of Personality and Social Psychology,* 1975, *32,* 92–101.

Epstein, R. Authoritarianism, displaced aggression, and social status of the target. *Journal of Personality and Social Psychology,* 1965, *2,* 585–589.

Flowers, L. *Personal communication to Rubin and Peplau* (1973).

Foxman, J., & Radtke, R. C. Negative expectancy and the choice of an aversive task. *Journal of Personality and Social Psychology,* 1970, *15,* 253–257.

Godfrey, B. W., & Lowe, C. A. Devaluation of innocent victims: An attributional analysis within the just world paradigm. *Journal of Personality and Social Psychology,* 1975, *31,* 944–951.

Hardy, J. E. *Just world theory, religiousness and compassion.* M.A. Thesis, University of Western Ontario, 1972.

Jones, C., & Aronson, E. Attribution of fault to a rape victim as a function of respectability of the victim. *Journal of Personality and Social Psychology,* 1973, *26,* 415–419.

Kirby, D. M., & Gardner, R. C. Ethnic stereotypes: Norms on 208 words typically used in their assessment. *Canadian Journal of Psychology,* 1972, *26,* 140–154.

Kirkpatrick, C. Religion and humanitarianism: A study of institutional implications. *Psychological Monographs,* 1949, *63* (9, Whole No. 304).

Kirscht, J. P., & Dillehay, R. C. *Dimensions of authoritarianism.* Lexington: University of Kentucky Press, 1967.

Kübler-Ross, E. *On death and dying.* New York: Macmillan, 1969.

Lao, R. C. Internal-external control and competent and innovative behavior among Negro college students. *Journal of Personality and Social Psychology,* 1970, *14,* 263–270.

Lerner, M. J. The desire for justice and reactions to victims. In J. Macaulay & L. Berkowitz (Eds.), *Altruism and helping behavior.* New York: Academic Press, 1970.

Lerner, M. J. Observer's evaluation of a victim: Justice, guilt, and veridical perception. *Journal of Personality and Social Psychology,* 1971, *20,* 127–135.

Lerner, M. J. "Belief in a just world" versus the "authoritarianism" syndrome . . . but nobody liked the Indians. *Ethnicity,* 1978, *5,* 229–237.

Lerner, M. J., & Matthews, G. Reactions to suffering of others under conditions of indirect responsibility. *Journal of Personality and Social Psychology,* 1967, *5,* 319–325.

Lerner, M. J., & Miller, D. T. Just world research and the attribution process: Looking back and ahead. *Psychological Bulletin,* 1978, *85,* 1030–1051.

Lerner, M. J., & Simmons, C. H. Observer's reaction to the innocent victim: Compassion or rejection? *Journal of Personality and Social Psychology,* 1966, *4,* 203–210.

Macaulay, J., & Berkowitz, L. (Eds.) *Altruism and helping behavior.* New York: Academic Press, 1970.

Miller, F. D., Smith, E. R., Ferree, M. M., & Taylor, S. E. *Innocence, culpability, and identification with the victim: A balance theory interpretation of the just world.* Unpublished manuscript, Harvard University, 1973.

Mitchell, H. E., & Byrne, D. *Minimizing the influence of irrelevant factors in the courtroom: The defendant's character, judge's instruction and authoritarianism.* Paper presented at the annual meeting of the Midwestern Psychological Association, Cleveland, May 1972.

Mitchell, H. E., & Byrne, D. The defendant's dilemma: Effects of jurors' attitudes and authoritarianism on judicial decisions. *Journal of Personality and Social Psychology,* 1973, *25,* 123–129.

Noonan, J. R., Barry, J. R., & Davis, H. C. Personality determinants in attitudes toward visible disability. *Journal of Personality,* 1970, *38,* 1–15.

Rokeach, M. The H. Paul Douglas Lectures of 1969. Part I. Value systems in religion. Part II. Religious values and social compassion. *Review of Religious Research,* 1969, *11,* 3–38.

Rotter, J. B. Generalized expectancies for internal versus external control of reinforcement. *Psychological Monographs,* 1966, *80,* (Whole No. 609).

Rubin, Z., & Peplau, L. A. Who believes in a just world? *Journal of Social Issues,* 1975, *31,* 65–90.

Smith, R. E., Keating, J. P., Hester, R. K., & Mitchell, H. E. Role and justice considerations in the attribution of responsibility to a rape victim. *Journal of Research in Personality,* 1976, *10,* 346–357.

Sorrentino, R. M., & Boutilier, R. G. Evaluation of a victim as a function of fate similarity/dissimilarity. *Journal of Experimental Social Psychology,* 1974, *10,* 84–93.

Sorrentino, R. M., Hancock, R. D., & Fung, K. K. Derogation of an innocent victim as a function of authoritarianism and involvement. *Journal of Research in Personality,* 1979, *13,* 39–48.

Sorrentino, R. M., & Hardy, J. E. Religiousness and derogation of an innocent victim. *Journal of Personality,* 1974, *42,* 372–382.

Steiner, I. D., & Johnson, H. H. Authoritarianism and "tolerance of trait inconsistency." *Journal of Abnormal and Social Psychology,* 1963, *67,* 388–391.

Vidmar, N. Retributive and utilitarian motives and other correlates of Canadian attitudes toward the death penalty. *Canadian Psychologist,* 1975, *15,* 337–356.

Vidmar, N., & Rokeach, M. Archie Bunker's bigotry: A study in selective perception and exposure. *Journal of Communication,* 1974, *24,* 36–47.

Zuckerman, M., Gerbasi, K. C., Kravitz, R. I., & Wheeler, L. *The belief in a just world and reactions to innocent victims.* Unpublished manuscript, University of Rochester, 1974.

V SOCIAL CONSTRAINTS ON HELPING

14 The Effects of Group Size on Helping Behavior

Bibb Latané
Steve A. Nida
The Ohio State University

David W. Wilson
Texas A&M University

One of the most consistent findings in social psychological research in the last decade has been that of the decreasing probability of an individual's offering help in an emergency situation as the size of the group in which he or she witnesses the event increases. In this chapter we summarize the empirical evidence for this phenomenon and discuss a number of methodological and theoretical issues that are relevant to this area of research.

HISTORY OF INTEREST IN THE PROBLEM OF GROUP SIZE AND HELPING

In 1970 Latané and Darley published a monograph reporting the results of a program of research on bystander intervention in emergencies that provided strong support for the general proposition that "the presence of other people serves to inhibit the impulse to help [p. 38]." Their work elicited a lot of interest, and it stimulated a good deal of subsequent research in this area.

We think there are at least four reasons for the interest generated by this research. First, with its high degree of mundane realism (Aronson & Carlsmith, 1968), it spoke to an issue of widespread public concern—the alarm created by the failure of 38 witnesses to report to the police the murder of Catherine Genovese. Because the research problem corresponded to a real world problem, readers gained insights into a type of situation that could potentially confront anyone. Latané and Darley (1970) offered a plausible scientific explanation of the dynamics of the emergency situation, suggesting that such vague and frightening concepts as "alienation" and "apathy" may not be necessary to understand events such as the Genovese incident.

A second reason for the widespread attention accorded the bystander-intervention research stems from the high level of experimental realism (Aronson & Carlsmith, 1968) in the research procedures. Participants found themselves in highly involving, serious, and realistic settings, and they were faced with choices among reasonable courses of action. By engaging participants in a meaningful situation the research seems to have avoided many of the artificialities of the laboratory environment without sacrificing experimental control.

A third focus of interest has been on the theoretical framework itself. Latané and Darley posited a decision tree that bystanders must climb if they are to intervene, the tree branching according to whether one notices the event, interprets it as an emergency, feels personally responsible for dealing with it, and possesses the necessary skills and resources to act. They painted a sympathetic picture of the unfortunate bystander, forced to choose among courses of action not only hurriedly, but also on the basis of incomplete information and unfavorable cost and reward schedules. They proposed three psychological processes—social influence, audience inhibition, and diffusion of responsibility—that lead bystanders to be less likely to act when others are present.

A final factor was the discovery of a previously unknown phenomenon: the social inhibition of helping. Contrary to common opinion and the predictions of colleagues, people are less likely to go to the aid of another if exposed to the emergency in the presence of others than if they are alone; many were surprised to find no support for their belief in "safety in numbers." The discovery of such a powerful phenomenon was valuable in its own right, but it also occasioned the need for experiments designed to determine the generality of the effect, explore its boundary conditions, and discover exceptions. As we shall see, many experiments of this sort have been reported, but the exceptions are remarkably few.

METHODOLOGICAL PROBLEMS IN STUDYING THE RELATIONSHIP BETWEEN GROUP SIZE AND HELPING

Two general classes of dependent measures have been used in this area of inquiry: the time required to help and the probability of helping. Probability measures—the proportion of bystanders who intervene, or the simple probability of helping—seem basically more useful than latency measures, and in this chapter we concentrate on them. The victim, bystanders, and other observers are more likely to remember and care about whether help was given than how long it took to do so; although speed might affect the success of some attempts to help, no intervention can succeed unless first attempted. It seems, therefore, that whether or not a bystander tries to help is psychologically more meaningful than how long he or she takes.

It is of course impossible to separate completely the probability of response from measures of time because the probability of response must refer to some point in time following the initiation of the need for help. Empirically, however, it seems that persons tend to help either quickly or not at all. Darley and Latané (1968), for example, found that 95% of the subjects who responded acted within 3 minutes, and Latané and Rodin (1969) found that 90% of all subjects who intervened did so within 90 seconds after the emergency. And although there were 3 minutes in which to respond in an experiment by Smith, Smythe, and Lien (1972), 90% of all responding subjects did so within 30 seconds; across all conditions 33% of those available to respond during the first minute did so, as compared to an average of less than 2% of those who had not yet responded during the remaining 2 minutes. Failing to help early presumably makes it more difficult to help later. A consequence of this fact, then, is that experimenters who choose appropriate time limits are likely to get probability of response measures that accurately represent a subject's propensity to help. These measures make it easier to compare results from different experiments because they are not as subject to such arbitrary variables as the time physically required to perform the helping act.

Finally, probability measures facilitate making the appropriate comparisons between individuals acting alone and in groups. Until someone responds to an emergency, the need for help continues. Once someone has acted, however, the situation changes and any action by others no longer has the same meaning. If, for example, one person reports a fire, it may be harmfully redundant for another to do the same. The overall percentage of individuals responding would therefore be misleading, and it is necessary instead to consider the group as the unit of analysis. Consequently, most research on helping in groups reports not the total proportion of individuals who take some helping action but the proportion of groups that contain at least one helper. This procedure, however, raises an important issue: Groups may seem to be more likely to respond than individuals, even if the individuals in the group are inhibited, merely because more individuals are available.

As a solution to this problem Latané (1977) has suggested calculating the *effective individual probability* of helping. Given the proportion of groups helping, one can derive the individual probability of helping necessary to obtain the observed number of groups helping. The formula is:

$$P_I = 1 - \sqrt[N]{1 - P_G}$$

where P_I is the effective individual probability of helping, and P_G is the proportion of groups of size N in which at least one person helps. The formula can be easily derived from a simple binomial independent trials model and is based on the null hypothesis that being in a group has no effect. With this formula the data are converted into a form that can be directly compared to the data of the remaining conditions, and the statistical significance of such comparisons can be assessed by chi-square using the maximum likelihood techniques described by Fienberg and Larntz (1971). The formula is particularly useful in that it makes it possible to compare effective individual rates of helping across conditions involving groups of different sizes.

Comparing the probability of helping of individuals and groups is not very informative when situational factors are such that either nobody helps or everyone helps. Under these circumstances real differences have no room to reveal themselves, and the lack of apparent differences is ambiguous. A related problem is that when a very high proportion of groups contains at least one responder or when group size is even moderately large, small changes in P_G lead to large changes in the effective individual probability of response. Consequently, with small sample sizes and a high probability of group response, the discontinuity of probabilities may make it impossible to get a precise estimate of effective individual probability. It is therefore important in this line of research to design experimental settings that elicit an intermediate level of helping and to use reasonably large sample sizes (i.e., 15–25 cases per condition) in order to have a reasonable chance to produce conclusive results. Occasionally in our treatment of the literature we have combined data from conditions that did not lead to significantly different response rates in order to gain adequate sample sizes.

It should be noted that in many helping studies "groups" consist of only one real subject and one or more confederates or "presumed" others. In these studies, of course, the proportion of individuals helping can validly be compared to the proportion of individuals in "groups" helping because in every case there is only one available person who can actually help.

EVIDENCE FOR THE GROUP SIZE PHENOMENON

Instead of presenting a comprehensive review of the group size and helping literature, we have chosen to summarize in tabular form the massive evidence that has accumulated over the past decade of experimentation. We have attempted to include in this survey every published or unpublished article that has developed data relevant to the relationship between group size and helping. We are aware of some 4 dozen published or unpublished studies from nearly 3 dozen different laboratories reporting data from over 5000 persons faced with the opportunity to help either alone or in the presence of others. With very few exceptions, individuals faced with a sudden need for action exhibit a markedly reduced likelihood of response if other people actually are, or are believed to be, available to act.

We have classified each study into one of two general categories. The first category consists of those studies in which the helping behavior of persons exposed to an event by themselves is compared to that of individuals who were tested in the presence of confederates or who believed other, unseen, persons to be present (Table 14.1). The second general category consists of studies in which single individuals are compared to actual groups (Table 14.2). Each entry lists (in increasing order of the alone-helping rate) the reference, a brief description of the type of emergency facing participants in that study, and the resulting data.

In Table 14.1 we have listed 56 published and unpublished comparisons of helping by persons who were alone versus those who were tested in the presence of confederates or who believed other, unseen, persons to be present. In 48 of these 56 comparisons there was less helping under the latter conditions, a result that would be expected to occur by chance well less than one time in 51 million. Overall, some 75% of people tested alone helped, but fewer than 53% of those tested with others did so.

Table 14.2 lists 37 comparisons between persons tested alone and in actual groups ranging in size from 2 to 8 people. In four cases the comparison is indeterminate whereas in 31 the effective individual probability of helping was less than the alone-response rate, a proportion that would occur by chance less than one time in 16 million. Overall, about 50% of the persons exposed to the emergencies alone offered help; the effective individual response rate for persons who viewed the emergencies in groups, on the other hand, was only 22%.

It is clear that the social inhibition of helping occurs in both laboratory and field settings employing a wide variety of emergencies designed by a multitude of independent researchers. It is indeed a robust social psychological phenomenon, perhaps as thoroughly replicated and documented as any in our field.

THEORETICAL ISSUES

Why should the actual or believed presence of others inhibit helping? In the following sections, we shall discuss the original theoretical perspective offered by Latané and Darley (1970) and then consider a number of extensions, elaborations and modifications that have been suggested over the ensuing decade.

Latané and Darley (1970) originally characterized emergencies as being: (1) threatening so that one can only avoid loss, not achieve gain; (2) unusual and rare so that people have little experience in intervention; (3) different one from another so that it is difficult to build up a store of cultural prescriptions as to how to deal with them; (4) unforeseen so that one cannot plan how to cope; and (5) requiring immediate action so that one has little time to think. Faced with situations from which they can gain no benefit, unable to rely on past experience, on the experience of others, or on forethought and planning; denied the opportunity to consider carefully their course of action, bystanders to an emergency are in an unenviable position. It is perhaps surprising that anyone should intervene at all.

It is especially surprising, Latané and Darley maintained, when one considers the many costs and few rewards for helping in an emergency. In fact, in many

TABLE 14.1

Social inhibition: Alone Subjects Compared to Individuals in Presence of Confederates or with Others Believed Present (n's in Parentheses).

Study	Situation	Confederates or others believed present	Hypothetical proportion of groups helping	Percent of Ss in groups helping	Percent of alone subjects helping
Byeff, 1970	Fall	1	73%	48% (44)	47% (30)
Ross & Braband, 1973	Smoke	1 normal	26%	14% (14)	50% (14)
		1 blind	87%	64% (14)	(50%)
Shaffer et al., 1975	Theft	1	44%	25% (32)	54% (32)
Horowitz, 1971*	Seizure	3 service group	98%	65% (20)	55% (20)
		3 social group	59%	20% (20)	(55%)
Thalhofer, 1971*	Help child	"many"	99%	44% (96)	60% (96)
Krupat & Epstein, 1973	Request	"several"	?	58% (36)	61% (36)
Ross & Braband, 1973	Crash	1 normal	58%	35% (14)	64% (14)
		1 blind	48%	28% (14)	(64%)
Smith, Smythe & Lien, 1972	E faints	1 similar	10%	5% (20)	65% (20)
		1 dissimilar	58%	35% (20)	(65%)
Latané & Rodin, 1969	Crash	1	14%	7% (14)	69% (26)
Wilson, 1976	Explosion	2 don't help	74%	38% (61)	75% (69)
		2 1 helps	99%	83% (66)	(75%)
Latané & Darley, 1968	Smoke	2	27%	10% (10)	75% (24)
Levy et al., 1972	Demands to enter room	1	68%	43% (30)	77% (30)
		2	49%	20% (30)	(77%)
Sommerfreund & Goodstadt, 1971	Fire alarm	1 calm	68%	43% (14)	79% (14)
		1 worried	59%	36% (14)	(79%)
Bickman, 1971*	Crash	1 (can't help)	93%	74% (15)	80% (15)

(Continued) —

TABLE 14.1 (*Continued*)

Study	Event	No.	Condition	%	%	(n)	(%)	(n)
Beaman & Diener, 1976	E faints	1	(can help)	64%	40%	(15)	(80%)	
		1	(saw S)	94%	75%	(20)	80%	(20)
		1	(S saw)	80%	55%	(20)	(80%)	
Harris & Robinson, 1973*	Asthma	2		95%	63%	(30)	81%	(16)
Gaertner & Dovidio, 1977I*	Fall	2	(white victim)	98%	75%	(16)	81%	(16)
Schwartz & Clausen, 1970*	Seizure	4		98%	54%	(48)	84%	(49)
		3	and expert	96%	48%	(50)	(84%)	
Latané & Darley, 1970*	Seizure	1	friend	94%	75%	(28)	85%	(13)
Darley & Latané, 1968*		1	stranger	86%	62%	(26)	(85%)	
		4	strangers	84%	31%	(13)	(85%)	
Ross, 1969	Drug	3		82%	35%	(20)	90%	(20)
Teger & Henderson, 1971	Sounds of distress	1	nonhelping M	58%	35%	(20)	90%	(10)
		1	nonhelping F	99%	90%	(30)	(90%)	
		1	helping M or F	99%	90%	(30)	(90%)	
Schwartz & Gottlieb, 1976*	Theft & crash	5	(no com)	95%	45%	(11)	92%	(13)
		5	(saw S)	100%	86%	(14)	(92%)	
		5	(S saw)	87%	33%	(12)	(92%)	
Schwartz & Gottlieb, 1976	Theft, Crash	5		99%	62%	(13)	(92%)	
Ross, 1971	Smoke, Crash	2	peers	41%	16%	(12)	92%	(12)
		2	children	88%	50%	(12)	(92%)	
Staub, 1974	Crash	1	"nonemergency"	44%	25%	(12)	93%	(14)
		1	"emergency"	89%	67%	(12)	(93%)	
		1	"discourage"	94%	75%	(12)	(93%)	
		1	"encourage"	97%	82%	(11)	(93%)	
		1	"encourage plus"	100%	100%	(12)	(93%)	
Gaertner & Dovidio, 1977I*	Fall	2	(black victim)	76%	38%	(16)	94%	(16)
Latané & Darley, 1976*	Shock	1	(no com)	97%	83%	(19)	95%	(19)
		1	(saw S)	92%	72%	(19)	(95%)	
		1	(S saw)	92%	72%	(19)	(95%)	

(*Continued*)

TABLE 14.1 (*Continued*)

Latané & Darley, 1976	Shock	1		75%		50%	(19)	(95%)	(43)
Silverman, 1975	Crash	1		99%		92%	(40)	95%	(10)
Gaertner, 1975	Crash	3	(white victim)	100%		90%	(10)	100%	(10)
		3	(black victim)	76%		30%	(10)	100%	(10)
Clark & Word, 1972I	Crash	1		100%		100%	(20)	100%	(10)
Misavage & Richardson, 1974*	Broken tape	2		94%		60%	(10)	100%	(10)
Overall percentage helping				88%		53%	(1279)	75%	(774)

Note. All studies are laboratory experiments except those of Shaffer et al. (1975) and Teger and Henderson (1971).

M = males; F = females; S = subject; E = experimenter.

*Studies involving restricted communication among bystanders.

TABLE 14.2

Social Inhibition: Alone Subjects Compared to Actual Groups (n's in Parentheses).

Study	Situation	Group size	Percent of groups with one or more helpers	Effective individual probability of helping	Percent of alone subjects helping
Staub, 1970	Crash	2 (5-7 yrs)	30% (43)	16%	6% (48)
Clark & Word, 1974 I	Ambiguous shock	2	44% (16)	25%	16% (11)
Staub, 1970	Crash	2 (9-11 yrs)	20% (30)	11%	23% (35)
Latané & Elman, 1970	Money theft	2	19% (16)	10%	24% (25)
Solomon et al., 1978	Faint	2	19% (27)	10%	26% (35)
Clark & Word, 1972 II	Ambiguous crash	2	20% (10)	11%	30% (10)
		5	40% (10)	10%	(30%)
Piliavin et al., unpublished	Theft	2	19% (16)	10%	32% (28)
Freeman, 1974	Request for help	2-8	68% (56)	22%	39% (46)
Howard & Crano, 1974*	Book theft	3	36% (72)	-14%	43% (72)
Byeff, 1970	Fall		37% (30)	20%	47% (30)
Latané, 1970*	Request money, help	2-3	40% (355)	19%	47% (1736)
Moylan & Greenwood, 1972*	Beer theft	2-4	33% (18)	14%	47% (19)
Clark & Word, 1974 I	Some ambiguity	2	62% (16)	39%	53% (19)
Ross & Burke, 1973	Shock	2-3	50% (14)	25%	57% (14)
Solomon et al., 1978	Faint	2	52% (60)	30%	57% (49)
Latané & Darley, 1970*	Beer theft	2	56% (48)	34%	65% (48)
Allen, 1972*	Misinformation	2-3	69% (45)	38%	67% (45)
Latané & Rodin, 1969	Crash, strangers	2	40% (20)	23%	69% (26)
	Crash, friends	2	70% (20)	45%	(69%)
Solomon et al., 1978	Crash	2	45% (20)	26%	70% (20)
Freeman, 1974	Knock on door	2-8	54% (56)	16%	72% (46)
Latané & Darley, 1968	Smoke	3	38% (8)	15%	75% (24)

(Continued)

TABLE 14.2 (*Continued*)

Study	Condition	Group size	Two together	Alone (predicted)	Overall
Freeman, 1974	Lights go off	2-8	70% (56)	23%	76% (46)
Anonymous*	Fall in mall	2	65% (58)	43%	79% (33)
Piliavin et al., unpublished	Fall	2	59% (17)	36%	79% (29)
Solomon et al., 1978*	Fall in laundry	2	75% (16)	50%	81% (16)
Konecni & Ebbesen, 1975 I*	Fallen confederate	2	71% (14)	46%	86% (14)
		2	53% (15)	31%	(86%)
Darley, Teger, & Lewis, 1973	Crash, facing	2	80% (10)	55%	90% (10)
	Crash, not facing	2	20% (10)	11%	(90%)
Clark & Word, 1974 I	Unambiguous shock	2	100% (24)	?	93% (30)
Staub, 1974	Crash	2	60% (15)	37%	93% (14)
Clark & Word, 1972 I	Crash	2	100% (20)	?	100% (10)
Clark & Word, 1972 II	Unambiguous crash	2-5	100% (20)	?	100% (10)
Misavage & Richardson, 1974	Broken tape	3	90% (10)	54%	100% (10)
Piliavin et al., 1969, 1972, 1975*	Fall in subway	8-20	71% (263)	6-14%	?
Overall percentage helping			50% (1291)	22%	50% (2028)

Note. All studies involve full communication in the sense that subjects are in each other's presence. Data from Piliavin et al. studies are not included in totals since there was no alone condition.

*Field studies.

cases it would seem that the major motivation for acting may by the psychological costs of not helping: empathic distress, embarrassment, shame, guilt, and the knowledge that one did not live up to the responsibility each of us bears to keep and protect our fellow people. There may also be psychological costs for giving help, but intervention tends to involve material costs as well: time and effort of course, but also possible physical danger, or potentially complicated legal involvement in the matter. Although costs may tend to be high, the rewards usually available in emergencies are not: the mention of one's name in the newspaper or on the evening news (if lucky), but more often little more than a hurried "thank you." This lack of rewards and prevalence of costs mean that the bystander to an emergency is faced with a choice among several courses of action—all of them bad. As Latané and Darley documented, this avoidance-avoidance conflict may lead bystanders to be motivated primarily to find ways of avoiding the choice, and several are available as they work their way through the sequence of steps or decisions that must be made before intervention takes place.

Before a bystander can intervene, he or she must notice the event, interpret it as an emergency, and decide that it is his or her personal responsibility to offer assistance. Furthermore the bystander must decide specifically what type of help can be given and how to go about carrying out that intervention. A negative decision at any step in this sequence will result in a failure to intervene: for example, if the individual is too wrapped up in his thoughts to notice the event, or if he decides that the person lying in a doorway is really a drunk, not a coronary victim, or if he decides that help is already on the way, help will not occur.

Within this theoretical framework, Latané and Darley (1970) discussed three social psychological processes that might occur when an individual is ir the presence of other people. Each of these processes can help explain part of the observed phenomenon of social inhibition of helping; all appear to be necessary to give a full account.

Audience Inhibition

There exist rules of public behavior, and people usually feel ashamed and embarrassed when they violate them. Because we are taught to mind our own business and not to stare at other people, we may as a consequence not even notice their need for help when it occurs. Even if an emergency is noticed, however, a person may feel embarrassed about intervening in front of other people. What if the need for help is misinterpreted? And what if a foolish course of intervention is initiated? The individual runs the risk of losing face, and the more people that are present, the greater is this risk. The presence of others can inhibit helping when an individual is fearful that his behavior can be seen by others and evaluated negatively, making him or her a fool in the public eye.

298 LATANÉ, NIDA, AND WILSON

Social Influence

Many apparent helping situations are ambiguous as to whether help is actually needed and as to what kind of action is called for. In order to help define a situation we look to other people, observe their reactions and behavior, and thus gauge our own actions on the basis of theirs. We are likely to find out how others interpret situations by watching their facial expressions and behavior rather than by talking to them, especially when among strangers in public places. If, in the midst of a crisis, a bystander is nonchalantly whistling or otherwise passively ignoring the stiuation, one would be likely to infer that there is no reason to intervene or that passive nonchalance is the socially appropriate behavior. This process can be thought of as the modeling of *inaction,* hence providing a conceptual mirror image of the modeling of altruistic *action* as discussed in the chapters by Rushton and by Grusec in this volume.

In public, people generally want to appear calm and collected. If everyone in a group tries to appear calm and at the same time looks to others for a definition of the situation, *each* may be misled into believing that action is inappropriate; until someone acts, then, each person sees only inaction and may be led not to help. The presence of others can thus inhibit helping when individuals see the behavior of others and interpret the situation as less critical than it actually is, or decide that inaction is the expected pattern of behavior.

Diffusion of Responsibility

Even when others cannot see you or you them, the knowledge that they are present and available to respond allows you to diffuse responsibility for helping to them. If you were to observe an emergency situation alone, the entire onus for action would lie on your shoulders—the presence of others should lighten this load and lead you to feel less personally responsible. Latané and Darley (1970) suggested that diffusing responsibility can be viewed as a means of reducing the psychological costs associated with nonintervention. When others are present, such costs are shared and nonintervention becomes more likely.

Not One, Not Two, But All Three

Each of these three psychological processes involves differing preconditions and each requires a different direction or channel of communication among the bystanders to an emergency, and thus it is possible empirically to isolate their effects (Latané and Darley, 1976). For example, diffusion of responsibility is the only process that can be operative when bystanders cannot see or be seen by each other, as in the restricted communication experiments cited in Table 14.1, and the existence of strong social inhibition effects demonstrates the independent operation of that process.

That diffusion is not the only process is illustrated nicely in a recent study by Petty, Williams, Harkins and Latané (1977). In that experiment, diffusion of responsibility was not likely to affect behavior because the behavior in question involved, not an emergency, but the opportunity to get something for nothing— namely a coupon good for a free "Quarter Pounder with Cheese." As in the emergency studies, the presence of others inhibited elevator passengers from helping themselves to these coupons, demonstrating the independent effects of seeing and being seen by others.

Figure 14.1, displays the results of an experiment designed to determine whether the three social psychological processes we have suggested are independent and additive (Latané & Darley, 1976). That experiment varied the processes allowed to operate by varying the channels of communication available between two bystanders to an emergency. In order for audience inhibition to have an effect, the other bystander must be able to tell what the individual does, but not vice versa. If social influence is to operate, on the other hand, the individual must be able to tell what the other bystander does, but it is not necessary that the other can reciprocate. Finally, of course, diffusion of responsibility does not require that either party see the other—only that each individual believe that another person is available to help.

As can be seen in Fig. 14.1, the results provide strong support for the independent and additive operation of each process. There is a substantial and significant decline in the rate of helping as one moves from the alone condition in which

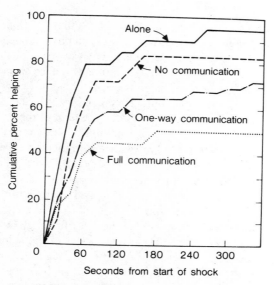

FIG. 14.1.   Cumulative response curve from Latané and Darley (1976).

none of the processes can operate, to the no communication condition with one process, the one-way communication conditions with two processes, and finally to the full communication treatment with all three processes operating. In short, the proposal of three distinct processes as contributing to the decreased likelihood of helping in groups should not be considered unparsimonious.

THEORETICAL ELABORATIONS

In the decade since the original publication of the Latané and Darley (1970) experiments, a number of other theorists have developed interesting and enlightening approaches to helping behavior. Generally speaking, these models build on the overall framework proposed by Latané and Darley but expand or elaborate on specific aspects of the psychological processes that underlie the decision to help or not to help, and we think that each contributes to our understanding of these processes. It is interesting that several of these theoretical elaborations can be seen as focusing on affective or emotional aspects of the intervention process, others on cognitive or rational aspects, and still others on the normative, conative or moral side. These differing emphases loosely correspond to the Freudian triumvirate of id, ego and superego.

Approaches Emphasizing Emotional Factors

Piliavin and Piliavin (cited in Piliavin, Piliavin & Rodin, 1975) posit that observing an emergency produces arousal, which has both physiological and cognitive components (Schachter, 1964). This arousal is an aversive state by which the bystander is motivated for selfish, egoistic reasons to reduce so as to incur as few net costs as possible. Therefore, redefining the situation (as with Latané and Darley, 1970, Experiment 10) or simply leaving the scene of the incident, as well as helping, can be ways of reducing arousal. In several of their experiments the Piliavins and their colleagues vary the condition of the victims (having blood ooze from his mouth or afflicting him with a birthmark) in ways that should increase affective arousal (Piliavin & Piliavin, 1972; Piliavin, Piliavin, & Rodin, 1975). Somewhat surprisingly, these manipulations *decreased* rather than increased helping, presumably because the associated increase in the cost of helping led bystanders to avoid the victim.

Also concentrating on the motivational basis for helping, Coke, Batson and McDavis (1978) have presented a two-stage model of empathic mediation of helping (see also Batson & Coke, Chapter 7). According to this model, a cognitive process—taking the perspective of a person in need—serves to increase the potential helper's empathic emotion, thereby increasing motivation to help. Although the motivation to help is determined by both cognitive and affective processes, cognitive perspective-taking affects helping only indirectly, by means of its effect on empathic emotion. The result, however, may be a truly altruistic motivation for helping in which the helper is actually concerned with eliminating the distress of another rather than his own negative arousal. Coke et al. (1978) reported two experiments that converge to support the suggestion that empathic emotion does mediate the effect of cognitive perspective-taking on behavior.

Do these models of the development and importance of empathic emotion have any implications for our primary concern with group size effects? We suspect they do. As Zajonc (1965, 1980) maintains, the mere presence of other bystanders may constitute an additional source of arousal. Although this would suggest that the presence of others would lead to increased empathic distress and hence helping, we speculate that bystanders may actually be led to label their arousal as due to the other bystanders rather than to the distress of the victim. Increases in the number of other bystanders would then be accompanied by an escalated probability that such mislabeling would occur, decreasing the likelihood that empathic emotion (and helping) will eventually result.

Approaches Emphasizing Cognitive Factors

Lynch and Cohen (1978) provide a cognitive approach to understanding helping by applying a subjective expected utility (SEU) model to the process of deciding whether or not to help. The basic premise of their position is that situational factors affect helping by affecting the salience of the various consequences of acting or not acting, the utility or subjective evaluation of those consequences, and/or their subjective probability. People select courses of action whose salient consequences yield the greatest utility as compared to the salient consequences of other behavioral alternatives. Thus, the Lynch and Cohen formulation represents an extended elaboration of the Latané-Darley cost-reward model discussed earlier, with costs and rewards reflected in the subjective evaluations of the consequences following from helping or not helping.

Lynch and Cohen provide an extended SEU analysis of Darley and Latané's (1968) classic seizure study, demonstrating that the subjective expected utility of helping should decrease and helping be rendered less attractive as the number of other bystanders increases. For example, although the probability of experiencing "embarrassment over disrupting experiment if help not appropriate" may be constant as group size increases, the negative utility should increase with more witnesses, and the resulting $P \times U$ product should become increasingly negative. Likewise, the costs of nonintervention (for example, the SEU on incurring guilt and/or punishment) would also be affected by the addition of further bystanders. Two questionnaire studies providing a precise test of the model led Lynch and Cohen to conclude that the probability and utility of a given consequence do combine multiplicatively, but that the $P \times U$ products for different consequences do not combine additively; an averaging model proved more appropriate.

Another cognitive model (Fishbein, 1967) has been successfully used by both Pomazal and Jaccard (1976) and Zuckerman and Reis (1978) to predict altruistic behavior, namely, donating blood. Specifically, the Fishbein model holds that behavior is determined by one's intention to perform that behavior, thus suggesting that the simple question of "what would you do?" can be a useful predictor of helping behavior, at least in the context of blood donations. A major characteristic of this situation, as with the situations provided by Lynch and Cohen, is the lack of time pressure that accompanies the typical emergency. As a result, there is ordinarily more opportunity for a coherent cognitive structure (i.e., intention and its determinants) to emerge as a clearly identifiable and accurate predictor of helping behavior. Whether such cognitive processes operate in the same fashion (if at all) under the stressful circumstances of a real emergency remains, however, an open question.

Approaches Emphasizing Normative Factors

Schwartz (1973, 1977, Chapter 9) distinguishes two types of normative explanation of helping behavior—those that involve social norms and those that involve personal norms. The first suggests that behavior is governed by the social expectations that others hold as to what we should do. Special circumstances will activate specific norms—such as those of equity (Hatfield, Walster, & Piliavin, 1978) or social responsibility (Berkowitz, 1972)—and people will behave in accordance with these rules. From this sociological perspective, the presence of other people is seen as simply another factor capable of selectively activating or deactivating a given norm. In most situations, however, we would expect people to behave more normatively the greater the extent to which their behavior is monitored by others—i.e., the more people are present. This expectation is not confirmed by the data relating group size and helping, at least if we make the natural assumption that social norms prescribe helping. Latané and Darley (1970) discussed a number of other problems generally associated with normative explanations, pointing out that there exist so many different norms that virtually any behavior can be explained in this ad hoc fashion; as a result, social norms may not explain very much at all.

Schwartz' (1977) own theorizing is concerned with *personal* norms. Although personal norms (the activation of which is likely to foster helping) may often be consistent with prevailing social norms, they are internal rather than external rules—"self-expectations for specific action in particular situations [p. 227]." Schwartz describes the processes associated with norm construction, norm activation, and defending oneself against those norms.

The relevance of this theory to the group size phenomenon is not entirely clear, however, for it is much more general. Schwartz (e.g., 1973, 1977) has indicated that if the personal norms relevant to helping are to be activated, the individual must feel some personal responsibility to become involved in the situation calling for help. It is perhaps reasonable to view the group size effect as resulting from this step of the norm activation process: the amount of felt responsibility may simply decrease as the number of other potential helpers increases. Schwartz (1979) himself says, though, that "in general, the personal norms aspect is not enlightening for differentiating helpers from nonhelpers—because the overwhelming number of participants consider it their moral obligation to help." A second process that may be involved is "responsibility denial"; that is, the opportunity to neutralize responsibility can decrease the likelihood of helping (see the chapter by Schwartz in this volume). From this perspective, it would seem that increasing group size should enhance the probability of responsibility denial.

Schwartz (1973) links personal norms to the self-concept: "anticipation or actual violation of the norm result in guilt, self-deprecation, loss of self-esteem; conformity or its anticipation result in pride, enhanced self-esteem, security [p. 353]." This idea appears remarkably similar to the process specified by objective self-awareness theory (Duval & Wicklund, 1972), in which an individual compares his self-concept to some internally held standard, experiencing pleasure or displeasure depending on the direction of the discrepancy observed between the self-concept and the standard.

Wegner and Schaefer (1978) analyze helping behavior in terms of objective self-awareness theory. Dealing specifically with group size effects, they propose that increasing the number of bystanders to an emergency decreases the probability of their experiencing objective self-awareness, which in turn decreases the probability of intervention. Following the Gestalt figure-ground principle, witnesses to an emergency should focus their attention on the role of whichever subgroup, bystander or victim, is smaller. A lone bystander would be likely to focus attention on himself and become objectively self-aware and help, but the presence of several bystanders should lead each to focus attention on the victim, decreasing self-awareness and, consequently, helping. In a complementary fashion, Wegner and Schaefer claim, increasing the number of victims should focus attention on the bystander subgroup, leading to more helping. It is interesting that while Coke et al. assume that attending to the victim should increase helping, Wegner and Schaefer predict the opposite result.

Although we find Wegner and Schaefer's explanation ingenious and are persuaded that focusing attention on one's internal standard of behavior is indeed likely to facilitate helping, we do not find it plausible that increasing the number of victims should decrease the amount of attention paid to them or that focusing attention on the victim should decrease the amount of help given. Wegner and Schaefer (1978) did find that a group of observer-subjects, given a written account of the experimental situation, judged that more attention would be focused on a specific victim if he was alone rather than a member of a three-victim group. It would seem, however, that the amount of attention paid to the *entire* group of victims would be more than that paid to any single member of the victim group. Furthermore, it is not clear how this theoretical position might deal with victimless emergencies. Wegner and Schaefer do present data supporting their predictions: increasing the number of bystanders decreases helping whereas increasing the number of victims increases helping. However, we think their results can be more parsimoniously interpreted by means of social impact theory.

Social Impact Theory

As a final theoretical elaboration that contributes to our understanding of the social inhibition of helping we present Latané's theory of social impact (Latané, 1973, 1976, 1978, 1981; Latané & Nida, 1980)—a broad theory of social behavior that attempts to specify the direction and amount of effect that the presence or actions of other people can have on an individual. According to Latané (1981) social impact refers to "any of the great variety of changes in physiological states and subjective feelings, motives and emotions, cognitions and beliefs, values and behavior that occur in an individual human or animal as a result of the real, implied, or imagined presence or actions of other individuals [p. 343]."

Impact is considered to be a result of the operation of social forces in a force field. The first principle of social impact theory states that the amount of impact experienced by a target in a multiplicative force field where other people are affecting him is a multiplicative function of the strength or salience (S), the immediacy or closeness (I), and the number (N) of persons who are the sources of impact: Impact = f(SIN). Since the present issue is the relationship between group size and helping, the third component (N) is the one of most concern here: the greater the number of other people affecting an individual, the greater the amount of impact he or she will experience. The processes of audience inhibition and social influence as we have described them should operate in such a multiplicative social force field. In other words, the individual bystander to an emergency should experience greater levels of audience inhibition and social influence as the number of other bystanders increases.

A second principle of social impact theory is a generalization of the concept of diffusion of responsibility. When other people stand with the individual in a divisive force field as the target of social forces coming from outside the group, increases in the strength, immediacy, or number of other people (i.e., other targets) should lead to a diminution or division of impact, with each target experiencing less impact than he or she would if alone. For example, the person witnessing an emergency simply feels less responsibility to intervene the greater the number of other witnesses who are present.

Finally, Latané (1981) hypothesizes that the addition of other sources in a social force field should result in marginally decreasing impact. That is, the first other person in a multiplicative social situation should have a greater effect than, say, the hundredth. As a parallel to Stevens's (1957) psychophysical law,

Latané's psycho*social* law states that social impact (I) should be equal to some root (t) of the number of sources (N), times a scaling constant (s) that reflects the specific situation and the impact of a single person. The theory maintains, furthermore, that the absolute value of the exponent t should be smaller than one—in other words, impact is proportional to some root of the number of people present: $I = sN^t$, $t < 1$. In divisive social situations, of course, $I = s/N^t$, which is equivalent to: $I = sN^{-t}$—the formula is the same but the sign of the exponent has changed.

In a multiplicative force field the degree of audience inhibition or social influence should grow as a power function of the number of people present, decreasing the individual's likelihood of giving help. In a typical conformity study (Gerard, Wilhelmy, & Conolley, 1968), for example, a power function accounts for 80% of the variance in means (i.e., conformity increases with increases in the number of other "conformers"). And in a study of imitation, Milgram, Bickman, and Berkowitz (1969) found that the greater the number of confederates standing on a street looking at an upstairs window, the greater was the likelihood that passersby would stop and join the group; in this case a power function accounted for 90% of the variance in imitation. Finally, Latané and Harkins (1976) found that anticipated tension and nervousness about performing before an audience increased as a power function of the number of people in the audience.

A number of experiments have been designed to test implications of social impact theory in helping situations. For example, the data of an experiment by Freeman (1974), in which persons in groups of different sizes were given the chance to report a power failure, follow an inverse power function (Fig. 14.2). Consistent with the theory, a negatively accelerated power function of the form $I = .77N^{-.81}$ accounts for an impressive 96% of the variance in means. Note that the sign of the exponent is negative as should be the case with divisive force fields, and its absolute value is less than one, showing marginally decreasing impact.

Other research also supports the theory. For example, Latané and Dabbs (1975) gave elevator riders the opportunity to help a fellow passenger who "accidentally" dropped some pencils or coins; the individual probability of response decreased as the number of people available to respond increased, a result more describable by an inverse power function having an exponent of about .5. In a study of tipping in restaurants (Freeman, Walker, Borden, & Latané, 1975), it was found that increasing the number of people dining together led to less tipping; in this case an inverse power function with an exponent of about .2 accounted for about 95% of the variance in mean percentage tipped.

In sum, the theory of social impact provides a more precise and quantitative indicator of inhibition of helping that occurs in group settings. In addition, however, the theory provides a general framework by which we can both understand the processes underlying the social inhibition of helping and see it as only a

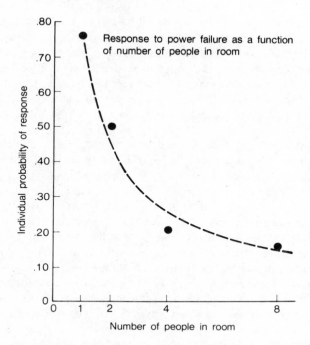

FIG. 14.2.   Response to power failure as a function of number of people in room (from Freeman, 1974).

single instance of a more general social phenomenon. Although the theory is sufficiently integrative to deal with the helping situation, it nevertheless leads to specific predictions; furthermore, social impact theory offers the distinct advantage of being able to account for the different ways in which increasing the number of other people can have opposite effects on the individual.

Finally, to put Wegner and Schaefer's (1978) experimental situation in terms of social impact theory, we would maintain that the single victim–multiple bystanders condition constitutes a divisive social force field conducive to the diffusion of responsibility as we have already described it. The situation involving multiple victims and a single bystander, however, corresponds to a multiplicative force field in which a higher level of helping is to be expected because of the higher level of social impact created by the presence of three victims (rather than one).

The Likelihood of Receiving Help

Thus far we have been dealing with the question of why an individual is less likely to help if part of a group than if alone. The victim of an emergency is concerned with a different issue, however—whether *anyone* will offer assistance—and is likely to assume that the more people available to respond, the greater the chance of finding at least one to do so. Latané and Darley (1970) viewed the victim's probability of going unhelped as simply the product of each individual bystander's probability of not helping (if the individual probabilities are assumed to be equal, this reduces to a simple binomial model). They treated the question of whether the increases in probability of *receiving* help due to the increased availability of helpers is great enough to outweigh the decrease in each helper's individual probability of *giving* help as an empirical issue.

According to Tables 14.1 and 14.2, very often the victim is actually *less* likely to get help as the number of helpers increases. In Table 14.1, in those studies involving full communication and confederates or others who are believed to be present the percentage of alone subjects helping exceeds the hypothetical proportion of groups helping in 21 out of a total of 32 comparisons; in 9 of these the reverse occurs, whereas in 2 the percentages are equal. Treating the comparison as the unit of analysis, we performed a matched-pairs t test comparing the hypothetical proportion of groups helping and the percentage of alone subjects helping. The resulting t of 3.00 ($df = 31$, $p < .01$) indicates that the victim is indeed less likely to receive help when groups are present (mean percentage = 70%) than when there is a single bystander (mean percentage = 82%).

We would expect, however, that such an effect should not be as strong when communication among bystanders is restricted. For the asterisked studies in Table 14.1, the percentage of alone subjects helping exceeds the hypothetical proportion of groups helping in only 7 out of 23 cases, whereas the reverse occurs in 15 comparisons; in one case the percentages are equal. A matched-pair t test performed on the asterisked data of Table 14.1 produces a nonsignificant t ($df = 22$) of 1.49. In studies involving restricted communication, then, the victim actually fares a little better in front of groups (mean percentage helping = 89%) than with single bystanders (mean percentage helping = 84%).

When actual groups are considered (Table 14.2), the victim once again appears to have a greater likelihood of receiving help when there is a single witness. The percentage of alone subjects helping exceeds the percentage of groups with one or more helpers in 26 of 36 instances, with the reverse occurring in 8 comparisons and equal percentages occurring in 2 cases. The matched-pairs t for Table 14.2 is 2.16 ($df = 35$, $p < .05$), indicating again that the likelihood of a victim's receiving aid is reliably lower in the presence of groups (mean percentage = 55%) than with individual bystanders (mean percentage = 62%). When all of the data in the tables are considered, this difference (69% versus 74%) is in the same direction and is again reliable: $t = 2.64$ ($df = 90$, $p < .01$). In general, a victim does seem to stand a slightly greater chance of receiving assistance when only a single individual witnesses his plight.

Grofman (1974) noticed that, in several of the early studies involving noncommunicating groups, an exponential model in which the probability of helping remains constant regardless of the number of bystanders present provided a good fit to the data. Grofman also noted that an exponential model—in this case one in which the likelihood of helping decreases as the square of the number of witnesses to the emergency—seemed to offer a satisfactory fit to the data of experiments involving communicating strangers as bystanders. Although Grofman's approach is descriptive rather than explanatory, his observation suggests that individual bystanders may act so as to regulate group output. As a precise form of diffusion of responsibility, it is possible that people in noncommunicating groups decrease their own likelihood of helping sufficiently to maintain the victim's chance of receiving aid at a constant level—a notion supported by our analysis of the studies involving restricted communication.

Morgan and Leik (described in Morgan, 1978) focus on the length of time that can be expected to elapse before at least one member of a group of bystanders will intervene in a situation calling for help. The basic equation of their model is:

$$R = (G/N) + I,$$

where R represents the individual's felt responsibility, G refers to the net expected group benefits, and I stands for the net expected individual benefits of helping. It is also assumed that R increases over time, but it is not specified whether this increase results from changes in G, I, or both. An individual will intervene whenever R exceeds his threshold for response, but different individuals have different thresholds for response. Thus, increasing the number of bystanders (N) should result in a decrease in R but a concurrent increase in the likelihood that that group will contain a person with a low threshold. A series of further equations is used to derive expected response latencies. Depending on the values assumed for G and I, expected response latency sometimes increases with group size, sometimes decreases with group size, and sometimes first increases and then decreases with group size.

Morgan's (1978) subjects had to decide whether to respond to someone knocking on the door while they solved mathematics problems. When the costs of intervening were low (i.e., when subjects had an unlimited amount of time to work on their task), no effect of group size on the length of time before someone intervened was observed. When subjects had only 10 minutes to work on the problems (i.e., when costs were high), however, response latencies tended to increase with increases in group size. Consistent with prediction, curves generated by the Morgan-Leik model provided a good fit to the data of both of these conditions.

The apparent flexibility of the model is no doubt responsible for Morgan's contention that it has considerable potential for integrating results from a range of studies, including those producing inconsistent findings. Although this characteristic may seem impressive, such flexibility is unfortunately made possible only by the numerous free parameters contained within the model; in this sense, then, the model may be *too* flexible to be especially useful. A further limitation of the model is its failure to deal with theoretical processes other than the diffusion of responsibility; despite its apparent flexibility, it cannot deal with the issues of audience inhibition and social influence. And, despite its complexity, the Morgan-Leik model emerges as the theoretical equivalent of the original Latané and Darley treatment of diffusion of responsibility, with the exception of the former's mechanism for dealing with individual differences (i.e., the notion of individual response thresholds).

CONCLUSIONS

In this chapter we have attempted briefly to portray the current status of some ten years of theory and research on the relationship between group size and helping in emergencies. We have discussed methodological concerns, summarized the available data, and surveyed a number of relevant theoretical positions. The two conclusions that follow from this exercise are straightforward. First, there is little doubt that an individual's likelihood of giving help decreases as the number of other bystanders also witnessing an emergency increases. The evidence for this group size effect is vast, remarkably consistent, and is comprised of studies involving a wide variety of experimenters, experimental situations, and participant populations.

Our second conclusion is that the current theory relevant to this issue represents quite a complete array of emphases on the psychological processes that lead to helping. Some theorists stress the role of emotion in the decision to help. Others depict the decison to help as a rational process involving a calculated judgment of cost-benefit factors, and still others describe a moral or rule-following process that determines whether the individual will help. We also offered a description of the theory of social impact—quantitative in part, yet providing a general, integrative framework that subsumes group size effects as well as other social psychological phenomena. Finally, we discussed mathematical formulations relating the bystander's probability of helping to the victim's probability of receiving help.

It would be a mistake to consider any of these theoretical positions as either right or wrong. Each has its own unique emphasis and each highlights a different facet of the psychological process underlying helping. Although some of the theoretical positions are not explicitly concerned with the group size effect, each has implications for it. The factors mediating the social inhibition of helping are undoubtedly complex and likely involve several or all of the different types of processes emphasized in the various theories. We hope that the next decade of work on this topic as well as on prosocial behavior in general continues the movement toward developing integrative theory.

REFERENCES

Allen, H. Bystander intervention and helping on the subway. In L. Bickman & T. Henchy (Eds.), *Beyond the laboratory: Field research in social psychology.* New York: McGraw Hill, 1972.

Anonymous. Manuscript reviewed by first author.

Aronson, E., & Carlsmith, J. M. Experimentation in social psychology. In. G. Lindzey and E. Aronson (Eds.), *Handbook of social psychology* (Vol. 2). Reading, MA.: Addison-Wesley, 1968.

Beaman, A. L., & Diener, E. *The effects of evaluation apprehension and social comparison on emergency helping behavior.* Unpublished manuscript, 1976.

Berkowitz, L. Social norms, feelings, and other factors affecting helping and altruism. In L. Berkowitz (Ed.), *Advances in experimental social psychology* (Vol. 6). New York: Academic Press, 1972.

Bickman, L. The effect of another bystander's ability to help on bystander intervention in an emergency. *Journal of Experimental Social Psychology,* 1971, *7,* 367–379.

Byeff, P. *Helping behavior and audio and audio-video conditions.* Unpublished senior honors thesis, University of Pennsylvania, 1970.

Clark, R. D., & Word, L. E. Why don't bystanders help? Because of ambiguity? *Journal of Personality and Social Psychology,* 1972, *24,* 392–400.

Clark, R. D., & Word, L. Where is the apathetic bystander? Situational characteristics of the emergency. *Journal of Personality and Social Psychology,* 1974, *29,* 279–287.

Coke, J. S., Batson, C. D., & McDavis, K. Empathic mediation of helping: A two-stage model. *Journal of Personality and Social Psychology,* 1978, *36,* 752–766.

Darley, J. M., & Latané, B. Bystander intervention in emergencies: Diffusion of responsibility. *Journal of Personality and Social Psychology.* 1968, *8,* 377–383.

Darley, J. M., Teger, A. I., & Lewis, L. D. Do groups always inhibit individuals' responses to potential emergencies? *Journal of Personality and Social Psychology,* 1973, *26,* 395–399.

Duval, S. & Wicklund, R. A. *A theory of objective self awareness.* New York: Academic Press, 1972.

Fienberg, S. E., & Larntz, F. K. Some models for individual-group comparisons and group behavior. *Psychometrika,* 1971, *36,* 349–367.

Fishbein, M. Attitude and the prediction of behavior. In M. Fishbein (Ed.), *Readings in attitude theory and measurement.* New York: Wiley, 1967.

Freeman, S. M. *Group inhibition of helping in nonemergency situations.* Unpublished master's thesis, Ohio State University, 1974.

Freeman, S., Walker, M., Borden, R., & Latané, B. Diffusion of responsibility and restaurant tipping: Cheaper by the bunch. *Personality and Social Psychology Bulletin,* 1975, *1,* 584–587.

Gaertner, S. L. The role of racial attitudes in helping behavior. *Journal of Social Psychology,* 1975, *97,* 95–101.

Gaertner, S. L., & Dovidio, J. F. The subtlety of white racism, arousal, and helping behavior. *Journal of Personality and Social Psychology,* 1977, *35,* 691–707.

Gerard, H. B., Wilhelmy, R. A., & Conolley, E. S. Conformity and group size. *Journal of Personality and Social Psychology,* 1968, *8,* 79–82.

Grofman, B. Helping behavior and group size: Some exploratory stochastic models. *Behavioral Science,* 1974, *19,* 219–224.

Harris, V. A., & Robinson, C. E. Bystander intervention: Group size and victim status. *Bulletin of the Psychonomic Society,* 1973, *2,* 8–10.

Hatfield, E., Walster, G. W., & Piliavin, J. A. Equity theory and helping relationships. In L. Wispé (Ed.), *Altruism, sympathy, and helping.* New York: Academic Press, 1978.

Horowitz, I. A. The effect of group norms on bystander intervention. *Journal of Social Psychology,* 1971, *83,* 265–273.

Howard, W., & Crano, W. D. Effects of sex, conversation location, and size of observer group on bystander intervention in a high risk situation. *Sociometry*, 1974, *37*, 491–507.

Konecni, V. J. & Ebbesen, E.B. Effects of the presence of children on adults' helping behavior and compliance: Two field studies. *Journal of Social Psychology*, 1975, *97*, 181–193.

Krupat, E., & Epstein, Y. *I'm too busy: The effects of overload and diffusion of responsibility on working and helping*. American Psychological Association, Montreal, September, 1973.

Latané, B. Field studies of altruistic compliance. *Representative Research in Social Psychology*, 1970, *1*, 49–62.

Latané, B. *Theory of social impact*. Paper presented at meeting of Psychonomic Society, St. Louis, 1973.

Latané, B. *Theory of social impact*. Paper presented at Symposium on Social Influence. XXI International Congress of Psychology, Paris, 1976.

Latané, B. *On comparing individuals with groups: Comment on Misavage and Richardson, "The focusing of responsibility: An alternative hypothesis in help-demanding situations."* Unpublished manuscript, Ohio State University, 1977.

Latané, B. *The psychology of social impact*. Presidential Address, Society for Personality and Social Psychology, American Psychological Association, Toronto, 1978.

Latané, B. Psychology of social impact. *American Psychologist*, 1981, *36*, 343–356.

Latané, B. & Dabbs, J. M. Sex, group size, and helping in three cities. *Sociometry*, 1975, *38*, 180–194.

Latané, B., & Darley, J. M. Group inhibition of bystander intervention in emergencies. *Journal of Personality and Social Psychology*, 1968, *10*, 215–221.

Latané, B., & Darley, J. M. *The unresponsive bystander: Why doesn't he help?* New York: Appleton-Century-Crofts, 1970.

Latané, B., & Darley, J. M. *Help in a crisis: Bystander response to an emergency*. Morristown, NJ: General Learning Press, 1976.

Latané, B., & Elman, D. The bystander and the thief. Reported in B. Latané & J. M. Darley, *The unresponsive bystander: Why doesn't he help?* New York: Appleton-Century-Crofts, 1970.

Latané, B., & Harkins, S. Cross-modality matches suggest anticipated stage fright a multiplicative power function of audience size and status. *Perception and Psychophysics*, 1976, *20*, 482–488.

Latané, B., & Nida, S. Social impact theory and group influence: A social engineering perspective. In P. B. Paulus (Ed.), *Psychology of group influence*. Hillsdale, NJ: Lawrence Erlbaum Associates, 1980.

Latané, B., & Rodin, J. A lady in distress: Inhibiting effects of friends and strangers on bystander intervention. *Journal of Experimental Social Psychology*, 1969, *5*, 189–202.

Levy, P., Lundgren, D., Ansel, M., Fell, D., Fink, B., & McGrath, J. E. Bystander effect in a demand-without-threat situation. *Journal of Personality and Social Psychology*, 1972, *24*, 166–171.

Lynch, J. G., & Cohen, J. L. The use of subjective expected utility theory as an aid to understanding variables that influence helping behavior. *Journal of Personality and Social Psychology*, 1978, *36*, 1138–1151.

Milgram, S., Bickman, L., & Berkowitz, L. Note on the drawing power of crowds of different size. *Journal of Personality and Social Psychology*, 1969, *13*, 79–82.

Misavage, R., & Richardson, J. T. The focusing of responsibility: An alternative hypothesis in help-demanding situations. *European Journal of Social Psychology*, 1974, *4*, 5–15.

Morgan, C. J. Bystander intervention: Experimental test of a formal model. *Journal of Personality and Social Psychology*, 1978, *36*, 43–55.

Moylan, J. J., & Greenwood, J. *Thief! Thief!* Unpublished manuscript, 1972.

Petty, R. E., Williams, K. D., Harkins, S. G., & Latané, B. Social inhibition of helping yourself: Bystander response to a cheeseburger. *Personality and Social Psychology Bulletin*, 1977, *3*, 575–578.

Piliavin, J. A., & Piliavin, I. M. Effect of blood on reaction to a victim. Journal of *Personality and Social Psychology.* 1972, *23,* 353–36].

Piliavin, I. M., Piliavin, J. A., & Rodin, J. Costs, diffusion, and the stigmatized victim. *Journal of Personality and Social Psychology.* 1975, *32,* 429–438.

Piliavin, J. A., Piliavin, I. M., & Trudell, B. *Incidental arousal, helping, and diffusion of responsibility.* Unpublished data.

Piliavin, I. M., Rodin, J., & Piliavin, J. A. Good Samaritanism: An underground phenomenon? *Journal of Personality and Social Psychology.* 1969, *13,* 289–299.

Pomazal, R. J. & Jaccard, J. J. An informational approach to altruistic behavior. *Journal of Personality and Social Psychology,* 1976, *33,* 317–326.

Ross, A. S. *Stranger in a strange land.* Unpublished manuscript, 1969. 4–34.

Ross, A. S. Effect of increased responsibility on bystander intervention: The presence of children. *Journal of Personality and Social Psychology,* 1971, *19,* 306–310.

Ross, A. S., & Braband, J. Effect of increased responsibility on bystander intervention, II: The we value of a blind person. *Journal of Personality and Social Psychology,* 1973, *25,* 254–258.

Ross, A. S., & Burke, H. *Effect of visibility of the victim on bystander intervention.* Unpublished manuscript, 1973.

Schachter, S. The interaction of cognitive and physiological determinants of emotional state. In L. Berkowitz (Ed.), *Advances in experimental social psychology* ((Vol. 1). New York: Academic Press, 1964.

Schwartz, S. Personal Communication, August 9, 1979.

Schwartz, S. H. Normative explanations of helping behavior: A critique, proposal, and empirical test. *Journal of Experimental Social Psychology,* 1973, *9,* 349–364.

Schwartz, S. H. Normative influences on altruism. In L. Berkowitz (Ed.), *Advances in experimental social psychology* (Vol. 10). New York: Academic Press, 1977.

Schwartz, S. H., & Clausen, G. T. Responsibility, norms, and helping in an emergency. *Journal of Personality and Social Psychology,* 1970, *16,* 229–310.

Schwartz, S. H., & Gottlieb, A. Bystander reactions to a violent theft: Crime in Jerusalem. *Journal of Personality and Social Psychology,* 1976, *34,* 1188–1199.

Shaffer, D. R., Rogel, M., & Hendrick, D. Intervention in the library: The effect of increased responsibility on bystanders' willingness to prevent a theft. *Journal of Applied Social Psychology,* 1975, *5,* 303–319.

Silverman, I. *Prediction of high-risk prosocial behavior.* Paper presented at meeting of American Psychological Association, Chicago, August-September 1975.

Smith, R. E., Smythe, L., & Lien, D. Inhibition of helping behavior by a similar or dissimilar nonreactive fellow bystander. *Journal of Personality and Social Psychology,* 1972, *23,* 414–419.

Solomon, L. Z., Solomon, H., & Stone, R. Helping as a function of number of bystanders and ambiguity of emergency. *Personality and Social Psychology Bulletin,* 1978, *4,* 318–321.

Sommerfreund, J., & Goodstadt, M. S. *Social influence and bystander apathy to emergencies.* Paper presented at meeting of the Midwestern Psychological Association, Detroit, May, 1971.

Staub, E. A child in distress: The influence of age and number of witnesses on children's attempts to help. *Journal of Personality and Social Psychology,* 1970, *14,* 130–140.

Staub, E. Helping a distressed person: Social, personality, and stimulus determinants. In L. Berkowitz (Ed.), *Advances in experimental social psychology* (Vol. 7). New York: Academic Press, 1974.

Stevens, S. S. On the psychophysical law. *Psychological Review,* 1957, *64,* 153–181.

Teger, A. I., & Henderson, J. E. *An examination of the social influence hypothesis of bystander intervention in emergencies.* Paper presented at Eastern Psychological Association Meeting, 1971.

Thalhofer, N. N. Responsibility, reparation, and self-protection as reasons for three types of helping. *Journal of Personality and Social Psychology.* 1971, *19,* 144–151.

Wegner, D. M., & Schaefer, D. The concentration of responsibility: An objective self-awareness analysis of group size effects in helping situations. *Journal of Personality and Social Psychology.* 1978, *36,* 147–155.

Wilson, J. P. Motivation, modeling, and altruism: A person X situation analysis. *Journal of Personality and Social Psychology,* 1976, *34,* 1078–1086.

Zajonc, R. B. Social facilitation. *Science,* 1965, *149,* 269–274.

Zajonc, R. B. Compresence. In P. B. Paulus (Ed.), *Psychology of group influence.* Hillsdale, NJ: Lawrence Erlbaum Associates, 1980.

Zuckerman, M., & Reis, H. T. Comparison of three models for predicting altruistic behavior. *Journal of Personality and Social Psychology,* 1978, *36,* 498–510.

15 Constraints on Helping Behavior in an Urban Environment

Charles Korte
North Carolina State University

Do the conditions of city living lead to a reduction in the helpfulness shown toward a person who needs assistance? Our stereotype of urban behavior suggests that this is the case and this stereotype has in fact been fruitful for research into helping behavior, if one thinks of the several useful explanations for helpfulness that have derived from the analysis of urban unhelpfulness, e.g., the responsibility diffusion explanation (Darley & Latané, 1968), and the input overload explanation (Milgram, 1970). Yet, in spite of the obvious interest in the link between helping behavior and the conditions of city living, the growing body of research on helping behavior has done little to clarify (1) whether a person is less likely to be helped by others in a city versus a less urbanized environment; and (2) if people in cities are less helpful, whether this is in fact due to the influence of factors that have been postulated as leading to urban unhelpfulness. This chapter describes a series of studies conducted by the author and his colleagues, which have sought to examine in detail the influence that an urban context exerts on helping behavior. The results of these studies will be related to other research and theorizing that has been carried out in this area, in order to see what general conclusions can be drawn at this point.

HELPFULNESS: ARE THERE CITY-TOWN DIFFERENCES?

Exploration of a helpfulness-urbanization link must begin with a question that is commonly overlooked. Is the likelihood of helpful action actually lower in a more urban versus less urban environment? Much has been presumed about the behavioral differences of persons in urban vs. nonurban environments, but very

315

few studies have been carried out that evaluate this presumption. Added to this difficulty is the fact that helpfulness covers a wide variety of different *acts*— e.g., assistance in emergencies, favor-doing, donations, giving comfort—which are carried out in a variety of different *contexts*—e.g., within the family, between strangers in public, anonymous acts carried out in private. The few studies that have compared the levels of positive forms of social behavior in more urban and less urban places can be categorized according to the context of helpfulness, e.g., whether it occurred between relatives, friends, or strangers. A review of these studies (Korte, 1976, 1978, 1980) shows that urban-nonurban differences in social behavior occur only for helpfulness between *strangers*. There is no evidence that relatives and friends are less likely to help each other in the city as compared to what is found in smaller-sized places. Thus it appears that if there is a link between urbanization and helpfulness, it is most likely to be apparent in those forms of helpfulness that involve the response to a stranger in need of assistance.

The first study to compare helpfulness between strangers in cities and towns was conducted by Milgram (1970), who reported two measures on which urbanites were less helpful than their less urban counterparts: willingness to admit strangers at the door asking to use the telephone, and willingness to assist wrong number callers who seek information. Small town residents were clearly more helpful than the urban residents (New York City) on the first measure, 72% versus 27%, whereas they were only slightly more helpful on the wrong number measure.

In the first study (Korte & Kerr, 1975) in the series described in this chapter, the aim was to undertake a comparison of urban and nonurban locales which (1) excluded New York City as possibly an atypical urban locale; and (2) used several different measures of solicited and unsolicited helpfulness. This study compared helpfulness in Boston with that found in several small towns in eastern Massachusetts. Three measures of helpfulness were used. One was the wrong number technique, which tested the helpfulness of people who answered what was presumed to be a wrong number call. The second measure, the accidental overpayment technique (Feldman, 1968), involved buying small items in self-service stores, where the researcher would leave an amount of money on the counter as an exact change payment and signal to the clerk that this was being done, although, in fact, the money left exceeded the exact amount. The researcher would slowly leave the store allowing time for the clerk to collect the money left, the measure then being whether or not the clerk called the shopper back to correct the overpayment. The final measure was the lost postcard measure (Milgram, Mann, & Harter, 1965) in which stamped postcards bearing an important message were "lost" in urban and nonurban locales, in order to observe the return rate. Each of these measures was administered by a female researcher. For the wrong number measure, a total of 40 respondents were selected by randomly drawing names from the appropriate telephone directory.

Forty stores were used for the overpayment measure and they represented a cross-section of the stores where it was feasible to leave exact change for small items. For the lost postcard measure a total of 36 postcards were distributed in a wide variety of easily noticed spots. The sample sizes were low in this particular study, but there is some compensation in the fact that three different measures were administered to test for helpfulness differences between cities and small towns.

The results confirmed that city people were less helpful than their small town counterparts. The helpfulness shown toward the wrong number caller was rated on a 4-point scale and showed a lower level of helpfulness in the city than in the small towns. The same difference was evident with the second measure: 80% of town store clerks corrected the overpayment, versus 55% of the city clerks. Finally on the third measure, more postcards were returned in the small towns than in the city locale, 78% versus 61%. In light of the small sample size, a final analysis was done which used dichotomized versions of all the measures and compared the overall rate of helpfulness in Boston versus the small towns, combining all three measures. This comparison showed a significant difference in favor of the small towns on helpfulness, 78% versus 55%. Hence the results provided consistent support for a helpfulness-urbanization link and confirmed that one did not have to use New York City in order to demonstrate city-town differences in helping behavior. This first study also showed that city-town differences were consistent for measures of solicited as well as unsolicited help-fulness and for face-to-face as well as remote helpfulness. The reliability of city-town differences in helpfulness between strangers has become even clearer with the evidence of a number of recent studies that have used a variety of helpfulness measures, e.g., returning lost letters (Hannson & Slade, 1977; Kammann, Thomson, & Irwin, 1979; Krupat & Coury, 1975; except if the letter addressee suggests a deviant identity, when the city-town difference reverses; see Hannson & Slade, 1977), doing small favors (Merrens, 1973; Rushton, 1978), helping a lost child (Takooshian, Haber, & Lucido, 1977), responding to wrong number callers (Kammann, Thomson, & Irwin, 1979), and agreeing to survey interviews (House & Wolf, 1978). In a clear minority are two studies which failed to find city-town differences in helping behavior (Forbes & Gromoll, 1973; Schneider & Mockus, 1974). This reinforces the belief that there is some-thing to be explained in the helpfulness that occurs in cities versus towns. There are additional studies that have examined urban versus nonurban background as a predictor of helping behavior, usually in the context of a laboratory study (Darley & Latané, 1968; Gelfand, Hartman, Walder, & Page, 1973; Hannson, Slade, & Slade, 1978; Korte, 1971; Schwartz & Clausen, 1970; Weiner, 1976). For the most part, these studies test whether the impact of living and growing up in a city is evident even when urbanites are somewhat removed from a city environment, i.e., in a psychological laboratory. The results of these studies offer only limited support for what may be called an "urban personality" explanation of helpfulness: only Darley and Latané (1968) and Gelfand et al. (1973) found differences in the helpfulness between subjects with city versus town backgrounds, with the town subjects being more helpful.

URBAN UNHELPFULNESS: ADAPTATION TO ENVIRONMENTAL INPUT LEVELS?

The results described so far indicate that there is a decrease in helpfulness toward strangers in urban environments. This leads to the question of *why* this difference exists. The three most plausible explanations for this difference can be termed the situational explanation, the urban personality explanation, and the population bias explanation. The situational explanation attributes the lower levels of helpfulness in the city to the influence of immediate environmental factors, e.g., congestion, noise levels, and high crime rates, which are usually more common in cities and are seen as having the effect of reducing the likelihood of helping behavior. Hence, this analysis suggests that with these particular environmental factors present, anyone encountering a person in need of assistance would be less helpful. The urban personality explanation states that the fact of having lived a considerable period of time in a city makes one less ready to respond to a stranger needing assistance. In this account, the conditions of city living are viewed as producing fairly enduring habits, mannerisms, and perceptions that make the urbanite less helpful, even in circumstances that are decidedly nonurban. The third explanation, population bias, argues that a city environment or city living per se has not made urbanites less helpful but that among the population of people found in the city there is a greater preponderence of people whose personality, cultural background, or personal circumstances makes them less likely to respond to others who need assistance. The city is thus composed of people who to begin with are less likely to act in a helpful way toward strangers.

The population bias explanation is of uncertain usefulness to the question of urban unhelpfulness. A survey of the characteristics of the urban population by Fischer (1976) found urbanites to be younger, less often married, higher in socioeconomic status, more diverse in background, and forming smaller-sized families. None of these characteristics would seem to lead to less helpfulness, except for the case of helpfulness between socially dissimilar people; helpfulness is likely to be reduced in such cases, and instances of racial and ethnic dissimilarity are more common in an urban environment (Fischer, 1976). Population bias has in fact been used mainly to explain behavioral characteristics other than helpfulness, e.g., the sociability of suburbanites (Gans, 1967) and mental illness in center city areas (Srole, 1972). This explanation was not seen as a central one for the phenomenon of urban unhelpfulness and hence did not serve as a focus for studies described in this chapter.

The present series of studies turned first to an evaluation of a situational explanation of urban unhelpfulness. It was felt that this would lead to a furthering of our understanding as to the particular ways in which the conditions of city living might result in a reduction in helpfulness among urbanites. In addition, evaluation of the impact of situational factors can be readily carried out methodologically with easily interpretable quasiexperimental techniques. A subsequent study in this series, the last one described in this paper, sheds some light on the social background, or urban personality, explanation.

The particular situational explanation whose evaluation was the goal of the following study is Milgram's (1970) input overload hypothesis, which links helpfulness in an urban environment to the level of "inputs"—stimuli, demands, opportunities, etc.—that characterizes that environment. An environment with an excessively high level of inputs such as a large city is, according to this view, managed only by adopting tactics that reduce the stress of the social and physical bombardment. Among these adapations may be a reduced willingness to respond to strangers who need assistance, which makes every day life in a large city far more manageable than it would otherwise be. Milgram's analysis states that the adaptive adjustments occurred once a point of input "overload" was reached. This is an intuitively appealing idea, but it presents methodological difficulties, principally the one of verifying whether subjects in a naturalistic field setting are in a state of overload or not. To meet this problem, Milgram's explanation of urban unhelpfulness was put in a more testable form, which predicts a decrease in helpfulness with an increase in the input level.

Examination of the environmental input level hypothesis was carried out in a field study, in collaboration with Ido Ypma and Anneke Toppen (Korte, Ypma, & Toppen, 1975). This research was conducted in the Netherlands, which also afforded an opportunity to test the cross-cultural generality of the city-town differences in helping behavior that had been found in North America. The basic design of the study involved locating a number of street locales where conditions were equivalent except for the environmental input level, which would be either high or low. The pedestrians in these locales were tested on naturalistic measures of helpfulness to see if their response would differ according to input level. To measure input level, a four part measuring instrument was developed and validated (see Korte et al., 1975 for details) which consisted of recording four environmental features: sound level of the locale, traffic density, pedestrian density, and the number of visible establishments catering to the public (mostly stores). Twenty different locales were used in the study, 10 with high and 10 with low input levels, and these locales were located in the two major cities of the Netherlands (Amsterdam and the Hague) and in four towns. Locales were selected in pairs; a potential pair would be used if they appeared to differ in input level and if the two locales were near enough together so as to have a sufficient interchange of pedestrian traffic, hence reducing the chance that the pedestrians in the two locales differed in a significant way, e.g., personal characteristics or present activity. Meeting this test, the locale pair was then examined to see whether the two locales showed sufficient differentiation on the input level measure. This was administered four times (before and after each of the two visits to the site for collection of the helpfulness data), the standard of acceptance being that the pair differ on at least three out of the four parts of the measure.

Three different measures of helpfulness were then applied: a request to people for their cooperation in a short interview, an accidental dropping of a bicycle key which goes unnoticed by the dropper, and a slightly distressed person attempting, apparently unsuccessfully, to find his or her destination using a local street map. The measures were administered by two Dutch social psychology graduate students, one male and one female, who collected data simultaneously in the two locales of a locale pair, hence further controlling for unwanted variation between the high- and low-input locales. For the interview measure, 400 subjects were selected by picking every fifth bypasser. Two hundred subjects were tested on the dropped key measure, selected on the basis of their being the first bypasser after the fourth who was unaccompanied and at a proper distance to be the obvious person to call attention to the dropped key. Subjects for the map assistance measure were all persons (n = 1967) to walk past the map reader on 200 separate trials, the measure being the percentage of people stopping to help; the trial ended once a helper stopped to assist, or else if 3 minutes had elapsed without help.

The results of this study showed a clear effect of input level on helping behavior: for all three measures, greater helpfulness occurred in the *low* input level locales, with these differences significant for the interview measure ($X^2(3) = 11.0$, p<.05) and the map measure ($X^2(1) = 31.2$, p<.01). This then was clear evidence that helpfulness is quite responsive to the influence of the immediate level of environmental bombardment, illustrating at least a short-term (if not also a long-term) adaptation of helping behavior to environmental circumstances which would seem quite prominent in an urban environment. Hence, it could provide part of the explanation for the lower levels of helpfulness found in the city. Yet with that said, a quite unexpected result from this study must be introduced, which is that there were no significant differences in helpfulness between the city and town locales (high- and low-input locales combined). It is certainly an interesting outcome, one about which speculation is possible, though little can be confirmed at present. Fischer (1978) has suggested that perhaps urban unhelpfulness was suppressed in Holland by local factors, e.g., the importance of the tourist trade. House and Wolf (1978) argued that a more representative sample of the urban and town populations in Holland might have revealed a city-town difference. Both of these explanations may account for the failure of the city-town effect to generalize to Holland; my own view is that cities and towns in Holland may simply not be all that different in important ways for behavior differentiation to occur. Input level is certainly not necessarily the overriding factor causing behavioral effects in any setting; yet, even if it were, it was interesting to discover that, overall, Dutch towns and cities were not very different on the input level measures. Perhaps even more importantly, pervasive Dutch norms, such as civility toward others (Goudsblom 1967), may be able in a homogeneous society like the Netherlands to produce stable patterns of public behavior that are not eroded by environmental changes such as the growth of cities.

In any case, this second study gave considerable encouragement to a further analysis of the effect input level was having on helping behavior and further examination of cross-cultural differences in the urbanization-helpfulness link. The reliability of the input level effect has been confirmed by the positive results obtained by others in testing Milgram's input overload hypothesis, especially as it pertains to helping behavior. Psychological research has long been concerned with the behavioral effects of input overload (Cohen, 1978) and several studies, all carried out in the United States, have incorporated measures of helping behavior, within a laboratory context, and all have demonstrated lower helpfulness under conditions of high input (Krupat & Epstein, 1973; Matthews & Canon, 1975; Sherrod & Downs, 1974; Weiner, 1976). Two other studies have examined the effects of noise on helping behavior in a naturalistic setting and both have shown clearly a lowering of helpfulness as a result of noise (Matthews & Canon, 1975; Page, 1977).

ENVIRONMENTAL INPUT LEVEL: HOW DOES IT AFFECT PEDESTRIANS?

In further exploring the input level effect, it quickly became apparent that there are different explanations for why input level might have the effect that it does on helping behavior. Pedestrians walking down a street with a high input level, when confronted by a person needing assistance, and in contrast to their behavior in a low input level street, may be more likely to (1) not notice the need for assistance; (2) be too fatigued to help; (3) be in too much of a hurry to help, and/or (4) be committed to noninvolvement as an appropriate course of action in this locale. The first of these hypothesized explanations, the reduced environmental awareness factor, is an appealing one to consider, as it is part of the popular stereotype of urban behavior often cited as an explanation for a lack of helpfulness in an urban environment, i.e., adjustment to the city involves such an unusual degree of tuning out peripheral events that the urbanite is simply not aware of the episodes going on around him. This is one of the simplest explanations for the effects resulting from high input levels and could be an explanation for the lower levels of helpfulness obtained in the high-input level Dutch locales, particularly on the map assistance measure.

This analysis of the input level effect was examined in the next study carried out, which was conducted in a Scottish city (Dundee, population 250,000) in collaboration with Rosalyn Grant (Korte & Grant, 1980). The hypothesis to be tested was that an increase in the environment input level results in a lower awareness of objects and events in that environment. Confirmation of the hypothesis would thus support one means by which high input levels might inhibit helpfulness, i.e., by leading to a restricted awareness of events and objects in the immediate environment, which may include a situation where assistance is required. In the present study, as in the previous ones, naturalistic environmental conditions were used, in this case traffic noise, which was either at a high or low level during the time that subjects, randomly selected sidewalk pedestrians, were tested for their awareness of certain persons and objects that were in the stretch of street they had just passed through.

Selection of data-collection periods when traffic noise was high versus low was done so as to minimize any corresponding variation in other factors, particularly environmental conditions and population characteristics. Two sites were selected which showed a medium level of pedestrian density and a variation in traffic noise level during different times of day. Each site was used during a period of high traffic noise and low traffic noise and the significance of this difference in noise level was confirmed with decibel recording measurements. Care was taken to select time periods for data collection that did not correspond to commuting patterns and also so that pedestrian density would remain generally constant across the traffic noise variation. Background characteristics of the subjects, as well as their destination or activity at the moment, were also assessed and on none of these factors did subjects differ between the high- and low-input conditions (except for length of residence in Dundee, which did not correlate with the environmental awareness measures and hence did not pose a threat to the interpretation of the results). An environmental awareness test was carried out by using a stretch of sidewalk within which were placed several novel objects that would be striking and unusual: a stationary female either wearing a comical pink party hat, or else holding a bright yellow teddy bear, a group of brightly colored balloons tied to a tree or lamppost, and a large newspaper headline advertisement board with the brightly written words, "Attention—Project in Progress!". Introducing new items into the environment ruled out the possibility that awareness could be a reflection of familiarity or past experience with the environment. Subjects consisted of 80 pedestrians, randomly selected from the flow of pedestrians emerging from the "test" stretch of sidewalk. The main question asked of subjects tested their recollection of any or all of the test items that had just been passed by. Awareness of any particular item required that the subject be able to describe one of its details, e.g., the color of the balloons. An additional sample of 80 subjects were also studied unobtrusively, under conditions of high- versus low-traffic noise, in order to examine further influences which high input levels might have on pedestrians, specifically their walking speed and gaze behavior.

Measures were taken for each pedestrian of the time required to walk between two preselected points and the length of time during this period that the subject's gaze was directed straight ahead.

The results showed a clear difference in both environmental awareness and pedestrian behavior as a function of high- versus low-levels of traffic noise. Under conditions of low noise, subjects were aware of 56% of the test items, versus an awareness level of 35% when traffic noise was high ($X^2(1) = 7.2$, $p<.01$). Higher traffic noise also resulted in significantly ($p<.01$) faster walking speeds (20.2 vs. 24.1 secs) and more straight ahead gazing (53% vs. 33% of the time). Of course, these three effects may not be independent of each other, as the reduced awareness observed with high traffic noise may have resulted from the manner of walking—fast, looking straight ahead—shown by pedestrians in this condition. In any case, this third study confirmed that there is a definite alteration in the behavior and awareness of pedestrians as a result of increased levels of environmental input. Again, it shows a fairly fine-tuned responsiveness to the immediate environmental conditions, a short-term adaptation that can be expected to be more pervasive in cities, assuming that cities are generally characterized by higher levels of environmental input.

HELPFUL ENVIRONMENTS: FURTHER CROSS-CULTURAL AND INTRA-URBAN COMPARISONS

Taken together, the three studies described thus far, carried out in three different cultures, represent a successful investigation into one factor that has been suggested as an explanation for the level of helpfulness occurring in any particular environment, specifically an explanation for why helpfulness might be less likely in an urban environment. Several significant unresolved points remain though, which led to a fourth study in this series. First, there is the question of whether city-town differences in helping behavior occur in cultures other than the United States and Canada. Second, given that the various districts of a city differ in those environmental features that appear to influence the occurrence of helpfulness, we might expect differences between these districts in terms of level of helpfulness. The size of such differences should provide an interesting comparison to the differences obtained *between* urban and nonurban environments. These questions led to the fourth study, carried out in Turkey by Korte and Ayvalioglu (in press).

The first aim of this study was to see if the urban-nonurban difference in helpfulness could be replicated in Turkey. The previous attempt to replicate this difference in a culture other than the United States or Canada had negative results, as described earlier in the study carried out in the Netherlands. The cross-cultural generality of the urban unhelpfulness phenomenon would be considerably strengthened by evidence of this phenomenon in Turkey, a developing nation quite different from the cultures in which the urban helpfulness research has been done.

The second aim of this study was to evaluate differences in helpfulness between different districts within a city, particularly as they compare with city-town differences. Apart from several studies that compared cities with suburbs, only one study is available which compared the level of helpfulness in different areas within the city. This study (Korte et. al., 1975) measured helpfulness in four districts of Amsterdam, selected on the basis of survey results which identified these four districts as having strong stereotypes as regards the helpfulness shown toward strangers, i.e., two districts had highly favorable stereotypes and two had highly unfavorable ones. The subsequent measurement of helping behavior showed no differences at all between these districts on any of the three measures of helpfulness that were used. In the present study, the design of this Amsterdam study was basically replicated using Istanbul and Ankara for the intra-urban comparisons. These cities have urban districts that are quite parallel to those found in large cities of the developed nations, with one important exception. This exception is the presence of large squatter settlements (present in nearly all major cities of the developing world), which are districts of hastily built homes, erected illegally on unoccupied land in the city by homeless rural immigrants who convert them into fairly permanent settlements. Several observers of these squatter settlements, including those located in Turkey (Suzuki, 1964; Levine, 1973) and elsewhere (Abu-Loghod, 1961; Lewis, 1959), have argued that social behavior among the squatters does not show the usual "urban" characteristics and that in fact the urban squatters, retaining the attitudes, behavior, and social structures of their village origins, resemble the inhabitants of villages and small towns more than they resemble their fellow urbanites in the rest of the city. It might be expected then that the squatter settlements could prove an exception to the urban unhelpfulness phenomenon, and samples of squatter districts were included in the present study, as well as four other city districts for each of the two cities where the intra-urban comparisons of helpfulness were carried out.

In this study, three different measures of helpfulness were utilized, each one validated for use in Turkey by means of a short survey which confirmed that the measures were seen as measuring helpfulness in the eyes of Turkish people. The three measures were a request for change, a request for cooperation with a short interview, and the dropping of a box which could not readily be retrieved by the dropper. The data were collected by two Turkish researchers, one male and the other female, who carried out the study in four Turkish towns (scattered throughout Turkey) as well as in Istanbul and Ankara. Four hundred and fifty-six subjects, randomly selected sidewalk pedestrians, were tested on the interview measure, which consisted of a 4-point scale of helpfulness in response to the request. Similarly, a 4-point scale was used to score the response of 463 subjects to the change request measure. The dropped box measure, carried out with 474 subjects, was accomplished by exposing the subject to the hapless researcher carrying a load of three large boxes. Once the subject was quite close, the top box was allowed to fall, and the researcher would begin a fruitless effort to retrieve the dropped box. The response of subjects to this situation was rated on a 3-point scale of helpfulness.

In each city, six different research locales were used, two squatter settlements and four nonsquatter districts. The squatter settlements were selected in consultation with municipal housing officials on the basis of their representativeness. The four other districts were picked on the basis of results obtained from a stereotype study conducted in each of the two cities. In this study, four types of city districts (central city; centrally located, mixed commercial-residential; working class residential; and suburban) were described to subjects (n = 173) who were asked to nominate the one neighborhood or district (from a list) for each type that was most representative of that type. The same description of district types was used in Istanbul and Ankara, resulting in a selection of four districts in each city which represented a similar spectrum of locales.

Again, concern for the comparability of the different samples of subjects meant a preliminary examination of subject characteristics and the relation of these characteristics to the helpfulness measures. Subjects' sex was found to be associated with the likelihood of help on two of the three measures (interview request and dropped box; males were more helpful), so, given the occasional noncomparability of the samples in terms of their male-female composition, the comparisons described below using the interview and dropped box measure are based on the data for male subject only—all samples were composed of males to an overwhelming degree (73%), which appears to reflect Moslem norms that restrict the public activities of women.

Turning first to the important city-town comparison, the results were strikingly clear: On all three measures, helpfulness was significantly lower in the cities (with the squatter samples excluded) than in the towns. On the change request measure, subjects helped 56% of the time in cities, versus 84% in towns $(X^2(2) = 27.6, p<.01)$. Cooperation with the interview request was also significantly lower in the cities (77% vs. 93%, $X^2(2) = 11.7, p<.01$), with a similar result for the dropped box measure, where the rate of helpfulness was 55% in cities, 86% in towns $(X^2(2) = 25.5, p<.01)$. Thus, city-town differences, which had not previously been demonstrated in a non-North American society, were present in a strong form in this Turkish study. Turning to the helpfulness levels obtained in the four Istanbul and Ankara squatter settlements, the results were again quite clear and consistent: Helpfulness in the squatter districts was much higher than that found in the rest of these cities and was at a level basically equivalent to that obtained in Turkish towns. On all three measures, helpfulness in the squatter settlements was not significantly different from the town sample, although it was significantly higher than the city sample: change request measure, 89% vs. 56% ($X^2(2)$ = 37.8, p<.01), interview request measure, 94% vs. 77% ($X^2(2)$ = 10.6, <.01), and dropped box measure, 92% vs. 55% ($X^2(2)$ = 33.1, p<.01). This confirms a significant degree of intraurban variability in levels of helpfulness and also supports the view that in their social behavior, the squatter residents resemble town dwellers rather than city dwellers.

A further evaluation of intraurban differences in helpfulness was offered by the results comparing helpfulness in the four non-squatter districts. In this study, quite contrary to the results obtained earlier in Amsterdam, weak but consistent differences did occur between the four different types of districts. For the most part these differences were not statistically significant, yet the rank order of the four district types was identical for each of the three different measures of helpfulness, as well as for the separate Istanbul and Ankara samples. In all cases the least helpful district type was the suburban district, followed by the center city district, then the centrally-located, mixed commercial-residential district, with the working-class residential district the most helpful. The level of helpfulness obtained in the working-class residential districts was lower than that in both the squatter districts and the town samples for each of three measures of helpfulness, though these differences only reached statistical significance for the dropped box measure (significant for both comparisons) and the interview measure (significant only for the town–working-class district comparison).

This fourth study thus gives some evidence for the existence of consistent differences in helpfulness between different districts of Turkish cities. City-town differences were also confirmed, (as long as the squatter districts were excluded from the city sample): Even with the variation in helpfulness levels between the different districts, no urban districts, apart from the squatter settlements, matched the degree of helpfulness obtained in the Turkish towns. Finally, the results confirmed the hypothesized similiarity in social behavior between town dwellers and urban squatter residents in a developing nation.

CONCLUSIONS

The series of studies described in this chapter has been concerned with the question of whether, and, if so, for what reasons, the conditions of city living deter the offering of help to a stranger in need. These studies, as well as a growing number of others, have shown quite clearly a definite link between helping behavior and urbanization: Helpfulness is lower in cities than in towns. The cross-cultural generality of this observation, though, remains uncertain. This chapter has described the two studies done to date which have examined urban versus nonurban helpfulness in societies other than the U.S. and Canada and the results were mixed. Differences were observed in Turkey, a society quite different from those of North America, whereas no difference occurred in the Netherlands. These studies are too few in number to settle the issue, but they do suggest the inadequacy of any extreme view on the helpfulness-urbanization relationship, i.e., either that the relationship only occurs in highly developed, urbanized societies like the United States or that it is a universal relationship. Analysis of the possible reasons for the absence of urban-nonurban differences in helpfulness in the Netherlands could prove fruitful in furthering our understanding of helping behavior. Some of these reasons could be a less stressful and overloaded environment in Dutch cities, strong cultural norms pertaining to civility in public behavior, low crime rates, and the homogenity and cohesiveness of the urban population. Evidence of urban helpfulness should provoke useful research hypotheses just as the opposite evidence has done. Nevertheless, the more common pattern to be explained is that of *lower* levels of helpfulness in urban versus nonurban environments.

One explanation for urban unhelpfulness to which the studies in this chapter have lent support, among the many that are undoubtably relevant, is the environmental input overload explanation. As was demonstrated in the second study, people are less helpful toward a stranger in need when the environmental context has a high level of physical and social inputs. This supports Milgram's (1970) contention that the unhelpfulness of urbanities is in part an adaptation to overly demanding environmental conditions. Further, it was demonstrated in the third study that pedestrians do make a fine-tuned, perhaps unconscious, adjustment to high input levels with a quickened pace and with lowered visual scanning and environmental awareness. Thus assistance-seeking in the city is handicapped to begin with by the difficulties in capturing the attention and time of potential helpers.

Environmental factors thus appear quite relevant to the phenomenon of urban unhelpfulness. Nevertheless, it would be misleading to minimize the importance of other factors that probably also account for the degree of helpfulness found in cities. Some of these other factors are particularly evident in the results from the fourth study carried out in Turkey. A comparison of different parts of the city showed the crowded, busy, noisy squatter settlements to be the most helpful areas, whereas the least helpful areas were the quiet, sedate, suburban neighborhoods. This would certainly not make much sense if environmental input level were the only determinant of helpfulness levels in the city. The squatter-suburban contrast may reflect the influence of factors such as the local traditions toward the treatment of strangers, social class difference in public behavior, and the type of ongoing public activity that characterizes the area. A further understanding of the strikingly high levels of helpfulness toward strangers obtained in the Turkish squatter districts might have significant practical value if this knowledge can be applied to efforts at community development in urban neighborhoods, where often what is needed is a strengthening of local networks of assistance that lend protection and help to other persons present in the neighborhood (Jacobs, 1961; Newman, 1973). This question is guiding further research efforts being planned by the author and his collaborators.

In sum the present state of research on urban unhelpfulness has established the significance of environmental influences on helping behavior and points also to the importance of nonenvironmental factors. Certainly the phenomena of urban behavior should continue to illuminate out thinking about helping behavior and continue to serve as an important source of research hypotheses.

REFERENCES

Abu-Loghod, J. Migrant adjustment to city life: the Egyptian case. *American Journal of Sociology,* 1961, *67,* 22–32.

Cohen, S. Environmental load and allocation of attention. In A. Baum, J. Singer, & S. Valins (Eds.), *Advances in Environmental Psychology,* (Vol. 1) Hillsdale, N.J.: Lawrence Erlbaum Associates, 1978.

Darley, J., & Latané, B. Bystander intervention into emergencies: diffusion of responsibility. *Journal of Personality and Social Psychology.* 1968, *8,* 377–383.

Feldman, R. Response to compatriot and foreigner who seek assistance. *Journal of Personality and Social Psychology,* 1968, *10,* 202–214.

Fischer, C. *The Urban Experience.* New York: Harcourt, Brace, Jovanovich, 1976.

Fischer, C. Sociological comments on psychological approaches to urban life. In A. Baum, J. Singer, & S. Valins (Eds.), *Advances in Environmental Psychology,* (Vol. 1) Hillsdale, N.J.: Lawrence Erlbaum Associates, 1978.

Forbes, G., & Gromoll, H. The lost letter techniques as a measure of social variables: some exploratory findings. *Social Forces,* 1971, *50,* 113–115.

Gans, H. *The Levittowners.* New York: Vintage, 1967.

Gelfand, D., Hartman, D., Walder, P., & Page, E. Who reports shoplifters? A field experimental study. *Journal of Personality and Social Psychology,* 1973, *25,* 276–285.

Goudsblom, J. *Dutch society.* New York: Random House, 1967.

Hansson, R., & Slade, K. Altruism toward a deviant in city and small town. *Journal of Applied Social Psychology,* 1977, *7,* 272–279.

Hansson, R., Slade, K., & Slade, P. Urban-rural differences in responsiveness to an altruistic model. *Journal of Social Psychology,* 1978, *105,* 99–105.

House, J., & Wolf, S. Effects of urban residence on interpersonal trust and helping behavior. *Journal of Personality and Social Psychology,* 1978, *36,* 1029–1043.

Jacobs, J. *The death and life of great American cities.* New York: Vintage Books, 1961.

Kammann, R., Thomson, R., & Irwin, R. Unhelpful behavior in the street: City size or immediate pedestrian density? *Environment and Behavior,* 1979, *11,* 245–250.

Korte, C. Effects of individual responsibility and group communication on help-giving in an emergency. *Human Relations,* 1971, *24,* 149–159.

Korte, C. *The effects of an urban environment on social behavior.* Unpublished manuscript, St. Andrews University, 1976.

Korte, C. Helpfulness in the urban environment. In A. Baum, J. Singer, & S. Valins (Eds.), *Advances in Environmental Psychology,* Vol. I. Hillsdale, N.J.: Lawrence Erlbaum Associates, 1978.

Korte, C. Urban-nonurban differences in social behavior and social psychological models of urban impact. *Journal of Social Issues,* 1980, *36,* 29–51.

Korte, C., & Ayvalioglu, N. Helpfulness in Turkey: cities, towns, and urban villages. *Journal of Cross-Cultural Psychology,* in press.

Korte, C., & Grant, R. Traffic noise, environmental awareness, and pedestrian behavior. *Environment and Behavior,* 1980, *12,* 408–420.

Korte, C., & Kerr, N. Response to altruistic opportunities under urban and rural conditions. *Journal of Social Psychology*, 1975, *95*, 183–184.

Korte, C., Ypma, I., & Toppen, A. Helpfulness in Dutch society as a function of urbanization and environmental input level. *Journal of Personality and Social Psychology*, 1975, *32*, 996–1003.

Krupat, E., & Coury, M. *The lost-letter technique and helping: An urban-nonurban comparison.* Paper presented at American Psychological Association Convention, Chicago, 1975.

Krupat, E., & Epstein, Y. *I'm too busy: The effects of overload and diffusion of responsibility on working and helping.* Proceedings of the American Psychological Association, 1973, *8*, 293–294.

Levine, N. Old culture, new culture: A study of migrants in Ankara, Turkey. *Social Forces*, 1973, *51*, 355–368.

Lewis, O. *Five families.* New York: Basic Books, 1959.

Matthews, K., & Canon, L. Environmental noise level as a determinant of helping behavior. *Journal of Personality and Social Psychology*, 1975, *32*, 571–577.

Merrens, M. Nonemergency helping behavior in various sized communities. *Journal of Social Psychology*, 1973, *90*, 327–328.

Milgram, S. The experience of living in cities. *Science*, 1970, *167*, 1461–1468.

Milgram, S., Mann, L., & Harter, S. The lost-letter technique: A tool of social research. *The Public Opinion Quarterly*, 1965, *29*, 437–438.

Newman, O. *Defensible space.* New York: Collier Books, 1973.

Page, R. Noise and helping behavior. *Environment and Behavior*, 1977, *9*, 311–334.

Rushton, J. P. Urban density and altruism: Helping strangers in a Canadian city, suburb, and small town. *Psychological Reports*, 1978, *43*, 887–900.

Schneider, F., & Mockus, Z. Failure to find a rural-urban difference in incidence of altruistic behavior. *Psychological Reports*, 1974, *34*, 294.

Schwartz, S., & Clausen, D. Responsibility, norms, and helping in an emergency. *Journal of Personality and Social Psychology*, 1970, *16*, 299–310.

Sherrod, D., & Downs, R. Environmental determinants of altruism: The effects of stimulus overload and perceived control on helping. *Journal of Experimental Social Psychology*, 1974, *10*, 468–479.

Srole, L. Urbanization and mental health: Some reformulations. *American Scientist*, 1972, *60*, 576–583.

Suzuki, P. Encounters with Istanbul: Urban peasants and rural peasants. *International Journal of Comparative Sociology*, 1964, *5*, 208–216.

Takooshian, H., Haber, J., & Lucido, D. Who wouldn't help a lost child? You maybe. *Psychology Today*, 1977, *10*, 67.

Weiner, F. Altruism, ambience, and action: The effects of rural and urban rearing on helping behavior. *Journal of Personality and Social Psychology*, 1976, *34*, 112–124.

Wirth, L. Urbanism as a way of life. *American Journal of Sociology*, 1938, *44*, 1–24.

16

The Nature and Organization of Altruistic Behavior Among Preschool Children

F. F. Strayer
Laboratoire D'Ethologie Humaine,
Department de Psychologie
Université du Québec à Montréal

Although experimental research on prosocial behavior among young children has increased substantially during the past decade (Rushton, 1976), only a few studies have examined naturally occurring altruistic activity within the socially stable context of the early peer group. Because of this relative lack of descriptive research, we still have very little normative information concerning spontaneous altruistic activity in natural settings. For example, what are the diverse forms of prosocial behavior that occur among familiar peers engaged in unstructured play? What are the relative rates of these altruistic gestures? Are some children generally more altruistic than others within the peer group? Do children have individualized prosocial styles, where they selectively engage in only certain forms of altruistic behavior? Does the young child discriminate among potential recipients for his altruistic acts? Are individual differences in prosocial behavior related to differences in specific roles which children assume within their peer group?

Answers to these questions require the use of observational research methods which provide a detailed description of naturally occurring altruistic behavior. Preliminary advances have been made in the elaboration of naturalistic procedures for the analysis of spontaneous prosocial behavior. Yarrow and Waxler (1976) recorded *Helping, Sharing* and *Comforting* activities among a large sample of preschool children. They found that *Helping* was the most frequent form of prosocial response, and suggested that there were fewer occasions for either *Sharing* or *Comforting* in the natural free-play context. In addition, to determine whether some children were generally more altruistic, rates of these three categories were compared. These analyses revealed positive, but relatively low correlations between the three classes of altruistic activity. The question of generality versus specificity in preschool altruism was addressed more directly in a recent naturalistic study by Strayer, Wareing and Rushton (1979). *Giving, Cooperating, Helping,* and *Comforting* directed toward peers were distinguished from similar activities directed toward adults in the preschool environment. *Giving* and *Cooperating* were the most frequent forms of altruistic activity, each occurring more than seven times as often as *Helping* or *Comforting*. Analyses of individual differences in rates of activity revealed high correlations between behavioral categories directed toward each class of social target. Altruism in this preschool group was specific with respect to its adult or peer orientation, but general with respect to the various forms of behavior that were directed toward peers and toward teachers.

Although these two preliminary studies contribute at both a methodological and a conceptual level to developmental research on prosocial behavior, they fail to provide convergent normative information on the nature of preschool altruism. In each investigation different criteria were employed for the description of observed prosocial activity. If we assume that the *Helping* category used by Yarrow and Waxler (1976) regrouped both the *Helping* and *Cooperating* activities described by Strayer et al. (1979), then a more coherent, but tentative picture of preschool altruism emerges. In both studies, mutual activity directed toward a common goal appears to be the modal form of altruism. Collective use and exchange of objects occurs less frequently, but more often than overt expressions of concern for the distress of other group members.

This interpretation must remain tentative, inasmuch as we still lack an adequate empirical basis for generalizations about prosocial activity during the preschool years. A more complete understanding of preschool altruism requires information from a larger sample of preschool children observed in more diversified social contexts. Immediate ecological and demographic features of different preschool groups may influence both the form and organization of prosocial behavior. Confronted with such possible sources of variation, it is essential to develop a more unified approach to descriptive research, which places less emphasis upon demonstrating significant relationships between particular behaviors in a single study, but instead attempts to provide a comparative evaluation of the nature and organization of prosocial activity in different social settings. The research described in the following section contributes to this comparative perspective by examining altruistic activity in three preschool peer groups.

Participants

The 54 children who participated in these studies ranged in age from 3 to 6 years. The first group contained 12 boys and 14 girls (mean age = 51.4 months, SD = 7.12) who attended an English speaking preschool at the University of Waterloo. The remaining two groups attended a French speaking community preschool near downtown Montréal. Both of these groups contained 7 boys and 7 girls. The younger children were in the Sallopette group (mean age = 45.6 months, SD = 4.85), while the older were in the Saltimbanque group (mean age = 62.6 months, SD = 6.34).

ALTRUISM INVENTORY

The descriptive system used in in the present research was a revised version of the inventory described by Strayer et al. (1979). Four classes of activity were defined in terms of specific forms of behavior observed during prosocial interaction among preschool children. *Object Activities* included five behavioral categories: *Offering* described attempts to give an object that led to explicit rejection, or to an implicit refusal by failure to acknowledge the potential gift (see Fig. 16.1). *Giving* was coded when an object was transferred from one individual to another (see Fig. 16.2). Sharing was defined as allowing another child to use personal objects. In this simplest form, *Sharing* was not accompanied by either *Giving* or *Offering* gestures. *Exchanging* was defined as the alternate transfer of a single object between two individuals (see Fig. 16.4). This category was distinguished from *Giving* to avoid multiple coding of repeated object transfer. When a single object changed hands repeatedly, each participant was coded as having engaged in a single episode of *Exchanging*. The fifth category of *Object Activity* included instances where two different objects were simultaneously transferred between two children. Such transfers were coded as *Trading*.

The second class of altruistic behavior included *Cooperative Activities*. *Task cooperation* was defined as mutual activity: carrying toys to a play area, or moving furniture in the playroom. These activities usually preceded the start of a play bout. *Play cooperation* included similar goal-directed activity that occurred during the course of a play sequence. For example, in Fig. 16.4, two boys engage in *Play cooperation* as they exchange roles while playing with a wagon.

Helping Activities comprised the third general class of prosocial activity. Helping was distinguished from cooperation because the behavioral activity of the helper was different from that of the recipient. *Task help* was defined as assisting another person to accomplish a specific goal, as in tying shoelaces, or putting on a piece of clothing (see Fig. 16.5). *Play Help* included similar activities that occurred during sequences of play, such as covering someone with a blanket while playing house, or pulling someone in a wagon while playing horse and buggy. If children alternated roles in such play bouts, the sequence was scored as *Play cooperation* because both performed the same type of activity.

The final class of altruistic behavior comprised *Empathic Activities*. This class was subdivided into three behavioral categories. *Looking at upset peer* included visual orientation toward a distressed child. *Approaching upset peer*

FIG. 16.1.   An illustration of *Offering*.

FIG. 16.2.   An illustration of *Giving*.

FIG. 16.3. An illustration of *Exchanging*.

FIG. 16.4. An illustration of *Play cooperation*.

FIG. 16.5.   An illustration of *Task Help*.

entailed attaining personal distance (approximately one meter) with a distressed child. Finally, *Comforting* included activities that seemed intended to lessen the discomfort of the distressed peer. The episode in Fig. 16.6 was coded as *Looking* and *Comforting,* but not as *Approaching,* because the two children were already within personal distance before the onset of crying.

The reliability of this coding system was evaluated in two different ways. First, two observers coded 2 hours of videotaped free-play. Agreement coeffi-

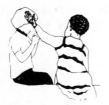

FIG. 16.6. An illustration of empathic *Looking* and *Comforting*.

cients were calculated using the standard formula of total agreements divided by the average number of total observations. The second reliability index compared rate estimates obtained by two observers who coded two 5 min samples for each of 12 children. Agreement indices for the different classes of behavior ranged from 85% to 95%, while rate correlations ranged from .87 to 1.00.

SAMPLING METHODS AND SETTINGS

Children at the Waterloo center were videotaped daily during free-play periods throughout a 6 week period. Although free-play was officially scheduled for an entire hour, the last 10 to 15 min. of each period were usually reserved for cleaning the playroom. The present data are based upon observations obtained during the first 45 to 50 min of each videotape. Thus, approximately 21 hours of recorded interaction drawn from a total sampling of 30 hours were used in these analyses. The Waterloo center contained one large playroom and two smaller special activity rooms. The large room was equipped with a permanently installed video system. Inasmuch as children had free access to all three rooms during the observation period, records of individuals present during each 3-min interval of videotape were obtained to determine the total time that each child was available for observation. These latter time estimates permitted calculation of individual rate measures for each form of prosocial behavior.

Members of the Sallopette and Saltimbanque groups were filmed using portable video equipment. Approximately one hour of free-play activities was recorded for each of these 28 children. The use of repeated 5 min focal periods provided a well-balanced sampling of all children throughout the 6 week observational session. To correct for minor variation in total sampling time, rate scores were again used as the basic analytic measure.

INDIVIDUAL DIFFERENCES IN THE NATURE OF PRESCHOOL ALTRUISM

A total of 1594 altruistic behaviors were coded from the video records obtained at Waterloo. Nearly 53 prosocial acts occurred during a typical period of free-play at this center. Substantially fewer altruistic events were coded from video records obtained at the French preschool. A total of 239 altruistic acts were observed among members of the Sallopette, while 252 were recorded for the older Saltimbanque group. This difference in the absolute frequency of prosocial activity directly reflects the different sampling methods used at each location. All children present on each videotape were continuously scanned at Waterloo. This procedure produced an average of 4.8 hours of observation for each group member. In contrast, members of the Sallopette and Saltimbanque groups were observed for an average of 1.1 hours. In spite of the large differences in total recorded behavior, the rates of prosocial activity were quite similar at each center.

Table 16.1 shows the mean rate of each category of altruistic behavior for each preschool group. Inasmuch as they control for differences in total sampling time and size of group, these descriptive statistics permit a direct comparison of the form and relative frequency of prosocial activity at each preschool. With the exception of *Trading* and *Comforting,* all forms of altruism described in our behavioral inventory were evident in each social setting. Four categories of behavior, *Giving, Offering, Sharing,* and *Play cooperation,* comprised the majority of prosocial activity in each group. However, there were also group differences in the nature of observed altruism. *Play helping* occurred much more frequently in both French groups, whereas empathic *Looking* was observed more often among the youngest Sallopette children. Table 16.1 also shows that there

TABLE 16.1
Descriptive Summary of Twelve Forms of Altruistic
Behavior at Three Preschool Centers

	Sallopette		Waterloo		Saltimbanque	
	Mean	S.D.	Mean	S.D.	Mean	S.D.
Giving	2.06	2.01	4.95	3.77	4.83	3.98
Offering	1.29	1.16	1.97	1.40	1.02	.132
Sharing	1.93	1.85	1.27	.97	1.80	1.11
Exchanging	.05	.83	.71	.55	.31	.64
Trading	—	—	.29	.31	—	—
Task Cooperation	.51	.64	.83	.87	.84	1.02
Play Cooperation	4.37	3.41	2.06	2.18	4.08	3.77
Task Help	.62	.82	.06	.14	.85	.78
Play Help	2.45	2.74	.16	.32	1.65	1.63
Looking	1.85	1.45	.47	.39	.57	.67
Approaching	.50	.75	.07	.14	.17	.29
Comforting	.19	.37	—	—	.11	—

Note: Rates reflect mean frequency per hour. Dashes indicate that a particular form of activity was not observed at one of the centers.

was considerable variability between individuals in the rate of the various forms of prosocial activity. The relatively large standard deviations for each altruistic category reflect that on each measure some children were usually considerably above the group average, whereas others had very low rates of responsiveness. To determine whether such individual differences supported the notion that certain group members could be characterized as generally more altruistic than others, these category measures were regrouped according to class of prosocial activity, and analyzed using correlational procedures. Prior to analysis, a root transformation normalized the skewed distribution of individual rate scores. The resulting Pearson product–moment correlations are shown in Table 16.2.

Although the pattern of association between altruistic classes indicates that a high score on one prosocial measures is correlated with a higher rate of responsiveness for at least one other form of activity, the overall results do not justify

TABLE 16.2
Correlations Between Classes of Altruistic Activity

Altruistic Class	1	2	3	4
1. Object Activity	—			
2. Cooperative Activity	.45**	—		
3. Helping Activity	-.02	.51**	—	
4. Empathic Activity	-.15	.11	.44**	—

**p .01, df = 52, one-tailed test.

the derivation of a unitary altruistic index reflecting a generalized disposition to engage in prosocial activity. A principal component analysis of these inter-class correlations is shown in Table 16.3. This second analysis suggests the possibility of a more limited degree of behavioral generality where preschool children can be characterized according to their particular styles of altruistic activity. Some children may be more responsive to the needs of others, which leads to a higher probability of *Helping Activity* that is associated with increases in both *Empathic* and *Cooperative Activities*. In contrast, other children may be more oriented toward responding to collective goals, which leads to a higher rate of *Cooperative Activity* that is associated with increased *Object Activity*. Similar analyses conducted separately for each preschool group revealed the same two-factor structure in each social context. These analyses indicated that the two somewhat overlapping prosocial styles identified in the first analysis were most characteristic for the oldest Saltimbanque children. For the youngest Sallopette group, *Helping Activity* was uncorrelated with the Goal Orientation Factor. Thus, among these latter children, the two prosocial styles seemed more sepa-rate. Finally, at Waterloo, *Empathic Activity* was the only form of behavior that correlated with the Need Orientation Factor, whereas the other classes of altruis-tic activity correlated significantly with the Goal Orientation Factor. These final results, in conjunction with the lower average rate of both *Helping* and *Empathic Activity* at Waterloo, suggest that the altruistic style of children at this center was organized more in terms of mutual goals, and less in terms of responding to the personal needs of other group members.

SOCIAL CONSTRAINTS ON PROSOCIAL STYLES

The nature of group differences in prosocial styles was clarified by examining how children differentially distributed altruistic activity to adults and peers in their preschool setting. Table 16.4 shows the relative frequency and hourly rate

TABLE 16.3
Principal Component Analysis of Altruistic Activity

	Varimax Factors	
	Need Orientation	Goal Orientation
1. Object Activity	-.17	.62**
2. Cooperative Activity	.37*	.82**
3. Helping Activity	.88**	.22*
4. Empathic Activity	.52**	-.10
Eigen Value	1.77	1.34
Variance	44.3%	33.4%

*p .05, df = 52
**p .01, df = 52

of each class of altruistic activity directed toward peers and adults. Although the mean rates of activity differ across settings, inspection of the relative frequencies shows that *Object* and *Cooperative Activities* were the predominant forms of peer-directed prosocial behavior, and that *Object Activity* was the most frequent form of prosocial response to adults. Table 16.4 also shows important group differences in the selection of adult and peer targets for altruistic gestures. In both French groups, over 90% of all activity was directed to peers, but at Waterloo, nearly 40% of prosocial behavior was adult-directed. Because the student/teacher ratio was similar at each of the three centers, these group differences cannot be explained in terms of differential access to adults during free-play.

Inasmuch as rates of prosocial activity differed as a function of the type of social target, a second correlational analysis examined the organization of adult- and peer-directed altruistic activities. The results of this analysis are presented in Table 16.5. Peer-directed prosocial behaviors were more convergent in this second analysis, whereas certain adult-directed behaviors were also significantly intercorrelated. Perhaps more interestingly, peer-directed *Helping* and *Empathic Activities* were negatively associated with forms of adult-directed behavior. A principal components analysis of this correlation matrix again revealed a simple two-factor structure underlying individual differences in altruistic behavior. However, these latter factors were slightly different than those identified in the preceding analysis. The Goal Orientation Factor in Table 16.6 regroups only peer-directed prosocial behaviors. This result indicates that the prosocial style organized in terms of mutual goals was predominantly a peer-oriented style. In contrast, the Need Orientation Factor regrouped both adult-directed *Object* and

TABLE 16.4
Distribution of Altruistic Activity as a Function of Social Target

	Sallopette		Waterloo		Saltimbanque	
	% Total	Mean Rate	% Total	Mean Rate	% Total	Mean Rate
PEER DIRECTED						
Object Activity	31	5.04	37	4.79	45	7.25
Cooperative	29	4.67	19	2.49	29	4.79
Helping	18	2.99	1	0.19	15	2.43
Empathy	16	2.54	4	0.54	5	0.86
ADULT DIRECTED						
Object	5	0.80	34	4.41	4	0.71
Cooperative	1	0.21	3	0.40	1	0.13
Helping	0	0.07	0	0.03	1	0.07
PEER ALTRUISM	93	14.55	62	8.01	94	15.33
ADULT ALTRUISM	7	1.08	38	4.84	6	0.91
TOTAL ALTRUISM		16.33		12.85		16.24

Note: Rates reflect average frequency per hour.

TABLE 16.5
Correlations between Classes of Altruistic Activity Directed
Toward Adults and Peers

Altruistic Class	1	2	3	4	5	6	7
1 Peer Object Activity	—						
2 Peer Cooperative Activity	.62**	—					
3 Peer Helping Activity	.23*	.54**	—				
4 Peer Empathic Activity	-.03	.15	.45**	—			
5 Adult Object Activity	.13	-.16	-.44	-.33	—		
6 Adult Cooperative Activity	.32**	.22	-.25	-.29	.54**	—	
7 Adult Helping Activity	.03	.04	.04	-.11	.11	.25*	—

*$p < .05$, df = 52, one-tailed test.
**$p < .01$, df = 52, one-tailed test.

Cooperative Activities and peer-directed *Helping* and *Empathic Activities*. The prosocial style organized in terms of personal needs was expressed in two divergent orientations. Some of these children adopted a peer strategy, characterized by increased *Helping* and *Empathic Activities* to group members; others were more oriented toward adults and more likely to engage in *Object* and *Cooperative Activities* with teachers. If we assume that the role differentiation that defined both *Helping* and *Empathic Activities* was in a sense parallel to role differentiation that characterizes adult-child interaction, then both of these latter prosocial styles may reflect an adult orientation in the organization of preschool atruistic activity.

TABLE 16.6
Principal Component Analysis of Altruistic Activity
Directed Toward Adults and Peers

	Varimax Factors	
	Need Orientation	Goal Orientation
1 Peer Object Activity	.19	.65**
2 Peer Cooperative Activity	-.11	.94**
3 Peer Helping Activity	-.60**	.53**
4 Peer Empathic Activity	-.50**	.13
5 Adult Object Activity	.77**	.05
6 Adult Cooperative Activity	.74**	.33
7 Adult Helping Activity	.18	.10
Eigen Value	2.29	1.97
Variance	32.7%	28.1%

*$p < .01$, df = 52

THE SOCIAL ORGANIZATION OF PEER-DIRECTED ALTRUISM

The preceding analyses suggest that aspects of the immediate social context have important influences on both the form of preschool altruism and the organization of prosocial response styles. However, a more complete consideration of social constraints on naturally occurring altruism requires an analysis of the pattersn of social exchange among members of each stable social group. The extent to which peer-directed altruism was organized according to principles of reciprocity was examined from two different perspectives. An initial measure of general reciprocity in prosocial behavior was computed by correlating the total activity initiated by each group member with the total activity received. This index of prosocial reciprocity was uniformly high in each of the three groups ($r = .82$ for the Sallopette; $r = .79$ for Waterloo; and $r = .88$ for the Saltimbanque). In each group, children who initiated more altruistic gestures towards their peers received significantly more altruistic responses from members of their social group. A second reciprocity index was developed to examine individual differences in reciprocity among group members. This measure correlated the rates of initiated and received behaviors separately for each individual across dyadic contexts. By computing the average common variance in these individual dyadic distributions, it was possible to extract a single correlation coefficient which reflected the average level of dyadic reciprocity in each preschool group. These dyadic reciprocity indices were slightly lower than the general reciprocity measures, but still uniformly high for each social group ($r = .69$ for the Sallopette; $r = .69$ for Waterloo; and $r = .74$ for the Saltimbanque). Although individuals varied in their level of dyadic reciprocity, the majority of children in each group distributed altruistic activity to specific peers in a fashion that was significantly correlated with their rate of receiving prosocial behaviors from these same group members.

A second question about the social organization of peer-directed altruism concerned whether children selected certain peers as preferred prosocial partners. To determine whether children discriminated among peers when initiating prosocial activity, chi-square analyses were conducted to examine the dyadic distribution of each group member's activity (Strayer, 1980). In addition, by noting which social targets received more than their expected frequency of prosocial gestures ($X^2 > 3.84$), it was possible to identify the significant altruistic preferences of each group member. The results of these analyses are summarized in Table 16.7. Over two-thirds of the children in each preschool group showed nonrandom deployment of altruistic activity. Those children who failed to discriminate among peer group members when initating prosocial gestures were without exception individuals with lower absolute rates of peer-directed altruism. In general, children directed altruistic gestures to an average of nearly seven members of the peer group, but usually selected an average of only two peers as

TABLE 16.7
Dyadic Distribution of Peer Altruism

	Sallopette	Waterloo	Saltimbanque
Percentage of Children with nonrandom distributions of Prosocial Activity	71%	77%	79%
Average Number of Altruistic Targets per Child	7.0	8.5	6.7
Average Number of Significant Social Preferences	1.5	1.4	2.1
Percentage of Children Never Chosen as Significant Altruistic Target	21%	46%	7%

preferred altruistic partners. The nature of these altruistic preferences did not entail a complete, or systematic discrimination against certain individuals in the group. At each preschool, all children received some altruistic gestures. However, not all children were selected as preferred prosocial partners. (Although in contrast, some individuals appeared frequently as the preferred altruistic target of many children within their group.)

The last set of question in this research concerned whether individual differences in levels of prosocial popularity were related to how children organized their own altruistic activity. Table 16.8 shows the correlations between the frequency of being chosen as a preferred prosocial partner and other individual measures of altruistic activity. In each preschool group, preferred targets initiated significantly more altruistic activity toward peers, and distributed these gestures in a manner which more closely paralleled their receipt of altruism from other group members. In addition, these preferred children were more discriminating

TABLE 16.8
Correlations between Popularity as a Prosocial Target and
Individual Differences in Organization of Altruistic Behavior

	Sallopette	Waterloo	Saltimbanque
Total Initiated Activity	.76**	.78**	.65**
Number of Social Targets	.57**	.63**	.27
Number of Social Preferences	.82**	.65**	.66**
Number of Reciprocal Relations	.83**	.88**	.84**
% Dyadic Reciprocity	.80**	.51**	.53*
Score on Goal Orientation Factor	.51*	.78**	.51*
Score on Need Orientation Factor	-.06	.13	-.01

**p .01, one-tailed test
*p .05, one-tailed test
Note: df = 12 for Sallopette and Saltimbanque group, and df = 24 for Waterloo.

in the distribution of their own prosocial activity. They had more altruistic preferences, and were more likely to reciprocate being chosen as a partner by other group members. Finally, inasmuch as these children had higher scores on the Goal Orientation Factor of prosocial styles, they were more oriented toward mutual goals shared with peers, than responsive to the expressed needs of particular individuals within their peer group.

SUMMARY AND CONCLUSIONS

The descriptive analysis of naturally occurring prosocial activity provides important insights concerning the form of altruistic gestures and the organization of altruistic profiles among preschool children. In each of the present settings, preschool altruism was characterized by a rich diversity of behavioral activity. However, the identification of diverse forms of prosocial activity did not lead to the inductive derivation of a generalized behavioral profile that could characterize the "young altruist" in the preschool group. Instead, children sampled from the repertoire of potential altruistic acts in a consistent fashion, which revealed two distinct prosocial styles. Although these styles may reflect important differences in the motivational basis for preschool prosocial behavior, at a descriptive level we can only claim that each is associated with a specific subset of altruistic activity. Future research should examine whether individual differences in prosocial styles remain stable during early childhood, and whether particular socialization experiences foster the development of one, or the other orientations among preschool children. At a speculative level, it seemed that those children who were characterized as more responsive to personal needs of others tended also to employ an adult/child role structure in many of their interactions with peers. These were the children who often assumed the attitude of an older sibling interacting with a younger, less competent child. Clearly, the development of such an attitude may be directly linked to demographic features of family, to patterns of social interaction at home, or to prior experience with the social demands of the preschool setting.

The present findings also demonstrate that altruistic activity is not merely organized at the level of individual response styles, but also in terms of recurrent patterns of dyadic exchange between members of a stable social unit. The discriminative deployment of altruistic gestures among potential recipients in the preschool setting suggests that prosocial activity may have important implications for the more general social adaptation of the young child, and for his integration into the stable stable peer-group. Previous analyses of peer-group social ecology have shown that the organization of altruistic behaviors among peers is coordinated with the organization of other forms of cohesive social activity (Strayer, 1980; Strayer et al., 1979). Future research must examine the developmental processes underlying the emergence of altruistic preferences and reciprocal prosocial relations among preschool children. Undoubtedly, such research should continue to explore the organization of preschool altruism in conjunction with other forms of behavioral exchange that determine the nature of social relationships among young children as well as begin to examine potential psychological factors, such as sociocognitive abilities and/or previous socialization experiences, which may influence the nature and organization of prosocial behavior.

ACKNOWLEDGMENTS

I would like to express my appreciation to Phil Rushton and Sue Wareing who collaborated during the initial development of some of the analytic approaches included in this report. In addition, I would like to thank Dianne Cox, Pat Harris, Michèle Pontbriand and Sue Wareing for help with the tedious task of video decoding, Teresa Blicharski for her fine illustrations of our behavior categories, and Roger Gauthier for moral support with a cranky computer. These research projects were supported by grants from the Spence Foundation, Le Conseil de Recherche en Sciences Humaines, and le Ministère de l'Education du Québec. A preliminary report of the Waterloo data were used by Sue Wareing in a master thesis presented to the Psychology Department at York University.

REFERENCES

Rushton, J. P. Socialization and altruistic behavior of children. *Psychological Bulletin,* 1976, *83,* 898–913.

Strayer, F. F. Social ecology of the preschool peer-group. In W. C. Collins (Ed.), *The Minnesota Symposium on Child Psychology, Vol. 13,* Hillsdale, New Jersey: Lawrence Erlbaum Associates: 1980.

Strayer, F. F., Wareing, S., & Rushton, J. P. Social constraints on naturally occurring preschool altruism. *Ethology and Sociobiology,* 1979, 1, 3–11.

Yarrow, M. R., & Waxler, C. Z. Dimensions and correlates of prosocial behavior in young children. *Child Development,* 1976, *47,* 118–125.

VI Consequences of Helping

17

Kidney Donors Revisited

Carl H. Fellner
University of Washington School of Medicine

John R. Marshall
University of Wisconsin Medical School

> *Mankind's common instinct for reality . . . has always held the world to be essentially a theatre for heroism* [p. 281].
>
> —William James, 1958

The living organ donor presents an entirely new phenomenon in medicine. He or she may have only a transitional role and may disappear with improving immunosuppressive techniques and better utilization and preservation of cadaver organs. Of course, we shall be happy to see them go, but for the time being, they are still with us and raise some very important behavioral and ethical problems.

In 1968, we published our first papers on the living, genetically related donors, reporting on a phenomenological study of 12 living donors (Fellner & Marshall, 1968; Fellner & Marshall, 1970a; Fellner & Marshall, 1970b). Elapsed time between surgery and interview varied from 5 weeks to 18 months, with a mean of 9 months, and all of the donated kidneys were functioning well except in one instance where the donor had experienced the death of the recipient, her sister, and with it the disappearance of the grafted kidney. In 1977, we published our findings from investigating our original cohort of donors 9 years later when only 5 of the recipients still survived (Marshall & Fellner, 1977). In the intervening years we have gradually added donors, potential donors, and other family members. Our initial conclusions about donorship had been based on a sample in which the act of donating an organ was relatively recent and the organ still was operational in most instances. With our larger sample, plus an additional survey in 1976, of 148 donors, patients of Dr. Tom Marchiero of the University of Washington Medical School, who had undergone nephrectomy from 1 to 8 years earlier, we now have prospective donors, recent donors and also donors (approximately 35%) who have found themselves in the situation where the donated organ is no longer functioning and where the recipient has died or is being maintained on dialysis. A few have received second or third grafts.

Throughout these studies the object of our investigations remained unchanged: a phenomenological inquiry into the process of decision making of the donors (or potential donors), the experience of donorship, and the impact of donorship and the fate of the donated organ on the subsequent life of the donors. The method used in our inquiries was one of phenomenology, meaning that we approached our subjects without preformed hypotheses or presuppositions and accepted their statements as coming from persons who are inherently free, spontaneous, creative and caring, and who expressed their thoughts and feelings much as they experienced them. In other words, we were trying to understand without using a favored form of reference, collecting our data with the sole goal of apprehending and understanding. Attempts at explanation followed only afterwards and were by necessity, somewhat reductionistic.

The questionnaires and interviews focused on the following areas of inquiry: (1) the decision making process towards becoming a donor; (2) informed consent; (3) postoperative complications and long term complications from the operation; (4) impact on the donor's life and feelings; (5) self-evaluation of donorship, i.e., in retrospect, how would the donor make his decision now; (6) the meaning to the donor of his act of donating, then and now.

THE DECISION MAKING PROCESS

There are three systems involved in this process: the medical selection system, the donor's self-selection, and the family selection system.

Medical Selection

The medical selection works in this way: When a transplant situation arises, all possible donor relatives of the patient are asked to come to the clinic for blood test (ABO typing). Great care is taken at this point by the medical staff to inform the volunteer subjects that this is an exceedingly preliminary procedure and no commitment whatsoever is involved by their appearing at this clinic, or elsewhere, to have their blood samples drawn. Those potential donors who are not ruled out on the basis of blood grouping are then asked to come to the renal clinic for a brief history-taking and complete physical examination, including routine laboratory studies.

Somewhat later, those among the possible donors who still remain are asked to return to the clinic for histocompatibility tests. The results of the mixed culture tests (MLCT) are not known until several weeks later and may have to be repeated before they can be conclusively read. Only after this stage does it become possible for the renal transplant team to select from among the available possible donors the most suitable one. He or she is then asked to come to the special studies unit at the hospital for a complete work-up and careful evaluation of renal status. During this brief hospitalization they are evaluated independently by at least three of the team physicians. Only at the end of this evaluation and after intensive, repeated briefing on the risks involved and the chances for success is the potential donor asked to make a decision giving his or her informed consent. A final chance to refuse at any time in a dignified and comfortable manner is offered by the team's expressed willingness to supply a plausible medical excuse to the recipient and family.

Donor Self-selection

The medical selection system as described, assumes that the future donor will make his or her decision only at the conclusion of the medical work-up and after intensive and repeated briefing. It is assumed that the decision will occur only at the end of adequate information-gathering and a weighing of the pros and cons. Actually, members of the renal transplant team are aware that most of the potential donors are ready to make a commitment earlier than that and have to be held off until the team has made its selection. It was thought that this point of commitment was reached during the evaluation process, but there seems now to be enough evidence to suggest that in most instances the decision to donate was made immediately, when the person was first contacted. Most donors interviewed stated that they had made their decision immediately when the subject of the kidney transplant was first mentioned over the telephone, "in a split-second," "instantaneously," and "right away." Some said they just went along with the tests hoping it would be someone else. They could not recall ever really having made a clear decision, yet they never considered refusing to go along either. As it became clear to each of them toward the end of the selection process that they were going to be the person most suited to the donor, each finally had committed themselves to the act. However, this decision too, occurred before the sessions with the team doctors in which all the relevant information and statistics were put before these individuals and they were finally asked to decide. Subsequent work by Simmons, Klein and Simmons (1977) confirmed that a large majority of their donors experienced a similar decision-making process. They found 88% of their donors reported considering the donation as soon as they heard about the need, and 78% know immediately that they would donate without thinking it over.

Of all the subjects who made their initial decision on the telephone upon first hearing of the possibility of the kidney transplant, hardly anyone had consulted his or her spouse. When questioned about this particular circumstance, each explained that the spouse later on had either been neutral or had reinforced the decision; they "knew it would be OK." To the hypothetical question of "What would you have done if your spouse had said no?", each answered, "I would have gone ahead and done it anyway."

The immediacy of the decision making with regard to donorship often contrasts markedly with the usual way in which the person makes other important decisions. When questioned more closely about this seeming paradox, all of our subjects clearly expressed their opinion that this was a rather special situation and could not be compared to ordinary decision making.

The Family System of Donor Selection

In our own investigations, the role the family plays in the selection of a donor from within its midst was very difficult to demonstrate. In retrospect, this difficulty arose in past from the general bias, which we shared at the beginning of our investigation, that the family would tend to select a likely donor as a sacrifice or scapegoat under the threat of family ostracism. We could not demonstrate such dynamics in our sample, except possibly in one case. What we did see, once we had become aware of this possibility, was that a family would exclude certain members from participation. This was most commonly done at the initial contact and was made possible by the rather haphazard communication between the medical staff and the family of the recipient. In only few cases were the donors given the first communication about the possibility of renal transplantation by a member of the transplant team, or by the family physician. Most heard about it first from a family member. Usually, the communication was by telephone call, the informant telling the future donor about the seriousness of the recipient's illness. He or she explained that the doctors were considering a kidney transplantation and that all close relatives would be invited in the near future to come to the clinic or the hospital for blood samples to be taken for initial tests. Usually, the informant followed this up with a brief discussion of which family members should be asked to participate, which should not, and for what reasons. The same route was used subsequently to transmit the results of tests, to make further appointments, and could also be used to discourage further participation. Thus, it becomes possible for one family member to assume the role of intermediary and to exert great influence on donor selection.

In one family, the father successfully dissuaded his two sons from coming for initial blood tests, his wife from participating beyond the halfway point, and ended up himself as the triumphant donor. In another family, where the recipient was a young girl, the only possible donors were her parents and an older brother. The father was excluded on the basis of his blood group. The mother and her oldest son then entered into a competitive struggle in which the mother tried very hard to dissuade the son from participating even in the preliminary tests. She subsequently attempted to enlist the help not only of her husband but also of friends and of the medical team to get him to withdraw from participation. Her argument was that her son was still too young to give up a kidney: that his life was all ahead of him, whereas she had already lived the better part of hers. The son finally "won" on the basis of tissue compatibility testing.

One woman became the donor to her son after convincing her daughter that she had to bring up her own children first. Two other daughters insisted upon going ahead with medical workups at their homes in another state. The mother then proceeded to control the selection process by getting her doctor to call and stop their medical screening. This occurred after she had passed successfully several of the initial tests but before she had been screened by the renal transplant team. In another family, the recipient was an only child and the mother became the donor. Only much later was it revealed that the father, who was never considered as a possible donor because of his age, was not the real father at all. The mother had been divorced and would not even consider notifying her first husband because, as she said, "We don't want him in on this." Our view is that the family system of donor selection is at its most efficient very early in the selection process and works primarily in the direction of excluding some family members from participation. Once the potential donors are known and made available to the renal team, the power of the family system to influence the medical selection process diminishes greatly.

Because of the complexity of these selection processes, it is not possible to give accurate estimates about the refusal (nonvolunteer) rates at any particular stage in the process. In addition to the family maneuvers, slightly different procedures at different institutions and occasional complex excuses by possible donors further complicate such a guess. Simmons et al. (1977) reported an overall nonvolunteer, nondonor average rate of 43% of eligible donors: father and mother, 14%; daughter, 33%; son, 34%; and sister and brother, 52 and 54%, respectively.

Simmons, Hickey, Kjellstrand, and Simmons (1971) approached the study of family tensions engendered by the need for a kidney transplant by focusing to a large extent on nondonors, i.e., family members who could have donated but did not. They report that many experienced great feelings of ambivalence and long periods of indecision, even to the point of volunteering and then withdrawing. In addition, they also reported that in their sample they found the spouses of the recipient or donor to be freer than the actual blood relations to play more "selfish" roles, and to apply pressure on the family; the spouse of the recipient pressuring for donation, the spouse of the would-be donor against it.

INFORMED CONSENT

Reference has already been made to the description of the donor self-selection to the contrast between ordinary, rational decision-making process, and to the immediate "irrational" decision described by most of the donors. The former model no doubt forms the basis for the ethical guidelines adopted by the American Medical Association and defines the necessary and sufficient conditions that must be met in the selection of a living kidney donor (American Medical Association Judicial Comment, 1968). This is usually referred to as "informed consent." It is stressed that the decision to donate an organ must be a reasoned, intellectual decision, not an emotional one, arrived at entirely voluntarily, free from pressure, and based on full awareness of all relevant information. However, the speed of decision, the apparent lack of conscious, intellectual weighing of alternatives by our donors and the failure to seek the kind of information we postulate they should be seeking, does not necessarily mean that the decision to donate a kidney was not based logically on other identifiable influences.

Shalom H. Schwartz (1970) felt that a moral decision-making model might apply. In this conceptual framework, the person must first be aware that their own actions can affect another person. Secondly, the person must ascribe some responsibility to him or herself, and the third condition is that the person must accept the moral norm at issue; that is, in this case, he or she must perceive donation as an act of virtue.

If we view the donor's decision making along these lines, we find that all relevant data are immediately available to him. The possibility of saving a life is always part of the initial communications to the potential donor: e.g., "George is terribly sick and the doctors said he will die unless we give him a new kidney." The potential donor may not know in detail what donating a kidney will do for the recipient, but he or she clearly believes that it is a question of life and death.

Ascription of responsibility for this action is probably also immediate, since the potential donor has been contacted because he is one of a very few people, the immediate blood relatives, who could carry out this action. Personal responsibility cannot be ascribed away from the self, except in a very limited way, i.e., to other possible donors. (One such instance occurred when a donor, brother of the recipient, hesitated for a while before committing himself because he felt that the son of the recipient should be asked first. This son had never been mentioned by the recipient because he was the product of a previous marriage, and there was "bad blood between them because of the divorce.") From our discussion of the family system of donor selection, it appears likely that the parental role, and especially the mother role, intensifies the ascription of responsibility to the self. And finally, it is unquestionably normative for people to take action that would save the life of a close family member.

SUBJECTIVE MOTIVATIONS

The donor's reason for volunteering has been studied, with regard to the genetically related volunteer, by Eisendrath, Gultman, and Murray (1969), Simmons et al. (1971), Cramond (1967), and Kemph (1971). To our knowledge, Sadler, Davidson, and Kountz (1971) were the only ones who studied exhaustively the genetically unrelated volunteer. We presumed that, when the donor belongs to the family, it is only natural to assume that altruism or love or pity or similar feelings are motivating forces. It was only after hearing Dr. Sadler's account of the unrelated donors and donor candidates, who had absolutely no personal knowledge of the recipient and who did not seem to care about the fate of the recipient or of the grafted organs, that we began to re-examine our own data and to take a fresh look at other published accounts of donors. We began to believe that a significant part of the immediate motivation of most of the donors was not pity for the other, not primarily a wish to help, nor a social idealism involving aid to another human being, but rather an inner imperative. The occasion for their action is indeed the call to help another, but they are doing it for their own sake, for themselves. Eisendrath et al. (1969) summarize this as follows:

> In most instances, no real decision-making problem existed for the donor. Most commonly, he stated that he must give to save the life of the potential recipient or he could not face himself. In a sense, he is 'called.' It is not always a call about which he is enthusiastic, but it is one that he believes he is unable to refuse.

Quotes from patients in our own group are quite similar. A 60-year-old woman: "People say to me: what a brave thing to do. I say, there was no bravery connected. It was just a thing I had to do." A 22-year-old man: "I had never done anything like this before. Just drifting along with the tide. First time I did something worthwhile. Something that had to be done." A 25-year-old woman: "I had to do it. It was no heroic act. I just felt I had to do it." A 43-year-old woman: "Not a great thing, but the right thing to do." A 31-year-old man: "I had to do it. I couldn't have backed out, not that I had the feeling of being trapped, because the doctors offered to get me out. I just had to do it." A 27-year-old man: "I never was particularly close to my sister (the recipient), but I had to do it anyway."

Thus, the awareness of consequences as expressed by our subjects concerned not only the fate of the sick family member but often included an appreciation of what would happen to the potential donor's own self-concept if he or she refused to participate: "I would feel very guilty if I had said no," or "How could you live with your conscience if you had done nothing and the poor fellow died?" An expression of awareness, at the time of decision making, of possible positive consequences of participation on the donor's self-concept was very difficult to elicit.

DISSONANCE

We have already mentioned that, as far as the medical team was concerned, the donor's initial decision to volunteer was not immediately accepted by them and was not regarded as a binding commitment until the actual moment of surgery. In fact, the initial decision had to be defended and maintained by the donor through out the long waiting period, often many months, that still separated him from the act. There was nothing unexpected in the way our subjects handled their "cognitive dissonance." This term pertains to the tension state that is always created, to a greater or lesser degree, in the mind of the decision maker by his or her knowledge of facts that are inconsistent with or contradictory to the decision (Festinger, 1964). Reduction of dissonance can be achieved in several ways, mostly by increasing the attractiveness of the chosen alternative and decreasing the attractiveness of the rejected alternative, thus strengthening the subject's main tendency to justify the decision. In all our cases, the postdecision dissonance was handled rather as predicted by theory. During this period, there was almost no further consideration of the donor's decision. As one donor put it, "What was there to think about? I made the decision, it was the right one, and that was that." No new information that might bear on the decision is acknowledged or processed. One donor stated, "My major goal was to think as little as possible and to get it over with." Thus, though most donors describe the waiting period as one of high stress and anxiety, they managed to remain committed to their course of action, even in instances where the final act (surgery) had to be postponed for long periods of time. The longer the time span during which this dissonance had to be dealt with, the higher were the levels of anxiety.

POST-OPERATIVE PHENOMENA

From the medical point of view the situation is quite simple: The donor has lost one of his or her kidneys and the total renal function has now to be carried by the remaining kidney which will be quite adequate for functioning and presumably not restrict the donor in any way. Few of the transplant programs pay subsequent attention to the donor unless he or she comes forward and demands further care for complications. On occasion, there have been discussions between transplant teams and insurance carriers with regard to whether or not there is an increase in vulnerability. Thus, the medical significance is restricted to the loss of one kidney and its possible negative aspects and historically physicians had no interest in possible positive aspects.

IMPACT ON DONOR'S LIFE AND FEELINGS

From the donor's subjective point of view, the rewards seem to be twofold: first, the satisfaction of rapid improvement in the recipient; second, more lasting and independent of the fate of the transplanted kidney, an important increase in self-esteem and a stronger feeling of self.

Other investigators in this field report similar findings to ours. Eisendrath et al. (1969) state that "replies (of 65 donors) were quite consistent, irrespective of the result of the transplant. There was unanimity of belief that the donor would do it again and that each had derived some sense of worthwhile accomplishment in helping to save a life. Sometimes the answers were "moving." Sadler et al. (1971) also confirm positive changes in life style resulting from donorship, adding that these persisted 5 years later. Fox (1970), in a survey article, refers to the increasing evidence suggesting that, for a significant number of donors,

> the act of making such a gift becomes a transcendent experience, akin to a religious one. Many donors testify that giving an organ was the most important, meaningful, ans satisfying act of their lives: one that increased their self-knowledge, enhanced their feeling of self-worth, gave them a sense of 'totality,' belief and commitment, and increased their sense of unity with the recipient, people in general and with humanity.

In 1977, when Dr. Marshall re-interviewed 10 of our original group of 12 early donors after an interval of 9 years, we found all of them to be in good general health. Several had minor physical complaints referable to the operative site such as "twinges" on bending or itching or irritation of the scar. All but one donor denied any sense of increased vulnerability, saying they had placed no limitations on their lives. They stated they seldom thought about having only one kidney and virtually never worried about its injury or failure. The exception was a man whose brother had died 4½ years after the donation. He noted "constant pain in the wound site that hasn't improved." He also stated his "sex life" was diminished and wondered if this was due to the surgery, adding, "My wife says I aged a great deal."

In the original study all of the subjects had noted changes in their attitudes and feelings about themselves. They initially related these feelings to the extraordinary attention they had received from family, friends and local news media. Later, however, they began to consider these changes more permanent, even though the additional external attention had almost ceased. The donors felt it was natural that people forgot, and several expressed relief at no longer being considered "special." Feelings were mixed. However, most admitted to being pleased when family members spoke of the donation. One man described with pleasure how his customers still asked about him. Another noted that she often "accidentally" mentioned it to new friends.

The permanence of the subjective changes was strongly confirmed. These changes ranged from minor ones, such as that reported by one individual, who noted, "Giving the kidney has made me more confident in myself" to very substantial ones. A 40-year-old man stated that "It changes you, you drop your walls, you're more understanding and compassionate of people." This man felt that he had been saved by God from a severe childhood accident for a reason, and he continues to believe this. "I have paid my debt," he said happily. A 68-year-old mother stated, "I'm more confident, more courageous and self-assured. Criticism is not so painful because you know you did something good. It was a

wonderful feeling of joy, it made me think deeper.'' A 34-year-old who originally felt she was chosen to ''teach her'' because she was a ''real snot'' said,
''Life is good. I feel rewarded, you appreciate things more, I am more careful of
people.'' It was particularly striking that many of our subjects used identical or
very similar phrases to those they had used 9 years before. The subjects were
amused when this was pointed out to them but felt the expressions best described
how they felt.

Thus, we can affirm that the positive consequences of donorship for the donor
stand the test of time. There is, however, one restriction we should make, namely
that with the passage of the years there is a certain leveling of the sense of
specialness and uniqueness experienced by the donor, often couched in terms like
''life just goes on, and one sometimes forgets that it even happened.'' The
importance of a sense of duty is stressed to a larger degree with the passage of the
years and in retrospect might have a more important place in the original decision
making.

SELF-EVALUATION OF DONORSHIP

We were extremely curious about this question: how would our respondents, and
especially the 35% of donors whose donated kidneys no longer survived, answer
if looking back and knowing all they know now, they were to decide whether
they would go through all of it again? The answer was uniformly in the affirma-
tive. What was then the right thing to do, remained the right thing to do now, and
they would do it again. Even our most ambivalent donor, a 33-year-old man who
donated his kidney three years earlier to his younger brother who rejected it and
since had a cadaveric transplant that is working well, had this to say, ''Yes, I
think I would probably become a donor again, but I would tell others not to. I
never felt it was a heroic venture, but I love my brother, and I wanted to help
him. I did then, and it still does make me feel good to know I did it. It probably
was an important thing to do.'' We can safely say this about even those donors
who have considerable ambivalent feelings because their act of sacrifice proved
to be in vain: they still believe that they did the right thing, that it was a
worthwhile act, that they still feel good about having done it, and that they
would, given the circumstances, do it again.

A VERY SPECIAL FAMILY

We would like to tell you now about a rather special family of donors, the Jones
family whom Dr. Carl Fellner had occasion to interview the summer of 1975,
and has seen on a number of occasions since. The parents were at that time, 51
and 57 years, respectively, and they had four children. Of the four, three had a

genetic metabolic disease, cystinosis, also called Lignac's Disease. This anomaly is carried by recessive genes and manifests itself after the first year in childhood. The oldest son, Rick, was a healthy boy, and the second son, Bill, showed the symptoms of this disease at age two or three, eventually dying at age ten. The third child, Ron, and the fourth child, Jane, both have cystinosis. Initially, of course, the parents had not been aware that they were carriers of the disease. When their second child Bill fell ill, the sophisticated treatment methods of hemodialysis and kidney transplant had as yet not been introduced into the practice of medicine, and he died in 1963. Then in 1968, when the next boy, Ron, had reached the critical stage of his illness, hemodialysis and renal transplantation were available to the public and he received a kidney transplanted from his father. At the time, both his father and mother had been competing for donorship, and the mother was actually the better match, but in the end found not acceptable because of a kidney infection. The father's kidney functioned well for Ron over the next few years, but when he reached the age of 15, the doctors decided to withdraw certain medications, letting his body reject the kidney and beginning hemodialysis. This decision was made in order to encourage his growth pattern to re-establish itself since, with the transplant and the necessary medication, he had stopped growing at age eight. Then in 1975, Ron received a second kidney tranplanted from his older brother, Rick, and that kidney has worked exceedingly well to date; Ron requires little medication and has grown considerably. He is going to school, working at the same time, and in general, doing very well.

The girl, Jane, did less well than her brother. Her first transplant, a kidney donated by her mother in 1970, was a good match, but Jane developed post-transplant complications fairly rapidly and rejected 3 months later. She then was on hemodialysis for five years. Her physicians attempted a cadaver kidney transplant in April, 1975, but it rejected instantly and the kidney had to be removed the next night. Since then, Jane has continued on the hemodialysis machine, has completed high school, and is doing quite well. She is working towards an independent life even though she has remained dwarfed and is physically at the developmental stage of a 10-year-old girl.

The extended family has also been involved in the Jones' struggle to keep these two youngsters alive and well. The father had three sisters, of whom one is surviving but is prevented from being a donor by her diabetes, though she has offered. Her oldest daughter has also offered to become a kidney donor, but in view of the virulent reaction to Jane's last transplant, no further transplants have been considered.

In the interim, Mrs. Jones had the following things to say, addressing first the period of time when they were waiting to donate a kidney to her son in which she had the better match but was told that she had an infection; "I was told that never could I be a donor because of the infection, and when I was told that, then my whole world fell through, because I wanted so much to be able to do this. Later, after a couple of years, it was cleared up, and I was able to give to our little girl.'' With regard to the rapid rejection of her donated kidney by her daughter in 1970, she said: ''At first it was very difficult emotionally on a comparative level. My husband had given to my son, and it was working more or less all right. My kidney was rejected, and I could not get the satisfaction of a parent giving that a child might live. I felt robbed of that satisfaction.'' She went then on to say that there were questions, that she took this problem to the Lord, and it disappeared.

With regards to their feelings and attitudes about themselves as donors, Mr. Jones said, ''I'm glad I could do it; I'm sorry it didn't last; I'm sorry it wasn't better.'' He went on to say that now the whole thing isn't a big deal anymore, not as important as it was at the time when it happened. However, he agreed with his wife when she said that, ''I think it is a big thing we have done. I have done what the Lord called for, to lay our lives on the line for our children and I feel good that we did this. I feel good in myself that I was able to do this.'' Further, Mr. Jones added, ''I'm glad that I could do this, that there was nothing wrong with my kidneys, that I was in a position to give my kidney to my son.'' They both agreed that becoming donors was ''a big climax in our lives.'' They added, ''If we had chosen not to do it, we would have been less the people we are now. We would have lost a certain amount of respect for ourselves, felt that there was something really lacking in us.'' They also expressed the feeling that if their children should die, and that's up to the Lord, they have done all they could. ''We could not have gone any other way; neither one of us ever sat down and personally talked this out together—it was automatic.'' Asked whether, knowing all they know now and looking back over events, would they donate their kidney over again, father said, ''Seeing the day-to-day battle of our children just to survive; at one time there, watching Jane, I would have given my remaining kidney and offered to go on the kidney machine myself for survival so that she would have a better time of it. The average person would not understand that, but we are looking for more.'' Retrospectively evaluating their actions, Mrs. Jones said, ''Through Jane's physical plight we all have grown as individuals through self-sacrifice and endurance. We have become more meaningful people and more helpful to others. We, as well as Jane, have deeper and richer characters.''

The oldest son, Rick, became a donor to his brother in 1975, and this transplant proved to be an excellent match, leading to a very rapid improvement in his brother. When his brother needed a second transplant and Rick had attained the age of 18, he was permitted to become the donor. He described his disappointment when earlier he had not been permitted to donate a kidney to his sister because he was still a minor. He said that he had been looking forward very much to that opportunity and yet felt that it was not such a big thing to do anyway. ''My brother needed a new kidney; I was the only one left in the family who had one to give.'' He also stated that, ''Some say I'm a very brave person, but bravery had nothing to do with it. Others say I must love my brother a lot, but it seemed like the thing to do at the time, and I'm glad I did it.'' Answering the question, whether he had ever done anything else in his life that could compare in importance with the action of donating one of his kidneys, he said, "Sure! I don't see it as that big a thing. Becoming a Christian changed my life forever; giving a kidney just slowed me down for a couple of weeks." He also said that, "You can't really equate me with most other donors. My whole family has been in and out of the hospital my whole life. It's been our second home. Operations are just a way of life here. Most people associate the hospital with terrible illness and dreadful things; we look at it as part of the regular course of events."

We hope that these quotes from our interviews will give a flavor of this rather unique family. But we also present them because many of their sentiments are not unique. The same feelings about decision making to become donors, about the experience of donorship and the moral consequences of donorship are expressed in very similar words by most of the donors we have interviewed.

MEDICAL ATTITUDES TOWARDS THE LIVING DONOR

Renal transplantation as an accepted medical procedure in end stage renal disease is exemplified by the existence of over 300 transplant teams throughout the world who have performed a total, as of May, 1976, of 25,108 transplants on 22,261 recipients of whom 10,300 are alive with functioning grafts. The source of the transplanted organ has remained controversial, between the genetically related living volunteer donor versus the kidney of cadaveric origin. This controversy is noticeable in the changing statistical trends evident in the reports of the Human Renal Transplant Registry (1975) which show an increase towards utilization of donor kidneys received from siblings and parents between the years 1965 and 1973, and then a reverse towards increasing use of cadaveric organs. The controversy is perhaps more clearly visible when we focus on individual transplant teams. The percentages in the use of cadaveric sources of kidneys differ regionally from the United States with 52.6% to Europe 70.8%, and Australia 98.3%. Thus, different transplant teams have different preferences for graft kidneys coming either from the live donor or from cadaveric origin. The rationale for these preferences is difficult to elucidate. As far as outcome is concerned, measured in functional survival of graft, the percentages are slightly more favorable for grafts from living relatives, especially in certain age groups such as the pediatric recipient. Unfortunately, we do not possess at this point sufficiently refined statistics that would also take into account the extent of tissue matching, and that seems to be the most significant single variable permitting prediction of graft survival. We can, however, state clearly that a key variable in giving preference to the cadaveric kidney over the live donor one is concern over the ethical and moral issue, i.e., whether or not a transplant team finds it justifiable to injure one person, the donor, by taking away a healthy organ in order to help another person, the recipient.

The dilemma for the surgeon is a very real one, because the practical decision is always his or hers. It is the surgeon and the transplant team who have to weigh and balance risks and advantages of such an intervention, who have to be the advocates for both donor and recipient. In interviewing transplant surgeons, we were invariably impressed by their anguish and concern about operating on a healthy, intact donor. Actually, the most puzzling aspect of our investigation has been the striking contrast between the naturalness, relative calm and equanimity of the volunteer donor, and the uncomfortableness of the transplant team. How is this to be understood? The most obvious answer is that we are dealing here with a difference in values: the transplant team who originally started out as the caretakers of one patient, are now caught in the position of having to assume responsibility for two. In operating on the donor, they expose him or her to the risks of a major operation to remove a healthy organ. The transplant team attempts to resolve this dilemma by falling back to the vantage point of the scientists, with objectivity, logic and detachment. To a scientific view, the subjective-relative experience of the donor remains opaque: he or she gives up a kidney but gets nothing in return.

There are two modes of truth: to be understood, each of them calls for a different cognitive approach. The "lived world" (Lebenswelt) calls for the descriptive-revealing methods of phenomenology, whereas the "scientific world" calls for the detachment, objectivity and neutrality of scientific methods. Our donors, as people, are directly aware of their own active intentions and of their objectives in their very acts. Examined by the methods of phenomenology, they reveal an existential situation and a world where meaning is expressed in action. The transplant teams, on the other hand, are governed by the pursuit of scientific truth, detached from the object of their investigation. The donor is observed as a thing out there, in itself. His or her life-world is discounted as subjective and impressionistic, therefore confused, unstable and unreliable. We propose that it is this difference in experiencing, of viewing, of understanding, that is at the heart of the contrast we found between the position of the donors and the conflict and anguish of the transplant team. In the foregoing, we have tried to compare what can be termed the *signification* of renal donorship, that is, the interpretation given to such an event by the observer, with the *meaning* of the act of donorship as it is expressed by the donor, themselves. We believe that such a comparison is necessary since a truly objective evaluation needs to take into account the totality of the phenomenon. If the meaning of this event were not included, we would be restricted to the signification alone, based as it were on the equally subjective opinion of the observer. Therefore, we take the position that any discussion regarding the utilization of the living, genetically related volunteer donor versus transplant kidneys of cadaveric origin needs to pay attention to the confusion that exists between meaning and signification, between "Lebenswelt" and the "objective" world, as revealed by the phenomenologic and the scientific methods.

SUMMARY

In the foregoing we have offered you the results of questionnaires and interviews of a large number of donors, many of them looking back on their experience with the knowledge that unfortunately their sacrifice proved to be in vain, either soon after transplant or in the long run. We have contrasted the evaluation of these donors as to the meaning of their action and the impact it had on their lives, which was judged by all of them in a very positive way, with the interpretation and judgment of the observers who look upon the event from the outside. We believe our observations to be in the nature of significant data that need to be taken into account in any discussion of the ethical and moral issues of renal transplant from the living human donor.

REFERENCES

American Medical Association Judicial Comment: Ethical guidelines for organ transplantation. *Journal of the American Medical Association,* 1968, *205,* 89–90.

Cramond, W.A. Renal homotransplantation—some observations on recipients and donors. *British Journal of Psychiatry,* 1967, *133,* 1223–1230.

Eisendrath, R.M., Gultman, R.D. & Murray, J.E. Psychological considerations in the selection of kidney transplant donors. *Surgery, Gynecology and Obstetrics,* 1969, *129,* 243–248.

Fellner, C., & Marshall, J.R. Twelve kidney donors. *Journal of the American Medical Association,* 1968, *206,* 2703–2707.

Fellner, C., & Marshall, J.R. The myth of informed consent. *American Journal of Psychiatry,* 1970, *129,* 1245–1251. (a)

Fellner, C., & Marshall, J. R. Kidney donors. In J. Macaulay & L. Berkowitz (Eds.), *Altruism and helping behavior.* New York: Academic Press, 1970. (b)

Festinger, L. *Conflict, decision, and dissonance.* Stanford, Calif.: Stanford University Press, 1964.

Fox, R. C. A sociological perspective on organ transplantation and hemodialysis. *Annals of the New York Academy of Sciences,* 1970, *169,* 406–428.

James, W. *Varieties of religious experience,* 1902. (Mentor Edition, New York, 1958).

Kemph, J.P. Psychotherapy with donors and recipients of kidney transplants. *Seminars in Psychiatry,* 1971, *3,* 145–158.

Marshall, J.R., & Fellner, C. Kidney donors revisited. *American Journal of Psychiatry,* 1977, *134,* 575–576.

Sadler, H.H., Davison, L.C., & Kountz, S.L. The living, genetically unrelated kidney donor. *Seminars in Psychiatry,* 1971, *3,* 86–101.

Schwartz, S.H. Moral decision making and behavior. In J. Macauley & L. Berkowitz (Eds.), *Altruism and helping behavior.* New York: Academic Press, 1970.

Simmons, R.G., Hickey, K., Kjellstrand, C.M., & Simmons, R.L. Donors and un-donors: family tension in the search for a kidney donor. *Journal of the American Medical Association,* 1971, *215,* 909–912.

Simmons, R.G., Klein, S.D., & Simmons, R.L. *Gift of life: the social and psychological impact of organ transplantation.* New York: Wiley, 1977.

The 12th Report of the Human Renal Transplant Registry. *Journal of the American Medical Association,* 1975, *233,* 787–796.

18

Extending Altruism Beyond the Altruistic Act: The Mixed Effects of Aid on the Help Recipient

Jeffrey D. Fisher
University of Connecticut

Bella M. DePaulo
University of Virginia

Arie Nadler
Tel-Aviv University

Receiving help is an integral component of the educational process, the health care system, the psychotherapeutic process, the welfare system, and the recurrent patterns of day-to-day life. Those who require aid on a more transient basis, as well as the depressed, the ailing, and the poor, may all function more effectively if they can obtain the resources that they need. An enormous amount of research effort has been channeled into studying the conditions under which people are more or less likely to provide help to the needy. Indeed, the contents of this volume provide compelling evidence of the breadth and depth of the interest in this issue, which is of both theoretical and practical significance. By now, whole bodies of literature exist on the precursors of altruism, the socialization of altruistic motivations, and the mediators and facilitators of altruistic behaviors. In contrast, the "other side" of the helping paradigm, the psychology of receiving help, has received relatively less research attention.

Underlying the intensive research activity on the psychology of giving help is an assumption that giving is good, and that helping relationships should be encouraged as a palliative for those in need. This assumption accords well with the liberal tradition in western culture (cf. Gergen, 1974). In line with these beliefs, people who give help may enjoy an increment in self-esteem, as well as other benefits (Fisher, Nadler, Hart, & Whitcher, 1981). Further, benefactors in a wide variety of helping contexts, including teachers, caseworkers, clinicians, foreign aid officials, nurses, neighbors, and friends, often expect that the recipient of their philanthropy will be duly appreciative. For their part, too, recipients may often feel that gratitude is the most appropriate reaction to aid.

Although help is frequently welcomed wholeheartedly and viewed as something of instrumental value which reflects donor liking and concern, there is growing evidence to suggest that the domain of recipient reactions to aid is not comprised solely of favorable responses. Included among the many classes of reactions to help that have been documented in the literature are feelings of tension and obligation, decrements in self-esteem and social status, and derogations of the helper, the help, and the helping institution. In fact, some of the same aid-related conditions (e.g., donor-recipient similarity, high donor resources) observed to elicit a high degree of helping in the aid-giving literature, have been found to lead to quite negative reactions in the help recipient (Fisher & Nadler, 1974, 1976).

Research paradigms employed in the study of recipient reactions to aid include as their most fundamental elements a donor, aid, a recipient, and a helping context. Aspects of each of these components of a helping interaction have important implications for the recipient's reactions. For the purpose of this paper, *donor characteristics* include behaviors and attributes of the donor as perceived by the recipient, and *aid characteristics* incorporate aspects of the help as experienced by the recipient. *Recipient characteristics* include fixed dispositions or skills and temporary emotional or cognitive states, and *context characteristics* incorporate a variety of situational factors surrounding the aid transaction (e.g., whether or not there are opportunities for the recipient to repay the donor) (Gergen, 1974).

The specific responses to aid which may occur in a particular helping setting can be classified into three categories: *external perceptions* (e.g., evaluations of the donor and the aid), *self-perceptions* (e.g., changes in self-concept), and *behavioral responses* (e.g., reciprocity to the donor). Although the most frequently studied reactions to aid include evaluative responses of various types and assessments of whether recipients reciprocate to donors, the categories of reactions to help delineated above also encompass many relatively unresearched dimensions (e.g., whether aid affects the recipient's future desire to engage in the task on which dependency occurred, whether help fosters future dependency). Such reactions may be quite important, and should receive more research attention.

In extant research, a number of theoretical frameworks have been employed to predict the relationship between various donor, aid, recipient and context characteristics on the one hand, and the several modes of recipient reactions to help on the other. Most of these formulations have been "borrowed" from other areas of social psychology, and have been adapted by researchers to the present context. The adequacy of these theories for conceptualizing reactions to aid has been discussed in detail elsewhere (Fisher, Nadler, & Whitcher, in press). Overall, each has been able to predict the consequences of at least some of the conditions that may be associated with aid, for at least several of the potential modes of recipient response. We will briefly (and necessarily somewhat incompletely) discuss the rationale and predictions associated with each of these formulations below. For more thorough coverage, the reader is referred to Gross, Wallston, and Piliavin (1979) and Fisher et al. (in press).

Equity theories (e.g., Adams, 1963; Blau, 1964; Gouldner, 1960; Greenberg, 1980; Homans, 1961; Walster, Berscheid, & Walster, 1973) suggest that the recipient's perception of the amount of inequity between him or herself and the donor is the critical variable in determining reactions to help. According to these formulations, inequity is an aversive state that is experienced when one party in a relationship has a more favorable ratio of outcomes to inputs than the other. Further, the amount of perceived inequity or indebtedness associated with help is determined by both the objective value of the aid, and other situational conditions associated with receiving help (such as whether help is accidental or intentional). For example, when a unit of help is intentional rather than accidental, perceived inequity is greater because the donor is viewed as having made more of a sacrifice (Walster et al., 1973). Recipients may alleviate feelings of inequity or indebtedness by reciprocating to the donor in equal measure—a restoration of actual equity, or by derogating the donor and/or the aid—a restoration of psychological equity.

In contrast to equity notions, *reactance theory* (Brehm, 1966) suggests that reactions to help are determined primarily by the degree to which recipients feel that their freedoms have been restricted by aid. According to a reactance formulation, people prefer to maximize their freedom of choice, and any reduction in perceived freedom arouses a motivational state (reactance) which is characterized by negative feelings, and which is directed toward the reestablishment of the lost freedoms. Applied to the aid recipient, to the extent that help limits the recipient's present or future actions (e.g., because they will have to act kindly toward the benefactor), it will arouse reactance. Recipients can reduce reactance by acting as though their behavior has not been restricted by help (e.g., by avoiding any actions based on perceived obligation toward the donor, and/or by derogating the source of the threat).

Other studies have employed *attribution theories* (Jones & Davis, 1965; Kelley, 1967) to conceptualize reactions to help. These may be used to predict the conditions under which recipients (1) will make attributions of the donor's motives for giving help (theory of correspondent inference), and (2) will make internal or external attributions for their own need for help (theory of external attribution). The preconditions necessary for making attributions according to these two formulations are described in detail elsewhere (Jones & Davis, 1965; Kelley, 1967). Beyond predicting when attributions will be made for a prosocial act, the two theories provide no explicit conceptual links between the recipient's attributions and their other reactions to aid. However, some empirical links can be derived from research to be reviewed in this paper.

A final set of studies have employed *threat to self-esteem* models (e.g., Fisher et al., in press; Gergen & Gergen, 1974a) for prediction. Unlike equity, reactance, and attribution theories, these formulations posit that it is the self-related consequences of aid (i.e., the effects of receiving help for one's self-concept), that are critical in determining the recipient's reactions. Specifically, it is assumed that aid potentially contains a mixture of self-supportive qualities (e.g., instrumental value, evidence of caring and concern), as well as self-threatening qualities (e.g., evidence of failure, inferiority, and dependency). Further, specific aspects of the helping situation (e.g., whether the donor belittles the recipient, or treats him/her with dignity), determine whether the potentially supportive or threatening aspects are more salient in a particular instance. To the extent that a receipt of aid is predominantly supportive, a cluster of essentially positive responses (e.g., favorable evaluations of the donor and the aid, high acceptance of help) occur. However, to the extent that aid is predominantly self-threatening, a cluster of essentially negative reactions (e.g., unfavorable donor and aid evaluations, high refusal of aid) are evidenced.

Having provided some background on the conceptual perspectives and the general parameters of the field, we move to the major purpose of this chapter, which is to present a comprehensive discussion of past research on recipient reactions to aid. The review is organized in four separate sections, which correspond to the four basic components of the aid transaction (i.e., donor characteristics, aid characterisitics, recipient characteristics, and context characteristics). Within each section, variables that have been found to have systematic effects on recipients' reactions are delineated, and the conceptual rationale behind relevant studies are discussed. Finally, more specific information concerning the details of the studies is presented in summary tables at the end of each section.

DONOR CHARACTERISTICS

A number of investigations have focused on the effect of the helper's general characteristics (e.g., friend or foe) and more specific motivations (e.g., humanitarian vs. manipulative intents) on the recipient's reactions to aid. From the recipient's perspective, these factors would seem to be very important: to be dependent on someone who has negative qualities and manipulative intents can be a very uncomfortable experience. Thus, it is not surprising that research on donor characteristics demonstrates that they can have important consequences for recipient responses.

One group of studies has focused on the effects of the donor's preexisting relationship with the recipient on the recipient's reactions to aid. In this regard,

Nadler, Fisher, and Streufert (1974) and Gergen and Gergen (1971) have found that help from a donor who is an "ally" or whose general qualities are liked and respected tends to lead to positive effects (e.g., enhanced attraction, constructive use of aid), and can generally be viewed as a means of improving relationships that are already at least moderately favorable. In contrast, aid from an "enemy" or a donor believed to have negative characteristics leads to no change in the status of the relationship, or may even elicit negative effects. Both Nadler et al. (1974) and Gergen and Gergen (1971) have explained their findings in terms of threat to self-esteem models. In both cases, it was assumed that help from an other characterized by positive characteristics was supportive, and thus permitted recipients to react constructively. In contrast, help from an other with negative qualities was threatening, which elicited various defensive reactions. On an applied level, these studies suggest that at least in the short run, it may be difficult to improve relationships with others who are negatively disposed toward one by engaging in prosocial acts.

Whether the donor consists of a single individual or nation, or a group of individuals or nations organized to provide benefits may also elicit differential reactions to help. For example, research on international aid has compared reactions to help given by a single donor nation (bilateral aid) with reactions to help given by groups of nations through agencies like the United Nations (multilateral aid). There are several significant qualities that differentiate bilateral from multilateral aid. In general, multilateral aid is less likely to be coupled with restrictive contingencies, such as threatening demands for political concessions. Too, the inferiority-superiority relationship between the donor and the recipient may be obscured in the case of multilateral aid, because the recipient is frequently a member of the donor organization. Based on threat to self-esteem and reactance models, it could be predicted that recipients would respond more favorably to aid in multilateral than in bilateral relationships. These predictions have been confirmed in several studies (Andreas, 1969; Gergen & Gergen, 1974a). Future research should determine the conditions under which this pattern of effects holds in other settings (e.g., when does help from the United Fund have a greater potential for favorable reactions than help from an individual source?)

Research attention has also focused on the effects of specific attributions that recipients make for a donor's prosocial act. An initial question involves specifying the conditions under which such attributions occur. Instructive in this regard are a group of studies that have compared recipient attributions for aid which is voluntary and deliberate, with those for involuntary and nondeliberate help. Attribution theories stipulate that for attributions to be made an actor (in this case, the helper) must have knowledge of his/her act, and the act must not be dictated by external factors (e.g., one's role). Thus it would seem that help which is voluntary and deliberate would be more likely to lead to attributions about the donor's intents than involuntary and nondeliberate aid. It has been found, as expected, that donors who gave help voluntarily and deliberately were more often seen as altruistic (Enzle & Schopflocher, 1978), motivated to help, and concerned about the recipient (Greenberg & Frisch, 1972).

A second group of studies has sought links between the attributions made for a donor's act, and the recipient's other reactions to aid. For example, equity theories have been used to predict that (positively attributed) voluntary and deliberate aid leads to greater perceived inequity than (negatively attributed) involuntary and nondeliberate help. This is because voluntary and deliberate help leads to recipient perceptions of more donor input to the relationship. Thus, in line with equity theories voluntary and deliberate aid should elicit stronger feelings of obligation, and lead to more reciprocity, than nondeliberate and involuntary help. In accord with these predictions, it has been found that recipients of the former types of aid generally feel greater obligation to the donor (Greenberg & Frisch, 1972), engage in greater reciprocity (Goranson & Berkowitz, 1966; Greenberg & Frisch, 1972; Gross & Latané, 1974; Leventhal, Weiss, & Long, 1969; Nemeth, 1970), and report more attraction to their donor (Goranson & Berkowitz, 1966; Gross & Latané, 1974; Nemeth, 1970). The findings for attraction, which can be interpreted as a form of reciprocity in accord with equity theories, could also be interpreted as a failure to support the equity assertion that help which elicits feelings of inequity will lead to derogation of the donor.

The generally positive attributional consequences of aid which is rendered voluntarily or deliberately are paralleled in the case of aid which is provided at considerable cost to the donor. Attribution theories assume that actions are more likely to be judged to reflect personal attributes, motives, or intentions when negative outcomes (e.g., costs, risks) are incurred. In accord with this, it has been predicted and found that individuals who are offered costly help are more likely than recipients of less costly aid to perceive their benefactors as generous, caring and concerned individuals (Fisher & Nadler, 1976; Greenberg & Frisch, 1972). Knowledge that such an other has provided one with aid can also have a self-supportive component for the recipient (Fisher & Nadler, 1976; Nadler & Fisher, 1978).

As with help which is intentional and deliberate, equity theories would again predict that high cost aid should elicit more feelings of obligation to the donor and more subsequent reciprocity than low cost help. In line with these predictions, it has been found that recipients of high cost aid do feel more obligated toward their donors than recipients of low cost aid (Muir & Weinstein, 1962; Tesser, Gatewood, & Driver, 1968). (Such feelings of obligation may cause people to avoid *seeking* help which is costly, cf. Castro, 1974; DePaulo & Fisher, 1980.) Recipients of high cost aid also devote their postaid efforts toward reciprocating to their donors rather than engaging in self-help behaviors to avoid future dependency (Fisher & Nadler, 1976; Gergen, Ellsworth, Maslach, & Seipel, 1975; Greenberg & Bar-Tal, 1976; Pruitt, 1968), and they like their donors more than recipients of low cost aid (Gergen et al., 1975). Again, the findings for donor liking can be interpreted either in line with equity models, or as a failure to support this formulation.

Several donor characteristics can serve as potential modifiers of the relationships discussed thus far. For example, it appears that various types of aid may become more threatening to the recipient when the donor is a social comparison other (cf. Festinger, 1954). That is, when the donor is someone with whom the recipient compares his or her own abilities, the receipt of aid (however well motivated) may serve to highlight the recipient's failure and dependency relative to this individual, and lead to an internal attribution of failure. A series of studies by Fisher and Nadler supports this formulation (Fisher, Harrison, & Nadler, 1978; Fisher & Nadler, 1974; Nadler, Fisher, & Streufert, 1976). Corroborating evidence is also available from the observation of Weiss (1969) that welfare recipients report being more ''bothered'' by welfare agents when interviewed by a similar than a dissimilar interviewer, and from the finding of Clark, Gotay, and Mills (1974) that less aid is accepted from a similar than from a dissimilar other when no opportunity for reciprocity is envisioned.

However, the potentially threatening effects of aid from a social comparison other might be mitigated or even reversed when the other is a close friend or someone with whom the recipient has a long-term relationship. In a study by DePaulo (1978a) respondents indicated a preference for seeking help from same-age, same-sex others who liked the recipient and who often were close friends. This may be because relationships among friends and family members, compared to less enduring associations with similar others, tend to be characterized by feelings that the other is ''obligated'' to help (Bar-Tal, Bar-Zohar, Greenberg, & Hermon, 1977). Too, there is evidence that they are governed more by norms of mutual responsiveness to the needs of others, whereas short-term relationships with similar others are characterized more by norms of economic exchange in which benefits are conferred in response to benefits received (Clark & Mills, 1979). Aid from a social comparison other might also be less threatening than aid from a nonsocial comparison other when the noncomparison other is of lower status than the recipient. DePaulo (1978b) and Druian and DePaulo (1977), for example, have shown that adults are more reluctant to seek or accept help from a child than from another adult. This occurs even when the child is as competent to help as the adult helper and more competent at the task than the recipient.

Finally, it appears that the physical attractiveness of the donor may also moderate reactions to help. In this regard, research suggests that a given type of aid may be less likely to be sought from physically attractive than unattractive others (Nadler, 1979; Stokes & Bickman, 1974). Perhaps this occurs because one risks a greater loss of esteem in admitting one's need for assistance to another who enjoys an enviable social status; alternatively, needy individuals may feel that especially attractive others are less likely to comply with their help request.

FISHER, DEPAULO, AND NADLER

However, Stokes and Bickman (1974) showed that when the donor is obligated by external constraints (e.g., role requirements) to answer a request for help, help-seeking is not influenced by the donor's physical attractiveness. This suggests that certain potentially threatening characteristics of the donor may be mitigated for the recipient if the donor is acting "in role."

Summary

Overall, it appears that general qualities of the donor and perceptions of specific donor motives affect a series of recipient reactions to aid. (See Table 18.1). When general qualities of the donor are favorable (e.g., when the donor is an ally, or an individual the recipient respects), aid tends to have positive effects. In contrast, when general donor qualities are unfavorable, aid may have negative consequences. In line with attribution theories, a number of factors determine whether recipients will make attributions of intent for a donor's prosocial act. To the extent that attributions of positive intent (e.g., altruistic motives) are made, help tends to elicit liking for the donor, feelings of obligation toward them, and reciprocity behavior. Finally, under certain conditions (e.g., when the donor is a social comparison other), aid may become self-threatening even when donor characteristics are otherwise positive.

CHARACTERISTICS OF AID

Several aid characteristics have been shown to have important consequences for the recipient's reactions to help. Past research in this area has had two primary foci: the effects of variations in the amount of help that needy individuals are given, and the effects of a number of different costs of help to the recipient.

The amount of help that is offered is probably one of the most important characteristics of aid to a person in need. Clearly, larger amounts of aid contain more instrumental benefits and may be perceived as reflecting more donor sacrifice and concern. Thus, it is not surprising that greater amounts of help lead to stronger perceptions that the donor is truly motivated to help (Greenberg & Frisch, 1972), and are more likely to be accepted (Freeman, 1977; Rosen, 1971).

The most common recipient reactions studied as a function of the amount of help given are feelings of indebtedness, and willingness to reciprocate. Equity theories would predict that, other things being equal, more aid should lead to greater inequity/indebtedness, and occasion higher reciprocity. In line with this model, experiments demonstrate that feelings of indebtedness (Greenberg & Frisch, 1972; Tesser et al., 1968) and reciprocity behavior increase as a direct linear function of the amount of help received (Berkowitz & Friedman, 1967; Greenberg & Bar-Tal, 1976; Greenberg & Frisch, 1972; Kahn & Tice, 1973; Pruitt, 1968; Stapleton, Nacci & Tedeschi, 1973). In addition, when no opportu-

TABLE 18.1
Donor Characteristics

Author & Date	Sex	N	Population	Type of Task	Aid Manipulation	Donor Characteristic	Operationalization of Donor Characteristic	Findings
Andreas (1969		5 Newspapers	India, Pakistan, United States	Newspaper Editorials	Content analysis of editorials discussing international assistance	Multilateral vs bilateral aid programs	Editorialists' descriptions	Bilateral aid viewed as more manipulative than multilateral aid
Bar-Tal Bar-Zohar Greenberg & Hermon (1977)	M-F	100	Undergraduates	Role-play questionnaire	Subjects are to imagine calling another person and asking for a ride	Parent, sibling friend, acquaintance, stranger	Role-play instructions	The closer the relationship between donor and recipient, the more recipients believed that the donor was obligated to help
Castro (1974)	M	90	Undergraduates	Forming words from letters	Partner (donor) sends subject extra letters	Provider of high or low cost aid	Donor loses five points (high cost) or one point (low cost) for sending the letters	Subjects are especially reluctant to seek high cost aid when it cannot be repaid
Clark, Gotay & Mills (1974)	M-F	42	Undergraduates	Creating an object from balloons	Partner (donor) offers to help the subject blow up balloons	Similar or dissimilar to recipient	Subjects are told that their answers to the value questionnaire were very similar/dissimilar to their partner's	When there is no opportunity to reciprocate, subjects accept less help from a similar than from a dissimilar other

(Continued)

375

TABLE 18.1 (Continued)

Author & Date	Sex	N	Population	Type of Task	Aid Manipulation	Donor Characteristic	Operationalization of Donor Characteristic	Findings
Clark & Mills (1979) (Study 1)	M	96	Unmarried undergraduates	Forming words from letters	Subjects are induced to send help to an attractive female subject (donor) who eventually does or does not return some of it	Donor is open to a communal or exchange relationship	Donor is said to be unmarried or married	Receiving help after giving help increases subject's liking for the donor when an exchange relationship is preferred but decreases liking when a communal relationship is desired
DePaulo (1978a)	M-F	303	Junior high school students, high school students, undergraduates, adults	Role-play questionnaire	Descriptions of hypothetical aid situations	Age, sex, stranger, acquaintance, friend, liking for recipient	Subjects indicate the type of donor they would prefer to seek help from	Subjects prefer to seek help from same-age, same-sex donors who like them and who are close friends
DePaulo (1978b) (Study 1)	F	139	Adults	Telephone survey	Willingness to accept free art lessons from talented children/adults	Age	Artists are described as children or adults	Subjects were less willing to accept help from the children than from the adults

Study	Sex	N	Population	Task	Procedure	Independent variable	Manipulation	Results
DePaulo & Fisher (1980)	F	62	Under-graduates	Recognition of overt and covert cues of emotion	Help-seeking from an expert helper	Provider of high or low cost aid	Helper's schedule indicates that she is busy working on her dissertation (high cost) or has no special plans (low cost)	Subjects were especially reluctant to seek high cost help
Druian & DePaulo (1977)	F	26	Under-graduates	Spelling test	Subjects can ask to use the helper's answer	Age	Helper is described as 19 or 10 years old	Subjects seek less help from the child than from the adult
Enzle & Schopflocher (1978)	M	41	Under-graduates	Proof-reading	Donor helps the subject with the task after finishing his own task	Provider of voluntary/involuntary aid	Experimenter tells the donor to help (involuntary) or doesn't say anything (voluntary)	Subjects perceive the donor of voluntary help as more altruistic
Fisher, Harrison, & Nadler (1978)	M	62	Under-graduates	Pattern-recognition tasks	Partner (donor) suggests a way to detect the patterns	Social comparison other/non-social comparison other	Donor's background is similar to the subject's or the donor has significantly more task-relevant experience	Recipients of help from a social comparison helper feel less self-confident and less intelligent; recipients of help from a non-comparison other feel more confident and intelligent

(Continued)

TABLE 18.1 (*Continued*)

Author & Date	Sex	N	Population	Type of Task	Aid Manipulation	Donor Characteristic	Operationalization of Donor Characteristic	Findings
Fisher & Nadler (1974)	M	64	Undergraduates	Stock market stimulation	Partner (donor) sends subject chips which can be used for further investments	Social comparison other/non-social comparison other	Donor endorses attitudes that are 100% similar or dissimilar to the subject's	Recipients of aid from a social comparison helper have lower self-esteem and self-confidence; recipients of aid from a non-comparison helper have higher self-esteem and self-confidence
Fisher & Nadler (1976)	M	64	Undergraduates	Stock market simulation	Partner (donor) sends subject chips which can be used for further investments	Low resources (helping is costly) high resources (helping is not costly)	After several playing periods, donor has 12 (low resources) or 60 (high resources) chips left	Recipients of costly aid perceive their donors as more generous and less desirous of power; experience enhanced self-concept and engage in less self-help

Study	Sex	N	Sample	Method	Task	Variables	Measures	Findings
Gergen Ellsworth, Maslach, & Seipel (1975)	M	180	Undergraduates in Japan, Sweden, and the United States	Decision-making game involving wagering money	Donor sends subject chips redeemable for money	Low resources (helping is costly)/high resources (helping is not costly)	After several trials, donor has 26 (low resources) or 66 (high resources) chips left	Recipients of costly help evaluate the donor more positively and return more help
Gergen & Gergen (1971)	M-F	About 60	Officials working in international assistance programs	Interview	Respondents are asked about the importance of various factors in the aid process	Attitude toward recipient nation and types of motives	Respect for recipient country, aggressiveness, selflessness of motives	Less favorable reactions to aid from donor nations perceived as aggressive, as having selfish motives, and as lacking respect for the recipient nation
Gergen & Gergen (1974a)	M-F	10,331	Large representative samples of citizens of 37 nations	Public opinion survey	Foreign aid received from United States and other nations	Types of motives	Imperialistic, domineering, aggressive	Less favorable reactions to aid from donor nations perceived as imperialistic, domineering, or aggressive

(Continued)

TABLE 18.1 (*Continued*)

Author & Date	Sex	N	Population	Type of Task	Aid Manipulation	Donor Characteristic	Operationalization of Donor Characteristic	Findings
Gergen & Gergen (1974b)				Lab studies, field studies, interviews	International assistance	Bilateral vs. multilateral aid	Aid from U.S.A. (bilateral) vs. I.D.A. (multilateral)	Bilateral aid leads to more attributions of ulter motivation, stresses inferiority of recipient more and generally leads to more negative reactions
Goranson & Berkowitz (1966)	F	84	Undergraduates	Clerical	Donor helps the subject with the task after finishing her own task	Provider of voluntary/involuntary aid	Donor volunteers to help or is instructed to help	Recipients show more reciprocity and more attraction to a donor who helped voluntarily
Greenberg & Bar-Tal (1976) (Study 1)	M	67	Undergraduates	Puzzle	Subject asks donor for some pieces that he's missing	Provider of high or low cost aid	Donor does (high cost) or does not (low cost) say that it took a while to find the requested pieces	Recipients spend more time studying information that might benefit the high cost donor

Page 380

Study	Sex	N	Population	Task	Manipulation	Independent variable	Donor description	Findings
Greenberg & Frisch (1972)	M	60	Undergraduates	Predicting company sales in a business simulation	Donor sends graphs that the subject needed	Provider of voluntary/involuntary aid	Donor realizes (voluntary)/doesn't realize (involuntary) that the graphs will be useful to the subject	Recipients perceive voluntary donors as more concerned and more motivated to help, and they reciprocate to them more
Gross & Latane (1974)	M-F	312	Undergraduates	Clerical	Donor helps the subject with the task after finishing own task	Provider of voluntary/involuntary aid	Donor volunteers to help or is instructed to help	Recipients like voluntary donors better and reciprocate to them more
Leventhal, Weiss, & Long (1964)	M	54	Undergraduates	Proof-reading	Donor divides the reward money between himself and the subject	Provider of voluntary/involuntary aid	Donor chooses the allocation plan (voluntary) or draws a set of allocation instructions at random (involuntary)	Recipients reciprocate more to the voluntary donor
Muir & Weinstein (1962)	F	120	Adults	Interview	Descriptions of hypothetical aid situations	Provider of high cost aid	Donor is described as "going out of his way" to do the favor	Recipients report feeling more obligated than usual to a high cost donor
Nadler (1979)	F	40	Undergraduates	Vocabulary test	Subjects have "consultation forms" they can use to ask their partners for help	Physically attractive/unattractive	Donor and recipient exchange photographs	Subjects seek less help from the attractive helper (if they expect to meet her)

(Continued)

TABLE 18.1 (*Continued*)

Author & Date	Sex	N	Population	Type of Task	Aid Manipulation	Donor Characteristic	Operationalization of Donor Characteristic	Findings
Nadler & Fisher (1978)	M	40	Undergraduates	Stock market simulation	Partner (donor) sends subjects chips which can be used for further investments	High/low expertise	Donor has had two prior courses (high expertise) or no prior courses (low expertise) relevant to investment skills	Recipients of aid from expert donors perceive themselves as having less ability; recipients of aid from non-experts perceive themselves as having more ability
Nadler, Fisher, & Streufert (1974)	M	48	Undergraduates	Simulated international conflict	Donor offers a large number of vaccine units to the subject's nation whose population is suffering from a disease	Ally/enemy	Subjects read historical description of conflict which describes eventual donor as enemy or ally	Aid from an ally leads to positive shifts in recipient's perceptions of the donor and negative shifts in their perceptions of enemy non-donors; aid from an enemy has essentially no effects

Nadler, Fisher, & Streufert (1976)	M	90	Undergraduates	Stock market simulation	Partner (donor) sends subject money which can be used for further investment	Donor-recipient social comparability	Attitudinal similarity	Aid from a similar other was threatening; aid from a dissimilar other was supportive
Nemeth (1970)	M-F	120	High school students	Proof-reading	Donor helps subject with the task after finishing own task	Provider of voluntary/involuntary aid	The experimenter tells the donors that they can provide help (voluntary) or they must provide help (involuntary)	Recipients like voluntary donors better and reciprocate to them more
Pruitt (1968)	M	77	Undergraduates	Variant of Prisoner's Dilemma	Donor decides how to divide money between himself and the subject	Provider of high or low cost aid	Donor gives subject 80% (high cost) or 20% (low cost) of his resources	More reciprocity to the donor of more costly help
Stokes & Bickman (1974)	F	80	Undergraduates	Perception task	Subject can ask a person sitting nearby for help	Physically attractive/unattractive; in helper role/not in helper role	Helper described as an experimenter (role) or a subject (non-role)	Less help-seeking from the attractive helper, but only when she was not in the helper role

(Continued)

TABLE 18.1 (*Continued*)

Author & Date	Sex	N	Population	Type of Task	Aid Manipulation	Donor Characteristic	Operationalization of Donor Characteristic	Findings
Tesser, Gatewood, & Driver (1968)	M	126	Undergraduates	Role-play questionnaire	Descriptions of hypothetical aid situations	Provider of high or low cost aid	Varies with the scenario; in one situation, the donors' financial situation was manipulated	Recipients feel more indebted to donors of more costly aid
Weiss (1969)	F	680	Black welfare mothers	Interview	Welfare	Interviewer-recipient similarity	Similarity in terms of SES, education, and age	Ss told similar interviewers they were "bothered" about being on welfare more than dissimilar interviewers

nity for material reciprocation is available, recipients offered relatively large amounts of help report more attraction to the donor than recipients of smaller amounts of aid (Berkowitz & Friedman, 1967; Freeman, 1977), and express a greater desire to interact with the donor in the future (Freeman, 1977; Greenberg & Frisch, 1972). These latter findings may be interpreted as a form of reciprocity (in line with equity theories), but may also be interpreted as failures to support the equity prediction that help which elicits feelings of inequity will lead to derogation of the donor.

A second series of studies on aid characteristics has focused on the effects of various costs of help to the recipient. One important cost from the recipient's perspective is the expectation that he/she will be penalized for obtaining help by receiving less credit for successful outcomes. The importance of this type of cost was demonstrated in an experiment by DePaulo and Fisher (1980), in which subjects expecting decreased credit for work done with the aid of a helper sought substantially less help. This contingency between receiving aid and ascribing credit is in force in many real-world helping situations, and hence may be a major impediment to obtaining necessary assistance.

Another type of cost with which recipients are often faced involves donor-initiated stipulations on the use of aid (e.g., U.S. government restrictions on purchasing certain types of goods with food stamps). According to reactance formulations, to the extent that a receipt of help restricts one's freedom, it should be aversive and lead to negative reactions. In a variety of laboratory and field contexts, this prediction has been supported. For example, in their interviews with foreign aid officials, Gergen and Gergen (1971, 1974a) concluded that recipients interpret stipulations by the donor as threatening evidence that they are perceived as too incapable or dishonest to run their own affairs, and feel best about themselves when permitted some input into the design and administration of aid programs. Aid "with strings attached" has other negative consequences as well. For example, studies have found that such help is less frequently accepted (Gergen, Morse & Kristeller, 1973; Rosen, 1971) and that donors of restrictive aid are evaluated more unfavorably (Gergen et al., 1973; Ladieu, Hanfman, & Dembo, 1947) than those who allow recipients to determine how they will use aid. Survey data (Gergen & Gergen, 1971) further suggests that recipients work less constructively to implement aid programs which they feel they have no hand in designing. Additionally, it has been shown that when the receipt of aid implies the loss of important freedoms, recipients are less willing to reciprocate (Brehm & Cole, 1966; Worchel, Andreoli, & Archer, 1976).

Aid might also be aversive to the recipient when the task on which it is offered is one which is very ego-involving (a "central" task). According to threat to self-esteem models, help on such tasks should be viewed as signaling inadequacy in an area important to one's self-image, and should be refused entirely if possible. When such aid cannot be avoided, recipients will respond in a variety of negative ways. In line with these predictions, cross-cultural questionnaire research by Gergen et al. (1973) demonstrated that recipients are less accepting of aid on tasks they feel pride in than on tasks they do not. Further, Morse (1972) found that subjects who receive help on central tasks allow the donor to influence them less, and display greater counter-conformity to the donor than noncentral aid subjects. It appears that the threat associated with help in ego-involving contexts is particularly disturbing to high self-esteem subjects, who are especially likely to seek less aid on central than on noncentral tasks (Tessler & Schwartz, 1972; Wallston, 1976). An interpretation for these last findings is offered in the "recipient characteristics" section of this paper. (See the discussion of "cognitive consistency" formulations and their predictions concerning the effects of threatening aid on high- and low-self-esteem individuals.)

Aid is also costly in a psychological sense when it is administered in settings in which the recipient believes that few others need help. Attribution notions predict that in such contexts, help is very likely to lead to a threatening internal attribution of failure. In line with this reasoning, Tessler and Schwartz (1972) report data suggesting that aid which is low normative is in fact more threatening than help which is high normative. Also, and in line with predictions based on threat to self-esteem models, such help is solicited less than aid which is highly normative. Other studies (e.g., Broll, Gross, & Piliavin, 1974; Gross, Fisher, Nadler, Stiglitz, & Craig, 1979; Nadler & Porat, 1978) similarly offer at least qualified support for the finding that low as opposed to high perceived normativeness of aid inhibits help-seeking.

A final condition which leads to higher costs to recipients is when help must be requested by them rather than being offered by the donor. Using an attributional analysis, it has been predicted that requesting help would lead to an internal attribution of failure because it is tantamount to an open admission of inadequacy. In contrast, accepting an offer of help from another individual would not stress personal responsibility for failure, and might even be supportive inasmuch as the offer indicates donor concern. As expected, it was found that requesting aid is more self-threatening than accepting an offer of help (Berman, Piliavin, & Gross, 1971). Also, and in line with the link between self-threat and reactions to aid posited by threat to self-esteem models, it has been observed that donors are evaluated more favorably and that more help is utilized in "offer" than in "request" conditions (Broll et al., 1974). Similar results were reported by Piliavin and Gross (1977) in a field experiment involving welfare recipients.

Summary

Specific characteristics of aid figure prominently in determining the recipient's reactions. (See Table 18.2). Individuals offered larger amounts of aid accept more help, feel more indebted, reciprocate more frequently, and perceive their helpers as more motivated and concerned than those offered smaller amounts of aid. Aid which is costly to the recipient breeds predominantly negative reactions.

TABLE 18.2
Aid Characteristics

	Subjects						
Author & Date	Sex	N	Population	Type of Task	Aid Manipulation	Aid Characteristic	Operationalization of Aid Characteristic	Findings

Author & Date	Sex	N	Population	Type of Task	Aid Manipulation	Aid Characteristic	Operationalization of Aid Characteristic	Findings
Berkowitz & Friedman (1967)	M	345	High school students	Supervisor-worker simulation	Worker can help supervisor to win contest	Amount of help received	Worker (donor) works very hard for subject (high help) or not very hard (low help)	More attraction to donor in high than low help conditions; also more reciprocity in high than low help conditions for entrepreneurial middle class subjects
Berman et al. (1971)	M	44	Undergraduate business majors	Business computer game	Hints about allocating money	Locus of help initiation	Help is requested (show card to request aid) vs. offered at intervals yoked to requests	More negative affect in request conditions than offer conditions, before Ss receive performance feedback
Brehm & Cole (1966)	M	60	Undergraduates	Impression formation task	Confederate gives subject a drink	Extent to which aid implies the loss of an important freedom	Ability to rate other "freely" (i.e., without regard to their aid) is either important or unimportant	Less reciprocity to the extent that aid threatens important behavioral freedom

(Continued)

TABLE 18.2 (*Continued*)

Author & Date	Subjects			Type of Task	Aid Manipulation	Aid Characteristic	Operationalization of Aid Characteristic	Findings
	Sex	N	Population					
Broll, Gross, & Piliavin (1974)	F	104	High school students and college undergraduates	Difficult logic problem	Subjects can receive aid in solving logic problem	Normativeness of help	Subjects told 98% (normative) or 30% (nonnormative) of previous subjects needed help	More aid accepted when normative only when Ss offered incentive for doing well
						Locus of help-initiation	Help is offered by helper at regular intervals, or Ss may request aid when they wish	Ss in "offer" condition obtained more help and liked the helper more than "request" subjects
DePaulo & Fisher (1980)	F	62	Undergraduates	Recognition of overt and covert cues of emotion	Help-seeking from an expert helper	Cost to the recipient of seeking aid	Receiving half (high cost) vs. full credit (low cost) for work when help is sought	Less help-seeking when high than low cost to the recipient
Freeman (1977)	M-F	81	Undergraduates	Internation stimulation	Donor offers subject chips redeemable for money	Amount of help given and obligation to repay it	S offered several amounts of aid coupled with several repayment arrangement requests varying in favorability, which he/she must choose from	Aid providing largest benefit at lowest cost most likely to be accepted, elicits greatest attraction and preference for the donor nor as a partner

| Gergen & Gergen (1971) | M-F | About 60 | Interview | Officials working in international assistance program | Respondents are asked about the importance of various factors in aid process | Amount of help received ⎯ Stipulations on the use of aid | Larger or smaller amounts of help received ⎯ Extent to which donor demands that aid be used according to certain proscriptions | In general, more aid leads to better reactions; but sometimes a small amount of aid is worse than none at all since it serves to frustrate ⎯ Aid with stipulations is threatening; recipients act more constructively to implement programs they "have a hand in designing" |
| Gergen & Gergen (1974a) | M-F | 10,331 | Public opinion survey | Large, representative samples of citizens of 37 different nations | Foreign aid received from U.S. and other nations | Stipulations on the use of aid | Extent to which donor perceived as "domineering" | Aid perceived as more exploitative to the extent that donor viewed as domineering |

(Continued)

TABLE 18.2 (*Continued*)

| Author & Date | Subjects | | Type of Task | Aid Manipulation | Aid Characteristic | Operationalization of Aid Characteristic | Findings |
	Sex	N					
Gergen, Morse, & Kristeller (1973)	M-F	579	15-25 year olds from six nations	Role-play questionnaire	Descriptions of hypothetical aid situations	Centrality of task on which help was given — Stipulations on use of aid	Extent to which task on which help is offered is one subject "takes pride in" — Extent to which there are stipulations on an aid offer	More aid acceptance on tasks recipients "feel no pride in," Aid with stipulations on use is less acceptable and leads to lower evaluations of donor
Greenberg & Bar-Tal (1976) (Study 2)	M	48	Undergraduates	Puzzle	Confederate assists in solving S's puzzle	Amount of help received	C helps for four minutes and assembles six pieces (high help) or for two minutes and assembles three pieces (low help)	Recipients remember more information to help C in high than low help condition

	Sex	N	Population	Task/Setting	Manipulation	Dependent variable	Operationalization	Results
Greenberg & Frisch (1972)	M	60	Undergraduates	Predicting future sales totals in business simulation	Partner sends S units of data on past sales	Amount of help received	Subject receives one (low help) or four units of missing data (high help) from previous year	High help leads to more favorable attributions about the donor, to greater indebtedness and reciprocity, and to a greater desire for future interaction with him
Gross, Fisher, Nadler, Stiglitz, & Craig (1979)	F	23	Residents of the Lafayette, IN community (Adults)	Adjustment problems in everyday life	Subjects can receive help with "women's problems" from group of mental health professionals	Normativeness of aid	Subjects told that "many women" have problems (high normative); or that such problems are relatively rare (low normative)	High normativeness appeals elicited more help-seeking only among women with high expressed inclusion scores on FIRO-B
Kahn & Tice (1973)	F	180	Undergraduates	Supervisor-worker simulation	Supervisor can help subject earn experiment credits	Amount of help received	Supervisor helps subject earn one or five research credits	Reciprocity increased as a positive function of aid received
Ladieu, Hanfman, & Dembo (1947)	M	113	People injured or partially incapacitated by disease (Adults)	Interview responses to questions about helping relationships	Various types of aid typically given to this population	Extent to which help restricts one's freedom	Any characteristic of help which interferes with the recipient's freedom	To the extent that help restricts the recipient's freedom, the donor is evaluated negatively

(Continued)

TABLE 18.2 (Continued)

Author & Date	Subjects			Type of Task	Aid Manipulation	Aid Characteristic	Operationalization of Aid Characteristic	Findings
	Sex	N	Population					
Morse (1972) (Study 2)		60	Undergraduates	Puzzle	Students are shown a picture of the completed puzzle	Centrality of the task	Students told puzzle was a test of eye-hand coordination (non-central) or a test of intelligence (central)	Recipients of aid on central tasks are more resistant to the donor's influence, and display more counter conformity
Nadler & Porat (1978)	M-F	32	High school students	Test of general knowledge	Subject can consult with E and get test answers	Normativeness of help ——— Anonymity	Subjects told that 10% or 90% of previous subjects able to answer all items correctly ——— Subjects required to write name and address on test, or not	Subjects believing need for help is high normative (i.e., 90% group) seek more help than low normative (i.e., 10% group) but only when anonymous
Piliavin & Gross (1977)	F	290	AFDC recipients in Minneapolis metropolitan area	Social service delivery system	Individual's can receive various types of financial and other services	Locus of help-initiation	Help is initiated by caseworker at regular intervals, or must be requested by recipient	Worker-initiated condition led to more aid than client-initiated condition

Study	Sex	N	Task	Manipulation	Independent variable	Operationalization	Results
Pruitt (1968)	M	77	Variant of Prisoner's Dilemma	Donor decides how to divide money between himself and subject	Amount of help received	Other gave S $.80 or $.20	Reciprocity increased as a positive function of aid received
Rosen (1971)	M-F	160	Role play of a handicapped student interviewing for a scholarship	Scholarship to attend college	Stipulations on the use of aid Amount of help	Must report grades each semester; or participate in elaborate publicity campaign $300 or $2000	Aid "with strings attached" is less frequently accepted Larger amounts of help are more frequently accepted
Stapleton, Nacci, & Tedeschi (1973)	F	65	Probability estimates	"Other" can give S points redeemable for experimental credit	Amount of help received	"Other" helps S 1, 5, or 9 times	Reciprocity increased as a positive function of aid received
Tesser, Gatewood, & Driver (1968)	M	126	Role play questionnaire	Descriptions of hypothetical aid situations	Value of aid to recipient	Aid described to be of great, moderate, or low subjective value to recipient	Perceived indebtedness is a positive function of the value of aid
Tessler & Schwartz (1972)	F	48	Rating dialogues for neuroticism	Subjects can consult a set of guidelines on identifying neuroticism	Centrality of the task Normativeness of help on the task	Task performance related to intelligence and mental health (high centrality) or not (low centrality)	High self-esteem individuals sought less help on central than non-central task

(Continued)

TABLE 18.2 (Continued)

| Author & Date | Subjects | | Population | Type of Task | Aid Manipulation | Aid Characteristic | Operationalization of Aid Characteristic | Findings |
	Sex	N						
							Subjects told that 65% (high normative) or 10% (low normative) of others have needed help	Subjects sought help sooner and more often in high than low normativeness conditions
Wallston (1976)	M	99	High school students and undergraduates	Rating dialogues for neuroticism	Subjects can consult an assistant for help in identifying neuroticism	Centrality of the task	Description of task as male or female (i.e., as sex role appropriate or not)	"Traditional" males with high self-esteem sought less help on central (male) task
Worchel, Andreoli, & Archer (1976)	F	120	Undergraduates	Identifying disturbed persons in photographs	Money won for performing task	Importance of freedoms lost due to aid	Accurate ratings of favor-doer either important or unimportant	When lost freedom is important, less liking and less reciprocity to donor than when freedom lost unimportant

Costly help includes aid which: (1) is low normative, (2) occurs on central tasks, (3) restricts important behavioral freedoms, (4) decreases the rewards that recipients expect to receive for successful task outcomes, and (5) must be actively sought by recipients.

CHARACTERISTICS OF THE RECIPIENT

So far it has been shown that reactions to aid depend on the kind of person who is giving the help and the type of help that is being given. The next set of studies to be discussed demonstrates that reactions to aid are also importantly determined by the kind of person who is receiving the help. The types of recipient characteristics that have been studied include a number of personality dimensions, other individual difference characteristics (e.g., need state), and demographic variables.

One personality trait that has frequently been related to reactions to help is self-esteem. Two different theoretical formulations yield divergent predictions about the effects of self-esteem on reactions to aid. A ''cognitive consistency'' formulation (Bramel, 1968) suggests that negative information about oneself (e.g., that one has failed on a central task) is more inconsistent and therefore more disturbing for high than for low self-esteem individuals. In contrast, a ''vulnerability'' formulation (cf. Tessler & Schwartz, 1972) suggests that because individuals with low self-esteem possess relatively few positive cognitions about themselves (i.e., because they are more vulnerable), they will be more disturbed by self-threatening information than high self-esteem individuals.

Research has generally supported the consistency formulation. For example, Nadler, Altman, and Fisher (1979) observed that subjects whose self-concept had been bolstered by an experimental manipulation experienced subsequent aid as threatening, whereas those whose self-concept had been lowered found aid to be supportive. Further, in a replication and extension of Fisher and Nadler's (1974) finding that aid from a social comparison other is threatening (discussed in the section on donor characteristics), Nadler et al. (1976) reported that this response was limited to high self-esteem individuals. Also in line with the assumption that high self-esteem individuals are especially responsive to the self-threat in aid, it has been observed that high (but not low) self-esteem individuals avoid seeking help on ego-involving tasks (Tessler & Schwartz, 1972; Wallston, 1976). Finally, it has also been shown that after receiving help on one task, high self-esteem subjects perform especially well on a subsequent task, presumably in an effort to avoid any further need for help (DePaulo, Brown, Ishii, & Fisher, (in press).

Several other individual difference characteristics also determine whether aid is experienced as threatening or supportive. These include the recipients' level of sensitivity to certain types of nonverbal cues, and their need state. Concerning the former variable, it would seem reasonable to assume that individuals who are particularly attuned to covert nonverbal cues (e.g., signs of annoyance that a donor might "leak" while overtly expressing an affable willingness to help), might be particularly likely to experience aid as aversive. In research by DePaulo and Rosenthal (1979) and DePaulo and Fisher (in press), evidence has accumulated which supports this assertion. Specifically, it has been found that those who are especially sensitive to covert nonverbal cues are reluctant to seek aid, presumably because they are too tuned-in to threatening feedback from others.

The recipient's need state also determines whether help is threatening or supportive. Although it might be hypothesized that individuals most in need of help would respond to aid in the most favorable manner, at least five different studies have reported just the opposite result: low need recipients responded more positively than did high need recipients (Calhoun, Dawes, & Lewis, 1972; Franklin, 1975; Mikesell & Calhoun, 1971; Morse & Gergen, 1971; Rosen, 1971). Morse and Gergen explain that while the non-needy have less urgent needs for help, they also have lower expectations for receiving it. Therefore, aid constitutes more of a positive disconfirmation (i.e., a pleasant surprise) to low-than high-need recipients, and is thus more supportive. There are several other potential explanations for this pattern of effects. First, it might be that while low need individuals can attribute their receipt of aid to something positive about themselves or the donor (either of which would be supportive), high need individuals are more likely to attribute it to their desperate situation. Second, it could be that low need individuals (*because* of their low need) can find the grossly inadequate levels of aid typical of many helping programs to be useful, rather than merely frustrating.

Additional recipient characteristics that affect attitudes toward aid and willingness to seek help include locus of control, achievement orientation, and authoritarianism. These findings, like other data for recipient characteristics, suggest that in certain situations it may be beneficial to "tailor" aid programs to the population in question. In effect, the same type of aid that may be helpful to one kind of recipient may be detrimental to another, so that the use of several "tailored" aid programs may be necessary to insure success for both groups. In the following discussion, in each case the general types of beliefs and behaviors characteristic of the personality variable in question seem to predict reactions to aid.

In one study, Fischer and Turner (1970) hypothesized that since internals believe that their own actions can produce meaningful changes while externals believe that outcomes are determined by fate or chance, more positive attitudes toward initiating help-seeking behaviors should characterize internals than externals. This hypothesis was corroborated: Internals did in fact hold more favorable attitudes toward help-seeking than externals. Similarly, individuals who have a high need for achievement (like internals) believe that their own efforts can produce successful outcomes; however, for these people it appears that success is most highly valued if obtained completely independently. In line with this hypothesis, Tessler and Schwartz (1972) found that high-need achievers seek less help than low-need achievers. Finally, because high authoritarians tend to be less accepting of their own personal weaknesses and less open to change than low authoritarians, it would be reasonable to predict that they would also be more resistant to seeking help. Fischer and Turner (1970) corroborated this line of reasoning: They found that high authoritarians are more reluctant to seek help than low authoritarians.

Relationships between demographic characteristics and reactions to aid similarly reflect internalized values and beliefs. This literature is reviewed in a recent paper by Gourash (1978), so the discussion here will be selective. For example, women are socialized to feel more comfortable than men in contexts characterized by dependency (cf. Hoffman, 1972; Stein & Bailey, 1973), and in line with this, studies of sex differences in help-seeking consistently find that women are more favorably disposed toward seeking and receiving help than men (Anderson & Anderson, 1972; DePaulo, 1978a,b; Fischer & Turner, 1970; Phillips & Segal, 1969). Furthermore, there is evidence to suggest that help-seeking is positively related to femininity (especially among females) and negatively related to masculinity (particularly among males) (DePaulo, 1978b).

A second demographic characteristic for which internalized values appear to predict reactions to aid is social class. Several studies relating this variable to reactions to aid have been performed by Berkowitz and his colleagues (Berkowitz, 1968; Berkowitz & Friedman, 1967). These investigations hypothesized that members of the entrepreneurial class, who are concerned with the exchange of money and services, would be likely to adhere to an exchange norm dictating reciprocity to others in accordance with the amount of benefit received. In contrast, the bureaucratic middle class base their reciprocity on another set of values. These individuals tend to be responsive to rules and regulations (such as the societal norm dictating that people should help those in need, even when the needy have little to offer in return). Therefore, they would tend to give to the needy regardless of prior receipts from them. The results of two studies of reciprocity behaviors support this hypothesis: for American entrepreneurs, more than American (Berkowitz & Friedman, 1967) or English (Berkowitz, 1968) bureaucrats, reciprocity was proportional to the amount of aid previously received.

Summary

A number of recipient characteristics have important effects for reactions to aid (see Table 18.3). Specifically, high self-esteem individuals, externals, people with high achievement motivation, and high authoritarians have been found to hold more negative attitudes toward seeking help and/or were relatively unlikely to seek aid. In addition to personality dimensions, other individual differences

TABLE 18.3
Characteristics of the Recipient

Author & Date	Subjects			Type of Task	Aid Manipulation	Recipient Characteristic	Operationalization of the Recipient Characteristic	Findings
	Sex	N	Population					
Anderson & Anderson (1972)	M-F	Nationwide survey (exact N unspecified)	United States citizens	Survey and archival records	Use of health services (self-report and archival records)	Sex		Females use health services more than males
Berkowitz (1968)	M	192	English adolescents	Supervisor-worker simulation	Worker (donor) works very hard for the subject (high help) or not very hard (low help)	Bureaucratic middle class or working class	Criterion was father's occupation and education	Bureaucrat's reciprocity was relatively unaffected by the amount of aid previously received; entrepreneurial class individuals were influenced by the amount of aid received
Berkowitz & Friedman (1967)	M	345	High school students	Supervisor-worker simulation	Worker (donor) works very hard for the subject (high help) or not very hard (low help)	Bureaucratic middle class, entrepreneurial middle class, or working class	Criterion was father's occupation and education	Bureaucrats' and working class reciprocity was less affected by the amount of help previously received than was the entrepreneurs'

Study	Sex	N	Population	Method	Measure	Variable	Instrument	Results
Calhoun, Dawes, & Lewis (1972)	M-F	36	Adult outpatients at a psychology clinic	Questionnaire about the client's psychological problem	Self-report scale of attitudes toward seeking professional help	Need state	Self-reported severity of problem	Clients who perceived their problems as more severe reported less favorable attitudes toward seeking professional help
DePaulo (1978a)	M-F	303	Junior high school students, high school students, undergraduates, and adults	Role-play questionnaire	Descriptions of hypothetical aid situations	Sex		Females were more willing to seek help than males
DePaulo (1978b) (Study 2)	M-F	123	High school students	Paper-and-pencil survey	Expressed willingness to accept free art lessons from children	Sex, sex-role orientation	Bem Sex Role Inventory; Spence Personal Attributes Questionnaire	Females expressed more interest in accepting help than did males. Favorability of attitudes toward accepting help were positively related to femininity (for females) and negatively related to masculinity (for males)

(Continued)

TABLE 18.3 (*Continued*)

Author & Date	Subjects			Type of Task	Aid Manipulation	Aid Characteristic	Operationaliza- tion of Aid Characteristic	Findings
	Sex	N	Population					
DePaulo, Brown, Ishii, & Fisher (in press)	F	78	Undergraduates	Pattern recog- nition tasks	Partner (donor) suggests a way to detect the patterns	High/low self- esteem	Coopersmith self-esteem inventory	After receiving help, high self- esteem subjects performed better than lows on a subsequent task
DePaulo & Fisher (in press)	F	62	Undergraduates	Recognition of overt and covert cues of emotion	Help-seeking from an expert helper	Sensitivity to face and body cues of emotion	Profile of Non- verbal Sensitivity	Subjects who asked for less help were rela- tively more sen- sitive to body (covert) than to face (overt) cues
DePaulo & Fisher (1980)	F	62	Undergraduates	Recognition of overt and covert cues of emotion	Help-seeking from an expert helper	Involvement in the task (task "centrality")	Academic major	Less help-seeking among subjects majoring in areas in which inter- personal sensi- tivity is highly valued
DePaulo & Rosenthal (1979)	M-F	39	Undergraduates	Recognition of overt and covert cues of emotion	Descriptions of hypothetical aid situations	Sensitivity to face and body cues of emotion	Profile of Non-verbal Sensitivity	Subjects reluc- tant to seek help were relatively more sensitive to body (covert) than to face (overt) cues

Study	Sex	N	Population	Measure	Procedure	Variable	Operationalization	Results
Fischer & Turner (1970)	M-F	960	High school students, nursing students, and undergraduates	Self-report scale of attitudes toward seeking professional help	Statements describing attitudes toward seeking professional help	Sex, authoritarianism, internal/external locus of control	F-scale, Rotter I-E	Females and internals hold more positive attitudes toward seeking help; authoritarians expressed more negative attitudes about help-seeking
Franklin (1975)	M-F	191	Undergraduates	Applying for financial aid	Subjects received or were denied aid	Confirmation/disconfirmation of expectancies	Aid for high need individuals is a confirmation of expectancies; help for low need individuals is a positive disconfirmation	Low need individuals who received help were more attracted to the university (the helping institution) than high need recipients
Mikesell & Calhoun (1971)	F	46	Undergraduates	Scale of attitudes toward professional help	Role-play of attitudes toward seeking help for moderate or severe psychological disturbances	Need state	Role-play	Subjects reported less favorable attitudes toward seeking help for severe than for moderate disturbances
Morse & Gergen (1971)	M	88	Undergraduates	Internation simulation	Money to implement projects; if granted S gets monetary reward	Confirmation/disconfirmation of expectancies	Aid for high need individuals is a confirmation of expectancies; help for low need individuals is a positive disconfirmation	Low need individuals responded more favorably to aid than high need individuals

(Continued)

TABLE 18.3 (*Continued*)

Author & Date	Subjects			Type of Task	Aid Manipulation	Recipient Characteristic	Operationalization of the Recipient Characteristic	Findings
	Sex	N	Population					
Nadler, Altman, & Fisher (1979)	M	40	Undergraduates	Stock market simulation	Partner (donor) sends subject money which can be used for further investments	Positive/negative self-regard	Positive/negative feedback on a personality test	Aid recipients with positive self-regard (compared to no-aid control) have more negative affect and self-perception; recipients with negative self-regard respond more positively to aid
Nadler, Fisher, & Streufert (1976)	M	90	Undergraduates	Stock market simulation	Partner (donor) sends subject money which can be used for further investments	High/low self-esteem	Coopersmith self-esteem Inventory	For high self-esteem subjects, aid from a similar other had negative effects on self-perceptions and aid from a dissimilar other had positive effects

Study	Sex	N	Subjects	Method	Manipulation	Independent variable	Dependent measure	Results
Nadler, Sheinberg, & Jaffe (in press)	M	38	Adult paraplegics	Interview and attitude scales	Descriptions of hypothetical aid situations	Acceptance (noncentrality)/nonacceptance (centrality) of physical disability	Linkowski Acceptance of Disability Scale	Paraplegics who do not accept their disability are less likely to seek help and less likely to anticipate positive affect when being offered help
Phillips & Segal (1969)	M-F	278	Adults	Interview	Use of health services, as indexed by physicians' records and clinic and hospital records	Sex		Controlling for number of physical illnesses and psychiatric symptoms, women seek more medical care than men
Rosen (1971)	M-F	160	Undergraduates	Role-play of a handicapped student interviewing for a scholarship	Student is offered $2000 (high value) or $300 (low value) with or without behavioral constraints (high/low cost); subjects decide whether to accept or reject the offer	Need state	Parents can/cannot finance the handicapped student's education	Needy subjects less likely to accept low value and low cost aid

(Continued)

403

TABLE 18.3 (Continued)

| Author & Date | Subjects | | | Type of Task | Aid Manipulation | Recipient Characteristic | Operationaliza- tion of the Recipient Characteristic | Findings |
	Sex	N	Population					
Tessler & Schwartz (1972)	F	48	Undergraduates	Rating dia- logues for neuroticism	Subjects can con- sult a set of guidelines on identifying neuroticism	Self-esteem, achievement motivation	Rosenberg Self- esteem Scale, Achievement Risk Preference Scale	High self-esteem subjects sought help less when task success was described as de- pendent on IQ and mental health ("central" task); high need achievement sub- jects sought less help
Wallston (1976)	M	99	High school students and undergraduates	Rating dialogues for neurocism	Subjects can con- sult with an assistant for help in identify- ing neuroticism	Self-esteem, sex- role ideology	Sherwood Self- Concept Scale, Wallston Sex- Role Ideology Scale	High self-esteem "traditional" males sought less help when the task was des- cribed as a Male" (central) task than when it was described as a "female" task

have strong consequences for reactions to help. Here it has been found that individuals in greater need, and people who are sensitive to covert emotional cues experience help as more aversive. Also, females appear to be more comfortable with helping relationships than males, and middle class bureaucrats react differently to help than members of the entrepreneurial class.

CONTEXT CHARACTERISTICS

Characteristics of the helping context that have been shown to affect reactions to aid include information available to recipients concerning the nature of their problem, the potential for recipients to reciprocate to the donor, and whether aid constitutes a confirmation or a disconfirmation of expectancies.

It has been suggested that information concerning the nature of one's problem could have important implications for one's attempts to deal with it (cf. Fisher & Farina, 1979). One series of studies measured the effects of contextual information which led people to believe either that mental disorders are essentially diseases like any other (a medical model view), or that they reflect learned patterns of behaviors (a social learning view). Compared to individuals exposed to information emphasizing a social learning view, subjects exposed to a medical model view felt less able to control their emotional problems, and were less likely to engage in self-help involving thinking about ways to improve their situation (Farina, Fisher, Getter, & Fischer, 1978; Fisher & Farina, 1979). In addition, subjects embracing a medical model view were more likely to use alchohol or drugs (i.e., to engage in "medical" forms of self-help) when depressed. That situationally available information about the problem necessitating help affects coping strategies may also have implications for alcoholics, the elderly, and others.

A second context characteristic which has received a great deal of research attention is the potential for the recipient to reciprocate to the donor. Equity theories predict that in the absence of an opportunity to reciprocate help, the recipient should experience affective distress, and could attempt to restore psychological equity by derogating the donor and/or the aid. It has been shown that one's affective state and attraction toward the donor do suffer during an interaction in which no return of help is possible, and that more positive feelings and higher donor attraction are evidenced when the recipient is given the opportunity to repay the donor (Castro, 1974; Gross & Latané, 1974). Also, in line with the assumption that people avoid aversive feelings of inequity, it has been found that individuals are less likely to ask for and accept needed help when they see no opportunity for reciprocity than when reciprocity is possible (Castro, 1974; DePaulo, 1978a; Greenberg & Shapiro, 1971; Morris & Rosen, 1973), particularly if the potential donor is a similar other (Clark et al., 1974).

In several of these studies, reactions to aid were measured for subjects who were afforded no opportunity to reciprocate, an opportunity to help a third person who had not previously aided them, or an opportunity to reciprocate directly to the donor. Data from this research could suggest whether feelings of inequity are a general state that can be alleviated through any act of reciprocity, or a specific state of obligation toward the donor. If individuals are motivated to reciprocate equally to the donor and a third party, and if manifestations of inequity (e.g., negative feelings and donor evaluations) are alleviated equally in both cases, then the case for inequity as a general state would be strengthened.

Based on extant research, it appears subjects evaluate their donors more positively (Gross & Latané, 1974; Shumaker & Jackson, 1979) and/or engage in more reciprocity (Goranson & Berkowitz, 1966; Gross & Latané, 1974; Shumaker & Jackson, 1979) when they are allowed to reciprocate directly to them than when they can help a third person. However, there is also evidence that the opportunity to aid a third person can lead to greater recipient liking for the actual donor than no opportunity at all to reciprocate (Castro, 1974; Gross & Latané, 1974). Thus, at this point it is unclear whether inequity is an aversive state related to feelings of injustice with a particular other, or a more general condition stemming from feelings of injustice with others in general.

Overall, then, it appears that recipients respond more favorably when they can reciprocate help than when they cannot. Beyond this, it has also been found that the *amount* of reciprocation requested by the donor moderates the favorability of the recipient's reactions. In this regard, Gergen et al. (1975) have observed a curvilinear relationship between the magnitude of obligation to repay aid imposed by the donor, and recipient liking for the donor. As might be expected on the basis of equity theories, it was found that donors who asked for a greater than equal return of the benefit as well as donors who required no repayment at all were not well liked. Donors who requested an equal return were liked the most, presumably because they offered their beneficiaries an opportunity to restore equity. It should be noted, however, that in one study in which recipients role played reactions to aid (Gergen et al., 1973) and in another in which subjects selected one of several offers differing in level of obligation (Freeman, 1977), recipients responded most positively to aid which demanded the least reciprocation.[1]

A third context characteristic which has been studied is whether aid constitutes a confirmation or a disconfirmation of expectancies (i.e., whether it is expected or unexpected). An attributional analysis suggests that expectancies may have important implications for reactions to aid. Thus, for example, help that is not expected (a positive disconfirmation) tends to be attributed to donor liking and concern. Accordingly, Franklin (1975), Morse (1972), and Morse and

---

[1]The methodologies employed in the latter two studies (i.e., within subjects designs and role-playing) could have made them especially susceptible to demand characteristics, so that the data should be interpreted cautiously.

Gergen (1971) have found that such aid leads to relatively high attraction to the donor. In contrast, a failure to receive expected help (a negative disconfirmation) tends to be perceived as a personal rejection, and leads to relatively low attraction. More moderate responses are engendered by aid that results in a confirmation of expectancies (i.e., the receipt of expected help or the failure to receive aid which is not anticipated), as this kind of help has little attributional value for the recipient. In terms of the behavioral effects of aid as a function of expectancy, it has been observed that recipients reciprocate more (Morse, Gergen, Peele, & van Ryneveld, 1977) and allow donors to exert significantly more influence on them (Morse, 1972) when aid is unexpected than when it is expected. However, although aid that is unexpected can lead to more positive behaviors than help that is expected, this is probably true only when it is appropriate to the context. When help is both unexpected and in violation of situational norms (i.e., when it appears to be inappropriate or "odd" behavior), the donor may be derogated rather than appreciated (Morse et al., 1977).

The appropriateness of aid may be important in determining reactions to help in other contexts as well. When the task is competitive rather than cooperative, or when the setting is formal rather than informal, an offer of assistance may be perceived as inappropriate. In these situations, derogations of the donor's character, defensive attributions of the donor's intent, or reluctance to reciprocate may result (Kiesler, 1966; Schopler & Thompson, 1968; Worchel & Andreoli, 1974). A receipt of help may also be resented if it directly follows one's giving of help to another in the context of an intimate relationship. This is because the norms of such relationships suggest that help is more appropriately rendered in response to needs than in response to benefits received (Clark & Mills, 1979). The appropriateness of an aid offer is also determined by the relative competences of the donor and the recipient. Peer-tutoring studies show that satisfaction with the helping relationship as well as perceived and actual performance are all augmented when the tutor is relatively more competent than the tutee (Rosen, Powell, & Schubot, 1977).

Finally, there is evidence that reactions to help may be moderated by whether or not the recipient expects to ever meet the donor. Specifically, it has been suggested that recipients who expect to meet their donor may experience more embarrassment about the acknowledgment of inferiority that receiving help often implies. In line with threat to self-esteem models, it has been shown that recipients who anticipate a meeting with their donors are less likely to seek aid (Nadler, 1979), and more likely to defensively attribute the donor's motivation to help to external constraints. Barring the possibility of external attributions, they are more likely to derogate the donor (Worchel & Andreoli, 1974). It has also been found that the effects of not expecting to meet the donor are similar to the effects of recipient anonymity: Anonymous recipients, who risk relatively little loss in public self-esteem, seek more help than their more identifiable and more vulnerable counterparts (Nadler & Porat, 1978; Shapiro, 1978).

Summary

Characteristics of the context of the helping interaction are important determinants of reactions to aid (see Table 18.4). Contextual cues that provide information to the recipient about the nature of the problem may suggest coping strategies for self-help. Contexts that provide opportunities for reciprocity (even to a third party) mitigate some of the potentially aversive consequences of aid. They lead to less rejection of help, more aid-seeking, more attraction toward the donor, more positive evaluation of the aid, and more willingness to be influenced by the donor. Whether aid constitutes a confirmation or a disconfirmation of expectancy is another important contextual characteristic. The receipt of unanticipated aid, if appropriate to the context, produces appreciative recipient responses and attributions of kindly donor intent, whereas the receipt of expected help has milder evaluative consequences. Finally, contexts in which recipients retain their anonymity or are afforded no opportunity to meet their helpers appear to render aid less threatening.

CONCLUSIONS

The studies reviewed in this paper suggest that differences in donor, aid, recipient, and context characteristics lead to differential reactions to help. Specifically, for each of these four components of an aid transaction, certain conditions lead to predominantly positive reactions on the part of the recipient, while others elicit mostly negative responses. Although the study of recipient reactions to aid is relatively recent, our review indicates that there are a number of relatively consistent patterns of effects which can form the bedrock of a social psychology of the aid recipient. This data base is quite provocative within social psychology because it is significant at both a conceptual and an applied level. Coexisting with these consistent patterns of effects, however, are numerous issues which are at present unresolved, and which should serve as a focus for future research.

One theme that recurs throughout the literature on reactions to help is that a receipt of aid constitutes a "mixed blessing." Although it can communicate a donor's liking and concern, provide instrumental benefits and hence constitute a supportive experience for the recipient, there have now been documented perhaps a surprisingly large number of conditions under which aid is relatively more threatening than supportive. Perhaps then we should reevaluate the common assumption that helping is a uniformly positive act that should always be encouraged, and begin an examination of those helping contexts likely to lead to positive and negative recipient reactions.

We should also consider the question of why we tend to encourage helping in others, while often experiencing the receipt of aid as aversive. In this regard, a normative analysis suggests that there may be sets of conflicting (but strongly

TABLE 18.4
Context Characteristics

Author & Date	Subjects			Type of Task	Aid Manipulation	Context Characteristic	Operationalization of Context Characteristic	Findings
	Sex	N	Population					
Castro (1974)	M	90	Undergraduates	Forming words from letters	Partner (donor) sends subject extra letters	Opportunity for reciprocating aid	Subjects had opportunity to reciprocate to original donor, to a third person, or no opportunity to reciprocate	Reciprocation to donor leads to higher liking for donor and to greater willingness to request future help than no reciprocity; opportunity to aid 3rd party leads to more donor liking than no opportunity to reciprocate
Clark, Gotay, & Mills (1979) (Study 2)	M-F	42	Undergraduates	Creating an object from balloons	Partner (donor) offers to help the subject blow up balloons	Opportunity for reciprocating aid	Subjects had opportunity/no opportunity to reciprocate to original donor	When there is no opportunity to reciprocate, Ss accept less help from a similar than from a dissimilar other

(Continued)

TABLE 18.4 (Continued)

Author & Date	Subjects			Type of Task	Aid Manipulation	Context Characteristic	Operationalization of Context Characteristic	Findings
	Sex	N	Population					
Clark & Mills (1979) (Study 2)	F	72	Undergraduates	Forming words from letters	Partner (donor) sends subject extra letters	"Communal" vs. exchange relationship between donor and recipient	"In communal" conditions, other is presented as potentially accessable for a close relationship; in exchange conditions, the other is presented as relatively inaccessable	Following the receipt of aid from other, an offer to reciprocate is resented in a communal relationship, but not in an exchange relationship
DePaulo (1978a)	M-F	303	Junior and high school students, undergraduates and adults	Role-play questionnaire	Descriptions of hypothetical aid situations	Opportunity to reciprocate aid	Donor is described as likely/unlikely to request reciprocation	Less help-seeking when S is unable to reciprocate
Farina et al. (1978) (Study 1)	M-F	119	Undergraduates	Questionnaire	Beliefs about the efficacy of various types of help for mental disorders	Information about the nature of mental disorders	Subjects led to believe mental disorders are a "disease" or a product of social learning	Medical model group believed they were less able to control problems than social learning group
(Study 2)	M-F	286	Undergraduates	Questionnaire	Same as Study 1	Same as Study 1	Same as Study 1	Same as Study 1
(Study 3)	F	38	Undergraduates	Psychotherapy session	Psychotherapy	Same as Study 1	Same as Study 1	Medical model group less likely to engage in self-help than social learning group

410

Fisher & Farina (1979)	M-F	81	Undergraduates	Questionnaire	Beliefs about the efficacy of various types of help for mental disorders, and self-reports of forms of help utilized	Information about the nature of mental disorders	Classes taught that mental disorders are a "disease" or a product of social learning	Medical models less likely to think about cause and solution of problems, more likely to drink and take drugs when depressed, than social learning group
Franklin (1975)	M-F	191	Undergraduates	Applying for financial aid	Subjects received or were denied aid	Confirmation/disconfirmation of expectancies	Aid for high need individuals is a confirmation of expectancies; help for low need individuals is a positive disconfirmation	Low need individuals who received help were more attracted to the university (the helping institution) than high need recipients
Freeman (1977)	M-F	81	Undergraduates	Internation simulation	Donor offers subject chips redeemable for money	Amount of repayment requested by the donor	Subjects informed that nothing need be returned to the donor (low obligation), that the aid had to be returned in kind (equal obligation), or that the aid must be returned with interest (high obligation)	Recipients liked the donor best who offered the highest benefit with the least obligation to repay

(Continued)

TABLE 18.4 (Continued)

Author & Date	Subjects			Type of Task	Aid Manipulation	Context Characteristic	Operationalization of Context Characteristic	Findings
	Sex	N	Population					
Gergen, Ellsworth, Maslach, & Seipel (1975)	M	180	Undergraduates in Japan, Sweden, and the United States	Decision-making game involving wagering money	Donor sends subject chips redeemable for money	Amount of repayment requested by the donor	Subjects informed that nothing need be returned to the donor (low obligation), that the aid had to be returned in kind (equal obligation), or that the aid must be returned with interest (high obligation)	Inverted-U shaped relationship between amount of obligation and attraction to donor
Gergen, Morse, & Kristeller (1973)	M-F	579	15-25 year olds from six nations	Role-play questionnaire	Descriptions of hypothetical aid situations	Amount of repayment requested by the donor	Subjects informed that nothing need be returned to the donor (low obligation), that the aid had to be returned in kind (equal obligation), or that the aid must be returned with interest (high obligation)	As obligation increases, liking for the donor decreases

Study	Sex	N	Population	Task	Manipulation	Condition	Results
Goranson & Berkowitz (1966)	F	84	Undergraduates	Clerical	Donor helps the subject with the task after finishing her own task	Opportunity to reciprocate aid	Possible to reciprocate to original donor or to 3rd party	Recipients show more reciprocity to donor than to 3rd party, when prior aid was given voluntarily
Greenberg & Shapiro (1971)	M-F	48	Undergraduates	Role-play of individuals with a handicap	Subjects can ask for help in meeting production quotas	Opportunity for reciprocating aid	"Reciprocity" subjects believed they would do very well on a subsequent task and that other would need their help; "No reciprocity" subjects believed themselves and other would do well, eliminating the opportunity to reciprocate	More resistance to seeking help in "no reciprocity" than in "reciprocity" condition
Gross & Latane (1974)	M-F	312	Undergraduates	Clerical	Donor helps subject with task after finishing own task	Opportunity for reciprocating aid	Subjects had opportunity to reciprocate to original donor, to a third person, or no opportunity for reciprocity	Opportunity to reciprocate to donor leads to more reciprocity and liking than opportunity to reciprocate to 3rd party or none at all. Evidence

(Continued)

TABLE 18.4 (Continued)

| Author & Date | Subjects | | Type of Task | Aid Manipulation | Context Characteristic | Operationalization of Context Characteristic | Findings |
	Sex	N					
							that aid to third party somewhat enhances donor attraction, and that an opportunity to reciprocate enhances affect
Kiesler (1966)	M	120	Forming words from letters	Donor sends subject some money (money is the reward for successful task performance)	Appropriateness of help to the context	Help occurred in a cooperative context (appropriate), or in a competitive context (inappropriate)	Appropriate help leads to greater attraction than inappropriate help
Morris & Rosen (1973)	M-F	56	Role-play of individuals with a handicap	Subject can ask for help in meeting production quota	Opportunity for reciprocating aid	There is either time (reciprocity conditions) or no time (no reciprocity conditions) to return the benefit	More latency in seeking help in no-reciprocity than in reciprocity conditions

Study	Sex	N	Sample	Setting	Manipulation	Variable	Operationalization	Findings
Morse (1972) (Study 1)		61	Undergraduates	Puzzle	Subjects are shown a picture of the completed puzzle	Confirmation/disconfirmation of expectancies	Subjects receive aid they don't expect (positive disconfirmation), or fail to receive aid they do expect (negative disconfirmation)	Positive disconfirmation leads to higher attraction, and less resistance to social influence than negative disconfirmation
Morse & Gergen (1971)	M	88	Undergraduates	Internation simulation	Money to implement projects; if granted, S gets monetary reward	Confirmation/disconfirmation of expectancies	Aid for high need individuals is a confirmation of expectancies; help for low need individuals is a positive disconfirmation	Low need individuals responded more favorably to aid than high need individuals
Morse, Gergen, Peele, & Van Ryneveld (1977)	M-F	60	High school students	Identification of hit songs and artists	"Hints" given by quizmaster	Expectancy for receiving help ---- violation/nonviolation of situational norms	Ss led to believe quizmaster generally gives hints, or generally does not ---- Rules of contest permitted or did not permit giving help	More reciprocity to quizmaster in "unexpected" than in "expected" help conditions ---- When aid is unexpected and a violation of a norm, donor attractiveness ratings are lower than in the other three cells

(Continued)

415

TABLE 18.4 (*Continued*)

| Author & Date | Subjects | | | Type of Task | Aid Manipulation | Recipient Characteristic | Operationaliza- of the Recipient Characteristic | Findings |
	Sex	N	Population					
Nadler (1979)	F	40	Undergraduates	Vocabulary test	Subjects have "consultation" forms they can use to ask their partners for help	Expectation of meeting donor	Expect to work in same room as donor later, or not	Subjects seek more help when they do not expect to meet the donor
Nadler & Porat (1978)	M-F	32	High school students	Test of general knowledge	Subject can consult with *E* to get test answers	Anonymity	Subjects required to write name and address on test, or not	If help is perceived to be high normative, subjects who are anonymous seek more aid than those who are identifiable
Rosen, Powell & Schubot (1977)	M-F	138	Undergraduates	Tutoring interaction	Subject receives aid from tutor	Relative competence of donor and recipient at task on which help is given	Tutor's pretest score equal, greater than, or less than tutee	Satisfaction with the helping relationship and perceived and actual performance are all augmented when the tutor is relatively more competent than the tutee

Study		N	Population	Task	Manipulation	Variable	Condition	Results
Schopler & Thompson (1968) (Study 2)	F	38	Undergraduates	Interview with a communicator	Subject receives a rose from communicator	Appropriateness of help to the context	Help occurred in an informal context (appropriate) or in a formal context (inappropriate)	Inappropriate aid inhibits reciprocity; appropriate aid facilitates it
Schumaker & Jackson (1979)	F	61	Undergraduates	Role-play of individuals with a handicap	Assistance in meeting production quota	Opportunity to reciprocate aid	Subjects given opportunity to aid donor, opportunity to aid 3rd party, or were blocked from reciprocating the aid	Subjects reciprocated more and evaluated the donor more favorably when allowed to reciprocate directly to the donor than when they reciprocated to a third person
Shapiro (1978)	F	60	Undergraduates	Ratings stories for neuroticism	Subjects can consult a set of guidelines on identifying neuroticism	Anonymity of help-seeking / Anonymity of task performance	Presence/absence of a confederate --- Subject will/will not meet the person who scores her answers	Help-seeking was most frequent when task performance was public and help-seeking was private
Worchel & Andreoli (1974)	F	148	Undergraduates	Answering questions	Help in alphabetizing computer forms	Cooperative vs. competitive situation	Ss cooperatively working against computer, or competing against each other	More external attribution for donor's act and derogation of donor in competitive than cooperative situations

socialized) norms pertaining to helping relationships in our society. On the one hand, the norm of social responsibility (cf. Berkowitz, 1972) dictates that needy individuals should be cared for by the more fortunate members of society. Yet at the same time, people in Western cultures are taught that independence is a virtue and that dependency is shameful (e.g., Blau, 1964; Heider, 1958; Weber, 1930).

Given the conflicting values about giving and receiving help, and the fact that aid is often quite threatening, it seems important that along with the traditional focus on factors that facilitate aid giving, future research on prosocial behavior should devote more attention to receiving aid. Such an approach would importantly contribute to the understanding of helping relationships at both the conceptual and applied levels.

REFERENCES

Adams, J.S. Toward an understanding of inequity. *Journal of Abnormal and Social Psychology,* 1963, *67,* 422–436.

Anderson, O. W., & Anderson, R. M. Patterns of use of health services. In H. D. Freeman, S. Levine, & L. G. Keeder (Eds.), *Handbook of medical sociology,* (2nd ed.). Englewood Cliffs, N. J.: Prentice-Hall, 1972.

Andreas, C. R. To receive from kings: An examination of government-to-government aid and its unintended consequences. *Journal of Social Issues,* 1969, *25,* 167–180.

Bar-Tal, D., Bar-Zohar, Y., Greenberg, M. S., & Hermon, M. Reciprocity in the relationship between donor and recipient and between harm-doer and victim. *Sociometry,* 1977, *40,* 293–298.

Berkowitz, L. Responsibility, reciprocity, and social distance in help-giving: An experimental investigation of English social class differences. *Journal of Experimental Social Psychology,* 1968, *4,* 46–63.

Berkowitz, L. Social norms, feelings and other factors affecting helping and altruism. In L. Berkowitz (Ed.), *Advances in Experimental Social Psychology, Vol. 6.* New York: Academic Press, 1972.

Berkowitz, L., & Friedman, P. Some social class differences in helping behavior. *Journal of Personality and Social Psychology,* 1967, *5,* 217–225.

Berman, A., Piliavin, I. M., & Gross, A. E. *Some effects of imposed versus requested help.* Unpublished honors thesis, University of Wisconsin, 1971.

Blau, P. M. *Exchange and power in social life.* New York: Wiley, 1964.

Bramel, D. Dissonance, expectation and the self. In R. Ableson, E. Aronson, T. M. Newcomb, W. J. McGuire, M. J. Rosenberg, & P. H. Tannenbaum (Eds.), *Source book of cognitive consistency.* New York: Rand-McNally, 1968.

Brehm, J. W. *A theory of psychological reactance.* New York: Academic Press, 1966.

Brehm, J. W., & Cole, A. H. Effect of a favor which reduces freedom. *Journal of Personality and Social Psychology,* 1966, *3,* 420–426.

Broll, L., Gross, A. E., & Piliavin, I. Effects of offered and requested help on help-seeking and reactions to being helped. *Journal of Applied Social Psychology,* 1974, *4,* 244–258.

Calhoun, L. G., Dawes, A. S., & Lewis, P. M. Correlates of attitudes toward help-seeking in outpatients. *Journal of Consulting and Clinical Psychology,* 1972, *38,* 153.

Castro, M. A. Reactions to receiving aid as a function of cost to the donor and opportunity to aid. *Journal of Applied Social Psychology,* 1974, *4,* 194–209.

Clark, M. S., Gotay, C. C., & Mills, J. Acceptance of help as a function of similarity of the potential helper and opportunity to repay. *Journal of Applied Social Psychology,* 1974, *4,* 224–229.

Clark, M. S., & Mills, J. Interpersonal attraction in exchange and communal relationships. *Journal of Personality and Social Psychology,* 1979, *37,* 12–24.

DePaulo, B. M. Help-seeking from the recipient's point of view. *JSAS Catalog of Selected Documents in Psychology,* (Ms. No. 1721). 1978, *8,* 62. (a)

DePaulo, B. M. Accepting help from teachers—when the teachers are children. *Human Relations,* 1978, *31,* 459–474. (b)

DePaulo, B. M., Brown, P. L., Ishii, S., & Fisher, J. D. Help that works: The effects of aid on subsequent task performance. *Journal of Personality and Social Psychology,* in press.

DePaulo, B.M. & Fisher, J.D. Too tuned-out to take: The role of nonverbal sensitivity in help-seeking. *Personality and Social Psychology Bulletin,* in press.

DePaulo, B.M., & Fisher, J. D. The costs of asking for help. *Basic and Applied Social Psychology,* 1980, *1,* 23–35.

DePaulo, B. M., & Rosenthal, R. Ambivalence, discrepancy, and deception in nonverbal communication. In R. Rosenthal (Ed.), *Skill in nonverbal communication.* Cambridge, MA: Oelgeschlager, Gunn & Hain, 1979.

Druian, P. R., & DePaulo, B. M. Asking a child for help. *Social Behavior and Personality,* 1977, *5,* 33–39.

Enzle, M. E., & Schopflocher, D. Instigation of attributional processes by attributional questions. *Personality and Social Psychology Bulletin,* 1978, *4,* 595–599.

Farina, A., Fisher, J. D., Getter, H., & Fischer, E. Some consequences of changing people's views regarding the nature of mental illness. *Journal of Abnormal Psychology,* 1978, *87,* 272–279.

Festinger, L. A theory of social comparison processes. *Human Relations,* 1954, *1,* 117–140.

Fischer, E. H., & Turner, T. L. Orientations to seeking professional help: Development and research utility of an attitude scale. *Journal of Consulting and Clinical Psychology,* 1970, *35,* 79–90.

Fisher, J. D., & Farina, A. Consequences of beliefs about the nature of mental disorders. *Journal of Abnormal Psychology,* 1979, *88,* 320–327.

Fisher, J. D., Harrison, C., & Nadler, A. Exploring the generalizability of donor-recipient similarity effects. *Personality and Social Psychology Bulletin,* 1978, *4,* 627–630.

Fisher, J. D., & Nadler, A. The effect of similarity between donor and recipient on reactions to aid. *Journal of Applied Social Psychology,* 1974, *4,* 230–243.

Fisher, J. D., & Nadler, A. Effect on donor resources on recipient self-esteem and self-help. *Journal of Experimental Social Psychology,* 1976, *12,* 139–150.

Fisher, J. D., Nadler, A., Hart, E., & Whitcher, S. *Helping the needy helps the self. Bulletin of the Psychonomic Society,* 1981.

Fisher, J. D., Nadler, A., & Whitcher, S. *Recipient reactions to aid: A conceptual review. Psychological Bulletin,* in press.

Franklin, B.J. Need, receipt or denial of aid, and attitudes toward the benefactor. *Journal of Social Psychology,* 1975, *97,* 261–266.

Freeman, H. R. Reward vs. reciprocity as related to attraction. *Journal of Applied Social Psychology,* 1977, *1,* 57.–66.

Gergen, K. J. Toward a psychology of receiving help. *Journal of Applied Social Psychology,* 1974, *44,* 187–294.

Gergen, K. J., Ellsworth, P., Maslach, C., & Seipel, M. Obligation, donor resources, and reactions to aid in three nations. *Journal of Personality and Social Psychology,* 1975, *3,* 390–400.

Gergen, K. J., & Gergen, M. International assistance from a psychological perspective. *1971 Yearbook of World Affairs,* Vol. 25. London: Institute of World Affairs, 1971.

Gergen, K. J., & Gergen, M. Understanding foreign assistance through public opinion. *1974 Yearbook of World Affairs,* Vol. 27. London: Institute of World Affairs, 1974. (a)

Gergen, K. J., & Gergen, M. Foreign aid that works. *Psychology Today,* 1974, *8,* 64–68. (b)

Gergen, K. J., Morse, S. J., & Kristeller, J. L. The manner of giving: Cross-national continuities in reactions to aid. *Psychologia,* 1973, *16,* 121–131.

Goranson, R. E., & Berkowitz, L. Reciprocity and responsibility reactions to prior help. *Journal of Personality and Social Psychology,* 1966, *3,* 227–232.

Gouldner, A. W. The norm of reciprocity: A preliminary statement. *American Sociological Review,* 1960, *25,* 161–178.

Gourash, N. Help-seeking: A review of the literature. *American Journal of Community Psychology,* 1978, *6,* 413–424.

Greenberg, M. S. A theory of indebtedness. In K. J. Gergen, M. S. Greenberg, & R. H. Willis (Eds.), *Social exchange: Advances in theory and research.* New York: Plenum Press, 1980.

Greenberg, M. S., & Bar-Tal, D. Indebtedness as a motive for acquisition of ''helpful'' information. *Representative Research in Social Psychology,* 1976, *1,* 19–27.

Greenberg, M. S., & Frisch, D. M. Effect of intentionality of willingness to reciprocate a favor. *Journal of Experimental Social Psychology,* 1972, *8,* 99–111.

Greenberg, M. S., & Shapiro, S. Indebtedness: An adverse aspect of asking for and receiving help. *Sociometry,* 1971, *34,* 290–301.

Gross, A. E., Fisher, J. D., Nadler, A., Stiglitz, E., & Craig, C. Initiating contact with a women's counseling service: Some correlates of help utilization. *Journal of Community Psychology,* 1979, *7,* 42–49.

Gross, A. E., & Latané, J. G. Receiving help, giving help, and interpersonal attraction. *Journal of Applied Social Psychology,* 1974, *4,* 210–223.

Gross, A. E., Wallston, B. S., & Piliavin, I. M. Reactance, attribution, equity and the help-recipient. *Journal of Applied Social Psychology,* 1979, *9,* 297–313.

Heider, F. *The psychology of interpersonal relations.* New York: Wiley, 1958.

Hoffman, L. W. Early childhood experiences and women's achievement motives. *Journal of Social Issues,* 1972, *28,* 157–176.

Homans, G.C. *Social behavior: Its elementary forms.* New York: Harcourt, Brace, and World, 1961.

Jones, E. E., & Davis, K. E. From acts to dispositions: The attribution process in person perception. In L. Berkowitz (Ed.), *Advances in Experimental Social Psychology,* Vol. 2. New York: Academic Press, 1965.

Kahn, A., & Tice, T. E. Returning a favor and retaliating harm: The effects of stated intentions and actual behavior. *Journal of Experimental Social Psychology,* 1973, *9,* 43-56.

Kelley, H. H. Attribution theory in social psychology. In D. Levine (Ed.), *Nebraska Symposium on Motivation.* Lincoln: University of Nebraska Press, 1967, 192-240.

Kiesler, S. The effect of perceived role requirements on reactions in favor doing. *Journal of Experimental Social Psychology,* 1966, *2,* 198–210.

Ladieu, G., Hanfman, E., & Dembo, T. Studies in adjustment to visible injuries: Evaluation of help by the injured. *Journal of Abnormal and Social Psychology,* 1947, *42,* 169–192.

Leventhal, G. S., Weiss, T., & Long, G. Equity, reciprocity, and reallocating the rewards in the dyad. *Journal of Personality and Social Psychology,* 1969, *13,* 300–305.

Mikesell, R. H., & Calhoun, L. G. *Attitudes toward seeking professional help as a function of causal attribution and severity of disturbance.* Paper presented at the meeting of the Southeastern Psychological Association, Miami, April 1971.

Morris, S. C., III, & Rosen, S. Effects of felt adequacy and opportunity to reciprocate on help-seeking. *Journal of Experimental Social Psychology,* 1973, *9,* 265–276.

Morse, S. Help, likeability, and social influence. *Journal of Applied Social Psychology,* 1972, *2,* 34–46.

Morse, S. J., & Gergen, K. J. Material aid and social attraction. *Journal of Applied Social Psychology,* 1971, *1,* 150–212.

Morse, S. J., Gergen, K. J., Peele, S., & van Ryneveld, J. Reactions to receiving expected and unexpected help from a person who violates or does not violate a norm. *Journal of Experimental Social Psychology*, 1977, *13*, 397-402.

Muir, D. E., & Weinstein, E. A. The social debt: An investigation of lower-class and middle-class norms of social obligation. *American Sociological Review*, 1962, *27*, 532-539.

Nadler, A. "Good looks do not help": Effects of helper's physical attractiveness and expectations for future interaction on help-seeking behavior. *Personality and Social Psychology Bulletin*, 1980, *6*, 378-383.

Nadler, A., Altman, A., & Fisher, J. D. Helping is not enough: Recipient's reactions to aid as a function of positive and negative self-regard. *Journal of Personality*, 1979, *47*, 615-628.

Nadler, A., & Fisher, J. D. *When giving does not pay: Recipient reactions to aid as a function of donor expertise*. Unpublished manuscript, Tel-Aviv University, 1978.

Nadler, A., Fisher, J. D., & Streufert, S. The donor's dilemma: Recipient's reaction to aid from friend or foe. *Journal of Applied Social Psychology*, 1974, *4*, 275-285.

Nadler, A., Fisher, J. D., & Streufert, S. When helping hurts: The effects of donor-recipient similarity and recipient self-esteem on reactions to aid. *Journal of Personality*, 1976, *44*, 392-409.

Nadler, A., & Porat, I. Names do not help: Effects on anonymity and locus of need attribution on help-seeking behavior. *Personality and Social Psychology Bulletin*, 1978, *4*, 624-626.

Nadler, A., Sheinberg, L., & Jaffe, Y. Seeking help from the wheelchair. In C. Spielberger & I. Sarason, *Stress and anxiety, Vol. 8*, Washington, D.C.: Hemisphere, in press.

Nemeth, C. Effects of free versus constrained behavior on attraction between people. *Journal of Personality and Social Psychology*, 1970, *15*, 302-311.

Phillips, D. L., & Segal, B. E. Sexual status and psychiatric symptoms. *American Sociological Review*, 1969, *34*, 58-72.

Piliavin, I. M., & Gross, A. E. The effects of separation of services and income maintenance on AFDC recipients' perceptions and use of Social Services: Results of a field experiment. *Social Service Review*, 1977, *9*, 389-406.

Pruitt, D. G. Reciprocity and credit building in a laboratory dyad. *Journal of Personality and Social Psychology*, 1968, *8*, 143-147.

Rosen, B. Evaluation of help by a potential recipient. *Psychonomic Science*, 1971, *23*, 269-271.

Rosen, S., Powell, E. R., & Schubot, D. B. Peer-tutoring outcomes as influenced by the equity and type of role assignment. *Journal of Educational Psychology*, 1977, *69*, 244-252.

Schopler, J., & Thompson, V. D. Role of attribution processes in mediating amount of reciprocity for a favor. *Journal of Personality and Social Psychology*, 1968, *10*, 243-250.

Shapiro, E.G. Help seeking: Effects of visibility of task performance and seeking help. *Journal of Applied Social Psychology*, 1978, *8*, 163-173.

Shumaker, S. A., & Jackson, J. S. The aversive effects of nonreciprocated benefits. *Social Psychology Quarterly*, 1979, *42*, 148-158.

Stapleton, R. E., Nacci, P., & Tedeschi, J. T. Interpersonal attraction and the reciprocation of benefits. *Journal of Personality and Social Psychology*, 1973, *28*, 199-205.

Stein, A. H., & Bailey, M. M. The socialization of achievement orientation in females. *Psychological Bulletin*, 1973, *80*, 345-356.

Stokes, S., & Bickman, L. The effect of the physical attractiveness and role of the helper on helping. *Journal of Applied Social Psychology*, 1974, *4*, 286-293.

Tesser, A., & Gatewood, R., & Driver, M. Some determinants of gratitude. *Journal of Personality and Social Psychology*, 1968, *9*, 233-236.

Tessler, R. C., & Schwartz, S. H. Help-seeking, self-esteem, and achievement motivation: An attribution analysis. *Journal of Personality and Social Psychology*, 1972, *21*, 318-326.

Wallston, B. S. The effects of sex-role ideology, self-esteem, and expected future interactions with an audience on male help-seeking. *Sex Roles*, 1976, *2*, 353-356.

Walster, E., Berscheid, E., & Walster, G. W. New directions in equity theory. *Journal of Personality and Social Psychology*, 1973, *25*, 151–176.

Weber, M. *The Protestant ethic and the spirit of capitalism*. London: George Allen and University, 1930.

Weiss, C. H. Validity of welfare mothers' responses. *Public Opinion Quarterly*, 1969, *32*, 622–633.

Worchel, S., & Andreoli, V. A. Attribution of causality as a means of restoring behavioral freedom. *Journal of Personality and Social Psychology*, 1974, *29*, 237–245.

Worchel, S., Andreoli, V. A., & Archer, R. When is a favor a threat to freedom: The effects of attribution and importance of freedom on reciprocity. *Journal of Personality*, 1976, *44*, 294–310.

VII OVERVIEW

19

Altruism and Helping Behavior: Current Perspectives and Future Possibilities

Richard M. Sorrentino
J. Philippe Rushton
The University of Western Ontario

Chapter 1 (Rushton & Sorrentino) provided the reader with a brief history of altruism up to the important decade of the 1960s when a great surge of research on altruism and helping behavior occurred. In this chapter, we examine some of the many contributions of the present book in light of research generated during that decade. By placing the contributions within their immediate historical perspective, it is hoped that the progress that has been made, as well as directions for future research will be elucidated.

If we were to choose one source, which was perhaps most representative of the issues during the 1960s, it would be Macaulay's and Berkowitz's (1970) *Altruism and Helping Behavior: Social Psychological Studies of Some Antecedents and Consequences.* It is no accident then, that many of the contributors to the present *Altruism and Helping Behavior* also appear in the original.

Among the chapters in that original volume we find the now classic research on bystander intervention in emergencies (Latané & Darley, 1970), the importance of social models for helping behavior (Bryan, 1970; Hornstein, 1970; Macaulay, 1970), several chapters on norms and the socialization of altruism (Aronfreed, 1970; Berkowitz, 1970; Darley & Latané, 1970; Kaufman, 1970; Schwartz, 1970), guilt, equity and justice notions of altruism (Freedman, 1970; Lerner, 1970; Rawlings, 1970; Schopler, 1970; Walster, Berscheid & Walster, 1970), and naturalistic studies of altrusim (Fellner & Marshall, 1970; London, 1970; Rosenhan, 1970). We will focus on some of the discoveries that researchers reported in that earlier volume, some of the challenging issues that remained at the end of it, and the progress that has been made since then as documented in the current volume. Obviously this chapter cannot be divorced from its authors' biases, nor, unfortunately, is there space to discuss all the issues we would have liked to have dealt with. With these caveats in mind, let us examine some of the salient issues.

DEFINING ALTRUISM

First, it might be noted that for their definition of altruism, Macaulay and Berkowitz (1970) chose, "behavior carried out to benefit another without anticipation of rewards from external sources [p.3]." This definition includes both the altruist's intentions and his or her behavior. It does, however, exclude such rewards from internal sources as self esteem and relief from guilt from primary concern. Such an exclusion has the practical advantage of avoiding both unobservable variables as well as the philosophical issue of whether there can ever be a truly unselfish act. To what extent though are the present contributors content with this definition of altruism?

As can be seen, there is little consensus from the authors; definitions in the current volume vary widely. The one that is perhaps most closely aligned with Macaulay and Berkowitz (1970) is that of Schwartz and Howard (Chapter 9). These authors also exclude material gain or social outcomes from their definition, but accept "anticipated self-reinforcement" as within the domain of altruism. They reject the notion, however, that anticipated self-reinforcement is the primary intention of altruistic behavior (Schwartz, 1980, personal communication). Departing from this approach at one extreme is Ridley and Dawkins (Chapter 1). Their definition is exclusively behavioral. Although an altruistic act must be at the "expense of the altruist," the intentions of the altruist are irrelevant. At the other extreme are several investigators arguing for a definition of altruism which completely excludes any trace of self-reward as the primary intention for the altruist. For Krebs and Russell (Chapter 7), the only acceptable definition is one which includes the "extent to which (motivating forces) give rise to the intention to benefit at some cost to the self and are devoid of self-interest." This definition is also implicit in Hoffman's (Chapter 3), and certainly Batson and Coke's (Chapter 8) chapters. Krebs and Russell suggest that too many definitions are motivated by "practical facility rather than theoretical appropriateness."

One of the strongest assertions against acceptance of altruism based on instrumental motives comes from Lerner and Meindl (Chapter 10). They not only challenge instrumental notions of previous justice theories, but also underline the pervasiveness of altruistic behavior in human society.

In the first place, it simply does not make sense to approach such enormous and important parts of our lives as if they were derivative or instrumental derivatives of other underlying, more powerful or basic personal agendas. There appears to be no more powerful and ubiquitous theme in human affairs than the personal and institutionalized concern with justice and deserving. Also, people voluntarily, if that term has any meaning at all, give away most of their resources and gain most of their "satisfaction" from doing for others. If this is true then it is highly doubtful that social psychologists will be able to invent a mechanism or set of mechanisms which provide a satisfactory explanation for how the weak and peripheral desires in our lives generate and control those events which dominate our private and social world. [p. 222]

It is unlikely that definitional problems will ever be solved in their entirety. It has been suggested that, to debate them too much, may be "to indulge in little more than an intellectual pillow fight [Krebs & Wispé, 1974]." Nonetheless, how a particular researcher defines altruism is likely to be an important determiner of how he or she conducts research. For example, Ridley and Dawkins, with their entirely behavioral definition are less likely to focus on internal mediators such as empathy, whereas those who focus on empathy as the only acceptable motivational construct are unlikely to focus on "apparent" altruistic behaviors mediated by, say, guilt reduction.

As for the editors, one of us (JPR), has elaborated in detail elsewhere (Rushton, 1980), the view that the *primary* focus of research attention should be on altruistic *behavior*, and that postulated motivators such as "empathy," and "norms of social responsibility," are hypothetical constructs, to be added only if they can account for the behavioral regularities more thoroughly. Rushton (1980) concluded, in this regard:

> Finally the behavioral definition also solves the endless, and fruitless, debate as to whether such a thing as *true* altruism exists. For example, it may be true that there will never be a total absence of *all* possible rewards, including such *internal* ones as the relief of guilt, pleasure for having lived up to an internal standard, reduction in a sense of injustice, or termination of a sympathetic feeling of pain for another . . . . however, let us note that there is a class of behaviors which are carried out that benefit others. Furthermore, these behaviors often are carried out in the absence of immediate reward and sometimes at some cost. Most people consider such behavior by their peers a virtue. It is useful to have a word for such behavior, and "altruism" is the one designated [p.10].

The other of us, on the other hand, (RMS), after reading the many arguments and substantive contributions in these pages, and after attempting to avoid the close link between the authors' definitions and their theoretical biases (e.g., genes don't think, empathy, emotion, and new justice theory are devoid of egoistic intentions), finds his sympathies lie with those who would define altruism as behavior directed toward the benefit of others at some cost to the self where no extrinsic *or intrinsic* benefit is the primary intent of the behavior. Such a definition, he feels, would avoid the confusion in the literature that Krebs and Russell (Chapter 7) point out. Also, by using the most stringent criteria for a definition of altruism, the onus is on investigators to demonstrate that they are indeed working with a truly altruistic act. For those who find this impractical, RMS recommends the term "prosocial behavior" or, simply, "helping." Several of the contributors appear to have already committed themselves to the more stringent criteria. Batson and Coke (Chapter 8) provide an ingenious technique and model for demonstrating that altruism can occur without egoism. Lerner and Meindl (Chapter 10) produce a testable model for a new justice theory which specifies a distinction between instrumental justice and altruistic justice, and Hoffman (Chapter 3) finds empathy to be a key to pure altruism. In essence, RMS feels that a stringent definition of altruism is already being put to the test and/or new models are being formulated.

In summary, it would appear that the diversity of definitions is still with us and that this is a healthy stimulus to debate and research.

THE ROLE OF MODELING AND SOCIALIZATION IN HELPING BEHAVIOR

The state of research on socialization processes in altruism and helping behavior was addressed in the Macaulay and Berkowitz (1970) volume. Aronfreed, for example, provided evidence that classical conditioning procedures could condition empathic affectivity in children, and that when children are made to empathize with another (by previously experiencing the pain or the pleasure the other is now facing) they are more likely than a control to help that person at a cost to themselves! Aronfreed suggested that empathy was the key to pure altruism. Here only children with the capacity to experience what the other child is experiencing, help that child. This would appear to rule out any form of selfish motivation. However, as Macaulay and Berkowitz pointed out, Aronfreed had not ruled out the possibility of vicarious reinforcement. That is, the children may empathize, but helping occurs in order to vicariously experience the pleasure of the reward or the relief from pain of the victim.

Most stress on socialization research in the Macaulay and Berkowitz volume, however, had been placed on the role of social models, the importance of which had been fairly well documented. The first chapter on this subject (Hornstein) demonstrated that if a similar model helped and felt good about it, then others were more likely to help. The second chapter (Macaulay) replicated this finding but also demonstrated that people would help if they saw a salient model actively refuse to help. Finally, Bryan demonstrated that children would behave generously or selfishly depending on how they had seen a model behave. Interestingly, Bryan also examined whether what the model *preached* ought to be done had any effects; it did not. The consensus from these studies appeared to be that models were important in eliciting or reinforcing social norms. (Hence Macaulay interpreted her finding that a model who ostentatiously refused to give elicited the norms to give anyway.) In these studies models had been treated primarily as though they were "situational" variables rather than forces of socialization. However, London (1970), and Rosenhan (1970), using a retrospective case study approach examined the socializing antecedents of real-life, natural altruists. London studied a group of German Christians who had been active in rescuing Jews from the Nazis during World War II, and Rosenhan studied a group of fully committed Civil Rights workers who had been active in the early, and particularly dangerous stages, of the Civil Rights Movement. He compared them to a control group of "partially committed." In both the London and Rosenhan studies there was clear evidence that each of the altruists has been exposed to at least one parent who themselves had been a strong altruist, and with whom the offspring had had strong emotional ties. Thus preliminary evidence had been provided that models were very important as socializers of altruism.

In the current volume socialization research plays a particularly significant part. In keeping with the earlier research, much of the current concern is also with the role of models, now with even more focus on their value in producing internal standards with the concomitant of durability and generalizability of behavior. Although the literature on the affects of modeling on *adult* helping behavior is sparse, many of the contributors provide an extremely rich source of data for modeling effects on children. From Grusec (Chapter 4), Rushton (Chapter 5), and Staub (Chapter 6), we can see that modeling indeed has important effects. Grusec provides a precise, objective, evaluation of laboratory and field research. Staub gives us rules of socialization in the home and educational settings backed with documented evidence. Rushton shows that television itself can be an important socializer. Although all these authors point out the limitations of present research, the important question of generalizability is also addressed and some promising results they report may lead to a resolution of this question in the 1980s. It would seem, for example, that although "one shot" laboratory experiments may or may not lead to generalizable effects; observational learning may have particularly generalizable effects when it is done in conjunction with other socialization procedures such as reasoning, the use of affective manipulations (reward and punishment) and the involving of the self-system. The verbal transmission of generalizable rules also seems important.

One intriguing avenue for future research stemming from modern socialization research is that involving social cognition. In this respect for example are the articulation of mechanisms for prosocial values. Grusec suggests that verbal exhortation could have longer-lasting effects than mere examples because while the former affects semantic memory, the latter only affects episodic memory (Tulving, 1972). She also invokes attribution theory and the self-concept to account for the internalization of altruistic values. Rushton suggests that television works as a socializer through the alteration of personal norms (a social cognition), and Staub presents a range of internal mechanisms involving personal norms, values, empathy and personality dispositions, all of which interact to produce behavior.

Another researcher who has concerned himself with socialization processes is Hoffman (Chapter 3). He too has attempted to specify some of the cognitive mechanisms that develop to mediate altruism. He provides the beginning of an integration of a biological-maturational approach, with socialization inputs, to account for the development of empathy.

Thus socialization research has become far more integrative and sophisticated with attempts to relate socialization procedures with possible genetic or early acquired predispositions to produce internalized mediators that subsequently come to guide behavior over both time and across situation.

INTERNAL MEDIATORS OF ALTRUISM AND HELPING BEHAVIOR

In the original Macaulay and Berkowitz volume, a number of underlying mechanisms had been postulated. For example, Schwartz's chapter had stressed the importance of personal norms for helping behavior while Aronfreed had argued for empathy as the true altruistic mechanism. Some support for the operation of both of these mechanisms might also have been gleaned intuitively from the case studies of the kidney donors studied by Fellner and Marshall, in that volume.

If it were merely a matter of empathy and norms as *the* underlying mechanisms of helping behavior, the research of the seventies might have had some clear cut resolvable issues. Instead, the Macaulay and Berkowitz volume provided a number of other underlying mechanisms to ponder. Freedman, for example, presented the case that if we wish to increase helping behavior, we have only to make the person feel guilty. Rawlings pushed the point further by demonstrating that the guilt might be direct (reactive guilt) or indirect (anticipatory guilt). Adding guilt to the list, does not simply increase the number of mediators that lead to helping. Rather it brings to the fore, yet another issue. Can it be assumed that seeing a person in need of help simply evokes some mechanism to help? Other chapters in that book said "no." Walster, Berscheid and Walster suggested that, if we are in some way responsible for a person suffering, that although in some cases we may help in order to restore justice, in others we may actually derogate the person in order to provide justification. Furthermore, the issue of derogation is not simply a matter of resolving guilt. Lerner brought this point home in his chapter on the desire for justice and reactions to victims. He provided evidence that if the victim is completely innocent in his or her suffering, another justice mechanism would be invoked, that is, the need to believe in a just world. This need may be restored by *derogating* an innocently suffering victim. Finally, Berkowitz showed the importance of another mediator—self-concern and mood. He demonstrated that if people were made to feel overly concerned with themselves that they would behave less generously than others—particularly if this self-concern resulted in negative affect toward the self.

A great deal of further information on just as many, if not more, internal mediators has been provided in the current volume. These are discussed in categories:

Norms

Schwartz and Howard (Chapter 9) continue to argue Schwartz's view that personal norms, representing internalized values of helping, are one of the significant determinants of altruism. Outside of these two authors, there is a growth (rebirth?) of the importance of personal or social norms by the other contributors. Clearly, several authors see the teaching of norms as an important component of the effects of socialization (e.g., Grusec, Hoffman, Rushton, & Staub), and Rushton (Chapter 12), considers internalized norms as one of the most important motivators of "the altruistic personality." One question is whether internalized norms will produce helping if empathy is absent? Staub (Chapter 6), for example, distinguishes between two types of prosocial goals: prosocial orientation and orientation toward duty or obligation. Perhaps these are similar to Rushton's (Chapter 12), empathic versus normative altruism, respectively. Insofar as the latter is devoid of empathic feelings, and the former includes them, it is possible that in certain circumstances the latter could interfere with helping when, as Staub states, "deviation from societal dictates or even from abstract moral absolutes is required to respond to someone's need." This might well be a view that Krebs and Russell (Chapter 7) would be sympathetic to if norms are defined narrowly as "specific rule following," for, to Krebs and Russell, the ability to role play, perceive the other's intention, and engage high levels of moral reasoning are the important determiners of true altruism. If on the other hand, norms are considered more widely, as any type of cognitive "rule" then they can incorporate both the "rules" of moral reasoning as well as those of empathy and role-taking (see Rushton, 1980). The interaction of norms and other mediators is likely to be a fruitful line of inquiry in the future.

The value of norms, as motivators of altruism, then, is still a question for debate and should carry over well into the next decade. Let us see if its competitor (or complement) has fared better.

Empathy

Although there was little mention of empathy outside of Aronfreed's (1970) chapter in the Macaulay and Berkowitz volume, no less than 11 of the contributors in this book make at least some mention of empathy. Krebs and Russell

(Chapter 7) provide a detailed conceptual and empirical analysis of the relationship between role-taking ability, empathy and altruism. Although they admit that, as yet, the evidence that role-taking leads to altruism does not have much empirical support they do a scholarly job of demonstrating why the situation has not really been adequately tested. As they state in their conclusions "The path from role-taking to altruism is tortuous and indirect." Batson and Coke (Chapter 8) provide fairly clear experimental evidence that empathy can and does, lead to altruism. Hoffman (Chapter 3) makes a similar case, but accepts the notion that empathy may have a "quasi-egoism" component. Lerner and Meindl (Chapter 10) consider empathy central to the development of the Identity relations and possibly to the Unit relations of their model.

While the link between empathy and altruism is encouraging, some notes of caution are also expressed by our contributors. In line with the previous discussion that norms may not be effective without empathy, empathy, in turn, may not be effective without internalized values (Schwartz and Howard, Chapter 9) and/or socialized norms (Staub, Chapter 6). Also, Grusec (Chapter 4) suggests that since the correlation between altruism and empathy, and altruism and role-taking ability appears stronger in younger children than older ones it is possible that level of empathy and role-taking ability may be less important in determining altruistic behavior in older children. She further suggests this may be because older children have experiences which mask or overcome the link between the ability to understand another's emotions and points of view and altruism. One must also consider Hoffman's (Chapter 3) cautions regarding overarousal of empathy and Rosenhan's, Salovey's, Karylowski's and Hargis's (Chapter 11) distinction between empathic joy and egocentric joy as other possible limitations to the utility of empathy for altruism.

Empathy approaches then, while extremely promising, also need to take account of the complementarity of normative factors as well as deal with some of the limitations stressed by present contributors.

Emotion

Both the mechanisms we have discussed so far, that is, personal norms and empathy, involve emotion. In the case of empathy, it is direct, as when a person matches his or her emotions with those of somebody in distress. In the case of personal norms, it is a little more indirect, that is, if one's own behavior does not match up, one censures onself, which produces an aversive state requiring redress; if one's behavior does match up then one congratulates oneself and feels a positive self-concept. There are, however, other ways in which affect can be generated and impact altruism. Rosenhan, Karylowski, Salovey, and Hargis (Chapter 11) provide a framework for understanding the nature and influence of emotion and attempt to pinpoint when experimentally induced "good moods" and "bad moods" lead to increases or decreases in altruism.

Overall Discussion of the Mechanisms of Helping

The issue of when a particular mechanism vis-a-vis other mechanisms is invoked, and exactly what effect it will have, remains to be resolved. To previous underlying mechanisms invoked (i.e., norm salience, empathy, guilt, instrumental justice, belief in a just world) when observing a person in need of help and/or suffering, we must now add emotion (Rosenhan, Salovey, Karylowski, & Hargis) noninstrumental justice (Lerner & Meindl), personal distress (Batson & Coke), and sympathy (Rosenhan et al.). Although many contributors attempt to specify when their particular mechanism or set of mechanisms is or is not invoked, there remains little apparent overlap between mechanisms.

Some readers of this volume, for example, will have noted that this issue has become increasingly more salient. There are striking similarities between the paradigms employed by investigators who study altruism and helping, and those who study victim derogation. Hoffman (Chapter 3) points out that the situation that should lead to the greatest empathy is where the victim is innocent in his or her suffering. Yet, according to Lerner (1970), this is precisely the situation that should be the greatest threat to one's belief in a just world. For the former, helping should occur due to empathy. For the latter, helping *or* derogation of the victim should occur depending on, for example, the cost of helping to the observer. Aderman, Brehm and Katz (1974) have shown that when the observer is *instructed* to empathize with the victim, they do not derogate and find the victim attractive. When, however, they use the Lerner and Simmons (1966) instructions, or they are instructed to attend closely to the victim's suffering, then they derogate. It seems, therefore, that *both* mechanisms are operating, depending on the observer's orientation. Yet neither just world theorists nor empathy theorists attempt to incorporate each other's viewpoints into their models even though the paradigms they employ are often strikingly similar (see for example, Sorrentino, Chapter 13, and Novak & Lerner, 1968, vis-a-vis Batson & Coke, Chapter 8). To add to the confusion, Hoffman (Chapter 3) and others argue that guilt is an important mechanism for helping, and indeed it is, as many studies have now shown. However, guilt has also been postulated to lead to derogation, as Sorrentino and others have argued (see Sorrentino, Chapter 13). Finally, observing a victim suffer could also lead to sympathy as Rosenhan et al. (Chapter 11) point out.

It seems clear, then, that several different mechanisms and behaviors may be evoked when one witnesses a person suffering and/or in need of help. Future research and theory which considers this could be beneficial.

PERSONALITY

Although our particular bias here is obvious (e.g., Rushton, Chapter 12; Sorrentino, Chapter 13), we still cannot help but point out the necessity for studies examining the role of individual differences. Aside from ourselves, several of the other contributors felt the same way, including Fisher, DePaulo and Nadler (Chapter 18), Krebs and Russell (Chapter 7), Schwartz and Howard (Chapter 9), and Staub (Chapter 6). In this section, we shall argue further that individual differences, while they may be one investigator's error term, can, to others, play a major role in furthering an understanding of helping behavior and altruism.

The use of individual differences, for example, can provide construct validity for any postulated mechanism of helping behavior. Take, for instance, Batson's and Coke's (Chapter 8) study using placebo effects to demonstrate that empathy is not egoistic. If the reader had any doubts that these investigators actually demonstrated that altruism did occur as a function of empathy in the unpleasant placebo condition, such doubts might be mitigated by replicating the experiment to demonstrate that those high on an empathy scale were more likely to help than those low on an empathy scale.

Individual differences can also help to determine if other mechanisms are operating in the same situation. From Sorrentino (Chapter 13), for example, it appears that while victim derogation may occur for many people, the actual mechanism for derogation is closely tied to the personality of the observer (e.g., guilt for High authoritarians, belief in a just world for Low authoritarians and Internals, belief in an unjust world for Externals). If we extend these findings to the helping literature, it seems logical that different mechanisms may lead to the same prosocial act but only if the mechanism is affecting the appropriate personality variable.

Individual difference variables can also aid in resolving important issues. Take Latané's, Nida's and Wilson's data (Chapter 14) illustrating the mathematically derived relation between an individual's probability of helping and the number of bystanders. An empathy theorist might at least expect that within this relationship persons High in empathy would still be more likely to respond than persons Low in empathy, as illustrated in Fig. 19.1a. Yet Latané et al. offer the intriguing hypothesis that any arousal due to empathy could be misattributed to the inaction of bystanders. This would have exactly the reverse effect, such that persons High in empathy would be even less likely to help than persons Low in empathy, as illustrated in Fig. 19.1b. An additionally intriguing possibility is suggested by Hoffman's (Chapter 3) analysis of empathic overarousal, "which suggests that beyond a certain point empathic distress may become so aversive that one's attention is directed to the self and not the victim." From this, it may be conjectured that the increased arousal due to the presence of bystanders may at some point lead the empathically aroused person to attribute this additional source of arousal to empathic overarousal. Thus, the Highly empathic person may be more likely to help than the Low, with a smaller number of bystanders, but as the number increases, the Lows and not the Highs are more likely to help. This possibility is illustrated in Fig. 19.1c (see also some data in Stotland, Mathews, Sherman, Hansson, & Richardson, [1978] supporting this). Thus, the study of individual differences may be used to settle specific controversies.

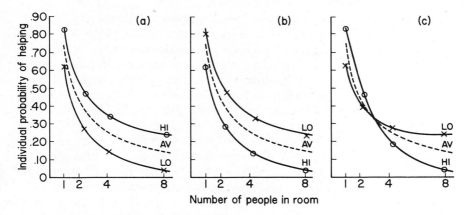

FIG. 19.1.   Three hypothetical relationships between helping and number of bystanders as a function of High (Hi) versus Low (Low) Empathy. (Note: Average (Av) is curve taken from Latané, Nida & Wilson (Chapter 14).

Although we have attempted to make a strong case for the importance of personality and individual differences either alone or in interaction with situational determinants, as we see in the next section, not all of the contributors would agree with us on this.

SOCIAL CONSTRAINTS ON HELPING

In Macaulay's and Berkowitz's previous volume, Darley and Latané (1970) challenged the importance of individual differences in internalized mediators for predicting altruism and helping behavior. Their specific focus was on norms, but their argument holds equally for empathy and other mediators. Their argument was that a person could draw on as many prosocial *or* antisocial norms as they pleased in order to fit any situation thus making them postdictive rather than predictive; that is, an instance of helping behavior occurs, and then we "explain" it by saying that empathy or a norm to help must have been in operation. In addition, they presented a series of studies designed to show that situational factors far outweigh individual difference factors; that is, predictions could be made whether a bystander would help better by knowledge of the number of other bystanders present than by knowledge of the bystander's internalized personal norms (Latané & Darley, 1970). Further evidence for the importance of situational factors can be found in the present volume.

Latané, Nida and Wilson (Chapter 14) demonstrate overwhelmingly, that, whether a person will go to the aid of someone in need depends very largely on the number of others there are around. This predictive relationship has now been demonstrated in so many studies (as their chapter makes amply clear) that it would appear there is only a little room left for individual differences. In terms of normative models or empathy explanations of helping, Latané, Nida and Wilson suggest that (1) since "responsibility denial" is also incorporated in the Schwartz and Howard model, an increase in bystanders would serve to increase the denial; and (2) empathic arousal would be misattributed to the presence of other bystanders thus *decreasing* the likelihood of helping on the part of empathic persons! They, therefore, do not believe that internalized norms to help or empathy will be of much use in predicting behavior.

Additional chapters by Korte (Chapter 15) and by Strayer (Chapter 16) also demonstrate that knowledge of the social situation a person is in helps to predict whether they will behave altruistically. In Korte's chapter it is knowledge of whether the person is in a large city or a small town, and within city, which part, that enables greater prediction of helping on a probability basis. In Strayer's chapter it is knowledge of the preschool organization that is important and what a child's sociometric position is that enables prediction (for example, whether another child had been altruistic to him or her just previously). Note, however, that, in the latter two chapters, at least, there is room for personality *interactions* with situations. For example is there an "urban personality" that increments the situational stressors in Korte's data? The evidence suggests that there is. And are there personality differences that lead to role positions in Strayer's preschool organization? Note for example, Strayer's finding of two different behavioral patterns of altruism.

Resolution of the personality x situation interaction for altruistic behavior, then, is another intriguing line for further research. Tentative beginnings have been made elsewhere (Rushton, 1980; Staub, 1980).

REMAINING ISSUES

Sociobiology

This is one of the most controversial topics for the social sciences that has emerged in the last decade (see for example, *Time,* August 1, 1979). The possibility of an innate component for altruism (Ridley & Dawkins, Chapter 2) brings this issue to the fore for social and developmental psychologists interested in helping behavior and altruism. Ridley and Dawkins (Chapter 2) suggest that one social psychological contribution to an integration is through the role of studying "manipulation," (that is, the persuasion by the recipient of altruism, of others). We feel that there may well be additional links between the sociobiology and psychology of altruism. For example, Hoffman (Chapter 3) states that empathy may be the mediating mechanism between genes for altruism and their expression in human behavior. Given that we are most likely to empathize with similar others (e.g., Batson & Coke, Chapter 8), then we would have an innate model of human altruism very similar to Ridley and Dawkin's notion of Relatedness, with:

	potential for		activated by		altruistic
innate mechanism	→	*empathy*	→	*similarity*	→	behavior .
(genes for altruism)		arousal		of potential		
				recipient		

Perhaps then, with human organisms we have a "green beard" effect (see Ridley & Dawkins) through the mediator of empathy.

Note also Lerner's and Meindl's (Chapter 10) distinctions among Identity, Unit, and Non-unit relations. For Identity relations, Lerner and Meindl feel altruism will occur due to empathic considerations; for Unit relations, reciprocal altruism will occur, and for Non-unit relations, false forms of altruism such as "mock equity" are likely to occur. The parallels between these different forms and those of Ridley and Dawkins' Relatedness, Reciprocal Altruism and Manipulativeness are rather striking.

All of these are intriguing conjectures; it will be interesting to see what the future will bring.

A Question of Values

In this final section, the sombre issue of caution in our approach to the application of principles of prosocial behavior might be raised. Fisher, DePaulo and Nadler (Chapter 18), for example, challenge the assumption that prosocial behavior will always have beneficial effects on the recipient. As they point out, there are a surprisingly large number of conditions under which aid is relatively more threatening than supportive. Conversely, we raise the question, will training children to be more prosocial usually have beneficial effects on them? Consider, for example, the kidney donors studied by Fellner and Marshall (Chapter 17). Although they apparently continued to feel good about their earlier decision, we might note that they *are* now minus a kidney. Thus it is a two-edged sword; altruism cuts both ways. Perhaps not always so. However, until we fully understand the precise nature of the underlying mechanisms facilitative to prosocial behavior, we might wish to proceed with some caution. A case in point is Rubin's and Peplau's (1973) advocacy of socialization practices which would attenuate one's belief in a just world. Yet Sorrentino (Chapter 13) provides evidence that personality correlates of this belief do not necessarily lead to the undesirable effects these authors suggest. In addition, correlates such as authoritarianism and religiosity could well be based on the normative component of Rushton's altruistic personality (Chapter 12). Should we then, also promote socialization of such mechanisms as empathy or guilt in children at this stage of knowledge? Although both have been demonstrated as mediators of helping and altruism, the former mechanism could at times lead to overarousal (Hoffman, Chapter 3) and a decreased likelihood to help (Latané, Nida & Wilson, Chapter 14). Guilt could also at times lead to derogation of the victim (Sorrentino, Chapter 13) and, in addition, one wonders what other effects socializing guilt may have on the later personality. Although we do not mean to side with Ayn Rand's (1964) extreme notion that altruism is evil, we feel it is interesting, and possibly important, to at least raise the question.

CONCLUSIONS

Because this chapter was not intended to review all the many significant contributions of the contributors, it has overlooked many intriguing and exciting developments that the reader will find. The mathematical formulation subsuming bystander intervention with other phenomena related to group size (Latané, Nida and Wilson, Chapter 14); the full implications of Lerner's and Meindl's new justice model for altruism (Chapter 10); the picture of social life in the preschool (Strayer, Chapter 16); and the compelling case studies of kidney donors (Fellner & Marshall, Chapter 17), are just a few of the many that will be found in this volume. We hope, however, that we have provided some additional integration, perspective, and questions for the research and theory of the 1980s. In any case, we look forward to a rich and exciting decade.

REFERENCES

Aderman, D., Brehm, S. S., & Katz, L. B. Empathic observation of an innocent victim: The just world revisited. *Journal of Personality and Social Psychology,* 1974, *29,* 342–347.

Aronfreed, J. The socialization of altruistic and sympathetic behavior: Some theoretical and experimental analyses. In J. Macaulay & L. Berkowitz (Eds.), *Altruism and helping behavior.* New York: Academic Press, 1970.

Berkowitz, L. The self, selfishness, and altruism. In J. Macaulay & L. Berkowitz (Eds.), *Altruism and helping behavior.* New York: Academic Press, 1970.

Bryan, J. H. Children's reactions to helpers: Their money isn't where their mouths are. In J. Macaulay & L. Berkowitz (Eds.), *Altruism and helping behavior.* New York: Academic Press, 1970.

Darley, J. M., & Latané, B. Norms and normative behavior: Field studies of social interdependence. In J. Macaulay & L. Berkowitz (Eds.), *Altruism and helping behavior.* New York: Academic Press, 1970.

Fellner, C. H., & Marshall, J. R. Kidney donors. In J. Macaulay & L. Berkowitz (Eds.), *Altruism and helping behavior.* New York: Academic Press, 1970.

Freedman, J. L. Transgression, compliance, and guilt. In J. Macaulay & L. Berkowitz (Eds.), *Altruism and helping behavior.* New York: Academic Press, 1970.

Hornstein, H. A. The influence of social models on helping. In J. Macaulay & L. Berkowitz (Eds.), *Altruism and helping behavior.* New York: Academic Press, 1970.

Kaufmann, H. Legality and harmfulness of a bystander's failure to interfere as determinants of moral judgment. In J. Macaulay & L. Berkowitz (Eds.), *Altruism and helping behavior*. New York: Academic Press, 1970.

Krebs, D. L., & Wispé, L. G. Rejoinder: On defining altruism. *Journal of Social Issues,* 1974, *30,* 194–199.

Latané, B., & Darley, J. M. Social determinants of bystander intervention in emergencies. In J. Macaulay & L. Berkowitz (Eds.), *Altruism and helping behavior*. New York: Academic Press, 1970.

Lerner, M. J. The desire for justice and reactions to victims. In J. Macaulay & L. Berkowitz (Eds.), *Altruism and helping behavior*. New York: Academic Press, 1970.

Lerner, M. J., & Simmons, C. H. Observer's reaction to the innocent victim: Compassion or rejection? *Journal of Personality and Social Psychology,* 1966, *4,* 203–210.

London, P. The rescuers: Motivational hypotheses about Christians who saved Jews from the Nazis. In J. Macaulay & L. Berkowitz (Eds.), *Altruism and helping behavior*. New York: Academic Press, 1970.

Macaulay, J. R. A shill for charity. In J. Macaulay & L. Berkowitz (Eds.), *Altruism and helping behavior*. New York: Academic Press, 1970.

Macaulay, J. R., & Berkowitz, L. (Eds.) *Altruism and helping behavior*. New York: Academic Press, 1970

Novak, D. W., & Lerner, M. J. Rejection as a consequence of perceived similarity. *Journal of Personality and Social Psychology,* 1968, *9,* 147–152.

Rand, A. *The virtue of selfishness*. New York: New American Library, 1964.

Rawlings, E. I. Reactive guilt and anticipatory guilt in altruistic behavior. In J. Macaulay & L. Berkowitz (Eds.), *Altruism and helping behavior*. New York: Academic Press, 1970.

Rosenhan, D. The natural socialization of altruistic autonomy. In J. Macaulay & L. Berkowitz (Eds.), *Altruism and helping behavior*. New York: Academic Press, 1970.

Rubin, Z., & Peplau, L. A. Belief in a just world and reaction to another's lot: A study of participants in the national draft lottery. *Journal of Social Issues,* 1973, *29,* 73–93.

Rushton, J. P. *Altruism, socialization, and society*. Englewood Cliffs, N.J.: Prentice-Hall, 1980.

Schopler, J. An attribution analysis of some determinants of reciprocating a benefit. In J. Macaulay & L. Berkowitz (Eds.), *Altruism and helping behavior*. New York: Academic Press, 1970.

Staub, E. Social and prosocial behavior: Personal and situational influences and their interactions. In E. Staub (Ed.), *Personality: Basic aspects and current research*. Englewood Cliffs, N.J.: Prentice-Hall, 1980.

Stotland, E., Mathews, K. E., Sherman, S. E., Hansson, R. O., & Richardson, B. Z. *Empathy, fantasy, and helping*. Beverly Hills, Ca.: Sage, 1978.

Tulving, E. Episodic and semantic memory. In E. Tulving & W. Donaldson (Eds.), *Organization and memory*. New York: Academic Press, 1972.

Walster, E., Berscheid, E., & Walster, G. W. The exploited: Justice or justification. In J. Macaulay & L. Berkowitz (Eds.), *Altruism and helping behavior*. New York: Academic Press, 1970.

Author Index

Italics denote pages with bibliographic information

Subject Index

Heroism, 5
Home, promotion of positive behavior in the, 109–120
Homosexuality, 32–33
Honesty, 8, 9, 83
  tests of, 254–255, 256
Human nature, concepts of, 3–5

I

Inclusive fitness, 7, 30, 42–44
Individual differences
  altruism and, 249–283, 433–435
  derogation of innocently suffering victims and, 268–270
  preschool altruism and, 340–342
Induction, 117–120
  other-oriented, 80
Indulgence, abstinence from, 8
Industriousness, 8
Infanticide, 28
Injustice, 268
Integrity, 264 (see also Honesty)
Internal control, effects of, on victim derogation, 276–278, 280–281

J

Joy, affective aspects of, 237
Just world, derogation of victims in, 267–282
Justice, altruism and, 213–230

K

Kidney donors, 351–365
Kin selection, 26–28, 31, 33–34
"Kitty Genovese" incident, 3

L

Learning
  cooperative, in schools, 126–127
  experiential, 127–130
  participation and, 120–122, 128, 130

M

Machiavellianism, 263
Manipulation, 30–31, 35
Mimicry, empathic arousal and, 46, 47

Modeling
  altruism and, 12, 69–74, 428
  promoting positive behavior through, 123–124
Moral education, schools and, 128–130
Moral judgment, altruism and, 263
Moral reasoning, assessment of, 263, 264
Moral rules, testing for knowledge of, 255
Morality, empathic, 57
Motivation, altruistic, empathy as source of, 167–185

N

Natural selection, altruism and, 7, 19–37, 42–44
Negative State Relief Model, 242
Neo-Darwinism, 28
Norms of appropriate behavior, 261–264, 431

O

Obligation, orientation toward, 111
Overarousal, empathic (see Empathic overarousal)
"Overjustification effect," 68–69

P

Parental care, 8, 24, 26, 31, 33
Parent-offspring conflict, 31
Participation, learning by, 120–122, 128, 130
"Paternal" care, 33–34
Peer counseling, 130
Peer group, nature of, 124–125
Personality
  altruistic, 251–264
  positive behavior and, 110–113
Perspective-taking ability, altruism and, 78–80
Persuasion, 35
  verbal, altruism and, 74–78
Positive behavior
  personality and, 110–113
  promotion of, 109–131
Preschool altruism, 331–348
Prosocial behavior
  norms concerned with, 261
  operational definitions of, 154–155
Prosocial characteristics, attribution of, 81–85
Prosocial orientation, 111
Punishment, altruism and, 68–69